NAVAL LAW

NAVAL LAW

THIRD EDITION

JUSTICE
AND
PROCEDURE
IN THE
SEA SERVICES

BRENT G. FILBERT & ALAN G. KAUFMAN

Naval Institute Press   Annapolis, Maryland

Library of Congress Cataloging-in-Publication Data

Filbert, Brent G., 1961–
    Naval law : justice and procedure in the sea services /
Brent G. Filbert and Alan G. Kaufman. — 3rd ed.
        p.   cm.
    Includes bibliographical references (p. 359).
    ISBN 1-55750-462-8 (alk. paper)
    1. Military offenses—United States.   2. Courts-martial
and courts of inquiry—United States.   3. United States.
Navy—Regulations.   I. Kaufman, Alan G., 1956–   .
II. Title.
KF7650.F55   1997
343.73'0143—dc21   ·   97-31042

Printed in the United States of America on acid-free paper ∞
05 04 03 02 01 00 99 98   9 8 7 6 5 4 3 2
First printing

CONTENTS

CASES

FOREWORD

[The Supreme Court] has long recognized that the military is, by necessity, a specialized society separate from civilian society. [It] has also recognized that the military has . . . developed laws and traditions of its own during its long history. The differences between the military and civilian communities result from the fact that 'it is the primary business of armies and navies to fight or be ready to fight wars should the occasion arise.'

Toth v. Quarles, 350 U.S. 11, 17 (1955).

Naval Law begins with an interesting historical perspective of the development of the laws and traditions of the navy that have governed the officers, petty officers, and sailors who manned the ships, as well as the marines who sailed with the fleet to secure it against all enemies. But, more importantly, this book quickly leads to the study of modern military law. Knowledge and understanding of the laws and traditions of the naval service are absolutely essential to successful leadership of a modern military force.

The Supreme Court has also said: "An army is not a deliberative body. It is the executive arm. Its law is that of obedience. No question can be left open as to the right to command in the officer, or the duty of obedience in the soldier" (in *re Grimley,* 137 U.S. 147, 153 [1890]). This statement applies with equal force to a navy. No ship could steam successfully through turbulent seas caused by enemy fire or natural forces if there were any question as to the duty of the sailor to obey the lawful orders of the ship's officers and petty officers. But the right to command carries with it a corollary responsiblity. A commander must have the respect and trust of his or her subordinates. While there are many attributes of a good commander, all will agree that a primary trait is for a commander to treat everyone he or she commands with dignity and fairness. The following statement by Major General Kenneth J. Hodson in 57 Mil.L.Rev. 1, 16 (1972) illustrates this point: "I have said many times that discipline is enhanced far more by the belief that a soldier can get fair treatment than it is by any system of iron-fisted military justice that appears to be unfair."

The present laws and traditions that govern the naval forces have evolved over the years simply to give a commander the necessary tools to achieve good order, discipline, high morale, and esprit de corps while preserving dignity and fairness. Brigadier General John S. Cooke, Chief Judge of the United States Army Court of Criminal Appeals, speaking at the 1997 Judicial Conference of the United States Court of Appeals for the Armed Forces, aptly explained the role of the military justice system:

> By discipline, I mean not fear of punishment for doing something wrong, but faith in the value of doing something right.
> Military justice is key. . . . It establishes basic standards of conduct and behavior for all men and women who wear the uniform, and it establishes the procedures by which those standards are enforced. Military justice doesn't simply impose discipline through deterrence and punishment. Military justice inculcates and reinforces discipline by consistently applying two fundamental principles: each person, regardless of rank, is responsible and accountable for his or her actions; and, each person, regardless of circumstances, is an individual entitled to be treated fairly, with dignity and respect.

I can state without fear of contradiction that any midshipman who carefully studies and learns the lessons contained in this book will grow and mature into a leader that men and women will follow. Furthermore, *Naval Law* is a superb collection of history, laws, treaties, rules, and traditions of the naval service. It is a book that officers will keep and update as a reference. I commend the authors for this work and urge each midshipman to study it scrupulously.

Walter T. Cox III
Chief Judge
United States Court of Appeals for the Armed Forces

PREFACE

This book is designed as an introduction to military naval law. Although attorneys may find the text a helpful primer on military jurisprudence, it is primarily intended for use by midshipmen and others interested in the law of the sea services. It is not, however, an exhaustive account of law in the U.S. Navy and Marine Corps. Rather, it provides discussion, resources, and materials designed to assist in the study and comprehension of naval law in the classroom setting.

Naval Law focuses on four primary areas: the development and history of law for land and sea forces, constitutional and criminal law, administrative law, and international law. To make the subjects interesting and relevant to the student, actual cases, treaties, statutes, instructions, and regulations are used throughout the book. These materials, including the court opinions, have been edited to make them as understandable and germane as possible. Throughout the text, issues designed to promote both understanding and critical analysis of the material presented are posed to the reader. The study questions at the end of each chapter are intended to focus the student's attention on fundamental aspects of naval law and to challenge the student's understanding of these concepts.

In order to comprehend why the military justice system exists as it does today, the student must understand how military law developed. Thus chapter 1 provides an overview of the history of military justice by tracing the development of the U.S. Army and Navy legal systems. Chapter 2 introduces some of the principles of criminal law that are essential to the study of military justice. The standards discussed in this chapter provide the foundation for the student's understanding of cases and materials throughout the book.

Chapters 3 and 4 examine the forums and procedures used to dispose of military offenses. These chapters explore the court-martial and administrative forums as well as the rules and concepts relevant to disposition of crimes in the armed forces. Focusing primarily on what are termed "uniquely military" crimes, chapter 5 introduces the elements and basic tenets of these offenses and provides cases that question and apply the principles involved.

The rapidly evolving law of government ethics is considered in chapter 6, which traces the development of ethics rules and examines the reasons for the limits placed on government employees, including members of the armed forces. This chapter also provides the rules that most frequently affect naval personnel and discusses the interpretation of these regulations.

Chapters 7 and 8 examine the relationship between the armed services and the Constitution. Chapter 7 deals with the complex nature of search and seizure, introducing the basic concepts of the Fourth Amendment and providing cases that consider how the amendment applies in the military setting. The constitutional and statutory bases for the privilege against self-incrimination are considered in chapter 8. Through the use of court opinions, this section explores the tension between the constitutional rights of service members and the military's duty to fight and win wars.

Chapter 9 canvasses the many types of criminal and administrative investigations conducted in the U.S. Navy and Marine Corps, explaining and contrasting these probes by presenting excerpts from relevant statutes and instructions. Through study of situations in which a service member's freedom of movement may be curtailed, chapter 10 examines the law of apprehension and restraint. This chapter also considers offenses that may arise when a member of the armed forces is apprehended or restrained.

The final three chapters are devoted to the broad topic of international law. Chapter 11 deals with the nature and importance of international law and explains how customary and conventional law develops. The law of war is the focus of chapter 12, which considers the limits on the use of force, including the persons and institutions protected under international law. The final chapter addresses crimes committed during the course of hostilities. Following an overview of the development of war crimes law, this chapter examines actual cases, agreements, and conventions that pertain to offenses occurring during armed conflict.

The eight appendixes to the book are designed to augment and amplify the reader's understanding of the materials covered in the main body of the text. The first three appendixes, the Constitution of the United States, the Uniform Code of Military Justice, and the Manual for Courts-Martial (MCM) Maximum Punishment Chart, are resources fundamental to the study of military justice. Four of the remaining five appendixes relate to international law and law of war. Appendix 4 provides a summary of the Geneva Conventions, and appendix 5 is the full text of Hague Convention No. IV Respecting the Laws and Customs of War on Land. Although the rules of engagement are not separately covered in the text, it is important for the student to understand that they serve as a limit on the use of force in addition to the law of armed conflict. Thus the Standing Rules of Engagement for U.S. Forces make up appendix 6, and appendix 7 consists of the Desert Shield and Desert Storm Rules of Engagement. Finally, appendix 8 is a glossary of military justice terms.

We would like to thank Cynthia P. Campise, whose dedicated efforts and unending patience were crucial to the completion of this book. We would also like to acknowledge the research assistance of Major Daniel J. Lecce, U.S. Marine Corps.

NAVAL LAW

CHAPTER ONE

THE HISTORY AND BACKGROUND OF MILITARY JUSTICE

There are limits on the extent to which the essentially autocratic armed forces are able to adopt notions regarded as precious by a democratic society. And there are limits on the extent to which civilian society will accept whatever such adaptations the services attempt, however much in good faith they may be acting. The tension between *discipline*—regarded as indispensable in a military force—and *justice*—similarly respected in the civilian community—may help to determine where those boundaries lie.

William T. Generous, Swords and Scales

Introduction

The stated purpose of military justice in today's U.S. armed services is "to promote justice, to assist in maintaining good order and discipline, to promote efficiency and effectiveness in the military establishment, and thereby strengthen the national security of the United States." This statement contains two goals for the military legal system: justice and discipline. The development of military justice as we know it today is really a story of the competition of these two principles: a competition in which neither principle can yet claim victory. As you read this chapter, consider which of these concepts is the driving force behind the developments in military justice.

To grasp how both justice and discipline endure in military law, one must understand how the military legal system developed. This requires the study of both law and military history. Much as in the private sector, law in the armed forces evolves in response to changes in the constituency and institutions that it serves. Given this fact, it is not surprising that wars and combat operations profoundly impact military law. That said, many events not involving armed conflict, such as societal trends and domestic and international politics, also shape military jurisprudence.

In recent years, the effect of particular events on the military legal scheme has increased. In tracing the progression of military justice, question why certain incidents result in changes in the military legal system and others do not. Also, consider why it seems that particular events have an impact on the law more quickly and frequently today than in the past.

This chapter traces the evolution of law for land and sea forces. It does so by explaining how the justice systems for U.S. ground and naval forces developed and by identifying the factors and circumstances that influenced each legal scheme.

Development of Military Justice

The American military legal system now provides persons in the armed forces with many of the same rights and protections afforded the rest of society. This is a relatively new phenomena. Historically, the good of the service was the overriding purpose of military law. In *Rocks and Shoals,* James E. Valle explains that "the ultimate purpose of military law [was] not to guarantee any person any particular rights, or due process of law, or set of procedures, or even to ensure fundamental justice, but to maintain military discipline." It was not until codes such as the Uniform Code of Military Justice (UCMJ) were established that concern with individual justice became a significant part of military law.

Although army and naval justice were both premised on the need to sustain discipline, they each developed in significantly different ways. Brigadier Gen. James Snedeker, U.S. Marine Corps (Ret.), in *A Brief History of Courts-Martial,* describes this bifurcated development:

> On land, proceedings leading to punishment were based upon theories of vengeance and prevention by example; at sea, upon a theory of protection of the ships and cargoes in maritime commerce. On land, in an era when war was a normal state of existence among tribes and kingdoms, the rules were established and abolished

with the rise and fall of dynasties on shore; at sea, there was a continuous and growing body of rules recognized as international in character, independent of dynastic changes. On land, justice was administered for the most part by the same individuals in peace and war, the civil judges being military commanders; at sea, special courts set up by the world traders retained jurisdiction over maritime matters and had no authority over non-maritime affairs.

As you study military justice, consider whether differences still exist between the law for American land and naval forces. Also question if there still are reasons for treating soldiers and sailors differently. The quote from General Snedeker implies that naval justice evolved from custom and practice. Are custom and tradition still part of naval law? What about international law? Law of the sea? Law of armed conflict? See chapters 11 to 13.

Military Justice for Land Forces

Military law arose almost simultaneously with the establishment of organized armies. For instance, the *Magistri Militum,* the law of the legions of the Roman Empire, codified Roman military law and established tribunals to hear cases involving military offenders. In early German armies, the duke or military chief heard cases involving members of the army in time of war. The Germans later developed courts presided over by either the military commander or his delegate. These early Roman and German tribunals tried offenses which still exist under the UCMJ: desertion, mutiny, cowardice under fire, and assaulting a superior officer. Although these crimes still exist, the severe punishments prescribed for these offenses may not seem so familiar: decimation, denial of burial after execution, maiming, exposure to the elements, and civil disqualification.

During the Middle Ages, military commanders were also civil judges, a situation which often blurred the line between civil and military jurisdiction. Beginning in the fifth century, legitimate military codes began to emerge, and by the ninth century, such codes existed in many European nation-states. From these early sets of laws emerged what became known as articles of war. In 1621, the king of Sweden, Gustavus Adolphus, issued a comprehensive set of articles regulating the conduct of his soldiers and establishing a system to try offenders. The articles set up a regimental court-martial, presided over by the regimental commander, and a general court-martial, presided over by the royal marshal of Sweden, with senior officers sitting as members (jurors). The regimental court-martial tried cases such as theft, insubordination, cowardice, and other minor offenses, while the general court-martial heard cases of treason and other serious crimes. General Snedeker describes the Articles of War of Sweden:

> These Articles of War were the best that had been issued anywhere. The Swedish soldier was exemplary, but he did, of course, occasionally disobey. In one notable aspect, the military law of Gustavus differed widely from that of the Norman court of chivalry. Whereas, the latter sanctioned the trial by single combat, Gustavus forbade promotion of dueling under pain of death. His code of articles was comprehensive, containing 167 articles, and was carefully drafted. When it was translated and published in London in 1639, it greatly influenced the later English codes.

ENGLISH MILITARY JUSTICE FOR
LAND FORCES

Following the fall of the Roman Empire, the feudal system and age of chivalry emerged in Europe. During this period, feudal knights began to sit as judges on courts of chivalry. William the Conqueror introduced this system into England at the time of his conquest in 1066. His senior military officers soon became members of Britain's Court of Chivalry, which had jurisdiction over military cases. When the power of the Court of Chivalry effectively disappeared in the sixteenth century, courts roughly equivalent to today's court-martial appeared. General Snedeker described these early courts-martial:

In the early British courts-martial, the general or governor convening the court ordinarily sat as the president. The power of the court was plenary, and its sentences were executed without confirmation by any higher authority. Such a court was legally convened, however, only in time of war.

As the power of Britain expanded, the English army began issuing specific military ordinances during wartime or prior to expeditions. In 1385 it issued twenty-six articles of war effective during time of war. During the next several centuries, the British army continued to issue various articles of war; however, the authority to conduct courts-martial during peacetime remained unsettled. By 1640 the king and Parliament were at war, with each side maintaining its own armed force. It was during this dispute that Parliament enacted a military code to govern its army. This was the first set of military justice regulations enacted by a legislature.

In 1660 England established a standing army, resulting in a need to maintain discipline during times of peace. Partly because of the limited ability to punish offenders during peacetime, discipline in the British army became increasingly lax. In 1689 eight hundred English and Scottish dragoons mutinied, causing the British Parliament to pass the First Mutiny Act. This statute empowered courts-martial to prescribe punishments, including the death penalty, for mutiny or desertion, even during peacetime. By 1803 Parliament had assumed complete control over laws relating to military justice. To this day, Parliament retains cognizance over all military justice laws.

Until the twentieth century, discipline of the troops was the overriding purpose of the British military justice system. Thus, punishments were severe and procedural rights of service members were few. Why was this the case? The Duke of Wellington offered some insight on this issue in 1811 when he described the armed services of Britain: "None but the worst description of men enter the regular service. The scum of the earth who have all enlisted for drink."

U.S. MILITARY JUSTICE FOR LAND FORCES

Given that the U.S. legal system developed from the English, it is not surprising that early American military law mirrored the British. The Provisional Congress of Massachusetts Bay passed a set of articles of war on 5 April 1775—the first written code of military law in America. Massachusetts modeled these articles almost entirely on the British Articles of War of 1765. In June 1775, the Continental Congress appointed a committee to prepare rules and regulations for the government of the Continental army. George Washington sat as a member of this committee, which adopted a set of sixty-nine articles known as the American Articles of War. Another committee of the Continental Congress revised this code in 1776 to more closely match the British Articles of War of 1774. John Adams, Thomas Jefferson, and John Rutledge were members of this panel. These articles remained in effect until 1806, with one major revision in 1786.

Punishments in the U.S. Army during this period were severe, to say the least. For instance, the Continental Congress authorized up to one hundred lashes for violations of the Articles of War. George Washington, however, sought at least five hundred and unsuccessfully petitioned the Continental Congress to increase the number above the one hundred initially authorized. The extremely harsh penalties used by the U.S. Army continued following the adoption of the Constitution in 1789. The disciplinary record of the Legion Army, a force assembled to defeat the Indian tribes along the northwestern frontier of the United States, illustrates this point. The following is a statistical breakdown of three of the most common offenses and the punishments awarded in the Legion Army between July 1792 and August 1793:

	Desertion	Sleeping	Drunkenness
Number tried	112	18	13
Convictions	93	16	13
Acquittals	19	2	0
Death	19	5	NA
Average lashes	91	87.5	95
Conviction rate	92%	88%	100%

(See *American State Papers Military Affairs* 1 (1832): 67.)

While the severity of the penalties under the early American Articles of War may seen unusual when measured against today's standards, the tribunals established to try military offenders were markedly similar to the courts currently in use. That is not to say that the army's fledgling legal system did not experience difficulties. An episode at Fort McIntosh in 1786 illustrates the problems encountered by the army in developing its court-martial procedures. At that time the three types of courts-martial, general, regimental, and garrison, all provided for trial by jury. A general court-martial, however, required a jury of thirteen officers, while the other two types required only five. The large number of members necessary for a general court-martial imposed a heavy burden on commands and eventually led to the incident at Fort McIntosh, which had a long-lasting impact on U.S. military law. Desertions were rampant at the fort, and the major in command decided to make examples of captured deserters by trying them at court-martial. Because desertion was a capital offense only triable at general court-martial, the major did not have a sufficient number of officers (thirteen) to sit on the panel. Not to be deterred, he convened a general court-martial, with only five members, which sentenced two of the offenders to death. The major then requested that the secretary of war confirm the sentences. He refused to do so, and instead, overturned the convictions as illegal, stating that "to supersede the laws in this respect is to assume the sovereignty and annul the compact, which the public have made with the troops, that they shall be governed by the rules and articles of war." Congress responded by repealing the existing rules relating to army courts-martial and specifically providing that a general court-martial could consist of only five members.

Can you think of other situations in which Congress has passed legislation to remedy an inadequacy or flaw in the military legal system? Consider the reaction to the *Somers* mutiny discussed later in this chapter. Did perceived inadequacies in military justice prompt Congress to enact the UCMJ? Certain laws exist today which some might argue are outmoded and need to be stricken. Contemplate the following UCMJ articles: Article 114 (dueling), Article 134 (abusing a public animal), Article 134 (adultery), and Article 125 (consensual heterosexual sodomy). Do these provisions still serve a purpose? If not, why has Congress not repealed these articles?

In 1806 Congress enacted a new set of articles of war. From time to time throughout the next seventy years, Congress passed important legislation affecting the army's justice scheme (for example, Congress abolished use of the scourge in 1812); however, it did not enact a new collection of articles until 1874. This long hiatus in congressional action was largely due to the belief that the civilian and military legal systems were, of necessity, completely different animals. General William Tecumseh Sherman, a practicing lawyer before returning to military duties during the Civil War, had this to say about military justice:

It will be a grave error if by negligence we permit military law to become emasculated by allowing lawyers to inject into it the principles derived from their practice in the civil courts, which belong to a totally different system of jurisprudence. The object of the civil law is to secure to every human being in a community all the liberty, security, and happiness possible, consistent with safety of all. The object of military law is to govern armies composed of strong men, so as to be capable of exercising the largest measure of force at the will of the nation.

These objects are as wide apart as the poles, and each requires its own separate system of laws, statutes and common law. An army is a collection of armed men obliged to obey one man. Every enactment, every change of rules which impairs the principle, weakens the army, impairs its value, and defeats the very objects of its existence.

The 1874 code did not dramatically alter the army's legal system but did establish maximum punishments for all offenses in time of peace and established the one-officer summary court-martial. In 1916 Congress issued a revised version of the Articles of War and published its first Manual for Courts-Martial (MCM) to explain and amplify the articles.

World War I had a dramatic impact on the army's military justice system. During the war, the army commissioned more than two hundred thousand new officers and enlisted nearly four hundred thousand soldiers. The experience of this huge influx of personnel with the army's procedures resulted in meaningful changes to the army's legal system following the conflict.

During the war, a particular incident also raised questions about the fairness of the army's legal process. At Fort Sam Houston in 1917, black troops mutinied because of their treatment at the hands of the army and the local Texas community. Courts-martial convicted thirteen of the alleged mutineers and sentenced each of the soldiers to death. Article of War 48 provided that in time of war the local commander could execute sentences without approval of higher authority. Although the troops and the command were not engaged in combat operations, the commander carried out the executions almost immediately following the verdicts, without apprising any higher authority of the results of the trials. The Fort Sam Houston mutinies caused the army to thereafter provide mandatory review by the army judge advocate general (JAG) in cases involving death sentences or dismissal of officers. This incident and other troubling episodes, coupled with the overall experiences of soldiers in World War I, caused the army to overhaul its articles of war in 1920.

The Articles of War of 1920 provided significantly broader protections to accused than any of the previous codes. For example, the articles made defense counsel mandatory in all but summary courts-martial. A "thorough and impartial" pretrial investigation also became a prerequisite prior to a general court-martial. The articles further banned the upward revision of sentences and reconsideration of findings by commanders following trial. Although the Articles of War of 1920 afforded soldiers significantly more rights than ever before, the rules still contained many provisions that purposely limited the protections of accused and retained power in the hands of commanders. For instance, enlisted members were not eligible to sit on courts-martial and trial judges did not have to be attorneys. Also, the recommendations of the pretrial investigator were not in any way binding on the commanding officer.

The Articles of War of 1920, the rules that ultimately governed the army through World War II, resulted from significant events affecting the army, for example, World War I and the Fort Sam Houston mutinies. Do you see a trend in this regard? Does it surprise you that the move to change the Articles of War of 1916 came from within the army? Why do you think that the Articles of War of 1920 provided more procedural protections than did previous articles of war? Note that some of the provisions contained in the Articles of War of 1920 are still in place today. See Article 20, UCMJ (no right to defense counsel at summary court-martial) and Article 32, UCMJ (commanding officer may disregard the findings of the pretrial investigating officer).

Military Justice at Sea

As previously discussed, naval justice developed in a much different manner than did law for land forces. General Snedeker describes the origins of military justice at sea:

> A body of sea-law began to take shape under the Phoenicians [ca. 500 B.C.]. It was a unique system, independent and unchallenged, because its jurisdiction was in a region owned by no king or local chieftain. The mariners who lived aboard the galleys shared a common life and experience. Their dangers, trials, and tribulations were similar, regardless of their origin, race, or creed. Although the empires ashore rose and fell, one after another, the growing body of sea-law continued to mature, independent of dynastic changes.

Rhodes emerged as a prominent sea power about 300 B.C., and developed a set of maritime laws that endured for more than a thousand years. Unlike military law on land, which emanated from a particular king or tribal leader, custom and practice formed the basis for this code. This explains in large measure why the maritime laws of Rhodes survived for such an extended period. In the thirteenth century, Barcelona produced an extensive set of maritime laws known as the *Consulado del Mar,* or the Book of the Jurisdiction of the Sea. As with the earlier laws of Rhodes, the code of Barcelona also derived from custom and practice. Barcelona printed the *Consulado del Mar* in 1494, which by then consisted of some 250 chapters. Roughly at the same time, the island of Oleron, an English possession off New Rochelle in the Bay of Biscay, had produced its own code of the sea. Based on the Rhodes model, the laws of Oleron served as the maritime code of northwestern Europe for several centuries. Other areas also developed sets of laws regulating life at sea. For example, the city of Wisby on the Baltic Sea developed a code of maritime laws that gained widespread acceptance in the Baltic area during this period.

All of the codes discussed above evolved from custom, that is, deeds practiced over a long period of time that take on the force and effect of law. These customs developed from several sources, including accepted practices on board vessels, local maritime courts, local regulations, treatises, and legislation by guilds of sea traders. Each of these sets of law addressed many areas of maritime law, such as contracts, ship's liability, wages, and dismissal of crew members. Not surprisingly, these laws also dealt with discipline on board vessels, the dominating feature of which, early on, was their extreme severity. For example, a typical maritime ordinance in the fifteenth century provided that a second conviction for desertion would be punished by public flogging, and a third offense by death. For mutiny, a mariner was publicly beaten with rods, and for a second offense was condemned to death.

Compare the prescribed punishments discussed above with the events in the *Somers* mutiny below. Is it surprising that the commanding officer in that case considered the death penalty an appropriate measure? Also look at chapter 5 regarding authorized punishments for desertion under the UCMJ. Are punishment considerations different today than in the fifteenth and sixteenth centuries? Do custom and practice still form the basis for naval law? Consider the sources of international law and law of war discussed in chapters 11 to 13.

ENGLISH NAVAL JUSTICE

As England emerged as the dominant maritime nation, it developed naval laws and customs that influenced other nations, in particular the United States. At first, the maritime courts of the English seacoast towns determined the law on board the king's ships. As the British navy grew in strength, it sought to retain jurisdiction over its own vessels. As a result, a publication entitled the *Black Book of the Admiralty* was compiled during the first half of the fourteenth century. It stated that the administration of justice "according to the law and ancient customs of the sea" was among an admiral's duties. For several centuries, sailors of the Royal Navy were disciplined based on these accepted practices, which, unfortunately for the enlisted man, included flogging, branding, ironing, and keelhauling (drawing a man by rope under the ship from one side to the other, usually resulting in death).

By the seventeenth century, British admirals began to issue regulations upon assuming command of a fleet. In 1652, the British Parliament issued a code with universal and continuous authority over the Royal Navy. In 1653, a set of tactical standards, known as the *Fighting Instructions,* were promulgated to impose order on the handling of ships during engagements with the enemy. These two sets of rules were soon incorporated by the Parliament into the First Naval Disciplinary Act of 1661, a code of thirty-seven articles that spelled out the laws pertaining to naval forces. Over the next century, dispensing naval justice became an accepted feature of British officers in command. This ultimately created a considerable body of naval law that provided the basis for American naval law in the eighteenth and nineteenth centuries.

U.S. NAVAL JUSTICE

The Continental Congress found the existing body of English naval law to be invaluable when it set to work on drafting rules and regulations for the navy of the united colonies in 1775. John Adams, an admiralty lawyer and member of the naval committee for the Continental Congress, explained:

It would be in vain for us to seek our own invention or the records of warlike nations of [*sic*] a more complete system of military discipline. I was, therefore, for reporting the British Articles of War *totidem verbis* [verbatim]. (See Valle, *Rocks and Shoals,* 41.)

In the fall of 1775, the Continental Congress issued the first set of American naval articles, entitled the *Rules for the Regulation of the Navy of the United Colonies.* These articles set forth only a few specific offenses but provided that all other "faults, disorders, and misdemeanors committed on board ship should be punished according to the laws and customs in such cases at sea." While the rules essentially mirrored earlier British articles, they contained some unique provisions in the area of punishment. John Adams ensured that the articles urged officers to try more humane methods of punishing minor offenses, such as wearing badges and collars. The articles also specifically limited the maximum number of lashes imposed at captain's mast and court-martial. In including these provisions, Adams hoped to prevent the American navy from adopting European naval traditions, such as keelhauling, inflicting death by flogging, shooting men out of a cannon, and other barbarous practices. (See Valle, *Rocks and Shoals,* 41).

When the federal convention met in 1787, there was a heated debate concerning whether the Constitution should provide for a standing military. Because of their experiences with martial law under the British, the framers feared a strong army and navy. Consequently, the convention gave Congress, not the president, the power to raise and maintain a military, and in Article I, Section 8, Clause 14, the authority to "make rules for the government and regulation of the land and naval forces." Although the states ratified the Constitution in 1788, the president did not appoint a secretary of the navy until 1798, and Congress did not enact the *Rules and Regulations for the Government of the Navy* until 1800. Most of these articles, nicknamed by sailors "Rocks and Shoals," remained in effect until replaced by the UCMJ in 1950.

The navy under Rocks and Shoals used four proceedings to address offenses: the general court-martial, the summary court-martial, the court of inquiry, and captain's mast (all these tribunals still exist today in much the same form). Despite the existence of adequate forums to adjudicate crimes, the actual administration of naval justice during the nineteenth century was inefficient and uneven. Accepted procedures were in many instances incomplete and often were intentionally disregarded or negligently misinterpreted by officers. The single consistency in naval law during this period was the severity of punishment. The *Somers* mutiny, as described by Edward M. Byrne in *Military Justice,* illustrates the character of naval justice in the 1840s.

UNITED STATES V. MIDSHIPMAN PHILIP SPENCER
ON BOARD USS *SOMERS*
NOVEMBER 29, 1842

Acting Midshipman Philip Spencer, U.S. Navy, 18 years of age, must have regarded the USS *Somers* with awe when he first beheld her on 13 August 1842. The *Somers* was a beautiful new brig-of-war that had just been released from the shipyards some months ago. Although displacing 266 tons, she was so sharply built that she only carried a crew of 120. Designed for swiftness the brig was very top-heavy and carried only ten cannons.

Anyone observing this young midshipman would hardly envision him as the principal participant in the first recorded mutiny on board a United States vessel since the founding of our country.

An indolent, dull-witted boy in many ways, Spencer

attended Hobart College from 1838 to 1841, when he was withdrawn for academic failure. He next attended Union College, where he was one of the founders of Chi Psi fraternity. He especially enjoyed and originated some of the secret rituals for his fraternity. Shortly thereafter, he obtained an appointment as an acting midshipman in the United States Navy.

His father was perhaps instrumental in his appointment, as he was then secretary of war in President Tyler's cabinet. What the elder Spencer did not know, or chose to ignore, was that his son's highest dream was to become a famous and renowned pirate. During short tours on two previous U.S. vessels before he arrived on board the *Somers,* Spencer retained his dream—and often discussed it. However, the reasons given for Spencer's transfer from his previous ship were "drunkenness and scandalous conduct."

When Philip Spencer reported to the USS *Somers,* there was no United States Naval Academy. The navy had begun to realize, however, that there was a need for training future officers and had chosen to do so by setting up small schools in some of the principal cities of the east and utilizing vessels as "floating academies." The *Somers* was the first of such training ships.

As captain of the *Somers,* the navy had selected Commander Alexander Slidell Mackenzie, a well-known naval officer—author of his day and a man with wealth, power and influence in his own family. For example, his sister, Jane Slidell, was the wife of Commodore Matthew Calbraith Perry.

The *Somers* left on 13 September 1842 for a cruise to Africa, thence to travel to the West Indies, and finally home to New York. Spencer, for whatever reasons, was never accepted by his fellow officers and sought the comfort of the crew—many of whom he generously furnished with rum and cigars. For example, by 26 November 1842, Spencer had purchased ten pounds of tobacco and seven hundred cigars. Spencer had two intimate enlisted friends—Samuel Cromwell and Elisha Small.

During the voyage, it was apparent that Spencer's obsession with piracy had not ended. Outside his intimate circle, he discussed pirates and what a pirate ship the *Somers* would make. He discussed a pirate flag and what it would look like. After the captain criticized him for another matter, he stated he would like to throw the captain overboard. Whether these were just the rantings of an insubordinate dolt whose father happened to be in a position of importance, we shall never know.

However, Spencer did more than talk. He put his aspirations in writing.

A list, written in Greek, indicated whom he considered would join him, whom he considered doubtful, and who would not join in an apparent takeover of the ship. Only four names were listed as "certain" and those included Spencer himself. One man was never involved and James W. Wales, who was listed as "certain," first reported Spencer to the captain. An "E. Andrews" was listed. No such man was aboard the ship, but Spencer insisted the name was an alias for Small.

On 25 November 1842, Midshipman Spencer approached Purser's Steward Wales, listed as "certain" on his Greek list, and asked him to join in a mutiny. Spencer reportedly told Wales that he had twenty men in his group and that he planned to take over *Somers* and turn her into a pirate ship. All the officers were to be killed. He then threatened Wales not to divulge his plan and asked him to join the mutiny. Small was in the vicinity and appeared to be involved with Spencer in the plan, according to Wales.

Wales related the story to the captain who at first dismissed it as a joke, but as a precaution asked Lieutenant Gansevoort to investigate the matter. The lieutenant did develop that Spencer had asked another officer if he was familiar with the Isle of Pines, a well-known pirate haunt. That was the only corroborative evidence prior to the ordering of Spencer's arrest on 27 November 1842. It is worthwhile relating what occurred prior to Spencer's apprehension. At evening quarters the following transpired:

> Mackenzie: I learn, Mr. Spencer, that you aspire to the command of the *Somers*.
>
> Spencer: Oh, no, sir!
>
> Mackenzie: Did you not tell Mr. Wales, sir, that you had a plan to kill the commander, the officers, and a considerable portion of the crew of this vessel and convert her into a pirate?
>
> Spencer: I may have told him so, sir, but in joke.

Spencer was then searched and placed in irons. Small and Cromwell were arrested one day later. Later, the lieutenant interviewed Spencer, who admitted he had

this plot on every ship he had been attached to, but had never gone as far with it as he had on board the *Somers*. Spencer thought it was a "mania" with him. He also stated that "E. Andrews," the name on the list, stood for Small and not Cromwell.

The captain and his officers became convinced that a mutiny was possible at any moment and that the only way to avoid it was to hang the ringleaders. In truth, the evidence to this effect was, at its best, slim. Apparently Lieutenant Gansevoort had discussed the possibility of hanging the three captives with most of the officers and had majority approval. However, they felt they needed a reason for hanging the men at this time. They told the captain that if more prisoners were taken this would obstruct navigation (the prisoners were in irons on the quarterdeck) and increase the possibility of rescue of the prisoners. Captain Mackenzie then arrested four more men for mutiny (none of whom were ever convicted of any crime regarding the mutiny). Upon this basis, the captain then asked his officers "to take into deliberate and dispassionate consideration the present condition of the vessel and the contingencies of every nature that the future may embrace, throughout the remainder of our cruise, and enlighten me with your opinion as to the best course to be pursued."

The officers heard thirteen witnesses, all of whom were sworn and their testimony written down. They then signed these statements. Lieutenant Gansevoort, who had already expressed his opinion of the guilt of the accused on several occasions and had garnered most of the evidence, was the senior man present. The prisoners were not brought before the officers, nor did they know they were being tried. The captain had already begun to prepare a watch bill for the executions; however, the council still continued to hear evidence. The inquiry did not arrive at a decision and resumed the next day. By midmorning they had reached a decision. They recommended the three accused should be put to death based upon the fact that "it would be impossible to carry them to the United States" due to the possibility of further mutinous acts. Even before they were led away, both Cromwell and Spencer asserted Cromwell's innocence. The three were then hanged with the roll of drums and the thunder of cannon, as prescribed in the captain's watch bill.

When the *Somers* arrived in New York and the story was released, Commander Mackenzie was considered a hero. However, Secretary of War Spencer and Cromwell's widow began to raise questions about the nature of the proceedings. A court of inquiry was held and found Mackenzie blameless. Mackenzie was later tried for murder of the three men by a court-martial and acquitted.

Even in 1842 an accused was entitled to appear before the tribunal, make objections, plead, confront the witnesses against him and examine them and present a defense. See *Regulations for the U.S. Navy and Marine Corps,* 19 February 1841. Did Commander Mackenzie make an appropriate decision in denying these procedural protections to the accused? What does his decision tell us about the condition of naval justice in 1842? Can you think of recent instances in the military in which procedural rights of accused and suspects may have been inappropriately disregarded?

The *Somers* mutiny resulted in significant changes in both the navy and its justice system. The incident emphasized the need for developing a truly professional academy for naval officers and led to the formation of the United States Naval Academy. Frederic F. Van de Water, in his book *The Captain Called It Mutiny,* explained: "George Bancroft was the father of the professional school at Annapolis, but Alexander Slidell Mackenzie, in association with Philip Spencer, were among the academy's remoter forebears."

The *Somers* affair also brought to the public's attention the extreme use of flogging on board navy vessels. Commander Samuel Francis Du Pont, commanding officer of the frigate *Congress,* recorded the number of men flogged on board his ship during a single month in 1845:

December 1	3 men flogged
December 4	4 men flogged
December 5	6 men flogged
December 8	4 men flogged
December 11	3 men flogged
December 13	5 men flogged
December 15	3 men flogged
December 17	3 men flogged
December 20	2 men flogged
December 22	2 men flogged
December 26	2 men flogged
December 27	4 men flogged

(Valle, *Rocks and Shoals,* 78.)

Statistics such as those on board Commander Du Pont's ship moved Congress to abolish flogging five years later. Flogging was replaced by a punishment still in existence today—confinement on bread and water. The summary hangings on board the *Somers* also made the navy extremely reluctant to carry out death sentences. While the army and air force have executed 159 persons since 1930, the navy has not carried out a single execution since 1849.

The *Somers* case received intense public interest partly because Midshipman Spencer was the son of the secretary of war. Compare the *Somers* situation with the case of *United States v. Kelly,* which involved the secretary of the navy's son.

UNITED STATES V. YEOMAN SEAMAN APPRENTICE
CHAD E. KELLY
NAVY AND MARINE CORPS COURT OF MILITARY REVIEW
40 M.J. 558
JUNE 13, 1994

Consistent with his pleas, the appellant was found guilty of numerous offenses involving the theft and wrongful use of other service members' credit cards, including conspiracy to commit larceny, larceny, forgery, and stealing mail matter. He was sentenced by the military judge to a dishonorable discharge, confinement for 2 years, forfeiture of all pay and allowances, and reduction to pay grade E-1.

The issue before us is whether the appellant's case is closely related to that of Yeoman Seaman [YNSN] H. Lawrence Garrett IV, U.S. Navy, the son of the then-secretary of the navy, whose offenses were disposed of at nonjudicial proceedings under Article 15, UCMJ, and, if so, whether the disparate treatment between the two cases resulted from impermissible considerations and inappropriate actions rather than good and cogent reasons.

We conclude, first, that the appellant's and YNSN Garrett's cases are closely related. The appellant's crimes involved the theft of mail matter and use of stolen credit cards to steal goods and services. YNSN Garrett admitted driving the appellant to the mail room where the appellant was to steal or retrieve a stolen credit card that came from the mail. YNSN Garrett later was a principal to several thefts through use of the stolen credit cards. Undoubtedly, under the law of principals, YNSN Garrett was the actual thief of at least one of the cards and was active in their subsequent unlawful use. These acts were generally similar in nature and seriousness to the appellant's offenses.

In addition, the two cases arose from a common scheme. Even assuming that the appellant began stealing the cards on his own initiative in order to steal goods and services, YNSN Garrett and others certainly joined the scheme at some point. YNSN Garrett apparently aided the theft of one card, and he frequently benefitted from the theft and use of the cards. He ultimately became sufficiently involved in the criminal enterprise for us to find that this and the appellant's offenses arose from a common scheme in which both took part.

There is no reasonable question that the disposition and sentence in the two cases are widely disparate. The appellant received a federal criminal conviction, a punitive discharge, substantial confinement, and the loss of over $14,000 in pay. YNSN Garrett received an administrative punishment not considered a conviction, no punitive discharge, no confinement (only extra duties and restriction to a base for thirty days), and the loss of $880 in pay.

A central issue is whether this disparity in disposition and sentence is for good and cogent reasons. We conclude that such reasons are wholly absent in the record before us.

The government emphasizes the number and seriousness of the appellant's offenses and stresses that his punishment is appropriate. We agree entirely. The government's suggestion, however, that YNSN Garrett's offenses were minor and of a nature and seriousness that warranted disposition by an Article 15, UCMJ, proceeding is without any basis in experience or reason.* The evidence before us indicates that YNSN Garrett was a principal to the theft of at least one credit card from the mails. He stole gasoline and clothing on sev-

eral occasions, received stolen food and beverages on several occasions, and solicited the theft of an expensive vacuum cleaner. These offenses alone warrant trial by a special court-martial with authority to adjudge a punitive discharge and confinement of up to 6 months. Yet these offenses do not stand alone. He also confessed to multiple uses of marijuana, and the evidence indicates regular and steady use. Lastly, he lied under oath more than once to NIS agents, crimes that are also punishable under the UCMJ. Had YNSN Garrett been tried by a general court-martial for these crimes, the maximum sentence he could have received would have included a dishonorable discharge and confinement for twenty-three years. We conclude that nothing in this record justifies the disparity in disposition and sentence between these two cases.

The most difficult issue is whether the unreasonable disparity between the cases results from an unfortunate but relatively benign factor, such as poor judgment or inexperience in military justice matters on the part of the officers who directed the disposition of YNSN Garrett's case, or worse, from an impermissible factor.

We turn first to YNSN Garrett's transfer from San Diego to Washington, D.C. At the time of this transfer, he was a single Sailor who had been assigned to shore duty on a major staff in California immediately after receiving his initial military training—certainly a desirable assignment for most naval personnel in similar circumstances. After reports of the loss of credit cards at the Shore Intermediate Maintenance Activity and the opening of an NIS investigation, YNSN Garrett contacted his father to complain that his petty officers were harassing him, he wanted to attend college, and his romantic interests were unsatisfied. Complaints by young Sailors in the navy concerning their superior petty officers are hardly uncommon. As the secretary's own statement makes clear, higher educational opportunities were available in San Diego. YNSN Garrett's romantic prospects were a frivolous concern. From all of the circumstances, there is a reasonable inference that YNSN Garrett's true motive for wanting to leave San Diego was other than the reasons he related to his father. He certainly did not want to be caught by the growing investigation into the theft and wrongful use of the credit cards, and he probably thought that duty in Washing-

---

*YNSN Garrett has been administratively discharged from the navy.

ton would provide him a safe haven. Therefore, he sought his father's assistance.

We conclude that YNSN Garrett's transfer resulted solely from his status as the son of the secretary of the navy. His shore assignment was terminated well before the normal rotation date for reasons that are uncompelling. The only conclusion left to us is that he was transferred cross-country because the secretary mentioned his son's unhappiness to Admiral Boorda, the chief of naval personnel, and not because the needs of the Naval Service were furthered by the move. There is no evidence, however, that any of the officers who effected the transfer were aware of YNSN Garrett's suspected criminal involvement at the time of the transfer.

When the appellant disclosed YNSN Garrett's offenses, YNSN Garrett had been removed from the place where most of his crimes had been committed. While NIS was certainly able to continue the investigation of YNSN Garrett in Washington, we are convinced that, once he left San Diego, the eventual disposition of the charges against him was affected because those who had the responsibility to handle his case in Washington were more likely to be influenced by his status than others in a different location. The investigation in Washington, D.C., is replete with actions by naval and NIS personnel that demonstrate that YNSN Garrett's case was not handled in the normal course of military justice.

First, YNSN Garrett conversed with the secretary's military legal advisor, Commander Fagan, a member of the Judge Advocate General's Corps and an officer who represents the Naval Service rather than any particular officer or service member. This officer elected to obtain the telephone number of the NIS office where YNSN Garrett was being interrogated so that his mother could interrupt that interrogation. The evidence shows that the night before an NIS interrogation, that officer chose to provide a rights advisement to a military accused, to include advice regarding NIS interrogation techniques. Predictably, the following day, YNSN Garrett explained his close relationship with this lawyer to NIS special agents for whatever effect he thought that relationship might have on them.

Additionally, the commander, Naval Investigative Service Command, intervened in the investigation to further the perceived interests of the secretary. We find that, contrary to his assertions, Rear Admiral Williams did direct that Mrs. Garrett's or Commander Fagan's telephone call be put through during YNSN Garrett's interrogation. We also find that his actions in the case of YNSN Garrett were motivated by loyalty to a close personal friend, a desire to spare the secretary personal anguish and public embarrassment, and a desire to dispose of an awkward situation in the most expeditious manner possible instead of fulfilling his duty as the head of NIS to ensure that a complete and accurate investigation of YNSN Garrett's case was completed. This fact became obvious to the NIS agents who investigated YNSN Garrett's alleged offenses.

The NIS investigation ultimately went before Captain LeGrand, the senior military lawyer in the Bureau of Naval Personnel. His explanation for recommending that YNSN Garrett's case be disposed of at an Article 15, UCMJ, nonjudicial proceeding is unconvincing. First, he spoke of the low monetary value of the property and services YNSN Garrett obtained. The evidence before us does not indicate what that overall value was because no investigator was called upon to tally the total, however, it certainly was at least several hundred dollars. He next considered that the drug offenses were for use as opposed to distribution. Convincing evidence of record suggests numerous if not frequent and prolonged use of marijuana by YNSN Garrett. We note that in our experience, cases of multiple drug use, standing alone, are commonly referred to trial by special court-martial where, upon conviction, the accused often receives a punitive discharge and months of confinement. We are perplexed by the reference to YNSN Garrett's cooperation with NIS as a reason for leniency in light of his evasion and showings of deception or inconclusiveness in his polygraph examination results. In fact, by his own admission, YNSN Garrett lied under oath to NIS agents, an offense unmentioned by Captain LeGrand in his declaration. Finally, while YNSN Garrett's prior clean record was a legitimate factor to consider in the disposition of the charges against him, this factor pales substantially given the gravity of the offenses he faced. We also note that the appellant had a good record prior to his general court-martial with no prior disciplinary actions.

Captain LeGrand added that YNSN Garrett was a potential witness against the appellant. However, YNSN Garrett had lied under oath to NIS agents, and the appellant had already confessed. Consequently, both the usefulness and necessity for YNSN Garrett's testimony as a prosecution witness were in considerable doubt. Next, Captain LeGrand referred to the requirement to corroborate YNSN Garrett's admissions. Considering the seized charge card receipts, the potential testimony of YNSN Garrett's roommates, and the other incriminating admissions in the case, this requirement was one that any prosecutor could easily meet. Finally, he referred to the situs of any prosecution, a problem arising solely from YNSN Garrett's early transfer, and one which was easily remedied by transferring him back to San Diego for disciplinary action. In short, the reasons for recommending disposition of YNSN Garrett's offenses at an Article 15, UCMJ, nonjudicial proceeding are unconvincing, and, in light of other evidence in this case, the only rational explanation for the extremely lenient treatment YNSN Garrett received was his status as the son of the secretary. In his statement, Rear Admiral Williams acknowledges that he conversed with Captain LeGrand regarding factual information in the case prior to nonjudicial punishment being imposed on YNSN Garrett. Rear Admiral Williams did not further disclose the details of the conversation, and Captain LeGrand did not mention this conversation in his affidavit.

Anyone familiar with the NIS investigation in this case when YNSN Garrett's offenses were referred to an Article 15 nonjudicial proceeding in April 1992 must have been aware that when YNSN Garrett was transferred from San Diego, he had committed serious offenses and that the transfer took him away from the location of the witnesses and other evidence. Further, they must have known that YNSN Garrett was aware of his own misconduct when he pressed his father for a transfer. In the navy, it is common practice to transfer an accused for disciplinary action from a current location back to a previous command where the alleged offenses occurred. When senior naval officers recognized the effect of YNSN Garrett's transfer from San Diego, the expected result would have been his transfer back to San Diego where his alleged offenses could have been

fully pursued in the same course as though he had not obtained his transfer. The failure of responsible officers to follow this common practice is further evidence that YNSN Garrett received preferential treatment.

Finally, we note that YNSN Garrett was charged at the Article 15 proceeding with but one charge for two separate uses of marijuana. The evidence, however, indicated numerous uses. Only one larceny specification embraced his multiple larcenies. Only one specification of receipt of stolen property was drafted in spite of the evidence of several receipts. The charges did include one specification for soliciting the theft of an expensive vacuum cleaner, but no specification mentioned his false swearing to the NIS agents during his interrogation.

Although YNSN Garrett was punished for his offenses, he was not processed for administrative discharge following the Article 15 proceeding. Not only is it uncommon, but it is extraordinary that a Sailor could be found to have used marijuana repeatedly, to have stolen property using stolen credit cards taken from a navy mail room, to have received stolen property stolen by using these cards, to have asked another Sailor to steal a vacuum cleaner by using another Sailor's stolen credit card, and to have lied to NIS agents under oath and then be retained on active duty without being processed for discharge. In this case, that result is not inexplicable. Based on our experience, we state with confidence that, absent extraordinary circumstances, any other Sailor in the U.S. Navy who faced such charges would have been tried by court-martial.

In summary, we find that YNSN Garrett's transfer was based solely on his status as the son of the secretary. The decision that his offenses should be disposed of at an Article 15 proceeding and that he would not be processed for administrative discharge thereafter was based on the same status. We find that in YNSN Garrett's case the military justice process was infected throughout by senior naval officers who considered who the accused was rather than what he had done.

We conclude that the appellant's and YNSN Garrett's cases are closely related and that their punishments are widely disparate. We further conclude not only that the disparity is not supported by good and cogent reasons, but also that it occurred as the result of an impermissible factor.

In deciding what action to take in light of our conclusions, we state the obvious: we are reviewing the appellant's conviction and sentence and not those of YNSN Garrett. We have no authority under the UCMJ to take any action regarding YNSN Garrett. Therefore, we can attempt to balance the scales only by reducing the appellant's otherwise totally appropriate sentence. The government has argued that the appellant's sentence should be affirmed in spite of what has taken place. We cannot accept such a result. More importantly, the integrity and fairness of the military justice system cannot accept such a result. Preferential treatment of a suspect based on his family relationship to a high-ranking officer or civilian has no place in any reputable justice system. Therefore, we have decided to reduce the appellant's sentence substantially.

Upon reassessment, and considering the disparate treatment and the reasons therefor, and considering the unique circumstances for this case, we affirm only so much of the sentence as includes confinement for fifteen months, forfeiture of $420.00 pay per month for fifteen months and reduction to pay grade E-1.

Why do you think the military still has difficulty with unlawful interference with the administration of justice? Does the chain of command structure make such problems inevitable? In assessing the *Somers* and *Kelly* cases, consider Article 98, UCMJ:

Any person subject to this chapter who . . . knowingly and intentionally fails to enforce or comply with any provision of this chapter regulating the proceedings before, during, or after trial of an accused, shall be punished as a court-martial may direct.

Did Commander Mackenzie violate the spirit of this provision? What about Secretary Garrett? Rear Admiral Williams?

In 1862, Congress recognized the need to formally update existing naval justice laws. The changes included establishing maximum punishments for offenses. Unlike the army's system, which underwent a major overhaul after World War I, the navy was not the target of legal reform until following World War II. What do you think is the explanation for this difference? In his book *Swords and Scales,* William T. Generous suggests the following:

The navy did much less to rearrange the social patterns and customs of its population than the army did. During peacetime, both services made officers out of gentlemen and enlisted men out of lower class recruits. During the mobilization, the navy continued that practice by commissioning mostly college graduates. But the army selected its officers on the basis of merit. The result was that in the navy those who were likely victims of perceived court-martial abuse were the same who had been abused in civilian life. In the army, on the other hand, the scions of high society who were forced by circumstances to serve in the enlisted ranks complained at every real or fancied maltreatment. The overall consequence was great agitation for changes in military law, but much less, almost none, in the sea service.

The Uniform Code of Military Justice

World War II

During World War II, the United States expanded its armed forces to a maximum strength of more than twelve million men and women. As a consequence, the number of courts-martial during this period of hostilities was staggering: approximately two million court-martial convictions, with eighty thousand of those handed down by general courts-martial. This activity placed the military justice system under scrutiny by a great number of Americans who had no previous contact with its workings. The experience of many of these service members was not positive. Former president Gerald R. Ford Jr., at the time a member of the House of Representatives, had this to say about naval justice:

It seems to me that a general statement can be made with all honesty, that in the navy, at least, justice is sometimes forgotten in order to impose on people in the service punishment of some kind or other. I am particularly concerned about the fact that in courts-martial, too often a court-martial board does not determine the guilt or innocence of the accused; but rather seeks to award punishment of one sort or another. I can recall hearing conversations between members of boards along this line: "What does the Old Man want us to do?"

Several studies conducted by the services after World War II confirmed the sentiments expressed above. As a result, calls for reform and unification of the systems into a single scheme increased. Congress responded by significantly revising the army's Articles of War under the Elston Act of 1948 but did not modify the navy's legal scheme. The move to reform military justice gained momentum, however, and by 1949 it was clear that Congress would enact a uniform code. The unanswered question was, What would such a code contain?

Adoption of a Uniform Code of Military Justice

In 1949, the newly established secretary of defense appointed a committee to draft a code applicable to all the services. This draft provided the basis for the code ultimately adopted by Congress in 1950.

Unlawful influence by commanders in the trial process was the major issue debated by Congress in considering passage of the UCMJ. Those who feared such influence argued that commanders should be totally removed from the court-martial process. Proponents of this view emphasized justice as the most important aspect of the new code. Others, such as Colonel Frederick Bernays Wiener of the army, argued to Congress that "if you trust [the line officer] to command, if you trust him with the lives and destinies of these millions of citizens under his command . . . you can certainly trust him with the appointment of a court." Thus, opponents of removing commanders from the process believed that discipline was the primary purpose of military justice. In the end, Congress resolved the controversy by reaching a compromise on this issue. The commander retained power to appoint counsel, the law officer (judge), and court members (jurors). However, the UCMJ provided that a neutral officer would conduct the pretrial investigation, qualified defense counsel

would represent the accused, and the all-civilian Court of Military Appeals (now the Court of Appeals for the Armed Forces) would provide appellate review of court-martial decisions.

As you will see in later chapters, the tension between the concepts of justice and discipline continues to this day. Which principle dominates the UCMJ? Which of the above arguments is most appealing? Have developments in the law and in society altered the principles underlying the UCMJ?

Although the UCMJ contains many uniquely military provisions, it clearly moved military justice much closer to civilian criminal law. Some would argue that as this trend continues, the authority of commanding officers is diminished and that this is hurting the morale of service members. Do you agree with this assessment?

A second area of intense debate in enacting the UCMJ focused on just how uniform the code would be. The U.S. Army's Articles of War influenced Congress to a much greater degree than did the U.S. Navy's articles; however, the navy and Marine Corps pushed hard to retain unique aspects of the existing naval justice scheme. Colonel Melvin Maas, national president of the Marine Corps Reserve Association, argued this point before Congress:

And we want to point out to you that while this bill is a compromise of the naval justice system and the Articles of War, that there is a definite difference in disciplinary control that is required at sea and the disciplinary control required on land. Therefore, the types of punishments may be quite different, of necessity. A relatively minor infraction at sea may become a very major thing from a disciplinary standpoint. A minor infraction may endanger the lives of all those on the ship, and it may involve a whole flotilla of ships. It is very rare that such a situation could exist in any other type of organization . . . Therefore, it is necessary for discipline at sea to be very much more rigid and very much more drastic than is necessary on shore. That is recognized, gentleman, through the ages in maritime law as well as in naval law.

Congress enacted several provisions which distinguished between personnel attached to or embarked in a vessel and members at shore commands. Consider these provisions contained in Article 15, UCMJ:

> Except in the case of a member attached to or embarked in a vessel, punishment may not be imposed upon any member of the armed forces under this article if the member has, before the imposition of such punishment, demanded trial by court-martial in lieu of such punishment.
>
> Any commanding officer may . . . impose . . . upon a person attached to or embarked in a vessel, confinement on bread and water or diminished rations for not more than three consecutive days.

Do you agree that the disciplinary concerns are different for ships than for shore commands? If yes, do increased punishments and fewer procedural rights help commanders at sea instill discipline? Take a look at the punishments awardable at courts-martial and nonjudicial punishment in chapters 3 and 4.

From 1951 to 1968, Congress enacted only relatively minor changes to the UCMJ. In 1968, however, Congress significantly modified the code. These changes came about because of the continuing tension between military discipline and civilian concepts of fairness and due process. For example, the 1968 act did away with law officers and replaced them with military judges and required that all defense counsel meet certain qualifications in order to represent military accused. Also, in 1968 the navy created a separate and distinct corps of lawyers entitled the Judge Advocate General's Corps (JAG Corps).

Summary

The struggle between justice and discipline still continues in the U.S. military. Procedural fairness, a secondary concern of military law since the birth the American armed forces, now has a legitimate place in military jurisprudence. Meanwhile, discipline, while still a primary objective of the military legal system, no longer dominates as it once did. Where this trend will take military law is unclear. What is clear is that important military, political, and societal events will continue to shape the services' justice system.

Study Questions

1. How did military justice for naval forces develop? How was its evolution different than the development of military law for land forces?

2. What impact did the British system have on the U.S. military legal system? Is the influence of the English system still present today?

3. How did the U.S. Army develop its legal system? How did its development differ from the U.S. Navy's?

4. What effect have significant events, that is, wars, disasters, scandals, and so on, had on military law in the United States? Do such incidents still result in changes in military jurisprudence?

5. Is there a trend in U.S. military law toward "civilianization"? If yes, what are the positive and negative aspects of such an inclination?

6. What caused Congress to enact the UCMJ? Has the code been significantly modified since it was adopted?

7. Which of the two principles, justice or discipline, dominates American military justice today? Does the UCMJ properly balance the two concepts?

CHAPTER TWO

FUNDAMENTALS OF MILITARY JUSTICE

Military law is a vital element in maintaining a high state of morale and discipline. Members of the armed forces must have a clear understanding of the standards of conduct to which they must conform, and they must also have confidence that the system of justice will operate in a fair and just manner.

—Senator Sam Nunn, "The Fundamental Principles of the Supreme Court's Jurisprudence in Military Cases," *Wake Forest Law Review* 29 (1994): 557

Introduction

As military justice has continued to move toward civilian criminal law, the fundamental legal principles of civilian criminal jurisprudence have become part of the military justice system. It is, therefore, necessary for the student of military law to grasp the concepts and principles that underlie American criminal law. It is also important to understand that many of the laws, rules, and regulations that make up military law are unique to the armed forces. The concepts and sources that form the foundation of military criminal law are the focus of this chapter.

Unlike their civilian counterparts, military personnel are an integral part of the justice system. For instance, officers and enlisted persons routinely serve in a police function as members of security forces and as investigators of minor criminal offenses. Officers also act as legal advisors, making them responsible for all aspects of military law, including consulting with the commanding officer on legal matters affecting the command. Both enlisted members and officers sit as members of courts-martial, as well. To carry out these important roles in the military legal system requires an understanding of the sources of law in the armed forces and the principles that underlie the military legal system.

Sources of Military Law

As discussed in chapter 1, military justice for naval forces originated from custom and practice. Today the sources of military law are firmly established and modified not by practice but by changes to the sources themselves. That is not to say, however, that developments in the military and in society do not eventually cause changes in military justice practice. To the contrary, the military legal system is continually modified in response to developments in both areas. Also, understand that other areas of law important to the armed services, for example, international law, are still made and altered by accepted uses and practice. See chapter 11.

U.S. Constitution

Article 1, Section 8 of the U.S. Constitution states: "Congress shall have the power . . . to make rules for the government and regulation of the land and naval forces." Article 2, Section 2, appoints the president as the "Commander-in-Chief of the Army and Navy of the United States." The result of these provisions is that Congress enacts laws governing the military, while the executive branch controls its operations. The Supreme Court in *Ex Parte Milligan,* 71 U.S. 2 (1866) explains this relationship:

> The power to make the necessary laws is in Congress; the power to execute in the president. Both powers imply many subordinate and auxiliary powers. Each includes all authorities essential to its due exercise. But neither can the president, in war more than in peace, intrude upon the proper authority of Congress, nor Congress upon the proper authority of the president. Both are servants of the people, whose will is expressed in the fundamental law. Congress cannot direct the conduct of campaigns, nor can the president, or any commander under him, without the sanction of Congress, institute tribunals for the trial and punishment of offenses.

Chief Justice of the Supreme Court John Marshall, himself an officer on General Washington's staff, de-

clared in *Marbury v. Madison,* 1 Cranch 137 (1803), that the judiciary has the authority to strike down laws that are repugnant to the Constitution. Thus all laws and regulations affecting the military must be in line with the Constitution. Federal and military courts continually construe the military's laws and regulations to assess the constitutionality of such provisions. See appendix 1 for the full text of the Constitution.

The Uniform Code of Military Justice

As discussed in chapter 1, the UCMJ is applicable to all service personnel "in all places." Also known as the "code," the UCMJ is divided into twelve subchapters, addressing every aspect of military justice, including: jurisdiction, investigations, apprehension and restraint, courts-martial, nonjudicial punishment, sentences, and appeals. The UCMJ also sets forth all military crimes in what are known as the punitive articles. See appendix 2 for the full text of the UCMJ.

Manual for Courts-Martial

Congress, in enacting the UCMJ, recognized that it could not write a rule for every aspect of military justice. Consequently, it delegated to the president the following authority:

> Article 36. President May Prescribe Rules. (a) Pretrial, trial, and post-trial procedures, including modes of proof, for cases arising under this chapter triable in courts-martial, military commissions, and other military tribunals and procedures for courts of inquiry, may be prescribed by the President by regulations which shall, so far as he considers practicable, apply the principles of law and the rules of evidence generally recognized in the trial of criminal cases in the United States district courts, but which may not be contrary to or inconsistent with this chapter.

Thus, in delegating significant authority to the executive branch to establish the rules and the procedures for courts-martial.

The president responded to the authority vested in him by Congress by promulgating the Manual for Courts-Martial. The MCM is the basic directive implementing the UCMJ, and it is available on all ships and stations in the naval service. Every officer has a responsibility to have a working knowledge of the MCM because it provides regulations which explain, amplify, and implement the UCMJ. For example, the MCM explains the elements to military offenses, contains the Military Rules of Evidence (MRE) and the Rules for Courts-Martial (RCM), and provides the maximum punishments for each offense under the UCMJ. See appendix 3 for the MCM Maximum Punishment Chart. The MCM is an executive order signed by the president and is applicable to all military branches. The most recent version of the MCM became effective in 1995.

Manual of the Judge Advocate General

There are certain matters peculiar to the individual services that the MCM cannot adequately address. Consequently, the UCMJ and MCM permit the "secretary concerned" to prescribe regulations in certain areas. For example, the secretary of the navy, under Article 23 of the UCMJ, has the authority to designate other commanding officers or officers in charge who may convene a special court-martial, in addition to those specifically enumerated in that article. Another example of this delegated authority is the Manual of the Judge Advocate General (the JAG Manual), a directive of the Department of the Navy, signed by the judge advocate general of the U.S. Navy and approved by the secretary of the navy. The JAG Manual, applicable only to the U.S. Navy and Marine Corps, contains many of the regulations specific to naval military justice, and is, therefore, a significant source of law for the navy and Marine Corps. It contains important regulations concerning administrative matters, such as claims, legal assistance, and nonjudicial punishment. This resource is particularly important for officers because it provides the rules and guidelines for conducting administrative investigations (known as JAG Manual investigations).

Service Regulations

Numerous other regulations and orders are promulgated by commanders, ranging from the secretary of the navy to commanding officers of U.S. Navy and Marine Corps units. Chapter 5 spends considerable time addressing the legal status of these regulations.

Court Decisions

Opinions from courts that decide cases involving members of the armed forces also provide an important source of military law. Military criminal courts (trial and appellate) only address military justice matters. A court-martial is the military equivalent of a civilian criminal trial court. A court of criminal appeals for each branch of the service is the first level of appeal from special and general courts-martial (these courts were known as Courts of Military Review until 1994). Thus the naval services (the navy and Marine Corps) have the Navy–Marine Corps Court of Criminal Appeals. Above the court of criminal appeals is the Court of Appeals for the Armed Forces, which hears cases from all branches (until 1994, the Court of Military Appeals). An appeal from this forum is to the highest appellate court in the land, the U.S. Supreme Court. Other federal courts also consider military law issues. Federal courts consider and rule, for example, on such issues as the military's policy on homosexuality, treatment of refugees, women in combat, and administrative separation of personnel. Because these courts continually interpret military rules and activities, their decisions provide an important source of laws for the armed forces. See chapter 3 for a full discussion of military courts.

Throughout this book the reader will note that cases are described as follows: *United States v. Cotten*, 10 M.J. 260 (C.M.A. 1981). This means that the case of *United States v. Cotten* may be found on page 260 of volume 10 of the *Military Justice Reporter.* The parenthetical information indicates that the Court of Military Appeals (now the Court of Appeals for the Armed Forces) decided the case in 1981.

Fundamentals of Criminal Law

Mens Rea

UNITED STATES V. THOMAS O. BASTIAN, JUNIOR, PRIVATE,
U.S. MARINE CORPS
UNITED STATES NAVY COURT OF MILITARY REVIEW
47 C.M.R. 203
MARCH 26, 1973
Opinion: Evans, Judge

Appellant was convicted of wrongful appropriation of a truck belonging to his friend, Lance Corporal Haney, in violation of Article 121, UCMJ.

Appellant asserts the evidence is insufficient to establish his criminal intent with respect to the wrongfulness of the taking. Lance Corporal Haney testified that on the night in question he went on liberty with appellant using Haney's truck for transportation. After visiting several bars Haney decided to stay ashore for some time and gave appellant 200 yen for transportation back to the base. Since he knew appellant did not have a driver's license he never had authorized him to drive the truck on a public street.

Appellant testified that after visiting several bars with Haney, he decided to return to the base alone, since Haney intended to visit another bar. After they had separated, appellant became concerned about Haney's welfare and commenced to look for him on foot. Later he came to the area where the truck was parked. He started the vehicle and drove it for about an hour along the street trying to locate the owner. Subsequently he hit a pole while avoiding another vehicle.

Appellant maintains since he took the vehicle for the purpose of assisting its owner, the taking was not wrongful within the meaning of Article 121, UCMJ. As we view appellant's testimony, his alleged pure motive does not obviate the fact that the taking was wrongful,

that is, his self-justification, a matter of motive, constitutes no defense to wrongful appropriation.

Appellant's motive was pure only to the extent he desired to help the owner as opposed to protecting the truck. Since he was not a licensed driver the probability of the owner recovering the property was reduced. Indeed, there was evidence one week expired before the owner finally found his damaged property in a navy salvage yard. This is the result Article 121, UCMJ aims to avoid. Additionally, appellant does not assert he was laboring under the mistaken belief he was authorized to drive the vehicle; or he took it with an innocent purpose to protect it for the benefit of the owner. In short, appellant's possession of the truck was wrong. We consider the evidence clearly shows appellant had at the time of the wrongful taking the necessary mens rea or criminal state of mind to commit the offense of wrongful appropriation.

Black's Law Dictionary 1136 (5th ed., 1979) describes mens rea as "a guilty mind; a guilty or wrongful purpose; a criminal intent." Does the court's analysis of mens rea comport with the description in *Black's Law Dictionary?* Is evidence of mens rea on the part of the accused necessary at nonjudicial punishment? At administrative separation hearings? See chapter 4.

Specific Intent

UNITED STATES V. JAMES J. GREENE, AVIATION STRUCTURAL
MECHANIC (HYDRAULIC) THIRD CLASS, U.S. NAVY
UNITED STATES COURT OF MILITARY APPEALS
20 U.S.C.M.A. 297; 43 C.M.R. 137
JANUARY 29, 1971
Ferguson, Judge

The accused was convicted by general court-martial, convened at Luzon, Republic of the Philippines, of one specification each of willful damage to military property of the United States by burning and simple arson, in violation of Articles 108 and 126, UCMJ. The object the accused was charged with burning was an SP-2H aircraft, located at the Naval Air Station, Whidbey Island, Washington.

The issue in this case is whether the law officer erred to the prejudice of the accused by failing to instruct the court-martial on the effect of intoxication upon the element of willfulness and maliciousness involved in simple arson.

Article 126(b), UCMJ, defines simple arson as follows:

> Any person subject to this chapter who willfully and maliciously burns or sets fire to the property of another, except as provided in subsection (a) [aggravated arson], is guilty of simple arson and shall be punished as a court-martial may direct.

In *United States v. Krosky*, 418 F.2d 65, 67 (6th Cir. 1969), the court defined "willfully" as follows:

An act is done "willfully" if done voluntarily and purposely with the specific intent to do that which the law forbids; that is to say, with bad purpose either to disobey or to disregard the law. Willfulness includes an evil motive.

Of particular importance to the question before us is our holding in *United States v. Groves,* 2 U.S.C.M.A. 541, 10 C.M.R. 39 (1953). Groves was charged, among other offenses, with "willfully damaging military property" under Article 108, UCMJ. The record was replete with evidence that Groves was deeply intoxicated at the time of the commission of the charged offense. Finding that specific intent was an element of the offense of willful damage to military property, we reversed his conviction for that offense because the law officer gave no instruction to the court as to the possible legal effect of intoxication upon Groves' ability to entertain a specific intent.

We hold, therefore, that intoxication having been raised by the evidence, it was error, prejudicial to the substantial rights of the accused, for the law officer to fail to instruct on the affirmative defense of intoxication.

Black's Law Dictionary defines specific intent as the "purpose to use particular means to effect certain results." In addition to possessing mens rea, an accused must have a specific intent for certain offenses. What was the specific intent element in *Greene?* Why was the court concerned with the issue of whether arson is a specific intent offense?

Standard of Proof

UNITED STATES V. RUSSELL OWEN COTTEN, ELECTRICIAN'S MATE FIREMAN, U.S. NAVY
UNITED STATES COURT OF MILITARY APPEALS
10 M.J. 260
FEBRUARY 9, 1981
Fletcher, Judge

The appellant was convicted at a special court-martial convened by Commanding Officer, U.S. Naval Station, Norfolk, Virginia, of 13 specifications of sale, transfer, and possession of both marijuana and lysergic acid diethylamide, in contravention of Article 92, UCMJ.

As part of his general instructions to the court-martial members trying appellant, the military judge quoted the following language:

> By reasonable doubt, it is intended not a fanciful and ingenious doubt or conjecture but substantial, honest, conscientious doubt suggested by the material evidence, or lack of it, in the case. It is an honest, substantial misgiving generated by insufficiency of proof of guilt.

This followed a prior reference in the military judge's preliminary instructions that reasonable doubt was defined as "substantial" doubt. After the general instructions, the defense counsel entered a strong objection to this equation of "reasonable doubt" with so-called "substantial doubt." As an alternative, the defense counsel proffered an instruction which had no reference to "substantial doubt." The defense counsel's objection was overruled and his offered instruction rejected. We conclude this equation was improper and prejudicial to the appellant.

Very early in the history of this Court we ruled that absent a request a law officer had no duty to define "reasonable doubt." All that the code and manual required was that he inform the court members that the guilt of the accused must be "established beyond reasonable doubt" and that any "reasonable doubt must be resolved in favor of the accused." "Beyond reasonable doubt" is the constitutionality required standard. As such, a proper instruction on this issue "is indispensable, for it 'impresses on the trier of fact the necessity of reaching a subjective state of certitude of the facts in issue,'" and is thus "a prime instrument for reducing the risk of convictions resting on factual error." We do not imply that some definition of reasonable doubt is [not] desirable or required in certain cases. Failure to explain reasonable doubt may constitute error where the request is appropriately made at trial. This instructional responsibility, however, calls for the finest exercise of the trial judge's craft and mere recourse to a thesaurus may result in unnecessary error.

We have recently made clear in *United States v. Salley,* 9 M.J. 189 (C.M.A. 1980), that the equation of "reasonable doubt" with "substantial doubt" is in disfavor with appellate courts generally and that any such reference to this equation should be avoided in military tribunals.

This was a highly contested drug case with controverted testimony from two government witnesses, and the appellant completely denied the charge on which he was ultimately convicted. In this case a proper jury understanding of "reasonable doubt" was essential. Here, however, the military judge made an absolute equation of "substantial doubt" with "reasonable doubt." This required the jury to make its decision based on a lesser evidentiary standard.

This text discusses standards of proof throughout. The "proof beyond a reasonable doubt" standard is not required in all proceedings in the military. What is the standard of proof at nonjudicial punishment? At administrative separation hearings? In line of duty determinations? See chapters 4 and 9.

Direct and Circumstantial Evidence

UNITED STATES V. DANIEL KIRBY, PRIVATE, U.S. ARMY
UNITED STATES COURT OF MILITARY APPEALS
37 C.M.R. 137
FEBRUARY 17, 1967
Kilday, Judge

The accused was convicted before a general court-martial convened at Fort Campbell, Kentucky, of desertion, in violation of Article 85, UCMJ.

The evidence shows the accused was absent without authority from Fort Jackson, South Carolina, for the period June 14 to December 3, 1965. On this latter date, he was apprehended by a Tennessee Highway Patrol comprised of a State officer and the deputy sheriff of Morgan County, Tennessee. When asked for identification, Kirby turned over Social Security and Selective Service registration cards, both bearing the name of Allen Ray Diamond. He carried no other indicia of identification.

It further appears that on September 20, 1965, during the unauthorized absence, the accused had registered for the draft in Casper, Wyoming, using the name of Diamond. In so doing, he listed his next of kin as Mrs. Marvin Watson, a sister, of Thomaston, Georgia. In keeping with Selective Service practices, a draft card was mailed to appellant's Casper, Wyoming, address. It was returned marked "Moved, left no address." Thereafter, the draft board received a change of address ostensibly from the accused giving his address as care of Gary D. Masters, General Delivery, Greensburg, Kansas. The draft registration card mailed to this second address was never returned.

The evidence further reflects while still in Casper the accused was given dental treatment on September 27, 1965, by a local oral surgeon. Here, again, he used the name of Allen Ray Diamond.

In a voluntary statement given to the commander of the Casual Detachment, Fort Campbell, the accused acknowledged using the name of Diamond explaining that he had secured a wallet containing this identification and had used it to obtain employment, being without any other means of identification. In Greensburg, Kansas, he had worked for a construction firm using this alias and then for a rancher under his true name. Accused further stated that he gave the name of Diamond to the apprehending officers so he could get home to see his family.

In testifying in his own behalf, accused admitted using the Social Security and draft registration cards but denied forwarding a change of address notice to the draft board. According to the accused, these items were given him by his traveling companions. He had not signed any of these cards. On the other hand, he did acknowledge having a sister in Thomaston, Georgia, whose married name was Watson. Finally, Kirby asserted he was just "goofing off" with the apprehending officers when he used the false name. According to him, his true identity was known to these officers.

The single issue is: Whether it was an error to not instruct the members that a higher standard of proof is required in cases based on circumstantial evidence.

The defense errs in saying that a stronger standard of proof is required in a circumstantial evidence case as compared with a direct evidence case. Under the circumstances of this case, where the instruction as a whole correctly conveys the concept of "reasonable doubt to the jury," as it does here, we can ask for nothing more. Accordingly, the defense's contention that the members should have been instructed that a stronger standard of proof was required is without merit.

Kirby is a case involving proof of desertion. What other types of circumstantial evidence might assist in proving the intent to desert? What direct evidence would be helpful? See chapter 5 for a discussion of desertion as a military crime.

Direct evidence is commonly defined as "that means of proof which tends to show the existence of a fact in question, without the intervention of the proof of any other fact." Circumstantial evidence is described as facts that "give rise to inferences" of other facts. According to the above cases, which type of evidence is more reliable? Which type of evidence are the following: urinalysis results, an eyewitness account, DNA test results, a bloody knife, and a paternity test result? Based on *Kirby,* does categorizing direct and circumstantial evidence make any difference?

Summary

To comprehend how the military legal system operates, one must first understand the fundamental concepts of military justice. This chapter has introduced many of these concepts. The principles discussed herein pertain to several facets of military law, including courts-martial, nonjudicial procedures, offenses, and investigations. As you study these areas of the law, consider where and how the tenets presented in this chapter apply. The next chapter concerns courts-martial—an area of the law in which the principles of military justice are particularly relevant.

Study Questions

1. What are the primary sources of military law?

2. Which of the following sources of military law is *only* applicable to U.S. Navy and Marine Corps personnel?

    a. The Manual for Courts-Martial

    b. The JAG Manual

    c. The Uniform Code of Military Justice

    d. The Military Rules of Evidence

    e. Decisions by the Court of Appeals for the Armed Forces

3. Who is the UCMJ applicable to and where? Which government body enacted the UCMJ?

4. Who promulgates the MCM? What does it contain? Who signs and who approves the JAG Manual?

5. Define mens rea. What is the difference between mens rea and specific intent?

6. What is a standard of proof? What does "proof beyond a reasonable doubt" mean? Where is this standard applicable?

7. Explain the difference between direct and circumstantial evidence. Which type, if either, is a better type of evidence?

CHAPTER THREE

COURTS-MARTIAL

It is the primary business of armies and navies to fight or be ready to fight wars should the occasion arise. But trial of soldiers to maintain discipline is merely incidental to an army's primary fighting function. To the extent that those responsible for performance of this primary function are diverted from it by the necessity of trying cases, the basic fighting purpose of armies is not served. . . . Military tribunals have not been and probably never can be constituted in such way that they can have the same kind of qualifications that the Constitution has deemed essential to fair trials of civilians in federal courts.

—*Toth v. Quarles,* 350 U.S. 11, 17 (1955)

Introduction

The above quotation from the U.S. Supreme Court highlights the underlying tension in the military courts-martial system between the mission of fighting forces and due process protections of service members. Unquestionably, the military's war fighting purpose affects the nature of courts-martial, resulting in trial and appellate courts that are very different from their civilian counterparts. Competing with the fundamental mission of the military is the requirement that courts-martial provide service members with rights and protections in line with the Constitution. The natural battleground for these often divergent interests is the military courtroom. It is here that judges must weigh the purpose of the military against the process due soldiers and sailors accused of crimes. As you read this chapter, consider how the balance between these two factors is reflected in courts-martial process and procedures.

Nature and Types of Courts-Martial

The following case describes the organization of trial and appellate courts in the military. It also considers the constitutionality of the military's court system.

ERIC J. WEISS V. UNITED STATES

SUPREME COURT OF THE UNITED STATES

114 S. CT. 752

JANUARY 19, 1994

TOGETHER WITH *HERNANDEZ V. UNITED STATES,* ALSO ON

CERTIORARI TO THE SAME COURT

Opinion: Chief Justice Rehnquist

We must decide in these cases whether the current method of appointing military judges violates the Appointments Clause of the Constitution.

Petitioner Weiss, a United States Marine, pleaded guilty at a special court-martial to one count of larceny, in violation of Article 121, UCMJ. Petitioner Hernandez, also a marine, pleaded guilty to the possession, importation, and distribution of cocaine, in violation of Article 112a, UCMJ.

It will help in understanding the issues involved to review briefly the contours of the military justice system and the role of military judges within that system. Pursuant to Article 1 of the Constitution, Congress has established three tiers of military courts. At the trial level are the courts-martial, of which there are three types: summary, special, and general. The summary court-martial adjudicates only minor offenses, has jurisdiction only over enlisted service members, and can be conducted only with their consent. It is presided over by a single commissioned officer who can impose up to one month of confinement and other relatively modest punishments. Arts. 16(3), 20, UCMJ. The special court-martial usually consists of a military judge and three court-martial members, although the code allows the members to sit without a judge, or the accused to elect to be tried by the judge alone. Art. 16(2), UCMJ. A special court-martial has jurisdiction over most offenses under the UCMJ, but it may impose punishment no greater than six months of confinement, three months of hard labor without confinement, a bad conduct discharge, partial and temporary forfeiture of pay, and a reduction in rank. Art. 19, UCMJ. The general court-martial consists of either a military judge and at least five members, or the judge alone if the defendant so requests. Art. 16(1), UCMJ. A general court-martial has jurisdiction over all offenses under the UCMJ and may impose any lawful sentence, including death. Art. 18, UCMJ.

The military judge, a position that has officially existed only since passage of the Military Justice Act of 1968, acts as presiding officer at a special or general court-martial. The judge rules on all legal questions, and instructs court-martial members regarding the law and procedures to be followed. The members decide guilt or innocence and impose sentence unless, of course, the trial is before the judge alone. No sentence imposed becomes final until it is approved by the officer who convened the court-martial.

Military trial judges must be commissioned officers of the armed forces and members of the bar of a federal court or a State's highest court. The judges are selected and certified as qualified by the judge advocate general of their branch of the armed forces. They do not serve for fixed terms and may perform judicial duties only when assigned to do so by the appropriate judge advocate general. While serving as judges, officers may also, with the approval of the judge advocate general, perform other tasks unrelated to their judicial duties. There are approximately 74 judges currently certified to preside at general and special courts-martial. An additional 25 are certified to preside only over special courts-martial.

At the next tier are the four Courts of Military Review, one each for the Army, Air Force, Coast Guard, and Navy–Marine Corps. These courts, which usually sit in three-judge panels, review all cases in which the sentence imposed exceeds one year of confinement, involves the dismissal of a commissioned officer, or involves the punitive discharge of an enlisted service member. The courts may review *de novo* both factual and legal findings, and they may overturn convictions and sentences.

Appellate judges may be commissioned officers or civilians, but each must be a member of a bar of a federal court or of a State's highest court. The judges are selected and assigned to serve by the appropriate judge advocate general. Like military trial judges, appellate judges do not serve for a fixed term. There are presently 31 appellate military judges.

The Appointments Clause of Article 2 of the Constitution reads as follows:

[The president] shall nominate, and by and with the Advice and Consent of the Senate, shall appoint Ambassadors, other public Minsters and Consuls, Judges of the Supreme Court, and all other Officers of the United States, whose Appointments are not herein otherwise provided for, and which shall be established by Law: but the Congress may by Law vest the Appointment of such inferior Officers, as they think proper, in the President alone, in the Courts of Law, or in the Heads of Departments.

We begin our analysis on common ground. The parties do not dispute that military judges, because of the authority and responsibilities they possess, act as "officers" of the United States. The parties are also in agreement, and rightly so, that the Appointments Clause applies to military officers.

It follows that those serving as military judges must be appointed pursuant to the Appointments Clause. All of the military judges involved in these cases, however, were already commissioned officers when they were assigned to serve as judges, and thus they had already been appointed by the president with the advice and consent of the Senate. The question we must answer, therefore, is whether these officers needed another appointment pursuant to the Appointments Clause before assuming their judicial duties. Petitioners contend that the position of the military judge is so different from other positions to which an officer may be assigned that either Congress has, by implication, required a second appointment, or the Appointments Clause, by constitutional command, requires one. We reject both of these arguments.

Petitioners' argument that Congress by implication has required a separate appointment is based in part on the fact that military judges must possess certain qualifications, including membership in a state or federal bar. But such special qualifications in themselves do not, we believe, indicate a congressional intent to create a separate office. Special qualifications are needed to perform a host of military duties; yet no one could seriously contend that the positions of military lawyer or pilot, for example, are distinct offices because officers performing those duties must possess additional qualifications.

Congress' treatment of military judges is thus quite different from its treatment of those offices, such as Chairman of the Joint Chiefs of Staff, for which it wished to require a second appointment before already-commissioned officers could occupy them. This difference negates any permissible inference that Congress intended that military judges should receive a second appointment, but in a fit of absentmindedness forgot to say so.

Petitioners' alternative contention is that even if Congress did not intend to require a separate appointment for a military judge, the Appointments Clause requires such an appointment by its own force. By enacting the Uniform Code of Military Justice in 1950, and through subsequent statutory changes, Congress has gradually changed the system of military justice so that it has come to more closely resemble the civilian system. But the military in important respects remains a "specialized society separate from civilian society," *Parker v. Levy,* 417 U.S. 733, 743 (1974). Although military judges obviously perform certain unique and important functions, all military officers, consistent with a long tradition, play a role in the operation of the military justice system.

Commissioned officers, for example, have the power and duty to "quell quarrels, frays, and disorders among persons subject to [the UCMJ] and to apprehend persons subject to [the UCMJ] who take part therein." Art. 7(c), UCMJ. Commanding officers are authorized to impose "non-judicial punishment" which includes restricting a service member's movement for up to 30 days, suspending the member from duty, forfeiting a week's pay, and imposing extra duties for up to two consecutive weeks. A commissioned officer also may serve as a court-martial member. When the court-martial is held without a judge, as it can be in both summary and special courts-martial, the members conducting the proceeding resolve all issues that would otherwise be handled by the military trial judge. Convening officers, finally, have the authority to review and modify the sentence imposed by courts-martial. Thus, by contrast to civilian society, non-judicial military officers play a significant part in the administration of military justice.

By the same token, the position of military judge is less distinct from other military positions than the office of full-time civilian judge is from other offices in civilian society. As the lead opinion in the Court of Military Appeals noted, military judges do not have any "inherent judicial authority separate from a court-martial to which they have been detailed. When they act, they do so as a court-martial, not as a military judge. Until detailed to a specific court-martial, they have no more authority than any other military officer of the same grade and rank." Military appellate judges similarly exercise judicial functions only when they are "assigned" to a Court of Military Review. Neither military trial nor appellate judges, moreover, have a fixed term of office. Commissioned officers are assigned or detailed to the position of military judge by a judge advocate general for a period of time he deems necessary or appropriate, and then they may be reassigned to perform other duties. Even while serving as military trial judges, officers may perform, with the permission of the judge advocate general, duties unrelated to their judicial responsibilities. Whatever might be the case in civilian society, we think that the role of military judge is "germane" to that of military officer.

In sum, we believe that the current scheme satisfies the Appointments Clause. It is quite clear that Congress has not required a separate appointment to the position of military judge, and we believe it equally clear that the Appointments Clause by its own force does not require a second appointment before military officers may discharge the duties of such a judge.

The Supreme Court in *Weiss* describes the military's court-martial system. What was the accused's basis to attack the constitutionality of the system? Do you think the current procedures for appointing military judges affects their fairness and neutrality? Can the military take action against a judge based upon his or her decisions? See Articles 26 and 37, UCMJ.

The Rules for Courts-Martial describe special and general courts-martial:

> RCM 201(f) Types of courts-martial.
> (1) General courts-martial.
> (A) Cases under the code.
> (i) Except as otherwise expressly provided, general courts-martial may try any person subject

to the code for any offense made punishable under the code. . . .
> (ii) Upon a finding of guilty of an offense made punishable by the code, general courts-martial may, within limits prescribed by this Manual, adjudge any punishment authorized. . . .
> (2) Special courts-martial.
> (A) In general. Except as otherwise expressly provided, special courts-martial may try any person subject to the code for any noncapital offense made punishable by the code and, as provided in this rule, for capital offenses.
> (B) Punishments.
> (i) Upon a finding of guilty, special courts-martial may adjudge, under limitations prescribed by this Manual, any punishment authorized . . . except death, dishonorable discharge, dismissal, confinement for more than 6 months, hard labor without confinement for more than 3 months, forfeiture of pay exceeding two-thirds pay per month, or any forfeiture of pay for more than 6 months.

The *Weiss* case focused on general and special courts-martial and appeals from those courts. The above sections from the RCM describe special and general courts-martial, as well. The following case discusses a forum, the summary court-martial, that is entirely unique to the military and considers the constitutionality of procedures used at that forum.

MIDDENDORF, SECRETARY OF THE NAVY V. HENRY
SUPREME COURT OF THE UNITED STATES
425 U.S. 25
MARCH 24, 1976
Opinion: Justice Rehnquist

In February 1973 plaintiffs—then enlisted members of the United States Marine Corps—brought this class action in the United States District Court for the Central District of California challenging the authority of the military to try them at summary courts-martial without providing them with counsel.

The UCMJ provides four methods for disposing of

cases involving offenses committed by servicemen: the general, special, and summary courts-martial, and disciplinary punishment administered by the commanding officer pursuant to Art. 15, UCMJ. General and special courts-martial resemble judicial proceedings, nearly always presided over by lawyer judges with lawyer counsel for both the prosecution and the defense. General courts-martial are authorized to award any lawful sentence, including death. Special courts-martial may award a bad-conduct discharge, up to six months' confinement at hard labor, forfeiture of two-thirds pay per month for six months, and in the case of an enlisted member, reduction to the lowest pay grade. Article 15 punishment, conducted personally by the accused's commanding officer, is an administrative method of dealing with the most minor offenses.

The summary court-martial occupies a position between informal nonjudicial disposition under Art. 15 and the courtroom-type procedure of the general and special courts-martial. Its purpose is to exercise justice promptly for relatively minor offenses under a simple form of procedure. It is an informal proceeding conducted by a single commissioned officer with jurisdiction only over noncommissioned officers and other enlisted personnel. The presiding officer acts as judge, fact finder, prosecutor, and defense counsel. The presiding officer must inform the accused of the charges and the name of the accuser and call all witnesses whom he or the accused desires to call. The accused must consent to trial by summary court-martial; if he does not do so, trial may be ordered by special or general court-martial.

The record of the trial is then reviewed by the convening officer and thereafter by a judge advocate.

The maximum sentence elements which may be imposed by summary courts-martial are: one month's confinement at hard labor; 45 days' hard labor without confinement; two months' restriction to specified limits; reduction to the lowest enlisted pay grade; and forfeiture of two-thirds pay for one month.

The question of whether an accused in a court-martial has a constitutional right to counsel has been much debated and never squarely resolved.

A summary court-martial is procedurally quite different from a criminal trial. In the first place, it is not an adversary proceeding. Yet the adversary nature of

civilian criminal proceedings is one of the touchstones of the Sixth Amendment's right to counsel.

The function of the presiding officer is quite different from that of any participant in a civilian trial. He is guided by the admonition in 79a of the MCM:

> The function of a summary court-martial is to exercise justice promptly for relatively minor offenses under a simple form of procedure. The summary court will thoroughly and impartially inquire into both sides of the matter and will assure that the interests of both the Government and the accused are safeguarded.

The presiding officer is more specifically enjoined to attend to the interests of the accused by these provisions of the same paragraph:

> The accused will be extended the right to cross-examine these witnesses. The summary court will aid the accused in the cross-examination, and, if the accused desires, will ask questions suggested by the accused. On behalf of the accused, the court will obtain the attendance of witnesses, administer the oath and examine them, and obtain such other evidence as may tend to disprove or negative guilt of the charges, explain the acts or omissions charged, show extenuating circumstances, or establish grounds for mitigation. Before determining the findings, he will explain to the accused his right to testify on the merits or to remain silent and will give the accused full opportunity to exercise his election.

We believe there are significant parallels between probation and parole revocation proceedings and the summary court-martial, which parallels tend to distinguish both of these proceedings from a civilian misdemeanor prosecution. When we consider in addition that the court-martial proceeding takes place not in civilian society, as does the parole revocation proceeding, but in the military community with all of its distinctive qualities, we conclude that a summary court-martial is not a "criminal prosecution" for purposes of the Sixth Amendment.

The Court of Appeals likewise concluded that there was no Sixth Amendment right to counsel in summary court-martial proceedings such as this, but applied due process standards of the Fifth Amendment which would have made the right to counsel depend upon the nature of the serviceman's defense. We are unable to agree that the Court of Appeals properly applied the standard in this military context.

We recognize that plaintiffs, who have either been convicted or are due to appear before a summary court-martial, may be subjected to loss of liberty or property, and consequently are entitled to the due process of law guaranteed by the Fifth Amendment. However, whether this process embodies a right to counsel depends upon an analysis of the interests of the individual and those of the regime to which he is subject.

In making such an analysis we must give particular deference to the determination of Congress, made under its authority to regulate the land and naval forces, that counsel should not be provided in summary courts-martial. As we held in *Burns v. Wilson,* 346 U.S. 137, 140 (1953):

> The rights of men in the armed forces must perforce be conditioned to meet certain overriding demands of discipline and duty, and the civil courts are not the agencies which must determine the precise balance to be struck in this adjustment. The Framers especially entrusted that task to Congress.

We thus need only decide whether the factors militating in favor of counsel at summary courts-martial are so extraordinarily weighty as to overcome the balance struck by Congress.

We first consider the effect of providing counsel at summary courts-martial. As we observed in *Gagnon v. Scarpelli,* 411 U.S. 778, 787 (1973):

> The introduction of counsel into a . . . proceeding will alter significantly the nature of the proceeding. If counsel is provided for the [accused], the State in turn will normally provide its own counsel; lawyers, by training and disposition, are advocates and bound by professional duty to present all available evidence and arguments in support of their clients' positions and to contest with vigor all adverse evidence and views.

In short, presence of counsel will turn a brief, informal hearing which may be quickly convened and rapidly concluded into an attenuated proceeding which consumes the resources of the military to a degree which Congress could properly have felt to be beyond

what is warranted by the relative insignificance of the offenses being tried. Such a lengthy proceeding is a particular burden to the armed forces because virtually all the participants, including the defendant and his counsel, are members of the military whose time may be better spent than in possibly protracted disputes over the imposition of discipline.

But if the accused has such a claim, if he feels that in order to properly air his views and vindicate his rights, a formal, counseled proceeding is necessary, he may simply refuse trial by summary court-martial and proceed to trial by special or general court-martial at which he may have counsel. Article 38(b), UCMJ, provides:

> The accused has the right to be represented in his defense before a general or special court-martial by civilian counsel if provided by him, or by military counsel of his own selection if reasonably available, or by the defense counsel detailed under Section 827 of this title.

It is true that by exercising this option the accused subjects himself to greater possible penalties imposed in the special court-martial proceeding. However, we do not find that possible detriment to be constitutionally decisive. We have frequently approved the much more difficult decision, daily faced by civilian criminal defendants, to plead guilty to a lesser included offense. In such a case the defendant gives up not only his right to counsel but his right to any trial at all. Furthermore, if he elects to exercise his right to trial he stands to be convicted of a more serious offense which will likely bear increased penalties. Such choices are a necessary part of the criminal justice system.

We therefore agree with the defendants that neither the Sixth nor the Fifth Amendment to the United States Constitution empowers us to overturn the congressional determination that counsel is not required in summary courts-martial.

Do you concur with the court's decision regarding defense counsel at summary courts-martial? What is the military's justification for not providing an attorney at such a proceeding? Generally, junior line officers sit as summary courts-martial. Would you have a difficult time wearing all the "hats" required of a

	SCM	SPCM	GCM
Jurisdiction	Minor offenses; enlisted only; voluntary	Non-capital or capital crimes if mandatory sentence does not exceed punishment limits	Non-capital or capital crimes
Composition	Summary court officer (commissioned officer, O–3 or above, same armed force)	MJ; TC; DC; at least three members NOTE: The accused may request trial by MJ alone rather than members	MJ; TC; DC; at least 4 members NOTE: In non-capital cases the accused may request trial by MJ alone rather than members
Standard of proof	Beyond reasonable doubt	Beyond reasonable doubt; 2/3 majority	Beyond reasonable doubt; 2/3 majority (3/4 majority for confinement greater than 10 years; unanimous for death penalty)
Counsel rights	No representation by military counsel	Representation by detailed military lawyer *or* requested military lawyer *and* civilian lawyer at your own expense	Representation by detailed military lawyer *or* requested military lawyer *and* civilian lawyer at your own expense
Maximum permissible punishment; enlisted	Confinement × 30 days (E-4 and below); reduction in rate to E-1 (E-5 and above only one paygrade); forfeitures of 2/3 pay per month for 1 month	Lesser of maximum permissible for offense or BCD; CHL × 6 months; forfeiture of 2/3 pay per month for 6 months; reduction in rate to E-1	Maximum permissible for the offense. This may include: death penalty DD, confinement for life; total forfeitures; reduction to E-1
Maximum permissible punishment; officer	Not applicable	Restriction × 60 days; forfeiture of 2/3 pay per month for 6 months; loss of lineal numbers	Maximum permissible for the offense. This may include: death penalty dismissal; confinement for life; total forfeitures; loss of lineal numbers

Figure 3-1 Courts-Martial Comparison

summary court officer (prosecutor, defense counsel, judge)?

In *United States v. Booker,* 5 M.J. 238 (C.M.A. 1977), a divided Court of Military Appeals held that before a record of a summary court-martial could be admitted to escalate or aggravate the sentence at a special or general court-martial, the prosecution must show that the accused had been advised of the right to consult with independent counsel before opting for summary court-martial, and that the accused affirmatively and personally waived in writing his or her right to object to summary court-martial. The *Booker* decision thus established the practice of making counsel available to provide advice on whether to accept or refuse summary court-martial. For the application of *Booker* to nonjudicial punishment, see *United States v. Mathews* in chapter 4.

Weiss and *Middendorf* describe the military's court-martial system. Figure 3-1 above compares the three types of courts-martial.

Convening Courts-Martial

Authority to Convene Courts-Martial

Who has authority to convene courts-martial in the navy and Marine Corps? The JAG Manual provides specific guidance on this matter:

JAG Manual 0120
    a. General courts-martial. The Secretary of the Navy, acting under Article 22(a)(8), UCMJ, has authorized the following officers . . . to convene general courts-martial:

(1) All flag or general officers, or their immediate temporary successors, [and those superior to such officers] in command of units or activities of the Navy or Marine Corps.

b. Special courts-martial. The Secretary of the Navy, acting under Article 23(a)(7), UCMJ, has authorized the following officers . . . to convene special courts-martial:

(1) Commanding officers of all battalions and squadrons, including both regular and reserve Marine Corps commands.

(2) Any commander whose subordinates in the operational or administrative chain of command have authority to convene special courts-martial.

(3) All commanders and commanding officers of units and activities of the Navy.

c. Summary courts-martial. Those officers who are empowered to convene general and special courts-martial may convene summary courts-martial. In addition, the Secretary of the Navy has empowered all commanders, commanding officers, and officers in charge . . . to convene summary courts-martial.

May the authority to convene courts-martial be delegated? The RCM answers this question:

RCM Rule 504(b)(4): Delegation prohibited. The power to convene courts-martial may not be delegated.

Procedures for Convening Courts-Martial

CONVENING ORDERS

RCM 504(d) Convening orders.

(1) General and special courts-martial. A convening order for a general or special court-martial shall designate the type of court-martial and detail the members and may designate where the court-martial will meet.

(2) Summary courts-martial. A convening order for a summary court-martial shall designate that it is a summary court-martial and detail the summary court-martial, and may designate where the court-martial will meet.

Figure 3-2 provides an example of a convening order for a general court-martial.

---

20 October 1997

COMMANDER, NAVAL SURFACE FORCE ATLANTIC

NORFOLK, VIRGINIA

GENERAL COURT-MARTIAL CONVENING ORDER 51-94

A general court-martial is hereby convened. It may proceed at Naval Legal Service Office, Norfolk, Virginia, to try such persons as may properly be brought before it. The court will be constituted as follows:

MEMBERS

Captain Mark E. PERRAULT, U.S. Navy
Commander Robert J. DOONAN, U.S. Navy
Lieutenant Commander Joseph W. KINSEY, U.S. Navy
Lieutenant Commander Michael F. HAGEN, U.S. Navy
Lieutenant Richard H. ENDERLY, U.S. Navy
Ensign Kenneth G. TUEBNER, U.S. Naval Reserve
Chief Warrant Officer (CWO-2) Stanley C. S BOLLINGER, U.S. Navy

/S/
R. E. NICHOLSON
Vice Admiral, U.S. Navy
Commander, Naval Surface Force Atlantic

Figure 3-2

CONVENING GENERAL COURTS-MARTIAL

There are unique procedures for convening a general court-martial. The military does not have a grand jury process. Instead, a pretrial investigative procedure is used under Article 32, UCMJ:

Art. 32, UCMJ. Investigation

(a) No charge or specification may be referred to a general court-martial for trial until a thorough and impartial investigation of all the matters set forth therein has been made.

(b) The accused has the right to be represented at that investigation by counsel. Full opportunity shall be given to the accused to cross-examine witnesses against him if they are available and to present anything he may desire in his own behalf, either in defense or mitigation, and the investigation officer shall examine available witnesses requested by the accused.

RCM 405. Pretrial Investigation

(c) Who may direct investigation. An investigation may be directed under this rule by any court-martial convening authority.

RCM 407. Action by commander exercising general court-martial jurisdiction

(a) Disposition. When in receipt of charges, a commander exercising general court-martial jurisdiction may:

(1) Dismiss any charges;

(2) Forward charges (or, after dismissing charges, the matter) to a subordinate commander for disposition; . . .

(4) Refer charges to a summary court-martial or a special court-martial for trial; . . .

(6) Refer charges to a general court-martial.

Based on the above rules, a commanding officer who is not a general court-martial convening authority may not convene a general court-marital. How may such a commander have a case tried at general court-martial? Note that the general court-martial convening authority is not bound by the recommendation of the pretrial investigating officer. As noted above, the Article 32 pretrial investigation is essentially equivalent to the grand jury system used in civilian criminal law. Which procedure is most fair to the accused? Why does a commander with general court-martial convening authority have so many options available in disposing of charges? Compare this authority with the powers of commanders prior to the UCMJ. Has the power to dispose of cases diminished?

Jurisdiction

Generally

EX PARTE MILLIGAN
SUPREME COURT OF THE UNITED STATES
71 U.S. 2
DECEMBER, 1866 TERM
Opinion: Justice Davis

Lamdin P. Milligan, a citizen of the United States, and a resident and citizen of the State of Indiana, was arrested on the 5th day of October, 1864, at his home in the said State, by the order of Brevet Major-General Hovey, military commandant of the District of Indi-

ana, and by the same authority confined in a military prison, at or near Indianapolis, the capital of the State. On the 21st day of the same month, he was placed on trial before a "military commission," convened at Indianapolis, by order of the said general, upon the following charges; preferred by Major Burnett, judge advocate of the Northwestern Military Department, namely:

1. "Conspiracy against the government of the United States";

2. "Affording aid and comfort to rebels against the authority of the United States";

3. "Inciting insurrection";

4. "Disloyal practices"; and

5. "Violation of the laws of war."

Under each of these charges there were various specifications. The substance of them was, joining and aiding, at different times, between October, 1863, and August, 1864, a secret society known as the Order of American Knights or Sons of Liberty, for the purpose of overthrowing the government and duly constituted authorities of the United States; holding communication with the enemy; conspiring to seize munitions of war stored in the arsenals; to liberate prisoners of war; resisting the draft . . . "at a period of war and armed rebellion against the authority of the United States, at or near Indianapolis, in Indiana, a State within the military lines of the Army of the United States, and the theater of military operations, and which had been and was constantly threatened to be invaded by the enemy."

The controlling question in the case is this: Did the military commission have jurisdiction, legally, to try the accused? Milligan, not a resident of one of the rebellious states, or a prisoner of war, but a citizen of Indiana for twenty years past, and never in the military or naval service, is, while at his home, arrested by the military power of the United States, imprisoned, and, on certain criminal charges preferred against him, tried, convicted, and sentenced to be hanged by a military commission, organized under the direction of the military commander of the military district of Indiana. Had this tribunal the legal power and authority to try and punish this man?

No graver question was ever considered by this court, nor one which more nearly concerns the rights of the whole people; for it is the birthright of every American citizen when charged with crime, to be tried and punished according to law. The power of punishment is, alone through the means which the laws have provided for that purpose, and if they are ineffectual, there is an immunity from punishment, no matter how great an offender the individual may be, or how much his crimes may have shocked the sense of justice of the country, or endangered its safety. By the protection of the law human rights are secured; withdraw that protection, and they are at the mercy of wicked rulers, or the clamor of an excited people. If there was law to justify this military trial, it is not our province to interfere; if there was not, it is our duty to declare the nullity of the whole proceedings. The decision of this question does not depend on argument or judicial precedents, numerous and highly illustrative as they are. These precedents inform us of the extent of the struggle to preserve liberty and to relieve those in civil life from military trials.

It is claimed that martial law covers with its broad mantle the proceedings of this military commission. The proposition is this: that in a time of war the commander of an armed force (if in his opinion the exigencies of the country demand it, and of which he is to judge), has the power, within the lines of his military district, to suspend all civil rights and their remedies, and subject citizens as well as soldiers to the rule of his will; and in the exercise of his lawful authority cannot be restrained, except by his superior officer or the president of the United States.

If this position is sound to the extent claimed, then when war exists, foreign or domestic, and the country is subdivided into military departments for mere convenience, the commander of one of them can, if he chooses, within his limits, on the plea of necessity, with the approval of the Executive, substitute military force for and to the exclusion of the laws, and punish all persons, as he thinks right and proper, without fixed or certain rules.

This nation, as experience has proved, cannot always remain at peace, and has no right to expect that it will always have wise and humane rulers, sincerely attached to the principles of the Constitution. Wicked men, ambitious of power, with hatred of liberty and contempt of law, may fill the place once occupied by Washington and Lincoln; and if this right is conceded, and the calamities of war again befall us, the dangers to human liberty are frightful to contemplate. If our fathers had failed to provide for just such a contingency, they would have been false to the trust reposed in them. They knew—the history of the world told them—the nation they were founding, be its existence short or long, would be involved in war; how often or how long continued, human foresight could not tell; and that unlimited power, wherever lodged at such a time, was especially hazardous to freemen. For this, and other equally weighty reasons, they secured the inheritance they had fought to maintain, by incorporating in a written constitution the safeguards which time had proved were essential to its preservation. Not one of these safeguards can the president, or Congress, or the judiciary disturb, except the one concerning the writ of habeas corpus.

It is essential to the safety of every government that, in a great crisis, like the one we have just passed through, there should be a power somewhere of suspending the writ of habeas corpus. In every war, there are men of previously good character, wicked enough to counsel their fellow-citizens to resist the measures deemed necessary by a good government to sustain its just authority and overthrow its enemies; and their influence may lead to dangerous combinations. In the emergency of the times, an immediate public investigation according to law may not be possible; and yet, the peril to the country may be too imminent to suffer such persons to go at large. Unquestionably, there is then an exigency which demands that the government, if it should see fit in the exercise of a proper discretion to make arrests, should not be required to produce the persons arrested in answer to a writ of habeas corpus. The Constitution goes no further. It does not say after a writ of habeas corpus is denied a citizen, that he shall be tried otherwise than by the course of the common law; if it had intended this result, it was easy by the use of direct words to have accomplished it. The illustrious men who framed that instrument were guarding the foundations of civil liberty against the abuses of unlimited power; they were full of wisdom, and the lessons of history informed them that a trial by an established court, assisted by an impartial jury, was the only sure way of protecting the citizen against oppression and wrong. Knowing this, they limited the suspension to one great right, and left the rest to remain forever inviolable. But, it is insisted that the safety of the country in time of war demands that this broad claim for martial law shall be sustained. If this were true, it could be well said that a country, preserved at the sacrifice of all the cardinal principles of liberty, is not worth the cost of preservation. Happily, it is not so.

It will be borne in mind that this is not a question of the power to proclaim martial law, when war exists in a community and the courts and civil authorities are overthrown. Nor is it a question what rule a military commander, at the head of his army, can impose on states in rebellion to cripple their resources and quell the insurrection. The jurisdiction claimed is much more extensive. The necessities of the service, during the late Rebellion, required that the loyal states should be placed within the limits of certain military districts and commanders appointed in them; and, it is urged, that this, in a military sense, constituted them the theater of military operations; and, as in this case, Indiana had been and was again threatened with invasion by the enemy, the occasion was furnished to establish martial law. The conclusion does not follow from the premises. If armies were collected in Indiana, they were to be employed in another locality, where the laws were obstructed and the national authority disputed. On her soil there was no hostile foot; if once invaded, that invasion was at an end, and with it all pretext for martial law. Martial law cannot arise from a threatened invasion. The necessity must be actual and present; the invasion real, such as effectually closes the courts and deposes the civil administration.

It is proper to say, although Milligan's trial and conviction by a military commission was illegal, yet, if guilty of the crimes imputed to him, and his guilt had been ascertained by an established court and impartial jury, he deserved severe punishment. Open resistance to the measures deemed necessary to subdue a great rebellion, by those who enjoy the protection of government, and have not the excuse even of prejudice of section to plead in their favor, is wicked; but that resistance becomes an enormous crime when it assumes the form of a secret political organization, armed to oppose the

laws, and seeks by stealthy means to introduce the enemies of the country into peaceful communities, there to light the torch of civil war, and thus overthrow the power of the United States. Conspiracies like these, at such a juncture, are extremely perilous; and those concerned in them are dangerous enemies to their country, and should receive the heaviest penalties of the law, as an example to deter others from similar criminal conduct. It is said the severity of the laws caused them; but Congress was obliged to enact severe laws to meet the crisis; and as our highest civil duty is to serve our country when in danger, the late war has proved that rigorous laws, when necessary, will be cheerfully obeyed by a patriotic people, struggling to preserve the rich blessings of a free government.

The military trial of Milligan was contrary to law. He was entitled to be discharged from custody.

Why did the military tribunal not have jurisdiction over Milligan? The discussion in *Milligan* discloses the limited nature of courts-martial jurisdiction under the law of the United States. The following section from the MCM sets forth the general requirements for jurisdiction of courts-martial today:

RCM 201. Jurisdiction in general
(a) Nature of courts-martial jurisdiction.
(1) The jurisdiction of courts-martial is entirely penal or disciplinary.
(2) The code applies in all places.
(3) The jurisdiction of a court-martial with respect to offenses under the code is not affected by the place where the court-martial sits. The jurisdiction of a court-martial with respect to military government or the law of war is not affected by the place where the court-martial sits except as otherwise expressly required by this Manual or applicable rule of international law.
(b) Requisites of court-martial jurisdiction. A court-martial always has jurisdiction to determine whether it has jurisdiction. Otherwise for a court-martial to have jurisdiction:
(1) The court-martial must be convened by an official empowered to convene it;
(2) The court-martial must be composed in accor-

dance with these rules with respect to number and qualifications of its personnel. As used here "personnel" includes only the military judge, the members, and the summary court-martial;

(3) Each charge before the court-martial must be referred to it by competent authority;

(4) The accused must be a person subject to court-martial jurisdiction; and

(5) The offense must be subject to court-martial jurisdiction.

RCM 201(b) sets forth the five prerequisites for a court-martial to have jurisdiction over a case. Convening courts-martial is discussed in the preceding section. The proper composition of courts-martial is discussed below. Referral of charges to a particular court-martial rests with commanders who have authority to convene the type of court-martial at which the charged is to be tried. The final two conditions, jurisdiction over the person and offense, are discussed in the next two subsections.

Jurisdiction over the Accused

STATUS OF ACCUSED

The following UCMJ provision describes those individuals subject to jurisdiction of courts-martial:

Article 2, UCMJ. Persons subject to this chapter
(a) The following persons are subject to this chapter:
(1) Members of a regular component of the armed forces.
(2) Cadets, aviation cadets, and midshipmen.
(3) Members of a reserve component while on inactive-duty training.
(4) Retired members of a regular component of the armed forces who are entitled to pay. . . .
(7) Persons in custody of the armed forces serving a sentence imposed by a court-martial. . . .
(9) Prisoners of war in custody of the armed forces.

The jurisdiction of the military begins when a service member begins active duty. Hence reserve personnel are subject to court-martial for offenses committed while on active duty. When does court-martial jurisdiction terminate? The discussion to RCM 202 explains:

Termination of jurisdiction over active duty personnel. The delivery of a valid discharge certificate or its equivalent ordinarily serves to terminate court-martial jurisdiction.

Does the military have jurisdiction over a service member who commits an offense during a prior enlistment? The following case addresses this issue.

HIRSHBERG V. COOKE, COMMANDING OFFICER
UNITED STATES SUPREME COURT
336 U.S. 210
FEBRUARY 28, 1949
Opinion: Justice Black

This case raises important questions concerning the statutory jurisdiction of general courts-martial of the navy.

In 1942 the accused was serving a second enlistment in the navy. Upon the surrender of the United States forces on Corregidor the accused became a war prisoner of Japan. After liberation in September, 1945, the accused was brought back to the United States and hospitalized. He was restored to duty in January, 1946. March 26, 1946, he was granted an honorable discharge because of expiration of his prior enlistment. The next day he re-enlisted, obligating himself to serve four years "subject to such laws, regulations, and articles for the government of the navy as are or shall be established by the Congress . . . or other competent authority."

About a year later, the accused was served with charges directing his trial by a general court-martial of the navy. The specifications included charges that during his prior enlistment the petitioner had maltreated two other naval enlisted men who were also Japanese prisoners of war and who were members of groups of prisoners working under petitioner's charge. The accused filed a plea in bar of the trial, one ground being that the court-martial was without jurisdiction to try him for alleged offenses committed during a prior enlistment at the end of which he had received an honorable discharge. His plea was overruled. The accused then brought this habeas corpus proceeding in a federal district court charging that the court-martial judgment was void because of want of statutory power to convict him for an offense committed if at all during his prior enlistment.

Court-martial authority to try and to punish petitioner for his prior enlistment conduct primarily depends on the language in Article 8 of the Articles for the Government of the Navy, which particularly provides that "such punishment as a court-martial may adjudge may be inflicted on any person in the navy . . . guilty of . . . maltreatment of, any person subject to his orders. . . ." The government contends that this language given its literal meaning authorized the court-martial to try and to punish petitioner for conduct during a prior enlistment. It is pointed out that the accused was "in the navy" when the offense was committed and when he was tried; this language it is argued brings his case under the Article. In aid of this interpretation the government emphasizes that during the whole period of time involved, the accused was continuously "in the navy" except for an interval of a few hours between his honorable discharge and his re-enlistment.

Obviously Article 8, which subjects to court-martial jurisdiction persons "in the navy," supports an argument that the accused was subject to trial by this court-martial. It is equally obvious that the language of Article 8 supports an argument that this court-martial could not try the accused for an offense committed prior to his honorable discharge. Under these circumstances the manner in which court-martial jurisdiction has long been exercised by the army and navy is entitled to great weight in interpreting the Articles.

The question of the jurisdiction of a naval court-martial over discharged personnel was submitted by the secretary of the navy to the attorney general in 1919. The precise question of whether re-enlistment could revive jurisdiction of a military court was not considered, but as to the power of military courts over discharged personnel in general the attorney general reached the conclusion that a person discharged from the navy before proceedings were instituted against him "for violations of the Articles Governing the Navy" could not "thereafter be brought to trial . . . for such violations, though committed while he was in the service." 31 Op.

Atty. Gen. 521, 529. This conclusion of the attorney general relied on statements of the judge advocate generals of the army and navy that their offices had "from the beginning and uniformly held that a person separated from the service ceases to be amenable" to military and naval jurisdiction. Previous to the attorney general's 1919 opinion neither the navy nor army had ever claimed court-martial power to try their personnel for offenses committed prior to an honorable discharge where proceedings had not been instituted before discharge. The government concedes that the army has always so construed its court-martial jurisdiction whenever the question arose. And the government concedes that the navy also followed this view of its jurisdiction until 1932.

This revised naval interpretation was given in 1932. Before that time, both army and navy had for more than half a century acted on the implicit assumption that discharged servicemen, whether re-enlisted or not, were no longer subject to court-martial power. The attorney general of the United States had proceeded on the same assumption. Under these circumstances, little weight can be given to the 1932 separate effort of the navy to change the long-accepted understanding of its statutory court-martial power. For should this belated naval interpretation be accepted as correct, there would be left outstanding an army interpretation of its statutory court-martial powers directly opposed to that of the navy. Since the army and navy court-martial powers depend on substantially the same statutory foundations, the opposing interpretations cannot both be right, unless it be assumed that Congress has left each free to determine its own court-martial boundaries. We cannot assume that Congress intended a delegation of such broad power in an area which so vitally affects the rights and liberties of those who are now, have been, or may be associated with the Nation's armed forces.

Does is seem equitable that Chief Hirshberg was not subject to court-martial jurisdiction even though he was still on active duty? The case was a focal point of the legislative hearings on enactment of the UCMJ. The following discussion regarding *Hirshberg* took place during the House of Representatives hearings:

Mr. Elston. I would like to ask you this question. I think it was since you completed your hearings that a case has been decided by the Supreme Court of the United States.

Dr. Morgan. The Hirschberg [*sic*] case?

Mr. Elston. Yes. To the effect that person who has left the service, that is, who has been separated from the service, cannot be tried subsequently by a military court for an offense committed prior to such separation.

Mr. Kilday. Even though he has reenlisted?

Mr. Elston. Even though he has reenlisted?

Dr. Morgan. That is right.

Mr. Elston. Now, you have not anything in your bill covering that . . . [even though he] may have even committed a murder within 3 days of his separation from the service?

Dr. Morgan. That is right. We have not covered that.

Mr. Elston. He reenlists and cannot be tried for it.

Dr. Morgan. That is right.

Mr. Elston. I think this committee can write something into the law that will take care of that ridiculous situation.

In light of *Hirshberg,* Congress enacted the following UCMJ provision:

Art. 3. Jurisdiction to try certain personnel

A person who is in a status in which the person is subject to this chapter and who committed an offense against this chapter while formerly in a status in which the person was subject to this chapter is not relieved from amenability to the jurisdiction of this chapter for that offense by reason of a termination of that person's former status.

The above provision is limited in scope in that it only applies to serious offenses and in situations in which other federal or state courts do not have jurisdiction to try the case. *United States v. Clardy,* 13 M.J. 308 (C.M.A. 1982), finally resolved the issue of whether a service member could be tried for offenses committed during a prior enlistment where there was no break in active service. *Clardy* held that court-martial jurisdiction exists over a service member who

is discharged solely for the purpose of reenlistment and his military status in the active service did not change.

FORMER JEOPARDY

"Former jeopardy" (also commonly termed "double jeopardy") prohibits the retrial of an accused for the same offense by the same authority. Consider the application of the former jeopardy rule in the following case.

UNITED STATES V. DAVID P. SCHNEIDER, MAJOR U.S. ARMY
UNITED STATES COURT OF MILITARY APPEALS
38 M.J. 387
SEPTEMBER 30, 1993
Opinion: Ryan, Circuit Judge

A general court-martial sitting at Fort Leavenworth, Kansas, convicted appellant, Major David P. Schneider, of attempted premeditated murder, conduct unbecoming an officer by committing adultery, and conduct unbecoming an officer by committing perjury in a state court, in violation of Articles 80 and 133, UCMJ, respectively.

In 1987, appellant moved to California with his wife and two children, pursuant to his assignment to the Lawrence Livermore National Laboratory. At the Laboratory, he worked with a woman named Paula, and by April 1989, their relationship had become sexual.

In 1989 appellant was assigned to attend the U.S. Army Command and General Staff College at Fort Leavenworth, Kansas, and moved with his family into government quarters there. In August 1989, he met with an insurance agent and purchased an additional $150,000 in life insurance coverage on his wife. He was the beneficiary of this policy, which had an effective date of October 1, 1989. That same summer, appellant sold the former family home in California and used the proceeds to purchase a home in Tracy, California; he convinced his wife that her name should not be on the deed. He then spent Labor Day weekend with Paula in California.

The incident out of which the specification of attempted murder arose occurred on October 20, 1989.

That night, appellant's wife awoke with intense pain in her head and was pulled to a sitting position in her bed. She saw appellant, visibly shaken, standing next to the bed. The toilet tank lid from the bathroom lay broken on the floor near his feet. She felt a baseball-sized lump on her head, which was "oozing." She brushed small pieces of porcelain from her hair. He then assisted her to the bathroom, and she sat on the toilet. When she began shaking, he helped her to the bathroom floor and covered her with a quilt. Appellant told his wife, repeatedly, "You must have hit your head." Although appellant suggested taking her to a doctor, his wife wanted only to go back to bed. The next morning, he took her to the medical facility and there told medical personnel that Debbie was sleepwalking, picked up the toilet tank lid, tripped, and hit her head. Other evidence at trial, however, indicated that his wife had never walked in her sleep.

Two weeks later, on November 4, appellant and his wife were to attend the Armor Ball. Appellant made arrangements for a "romantic" night at Embassy Suites Hotel. At appellant's insistence, he and his wife left prior to the end of the ball in order to go to the hotel. Upon arriving, appellant learned that, although he had asked for an eighth-floor room when making reservations, he was given a room on the seventh floor instead.

They nonetheless took the elevator to the eighth floor, where they were observed by two 16-year-old girls. The girls saw appellant and his wife walk side by side down the hallway. One girl then saw appellant make vigorous hand movements in front of his wife as she faced him with her back to a rail overlooking an interior courtyard. The girl observed appellant put his left arm around his wife at the point where the rail met her back, put his right hand on her chest, and flip her over the rail. The wife fell some 70 or 80 feet, and hit a table on the atrium floor. The girl watched appellant look over the railing, say nothing ("he didn't yell for someone to call an ambulance"), then walk to the elevator, and walk back to the railing. He then walked back to the elevator and proceeded down. When he reached the atrium floor, appellant was cool and collected. His wife's pelvis was fractured in thirteen places; both left and right femurs were broken in several places; a bone

penetrated her abdominal cavity, damaging her colon; and an ankle and several ribs were fractured.

On December 4, one month after the ball and two days after his wife returned home from the hospital, appellant told his wife that he did not love her any more and was getting a divorce. On December 5, he admitted to police that he had had an affair with Paula and that he loved her and hoped to marry her when his divorce was final.

Appellant was charged by state authorities with first-degree assault, in violation of Section 565.050, Revised Statutes of Missouri, for the incident at the Embassy Suites Hotel. At the state trial, appellant testified that the incident at the Embassy Suites Hotel occurred when he attempted to carry his wife across the threshold. He picked her up and was carrying her at high port when she told him that they were on the wrong floor. He then turned and tripped; his wife slipped from his grasp, causing her to fall over the balcony railing to the atrium floor. He testified that he did not intend to injure his wife. He was acquitted.

Shortly after the state case was concluded, military authorities charged appellant with specifications of attempted premeditated murder, conduct unbecoming an officer by committing adultery, and conduct unbecoming an officer by committing perjury. A court consisting of officer members found appellant guilty and sentenced him to dismissal, confinement for 23 years, and total forfeitures. The convening authority approved the sentence, except that he suspended forfeitures in excess of $400 pay per month until execution of the dismissal, provided that the suspended forfeitures be paid to appellant's now ex-wife.

The issue we consider is appellant's contention that his prosecution for conduct unbecoming an officer by wrongfully . . . testifying falsely under lawful oath before a jury sitting in the Platte County, Missouri, District Court was a violation of double jeopardy.

Appellant complains that in prosecuting him for falsely testifying, the military is merely attempting to do indirectly what it cannot do directly. We disagree. Plainly, the Fifth Amendment would have permitted the military to reprosecute appellant directly for first-degree assault or an equivalent offense under the Uniform Code of Military Justice. The Double Jeopardy Clause does not bar one sovereign from proceeding on a charge of which an accused has been acquitted by another sovereign. Since appellant could have been reprosecuted by the military for first-degree assault or its equivalent, he clearly could be prosecuted for the entirely separate offense of conduct unbecoming an officer, which was committed at a wholly distinct place and time.

Appellant's subordinate contention that his prosecution for falsely testifying was barred by army policy also fails. Para. 4-2, Army Regulation 27-10, *Military Justice,* provides the general rule:

> A person subject to the UCMJ who has been tried in a civilian court may, but ordinarily will not be tried by court-martial or punished under Article 15, UCMJ, for the same act over which the civilian court has exercised jurisdiction.

Paragraph 4-3 of the same regulation provides, however, that an officer exercising general court-martial jurisdiction may authorize disposition of a case under the UCMJ and the MCM despite a previous trial. The general court-martial convening authority here personally authorized appellant's trial on the falsely-testifying specification, after the requisite findings were made. And, as already pointed out, appellant was not, in any event, prosecuted for "the same act" for which he was tried by the State of Missouri. Thus, the military was in full compliance with its policy. There was no bar to appellant's prosecution for falsely testifying at his civilian trial, so the issue is without merit.

The following provision of the RCM specifically addresses jurisdiction over uniquely military crimes and discusses the former jeopardy principle:

RCM 201:
> (d) Exclusive and nonexclusive jurisdiction.
> (1) Courts-martial have exclusive jurisdiction of purely military offenses.
> (2) An act or omission which violates both the code and local criminal law, foreign or domestic, may be tried by a court-martial, or by a proper civilian tribunal, foreign or domestic, or, subject to regulations of the secretary concerned, by both.
> (3) Where an act or omission is subject to trial by court-martial and by one or more civil tribunals,

foreign or domestic, the determination which nation, state, or agency will exercise jurisdiction is a matter for the nations, states, and agencies concerned, and is not a right of the suspect or accused.

For former jeopardy to apply, the accused must be tried by the same authority. Courts-martial are under the authority of the United States and, therefore, may not retry members previously tried in other U.S. federal courts (military or civilian). Trials by the courts of a state or foreign country, however, are not under federal authority and will not bar subsequent trial by courts-martial. Nonetheless, the services have a policy to limit trial by courts-martial of members previously tried by state or foreign courts for the same offense to those unusual cases in which punishment imposed by the military is considered essential in the interests of justice, discipline, and proper administration within the military. Is *Schneider* the type of case contemplated by such a policy?

Jurisdiction over the Offense

UNITED STATES V. PRIVATE JOHN W. MAUCK, U.S. ARMY
UNITED STATES ARMY COURT OF MILITARY REVIEW
17 M.J. 1033
APRIL 16, 1984
Opinion: Yawn, Judge

Appellant is before this Court convicted of larceny, maiming, forcible sodomy and attempted murder, violations of Articles 121, 124, 125, and 80, UCMJ, respectively. He argues that the court-martial lacked jurisdiction over the subject matter of the charged offenses since they occurred off-post.

On or about 4 January 1982 Billy Ray Hutcherson and John W. Mauck reported to Redstone Arsenal, Alabama. Hutcherson and Mauck were assigned to the 8th Student Company. Several days after reporting to Redstone Arsenal, Mauck and Hutcherson became acquainted with each other. Prior to 22 January 1982, their acquaintance had grown into a friendship. Not long after coming to Redstone Arsenal, Hutcherson met Julie [F.], the dependent daughter of a military retiree. Julie's family lives only a short distance from the

Redstone Arsenal boundary line, near Gate 5. Julie had many friends who were service members. Moreover, Julie frequented and socialized at the Enlisted Man's Club and at other locations on Redstone Arsenal. On various occasions Julie talked with Hutcherson at the Enlisted Man's Club. Their acquaintance soon blossomed into an intimate friendship. Their resulting sexual acts all occurred at Redstone Arsenal. On the night of 21 January 1982, Hutcherson and Julie engaged in sexual intercourse in the 8th Student Company billets. On the morning of 22 January, Hutcherson may have told Mauck about the sexual affair that had occurred the previous evening with Julie. On the afternoon of 22 January, Mauck met Julie through his friend Hutcherson. Plans were made to go out on the town in Huntsville, Alabama, the evening of 22 January 1982. Since Mauck did not have a date, and since he was a good friend of Hutcherson, Julie agreed to arrange a blind date for Mauck. On the same afternoon of 22 January 1982, Mauck drove Julie to her home while Hutcherson showered and changed into civilian clothes. Upon returning to post, the three of them, all dressed in civilian clothing, went to dinner at the unit mess hall where they met service members Buck, a friend of Mauck and Hutcherson, and Linda [G.], a friend of Julie's. After dinner the five of them went to the Enlisted Man's Club where they consumed beer and danced. Some time later, all five left the Enlisted Man's Club and went to a local beverage store off post and purchased two quarts of Jack Daniels which they passed around inside the car. The party then went to the Sunshine Lounge, Huntsville, Alabama, where they continued to drink Jack Daniels. About midnight, Mauck learned that his blind date was not going to show up and he became very enraged. Consequently, Mauck and Hutcherson decided to drive Julie [F.] home. While en route Mauck and Hutcherson continued to argue with and execrate Julie for the failure of his blind date to show up. The argument became so intensified that Julie got out of the car twice. Finally, Mauck drove to an abandoned road approximately 15 feet outside the boundary line of Redstone Arsenal, at secured Gate 5. All parties exited the car, leaving the lights on. It was here that Julie was sodomized and brutally and violently beaten. Mauck and Hutcherson left Julie's naked, beaten, maimed, and

bloody body in the freezing rain. They believed Julie was dead. After everything occurred at Gate 5, Mauck and Hutcherson returned to Redstone Arsenal. On 3 February 1982, Mauck and Hutcherson were arrested by the Huntsville Police Department. On 19 February 1982, Mauck and Hutcherson were indicted by the Madison County Grand Jury for assault and sodomy of Julie [F.]. On 5 May 1982, Hutcherson was tried in the circuit court of Madison County and found guilty of assault in the second degree and sexual abuse in the second degree. Hutcherson was sentenced to serve fifteen years at hard labor in the Alabama penitentiary. In early July 1982, the District Attorney's Office of Madison County decided not to prosecute Mauck's case.

The basic law on this issue is found in *Relford v. Commandant,* 401 U.S. 355 (1971), and *O'Callahan v. Parker,* 395 U.S. 258, 89 S. Ct. 1683, 23 L. Ed. 2d 291 (1969). In *O'Callahan,* the Supreme Court held that courts-martial lack jurisdiction over the subject matter of an offense unless it is "service connected." Such jurisdiction was found lacking in *O'Callahan* because O'Callahan's offenses, attempted rape and related crimes, were committed off post while he was on pass and within the Territory of Hawaii; there was no connection between the offenses and his military duties; he was not in uniform; and his victim had no ties to the military. *Relford,* on the other hand, raped both a military dependent and an employee of the post-exchange on the post where he was stationed. A unanimous Court found the offenses service connected, and clarified *O'Callahan* by holding "that when a serviceman is charged with an offense committed within or at the geographical boundary of a military post and violative of the security of a person or of property there, that offense may be tried by a court-martial." The Court recognized, however, that some offenses perpetrated off post could be service connected, and, in particular, could include offenses committed upon or against civilians near a military post.

The border of a military post is not a demarcation line where court-martial jurisdiction ends. The fact that the appellant's crimes were not committed within the borders of Redstone Arsenal does not, when considered in the totality of the circumstances, exempt him from trial by court-martial. The appellant and his victim became acquainted as a result of his military status. Victim, a dependent daughter of a military retiree living just off the post, was a member of the military community. On the evening in question, they met and socialized on the post where the appellant was stationed, then left with other military personnel for additional socializing. Finally, after the offenses were committed, the appellant and his confederate returned to the post, leaving what they thought was a dead body "approximately 15 feet outside the boundary line" of the post.

We find that these offenses were committed "at the geographical boundary" of a military post and were violative of the security of persons therein, and that the appellant's conduct had a significant effect upon that enclave. We therefore hold jurisdiction existed and affirm the finding of guilt.

In *United States v. Solario,* 483 U.S. 435 (1987), the Supreme Court held that "jurisdiction of a court-martial depends solely upon the accused's status as a member of the armed forces, and not on the service-connection of the offense charged." Hence, the location of the offense is no longer a factor in deciding whether the military has jurisdiction. *Solario* significantly increased the number of cases that the military may try at courts-martial. Given this expanded jurisdiction, it is not surprising that the number of courts-martial cases grew rapidly following the *Solario* decision. However, the military drawdown caused by the end of the Cold War has since caused a downward spiral in the number of court-martial cases.

Trial Procedures

Participants at Courts-Martial

The RCM sets forth the personnel who make up a court-martial and their required qualifications:

Rule 502. Qualifications and duties of personnel of courts-martial

(a) Members.

(1) Qualifications. The members detailed to a court-martial shall be those persons who in the opinion of the convening authority are best quali-

fied for the duty by reason of their age, education, training, experience, length of service, and judicial temperament. Each member shall be on active duty with the armed forces and shall be:

(A) A commissioned officer;

(B) A warrant officer, except when the accused is a commissioned officer; or

(C) An enlisted person if the accused is an enlisted person and has made a timely request.

(2) Duties. The members of a court-martial shall determine whether the accused is proved guilty and, if necessary, adjudge a proper sentence, based on the evidence and in accordance with the instructions of the military judge. Each member has an equal voice and vote with other members in deliberating upon and deciding all matters submitted to them, except as otherwise specifically provided in these rules. No member may use rank or position to influence another member. No member of a court-martial may have access to or use in any open or closed session this Manual, reports of decided cases, or any other reference material, except the president of a special courts-martial without a military judge may use such materials in open session.

(b) President.

(1) Qualifications. The president of a court-martial shall be the detailed member senior in rank then serving.

(2) Duties. The president shall have the same duties as the other members and shall also:

(A) Preside over closed sessions of the members of the court-martial during their deliberations;

(B) Speak for the members of the court-martial when announcing the decision of the members or requesting instructions from the military judge; and

(C) In a special courts-martial without a military judge, perform the duties assigned by this Manual to the military judge except as otherwise expressly provided.

(c) Qualifications of military judge. A military judge shall be a commissioned officer on active duty in the armed forces who is a member of the bar of a Federal court or a member of the bar of the highest court of a State and who is certified to be qualified for duty as a military judge by the Judge Advocate General of the armed force of which the military judge is a member. In addition, the military judge of a general court-martial shall be designated for such duties by the Judge Advocate General or the Judge Advocate General's designee, certified to be qualified for duty as a military judge of a general court-martial, and assigned and directly responsible to the Judge Advocate General or the Judge Advocate General's designee. . . .

(d) Counsel.

(1) Certified counsel required. Only persons certified under Article 27(b) as competent to perform duties as counsel in courts-martial by the Judge Advocate General of the armed force of which the counsel is a member may be detailed as defense counsel or associate defense counsel in general or special courts-martial or as trial counsel in general courts-martial.

(2) Other military counsel. Any commissioned officer may be detailed as trial counsel in special courts-martial, or as assistant trial counsel or assistant defense counsel in general or special courts-martial. The Secretary concerned may establish additional qualifications for such counsel.

(3) Qualifications of individual military and civilian defense counsel. Individual military or civilian defense counsel who represents an accused in a court-martial shall be:

(A) A member of the bar of a Federal court or of the bar of the highest court of a State; or

(B) If not a member of such a bar, a lawyer who is authorized by a recognized licensing authority to practice law and is found by the military judge to be qualified to represent the accused upon a showing to the satisfaction of the military judge that the counsel has appropriate training and familiarity with the general principles of criminal law which apply in a court-martial.

The above rules apply only to general and special courts-martial. Summary courts are composed of one active-duty commissioned officer of the same armed force as the accused. See the section on Nature and Types of Courts-Martial and the *Middendorf* case

above for discussions of the procedures at summary courts-martial. Members (jurors) at general and special courts-martial are active-duty officers who are senior to the accused. Enlisted accused may elect to have one-third of the members be enlisted. Unlike most civilian jurisdictions, which require unanimous verdicts, only two-thirds of the panel have to agree on guilt or innocence. Note, however, where confinement may exceed ten years, a three-fourths majority is necessary, and, in capital cases, the verdict must be unanimous. See figure 3-1 for a comparison of the composition of members at special and general courts-martial.

RCM 502 above discusses the role and qualifications of defense counsel. The following case addresses the ethical responsibilities of defense counsel.

UNITED STATES V. PRIVATE ANGELA H. BRYANT, U.S. ARMY
UNITED STATES ARMY COURT OF MILITARY REVIEW
35 M.J. 739
SEPTEMBER 23, 1992
Opinion: Gravelle, Judge

Contrary to her pleas, the appellant was convicted by a military judge sitting as a special court-martial of two specifications of failing to go to her appointed place of duty, two specifications of disobeying the orders of a noncommissioned officer, and one specification of disrespect toward a noncommissioned officer, in violation of Articles 86 and 91.

In this case, we must decide whether the defense counsel's conduct in providing advice to his client regarding choice of forum, advice with which the counsel did not personally agree, amounted to ineffective assistance of counsel.

The appellant's court-martial occurred in Saudi Arabia. On appeal, she initially asserted that her defense counsel, MAJ D [then CPT D], was ineffective during the sentencing proceedings at trial and during the post-trial processing of this case. She has filed an affidavit with this court detailing her reasons for believing that her defense counsel was ineffective. The defense counsel has also filed an affidavit in reply. Based on these affidavits, the government has conceded that MAJ D was ineffective in his representation of the appellant during and after sentencing.

The defense counsel's affidavit also raised a troubling issue regarding his effectiveness during the pretrial phase involving a decision made by the appellant at trial. In his affidavit, the trial defense counsel asserted:

> Prior to trial, I made two trips out to the desert [in Saudi Arabia] where the 1st Armor [*sic*] Division was encamped to interview my client and prepare the case. I had no means of transportation nor communication and was forced to rely upon transportation provided by the 1st Armor [*sic*] Division. During these two visits, I focused my investigation on the guilt/innocence portion of the trial and expended a lot of energy attempting to convince the command to dispose of the charges either administratively or through nonjudicial punishment. . . .
>
> Despite my attempts to make the charges go away, I was notified several days prior to February 23, 1991 that we would be going to trial. I did not arrive at Log Base Echo until the late afternoon of February 22, 1991. The 1st Armor [*sic*] Division had just moved forward and it was well known that the ground war would be starting in the immediate future. Although I was well prepared for the guilt/innocence phase of the trial, I knew that I had done nothing to put together an extenuation and mitigation case.
>
> Moreover I was faced with a dilemma that I had never faced before—being torn between my loyalties as an officer and my loyalties as a defense counsel. I knew that the case against PVT Bryant was full of problems and that there was a chance for acquittal before a panel. I also knew that the ground war was to about start and that the 1st Armor [*sic*] Division needed each and every officer and noncommissioned officer to do their part. I am sorry to admit that CPT [D] the officer won over CPT [D] the defense counsel and I convinced PVT Bryant that she should choose to go judge alone. I knew that this was a classic case which warranted a panel. In fact, after trial the judge questioned me about why I did not go with a panel and indicated that he thought I would have done better with a panel. I gave my client advice which was in the best interest of the war effort and not in her best interest.

Appellate defense counsel, not surprisingly, assert that the trial defense counsel's actions amount to ineffective assistance of counsel. In addition, the appellant has submitted a new affidavit in which she asserts that MAJ D failed to call a number of witnesses to testify on the merits of the case on her behalf.

The government responds that we should not find ineffective assistance of counsel because it is human na-

ture for a defense counsel to second-guess his own decisions and trial tactics after an unfavorable trial result, that "speculation based on hindsight is not the proper standard" for determining whether MAJ D was ineffective, and that the advice was "not unreasonable under the circumstances and was well within professional norms." Assuming, arguendo, that the advice was erroneous, the government further argues that "the appellant was not prejudiced as a result of the counsel's actions because "the decision regarding forum was ultimately appellant's to make." Appellate government counsel argues that the record shows that the appellant knowingly, intelligently, freely, and unequivocally elected trial by military judge alone.

The Sixth Amendment right to counsel includes the right to effective representation of counsel. The appellant is entitled to effective representation of counsel before, during, and after trial. A counsel's performance is judged under standards set out in *Strickland v. Washington,* 466 U.S. 668 (1984), which are applicable in the military justice system. Under *Strickland,* a counsel's performance is presumed to be competent. To overcome this presumption, an appellant must point out specific errors made by his defense counsel that were unreasonable under prevailing professional norms.

We reject the government's arguments summarized above. We cannot agree that the defense counsel's advice to the appellant before trial was "not unreasonable under the circumstances and was well within professional norms." Nor can we agree that we should treat the contents of the defense counsel's affidavit as merely the product of human nature to second-guess his own performance and as "speculation based on hindsight." Finally, while the record of proceedings may ostensibly show that the appellant's choice of forum was knowingly, intelligently, and freely made, the defense counsel's affidavit shows the contrary. A component of a client's knowing and intelligent decisions prior to and at trial is the counsel's best advice, unencumbered by divided loyalties.

In our system of military justice, it is clear that the interests of the army are best served when the interests of the defense counsel's client are paramount in that counsel's mind. In the case before us, the defense counsel failed to understand, or lost sight of the fact, that a defense counsel's duty to the army is to provide his or her client with representation unclouded by the government's operational considerations.

We judicially note that the ground war against Iraq began during Operation Desert Storm on 24 February 1991, and that the First Armored Division was an active participant throughout. We also note that the trial of this case occurred on 23 February 1991. We find that the defense counsel's affidavit is believable, credible, and forthright, and we accept it as accurate. By the defense counsel's own admission, he placed what he perceived to be the army's interests over those of his client. We hold that the defense counsel provided ineffective assistance of counsel when he gave advice regarding the critical decision of choice of forum, advice that he himself did not agree with and which he was convinced was not in his client's best interest.

Do you agree that a military defense counsel's first obligation is to his or her client? Should operational commitments ever be taken into account by a defense counsel? Note that military defense counsel are members of various state and federal bars. Ethical violations on their part subject them to not only decertification as military attorneys but also to disciplinary action by their respective bars.

Sentencing

Following conviction of an accused at court-martial, a second phase of the trial, referred to as the "sentencing hearing," occurs. During this hearing, the court must decide on an appropriate sentence. The government and defense will usually introduce evidence during the sentencing phase that bears on the appropriate type and amount of punishment that the court should award. The following case considers the role of the convening authority in this process.

UNITED STATES V. PRIVATE FIRST CLASS GENE A. HILL,
U.S. ARMY
UNITED STATES ARMY COURT OF MILITARY REVIEW
18 M.J. 75
AUGUST 13, 1984
Opinion: McKay, Senior Judge

In accordance with his pleas, the appellant, Private Hill, was convicted by a military judge sitting as a spe-

cial court-martial of two specifications of distribution of marijuana in the hashish form, a violation of Article 134, UCMJ. The appellant argues that the military judge improperly prohibited Private Hill's defense counsel from developing facts relevant to the issue of the effect of illegal command influence upon the presentation of evidence favorable to Private Hill during the sentencing portion of his trial and, in a related vein, that Private Hill was denied a fair sentencing proceeding due to the presence of unlawful command influence.

During the sentencing portion of the appellant's trial, First Lieutenant David Sanders was called as a defense witness. Lieutenant Sanders, who was a member of Private Hill's battalion, testified that he was aware of the letter written and distributed by the Division Command sergeant major (hereinafter referred to as the Haga letter) and containing his thoughts on what a good noncommissioned officer should and should not do regarding testimony at courts-martial. Lieutenant Sanders further testified that his battalion commander, at an officers' professional development class, read and "interpreted" a policy letter from General Anderson indicating that although a witness called before a court-martial should testify truthfully, he should "not paint so rosy a picture that all of the effort and time expended in creating the . . . court-martial packet would be just wasted, by recommending that the soldier remain on active duty." Lieutenant Sanders averred that his battalion commander's "guidance" had not influenced his testimony. He testified that Private Hill could be rehabilitated and be of benefit to the army.

On redirect examination, Private Hill's defense counsel asked Lieutenant Sanders whether he knew what effect the Haga letter may have had on any of the other witnesses in the appellant's case. The trial counsel objected to the question and his objection was sustained. Although Lieutenant Sanders was examined further regarding the Haga letter and his battalion commander's statements, he was not permitted to answer the question regarding the effect of these matters on other witnesses. When the appellant's defense counsel attempted to delve deeper into Lieutenant Sanders' knowledge of the effect of command influence on the appellant's case, the military judge abruptly curtailed questioning, demanding that the defense counsel demonstrate the relevance to the appellant's trial of testimony regarding command influence. When the defense counsel's response—that, although Lieutenant Sanders had not been affected, others might have been—did not satisfy the military judge, he refused to allow further questioning regarding command influence.

Article 37, UCMJ, prohibits coercion or unauthorized influence on actual or prospective witnesses with respect to the content of their testimony. A finding that unlawful pressure has been brought to bear in violation of Article 37 triggers a rebuttable presumption that the recipient of the unlawful pressure was in fact influenced. Accordingly, if any prospective character witness for Private Hill heard, either directly or indirectly, General Anderson's message, the battalion commander's interpretation of the message, or the Division Command sergeant major's message, and reasonably understood them to be discouraging favorable character testimony, such discouragement would amount to unlawful pressure under Article 37, UCMJ, and would raise the presumption.

In this case, the military judge denied the defense counsel the opportunity to present evidence that potential witnesses were influenced not to testify on Private Hill's behalf. In a situation where the evidence of unlawful command influence within the 3d Armored Division was so squarely raised, the military judge's refusal to allow defense counsel to pose a question so fundamental to his case was error.

We can gain some insight into the information Lieutenant Sanders might have provided by examining Defense Appellate Exhibit M, an affidavit executed by Lieutenant Sanders a little more than two weeks after Private Hill's trial. This information exposes another serious problem in this case resulting from the conduct of General Anderson.

Referencing Private Hill's court-martial, Lieutenant Sanders stated that after the Haga letter had been disseminated throughout his battalion, it was discussed during a meeting of the battery commanders and the battalion staff. A point of the discussion was that a witness could refuse to answer the question of whether a convicted soldier should be retained in the army. The battalion command sergeant major, who attended the meeting, presented the letter the following day to the

battalion first sergeants, who, in turn, distributed the letter to the section chiefs. The letter was again discussed at a meeting among officers, noncommissioned officers, and enlisted members. The impression of the letter among those present was that no senior noncommissioned officer or officer should testify favorably before an administrative board or a court. The battalion commander's advice not to "embarrass the command by making a recommendation, in testimony, that the board or court should allow the individual to remain on active duty" was reiterated. Although members of the battalion were also made aware of a later letter from General Anderson, it was not perceived as a retraction of the Haga letter.

In light of the information contained in Lieutenant Sanders' post-trial affidavit, we believe it is clear that at least one witness who testified in Private Hill's behalf was adversely influenced by what was perceived as General Anderson's message. Staff Sergeant Noris Bodley, Private Hill's section chief, when asked whether Private Hill could be rehabilitated and retrained and still benefit the army, replied:

> Sir, in my opinion, and I hope it goes good on the record, I feel that PFC Hill can be rehabilitated due to the fact of my prior knowledge of PFC Hill. If he was a problem within the unit, within the personnel that works around him, myself, his platoon sergeant, platoon leader, then I can see where he would not benefit the army, but there's one thing the army doesn't tolerate, and that's drugs, so I wouldn't care to answer that as far as the army keeping him, but he can be rehabilitated.

We believe that Sergeant Bodley's concern for how he would sound "on the record" and his reluctance to opine whether Private Hill should be retained in the service can be attributed directly to the unlawful influence visited upon him by General Anderson, the Division Command sergeant major, and his battalion commander.

In *Hill* the court concluded that there was sufficient evidence of unlawful influence. How did the actions of Major General Anderson constitute illegal command influence? The UCMJ was designed to limit unlawful command influence; however, as *Hill* demonstrates, improper persuasion of witnesses and proceedings sometimes still occurs. See chapter 1 and, in particular, *United States v. Kelly.* Because commanders convene and review courts-martial, will it ever be possible to totally eradicate command influence?

Study Questions

1. What are the three types of courts-martial? What is the maximum permissible punishment that may be awarded at each?

2. What are the appellate courts in the military? How are trial and appellate judges appointed? Is the current system of appointing judges constitutional?

3. Which of the following is *true* regarding general courts-martial?

a. An Article 32, UCMJ, pretrial investigation is required before charges may be referred to a general court-martial.

b. A general court-martial may be convened by any commanding officer.

c. The minimum number of members needed to sit on a general court-martial is three.

d. The maximum punishment at a general court-martial is six months confinement, forfeiture of two-third's pay per month for six months, reduction in rate to paygrade E-1, and a bad conduct discharge.

e. All of the above are *true*.

4. What rights does a service member have at a special court-martial? At a general court-martial? At a summary court-martial? At which proceedings is military defense counsel detailed to an accused?

5. Which of the following is *false* regarding summary courts-martial?

a. A summary court-martial is composed of one commissioned officer in the paygrade 0-3 or above from the same armed force as the accused.

b. An accused has the right to refuse trial by summary court-martial.

c. An accused has the right to be represented by counsel at a summary court-martial.

d. All of the above are *false.*

6. Who has authority to convene the three types of courts-marital? May a commander delegate the authority to convene courts-martial?

7. When does jurisdiction over service members begin and terminate? May a member be tried for offenses committed during a prior enlistment?

8. When does the principle of former jeopardy preclude prosecution of a service member? Does former jeopardy apply to cases in which the court does not reach a verdict, that is, a finding of guilt or innocence?

9. Who are the participants at each of the three types of courts-martial? What is the minimum number of members (jurors) at a general court-martial? At a special court-martial?

10. Explain the concept of command influence. Can unlawful influence occur during the sentencing phase of a court-martial?

CHAPTER FOUR

NONJUDICIAL PROCEDURES

There is a strong implication that discipline is something the Captain does to men when they appear at mast. On the contrary, discipline is not something one man does to another. Discipline is a personal quality that each person has or does not have. Therefore, the purpose of "disciplinary action" at Captain's Mast is to convince men without discipline, or those who have a temporary lapse of discipline, that it is better to have it or develop it.

—USS *Enterprise* (CVN 65) Leadership Manual (1985)

Introduction

Discipline, order, morale, deterrence, expediency, operational readiness, and force planning are all factors that impact determinations about potential offenses. Balanced against these factors is the need to provide accused personnel with adequate procedural safeguards. Because of the multitude and nature of these interests, commanders require flexibility and discretion in selecting the best method to handle a possible offense. This explains to some degree why the military justice system contains such a varied mixture of administrative, disciplinary, and criminal measures. In *Parker v. Levy*, 417 U.S. 733 (1974), the Supreme Court commented on the military's wide range of potential sanctions:

> The Uniform Code of Military Justice regulates a far broader range of the conduct of military personnel than a typical state criminal code regulates of the conduct of civilians; but at the same time the enforcement of that code in the area of minor offenses is often by sanctions which are more akin to administrative or civil sanctions than to civilian criminal ones. The availability of these lesser sanctions is not surprising in view of the different relationships of the government to members of the military. It is not only that of lawgiver to citizen, but also

that of employer to employee. Indeed, unlike the civilian situation, the government is often employer, landlord, provisioner, and lawgiver rolled into one. . . . While members of the military community enjoy many of the same rights and bear many of the same burdens as do members of the civilian community, within the military community there is simply not the same autonomy as there is in the larger civilian community.

RCM 306(a) provides that a commander "has discretion to dispose of offenses by members of that command." A commander may elect to dispose of a suspected offense under RCM 306 by:

(2) Administrative action. A commander may take or initiate administrative action, in addition to or instead of other action taken under this rule. . . ;

(3) Nonjudicial punishment. A commander may consider the matter pursuant to Article 15, nonjudicial punishment.

This chapter focuses on nonpunitive measures, nonjudicial punishment, and administrative separations as ways to address potential misconduct by military members.

Nonpunitive Measures

Military criminal law monitors the behavior of service members to a much greater degree than does civilian criminal law. For example, the UCMJ makes it unlawful to be late for work, make unkind remarks about a supervisor, disobey the direction of a superior, perform work in a poor fashion, and act inappropriately outside of work. All of these violations of the UCMJ can result in the imposition of nonjudicial punishment or trial by court-martial. In many instances, however, such actions do not satisfy the commander's desires concerning discipline, morale, or operational readiness (that is, a commander may want to use other measures to address an offense). Nonpunitive measures provide alternatives to more

formal and harsh disciplinary action. These "administrative corrective measures" are not punishment and may be used for acts or omissions that are not criminal in nature, as well as for violations of the UCMJ.

Relationship to Nonjudicial Punishments

Paragraph 1g, Part 5, MCM, explains the relationship between nonpunitive measures and nonjudicial punishments:

Relationship of nonjudicial punishment to administrative corrective measures. [The regulations regarding nonjudicial punishment] do not apply to include, or limit use of administrative corrective measures that promote efficiency and good order and discipline such as counseling, admonitions, reprimands, exhortations, disapprovals, criticisms, censures, reproofs, rebukes, extra military instruction, and administrative withholding of privileges.

Based on the above, a commander may assign nonpunitive measures in lieu of, or in addition to, nonjudicial punishments under Article 15, UCMJ. See the Authority to Impose section below.

Types of Nonpunitive Measures

Nonpunitive measures encompass a wide range of actions aimed at correcting the performance of service members. These measures range from oral counseling (that is, a "chewing out," verbal encouragement, and so on) to limiting the liberty of a service member through after-hours instruction. The JAG Manual closely regulates the use of administrative corrective actions for navy and marine personnel. These regulations are referenced throughout this section.

EXTRAMILITARY INSTRUCTION
JAG Manual 0103 defines extramilitary instruction:

Definition. Extra military instruction (EMI) is defined as instruction in a phase of military duty in which an individual is deficient, and is intended for and directed towards the correction of that deficiency. It is a bona fide training technique to be used for improving the efficiency of an individual within a command or unit through the correction of some deficiency in that individual's performance of duty. It may be assigned only if genuinely intended to accomplish that result. It is not to be used as a substitute for judicial (court-martial) action or nonjudicial punishment, and must be logically related to the deficiency in performance for which it was assigned.

JAG Manual 0103 also sets specific limits on the assignment of extramilitary instruction:

Limitations. EMI shall be conducted within the following limitations:

(1) EMI normally will not be conducted for more than 2 hours per day.

(2) EMI may be conducted at a reasonable time outside normal working hours.

(3) EMI will not be conducted over a period that is longer than necessary to correct the performance deficiency for which it was assigned.

(4) EMI should not be conducted on the member's Sabbath.

(5) EMI will not be used for the purpose of depriving the member of normal liberty to which the member is otherwise entitled. A member who is otherwise entitled thereto may commence normal liberty upon completion of EMI.

(6) Authority to assign EMI that is to be performed during normal working hours is not limited to any particular grade or rate, but is an inherent part of that authority over their subordinates which is vested in officers and noncommissioned/petty officers in connection with duties and responsibilities assigned to them. This authority to assign EMI that is to be performed during normal working hours may be withdrawn by any superior if warranted.

(7) Authority to assign EMI to be performed after normal working hours is vested in the commanding officer or officer in charge. Such authority may be delegated, as appropriate, to officers and noncommissioned/petty officers, in connection with duties and responsibilities assigned to them.

JAG Manual 0103 forbids the use of extramilitary instruction as a form of punishment or to deny liberty. The regulation also attempts to ensure that extra military instruction is used to improve performance in a phase of military duty, and that assigned tasks logically relate to a deficiency. Outside of supervision by members of the chain of command, however, there are no formal means to ensure that abuses do not occur. This means that the U.S. Navy and Marine Corps must rely on its personnel to use good judgment in assigning nonpunitive measures. Is this a positive or negative aspect of the broad delegation of authority to impose corrective measures? What are the advantages or disadvantages to this approach?

JAG Manual 0103(5) essentially deems liberty a right of sailors and marines. If that is the case, who has authority to restrict this right? See the section on Nonjudicial Punishment below. Extramilitary instruction may not be assigned at unreasonable times outside of working hours. What times are considered unreasonable? Does it depend on the operational schedule of the ship or unit? JAG Manual 0103b(6) discusses assigning extramilitary instruction during working hours. Is assigning tasks designed to improve the performance during working hours really extramilitary instruction subject to the above limitations?

ADMINISTRATIVE WITHHOLDING OF PRIVILEGES

As in other parts of society, the military designates particular benefits as rights or privileges. The distinction between the two is significant because withholding a right triggers more process for the service member. See the section on Nonjudicial Punishment below. Consider the definition of a "privilege" and the rules regarding the withholding of liberty contained in JAG Manual 0104:

Privilege. A privilege is a benefit, advantage, or favor provided for the convenience or enjoyment of an individual. Examples of privileges that may be temporarily withheld as administrative corrective measures are: special liberty; exchange of duty; special command programs; access to base or ship libraries, base or ship movies, or enlisted or officers' clubs; base parking; and base or ship special services events. It may also encompass the withholding of special pay as well as commissary and exchange privileges, provided such withholding complies with applicable rules and regulations, and is otherwise in accordance with law. In all instances, unless properly delegated, final authority to withhold a privilege, however temporary, must ultimately rest with the level of authority empowered to grant that privilege.

Deprivation of liberty. Deprivation of normal liberty as a punishment, except as specifically authorized under the UCMJ, is illegal. Therefore, except as the specific result of punishment imposed under Article 15, UCMJ, or as the result of the sentence of a court-martial, it is illegal for any officer or noncommissioned/petty officer to deny to any subordinate normal liberty, or privileges incident thereto, as punishment for any offense. Lawful deprivation of normal liberty, however, may result from other lawful actions such as authorized pretrial restraint, or deprivation of normal liberty in a foreign country or in foreign territorial waters, when such action is deemed essential for the protection of the foreign relations of the United States. . . . Moreover, it is necessary to the efficiency of the naval service that official functions be performed and that certain work be accomplished in a timely manner. It is, therefore, not a punishment when persons in the naval service are required to remain on board and be physically present outside of normal working hours for work assignments that should have been completed during normal working hours, for the accomplishment of additional essential work, or for the achievement of the currently required level of operational readiness.

As a general rule, denial of liberty is a punishment that can be imposed only at nonjudicial punishment or at court-martial. However, JAG Manual 0104 refers to limiting liberty in foreign countries. This is known as placing a member in a "liberty risk" status to avoid embarrassing the United States. *United States v. Wilkes* in chapter 10 discusses the parameters of a legitimate liberty risk program.

Counseling
Extramilitary instruction
Administrative admonition/reprimand (not part of permanent service record)
Adverse conduct rating
Adverse efficiency rating
Transfer to another work section
Withholding of privileges

Figure 4-1 Administrative/Nonpunitive Measures

NONPUNITIVE CENSURE

JAG Manual 0105 explains the difference between punitive and nonpunitive censure:

General. "Censure" is a statement of adverse opinion or criticism of an individual's conduct or performance of duty expressed by a superior in the member's chain of command. Censure may be punitive or nonpunitive.

Nonpunitive censure may be issued by any superior in the member's chain of command, and may be either oral or in writing.

A nonpunitive letter is not considered punishment; rather, the letter is issued to remedy a noted deficiency in conduct or performance of duty. The contents of a nonpunitive letter are not limited to but may include the following: identification of conduct or performance of duty deficiencies, direction for improvement, language of admonishment, identification of sources of assistance, outline of corrective action, and the consequences of failing to correct the deficiencies.

A nonpunitive letter will be kept a personal matter between the member and the superior issuing the nonpunitive letter. The letter may not be forwarded to the Chief of Naval Personnel or the Commandant of the Marine Corps, quoted in or appended to fitness reports, included as enclosures to investigations pursuant to the Manual of the Judge Advocate General or to other investigations, or otherwise included in official departmental records of the recipient.

Nonpunitive censure is issued to remedy identified deficiencies in conduct or performance. Compare nonpunitive censure with a punitive letter of reprimand, discussed below under Nonjudicial Punishment. When is it wise to use nonpunitive censure? When should it be in writing? Figure 4-1 summarizes the nonpunitive measures available in the navy.

Nonjudicial Punishment

Article 15, UCMJ, authorizes nonjudicial punishment (also referred to as "captain's mast" in the navy and "officer hours" in the Marines Corps). Part 5, MCM, augments Article 15, as does chapter 1 of the JAG Manual. In contrast to nonpunitive measures, nonjudicial punishment is disciplinary in nature. This feature results in greater oversight of nonjudicial punishment proceedings and in broader procedural protections for accused.

Authority to Impose

Article 15 permits the secretaries of each service to determine which officers should have nonjudicial punishment authority. JAG Manual 0106 sets forth the officers in the navy and marines who possess Article 15 authority:

> Commander. Any commander or commanding officer . . . may impose nonjudicial punishment upon officers and enlisted persons of the command.
>
> Officer in charge. Any commissioned officer who is designated as officer in charge . . . may impose upon enlisted persons assigned to the unit admonition or reprimand and one or more of the punishments listed in Part 5, MCM.

Paragraph 1d, Part 5, MCM, provides guidance on when it is appropriate to impose nonjudicial punishment:

> (1) Commander's responsibility. Commanders are responsible for good order and discipline in their commands. Generally, discipline can be maintained through effective leadership including, when necessary, administrative corrective measures. Nonjudicial punishment

is ordinarily appropriate when administrative corrective measures are inadequate due to the nature of the minor offense or the record of the service member, unless it is clear that only trial by court-martial will meet the needs of justice and discipline. Nonjudicial punishment shall be considered on an individual basis. Commanders considering nonjudicial punishment should consider the nature of the offense, the record of the service member, the needs for good order and discipline, and the effect of nonjudicial punishment on the service member and the service member's record.

> (2) Commander's discretion. A commander who is considering a case for disposition under Article 15 will exercise personal discretion in evaluating each case, both as to whether nonjudicial punishment is appropriate, and, if so, as to the nature and amount of punishment appropriate. No superior may direct that a subordinate authority impose nonjudicial punishment in a particular case, issue regulations, orders, or "guides" which suggest to subordinate authorities that certain categories of minor offenses be disposed of by nonjudicial punishment instead of by court-martial or administrative corrective measures, or that predetermined kinds or amounts of punishments be imposed for certain classifications of offenses that the subordinate considers appropriate for disposition by nonjudicial punishment.

A commander may not delegate his or her authority under Article 15. However, the officer who is second in command, normally the executive officer, may award nonjudicial punishment if he or she succeeds to command during an official absence of the commander. How should this assumption of command be done? In writing? The above language indicates that a commander should exercise "personal discretion" in adjudicating each case. The executive officer in many cases will conduct his or her own inquiry prior to nonjudicial punishment. May the executive officer award punishment at such a proceeding? What about nonpunitive measures? Note, finally, that in a recent change to the JAG Manual, multiservice commanders are now authorized to impose nonjudicial punishment on naval members assigned to

```
REPORT AND DISPOSITION OF OFFENSE(S)
NAVPERS 1626/7 (REV 8-81) S/N 0104-LF-016-2624

To:  Commanding Officer. (Name of Unit)              Date of Report _____

1. I hereby report the following named person for the offense(s) noted:

NAME OF ACCUSED          | SERIAL NO. | SOCIAL SECURITY NO. | RATE/GRADE | BR. & CLASS | DIV/DEPT

PLACE OF OFFENSE(S)                    | DATE OF OFFENSE(S)
For EACH offense (Be Specific)         | For EACH offense (Be Specific)

DETAILS OF OFFENSE(S) (Refer by article of UCMJ, if known. If unauthorized absence, give following info: time and date of commencement, whether over
leave or liberty, time and date of apprehension or surrender and arrival on board, loss of ID card and/or liberty card, etc.)

List offenses separately, by Charge and Specification. Use sample speci-
fications (PART IV, MCM) for correct format and content. Include as much
information as necessary for clarity.  See figure 4-3 for example.

NAME OF WITNESS | RATE/GRADE | DIV/DEPT | NAME OF WITNESS | RATE/GRADE | DIV/DEPT
List ALL known witnesses, even if currently unavailable.

(Rate/Grade/Title of person submitting report)   (Signature of person submitting report)

I have been informed of the nature of the accusation(s) against me. I understand I do not have to answer any questions or make any statement regarding the
offense(s) of which I am accused or suspected. However, I understand any statement made or questions answered by me may be used as evidence against
me in event of trial by court-martial (Article 31, UCMJ).

Witness: _____         Acknowledged: _____
         (Signature)                   (Signature of Accused)

PRE-MAST RESTRAINT
[ ] PRETRIAL CONFINEMENT    RESTRICTED: You are restricted to the limits of _____ in lieu of arrest
[ ] NO RESTRICTIONS         by order of the CO. Until your status as a restricted person is terminated by the CO, you may not
                            leave the restricted limits except with the express permission of the CO or XO. You have been
                            informed of the times and places which you are required to muster.

(Signature and title of person imposing restraint)   (Signature of Accused)

INFORMATION CONCERNING ACCUSED
CURRENT ENL DATE | EXPIRATION CURRENT ENL. DATE | TOTAL ACTIVE NAVAL SERVICE | TOTAL SERVICE ON BOARD | EDUCATION | GCT | AGE
******INFORMATION FROM THE SERVICE RECORD OF THE ACCUSED****

MARITAL STATUS | NO. DEPENDENTS | CONTRIBUTION TO FAMILY OR OTRS ALLOWANCE (Amount required by law) | PAY PER MONTH (including sea or foreign duty pay, if any)

RECORD OF PREVIOUS OFFENSE(S) (Date, type, action taken, etc. Nonjudicial punishment incidents are to be included.)
List all prior court-martial convictions and non-judicial punishments.
Include type of action (NJP, SCM, etc.), nature of offense(s) including
UCMJ article violated and description of violation (eg. Violation of Ar-
ticle 86, UA from 5-8 JAN 95), date of offense, date of action, and pun-
ishment or sentence imposed.
```

Figure 4-2

their unit or staff. Prior to this modification, a multiservice commander only had Article 15 authority over members of his or her own service. This is a significant change, especially in light of the increased emphasis on joint warfare and operations.

The process for handling nonjudicial punishment cases is generally standardized in each of the services. Figures 4-2 and 4-3 are examples of the forms used to report and dispose of cases in the navy.

Figure 4-2 (cont.)

Jurisdiction

"Jurisdiction" is the authority to adjudicate a particular offense. The officer conducting nonjudicial punishment must have authority over both the service member and the offense. JAG Manual 0107 describes

the persons subject to nonjudicial punishment jurisdiction of U.S. Navy and Marine Corps officers:

General rule. When nonjudicial punishment is imposed, the accused must be a member of the command, or of the unit, of the officer imposing the punishment.

REPORT AND DISPOSITION OF OFFENSE(S)
NAVPERS 1626/7 (REV 8-81) S/N 0104-LF-016-2624

To: Commanding Officer: USS BENSON (DD-895)   Date of Report: 15 June 199X

1. I hereby report the following named person for the offense(s) noted.

NAME OF ACCUSED	SERIAL NO.	SOCIAL SECURITY NO.	RATE/GRADE	BR. & CLASS	DIV/DEPT
WILLIAMS, John P.	NA	888-88-8888	RDSN/E-3	USN	OPS

PLACE OF OFFENSE(S)	DATE OF OFFENSE(S)
Quarterdeck, USS BENSON (DD-895)	15 June 199X

DETAILS OF OFFENSE(S) (Refer by article of UCMJ, if known. If unauthorized absence, give following info: time and date of commencement, whether over leave or liberty, time and date of apprehension or surrender and arrival on board, loss of ID card and/or liberty card, etc.)

Charge: Violation of the Uniform Code of Military Justice, Article 134.

Specification: In that RDSN John P. WILLIAMS, USN, USS BENSON (DD-895), on active duty, did, onboard USS BENSON (DD-895), on or about 15 June 199X, unlawfully carry on or about his person a concealed weapon, to wit: a switch-blade knife.

NAME OF WITNESS	RATE/GRADE	DIV/DEPT	NAME OF WITNESS	RATE/GRADE	DIV/DEPT
Harold B. Johnson	YNC	X			
Robert A. Hudson	CWO2	ENG			

YNC, USN
(Rate/Grade/Title of person submitting report)

/s/ Harold B. Johnson
(Signature of person submitting report)

I have been informed of the nature of the accusation(s) against me. I understand I do not have to answer any questions or make any statement regarding the offense(s) of which I am accused or suspected. However, I understand any statement made or questions answered by me may be used as evidence against me in event of trial by court-martial (Article 31, UCMJ).

Witness: /s/ H. O. Kay, ENS., USN   Acknowledged: /s/ John P. Williams
         (Signature)   (Signature of Accused)

PRE-MAST RESTRAINT
☐ PRETRIAL CONFINEMENT
☒ NO RESTRICTIONS

RESTRICTED: You are restricted to the limits of _____ in lieu of arrest by order of the CO. Until your status as a restricted person is terminated by the CO, you may not leave the restricted limits except with the express permission of the CO or XO. You have been informed of the times and places which you are required to muster.

(Signature and title of person imposing restraint)   (Signature of Accused)

INFORMATION CONCERNING ACCUSED

CURRENT ENL. DATE	EXPIRATION CURRENT ENL. DATE	TOTAL ACTIVE NAVAL SERVICE	TOTAL SERVICE ON BOARD	EDUCATION	GCT	AGE
24 May 93	23 May 97	1 yr 1 mo	10 mos	HS	57	19

MARITAL STATUS	NO. DEPENDENTS	CONTRIBUTION TO FAMILY OR QTRS ALLOWANCE (Amount required by law)	PAY PER MONTH (including sea or foreign duty pay, if any)
Single	0	NA	$XXX.XX

RECORD OF PREVIOUS OFFENSE(S) (Date, type, action taken, etc. Nonjudicial punishment incidents are to be included.)

NONE

Figure 4-3

A member is "of the command," or "of the unit," if assigned or attached thereto. A member may be "of the command," or "of the unit," of more than one command or unit at the same time and, consequently, be subject to the nonjudicial punishment authority of both commanders. For example, members assigned to or attached to commands or units for the purpose of performing temporary duty (TDY) are subject to the nonjudicial punishment authority of the commanders of both the parent and TDY commands. Similarly, members assigned or attached to a detachment under the operational control of another command or unit by

PRELIMINARY INQUIRY REPORT

From: Commanding Officer   Date 20 June 199X

To: ENS David W. Willis, USNR

1. Transmitted herewith for preliminary inquiry and report by you, including, if appropriate in the interest of justice and discipline, the preferring of such charges as appear to you to be sustained by expected evidence

Remarks of Division Officer (Performance of duty, etc.)

Seaman Williams is a good worker who is learning his rate through on-the-job training. He needs occasional supervision, but works willingly when assigned a job. I consider him petty officer material, and this is his first offense.   /s/ LT Garry V. Brown

NAME OF WITNESS	RATE/GRADE	DIV/DEPT	NAME OF WITNESS	RATE/GRADE	DIV/DEPT

RECOMMENDATION AS TO DISPOSITION:

☐ REFER TO COURT MARTIAL FOR TRIAL OF ATTACHED CHARGES (Complete Charge Sheet: {DD Form 458} through Page 2)

☒ DISPOSE OF CASE AT MAST   ☐ NO PUNITIVE ACTION NECESSARY OR DESIRABLE   ☐ OTHER

Comment (Include data regarding availability of witnesses, summary of expected evidence, conflicts in evidence, if expected. Attach statements of witnesses, documentary evidence such as service record entries in UA cases, items of real evidence, etc.)

SN Williams was discovered to be carrying a switchblade knife with a 5" blade by YNC H. B. Johnson when he was the JOOD on 15 June. SN Williams was about to depart the ship on liberty at approx. 1630, when Johnson noticed a bulge in his front pocket. The knife was discovered when Johnson had Williams empty his pocket. YNC Johnson reported the incident to the OOD, CWO2 R. A. Hughes, who directed that Williams be put on report (Continued on attached sheet)

/s/ David S. Willis
(Signature of Investigation Officer)

ACTION OF EXECUTIVE OFFICER

SIGNATURE OF EXECUTIVE OFFICER

☐ DISMISSED   ☒ REFERRED TO CAPTAIN'S MAST   /s/ R. D. Line, LCDR, USN

RIGHT TO DEMAND TRIAL BY COURT-MARTIAL
(Not applicable to persons attached to or embarked in a vessel)

I understand that nonjudicial punishment may not be imposed on me if, before the imposition of such punishment, I demand in lieu thereof trial by court-martial. I therefore (do) (do not) demand trial by court-martial.

WITNESS   SIGNATURE OF ACCUSED

ACTION OF COMMANDING OFFICER

☐ DISMISSED
☐ DISMISSED WITH WARNING (Not considered NJP)
☐ ADMONITION: ORAL/IN WRITING
☐ REPRIMAND: ORAL/IN WRITING
☐ REST. TO _____ FOR ___ DAYS
☐ REST. TO _____ FOR ___ DAYS WITH SUSP. FROM DUTY
☒ FORFEITURE: TO FORFEIT $ 50.00 PAY PER MO. FOR 1 MO(S)
☐ DETENTION: TO HAVE $ _____ PAY PER MO. FOR (1, 2, 3) MO(S) DETAINED FOR ___ MO(S)

☐ CONF. ON _____ 1, 2, OR 3 DAYS
☐ CORRECTIONAL CUSTODY FOR ___ DAYS
☐ REDUCTION TO NEXT INFERIOR PAY GRADE
☐ REDUCTION TO PAY GRADE OF _____
☐ EXTRA DUTIES FOR ___ DAYS
☐ PUNISHMENT SUSPENDED FOR _____
☐ ART. 32 INVESTIGATION
☐ RECOMMENDED FOR TRIAL BY GCM
☐ AWARDED SPCM   ☐ AWARDED SCM

DATE OF MAST	DATE ACCUSED INFORMED OF ABOVE ACTION	SIGNATURE OF COMMANDING OFFICER
25 June 199X	25 June 199X	/s/ S. D. Dunn, CDR, USN

It has been explained to me and I understand that if I feel this imposition of nonjudicial punishment to be unjust or disproportionate to the offenses charged against me, I have the right to immediately appeal my conviction to the next higher authority within 5 days.

SIGNATURE OF ACCUSED	DATE	I have explained the above rights of appeal to the accused.
/s/ John P. Williams	25 June 9X	/s/ H. O. Kay 25 June 9X
		SIGNATURE OF WITNESS DATE

FINAL ADMINISTRATIVE ACTION

APPEAL SUBMITTED BY ACCUSED

DATED 28 June 199X

FORWARDED FOR DECISION ON 3 July 199X

FINAL RESULT OF APPEAL

Appeal denied by Commander, CRUDESGRU 8, 7 July 199X

APPROPRIATE ENTRIES MADE IN SERVICE RECORD AND PAY ACCOUNT ADJUSTED WHERE REQUIRED

DATE 25 June 199X   INITIALS HOK

FILED IN UNIT PUNISHMENT BOOK

DATE 25 June 199X   INITIALS HOK

NAVPERS 1626/7 (REV 8/81)(BACK)   US GPO 1982.539.003 2045 Region 3

Figure 4-3 (cont.)

virtue of operational orders, or other authorized means, are subject to the nonjudicial punishment authority of the commanders of both the parent and supported units.

Although a commander of a unit attached to a ship retains nonjudicial punishment authority, as a matter of policy, the commander refrains from exercising nonjudicial punishment power while embarked. Why does this rule exist? JAG Manual 0108 explains that the policy is a "necessary corollary to the ship captain's overall responsibility for the safety, well being, and efficiency of the ship." The commanding officer of a ship may, nevertheless, permit a commander of a unit attached to that ship to exercise nonjudicial punishment authority. When would this happen? Does it depend on the type of case? JAG Manual 0108 states that "certain types of offenses, or offenses committed by certain categories of personnel, may nonetheless be required to be referred to the commanding officer of the ship for disposition." What types of cases do you think would best be handled by the commander of the ship?

Commanders are authorized to use nonjudicial punishment for "minor offenses." Consider the JAG Manual, which addresses which crimes fit into that category:

> Minor offenses. Nonjudicial punishment may be imposed for acts or omissions that are minor offenses under the punitive articles. Whether an offense is minor depends on several factors: the nature of the offense and the circumstances surrounding its commission; the offender's age, rank, duty assignment, record, and experience; and the maximum sentence imposable for the offense if tried by general court-martial. Ordinarily, a minor offense is an offense for which the maximum sentence imposable would not include a dishonorable discharge or confinement for longer than one year if tried by general court-martial. The decision whether an offense is "minor" is a matter of discretion for the commander imposing nonjudicial punishment, but nonjudicial punishment for an offense other than a minor offense (even though thought by the commander to be minor) is not a bar to trial by court-martial for the same offense. However, the accused may show at trial that nonjudicial punishment was imposed, and if the accused does so, this fact must be considered in determining an appropriate sentence.

The following case considers the ramifications of a determination that an offense addressed at captain's mast is minor.

UNITED STATES V. JACK M. FRETWELL, LIEUTENANT,
U.S. NAVY
UNITED STATES COURT OF MILITARY APPEALS
11 U.S.C.M.A. 377; 29 C.M.R. 193
APRIL 8, 1960
Opinion: Latimer, Judge

The charges for which accused was tried grow out of events that occurred January 16, 1959. On that date accused was assigned as officer-of-the-deck for the midwatch aboard the aircraft carrier USS *Hancock*. He judicially confessed and there is no dispute that after having assumed and while on such duty he was found drunk in uniform, lying unconscious in a passageway of the ship. However, before accused entered his plea admitting his guilt, the defense moved to dismiss the charges on the ground of former punishment. It was stipulated that on January 23, 1959, the commanding officer of the USS *Hancock* imposed nonjudicial punishment upon accused under Article 15, UCMJ, for the same acts of misconduct that were the basis of the charges being tried, whereby he restricted accused to his stateroom for ten days and recommended that the commander, Fleet Air Alameda, issue accused a letter of reprimand. Accused served the imposed restriction, but the commander, Fleet Air Alameda, when the matter was referred to him for the recommended letter of reprimand, stated his belief that the nature of the alleged violations by accused more appropriately warranted trial by court-martial, for he considered the actions did not constitute minor offenses. Subsequently, charges were preferred against accused and forwarded, together with the recommendations of the commanding officer, USS *Hancock,* and the commander, Fleet Air Alameda, to the commandant of the Twelfth Naval District, who acted as convening authority and referred them for trial to the instant general court-martial. After the government and the defense had presented their respective arguments, the law officer denied the motion to dismiss.

At the outset, we deem it worthwhile to point out that we are not here concerned with a situation where true former jeopardy is asserted as the basis for relief. A plea in bar so predicated is available in the civilian and the military communities alike, for that fundamental protection to an accused is spelled out in the Fifth Amendment to the United States Constitution and Article 44, UCMJ, is to be borne in mind, however, that the right thereby extended to an accused concerns itself solely with prior judicial proceedings, as is clear from the terms of the last-mentioned Article. And there can be no doubt that the prior punishment visited upon accused in the case at bar is not of that nature. True it is that he was previously punished, but not judicially. To the contrary, the commanding officer of his ship undertook to discipline him under Article 15 of the code.

In Article 15(e), UCMJ, Congress provided:

> The imposition and enforcement of disciplinary punishment under this article for any act or omission is not a bar to trial by court-martial for a serious crime or offense growing out of the same act or omission, and not properly punishable under this article; but the fact that a disciplinary punishment has been enforced may be shown by the accused upon trial, and when so shown shall be considered in determining the measure of punishment to be adjudged in the event of a finding of guilty.

> Whether an offense may be considered 'minor' depends upon its nature, the time and place of its commission, and the person committing it. Generally speaking the term includes misconduct not involving moral turpitude or any greater degree of criminality than is involved in the average offense tried by summary court-martial. An offense for which the punitive article authorizes the death penalty or for which confinement for one year or more is authorized is not a minor offense. Offenses such as larceny, forgery, maiming, and the like involve moral turpitude and are not to be treated as minor. Escape from confinement, willful disobedience of a noncommissioned officer or petty officer, and protracted absence without leave are offenses which are more serious than the average offense tried by summary courts-martial and should not ordinarily be treated as minor.

Drunk and disorderly conduct, whether by an officer or by enlisted personnel, is a much more serious offense if committed aboard ship than otherwise and will permit imposition of six months' confinement and punitive separation from the service. And drunkenness on duty is one step further up the ladder of aggravated offenses, for it may be punished by punitive discharge and nine months' incarceration. Without doubt accused's actions here constitute an even more flagrant breach of the law. Not only was he both drunk aboard ship and while on duty but, as the board of review pointed out, his duty was as officer-of-the-deck and, as such, he was the direct representative of the commanding officer of the ship, which position carries great responsibility. It would be downgrading and belittling to the responsibility placed upon an officer-of-the-deck, whether on a ship at sea or, as here, in drydock, to conclude otherwise.

Rights of the Accused

Paragraph 3, Part 5, MCM, discusses the right to demand trial by court-martial:

> Except in the case of a person attached to or embarked in a vessel, punishment may not be imposed under Article 15 upon any member of the armed forces who has, before the imposition of nonjudicial punishment, demanded trial by court-martial in lieu of nonjudicial punishment. This right may also be granted to a person attached to or embarked in a vessel if so authorized by regulations of the secretary concerned. A person is "attached to" or "embarked in" a vessel if, at the time nonjudicial punishment is imposed, that person is assigned or attached to the vessel, is on board for passage, or is assigned or attached to an embarked staff, unit, detachment, squadron, team, air group, or other regularly organized body.

The above paragraph raises the issue of what, for purposes of the right to demand a trial, is a "vessel." The following case addresses this question.

UNITED STATES V. GLEN P. EDWARDS, AVIATION
BOATSWAIN'S MATE, U.S. NAVY
U.S. COURT OF APPEALS FOR THE ARMED FORCES
46 M.J. 41
FEBRUARY 28, 1997
Opinion: Gierke, Judge

This case involves the so-called vessel exception to Article 15, UCMJ. Article 15 empowers commanding officers to impose nonjudicial punishment on members of their commands. It also provides that "except in the case of a member attached to or embarked in a vessel, punishment may not be imposed upon any member of the armed forces under this article if the member has, before the imposition of such punishment, demanded trial by court-martial in lieu of such punishment."

The granted issue arose during appellant's sentencing hearing, when the prosecution offered evidence that appellant had received nonjudicial punishment for a short unauthorized absence and for carrying concealed weapons. The evidence reflected that when the nonjudicial punishment was imposed, appellant's unit was

USS *Constellation* (CV 64) located at Naval Shipyard, Philadelphia. Defense counsel objected, citing *United States v. Yatchak,* 35 MJ 379 (CMA 1992), and *United States v. Lorance,* 35 MJ 382 (CMA 1992). Defense counsel asserted that the USS *Constellation* was not in an operational status when the punishment was imposed, but was undergoing overhaul at the Philadelphia Navy Yard. Defense counsel argued that because the ship was not in an operational status, appellant was not "attached to or embarked in a vessel" within the meaning of Article 15. Thus, at the time the Article 15 was administered, appellant had the right to demand trial by court-martial and to consult with a lawyer before deciding whether to demand trial.

The military judge admitted the evidence of nonjudicial punishment without commenting on the merits of the defense objection. Defense counsel then asked, "Is the court stating that they believe the *Constellation* is an operational vessel?" The military judge responded that "it's the court's interpretation that the cases cited by the defense counsel refer to the issue of whether an accused is attached to or embarked on a vessel for the purposes of awarding confinement on bread and water at a court-martial," and that "the court interprets that holding to apply only to that punishment." Defense counsel asked that it be "noted on the record that we feel that because it's not an operational vessel for those purposes that we feel that at the very least *Booker* warnings should be given." See *United States v. Booker,* 5 MJ 238 (CMA 1977) (right to consult with counsel before deciding whether to demand trial). The military judge concluded the discussion by informing defense counsel that "your objection is made for the record."

In *United States v. Yatchak,* we construed the term "attached to or embarked in a vessel" as it appears in Article 15(b)(2)(A). We held that confinement on bread and water was not an authorized punishment in that case because the accused was not "attached to or embarked in a vessel" within the meaning of Article 15. We relied on several factors: (1) the sentence was imposed by a court-martial conducted ashore; (2) the sentence was imposed on a sailor assigned to a vessel undergoing long-term overhaul that would not be completed until several months after the trial; (3) the government and the defense agreed that the vessel "was never in an op-

erational status throughout the period of appellant's naval service"; and (4) the sentence was served in a shore facility.

Our review of the decision of the court below does not involve the legality of appellant's nonjudicial punishment, but only its admissibility in a subsequent court-martial. The jurisdiction of our Court does not extend to direct review of nonjudicial punishment proceedings.

In *United States v. Booker,* this Court held that evidence of previous nonjudicial punishment is not admissible unless the person being punished was advised of his or her right to confer with "independent counsel" before deciding whether to demand trial by court-martial. Of course, if the evidence relating to the nonjudicial punishment shows that the person being punished had no right to demand trial because attached to or embarked in a vessel," then *Booker* is inapplicable.

In determining whether appellant was "attached to or embarked in a vessel," two issues must be resolved: (1) Was appellant's relationship to the ship sufficient to satisfy what Congress intended by the words "attached to or embarked in," and thus sufficient to trigger the exception to the statutory right to demand trial and the ancillary right to consult with counsel before deciding whether to demand trial? And (2) Was the ship a "vessel" within the meaning of Article 15?

With respect to the first preliminary question, the legislative history of Article 15 is instructive in discerning what Congress meant by the words "attached to or embarked in." When Congress first enacted Article 15 in 1950, the statute contained no right to demand trial by court-martial. Instead, Congress merely empowered the service secretaries to, "by regulation, place limitations on the powers granted by this article with respect to . . . the applicability of this article to an accused who demands trial by court-martial." Paragraph 132, Manual for Courts-Martial, United States, 1951, set out the service regulations as follows:

> Pursuant to the authority of Article 15b, the following departmental regulations with respect to the applicability of Article 15 to persons who demand trial by court-martial are announced by the several Secretaries:
> Army and Air Force.—No disciplinary punishment under the provisions of Article 15 may be imposed upon

any member of the army or of the air force for an offense punishable thereunder if the accused has, prior to
the imposition of such punishment, demanded trial by
court-martial in lieu of such disciplinary punishment.

Navy and Coast Guard.—No member of the navy or
the coast guard may demand trial by court-martial in
lieu of punishment under the provisions of Article 15.

In 1962 Article 15 was amended in several respects, including the addition of a statutory right to demand trial
by court-martial, "except in the case of a member attached to or embarked on a vessel." This statutory
amendment had the effect of extending to members of
the navy and coast guard the right to demand trial by
court-martial in lieu of nonjudicial punishment, subject to the "vessel exception."

The legislative history of the 1962 amendment suggests that Congress intended the "vessel exception" to
apply only to "military members aboard ship." The
Senate adopted the amendments to Article 15 on the
representation of the Senate Armed Services Committee chairman that the amendment would give all military members a right to demand trial in lieu of nonjudicial punishment except "in some cases where a ship is
at sea."

When the proposed executive order implementing
the amendments to Article 15 was transmitted to the
president, it was accompanied by a memorandum from
Assistant Attorney General Norbert A. Schlei addressing the ambiguity of the vessel exception and the possibility that it might be applied to persons "considerably
removed from the vessel involved, and without regard
to whether actual boarding of the vessel is planned for
the immediate future." Mr. Schlei opined that such an
interpretation "would appear to be inconsistent with
the congressional intent." Mr. Schlei assured the president that "representatives of the air force [the executive
agent for promulgating the changes], on behalf of all
the services, state that the military services have no intention of denying an election to any member . . . unless he is either aboard [a] vessel or unless he is in the
immediate vicinity of a vessel and is in the process of
boarding." Mr. Schlei advised the president that the
services also intended to apply the vessel exception "to
members attached to vessels who are absent without authority in foreign ports." Mr. Schlei proposed to the

president that the implementing rules be issued as
drafted to avoid the considerable delay required to re-
draft them. Finally, Mr. Schlei informed the president
that "in order to avoid any misunderstanding concerning this matter," a copy of his memorandum would be
disseminated to the services for their guidance. The
president signed the proposed executive order as recommended by Mr. Schlei. We conclude from the foregoing
that both Congress and the President intended the "vessel exception" to be limited to situations such as where
service members were aboard a vessel, in the immediate
vicinity and in the process of boarding, or attached to
vessels and absent without authority in foreign ports.

Turning to the second preliminary question of fact,
we note that the term "vessel" has been defined by
Congress, and that the statutory definition has been incorporated into the Manual for Courts-Martial. RCM
103(20) expressly adopts "the definitions and rules of
construction in 1 USC §§ 1 through 5 and in 10 USC
§§ 101 and 801." The term "vessel" is defined in 1 USC
§ 3 as follows: "The word 'vessel' includes every description of watercraft or other artificial contrivance
used, or capable of being used, as a means of transportation on water." Nothing in the legislative history
or legal context suggests that Congress intended a different definition of "vessel" in connection with nonjudicial punishment. Based on this definition, we reject
the position taken by the court below that operational
status is irrelevant. We hold that a ship's operational status is relevant to a factual determination whether it is
"used or capable of being used, as a means of transportation on water." As in *Yatchak,* it is one of several
factors involved in determining whether withdrawing
the right to demand trial is consistent with the congressional intent behind the vessel exception.

We are mindful of the concerns of the court below
that "operational status" is "undefined," and that a ship
might become nonoperational under circumstances for
which the vessel exception should apply, such as a casualty at sea, accidental grounding or collision, or wartime damage. We have little difficulty defining "operational."

We also note that the Department of the Navy has issued no regulatory guidance to define the term "operational status" in the four years since this Court used

that term in *Yatchak* to limit the phrase "attached to or embarked on a vessel" under Article 15. While we must necessarily reserve judgment on the application of any such guidance to a particular case, we have no reason to doubt that the navy is capable of publishing guidance that would cover many reasonably foreseeable circumstances. Regardless of whether such guidance is published, we are confident that military judges and the courts of criminal appeals can apply their wisdom and experience in assessing whether the right to demand trial by court-martial was denied properly in a particular situation.

Edwards focuses on when an accused has the right to demand trial by court-martial. If an accused does have such a right, should he or she have access to counsel to assist in this decision? The following case addresses this question.

UNITED STATES V. JERRY L. MATHEWS, PRIVATE FIRST CLASS, U.S. ARMY

UNITED STATES COURT OF MILITARY APPEALS

6 M.J. 357

APRIL 9, 1979

Opinion: Fletcher, Chief Judge

The issue presented in this case examines whether or not the military judge erred in questioning the appellant concerning his waiver of both counsel and right to trial in relation to a prior Article 15, punishment.

The pertinent facts are clear. The appellant entered his plea of guilty, and the tendered plea was accepted by the trial judge. Prior to the presentation of any evidence at the hearing regarding extenuation and mitigation, the government offered for admission Record of Proceedings under Article 15, UCMJ, relating to the appellant. Upon inquiry by the trial judge, the defense counsel stated that he had no objection to its admission. The appellant then called two witnesses, one of which testified concerning the Article 15. Subsequent to hearing this witness, the trial judge had a bench colloquy with the appellant concerning his understanding of Article 15 procedures and rights exercisable under the law by the appellant. The trial judge on the record satisfied himself that the appellant had waived his right to consult with an attorney prior to his acceptance of an Article 15 proceeding.

Resolution of this issue requires evaluation of our language in *United States v. Booker,* 5 M.J. 238, 244 (C.M.A. 1977), as follows:

> We believe that the Supreme Court's and this Court's longstanding position of requiring that every reasonable presumption against waiver of the assistance of counsel be indulged mandates that the record affirmatively demonstrate a valid personal waiver by the individual of his right to trial in a criminal proceeding rather than having us infer or assume one solely on the basis of a single check in a box on a prepared form. If the exhibit does not affirmatively establish a valid waiver, the trial judge must conduct an inquiry on the record to establish the necessary information.

Under the facts of *Booker,* this language refers to the introduction of summary court-martial convictions during the hearing on extenuation and mitigation. As dicta, this language could be read to embrace within its concepts the admission of a record of a prior Article 15 punishment. We believe, and hereby hold, that the requirements set forth in *Booker* are likewise applicable to the introduction of a record of an Article 15 hearing in extenuation and mitigation at a court-martial.

Booker considered the right to consult with counsel prior to accepting or declining summary court-martial. The court in *Mathews* relied on that case in addressing the issue of the right to consult with counsel prior to deciding whether to accept or decline nonjudicial punishment. What is the effect of not making counsel available prior to nonjudicial punishment? Does it make the conviction null and void? JAG Manual 0109a explains the consequences:

> There is no right for an accused to consult with counsel prior to nonjudicial punishment; however, commanding officers are encouraged to permit an accused to so consult subject to the immediate availability of counsel, the delay involved, or operational commitments or military exigencies. Failure to provide the opportunity for an accused to consult with counsel prior to nonjudicial punishment does not preclude the imposition of nonjudicial punishment; it merely precludes the admissibility of the record of nonjudicial punishment in aggravation at a later court-martial (unless the accused was attached to or embarked in a vessel at the time of the imposition of nonjudicial punishment).

Limitations on Imposition

Paragraph 1f, Part 5, MCM, spells out specific restrictions on nonjudicial punishment:

f. Limitations on nonjudicial punishment.

(1) Double punishment prohibited. When nonjudicial punishment has been imposed for an offense, punishment may not again be imposed for the same offense under Article 15.

(2) Increase in punishment prohibited. Once nonjudicial punishment has been imposed, it may not be increased, upon appeal or otherwise.

(3) Multiple punishment prohibited. When a commander determines that nonjudicial punishment is appropriate for a particular service member, all known offenses determined to be appropriate for disposition by nonjudicial punishment and ready to be considered at that time, including all such offenses arising from a single incident or course of conduct, shall ordinarily be considered together, and not made the basis for multiple punishments.

(4) Statute of limitations. . . . nonjudicial punishment may not be imposed for offenses which were committed more than two years before the date of imposition.

Procedure

Paragraph 4a, Part 5, MCM, describes the procedures that occur prior to a nonjudicial punishment hearing:

Notice. If, after a preliminary inquiry . . . the nonjudicial punishment authority determines that disposition by nonjudicial punishment proceedings is appropriate . . . the nonjudicial punishment authority shall cause the service member to be notified. The notice shall include:

(1) A statement that the nonjudicial punishment authority is considering the imposition of nonjudicial punishment;

(2) A statement describing the alleged offenses, including the article of the code, which the member is alleged to have committed;

(3) A brief summary of the information upon which the allegations are based or a statement that the member may, upon request, examine available statements and evidence;

(4) A statement of the rights that will be accorded to the service member . . . ;

(5) Unless the right to demand trial is not applicable . . . a statement that the member may demand trial by court-martial in lieu of nonjudicial punishment; a statement of the maximum punishment; which the nonjudicial punishment authority may impose by nonjudicial punishment; a statement that, if trial by court-martial is demanded, charges could be referred for trial by summary, special, or general court-martial; that the member may not be tried by summary court-martial over the member's objection and that at a special or general court-martial the member has the right to be represented by counsel.

Paragraph 4b, Part 5, MCM, details the hearing procedures, including the determinations that the nonjudicial punishment authority must make:

(1) Personal appearance requested; procedure. Before nonjudicial punishment may be imposed, the service member shall be entitled to appear personally before the nonjudicial punishment authority who offered nonjudicial punishment, except when appearance is prevented by the unavailability of the nonjudicial punishment authority or by extraordinary circumstances, in which case the service member shall be entitled to appear before a person designated by the nonjudicial punishment authority who shall prepare a written summary of any proceedings before that person and forward it and any written matter submitted by the service member to the nonjudicial punishment authority. If the service member requests personal appearance, the service member shall be entitled to:

(A) Be informed in accordance with Article 31(b), UCMJ;

(B) Be accompanied by a spokesperson. . . ;

(C) Be informed orally or in writing of the information against the service member and relating to the offenses alleged;

(D) Be allowed to examine documents or physical objects against the member which the nonjudicial punishment authority has examined in connection with the case and on which the nonjudicial punishment authority intends to rely in deciding whether and how much nonjudicial punishment to impose;

(E) Present matters in defense, extenuation, and mitigation orally, or in writing, or both;

(F) Have present witnesses, including those adverse to the service member, upon request if their statements will be relevant and they are reasonably available. For purposes of this subparagraph, a witness is not reasonably available if the witness requires reimbursement by the United States for any cost incurred in appearing, cannot appear without unduly delaying the proceedings, or, if a military witness, cannot be excused from other important duties;

(G) Have the proceeding open to the public unless the nonjudicial punishment authority determines that the proceeding should be closed for good cause, such as military exigencies or security interests. . . .

(3) Evidence. The Military Rules of Evidence, . . . other than with respect to privileges, do not apply at nonjudicial punishment proceedings. Any relevant matter may be considered.

(4) Decision. After considering all relevant matters presented, if the nonjudicial punishment authority,

(A) Does not conclude that the service member committed the offenses alleged, the nonjudicial punishment authority shall so inform the member and terminate the proceedings;

(B) Concludes that the service member committed one or more of the offenses alleged, the nonjudicial punishment authority shall:

(i) So inform the service member;

(ii) Inform the service member of the punishment imposed; and

(iii) Inform the service member of the right to appeal.

The commander must decide on the guilt or innocence of the accused. The government must prove an accused's guilt at court-martial beyond a reasonable doubt. See chapter 3. JAG Manual 0110b describes the standard used to decide nonjudicial punishment cases in the U.S. Navy and Marine Corps:

Standard of proof. Captain's mast or office hours that results in nonjudicial punishment is not a criminal trial; it is a disciplinary proceeding. Its purpose is to determine whether an offense was committed by the member and, if appropriate, to provide punishment therefor.

Such punishment is designed for minor misconduct in a nonjudicial forum, without the permanent stigma of a record of "federal conviction." As such, the standard of proof by which facts must be established at mast or office hours is a "preponderance of the evidence," rather than "beyond a reasonable doubt," as it is at courts-martial.

Compare this standard with procedures used at administrative separation boards. See the section on Administrative Separation Procedures below. Note that an accused at nonjudicial punishment must be warned of the right to remain silent under Article 31(b), UCMJ. See chapter 8 concerning the right against self-incrimination. Is an admission of guilt at nonjudicial punishment admissible at a subsequent court-martial? The following case addresses that issue.

UNITED STATES V. CECIL D. JORDAN, LANCE CORPORAL, U.S. MARINE CORPS
UNITED STATES COURT OF MILITARY APPEALS
20 U.S.C.M.A. 614; 44 C.M.R. 44
JUNE 22, 1971
Opinion: Darden, Judge

A special court-martial consisting of a military judge alone convicted the appellant of assault with force likely to produce grievous bodily harm, burglary, and assault with intent to commit rape.

At the trial, the prosecution used the appellant's pretrial statement to impeach him while he was testifying before findings. He had made the pretrial statement after having been warned in compliance with Article 31, UCMJ, but without his having been notified of his right to counsel promulgated in *Miranda v. Arizona* and *United States v. Tempia*.

After completion of the government's case, Jordan was called to the witness stand by his own counsel. When asked on direct examination whether he had been at the victim's home at 227-Banchi Aza-Kin, Kin-Son, Okinawa, on October 29, 1969, Jordan replied, "No I wasn't." He was asked during cross examination if he had "Battalion Office Hours for this offense"; whether Lieutenant Colonel Harris, the battalion commander, had warned him of his rights under Article 31; and if he had voluntarily given a statement after the warning. In each instance, Jordan answered in the affirmative. When questioned about what he had told his battalion commander, Jordan replied, "I told him that I was there." He admitted having lied earlier on direct examination, "Because I got shook up." Jordan went on to explain that on the night in question he was "out getting drunk" and mistook the victim's residence for a house of prostitution.

His counsel now maintain that Jordan was improperly cross-examined regarding his prior out-of-court statement, since the government did not demonstrate compliance with *Miranda v. Arizona* and *United States v. Tempia* that the appellant was also first warned of his right to counsel before Lieutenant Colonel Harris questioned him.

Miranda and *Tempia* are apposite only if Jordan made a statement during a custodial interrogation. Such a determination depends not on whether he technically was in custody but on whether he was "otherwise deprived of his freedom of action in any significant way."

At the time Jordan gave the statement . . . he was the prime suspect, if not the only one. Other indications that the interrogation was custodial include the battalion commander's having read to him the charges on which he was later tried and the commander's having given him an Article 31 warning. Jordan could not have disregarded the call to battalion office hours without hazarding himself, and he hardly could have left the commander's office with impunity until he was dismissed. We, therefore, hold that Jordan was in a coercive situation for *Miranda* and *Tempia* purposes and that he should have been informed of his right to counsel. We do not hold that a member of the armed forces who is questioned by a superior in rank is subjected to custodial interrogation solely because the questioning is conducted by a superior. And a member of the armed forces is not in custody solely as a result of his status. Each case must be examined for indicia of a more significant deprivation of freedom than status as a member of the armed forces or questioning by a superior in rank. But questioning by a commanding officer or military police or investigators at which the accused is given an Article 31 warning strongly suggests that an accused is also entitled to a right to counsel warning under *Miranda* and *Tempia*.

Based on *Jordan,* would it be wise to provide both Article 31 and *Miranda* warnings to an accused at nonjudicial punishment? See *United States v. Tempia* in chapter 8.

Punishments

There are several types of punishments awardable at nonjudicial punishment. Paragraph 5c, Part 5, MCM, describes the nature of each of these punishments:

(1) Admonition and reprimand. Admonition and reprimand are two forms of censure intended to express adverse reflection upon or criticism of a person's conduct. A reprimand is a more severe form of censure than an admonition. When imposed as nonjudicial punishment, the admonition or reprimand is considered to be punitive, unlike . . . nonpunitive admonition and reprimand. . . . In the case of commissioned officers and warrant officers, admonitions and reprimands given as nonjudicial punishment must be administered in writing. In other cases they may be administered either orally or in writing.
(2) Restriction. Restriction is the least severe form of deprivation of liberty. Restriction involves moral rather than physical restraint. The severity of this type of restraint depends on its duration and the geographical limits specified when the punishment is imposed. A person undergoing restriction may be required to report to a designated place at specified times if reasonably necessary to ensure that the punishment is being properly executed. Unless otherwise specified by the nonjudicial punishment authority, a person in restriction may be required to perform any military duty.
(3) Arrest in quarters. As in the case of restriction, the restraint involved in arrest in quarters is enforced by a moral obligation rather than by physical means. This punishment may be imposed only on officers.
(4) Correctional custody. Correctional custody is the physical restraint of a person during duty or nonduty hours, or both, imposed as a punishment under Article 15, and may include extra duties, fatigue duties, or hard labor as an incident of correctional custody.
(5) Confinement on bread and water or diminished rations. Confinement on bread and water or diminished

Punishment	On Officers By				On Enlisted Personnel By	
	CO who is 0–3 or below	CO who is 0–4 or above	CO who is GCM CA	Officer who is Flag Rank	CO who is 0–3 or below (or any OIC)	CO who is 0–4 or above
Admonition or Reprimand *plus* one or more of the following	Written	Written	Written	Written	Oral or Written	Oral or Written
Confinement on B&W if attached to or embarked in a vessel (1)					3 days	3 days
Correctional custody					7 days	30 days
Restriction to limits with or w/o suspension of duty	15 days	30 days	30 days	60 days	14 days	60 days
Arrest in quarters			30 days	30 days		
Extra duties (2)					14 days	45 days
Forfeiture				1/2 per 2 months	7 days pay	1/2 for 2 months
Reduction in rate (3)					One grade	One grade

(1) Imposable only on E-3 and below.
(2) Limited to 2 hours per day.
(3) No reduction from pay grade E-7 or above in U.S. Navy. No reduction from pay grade E-6 or above in the Marine Corps.

Figure 4-4 NJP Punishment Chart

rations involves confinement in places where the person so confined may communicate only with authorized personnel. The ration to be furnished a person undergoing a punishment of confinement on bread and water or diminished rations is that specified by the authority charged with the administration of the punishment, but the ration may not consist solely of bread and water unless this punishment has been specifically imposed.

(6) Extra duties. Extra duties involve the performance of duties in addition to those normally assigned to the person undergoing the punishment. Extra duties may include fatigue duties. Military duties of any kind may be assigned as extra duty.

(7) Reduction in grade. Reduction in grade is one of the most severe forms of nonjudicial punishment and it should be used with discretion. As used in Article 15, the phrase "if the grade from which demoted is within the promotion authority of the officer imposing the reduction or any officer subordinate to the one who imposes the reduction" does not refer to the authority to promote the person concerned but to the general au-

thority to promote to the grade held by the person to be punished.

(8) Forfeiture of pay. Forfeiture means a permanent loss of entitlement to the pay forfeited. "Pay," as used with respect to forfeiture of pay under Article 15, refers to the basic pay of the person or, in the case of reserve component personnel on inactive-duty, compensation for periods of inactive-duty training, plus any sea or foreign duty pay. "Basic pay" includes no element of pay other than the basic pay fixed by statute for the grade and length of service of the person concerned and does not include special pay for a special qualification, incentive pay for the performance of hazardous duties, proficiency pay, subsistence and quarters allowances, and similar types of compensation. If the punishment includes both reduction, whether or not suspended, and forfeiture of pay, the forfeiture must be based on the grade to which reduced.

Maximum punishments depend up the rank/rate of both the accused and the nonjudicial punishment authority. Figure 4-4 sets forth the maximum punishments in the U.S. Navy and Marine Corps.

Note that Paragraph 5d, Part 5, MCM, limits the combinability of certain deprivations of liberty:

(1) Arrest in quarters may not be imposed in combination with restriction;

(2) Confinement on bread and water or diminished rations may not be imposed in combination with correctional custody, extra duties, or restriction;

(3) Correctional custody may not be imposed in combination with restriction or extra duties;

(4) Restriction and extra duties may be combined to run concurrently, but the combination may not exceed the maximum imposable for extra duties;

(5) Subject to the limits [in the subparagraphs above] all authorized punishments may be imposed in a single case in the maximum amounts.

Based on the above, may a commander combine bread and water with restriction? With correctional custody? Can restriction be combined with extra duties? If yes, what are the maximum number of days of restriction permissible?

Post Nonjudicial Punishment Actions

One of the primary purposes of nonjudicial punishment is to maintain discipline. To that end, the U.S. Navy and Marine Corps authorize publication of the results of Article 15 proceedings. JAG Manual 0115 describes the rules for dissemination of nonjudicial punishment information:

Publication. Publication of nonjudicial punishment results is rooted in the reasonable belief that it serves to deter other members of the organization from committing similar offenses and that it has salutary effects upon the morale of the organization. Accordingly, commanding officers may, if the interests of the rehabilitation of the offender, good order, high morale, and perceptions of fairness so warrant, establish a policy whereby the disposition of nonjudicial punishment cases should be announced. Announcement may be, for example, by any or all of the methods below:

Plan of the Day publication. The name, rate, offense(s), and disposition of the offender may be published in the plan of the day within one month of the imposition of nonjudicial punishment or, if the punishment is appealed, within one month of the date the appeal is denied, provided that the plan of the day is disseminated to military personnel only. If the plan of the day is disseminated to other than military personnel, nonjudicial punishment results may be published without the name of the accused.

Bulletin boards. The name, rate, offense(s), and disposition of the individual case may be posted within one month of the imposition of nonjudicial punishment or, if the punishment is appealed, within one month of the date the appeal is denied, on command bulletin boards for military personnel only. If command bulletin boards are accessible to other than military personnel, nonjudicial punishment results may be published without the name of the accused.

Daily formation (Marine Corps) or morning quarters (Navy). The name, rate, offense(s), and disposition of nonjudicial punishment cases may be announced at daily formations or morning quarters within one month of the imposition of nonjudicial punishment or, if the punishment is appealed, within one month of the date the appeal is denied.

Do you think the above actions deter misconduct on the part of other service members? Does publication of information violate the accused's privacy rights? For that matter, does a person ever have a right of privacy in his or her own misconduct?

Following nonjudicial punishment, the commander imposing punishment may take certain actions with respect to the punishment imposed. Paragraph 6, Part 5, MCM, describes these actions:

a. Suspension. The nonjudicial punishment authority who imposes nonjudicial punishment . . . may, at any time, suspend any part or amount of the unexecuted punishment imposed and may suspend a reduction in grade or a forfeiture, whether or not executed, subject to the following rules:

(1) An executed punishment of reduction or forfeiture of pay may be suspended only within a period of four months after the date of execution.

(2) Suspension of a punishment may not be for a period longer than six months from the date of the sus-

pension, and the expiration of the current enlistment or term of service of the service member involved automatically terminates the period of suspension.

(3) Unless the suspension is sooner vacated, suspended portions of the punishment are remitted, without further action, upon the termination of the period of suspension.

(4) Unless otherwise stated, an action suspending a punishment includes a condition that the service member not violate any punitive article of the code. The nonjudicial punishment authority may specify in writing additional conditions of the suspension.

b. Mitigation. Mitigation is a reduction in either the quantity or quality of a punishment, its general nature remaining the same.

c. Remission. Remission is an action whereby any portion of the unexecuted punishment is canceled. Remission is appropriate under the same circumstances as mitigation.

d. Setting aside. Setting aside is an action whereby the punishment or any part or amount thereof, whether executed or unexecuted, is set aside and any property, privileges, or rights affected by the portion of the punishment set aside are restored.

Following imposition of nonjudicial punishment, a service member has the right to appeal. Paragraph 7, Part 5, MCM, describes the appeal process:

a. In general. Any service member punished under Article 15 who considers the punishment to be unjust or disproportionate to the offense may appeal through the proper channels to the next superior authority. . . .

c. Format of appeal. Appeals shall be in writing and may include the appellant's reasons for regarding the punishment as unjust or disproportionate.

d. Time limit. An appeal shall be submitted within five days of imposition of punishment, or the right to appeal shall be waived in the absence of good cause shown. A service member who has appealed may be required to undergo any punishment imposed while the appeal is pending except that if action is not taken on the appeal within five days after the appeal was submitted, and if the service member so requests, any unexe-

cuted punishment involving restraint or extra duty shall be stayed until action on the appeal is taken. . . .

f. Action by superior authority.

(1) In general. In acting on an appeal, the superior authority may exercise the same power with respect to the punishment imposed as may be exercised . . . by the officer who imposed the punishment. The superior authority may take such action even if no appeal has been filed.

An appeal may be filed if the service member believes the nonjudicial punishment was "unjust or disproportionate." The chances of success on appeal from nonjudicial punishment are less than an appeal of a court-martial conviction. The relatively low standard of proof at nonjudicial punishment (preponderance of the evidence) partially accounts for the low success rate on appeal. The absence of formal rules of evidence at nonjudicial punishment also plays a part. What other factors may influence the decision of an appeal authority?

Administrative Separation Procedures

Relationship to Nonjudicial Punishment and Courts-Martial

In addition to courts-martial and nonjudicial punishment, the military has the option of administratively separating service members. In many instances, administrative separations result from commission of military crimes; however, unlike disciplinary proceedings, administrative separations relate solely to a service member's fitness for future useful service and do not focus on punishment or rehabilitation. Because an administrative separation may occur before or after, or even in the absence of, nonjudicial punishment or court-martial, it provides a commander with another method to dispose of suspected offenses. This section will center on administrative separations involving wrongdoing on the part of service members.

Procedure

The military employs two types of procedures to administratively separate service members: (1) the administrative board procedure and (2) the notification procedure. The selection of the separation procedure depends on the nature of the discharge. Thus a separation that results in an adverse characterization of discharge (other than honorable) or carries a negative stigma (homosexuality) or involves a service member with significant time in the military (six years of service) will entail more process. A hearing will be afforded service members in these categories (that is, an administrative board). Naval Military Personnel Manual 3640350 describes the procedural rights of service members (referred to as "respondents") appearing before such boards:

2. General Procedural Instruction.

a. The board functions as an administrative rather than a judicial body. Strict rules of evidence need not be observed; however, reasonable restrictions shall be observed concerning relevancy and competency of evidence.

b. While board proceedings . . . are not a judicial trial, they should be formalized to the extent of assuring a full opportunity for presentation of the respondent's case.

c. Witnesses. No authority exists for the issuance of subpoenas in connection with these hearings. . . . Attention is directed to the fact that military personnel on active duty may not be compelled to testify or produce evidence that will incriminate them.

3. Rights of the Respondent. A respondent who has elected an Administrative Board and whose case is presented to such Board has the following rights:

a. Respondents may appear in person, with or without counsel, or in their absence be represented by counsel, at all open proceedings of the Board.

b. Respondents may challenge a voting member of the board or the legal advisor, if any, for cause only.

c. Respondents may request the attendance of witnesses in their behalf at the Administrative Board. . . .

e. The respondent or respondent's counsel may question any witness who appears before the Board.

f. The respondent or respondent's counsel may present argument prior to the Board's closing for deliberation on findings and recommendations.

h. The respondent may testify in his or her own behalf, subject to the provisions of Article 31, UCMJ. If the respondent elects to remain silent, that fact shall not be considered by the board for any purpose on any issue before it. . . .

5. Findings and Recommendations.

b. The Board shall determine whether each allegation . . . is supported by a preponderance of the evidence. . . .

d. The Board shall make recommendations as to retention or separation.

e. If separation . . . is recommended, the board shall recommend characterization of service or description of service.

Compare the rights of a service member at a discharge board with the rights at nonjudicial punishment and courts-martial. In particular, compare summary courts-martial with discharge boards. A respondent at a discharge board is afforded counsel, while an accused at summary court-martial is not. See chapter 3. Does this protection relate to the discharge board's authority to recommend an other than honorable discharge? Also note the standard of proof at an administrative separation board, preponderance of the evidence. This is the same standard as in nonjudicial punishment proceedings, but lower than the measure of proof at courts-martial (beyond a reasonable doubt).

An administrative separation board provides a respondent with several procedural rights, including the right to counsel, to call witnesses, to cross-examine witnesses, to make argument, and to challenge board members for cause. The next case addresses the adequacy of these procedures.

LUIS PEREZ V. UNITED STATES
UNITED STATES DISTRICT COURT FOR THE NORTHERN
DISTRICT OF ILLINOIS, EASTERN DIVISION
850 F. SUPP. 1354
APRIL 14, 1994
Opinion: Williams, Judge

Plaintiff Luis Armando Perez ("Perez" or "PN2 Perez") has brought suit against the United States. Perez seeks a declaratory judgment finding that his administrative discharge from the U.S. Navy is void and that he has never been legally separated from the armed services. He also seeks an order compelling the secretary of the navy to formally vacate his administrative discharge and restore plaintiff to his pre-discharge status as a petty officer, second class in the United States Navy.

In August 1992 Perez was administratively discharged from the United States Navy ("navy") under Other Than Honorable Discharge by Reason of Misconduct Due to Commission of a Serious Offense. Plaintiff had served twelve years in the United States Navy at the time of his discharge. Having first enlisted in 1979, Perez worked as a petty officer on active duty and, at the time of his discharge, held the rank of petty officer second class. As defendants readily acknowledge, Perez was an outstanding sailor. Indeed, throughout his service with the navy, Perez received numerous excellent evaluation reports, and was regularly recommended for advancement. In July 1985, plaintiff married Petty Officer Kathleen Pedigo ("Pedigo") who, like plaintiff, was also on active duty at the time of the events in question. Together, they had one child, Blake Perez ("Blake"). On March 9, 1990, plaintiff and Pedigo were divorced and Pedigo was awarded custody of Blake. She subsequently requested, and was granted, permission to transfer to Italy. In late October 1990, Perez also requested a transfer to Italy to be near his son.

On Nov. 5, 1990, while at a military day care center in Italy, a day care worker, Marisa Minton, claimed to have found Blake imitating anal intercourse with another one of the children. Blake was four years old at the time. When Ms. Minton asked Blake about what he was doing, he reportedly said: "My daddy does it to me all the time. He hugs me and tells me not to tell my Mommy." After being informed of her son's statements and conduct, Pedigo claimed that Blake had twice be-

fore made comments to her indicating that he may have been sexually abused by his father. According to Pedigo, Blake told her in July 1990 that "Daddy touched my pee-pee" and on another occasion said that "Daddy puts his pee-pee in my mouth." Initially, the allegations against plaintiff were investigated by the Naval Criminal Investigative Service (NCIS). After this preliminary investigation, plaintiff's commanding officer, Personnel Support Activity, Great Lakes, Illinois ("commanding officer") preferred charges against Perez. Plaintiff was charged with one count of sodomy and six counts of indecent acts or liberties with a child.

In September 1991, the commanding officer convened a pretrial investigation ("Article 32 investigation") to determine whether a general court-martial was warranted under the circumstances. The investigation lasted three days and plaintiff was represented by military counsel throughout the proceeding. At the investigation NCIS Investigating Officer Ursala Pedrillo and Pedigo testified. Statements from the social worker and counselor involved with Blake Perez were admitted and made part of the record as were clinical notes of treatment, letters from the plaintiff to Blake, statements from people who had contact with Blake at the day care center. After the Article 32 hearing, the investigating officer, Ursula Pedrillo, recommended that charges not be referred to a general court-martial. Consequently, the commanding officer chose an administrative separation procedure, instead of convening a general court-martial or taking no action whatsoever.

In January 1992, an administrative discharge board was convened to hear the charges against plaintiff. Following the conclusion of the hearing, the board deliberated for ten minutes and found, by a vote of 3 to 0, that plaintiff had committed misconduct due to commission of a serious offense for which he should be separated from the navy with an other than honorable discharge. These recommendations, along with Perez' counsel's letter of deficiencies were then forwarded to Perez' commanding officer. The commanding officer adopted the recommendations, and on May 5, 1992, the chief of Naval Personnel ordered that Perez be separated from the naval service with an other than honorable discharge. PN2 Perez was ultimately discharged on August 5, 1992.

Plaintiff alleges that his due process rights were violated on several grounds. The court will address each in turn.

Plaintiff claims that the navy failed to notify him of the charges against him prior to his discharge hearing. Though plaintiff received the pre-hearing notice required under Naval Military Personnel Manual 3640300, this notice merely stated (in pertinent part) "you are being considered for an administrative discharge from the Naval Service by reason of Misconduct due to Commission of a Serious Offense." It did not detail the underlying charges. Nevertheless, after carefully reviewing the Administrative Record, the court finds that plaintiff was well aware of the nature of the charges against him at the time of the separation proceeding.

Initially, the court notes that by January 1992, when the separation proceeding began, plaintiff had been the subject of a 16-month investigation focusing on his alleged sexual abuse of his son. In addition to having received copies of the charge sheet detailing the alleged conduct, Perez was present throughout the three-day pretrial investigation hearing held in September 1991 where both live testimony and written evidence was offered regarding Perez' alleged sexual abuse of his son.

His familiarity with the charges against him is also evidenced by his lawyer's conduct at the January 1992 proceeding. At voir dire, his lawyer asked questions intended to elicit information about the board members' potential bias against accused sex offenders. Questioning focused on issues surrounding children, visitation with children by non-custodial parents, and the sexual abuse of children.

Finding substantial evidence in the record indicating that both plaintiff and his lawyer were well aware of the nature of the charges against him, the court rejects Perez' assertion that the navy failed to provide him with adequate notice of the basis for the discharge proceedings as meritless.

Perez claims that his due process rights were also infringed through the navy's denial of his "right" to confront his accusers and to a trial by jury. As discussed below, these Sixth Amendment rights do not apply in the administrative discharge context. Procedural due process generally requires notice and some form of pre-deprivation hearing. While the hearing should normally be sufficiently structured to allow the plaintiff an opportunity to be heard and to respond to the charges against him, it need not provide him with the same protections afforded defendants in criminal trials. Defendant's refusal to allow Perez to confront all of the witnesses' against him or provide him with a trial by jury did not violate procedural due process.

The Sixth Amendment to the United States Constitution requires that, "In all criminal prosecutions, the accused shall enjoy the right . . . to be confronted with the witnesses against him. . . ."

The plain language of the Sixth Amendment contemplates its application only in criminal proceedings. Furthermore, relevant case law makes it abundantly clear that Sixth Amendment rights do not attach in non-criminal proceedings.

Members of the armed forces may be subjected to "criminal prosecutions" through the Uniform Code of Military Justice. This was not the basis of plaintiff's discharge. Instead, plaintiff was the subject of an administrative discharge procedure. "An administrative military discharge is not criminal or quasi-criminal in nature, but is governed by traditional administrative law doctrine, tempered by reference to the unique circumstances of the military." *Schowengerdt v. United States*, 944 F.2d 483, 490 n.9 (9th Cir. 1991). Consequently plaintiff was not entitled to any Sixth Amendment protections in his discharge proceedings.

Note from *Perez* that an administrative discharge board is convened by the commander of the service member's unit. It is made up of at least three commissioned, warrant, or noncommissioned officers (of the grade E-7 or higher and senior to the respondent). A majority of the board must be commissioned or warrant officers, and at least one member of the board must be an officer of the grade O-4 or higher. As *Perez* holds, this system has been deemed to provide sufficient procedural protections for service members. Is there any guarantee, however, that a board will not be improperly influenced by the commander convening the board? Representation by counsel will guard against illegal influence to some degree; however, the counsel cannot protect against all abuses. The military must, therefore, rely upon its officers to act appropriately.

A nonhearing procedure, the notification procedure, is used for all separations not involving a negative characterization of service, homosexuality, or a member who has six or more years of service. If the notification procedure is used, a general discharge is the least favorable characterization of service. A service member processed using these procedures is entitled to the following rights under Naval Military Personnel Manual 3640200.5:

a. To consult with counsel.
b. To present verbal or written statements in your own behalf.
c. To obtain copies of documents . . . supporting the basis for the recommended separation. . . .
h. To a minimum of 2 working days to respond to this notice.

Is the process provided by the notification procedure sufficient to protect the interests of the service member? The decision below considers this question.

RIGOBERTO GUERRA, JR., PRIVATE, UNITED STATES ARMY V.
HUGH F. SCRUGGS, COLONEL, COMMANDING OFFICER,
7TH SPECIAL FORCES GROUP, UNITED STATES ARMY
UNITED STATES COURT OF APPEALS FOR THE FOURTH
CIRCUIT
942 F.2D 270
AUGUST 9, 1991
Opinion: Ervin, Chief Judge

Private Rigoberto Guerra brought suit against Col. Hugh F. Scruggs, commanding officer of the 7th Special Forces Group at Fort Bragg, and Michael Stone, secretary of the army, in the United States District Court for the Eastern District of North Carolina. He sought a temporary restraining order and a preliminary injunction to prevent his discharge from the army. Guerra challenged the procedures by which Col. Scruggs decided to discharge Guerra with a general discharge under honorable conditions for cocaine usage and absence from duty due to alcohol intoxication. Guerra alleged that the procedures violated the Due Process Clause and the Equal Protection Clause.

We find that the district court erred in granting the injunction in this case. Therefore, we reverse.

I

Private Guerra was a member of D Company, 2d Battalion, 7th Special Forces Group (Airborne), stationed at Fort Bragg. He received the Army Achievement Medal on two occasions and was named as the "Soldier of the Year" for Fiscal Year 1990 in his military organization at Fort Bragg. However, on October 29, 1989, Guerra missed a P.T. formation due to alcohol intoxication. On April 23, 1990, Guerra tested positive for cocaine use. Guerra accepted nonjudicial punishment pursuant to Article 15 of the UCMJ for his cocaine use.

Under Article 15, UCMJ, Guerra could have refused the nonjudicial proceedings and demanded trial by court-martial. If Guerra had made such a demand, he would have been entitled to a court-martial before any punishment could be imposed. Guerra did not demand a court-martial. Rather, he voluntarily accepted proceedings under Article 15. After the Article 15 proceedings were completed, Guerra received a notice of proposed separation from Captain Akers, commanding officer of D Company. Grounds for the proposed separation were the positive test for cocaine use and the missed P.T. formation due to alcohol intoxication. Captain Akers stated that he would recommend a general discharge. The notice of proposed separation informed Guerra of the following procedural rights:

You have the right to consult with a military counsel at no cost, and with civilian counsel at no expense to the government within a reasonable time (not less than 3 duty days).
You may submit written statements in your behalf.
You may obtain copies of documents that will be sent to the separation authority supporting the proposed separation.

In response to the notice of proposed separation, Guerra did not deny using cocaine, but instead pleaded that his mistake had been paid for by the Article 15 punishment. Guerra requested a hearing before an administrative elimination board. Because he had not served in the army for at least 6 years, he was not entitled to such a hearing. Guerra submitted ten statements from other soldiers in support of his plea of leniency. After reviewing these statements, Colonel Scruggs, commanding officer of the 7th Special Forces Group, approved the recommendation for a general discharge of Guerra.

The first factor to be considered is the nature and strength of Guerra's challenge to the military determination. Guerra raises essentially two constitutional challenges: (1) a Due Process challenge, and (2) an Equal Protection challenge. We will address each in turn.

The district court found that Guerra did have a liberty interest which afforded him due process rights. "Liberty" as referred to in the Due Process Clause of the Fourteenth Amendment includes the right of an individual to contract, to engage in any of the common occupations of life, to acquire useful knowledge and generally to enjoy those privileges long recognized as essential to the orderly pursuit of happiness by free men. From the broad notion of liberty has sprung the concept that "where a person's good name, reputation, honor, or integrity is at stake because of what the government is doing to him, notice and an opportunity to be heard are essential." *Wisconsin v. Constantineau*, 400 U.S. 433 (1971). The purpose of such notice and hearing is to provide the person an opportunity to clear his name. In the abstract, Guerra might have a liberty interest in his good name. The stigma attached to a general discharge related to a drug offense is well documented. However, merely having a liberty interest in one's good name does not make out a claim of a Due Process violation. Here, Guerra never denied that he had used cocaine. In fact, he voluntarily underwent disciplinary procedures under Article 15 without demanding a court-martial to contest the drug test results. Therefore, Guerra has failed to make out an essential element of his Due Process claim: he cannot show that the stated reason for his discharge, cocaine use, was untrue. Thus, we find that Guerra had no liberty interest.

Guerra also raised an Equal Protection claim challenging the requirement that a serviceman must serve in the army for six years before being entitled to a hearing. Guerra asserted that the six year requirement bears no rational relationship to a legitimate government objective and that it is arbitrary and capricious. Unless a statute or regulation impinges upon a fundamental right or involves a suspect classification, a minimal level of scrutiny is applied under the rational basis test. Since no fundamental right or suspect classifica-

tion is involved here, we must apply the rational basis test.

Under the rational basis test, a regulation need only bear some rational relationship to legitimate governmental purposes. The deference afforded to the government under the rational basis test is so deferential that even if the government's actual purpose in creating classifications is not rational, a court can uphold the regulation if the court can envision some rational basis for the classification.

In the case at bar, the army explained the reason for the six year requirement as follows:

> Six years is the maximum enlistment in the United States Army. So any soldier who has served beyond six years is by definition serving beyond his initial tour of enlistment. . . . The rights of the procedures that are afforded to those soldiers are not a recognition they possess a property right to continue service in the military, but merely out of the fact that they have served beyond that initial enlistment period.
>
> We are saying that we will afford these soldiers because of their term of service these procedures when they are considered for administrative elimination or separation from the service. And secondly, as expressed in AR 635-200 in its purpose paragraph, it is for the purpose of maintaining the readiness and the competence of a fighting force.
>
> The army has an investment by virtue of the time and the training possessed and invested in that soldier who serves six years or more. So it is not all for the soldier; it is there too to protect the investment of the service, again, a rational basis for determining what procedures are afforded to who [sic]. Under the exceedingly deferential rational basis test, this stated purpose of the 6 year classification is rational and does not violate the Equal Protection Clause.

Guerra's proposed discharge was at the request of Captain Akers, who was the commanding officer of Guerra's Company D. Apparently, he believed that Guerra's actions could not be tolerated in the military context. While we might conclude that the army should forgive Guerra and give him a second chance, we are not in a position to evaluate how this type of behavior impacts on a military unit, especially a special forces unit.

Why did Private Guerra not have a right to a discharge hearing in the first place? The commander in

Basis for Processing	Procedure	Least Favorable Discharge	Mandatory Processing	Counseling Required
Misconduct				
Pattern	Admin Board	OTH	No	Yes
Serious Offense	Admin Board	OTH	No (when a punitive disch would be auth by the MCM)	No
			Yes (resulted in death or serious bodily injury, or involved sexual perversion or aggravated sexual harass)	No
Drug Abuse	Admin Board	OTH	Yes	No
Homosexuality	Admin Board	OTH (if; by force, w/a person under 16, w/a subordinate, openly in public view, for compensation, aboard a naval vessel or a/c); otherwise type warranted by service record		No

Figure 4-5 Summary of Administrative Discharges and Procedures

Guerra elected to process the accused for a general discharge only. The army convicted Private Guerra of drug use at a nonjudicial proceeding. Therefore, the commander could have processed Private Guerra for an other than honorable discharge, but he elected not to do so. Because Private Guerra did not have six or more years of service, he was not entitled to a hearing procedure. This mirrors the procedures used by the navy and marines as well. See the Administrative Separation Procedures section above.

Characterizations of Discharge

When a member is administratively separated, his or her service is always characterized. There are four possible characterizations of service discussed below.

An honorable discharge is awarded when "the quality of the member's service has for the most part met acceptable standards of conduct and performance of duty." See Naval Military Personnel Manual 3610300.3.a. The vast majority of enlisted members who leave the service receive an honorable discharge.

A general discharge is issued when the performance of a service member "has been honest and faithful but significant negative aspects of the member's conduct or performance of duty outweigh positive aspects of the member's service record." See Naval Military Personnel Manual 3610300.3.b. A general discharge is "under honorable conditions," thereby entitling a member to virtually the same benefits received by virtue of an honorable discharge. Some grounds for discharge will result in a characterization of "type warranted by service record." This means that the member will receive either an honorable or general characterization, depending on his or her evaluation marks.

An other than honorable discharge is the most negative administrative discharge issued by the armed forces. It is issued if there "have been one or more acts or omissions that constitute a significant departure from expected conduct" (that is, the service member committed misconduct). See Naval Military Personnel Manual 3610300.3.c. Compare an other than honorable discharge with a bad conduct or a dishonorable discharge. Only a court-martial can award a bad conduct or dishonorable discharge. Which type of discharge sounds the most serious?

Note that an other than honorable discharge causes a member to lose entitlements to Veterans Administration benefits and the GI Bill. Because of the seriousness of receiving an other than honorable discharge, a service member always has the right to request an administrative board in cases in which it is a possible characterization.

Service members are in an entry level "status" for the first 180 days of uninterrupted active duty, and administrative discharge processing initiated during that period qualifies a member for an entry-level separation. However, service members who would otherwise be eligible for an entry-level characterization may receive one of the other types of administrative discharges, including an other than honorable characterization, if warranted by the circumstances of the case.

Grounds

There are numerous grounds for separating a service member. This section will consider those grounds relating to misconduct, and to separations on the basis of homosexuality. Although the focus of this section will be the basis for administrative discharge, procedural considerations such as counseling and mandatory processing are also discussed. Figure 4-5 summarizes the procedures used for each of the different grounds for discharge discussed in this section.

Misconduct

There are several grounds for separation which fall into the category of "misconduct." Members discharged under any of these bases may receive an other than honorable characterization. Naval Military Personnel Manual 3630600 explains one of these bases:

Misconduct due to a Pattern of Misconduct

(1) A pattern of misconduct is defined as discreditable involvement with civil and military authorities. The member must have violated counseling prior to initiating counseling. Such a pattern may include both minor and serious infractions as evidenced by:

(a) Two or more civilian convictions within the current enlistment.

(b) Two or more punishments under the UCMJ within the current enlistment.

(c) Any combination of two civilian convictions or punishments under the UCMJ within the current enlistment.

(d) Three or more periods of unauthorized absence of more than three days duration within the current enlistment.

Discharge processing for a pattern of misconduct requires documented counseling. For navy personnel, this is usually accomplished via a "page 13" service record entry. See the Counseling Requirement section below.

Misconduct for purposes of administrative separations can also be established by commission of a serious offense. Naval Military Personnel Manual 3630600 provides:

Misconduct Due to Commission of a Serious Offense (processing not mandatory).

An individual may be processed for administrative separation when a punitive discharge would be authorized by the Manual for Courts-Martial for the same or a closely related offense.

Misconduct Due to Commission of a Serious Offense (processing mandatory).

(1) An individual must be processed for administrative separation when the commanding officer believes by a preponderance of the evidence that the individual committed extremely serious misconduct that either resulted in or had the potential to result in death, or serious bodily injury.

(2) Sexual Perversion. An individual must be processed for administrative separation when an incident involves sexual behavior that deviates from socially acceptable standards of morality and decency.

(3) Sexual Harassment. An individual must be processed for administrative separation following punitive action if appropriate, on the first substantiated incident of sexual harassment involving any of the following circumstances:

(a) threats or attempts to influence another's career or job for sexual favors;
(b) rewards in exchange for sexual favors; or
(c) physical contact of a sexual nature. . . .

Note that a civilian conviction for an offense that could result in a punitive discharge under the MCM is also the basis for nonmandatory processing. Likewise, processing is mandatory for a civilian conviction for an offense involving death or serious bodily injury. See Naval Military Personnel Manual 3630600.1e and 3630600.1f. The military has significantly increased the number of situations in which processing is mandatory (drugs, serious offenses, sexual harassment, and so on). What has caused this to occur? Do you think the Tailhook debacle played a part? Mandatory processing clearly reduces the discretion of commanders. Is this a positive or negative trend?

It is not necessary that there be a nonjudicial or court-martial conviction for a member to be processed for commission of a serious offense. Thus a commanding officer may decide to forego punitive action (nonjudicial punishment or court-martial) and process the member immediately. Administrative processing under this category cannot be based on an offense for which a member was acquitted (found not guilty) at trial. Processing is not precluded, however, in situations in which a service member was tried but escaped conviction for reasons other than an acquittal. What if a service member is convicted at court-martial but not awarded a punitive discharge? May the military still process the member? The Naval Military Personnel Manual permits processing in such cases for offenses that are a "serious offense" as defined above.

Drug Abuse

Drug abuse in the military results in mandatory processing for separation. Naval Military Personnel Manual 3630600 defines three types of drug abuse:

Drug Abuse. The illegal or wrongful use or possession of controlled substance(s).

Drug Paraphernalia. All equipment, products, and materials that are used, or intended for use, or designed for use in injecting, ingesting, inhaling, or otherwise introducing into the human body controlled substances into the human body.

Drug Trafficking. The sale, transfer, or possession with intent to sell or transfer, controlled substance(s).

The navy and marines have a "zero tolerance" policy toward drug abuse. Does that policy mean that every service member convicted of a drug-related offense will be separated? Note that all service members processed for misconduct have a right to an administrative separation board. May a board retain a respondent even though the board found he or she committed misconduct?

Homosexuality

The military's current policy is that "homosexual orientation is not a bar to service entry or continued service. Homosexual conduct, however, is grounds for separation." Naval Military Personnel Manual 3630400 provides:

Basis for separation: Homosexual conduct is grounds for separation from the naval service. Homosexual conduct includes homosexual acts, a statement by a member that demonstrates a propensity or intent to engage in homosexual acts, or a homosexual marriage or attempted marriage. . . . Separation processing is mandatory if the commanding officer believes that, by a preponderance of the evidence that homosexual conduct . . . has occurred.

In cases involving the commission of homosexual acts, a service member may be retained if it is found that the acts were not accomplished by force or coercion, the member is unlikely to engage in future homosexual acts, and such acts were a departure for the member's usual and customary behavior. Likewise, in cases based on statements by the member that he or she is a homosexual or bisexual, retention may occur if it is found that the member is not a person who engages in, has a propensity to engage in, or intends to engage in homosexual acts.

The military's policy on separation of homosexuals has created significant controversy. Note that the current "don't ask, don't tell" policy instituted by President Clinton did not alter the military's basic policy of discharging homosexuals. It only affects the procedure for initiating investigations of homosexual conduct. The following case considers separation of a service member on the basis of a statement that the member is a homosexual.

JOSEPH C. STEFFAN V. WILLIAM J. PERRY,
SECRETARY OF DEFENSE
UNITED STATES COURT OF APPEALS FOR THE DISTRICT OF
COLUMBIA CIRCUIT
41 F. 3D 677
NOVEMBER 22, 1994
Opinion: Silberman, Judge

Joseph Steffan, a former navy midshipman who admitted to being a homosexual, appeals from the judgment of the district court sustaining the constitutionality of the regulations pursuant to which he was discharged from the Naval Academy.

Joseph Steffan enrolled in the Naval Academy in 1983 and successfully completed three of his four years of training, consistently being ranked near the top of his class. During the fall of his senior year, Steffan confided in two fellow midshipmen that he was a homosexual. One of the two reported Steffan's conversation to Academy officials and on the basis of this report the Naval Investigative Service began an investigation of Steffan's homosexuality. Steffan was informed of that inquiry by a fellow midshipman in March 1987. When questioned by Naval investigators, Steffan "invoked his right to remain silent," but did confide his homosexuality to a chaplain in the Academy. Subsequently, in a meeting with the commandant of the Academy, Steffan stated that he was a homosexual.

On March 24, 1987, the Academy convened a meeting of its Performance Board. At that hearing, Steffan was asked, "I'd like your word, are you a homosexual?" He replied, "Yes, sir." Steffan was then asked whether he had "anything else to add at this point," and he answered "no." Based on this hearing the Performance Board recommended to the commandant of the Academy that "Steffan be separated from the Naval Academy due to insufficient aptitude for commissioned service."

Following that meeting, Steffan, who was advised by counsel, reached an agreement with the navy, the terms of which were embodied in a "statement of understanding" signed by Steffan. Steffan acknowledged in the statement that based upon the recommendation of the Academic Board, the superintendent of the Academy would recommend his discharge. Steffan had been given a choice: either submit a "qualified resignation" or litigate and risk recommendation of a discharge. The official transcript of a midshipman who submits a "qualified resignation" reads "Resigned" rather than "Discharged" as the cause of separation. But the qualified resignation itself includes an acknowledgment by the midshipman that he will be recommended for discharge by the superintendent if he does not resign. Had Steffan chosen to appeal, presumably to the secretary of the navy, and had the secretary decided that discharge was in order, Steffan's transcript would have revealed "Discharged" as the reason for his termination. Steffan chose the first option and resigned from the Academy. The statement of understanding provided that by choosing to submit his resignation Steffan forfeited "his right to show cause to higher authority why he should not be disenrolled from the Naval Academy." The secretary of the navy accepted Steffan's resignation on May 28, 1987. Subsequently, the Naval Investigative Service terminated its uncompleted investigation into possible conduct-related criminal and regulatory violations by Steffan.

Roughly a year and a half after submitting his resignation, Steffan wrote the secretary of the navy seeking to withdraw his resignation and resume his studies at the Academy. The superintendent of the Academy "strongly" recommended to the secretary that he deny the request. The superintendent's letter noted that Steffan had made an informed decision to resign following the conclusion of all the hearings to which he was entitled under Academy regulations. As for the merits of Steffan's request, the superintendent pointed out that Steffan's admission that he was a homosexual constituted a basis for separation under the Academy regulations, and that the DOD Directives provided that "homosexuality" was incompatible with military service.

The secretary disapproved Steffan's request to withdraw his resignation "in accordance with the recommendation of the superintendent."

Steffan argues that the military regulations lack a rational basis because they are simply an attempt to cater to the prejudices of members of the military and because they "punish" homosexuals simply on the basis of their "status" and "thoughts" rather than on the basis of conduct. Steffan concedes, and this concession frames the dispute, that the military may discharge those who engage in homosexual conduct whether on or off duty. The government contends that the regulations are a rational attempt to exclude from the military individuals who engage in, or demonstrate a propensity to engage in, homosexual conduct. The government also asserts that admission into the military of those who engage in such conduct would undermine unit cohesion. And the government defends the regulations as an attempt to protect the privacy of service members.

The dispute between the parties is limited to the question of whether the regulations, by requiring the discharge of those midshipmen who describe themselves as homosexual, whether or not the Academy has information establishing that an individual has engaged in homosexual conduct or intends to do so, are rational. Steffan first argues that there is no necessary factual connection between such self-description and such conduct. But Steffan relies primarily on a more subtle and novel argument. Even if the government could rationally, as a factual matter, draw a connection between the statement and the conduct, other legal considerations prevent the government from so doing. The military may not, according to Steffan, "punish" homosexuals solely on the basis of their "status." Nor may the military presume that self-declared homosexuals will actually engage in homosexual conduct, for such conduct is illegal under the Code of Military Justice (sodomy is prohibited under Article 125, UCMJ). Such a presumption, that someone will actually break the law, is inconsistent, he argues, with our legal traditions.

We consider first whether the regulation has a rational factual basis. The appropriate question, it seems to us, is whether banning those who admit to being homosexual rationally furthers the end of banning those who are engaging in homosexual conduct or are likely to do so. The Academy can treat someone who intends to pursue homosexual conduct in the same manner as someone who engages in that conduct, because such an intent is a precursor to the proscribed conduct and makes subsequent homosexual conduct more likely than not. And the military may reasonably assume that when a member states that he is a homosexual, that member means that he either engages or is likely to engage in homosexual conduct. The inference seems particularly valid in this case because Steffan made no attempt to clarify what he meant by the term. He did not specify (nor was he asked by the Board) whether he had engaged in homosexual conduct in the past, whether he was presently engaged in homosexual conduct, whether he intended to engage in homosexual conduct in the future, or whether all three were true. Indeed, as we noted, he had previously invoked his right to remain silent when questioned on these subjects. Nor did Steffan ever indicate that his answer to the Board referred to homosexual orientation as a concept implicating only wants or thoughts unrelated to conduct, a meaning that he now suggests was a possible interpretation of the term and which the dissent embraces. He left it to the Board to draw what he apparently thought were the ordinary inferences the term homosexual suggests. These ordinary inferences are reflected in the Academy regulations and were the apparent bases for the Board's conclusions. The dissent's deconstruction of Steffan's terse response overlooks the obvious point that Steffan assumed that the Board would fully understand what he meant.

Admittedly, it is conceivable that someone would describe himself as a homosexual based on his orientation or tendencies (and, perhaps, past conduct), notwithstanding the absence of any ongoing conduct or the probability of engaging in such conduct. That there may be exceptions to the assumption on which the regulation is premised is irrelevant, however, so long as the classification (the regulation) in the run of cases furthers its purpose, and we readily conclude that it does.

The rule of law presupposes the creation of categories. The military thus may rely on presumptions that avoid the administratively costly need to adduce proof of conduct or intent, so long as there is a rational basis for believing that the presumption furthers that end. And the military certainly furthers its policy of discharging those members who either engage in, or are likely to engage in, homosexual conduct when it discharges those who state that they are homosexual. The special deference we owe the military's judgment necessarily affects the scope of the court's inquiry into the rationality of the military's policy. Whether a certain course of conduct is rational does not depend solely upon the degree of correlation that exists between a surface characteristic and a corresponding hidden trait. For the question whether the degree of correlation justifies the action taken, that is, whether it is rational, necessarily depends on one's assessment of the magnitude of the problem the action seeks to avoid. The military is entitled to deference with respect to its estimation of the effect of homosexual conduct on military discipline and therefore to the degree of correlation that is tolerable. Particularly in light of this deference, we think the class of self-described homosexuals is sufficiently close to the class of those who engage or intend to engage in homosexual conduct for the military's policy to survive rational basis review.

It is asserted that one does not choose to be homosexual and that therefore it is unfair for the military to make distinctions on that basis. But whether or not one's homosexuality is genetically predetermined, one's height certainly is. Steffan conceded at oral argument that the navy's maximum height restrictions are constitutional because they rationally further a legitimate naval purpose. That concession amounts to an admission that employment decisions based on a person's characteristics are subject to the same analysis as decisions based on a person's conduct.

To be sure, it would not pass even rational basis review for the military to reject service members because of characteristics, such as race or religion or the lack of inherited wealth, that have absolutely no bearing on their military service. Homosexuality, by contrast, is not irrelevant to homosexual conduct. And once Steffan concedes that the military may constitutionally seek to prevent the latter, his analogy to a hypothetical exclusion of those of a particular race or religion fails.

Nevertheless, Steffan, in order to make his point, would have us see homosexual status, which is all that he should be thought to have acknowledged, as conceptually unrelated to homosexual conduct. Although there may well be individuals who could, in some sense, be described as homosexuals based strictly on an inchoate orientation, certainly in the great majority of cases those terms are coterminous. Homosexuality, like all forms of sexual orientation, is tied closely to sexual conduct.

We recognize that the government's basic policy, that homosexuals (using the ordinary meaning) may not serve in the armed forces, is quite controversial. The issue is politically decisive. We think, however, that Steffan's claim that the government cannot rationally infer that one who states he or she is a homosexual is a practicing homosexual, or is at least likely to engage in homosexual acts, is so strained a constitutional argument as to amount to a basic attack on the policy itself.

Other cases have held the opposite of *Steffan.* In *Meinhold v. United States,* 808 F. Supp. 1455, 1458 (C.D. Cal. 1993), the court permanently enjoined the Department of Defense "from discharging or denying enlistment to any person based on sexual orientation in the absence of sexual conduct which interferes with the military mission of the armed forces of the United States." The Ninth Circuit concluded that separation could be based on a statement identifying oneself as a homosexual only when it was accompanied by evidence of conduct or intent. The court found that Petty Officer Meinhold's televised announcement that he was gay failed to provide any such evidence. As the court pointed out in *Steffan,* a declaration of homosexual status is still a basis for separation under the terms of the current Department of Defense policy (although *Meinhold* found this to be unconstitutional). Ultimately, the Supreme Court will have to resolve the issue of homosexuals in the armed services.

Service members discharged for homosexual conduct receive a type warranted by service record discharge characterization. However, an other than honorable discharge is possible in certain situations. Naval Military Personnel Manual 3630400.4 provides that an individual engaging in homosexual acts

ADMINISTRATIVE REMARKS
NAVPERS 1070/613 (REV. 10-81)
S/N 0108-LF-010-9991

SHIP OR STATION   USS ALWAYS GONE (CVN 72)

15 March 19XX

1. You are being retained in the naval service, however, the following deficiencies in your performance and/or conduct are identified:

> Here outline in a brief paragraph specific performance deficiencies such as failure to complete required PQS courses, poor attitude in the work center, lack of care in performing required tasks, failure to learn minimum required work skills necessary to complete assigned tasks, poor grooming habits, etc. Also outline conduct deficiencies such as lack of proper respect for supervisors, periods of UA from the work center, specific offenses for which the member has been punished at NJP or court-martial.

2. The following are recommendations for corrective action:

> Here specify how the member should correct the problems you outlined in the first paragraph. For example: "Adopt a more positive attitude toward your work and your supervisors. Obtain a reliable alarm clock and ask a friend to ensure that you are up each morning in time to make muster. Since many of your disciplinary problems appear to be related to alcohol abuse, acquire hobbies and pursue recreation activities which do not involve drinking."

3. Assistance is available through:

> Here indicate the availability of counseling from the member's leading petty officer, work center supervisor, leading chief, and division officer. If the member exhibits signs of drug or alcohol abuse, outline the availability of help from the command. Indicate that the Command master Chief and Chaplain are also available to provide counseling on personal problems. The member might also be referred to the Career Counselor if he is dissatisfied in his current rating and would like to discuss other options.

4. You are advised that any further deficiencies in your performance and/or conduct will terminate the reasonable period of time for rehabilitation that this counseling/warning entry infers and may result in disciplinary action and in processing for administrative separation. All deficiencies previously cited and/or misconduct during your current enlistment, both prior to and subsequent to the date of this action will be considered. Subsequent violation(s) of the UCMJ or conduct resulting in civilian conviction could result in an administrative separation under other than honorable conditions.

5. This counseling/warning entry is made to afford you an opportunity to undertake the recommended corrective action. Any failure to adhere to the guidelines cited above, which is reflected in your future performance and/or conduct, will make you eligible for administrative separation action.

Witnessed: _____   Acknowledged: _____
            M division officer   SN Juan Moore Chance

Name (Last, First, Middle)	SSN	BRANCH AND CLASS
CHANCE, Juan Moore	123-45-6789	USN

Figure 4-6 Summary of Administrative Discharges and Procedures

under the following circumstances may receive a negative discharge:

a. By using force, coercion, or intimidation;

b. With a person under sixteen years of age;

c. With a subordinate in circumstances that violate customary naval superior-subordinate relationships;

d. Openly in public view;

e. For compensation;

f. Aboard a naval vessel or aircraft;

g. In another location subject to naval control under aggravating circumstances that have an adverse impact on good order, discipline, or morale.

In all homosexuality separations, the service member has the right to an administrative board, even if an other than honorable characterization is not possible. Why does the military have this rule? See *Selland v. Aspin,* 832 F. Supp. 12 (D.C. 1993) (court noted stigmatizing nature of an honorable discharge on the basis of homosexuality). Finally, most homosexual conduct is still a violation of the UCMJ. See *Steffan* and Article 125, UCMJ (sodomy).

Counseling Requirement

Evidence that the member has previously been counseled concerning the basis for separation is a prerequisite for discharge processing in many separation cases. For example, counseling is required in separations for misconduct due to a pattern of misconduct. Failure to adhere to the counseling requirement will preclude administrative processing. The counseling must include: (1) notification concerning the deficiency or impairment to be corrected, (2) specific recommendations for corrective action, (3) assistance available to the member, (4) a comprehensive explanation of consequences for failure to successfully undertake the corrective action, and (5) a reasonable period provided to allow the member an opportunity to correct the deficiency. If counseling is required, it must be documented in writing in the member's service record. See figure 4-6 for an example of a navy page 13 counseling entry.

A counseling is like a contract with the service member in the sense that the government promises not to discharge the member if he or she complies with its provisions. What happens if the government breaches this contract? See *Perez* above, which relates to a service member's right to have the military comply with its own procedures.

Study Questions

1. What is purpose of nonpunitive measures? What are the types of nonpunitive measures? Who has authority to deprive a member of liberty?

2. What is the difference between punitive and nonpunitive censure?

3. Who has authority to impose nonjudicial punishment? May the authority be delegated?

4. What is a "minor offense" for purposes of nonjudicial punishment? Why is the definition important?

5. An enlisted accused attached to a vessel has the following rights at a nonjudicial punishment hearing *except:*

a. The right to examine any evidence on which the commanding officer intends to rely in deciding whether to make a finding on guilt or innocence.

b. The right to present matters in defense, extenuation, or mitigation.

c. The right to be fully represented at the hearing by military counsel and/or civilian counsel.

d. The right to speak privately with the commanding officer during the hearing about matters of a personal or embarrassing nature.

e. The right to be advised of his right to appeal, if nonjudicial punishment is awarded.

6. When does an accused have the right to refuse nonjudicial punishment?

7. What is the standard of proof at nonjudicial punishment?

8. What punishments may be awarded at nonjudicial punishment? What are the limitations on combining punishments?

9. HM3 McCoy (an E-4) was apprehended by shore patrol as a result of a bar brawl. He was returned to the USS *Enterprise* and put on report for being drunk and disorderly. Which of the following punishments may the commanding officer (an O-6) *not* award to HM3 McCoy?

  a. Three days bread and water, ten days restriction, and reduction in rate to E-3.

  b. Forty-five days restriction, forty-five days extra duty, and forfeiture of one-half month's pay for two months.

  c. Three days bread and water, forfeiture of one week's pay, and reduction in rate to E-3.

  d. Thirty days correctional custody, reduction in rate to E-3.

  e. None of the above; they are all permissible punishments.

10. What actions may a commander take following imposition of nonjudicial punishment? May a commanding officer ever increase the punishment following the hearing? What are a service member's appeal rights following nonjudicial punishment? What actions may the appeal authority take on an appeal?

11. How do administrative separations relate to nonjudicial punishment and courts-martial?

12. Describe the types of procedures used to administratively separate service members. When is the administrative board procedure used? When is the notification procedure appropriate? What are a service member's rights at a discharge board?

13. BM3 Smith is being processed for administrative separation under the notification procedure. The *least favorable* possible characterization of his discharge is:

  a. Discharge under other than honorable conditions.

  b. Discharge with a dishonorable discharge.

  c. Discharge with a general discharge.

  d. Discharge with an honorable discharge.

  e. Discharge with a bad conduct discharge.

14. Certain bases for administrative separation require mandatory processing. What are those bases?

15. When is processing mandatory for commission of a serious offense? What is a "serious offense" for purposes of administrative separation?

16. Assuming that each case has appropriately documented counseling, which of the following situations provides the grounds for separation due to misconduct: pattern of misconduct?

  a. Two nonjudicial punishments for unauthorized absence.

  b. Two civilian convictions for drunk and disorderly.

  c. Two court-martial convictions for assault.

  d. Three nonjudicial punishments for dereliction of duty.

16. How does the "don't ask, don't tell" policy affect separation of service members on the basis of homosexuality? Does a declaration of homosexuality provide grounds for administrative separation? When can a member separated for homosexuality receive an other than honorable discharge?

17. What are the requirements for a valid counseling? What grounds for administrative separation require a counseling? Which do not?

CHAPTER FIVE

MILITARY CRIMES

[The UCMJ] cannot be equated to a civilian criminal code. It, and the various versions of the Articles of War which have preceded it, regulate aspects of the conduct of members of the military which in the civilian sphere are left unregulated. While a civilian criminal code carves out a relatively small segment of potential conduct and declares it criminal, the UCMJ essays more varied regulation of a much larger segment of the activities of the more tightly knit military community.

—*Parker v. Levy,* 417 U.S. 733, 739 (1974)

Nature of Military Crimes

In the above quotation, the U.S. Supreme Court explains that the UCMJ regulates a much broader range of conduct than civilian codes in the society at large. The extensive reach of military criminal law is partly the result of the large number of purely military offenses in the UCMJ. These crimes generally have no civilian counterpart and exist solely because of the military's need to maintain good order and discipline. Some of the more common of these military-specific offenses are discussed in this chapter. They include absences, disrespect, orders violations, dereliction of duty, and fraternization. Because of the military's strong involvement in prohibiting and preventing drug use by service members, controlled substance crimes are also addressed.

To a large degree, the military and military courts have developed the law surrounding the crimes discussed in this chapter. The result of this is twofold. First, the principles used to interpret military offenses are in many ways unparalleled in civilian criminal law. This means that courts in the armed services primarily look to other military decisions to decide issues involving purely military offenses. Second, the purpose behind uniquely military crimes—the maintenance of good order and discipline in the armed services—is a primary consideration of courts in interpreting such offenses. As a result, military courts must weigh fairness to accused service members against the aim of preserving order and control over soldiers and sailors. In reading the cases below, consider how these two principles are reconciled in each opinion.

Absence Offenses

There are three types of absence offenses under the UCMJ: absence without leave (Article 86), desertion (Article 85), and missing movement (Article 87). These offenses are discussed below.

Absence without Leave

Paragraph 10c, Part 4 of the MCM explains the nature of Article 86:

> In general. This article [Article 86] is designed to cover every case not elsewhere provided for in which any member of the armed forces is through the member's own fault not at the place where the member is required to be at a prescribed time.

Paragraph 10b, Part 4 of the MCM provides:

> Article 86—Absence without leave
> b. Elements.
>   (1) Failure to go to appointed place of duty.
>   (a) That a certain authority appointed a certain time and place of duty for the accused;
>   (b) That the accused knew of that time and place; and
>   (c) That the accused, without authority, failed to go to the appointed place of duty at the time prescribed. . . .
>   (3) Absence from unit, organization, or place of duty.
>   (a) That the accused absented himself or herself from his or her unit, organization, or place of duty at which he or she was required to be;

> (b) That the absence was without authority from anyone competent to give him or her leave; and
>   (c) That the absence was for a certain period of time. (Note: If the absence was terminated by apprehension, add the following element)
>   (d) That the absence was terminated by apprehension.

Based on the elements listed above, what are the primary differences between the two types of absence without leave offenses? Which do you think is the most commonly violated? Which is most serious? See appendix 3, the MCM Maximum Punishment Chart. Failure to go to appointed place of duty requires that a specific time and place of duty be assigned to the accused and that the accused not appear as ordered. Thus the government must prove actual knowledge of the duty assignment. Actual knowledge is not an element of absence from unit, organization, or place of duty. How specific must the order to go be as to time and place? What are the best ways to ensure an order is sufficiently specific as to time and place?

INCEPTION AND TERMINATION
Paragraph 10c, Part 4 of the MCM provides:

> Duration. Unauthorized absence under Article 86(3) is an instantaneous offense. It is complete at the instant an accused absents himself or herself without authority. Duration of the absence is a matter in aggravation for the purpose of increasing the maximum punishment authorized for the offense.
>   Termination—methods of return to military control.
>   (a) Surrender to military authority. A surrender occurs when a person presents himself or herself to any military authority, whether or not a member of the same armed force, notifies that authority of his or her unauthorized absence status, and submits or demonstrates a willingness to submit to military control. Such a surrender terminates the unauthorized absence.
>   (b) Apprehension by military authority. Apprehension by military authority of a known absentee terminates an unauthorized absence.

(c) Delivery to military authority. Delivery of a known absentee by anyone to military authority terminates the unauthorized absence.

(d) Apprehension by civilian authorities at the request of the military. When an absentee is taken into custody by civilian authorities at the request of military authorities, the absence is terminated.

(e) Apprehension by civilian authorities without prior military request. When an absentee is in the hands of civilian authorities for other reasons and these authorities make the absentee available for return to military control, the absence is terminated when the military authorities are informed of the absentee's availability.

The above language addresses how absence without leave is terminated. The following case addresses the relationship between leave and unauthorized absence.

UNITED STATES V. MARCUS G. RINGER, SEAMAN
APPRENTICE, U.S. NAVAL RESERVE
UNITED STATES NAVY–MARINE CORPS COURT OF
MILITARY REVIEW
14 M.J. 979
NOVEMBER 17, 1982
Opinion: Byrne, Judge

Seaman Apprentice Ringer was convicted of unauthorized absence in violation of Article 86 of the UCMJ at a special court-martial.

Seaman Apprentice Ringer pled not guilty to one of the two unauthorized absence specifications. As to this specification, a service record entry showed his unauthorized absence began at 1900 on March 18, 1981, and terminated at 1415 on November 6, 1981, the dates alleged in the specification.

To rebut the government's service record entry, trial defense counsel offered a tattered leave authorization form. The form stated Seaman Apprentice Ringer was authorized fifteen days leave, beginning at 1530 on March 23, 1981, and ending at 0700 on April 6, 1981, a period of time located in the middle of his alleged unauthorized absence period.

The authorization to take leave was signed by Lieutenant Commander Griggs. Other completed boxes on the leave authorization, signed by Aviation Storekeeper

Third Class Wooten, state that Seaman Apprentice Ringer departed on leave at 1020 on March 18, 1981; five days before the leave was to take effect and approximately nine hours before the official documents previously mentioned declared him to be an unauthorized absentee.

To authenticate the leave authorization form, the defense counsel called his only witness, Petty Officer Wooten. One of Petty Officer Wooten's duties as a yeoman in the command's Supply Department was to state, on the form, the time and day of departure of navy personnel authorized leave and to then sign them out on leave on the form. Although Petty Officer Wooten did not specifically remember signing Seaman Apprentice Ringer out on leave, he did identify his own signature and that of Lieutenant Commander Griggs on the Leave Authorization.

Petty Officer Wooten also testified as follows:

> I remember the name "Ringer," sir, but as far as remembering signing, no, sir. It depends—like, I sign so many, like, you know, they come into the office and they say, "Sign my leave papers," they come in to pick up their leave papers and I turn it in to them, you know—well, they say, "I'm going on leave such and such a date" and I go ahead and just sign them out.

Did the statement that appellant departed on leave prior to the specified beginning date on his leave authorization authorize an early leave departure? It did not. Petty Officer Wooten's duties were to type up leave papers and sign navy personnel out on leave. There is no indication he possessed authority to authorize early departures. We conclude that Petty Officer Wooten's signature indicating an early departure on leave did not authorize additional leave beyond that specified in the Leave Authorization.

Did the sign-out of appellant on leave on March 18, 1981, effectuate a departure on leave five days later while appellant was in an unauthorized absence status? It did not. Initially, we note that the Leave Authorization form specifying the hour and date of departure states "Departed on Leave." Obviously, since Seaman Apprentice Ringer could not have departed on leave prior to 1530 on March 23, 1981 (the day and hour specified in his Leave Authorization for his leave to begin), a statement that he departed at an earlier time did not change his status.

Further, Petty Officer Wooten testified that the procedure used for checking navy personnel out on leave in the Supply Department of the command was to rely upon a statement from the individual taking leave as to when his leave began. Abuse of such a check-out system, no matter how lax, cannot be translated into a valid checkout for the day authorized. To hold otherwise would be to benefit those few personnel whose personal word cannot be relied upon—a circumstance that is counterproductive to the interests of high morale, good order and discipline in the naval service.

Did the approved leave authorization terminate appellant's unauthorized leave status? It did not. Once an unauthorized absence begins, it is presumed to continue until terminated by the exercise of military control over the absentee. The approved leave authorization did not, by itself, return Seaman Apprentice Ringer to military control.

Leave authorizations are always subject to revocation because of unexpected operational requirements or other military exigencies. They can also be revoked by placing a serviceman on restriction in lieu of arrest pending appropriate disciplinary action, which could well have happened to Seaman Apprentice Ringer if he had returned to military control from his unauthorized absence. Suffice it to say that there are many legitimate military reasons for revoking leave, either before the authorization date or during the leave period itself. To permit a service member to obtain irrevocable leave by absenting himself without authority would adversely affect the interests of high morale, good order and discipline in the military services.

Seaman Apprentice Ringer had certain acts that had to be completed before he would have been authorized to depart on leave: he had to terminate his unauthorized absence and he had to properly check out on leave sometime after the time specified for his leave to begin.

Since Seaman Apprentice Ringer did not terminate his unauthorized absence or properly check out on leave, the observation of the United States Court of Military Appeals applies to this case:

One who renders impossible the accomplishment of these procedures through his own unauthorized absence is without standing to complain.

Which type of absence without leave was Seaman Apprentice Ringer accused of having committed? Did you get a sense in reading the case that Seaman Apprentice Ringer was trying to pull the wool over the eyes of the command in leaving the ship early? See the section on Affirmative Defenses to Absence Offenses below regarding defenses to unauthorized absence. The following case considers how an unauthorized absence is terminated.

UNITED STATES V. PRIVATE MILTON B. COGLIN,
UNITED STATES ARMY
UNITED STATES ARMY COURT OF MILITARY REVIEW
10 M.J. 670
JANUARY 6, 1981
Opinion: Jones, Senior Judge

The issue raised below and again before this Court is whether appellant, by his presence on a military installation and his contacts with military personnel, terminated his absence at a time earlier than that charged.

At the completion of his tour of duty in Korea, the appellant was reassigned to Fort Carson, Colorado. Instead of reporting to his new duty station, he went to Fort Benning, Georgia, his place of assignment prior to Korea and an installation much closer to his home in Florida. The appellant remained at Fort Benning for two or three weeks, living wherever he could find a spare bed in the barracks (with permission of the room occupant but without permission of a unit commander or first sergeant). During his stay at Fort Benning, appellant sometimes wore his uniform and sometimes wore civilian clothes. The appellant went to Fort Benning to obtain a compassionate reassignment from Fort Carson. He spoke to an "E-7" at "personnel" who advised him of the appropriate procedure. Eventually the "E-7" told appellant that he did not have sufficient reasons to obtain a compassionate reassignment. Appellant contends that he advised the "E-7" of his absentee status.

The appellant went to finance with his records in an unsuccessful attempt to be paid, and he spoke to the current first sergeant of his former company in an effort to get reassigned to that unit, to no avail. He identified himself properly to the individuals at finance and to the first sergeant but he did not disclose to them that he was absent without leave. When he was unable to obtain pay or a compassionate reassignment, he departed Fort Benning and remained absent almost four more months before surrendering to military authorities at Fort Dix, New Jersey.

Supporting appellant's factual recitation was the stipulated testimony of a Sergeant Montgomery who was appellant's squad leader during most of appellant's tour of duty in Korea. Sergeant Montgomery was subsequently transferred to Fort Benning. By stipulation he testified that he saw appellant on several occasions during a two-week period shortly after he arrived at Fort Benning and that he advised appellant on how to obtain a compassionate reassignment. The stipulated testimony does not indicate whether Sergeant Montgomery knew appellant was AWOL when he was at Fort Benning. Assuming, as appellant maintains, that Sergeant Montgomery knew he was AWOL, it is significant that appellant states he left Fort Benning when Sergeant Montgomery advised him to turn himself in or he, the sergeant, would turn him in.

It has long been a principle of military law that an unauthorized absence may be terminated by any proper exercise of military control over an absentee. For a voluntary termination initiated by the absentee to become effective, several factors must be present.

First, the absentee must present himself to competent military authority with the intention of returning to military duty. He must present himself personally, a phone call being insufficient, but he need not report to a military installation; a recruiting office and a selective service office being sufficient for the purpose. Even a return to a military reservation does not automatically result in a termination as an absentee's casual presence on an installation for his own private purpose will not satisfy this requirement. Additionally, the competent military authority to whom the absentee must present himself must be someone with authority to apprehend, e.g., a commissioned officer, a noncommissioned officer, or a military policeman.

The second requirement that must be present for the termination of an absence is that the absentee must identify himself properly and must disclose his status as an absentee. Both identity as a member of the military and status as an absentee must be divulged. Furnishing

information on the former while at the same time concealing, misrepresenting or even remaining silent on the latter would not suffice to supply the requisite degree of knowledge. An exception to this requirement that the absentee must affirmatively divulge his identity and status would be in those situations where the competent military authority was already aware of the absentee's status or, having a duty to inquire, could have determined the status by reasonable diligence.

The final necessary requirement for the termination of an absence is that the military authority, with full knowledge of the individual's status as an absentee, exercises control over him. The measure of military control exercised may be as seemingly unimportant as referring the absentee to some other individual to solve his problem. Again an exception would occur if the military authority declined to exercise control over the absentee or was slow in the exercise of such control. In that event, the government would not be permitted to deny a termination of absence because of the failure to exercise control.

In applying the facts of the instant case to the requirements discussed above, we find a deficiency in each of the three categories. First, the appellant did not present himself to competent military authorities with the intention of terminating his absence and returning to military duty. His whole purpose at Fort Benning was a private one—to obtain a compassionate reassignment and to get paid. He spoke to the E-7, the first sergeant, Sergeant Montgomery, and others for these reasons only. An intention to return to duty would not have arisen until appellant obtained the reassignment.

Although the appellant apparently identified himself properly, we find, contrary to his contention, that he did not divulge his status as an absentee to the E-7. Appellant testified that he told the E-7 that he was "late reporting to Fort Carson." In evaluating appellant's testimony we are convinced that he misrepresented his true status to the E-7. Only through deception could he have continued his discussion for a 3 week period with an E-7 in personnel concerning a compassionate reassignment, issuance of a transportation request, and casual or partial pay without that noncommissioned officer turning him in. To accept appellant's examination, we would have to conclude that the E-7 advised him for this extended period without apprehending him or even counselling him to turn himself in. Our credulity does not stretch that far.

The appellant testified that he told Sergeant Montgomery, his former squad leader, that he was AWOL, and that Sergeant Montgomery responded that appellant should turn himself in or he (Sergeant Montgomery) would turn him in. The stipulated testimony of Sergeant Montgomery was silent as to his knowledge of appellant's status. Accepting appellant's statement that he divulged his absentee status to Sergeant Montgomery as true, appellant still did not submit to military control when Sergeant Montgomery attempted to exercise such control. He departed the post instead. The first sergeant and the E-7, having no knowledge of appellant's status, made no effort to exercise military control over him.

In summary, appellant did not present himself to competent military authority at Fort Benning with the intention of returning to military duty, did not disclose his status as an absentee to two of the three noncommissioned officers with whom he had dealings, and thwarted the attempted exercise of military control by the noncommissioned officer to whom he disclosed his status. Under these circumstances, the appellant did not terminate his absence by his interlude at Fort Benning.

What are the factors that will determine whether the military has exercised control over an absentee? Did you believe Private Coglin's contention that he had informed senior enlisted personnel of his AWOL status and that they did nothing to terminate his absence? Figure 5-1 demonstrates when an unauthorized absence terminates.

How does a civilian arrest affect unauthorized absence? Paragraph 10c, Article 4 of the MCM discusses control over military personnel by civilian authorities:

Control by civilian authorities. A member of the armed forces turned over to the civilian authorities upon request is not absent without leave while held by them under that delivery. When a member of the armed forces, being absent with leave, or absent without leave, is held, tried, and acquitted by civilian authorities, the

Situation	AWOL Terminates
Apprehension by military authorities	At the apprehension
Surrender to military authorities	At the surrender
Civilian arrest for AWOL	At the civilian arrest
Civilian arrest for civilian crime	When military is informed that the accused is available for pick-up

Figure 5-1 When AWOL Terminates

member's status as absent with leave, or absent without leave, is not thereby changed, regardless how long held. The fact that a member of the armed forces is convicted by the civilian authorities, or adjudicated to be a juvenile offender, or the case is "diverted" out of the regular criminal process for a probationary period does not excuse any unauthorized absence, because the member's inability to return was the result of willful misconduct. If a member is released by the civilian authorities without trial, and was on authorized leave at the time of arrest or detention, the member may be found guilty of unauthorized absence only if it is proved that the member actually committed the offense for which detained, thus establishing that the absence was the result of the member's own misconduct.

Desertion

Paragraph 9b, Part 4, MCM, provides the elements of desertion offenses under Article 85:

(1) Desertion with intent to remain away permanently.
  (a) That the accused absented himself or herself from his or her unit, organization, or place of duty;
  (b) That such absence was without authority;
  (c) That the accused, at the time the absence began or at some time during the absence, intended to remain away from his or her unit, organization, or place of duty permanently; and
  (d) That the accused remained absent until the date alleged.
  (Note: If the absence was terminated by apprehension, add the following element)
  (e) That the accused's absence was terminated by apprehension.
(2) Desertion with intent to avoid hazardous duty or to shirk important service.

Situation*	AWOL	Not AWOL	Duration
AWOL, civ. arrest; acquit.	X		For the entire period
AWOL, civ. arrest; no trial	X		For the entire period
AWOL, civ. arrest; convict	X		For the entire period
On Leave; arrest; acquit		X	Never AWOL
On Leave; arrest; No trial	X		Of accused "at fault" (for all the time over leave)
Leave; arrest; convicted	X		All the time over leave
Military turnover to civilians		X	Never AWOL

Figure 5-2 Relationship Between AWOL Status and Civilian Criminal Charge

(a) That the accused quit his or her unit, organization, or other place of duty;

(b) That the accused did so with the intent to avoid a certain duty or shirk a certain service;

(c) That the duty to be performed was hazardous or the service important;

(d) That the accused knew that he or she would be required for such duty or service; and

(e) That the accused remained absent until the date alleged.

Based upon the above elements, what are the differences between the two types of desertion? Which do you think is most common? Paragraph 9c, Part 4 of the MCM explains several aspects of desertion offenses:

(1) Desertion with intent to remain away permanently.

(a) In general. Desertion with intent to remain away permanently is complete when the person absents himself or herself without authority from his or her unit, organization, or place of duty, with the intent to remain away therefrom permanently. A prompt repentance and return, while material in extenuation, is no defense. It is not necessary that the person be absent entirely from military jurisdiction and control. . . .

(c) Intent to remain away permanently.

(i) The intent to remain away permanently from the unit, organization, or place of duty may be formed any time during the unauthorized absence. The intent need not exist throughout the absence, or for any particular period of time, as long as it exists at some time during the absence.

(ii) The accused must have intended to remain away permanently from the unit, organization, or place of duty. When the accused had such an intent, it is no defense that the accused also intended to report for duty elsewhere, or to enlist or accept an appointment in the same or a different armed force.

(iii) The intent to remain away permanently may be established by circumstantial evidence. Among the circumstances from which an inference may be drawn that an accused intended to remain absent permanently are: that the period of absence was lengthy; that the accused attempted to, or did, dispose of uniforms or other military property; that the accused purchased a ticket for a distant point or was arrested, apprehended, or surrendered a considerable distance from the accused's station; that the accused could have conveniently surrendered to military control but did not; that the accused was dissatisfied with the accused's unit, ship, or with military service; that the accused made remarks indicating an intention to desert; that the accused was under charges or had escaped from confinement at the time of the absence; that the accused made preparations indicative of an intent not to return (for example, financial arrangements); or that the accused enlisted or accepted an appointment in the same or another armed force without disclosing the fact that the accused had not been regularly separated, or entered any foreign armed service without being authorized by the United States. On the other hand, the following are included in the circumstances which may tend to negate an inference that the accused intended to remain away permanently: previous long and excellent service; that the accused left valuable personal property in the unit or on the ship; or that the accused was under the influence of alcohol or drugs during the absence.

(iv) Entries on documents, such as personnel accountability records, which administratively refer to an accused as a "deserter" are not evidence of intent to desert.

(v) Proof of, or a plea of guilty to, an unauthorized absence, even of extended duration, does not, without more, prove guilt of desertion.

(2) Quitting unit, organization, or place of duty with intent to avoid hazardous duty or to shirk important service.

(a) Hazardous duty or important service. "Hazardous duty" or "important service" may include service such as duty in a combat or other dangerous area; embarkation for certain foreign or sea duty; movement to a port of embarkation for that purpose; entertainment for duty on the border or coast in time of war or threatened invasion or other disturbances; strike or riot duty; or employment in aid of the civil power, in, for example, protecting property, or quelling or preventing disorder in times of great public disaster. Such services as drill, target practice, maneuvers, and practice marches are not ordinarily "hazardous duty or important service."

(b) Quits. "Quits" in Article 85 means "goes absent without authority."

(c) Actual knowledge. Requires proof that the accused actually knew of the hazardous duty or important service. Actual knowledge may be proved by circumstantial evidence.

Based on the above, a service member who only intends to desert the command and not the service still has violated Article 85(1). Also, the intent to remain away permanently may be formed at any time during the absence. When a member has been UA for thirty days (or less, if the command has evidence of a desertion intent), he or she is administratively declared a "deserter." This action is administrative, resulting in the issuance of a DD Form 553 (federal arrest warrant for deserters). The DD 553 is filed on the NCIC (National Crime Information Center) computer and is available to all law enforcement officials nationwide. The issuance of a DD 553 does not mean that a service member is guilty of desertion. Can it be used as evidence of intent to remain away permanently?

The following case considers the evidence required to prove desertion.

UNITED STATES V. THADDEUS E. THUN, SPECIALIST,
U.S. ARMY
UNITED STATES COURT OF MILITARY APPEALS
36 M.J. 468
APRIL 29, 1993
Opinion: Wiss, Judge

Despite not-guilty pleas, a military judge sitting alone as a general court-martial convicted appellant of desertion, in violation of Article 85, UCMJ.

The military judge convicted appellant of having "quit his unit, about to deploy . . . to Saudi Arabia, then a combat zone," at 0845 hours, January 18, 1991, "with intent to shirk important service, namely: participation in Operation Desert Storm . . . and did remain so absent in desertion until 1200 hours" that same day.

In this case, the statute that appellant was charged with violating reflects two essential elements, tailored to the specifics of this case: that appellant was absent from his unit without authority from 8:45 A.M. until noon on January 18, 1991, and secondly, that he did so with intent to shirk important service. The latter element of intent, in turn, requires that the service intended to be shirked was "important service," and that appellant had actual knowledge that he would be required for that important service.

Here, there was evidence that appellant, realizing for several weeks that he and his unit were marked as replacement troops in the United States' Operation Desert Storm, repeatedly made statements indicating that he did not want to be a part of such a mission and that he thought the whole effort was a misguided war over oil. Three military superiors of appellant testified that they had informed appellant, as well as other members of his unit, about the danger and the importance of their military duty regarding this mission.

The prosecution's evidence indicated that, on January 16, 1991, First Lieutenant Davenport, appellant's platoon leader, told appellant and others that their unit should "be prepared to deploy to Saudi Arabia no later than midnight" of January 17. On January 17, Davenport told the unit to continue to work, to pack their bags, and to make sure that everything was prepared for deployment the next day to Saudi Arabia and Operation Desert Storm.

At the formation at 6:30 A.M. on January 18, 1991, First Sergeant Ortiz told the unit that the last thing to be done before deploying was to weigh everyone's bags. After Ortiz had released the platoons, appellant's platoon sergeant, Sergeant First Class Anderson, ordered appellant and the rest of the platoon to return at 8:45 A.M. that same morning to weigh their bags for deployment. At that scheduled weigh-in, appellant's packed bag was present, but appellant was not. The evidence indicated that no one in appellant's immediate chain of command had given appellant permission not to be present, as he had been ordered to be.

We acknowledge that the time period of which appellant was convicted of being absent was unusually short for a charge of desertion. Nevertheless, it is not the duration of appellant's absence that is telling, but its timing. "It is well established in military law that absence without leave with knowledge of immediate overseas movement is sufficient [evidence] from which a court may find desertion predicated on the intent to shirk important service." *United States v. Hemp*, 1 U.S.C.M.A. 280, 287, 3 C.M.R. 14, 21 (1952). Under the particular facts of a given case, the imminence of the overseas duty may be the decisive factor in a desertion case.

What was the important service Specialist Thun was charged with shirking? What factors did the court examine to determine whether the accused had the intent to shirk important service? See Paragraph 9c, Part 4, MCM, above regarding the factors that will bear on the issue of the intent to desert and *United States v. Kirby* in chapter 2. Note the length of Specialist Thun's absence (less than four hours). How could the court find a violation of Article 85 when the accused was absent for such a short period?

Missing Movement

The below provisions from Paragraph 11b, Part 4, MCM, describe and explain the elements of missing movement:

(1) That the accused was required in the course of duty to move with a ship, aircraft or unit;
(2) That the accused knew of the prospective movement of the ship, aircraft or unit;
(3) That the accused missed the movement of the ship, aircraft or unit; and
(4) That the accused missed the movement through design or neglect. . . .
    c. Explanation.

(1) Movement. "Movement" as used in Article 87 includes a move, transfer, or shift of a ship, aircraft, or unit involving a substantial distance and period of time. Whether a particular movement is substantial is a question to be determined by the court-martial considering all the circumstances.
(2) Mode of movement.
    (a) Unit. If a person is required in the course of duty to move with a unit, the mode of travel is not important, whether it be military or commercial, and includes travel by ship, train, aircraft, truck, bus, or walking.
    (b) Ship, aircraft. If a person is assigned as a crew member or is ordered to move as a passenger aboard a particular ship or aircraft, military or chartered, then missing the particular sailing or flight is essential to establish the offense of missing movement.
(3) Design. "Design" means on purpose, intentionally, or according to plan and requires specific intent to miss the movement.
(4) Neglect. "Neglect" means the omission to take such measures as are appropriate under the circumstances to assure presence with a ship, aircraft, or unit at the time of a scheduled movement, or doing some act without giving attention to its probable consequences in connection with the prospective movement, such as a departure from the vicinity of the prospective movement to such a distance as would make it likely that one could not return in time for the movement.
(5) Actual knowledge. In order to be guilty of the offense, the accused must have actually known of the prospective movement that was missed. Knowledge of the exact hour or even of the exact date of the scheduled movement is not required. It is sufficient if the approximate date was known by the accused as long as there is a causal connection between the conduct of the accused and the missing of the scheduled movement. Knowledge may be proved by circumstantial evidence.

Actual knowledge of the movement is an element of missing movement. See the section on Specific Intent in chapter 2 regarding specific and general intent crimes. How would you prove actual knowledge? What is the difference between missing movement through neglect and design? Does knowledge of the movement have an impact on whether the offense was through neglect or design? The following case addresses what is a "substantial movement" for purposes of Article 87.

UNITED STATES V. GUILLERMO QUEZADA, OPERATIONS
SPECIALIST SEAMAN APPRENTICE, U.S. NAVY
UNITED STATES COURT OF MILITARY APPEALS
40 M.J. 109
AUGUST 17, 1994
Opinion: Sullivan, Chief Judge

Appellant was charged with and pleaded guilty to the following offense under Article 87:

> Specification: In that [appellant] did, at Naval Air Station North Island, San Diego, California, on or about 29 June 1991, through neglect, miss the movement of the USS *Independence* with which he was required in the course of duty to move.

Appellant asserts that his responses to the guilty-plea inquiry do not establish this military offense as a matter of law because he only admitted to missing an insubstantial movement of his ship, i.e., "an eight-hour dependents' cruise." He argues that Article 87 only prohibits missing the movement of a ship in the special military situations encountered in World War II.

We note that Article 87 states:

> Any person subject to this chapter who through neglect or design misses the movement of a ship, aircraft, or unit with which he is required in the course of duty to move shall be punished as a court-martial may direct.

The plain language of this codal provision centers on appellant's duty to move with a ship, not with the purpose of the ship's movement. Moreover, the prior experience of the navy with this type of military misconduct has not deterred this Court from giving this language its full and natural meaning.

Paragraph 11, Part 4, MCM, explains the word "movement" in Article 87, as follows:

> c. Explanation.
>> (1) Movement. "Movement" as used in Article 87 includes a move, transfer, or shift of a ship, aircraft, or unit involving a substantial distance and period of time. Whether a particular movement is substantial is a question to be determined by the court-martial considering all the circumstances. Changes which do not constitute a "movement" include practice marches of a short duration with a return to the point of departure, and minor changes in location of ships, aircraft, or units, as when a ship is shifted from one berth to another in the same shipyard or harbor or when a unit is moved from one barracks to another on the same post.

To the extent this explanation accurately reflects substantive military criminal law, we agree that the movement of an aircraft carrier for eight hours cannot in any reasonable sense be considered "minor."

Quezada holds that the purpose of the ship's movement does not control whether a movement is significant under Article 87. Given this holding, most movements by a ship will fall within the parameters of Article 87. In what situation will a movement not be substantial?

Affirmative Defenses to Absence Offenses

In criminal jurisprudence, an affirmative showing of certain facts will constitute a defense to some crimes. These sets of facts are known as affirmative defenses. Examples of affirmative defenses include self-defense, temporary insanity, and defense of others. Two affirmative defenses to absence offenses, impossibility and duress, are discussed below.

IMPOSSIBILITY

Paragraph 10c(6), Part 4, MCM, explains the defense of impossibility:

> Inability to return. The status of absence without leave is not changed by an inability to return through sickness, lack of transportation facilities, or other disabilities. But the fact that all or part of a period of unauthorized absence was in a sense enforced or involuntary is a factor in extenuation and should be given due weight

when considering the initial disposition of the offense. When, however, a person on authorized leave, without fault, is unable to return at the expiration thereof, that person has not committed the offense of absence without leave.

Note that "impossibility" refers to absences caused by misfortunes that are not foreseeable and occur through no fault of the absentee. What situations are foreseeable? Acts of nature, acts of third parties, and physical disability are three situations generally considered to be unforeseeable. Note also that the impossibility cannot arise after an absence without leave has already commenced.

DURESS

The following case considers the defense of duress.

UNITED STATES V. LANCE CORPORAL RIOFREDO,
U.S. MARINE CORPS
UNITED STATES NAVY–MARINE CORPS COURT OF
MILITARY REVIEW
30 M.J. 1251
MAY 11, 1990
Opinion: Strickland, Judge

Appellant was found guilty of an unauthorized absence of nearly 8 1/2 months in violation of Article 86, UCMJ.

Appellant asserted, both at trial and on appeal, that his absence was the result of duress. The duress defense was raised as a result of two confrontations between appellant and his staff noncommissioned officer-in-charge. Apparently, a less than amicable relationship existed between the two leading up to the first confrontation, which appellant described as follows:

Q. Did you ever have any physical altercations with Staff Sergeant Lowery?
A. Yes, I did, sir.
Q. How many times?
A. Twice, sir.
Q. Approximately when was the first one in relation to 22 June?
A. Approximately three weeks before, sir.
Q. And what happened?
A. I was physically struck by Staff Sergeant Lowery and thrown across a desk, and up against a wall, sir.

Q. And where did this happen?
A. In the back room of the chow hall, sir.
Q. And was it during the working day or, when did this happen?
A. It was towards the end of our working shift, sir.
Q. Were you alone in the room with Staff Sergeant Lowery?
A. Yes, sir.

Following this altercation, appellant reported the incident to his chain of command, up through and including the Battalion Sergeant Major. The command responded by formally counseling Staff Sergeant Lowery and placing a page 11 counseling entry in his service record book.

Subsequently, a second confrontation occurred off-base between appellant and Staff Sergeant Lowery. This occurred on 22 June 1988, the same day appellant is alleged to have commenced his unauthorized absence. This confrontation and its aftermath are recounted by appellant in this colloquy:

Q. And what happened that day?
A. I was sitting on my motorcycle in the parking lot of Rocking H Video out in town. Staff Sergeant Lowery ran into me there. He pulled me off my motorcycle and threw me on the ground. When I picked myself up off the ground I was struck on the left side of my face, which resulted in having a tooth of mine, my back tooth broken.
Q. Were you scared of Staff Sergeant Lowery?
A. Yes, sir.
Q. What did, were you supposed to go to work that day?
A. Yes, sir.
Q. And why didn't you go to work that day?
A. I felt threatened and I was scared of Staff Sergeant Lowery, sir.
Q. What did you do?
A. I packed my bags and I left, sir.
Q. Why didn't you, the second altercation with Staff Sergeant Lowery, why didn't you report that to somebody? Why did you leave?
A. In my opinion, sir, I felt that it was obvious that nothing was being done. I felt further threatened by Staff Sergeant Lowery for trying to cause more trouble.

Evidence was also presented that Staff Sergeant Lowery was significantly larger in stature than was appellant and that Lowery lifted weights. Further evidence indicated that Lowery had recently reported to the command and appellant believed he would remain indefinitely.

Appellant contends that he had a reasonably grounded fear of serious bodily harm, that his attempts to resolve the matter with his chain of command had not prevented his injury in the second attack, and that he, therefore, could not avoid the absence without subjecting himself to this threatened danger. The government asserts that there was no threat of immediate death or serious bodily harm and that appellant could have avoided his absence by reporting the matter to his chain of command.

We reject the government's argument that the harm threatened in this instance is not of sufficient magnitude to raise the duress defense. The threat of a beating and of an initiation has been held to be justification for a reasonably grounded fear of receipt of serious bodily injury. Serious injury had already been inflicted on appellant, particularly in the second assault, which caused one of appellant's teeth to be broken.

The question in this case is not whether appellant had a reasonably grounded fear of serious bodily harm, but whether appellant could have avoided commencing his unauthorized absence without subjecting himself to a further assault. Appellant argues that he could not have avoided this absence because reporting the first assault to his chain of command did not prevent the occurrence of the second assault. This case is distinguishable from past cases because in those cases the threat of serious bodily harm had been reported to the chain of command and no action was taken. In this instance, the command took positive action following appellant's report of the first assault. The action taken was not merely a perfunctory one, but rather was a formal counseling which resulted in an adverse entry in the service record book of his assailant, a Staff Sergeant. Such an entry has a lasting impact on the record of a staff noncommissioned officer.

The real issue in this case is not whether command action prevented the second assault, but whether appellant could have reasonably expected that the command would have taken action after the second assault which would have precluded the occurrence of further assaults. If there was such a reasonable expectation, appellant was obligated to inform his command instead of initiating self-help measures. Where one has a reasonable opportunity to avoid committing an offense without subjecting himself to the threatened harm, the defense of duress does not apply.

We believe that the testimony of record indicates that there was a reasonable expectation that the chain of command would have taken further action against Staff Sergeant Lowery had appellant reported the second assault and that the action taken would have precluded the occurrence of additional assaults. Given the strong command response to the first assault, we are convinced the command's response to the second assault would have been even stronger and that affirmative steps would have been taken to bring a halt to this matter. Instead of packing his bags and leaving, appellant could have immediately returned to base, sought whatever medical assistance he needed and promptly made the command aware of the situation. Such prudent action would have ensured that appellant not be required to go to work with Staff Sergeant Lowery later that day and would have enabled appropriate measures to be instituted by the command. Appellant's actions were not excusable where he had an opportunity to avoid his absence by seeking the assistance of his command. Under all of the facts and circumstances of this case we are convinced beyond a reasonable doubt that the duress defense did not exist.

Riofredo holds that the threat to the accused be immediate. What must the accused fear? Lance Corporal Riofredo was absent for eight months after leaving his command. What affect do you think the length of absence had on the court's decision?

Offenses against Authority

Under the UCMJ, there are two categories of crimes against authority, disrespect offenses and order violations. These two types of offenses are discussed below.

Disrespect Offenses

Disrespect is defined as behavior that detracts from the respect and/or authority due to another person. It may consist of acts, omissions, or language, and may refer to the "victim," in his or her capacity as an officer/noncommissioned officer/petty officer or as a private individual.

Paragraph 13b, Part 4, MCM, provides the elements of disrespect toward a superior commissioned officer under Article 89:

(1) That the accused did or omitted certain acts or used certain language to or concerning a certain commissioned officer;

(2) That such behavior or language was directed toward that officer;

(3) That the officer toward whom the acts, omissions, or words were directed was the superior commissioned officer of the accused;

(4) That the accused then knew that the commissioned officer toward whom the acts, omissions, or words were directed was the accused's superior commissioned officer; and

(5) That, under the circumstances, the behavior or language was disrespectful to that commissioned officer.

Paragraph 13c, Part 4, MCM, explains the elements of Article 89:

(1) Superior commissioned officer.

(a) Accused and victim in same armed force. If the accused and the victim are in the same armed force, the victim is a "superior commissioned officer" of the accused when either superior in rank or command to the accused; however, the victim is not a "superior commissioned officer" of the accused if the victim is inferior in command, even though superior in rank.

(b) Accused and victim in different armed forces. If the accused and the victim are in different armed forces, the victim is a "superior commissioned officer" of the accused when the victim is a commissioned officer and superior in the chain of command over the accused or when the victim, not a medical officer or a chaplain, is senior in grade to the accused and both

are detained by a hostile entity so that recourse to the normal chain of command is prevented. The victim is not a "superior commissioned officer" of the accused merely because the victim is superior in grade to the accused.

(c) Execution of office. It is not necessary that the "superior commissioned officer" be in the execution of office at the time of the disrespectful behavior.

(2) Knowledge. If the accused did not know that the person against whom the acts or words were directed was the accused's superior commissioned officer, the accused may not be convicted of a violation of this article. Knowledge may be proved by circumstantial evidence.

(3) Disrespect. Disrespectful behavior is that which detracts from the respect due the authority and person of a superior commissioned officer. It may consist of acts or language, however expressed, and it is immaterial whether they refer to the superior as an officer or as a private individual. Disrespect by words may be conveyed by abusive epithets or other contemptuous or denunciatory language. Truth is no defense. Disrespect by acts includes neglecting the customary salute, or showing a marked disdain, indifference, insolence, impertinence, undue familiarity, or other rudeness in the presence of the superior officer.

(4) Presence. It is not essential that the disrespectful behavior be in the presence of the superior, but ordinarily one should not be held accountable under this article for what was said or done in a purely private conversation.

Compare the above provisions with the following sections contained in Paragraph 15c, Part 4, MCM, pertaining to disrespect to a warrant, noncommissioned, or petty officer, Article 91:

(1) In general. Article 91 has the same general objects with respect to warrant, noncommissioned, and petty officers as Articles 89 and 90 have with respect to commissioned officers, namely, to ensure obedience to their lawful orders, and to protect them from violence, insult, or disrespect. Unlike Articles 89 and 90, however, this article does not require a superior-subordinate relationship as an element of any of the offenses denounced.

(2) Knowledge. All of the offenses prohibited by Article 91 require that the accused have actual knowledge that the victim was a warrant, noncommissioned, or petty officer. Actual knowledge may be proved by circumstantial evidence. . . .

(5) Treating with contempt or being disrespectful in language or deportment toward a warrant, noncommissioned, or petty officer. "Toward" requires that the behavior and language be within the sight or hearing of the warrant, noncommissioned, or petty officer concerned.

The above provisions define a "superior commissioned officer" for purposes of Article 89. Based on that definition, could an enlisted member of the navy be disrespectful to an army officer? If no, are there other orders offenses that may apply? See the sections on Failure to Obey a Lawful General Order or Regulation and Failure to Obey an Other Lawful Order below under Article 92. Note that the U.S. Navy and Marine Corps are considered part of the same armed force. The military continues to increase its emphasis on jointness among the different services. This trend has significantly increased joint operations, exercises, and commands. Is it time for Congress to amend the UCMJ to account for this significant trend in the nature of the armed services? Consider that the JAG Manual now permits a multiservice commander to impose nonjudicial punishment on all members of the command, regardless of service.

A superior officer need not be in the execution of his or her office, or even be present, at the time of the disrespectful conduct. Compare those rules with Article 91 discussed above. Why is there a difference between the two provisions?

Is it possible to lose the protections on one's rank through inappropriate or abusive conduct? Paragraph 13c, Part 4, MCM, discusses this situation:

Special defense, unprotected victim. A superior commissioned officer whose conduct in relation to the accused under all the circumstances departs substantially from the required standards appropriate to that officer's

rank or position under similar circumstances loses the protection of this article. That accused may not be convicted of being disrespectful to the officer who has so lost the entitlement to respect protected by Article 89.

The following case considers the defense commonly referred to as "abandonment of rank" as it applies to a victim who is a noncommissioned officer.

UNITED STATES V. AIRMAN BASIC BOBBY L. CHEEKS,
U.S. AIR FORCE
UNITED STATES AIR FORCE COURT OF MILITARY REVIEW
43 C.M.R. 1013
APRIL 21, 1971
Opinion: Brewer, Judge

The accused was tried by general court-martial with one specification alleging disrespectful and contemptuous language and deportment toward his superior noncommissioned officer and one specification of willful disobedience of an order issued by the same noncommissioned officer.

The specification in question alleges in pertinent part that on 24 July 1970, while confined as a prisoner in the detention facility at Shaw Air Force Base, South Carolina, the accused "was disrespectful and contemptuous in language and deportment toward Staff Sergeant Levon Skipper, his superior noncommissioned officer, who was then in the execution of his office, by saying to him, 'I'm not going to do a damned thing,' 'you don't tell me what to do,' 'Get fucked,' or words to that effect, and by slamming the cell block door and saying, 'You will see who goes to work,' or words to that effect."

At trial, it was the contention of defense counsel that on the occasion in question, as well as during a very substantial period of time prior thereto, Sergeant Skipper had systematically subjected the accused to vile and degrading verbal abuse, as a consequence of which the accused had been "provoked, harassed, badgered and baited" into the behavior alleged in the specification. Expanding on that theme here, appellate defense counsel urge that the repeated abuse visited upon the accused by Skipper, as overwhelmingly established by the evidence, was so patently reprehensible as to divest

Sergeant Skipper of his cloak of authority and thus strip him of any right, on the occasion in question, to be accorded the respect otherwise due him as a noncommissioned officer in the execution of his office. In order for us to properly assess that contention, a brief recitation of the evidence is essential.

The picture which this record portrays of Sergeant Skipper is nothing short of appalling. The uncontroverted evidence establishes a disgraceful history of sustained prisoner abuse on the part of Skipper. It was shown, and indeed acknowledged by Skipper, that on one prior occasion he had been punished under Article 15 for physically abusing a prisoner. On yet another occasion, while in a drunken rage, Skipper struck a prisoner in the face, knocking him to the ground, following which he kicked him repeatedly in the chest, shouting, "I'm going to stomp the hell out of you." The brutality and general dereliction shown by Skipper on that occasion resulted in a high level investigation which apparently resulted in some further disciplinary action of an undisclosed nature. Unsurprisingly, by the time of trial, Skipper was no longer performing duties of any kind in the confinement facility.

As regards this accused, Skipper was apparently content to restrict himself to verbal abuse. The record shows that he repeatedly cursed the accused and systematically ridiculed him by constantly addressing him as "Shits" or "Airman Shits." Becoming ever more sensitive to that degrading treatment, the accused frequently requested Skipper to address him properly. Skipper, however, continued to regularly address the accused in that loathsome fashion, professing that he "couldn't pronounce" the accused's simple and uncomplicated name of Cheeks. That pattern of abuse prevailed for a period of several months immediately prior to the episode which gave rise to the accused's alleged disrespectful behavior.

In the early morning hours of 24 July 1970, Sergeant Michael Mulliken, who was then performing supervisory duties at the confinement facility, assigned the accused to a buffer machine cleaning detail in a nearby building. Approximately 20 minutes later, the accused returned to the confinement facility and informed Mulliken that the buffer insert had worn out and that a new one would be needed. Mulliken instructed the accused to return to the situs of the cleaning detail and busy himself with other chores. Mulliken indicated that in the meantime he would attempt to locate a new buffer. A short while later, the accused returned once again to the confinement facility and inquired of Mulliken if he had yet located another buffer. On this occasion, for no apparent reason, Sergeant Skipper intervened, directing the accused to discontinue the cleaning detail to which he had earlier been assigned and to clean the latrine instead. Somewhat aggravated by that development, the accused nevertheless grudgingly complied.

Some fifteen minutes later, a Technical Sergeant Harris arrived at the confinement facility to obtain a prisoner detail for work at Base Operations. Whereupon, Sergeant Skipper directed the accused to accompany Sergeant Harris on that work detail. As recounted by several witnesses, Skipper addressed the accused as "Shits" on that occasion as he had on past occasions. According to one version, Skipper shouted, "Shits, fall out to go on detail." Another version recounts Skipper as saying, "Shits, get up here, you are going on detail now." All agree that Skipper used the word "Shits" at several junctures during the episode.

Angered by Skipper's continued insistence upon addressing him in that manner, the accused responded, "I'm not moving until you call me Cheeks." Thus triggered, the exchange quickly escalated in intensity, with Skipper and the accused "both yelling at each other." During the course of the exchange, it is undisputed that the accused did speak and behave in the manner alleged in the specification. As for Skipper, his demeanor during the exchange is variously described as "losing control of himself"; "swearing and cursing"; and "yelling and screaming and going crazy." One witness recounted that Skipper approached the accused in a menacing manner with uplifted "balled up fist" and that "it looked like he was going to hit him."

In the face of that overwhelming showing of Sergeant Skipper's own gross misconduct, we have no hesitation in concluding, as urged by appellate defense counsel, that during the course of the episode described, Skipper forfeited the special privilege which Article 91 confers upon a noncommissioned officer to be treated with respect in the execution of his office. Under those circumstances, the accused's behavior, as alleged in the specification, was without criminality and his conviction of the alleged offense of using disrespectful and contemptuous language to a superior noncommissioned officer cannot be permitted to stand.

We decline, however, to extend the application of that principle to the disobedience offense of which the accused was also convicted. While we recognize that some forms of misbehavior on the part of a noncommissioned officer in the purported execution of his office could conceivably rise to such magnitude as would divest him even of his authority to exact obedience from subordinates, we are satisfied that verbal abuse would not, standing alone, serve to vitiate a legitimate order. It is one thing to conclude, out of simple considerations of human dignity, that a superior forfeits his right to be treated with respect by a subordinate upon whom he has heaped verbal abuse. It is quite another matter, however, to conclude that a subordinate is vested with a license to disobey any order administered in a verbally abusive manner. We are simply not prepared to risk the devastation of discipline likely to be visited upon the military establishment as a consequence of such a conclusion. As cogently observed by Judge Finkelstein in his concurring and dissenting opinion in *United States v. Johnson,* "Words, no matter how hateful, when employed by a [superior] in an effort to require compliance with an order which may even involve hardship and possible death, would not excuse disobedience."

Here there can be no doubt that the order administered by Sergeant Skipper to the accused was, on its face, a perfectly valid one. Moreover, it is not open to controversy that however much the accused was verbally abused on that occasion, the order was administered by Skipper in the clear execution of his office. We conclude, therefore, that neither the provocative and abusive manner in which the order was administered, nor any other aspect of the attendant circumstances, would serve to legally excuse the accused's disobedience.

Note that abandonment of rank applies to disrespect offenses, but not to orders violations. The court in *Cheeks* refused to extend the defense to disobedience because of the "devastation of discipline" that such a ruling would cause. Does this distinction make sense?

Orders Offenses

Five types of orders offenses exist under the UCMJ: (1) willful disobedience of a superior commissioned officer, Article 90; (2) willful disobedience of a warrant, noncommissioned or petty officer, Article 91; (3) failure to obey a lawful general order or regulation, Article 92(1); (4) failure to obey an other lawful order, Article 92(2); and (5) dereliction of duty, Article 92(3). Each of these offenses is discussed below.

A fundamental principle of the law of military orders is that only lawful directives may be enforced. In order to be lawful, the order must relate to some military duty. This includes "all activities reasonably necessary to safeguard and protect morale, discipline and usefulness of the members of a command." See *United States v. Martin,* 5 C.M.R. 102 (C.M.A. 1952). The order may not, without such a valid military purpose, interfere with private rights or personal affairs, nor may it conflict with the statutory or constitutional rights of the person receiving the order. As a general rule, service members may assume that the orders issued to them are lawful. However, this assumption will not apply to a patently illegal order, such as one that directs a subordinate to perform an act of personal servitude for the superior, or directs the subordinate to commit a crime. See *United States v. Calley* in chapter 13 concerning an order to kill civilian noncombatants. The next case addresses the lawfulness of an order that affects the private life of a service member.

UNITED STATES V. MARC A. DUMFORD, SENIOR AIRMAN,
U.S. AIR FORCE
UNITED STATES COURT OF MILITARY APPEALS
30 M.J. 137
MAY 10, 1990
Opinion: Per Curiam

Appellant stands convicted of willfully disobeying the command of a commissioned officer not to engage in sexual activity without informing his partner that he was infected with the Human Immunodeficiency Virus (HIV) and taking precautions against spreading the virus. The only question is whether a valid military necessity existed as to scope because the order required appellant to warn civilians as well as service members.

Appellant argues that, as applied to consensual, non-deviant, sexual intercourse with a female civilian, the order restricts his personal rights. However, many states have enacted statutes limiting the personal liberties of those persons who carry HIV, statutes which are far more restrictive than the present order. This order did not prohibit sexual contact; rather, it set forth terms under which appellant could engage in such activities. Thus, even to the extent that the order may have limited appellant's freedom, it is not so broadly drawn as to warrant invalidating the order.

Appellant's argument that the order lacks any valid military purpose is also without merit. We are certain that, when a service member is capable of exposing another person to an infectious disease, the military has a legitimate interest in limiting his contact with others, including civilians, and otherwise preventing the spread of that condition.

WILLFUL DISOBEDIENCE OFFENSES

Paragraph 14b(2), Part 4, MCM, provides the elements of willful disobedience of a superior commissioned officer, Article 90:

(a) That the accused received a lawful command from a certain commissioned officer;

(b) That this officer was the superior commissioned officer of the accused;

(c) That the accused then knew that this officer was the accused's superior commissioned officer; and

(d) That the accused willfully disobeyed the lawful command.

Paragraph 15b(2), Part 4, MCM, provides the elements of willful disobedience of a warrant, noncommissioned, or petty officer, Article 91:

(a) That the accused was a warrant officer or enlisted member;

(b) That the accused received a certain lawful order from a certain warrant, noncommissioned, or petty officer;

(c) That the accused then knew that the person giving the order was a warrant, noncommissioned, or petty officer;

(d) That the accused had a duty to obey the order; and

(e) That the accused willfully disobeyed the order.

Note that the order involved in a willful disobedience charge must be personally and individually directed to the accused. Orders to a unit as a whole, oral or written, are not personal to the accused; therefore, "unit" or "group" orders are not punishable under Articles 90 and 91 (although they may be punishable under Article 92).

The definition of a superior commissioned officer used in Article 89 also applies to disobedience offenses. As with disrespect, willful disobedience of the order of a warrant, noncommissioned, or petty officer does not require "superior" status. See the discussion above regarding situations in which an enlisted member is subject to the authority and orders of one who is junior in rank.

The disobedience must be intentional, not a result of neglect or incompetence. Does the failure to immediately carry out an order constitute a willful disobedience? Consider the following case.

UNITED STATES V. SPECIALIST ALISA SCHWABAUER,
UNITED STATES ARMY
UNITED STATES ARMY COURT OF MILITARY REVIEW
34 M.J. 709
FEBRUARY 6, 1992
Opinion: Naughton, Senior Judge

In January 1991, the appellant and her husband, Specialist Steven P. Schwabauer deployed with their unit from Germany to Saudi Arabia for Operation Desert Shield/Storm. On 4 February 1991, Command Sergeant Major (CSM) Cook was approached by the appellant and her husband and asked whether he was available for a private conversation. After a short delay, the conversation began and the appellant and her husband told of the appellant's fears of being forward deployed as a member of a contact team engaged in repairing intelligence equipment and of going into combat. According to the stipulation of fact, they both stated words to the effect that "we are sick of this, we can't take any more, we want to quit the army." CSM Cook attempted to resolve the situation, but the appellant became emotional and upset. The appellant and her husband then placed their M16A2 rifles on a folded tent, dropped their bayonets on the ground, turned, and began walking away. CSM Cook ordered the appellant and her husband to "stop and come back here" but they continued to walk away. The appellant and her husband continued to walk for another several feet and CSM Cook again told them to "stop." They stopped walking after the second order, but did not return to CSM Cook.

The appellant contends that the short delay in compliance between CSM Cook's first order and second order to stop does not constitute disobedience and that the appellant was entitled to a reasonable time to comply with the order to stop. In *United States v. Wilson,* 17 M.J. 1032, 1033 (A.C.M.R. 1984), this Court stated, "That immediate compliance is required by any order which does not explicitly or implicitly indicate that delayed compliance is authorized or directed." A direct order to "stop and come back here" is clear and unambiguous. It requires immediate obedience. Under the circumstances of this case, there is nothing in CSM Cook's order that permitted or implied a reasonable time to obey or authorized delayed compliance.

In *Schwabauer,* the order given was meant for immediate execution. The ruling adheres to the principle that a declaration by the accused that he or she will not obey an order constitutes disobedience. What about the same declaration concerning an order that does not require action until some time in the future? Generally, such an order cannot be violated until the time for performance arrives. See *United States v. Williams,* 39 C.M.R. 78 (C.M.A. 1968).

FAILURE TO OBEY A LAWFUL GENERAL ORDER OR REGULATION, ARTICLE 92(1)

Paragraph 16b(1), Part 4, MCM, states the three elements to this offense:

(a) That there was in effect a certain lawful general order or regulation;
(b) That the accused had a duty to obey it; and
(c) That the accused violated or failed to obey the general order or regulation.

Paragraph 16c, Part 4, MCM, explains who has authority to issue general orders:

(1) Officers having general court-martial convening authority;
(2) General or flag officers in command; or
(3) Commanders superior to general court-martial convening authorities/flag officers in command.

An example of an officer who can issue general orders is the commanding general of Marine Corps Base Camp Pendleton, California, a brigadier general. As a general officer in command (and general court-martial convening authority), he has the authority to issue general orders and regulations. Other examples of general orders or regulations are SECNAVINST 5300.26B (sexual harassment), SECNAVINST 5300.28B (drug abuse paraphernalia), and Article 1165 of U.S. Navy Regulations (fraternization). These regulations are all issued by the secretary of the navy. Why is the authority to issue general orders limited to high-ranking officers?

Knowledge of the order is often a key issue in cases involving violation of an order. Consider the knowledge aspect of general orders as explained in Paragraph 16c, Part 4, MCM:

Knowledge. Knowledge of a general order or regulation need not be alleged or proved, as knowledge is not an element of this offense and a lack of knowledge does not constitute a defense.

Note that a directive must be "punitive" in nature to constitute a general order. Paragraph 16c(1), Part 4, MCM, explains, "Not all provisions in general orders or regulations can be enforced under Article 92(1). Regulations which only supply general guidelines or advice for conducting military functions may not be enforceable under Article 92(1)." Consider uniform regulations, classified material instructions, standard operating manuals, and safety instructions: which are punitive orders and which are guidelines? Will the language of the regulation affect whether it is punitive or advisory in nature?

FAILURE TO OBEY AN OTHER LAWFUL ORDER, ARTICLE 92(2)

This offense includes all other lawful orders not covered by Articles 90, 91, and 92(1). Its elements are:

(1) That a member of the armed forces issued a certain lawful order;
(2) That the accused had knowledge of the order;
(3) That the accused had a duty to obey the order; and
(4) That the accused failed to obey the order.

Paragraph 16c, Part 4, MCM, explains this offense:

(a) Scope. Article 92(2) includes all other lawful orders which may be issued by a member of the armed forces, violations of which are not chargeable under Article 90, 91, or 92(1). It includes the violation of written regulations which are not general regulations.

(b) Knowledge. In order to be guilty of this offense, a person must have had actual knowledge of the order or regulation. Knowledge of the order may be proved by circumstantial evidence.

(c) Duty to obey order.

  (i) From a superior. A member of one armed force who is senior in rank to a member of another armed force is the superior of that member with authority to issue orders which that member has a duty to obey under the same circumstances as a commissioned officer of one armed force is the superior commissioned officer of a member of another armed force for the purposes of Articles 89 and 90.

  (ii) From one not a superior. Failure to obey the lawful order of one not a superior is an offense under Article 92(2), provided the accused had a duty to obey the order, such as one issued by a sentinel or a member of the armed forces police. The order may be oral or in writing, and need not have been directed to the accused personally. This paragraph provides the ability to punish group-directed orders that may not be

punished as willful disobedience and lawful orders issued by an authority lacking rank or status to issue "general orders."

Article 92(2) provides a method to charge service members for orders violations that do not meet the criteria of willful disobedience or failure to obey a general order. When would this occur? Does this make violation of an other lawful order a lesser included offense of willful disobedience or a general order offense?

DERELICTION OF DUTY, ARTICLE 92(3)

Though dereliction of duty does not involve the violation of a direct order, it is so closely related to the overall concept of disobedience that it is included within Article 92. Its elements are:

(1) That the accused had certain duties;
(2) That the accused knew or reasonably should have known of the duties; and
(3) That the accused was (willfully)(through neglect or culpable inefficiency) derelict in the performance of those duties.

Paragraph 16c, Part 4, MCM, explains this offense:

(a) Duty. A duty may be imposed by treaty, statute, regulation, lawful order, standard operating procedure, or custom of the service.

(b) Knowledge. Actual knowledge of duties may be proved by circumstantial evidence. Actual knowledge need not be shown if the individual reasonably should have known of the duties. This may be demonstrated by regulations, training or operating manuals, customs of the service, academic literature or testimony, testimony of persons who have held similar or superior positions, or similar evidence.

(c) Derelict. A person is derelict in the performance of duties when that person willfully or negligently fails to perform that person's duties or when that person performs them in a culpably inefficient manner. "Willfully" means intentionally. It refers to the doing of an act knowingly and purposely, specifically intending the natural and probable consequences of the act. "Negligently" means an act or omission of a person who is under a duty to use due care which exhibits a lack of that degree of care which a reasonably prudent person would have exercised under the same or similar circumstances. "Culpable inefficiency" is inefficiency for which there is no reasonable or just excuse.

(d) Ineptitude. A person is not derelict in the performance of duties if the failure to perform those duties is caused by ineptitude rather than by willfulness, negligence, or culpable inefficiency, and may not be charged under this article, or otherwise punished. For example, a recruit who has tried earnestly during rifle training and throughout record firing is not derelict in the performance of duties if the recruit fails to qualify with the weapon.

The following case discusses the nature of dereliction of duty.

UNITED STATES V. ALLEN V. LAWSON, FIRST LIEUTENANT,
U.S. MARINE CORPS
UNITED STATES NAVY–MARINE CORPS COURT OF
MILITARY REVIEW
33 M.J. 946
OCTOBER 31, 1991
Opinion: Mitchell, Senior Judge

Appellant stands convicted by members at a contested general court-martial of failure to obey the lawful order of a superior officer to submit a roster of checkpoint marines before posting them and dereliction of duty by failing to post as a pair Lance Corporals Rother and Key at a tactical exercise road checkpoint. The charges arose during a tactical Combined Arms Exercise (CAX) conducted in the California desert.

On 30 August 1988, appellant was temporarily deployed with his battalion to a training site at Marine Corps Air-Ground Combat Training Center, Twenty-nine Palms, California (29 Palms). While there, he was detailed to post road guides along a route for a motorized night march. At the conclusion of the march, a road guide, Lance Corporal Rother, was not picked up. His unit did not report his absence to the battalion headquarters for about 1 1/2 days. When the situation was reported, the battalion commander, suspecting that Lance Corporal Rother had been left in the desert, ordered a massive search for him. The search was unsuccessful.

During the ill-fated CAX, appellant participated in mock tactical operations. Toward the end of training, he was assigned uncomplicated duties of (1) posting road guards in pairs along a route designated for a battalion-sized motorized night movement, (2) obtaining a roster of marines posted as road guides, and (3) providing the roster to Captain Edwards, the appellant's superior coordinator for this movement.

Appellant was Heavy Machine Gun Platoon Commander, 3d Battalion, 2d Marine Regiment (3/2). He had no prior desert training but had 20 months' experience as an infantry officer. The battalion commander, Lieutenant Colonel Robeson, was a new and inexperienced battalion commander. All company commanders were also new. Nonetheless, Lieutenant Colonel Robeson had stressed personnel accountability at all times because of harsh desert conditions and the number of key new people in the battalion. To conduct the critical movement, Lieutenant Colonel Robeson decided to use newly available terrain to move the battalion to the objective. Consequently, no plan for this movement had been written or practiced in advance. The exercise evolved as follows.

The CAX was to be conducted over two and one-half days. The first two days of objectives were taken. At the second objective, Lieutenant Colonel Robeson received and, in turn, gave a fragmentary order for a third objective. The battalion was very disorganized at this time. Timing afforded a period from 1730 to 2300 to jump off on the third objective. Lieutenant Colonel Robeson gave a short (fifteen-minute) brief to command personnel on the myriad of things to be done and decided to short-cut normal preparedness so that the battalion could get under way before dark. It was understood that appellant had some discretion in posting guides in that he could add road guides, but they all had to be posted in pairs and on the movement route.

Lieutenant Colonel Robeson's extant policy was that following briefings, officers were to ask questions of him if they did not understand something or had any doubts about the subject matter. The appellant claims he stayed after this brief and asked some questions, but he provided no details for the record. Lieutenant Colonel Robeson testified that the appellant did not stay and did not ask mission questions. We conclude that even if appellant asked questions, they were not on matters pertinent to the road guide operation. Road guide details were set out on maps that no one in the command had seen before this time. For purposes of battalion control, Lieutenant Colonel Robeson used a unique system of two command teams, gold and scarlet. The critical events occurred on the night of 30 August 1988.

Specifically, appellant was detailed to reconnoiter the route of advance and to post road guides at four predetermined checkpoints at major road intersections. He was to post two guides at each location, a buddy system. The road guides were to prevent convoys from turning from the line of advance and getting lost. Captain Edwards was detailed to place a unit in trace of the battalion and conduct road guide recovery operations. Captain Edwards tasked appellant with providing a list of names of guides and posting points to him for use as a checklist. The roster was to be delivered before appellant departed the area to post the road guides. Appellant understood these leadership obligations but did not discharge them.

In his briefing, Lieutenant Colonel Robeson initially said road guides could be singly posted because of vehicle space limitations, but later in the brief changed his mind on this and directed paired road guides. In any event, it was clear at the end of the briefing that guides were to be posted in pairs and not separated. This was consistent with established battalion policy and, at the moment, driven by darkness and desert safety concerns. Specific and detailed instructions for road guide posting and recovery operations were not given to Captain Edwards or appellant by the battalion commander. Appellant, however, knew that another battalion, 1st Battalion, 10th Marine Regiment (1/10), which was also to use the same route and follow his battalion, was also going to post road guides.

The terrain and scheme of maneuver for this movement, as revealed in the record, are as follows. The exercise was conducted in remote and rough desert terrain in California, during late August. The exercise covered a line of movement of approximately forty miles, largely through valleys surrounded by rugged mountains. It was a straightline exercise that did not contemplate revisiting terrain through which the ma-

neuvering commands had previously moved. There was no built-up area beyond the initial line of departure at day one that was within a minimum of about ten miles of any point on the route of advance. Maps reveal no apparent natural or artificial water sources. It is difficult to imagine a more remote, barren, and dangerous environment than the terrain over which this exercise was conducted. The fatal third movement covered about twenty-three miles of administrative and operational movement. Once a command passed a point, it left behind and alone in this environment anything that did not move with the commands that passed over the particular road assigned for that portion of the exercise. Thus, if Lance Corporal Rother was not picked up by his battalion and his whereabouts were totally unknown to the tracing battalion, he was on his own against the harsh desert.

At the outset of appellant's assignment things were not smooth. One company refused to provide guides as required, leaving appellant short two guides. Scarlet leader, the battalion executive officer (Major Holm), then in control, learned of this when he found appellant still at the second objective at 1845 and facing a 1900 launch time. Major Holm told appellant to go to the offending company, get the guides and immediately get on the road. At the time appellant had been talking with a Lieutenant Liddy. Lieutenant Liddy had advised appellant to go to the offending company and pick up the guides, make a list of all guides, and post a staff noncommissioned officer (SNCO) at the rear of battalion with the list to check the recovery. Appellant apparently was unable to locate the offending unit and did not know whether their guides were on the way. He did know that he was under orders to leave before dark. Appellant still did not know what to do (even though he had seventeen marines in his own platoon he could have used) when Major Holm found him. He finally got on the road twenty minutes late. Appellant left to post the road guides two marines short of the requisite manpower and without having made a list of road guides and their posts. Appellant did not provide any guide list to Captain Edwards.

Marines Rother, McAdams, Adamson and Key were designated guides by Kilo Company. Their executive officer briefed them on their duty and told them they were to stay in pairs. None of them saw appellant before departure, and their names were not taken by appellant when they reported to him. When they reported for guide duty they were simply told to board the vehicles and go.

Appellant put his best navigator, Sergeant Gardner, on the point of his column of several vehicles, while he stayed in the rear apparently because he thought that would enhance his control of his column. He told Sergeant Gardner that appellant was directed to post two guides at designated spots on the map. The column then departed on the mission. Before Checkpoint 1, Sergeant Gardner misread a rock formation and wrongly veered north (right) off the main road. The road began to thin out and soon looked nothing like a main road. He ultimately returned to the main road at Checkpoint 1 by cutting across rough terrain. Appellant followed Sergeant Gardner but stopped where the navigator turned to rejoin the main road. At first, appellant posted two guides, Lance Corporals Key and Rother at that spot, wrongly believing it to be Checkpoint 1. After scouting the bogus road for a distance, appellant became uncertain about the checkpoint. He returned to the site and picked up Lance Corporal Key. He left Lance Corporal Rother there posted at a rock about 200 yards off the main road and some four hundred yards from the designated Checkpoint 1.

Appellant then proceeded across open terrain to the real Checkpoint 1 where he joined Sergeant Gardner. He posted Lance Corporal Key there. He also drove down the plainly identifiable main supply road a short distance and talked with Sergeant Gardner, who was parked in front of an intersection sign that marked the checkpoint and, hence, the main road. We are convinced that by this time appellant knew that Lance Corporal Rother was not posted at the correct checkpoint. We also find that mission performance and speed of movement were the paramount concerns to him despite the safety emphasis in the battalion. He realized that he was behind schedule and he did not take the time to go back to Lance Corporal Rother and re-post him with Lance Corporal Key at Checkpoint 1. He did nothing about Rother until much later at the final assembly area when he realized that this was only an exercise and not real war and that safety concerns were important.

Appellant did not record Lance Corporal Rother's name or his location when he posted him at the rock. He ignored warnings about posting in pairs given by Lance Corporals Adamson and Key, reminding them that he was the senior. He did not give any instructions about the circumstances under which either guide could leave his post or how each was to consolidate for pick up after the battalion main column passed. Appellant told both guides to keep the battalion convoy on the main road, but did not tell Lance Corporal Rother where Checkpoint 1 was located (at that time appellant did not know). He told neither marine what course directions to give the battalion if it passed by him.

Appellant testified that he did not think Rother was in jeopardy because he was posted in close proximity to Lance Corporal Key. They were both left with chemical lights, rations, and water. Lance Corporal Key at Checkpoint 1 was about 400 yards from Lance Corporal Rother and could see him in daylight. At night, Lance Corporal Key could see Lance Corporal Rother's chemical light. We do not know whether Lance Corporal Rother saw Lance Corporal Key. The appellant apparently did not see Rother from Checkpoint 1 and it is unlikely that anyone not specifically looking at his position would see him in daylight or darkness. Appellant was not concerned that the guides might be afraid or in danger. Lost to his concern, however, was the effect of his changing the game plan in midstream when none of the necessary coordinating and guide recovery parties knew about it. This was the jeopardy of being left behind in the desert. At least the recovering party expected to look for and find guides on the main road. But what did they know of a second route? This danger should also have occurred to appellant when First Sergeant Floyd later asked him at Checkpoint 3 if appellant was posting his road guides in pairs. Appellant said he was doing that, implying that appellant knew it was an important policy, knew that he was not following orders, and knew that he did not want to admit that to the First Sergeant.

At 0700 on 31 August, appellant saw Major Holm, the battalion executive officer, and asked him if all marines had returned, a peculiar question to ask him, considering the known lack of accounting the previous night. Major Holm said everything was fine as far as he knew and that the march was smooth. Appellant did not discuss the failure to pair guides at Checkpoint 1 or the list deficiency. However, Lance Corporal Adamson, who had been a road guide during the battalion movement, noticed at weapon turn-in that Lance Corporal Rother's rifle card was still not claimed at the end of the exercise. He reported it to Platoon and was told that Lance Corporal Rother was gone on a guard detail. We conclude that this was an unfortunate misunderstanding.

The night of 31 August, the battalion commander met with his officers and stressed that three things were to be accounted for—"people, weapons and communication security material system gear"—and reports filed with him that night. At 1000 on 1 September, Lance Corporal Rother had still not turned in his weapon, so Lance Corporal Adamson reported this to his Company headquarters. At 1730, 1 September, appellant revealed Lance Corporal Rother's split posting at Checkpoint 1 when Captain Henderson, Lance Corporal Rother's company commander, confronted appellant about the missing Rother. Lance Corporal Rother was later found dead.

The circumstances in which the appellant found himself on movement night, while a somewhat pressured, fast-moving and confusing situation, are common to tactical operations and exercises of this size and kind. Some of appellant's difficulties were of his own creation, particularly his failure to pick two of his own men and mount out with a complete unit on time. The circumstances of this exercise were not, as the court members also decided by their findings, of such magnitude as to excuse appellant from responsibility for his failures to follow his orders. Likewise, without regard to the derelictions, criminal or otherwise, of other officers, staff noncommissioned officers and other marines involved in the fatal tactical movement, we are convinced, as were the court members, that appellant's failure to follow his orders with a good measure of plain common sense, was a key failure in a chain of events that could have been expected to and did result in leaving a marine in the desert, alone, at night, with no apparent capacity to link up to his own or any other command.

What duty was First Lieutenant Lawson derelict in performing? The MCM states that the "duty" can be imposed by regulation, order, or custom of the service. Who or what imposed the duty on the accused in *Lawson?* It is possible for a service member to be derelict in performance of a duty of which he or she was unaware. A "should have known" standard may be the basis for a dereliction of duty charge, making it possible to convict a member of dereliction of duty for failing to properly perform a task that he or she should have known about.

Drug Offenses

Article 112a, UCMJ

Because fitness of personnel is a fundamental concern in the military, the services aggressively investigate and prosecute drug offenses. Through urinalysis and investigation by military law enforcement officials, the armed forces have succeeded in making the use of controlled substances significantly lower among service personnel than in the rest of society. Article 112a of the UCMJ sets forth most of the military offenses involving controlled substances. Paragraph 37, Part 4, MCM, explains those offenses:

> (a) Any person subject to this chapter who wrongfully uses, possesses, manufactures, distributes, imports into the customs territory of the United States, exports from the United States, or introduces into an installation, vessel, vehicle, or aircraft used by or under the control of the armed forces, a [controlled] substance shall be punished as a court-martial may direct.

Paragraph 37 also describes the prohibited substances:

> (1) Opium, heroin, cocaine, amphetamine, lysergic acid diethylamide, methamphetamine, phencyclidine, barbituric acid, and marijuana, and any compound or derivative of any such substance.
>
> (2) Any substance not specified in clause (1) that is listed on a schedule of controlled substances prescribed by the President for the purposes of this article.
>
> (3) Any other substance that is listed in schedules I

through V of section 202 of the Controlled Substances Act (21 U.S.C. 812).

There are numerous controlled substances listed in schedules issued by the president or contained in the Controlled Substances Act, but most prosecutions in the U.S. Navy and Marine Corps involve marijuana, cocaine, methamphetamine, heroine, or lysergic acid diethylamide (LSD). The activities prohibited by Article 112a include the wrongful possession, use, distribution, introduction, and manufacture of such controlled substances. There are two fundamental elements for each drug offense: (1) that the accused possessed/used/distributed/introduced/manufactured a controlled substance, and (2) that the possession/use/distribution/introduction/manufacture was wrongful. Paragraph 37c(5), Part 4, MCM, explains the nature of "wrongfulness" in relation to drug offenses:

> Wrongfulness. Possession, use, distribution, introduction, or manufacture of a controlled substance is wrongful if it is without legal justification or authorization. It is not wrongful if such act or acts are: (A) done pursuant to legitimate law enforcement activities (for example, an informant who receives drugs as part of an undercover operation is not in wrongful possession); (B) done by authorized personnel in the performance of medical duties; or (C) without knowledge of the contraband nature of the substance (for example, a person who possesses cocaine, but actually believes it to be sugar, is not guilty of wrongful possession of cocaine).

Article 112a sets forth several offenses involving controlled substances. The following sections discuss some of these offenses.

POSSESSION
Paragraph 37c(2), Part 4, MCM, discusses the nature of possession:

> Possess. "Possess" means to exercise control of something. Possession may be direct physical custody like holding an item in one's hand, or it may be constructive, as in the case of a person who hides an item in a locker or car to which that person may return to retrieve it. Possession must be knowing and conscious. Possession inherently includes the power or authority to preclude control by others. It is possible, however, for more than one person to possess an item simultaneously, as when several people share control of an item. An accused may not be convicted of possession of a controlled substance if the accused did not know that the substance was present under the accused's control.

Based on the above, what factors determine whether an owner of a house in which drugs are found is guilty of possession of a controlled substance?

DISTRIBUTION
Paragraph 37c(3), Part 4, MCM, explains distribution under Article 112a:

> Distribute. "Distribute" means to deliver to the possession of another. "Deliver" means the actual, constructive, or attempted transfer of an item, whether or not there exists an agency relationship.

The above appears to define the term "distribute" very broadly. Does every transfer of a controlled substance amount to a distribution? If a sailor or marine is convicted of distribution, should the nature of the transfer affect the sentence awarded? Consider the following case.

UNITED STATES V. THOMAS R. RATLEFF, PRIVATE FIRST CLASS U.S. ARMY
UNITED STATES COURT OF MILITARY APPEALS
34 M.J. 80
FEBRUARY 21, 1992
Opinion: Cox, Judge

The accused used marijuana in the hashish form, on 18 December 1989, with PFC Jaundoo in the accused's room. The accused had accompanied PFC Jaundoo to the mess hall, where PFC Jaundoo had hidden a can with hashish in it. PFC Jaundoo extracted the can, then he and the accused went back to the accused's room. The accused ripped the can open, extracted the hashish, and gave it to PFC Jaundoo. The accused and PFC Jaundoo then smoked the hashish. The hashish was smoked by poking holes in a soft drink can, setting the hashish in an indentation made in the can, lighting the substance, and inhaling the resulting smoke into the lungs.

These facts formed the basis for specifications alleging use and distribution of hashish. Appellant asserts the facts do not support a conviction for distribution of hashish, arguing that this set of facts suggests only that he and PFC Jaundoo jointly possessed the hashish or that only Jaundoo could be found guilty of the distribution. We reject these arguments. The plain, ordinary construction of Article 112a of the code requires us to conclude that appellant "delivered" the hashish to his friend, a fact readily admitted by appellant.

MANUFACTURE OF A CONTROLLED SUBSTANCE

Paragraph 37c(4), Part 4, MCM, explains "manufacture" under 112a:

> Manufacture. "Manufacture" means the production, preparation, propagation, compounding, or processing of a drug or other substance, either directly or indirectly or by extraction from substances of natural origin, or independently by means of chemical synthesis or by a combination of extraction and chemical synthesis, and includes any packaging or repackaging of such substance or labeling or relabeling of its container. "Production," as used in this subparagraph, includes the planting, cultivating, growing, or harvesting of a drug or other substance.

The above definition is very broad in the sense that it includes labeling and packaging of a drug. Is such an expansive reading consistent with the interpretation of "distribution" discussed above?

USE OF A CONTROLLED SUBSTANCE

To "use" a controlled substance means to ingest it by smoking, snorting, eating, injecting, and so on. The vast majority of wrongful use cases come about because of the military's urinalysis program. Urinalysis essentially looks for the presence of certain chemical byproducts of illegal drugs (called "metabolites") in each specimen tested. If such metabolites are found, the laboratory sends a message back to the command reporting the positive result of the analysis. See OP-NAVINST 5350.4 series (the navy's drug testing instruction). What are the bases for conducting a urinalysis? Do Fourth Amendment considerations apply to urinalysis? See *Unger v. Ziemniak* in chapter 7 regarding the legal basis for ordering a urinalysis.

A positive urinalysis normally raises the inference of a wrongful use on the part of the accused. The burden is then on the sailor or marine to show that the collection or testing procedures were flawed or that his or her ingestion of the controlled substance was not wrongful (for example, the cocaine was unknowingly slipped in the member's drink or use of controlled substances is so out of character the ingestion could not have been wrongful). Courts-martial are sometimes reluctant to convict a member based only on a positive urinalysis. Why would this be? Does the answer have to do with the difference between direct and circumstantial evidence?

INTRODUCTION OF A CONTROLLED SUBSTANCE

This offense is committed by bringing a controlled substance onto a vessel, aircraft, vehicle, or installation used by or under the control of the armed forces. A sailor or marine is not guilty of introduction if he or she receives or distributes a controlled substance while already on board property of the armed forces. If a sailor borrows a friend's jacket that has LSD in the pocket, will she be guilty of introduction if she goes on board a navy ship? What factors will the court consider to decide this issue? Will knowledge on the part of the sailor be a consideration?

DEFENSES TO DRUG OFFENSES

As discussed above, wrongfulness is a necessary element of offenses under Article 112a. Besides the absence of wrongfulness, what other defenses may an accused raise? Consider the following case regarding the entrapment defense.

UNITED STATES V. STAFF SERGEANT ORLANDO CORTES,
UNITED STATES ARMY
UNITED STATES ARMY COURT OF MILITARY REVIEW
29 M.J. 946
JANUARY 3, 1990
Opinion: Neurauter, Judge

Appellant asserts that the special defense of entrapment was raised at his trial and that the government failed to prove beyond a reasonable doubt that he was not entrapped.

The Manual for Courts-Martial, United States, 1984, Rule for Courts-Martial 916(g) provides that "it is a defense that the criminal design or suggestion to commit the offense originated in the Government and the accused had no predisposition to commit the offense." The manual further provides that:

> The "Government" includes agents of the Government and persons cooperating with them (for example, informants). The fact that persons acting for the Government merely afford opportunities or facilities for the commission of the offense does not constitute entrapment. Entrapment occurs only when the criminal conduct is the product of the creative activity of law enforcement officials.

The latitude given the Government in inducing the criminal act is considerably greater in contraband cases (drugs, liquor)—which are essentially victim-less crimes—than would be permissible as to other crimes, where commission of the acts would bring injury to members of the public. Here, although appellant testified that SGT L approached him approximately ten times over a two-month period with requests to bring cocaine back to Fort Drum from New York City, appellant also stated that he just put SGT L off and said he would think about it. SGT L testified that when he asked appellant if he could "get some drugs for me," that appellant responded that he wasn't sure, he would let SGT L know, and that he (appellant) used to sell drugs but that he had "retired" from that. Finally, when asked by his trial defense counsel why he finally decided to purchase the cocaine and then distribute it at Fort Drum, appellant referred to pressures of his job, his family problems (appellant's divorce was pending at the time), and his financial situation.

At the time of the offense, appellant had served more than eight years in the army, was a staff sergeant, had been a noncommissioned officer more than three years, and was twenty-eight years old. SGT L, the government informant, was junior to appellant, and, according to the testimony of both appellant and SGT L, they were merely acquaintances, for they were neither friends nor did they work together. The record clearly establishes and appellant admits that, when the distribution took place, appellant bragged about the quality of the cocaine ("taste it, it's real good—it's the best in the city"), he stated there would be no problem supplying the buyer with cocaine on a regular basis, and he anticipated making at least $500.00 from the transaction. In addition, SGT L testified that appellant wanted him to sell drugs for appellant and was guaranteed at least $400.00 per week.

The establishment of a profit motive, in and of itself, does not establish the appellant's predisposition to commit the offense of distribution of cocaine. However, it is one factor which may be considered along with the other evidence in the case. Even accepting without question the testimony of appellant, SGT L, the government informant, did not practice any form of deceit, nor did he engage in any egregious activity in attempts to overcome appellant's resistance to distribute cocaine. Appellant did not convey to the informant an outright refusal to engage in such activity, and when the opportunity arose and the circumstances were favorable, appellant freely and willingly purchased the cocaine, transported it to Fort Drum, and distributed it to a police undercover agent. We are convinced beyond a reasonable doubt that, although the suggestion to commit the offense originated with the government, the appellant was, in fact, predisposed to commit the offense.

The court in *Cortes* stated that the government is given considerably more latitude in inducing criminal behavior in contraband cases than in crimes that might cause physical harm to others. Do you agree with this principle? Such a statement suggests the difficulty in successfully using the defense of entrapment in drug cases. What did the court say in *Cortes* about the accused's contention that he was not predisposed to commit the charged offense?

Fraternization

The military has historically relied upon custom and tradition to define the bounds of acceptable personal relationships among its members. The following case discusses the history and development of fraternization rules.

UNITED STATES V. DENNIS A. TEDDER,
CAPTAIN U.S. MARINE CORPS
UNITED STATES COURT OF MILITARY APPEALS
24 M.J. 176
JULY 6, 1987
Opinion: Everett, Chief Judge

Captain Tedder was the unit legal officer for a squadron. Lance Corporal Germaine Chiriboga, a 19-year-old woman marine in the same squadron, testified that in early November 1982 she had consulted appellant about allegations of homosexual conduct lodged against her. Subsequently, he had conversed with her while she was on watch as assistant staff duty officer. At this time, he mentioned that he frequented the Northwoods Tavern, a bar near the air station at Cherry Point, North Carolina, where both were stationed. According to Chiriboga, appellant told her that, if he saw her there, he would buy her a beer. She had responded that he could do so; and Tedder then informed her that he would probably be there the next weekend.

Accompanied by another woman marine lance corporal, she had gone to eat at the Northwoods on the next Saturday. After dinner, she went into the bar to see if appellant would arrive. Shortly thereafter, he and several friends entered the bar; and he approached her and stood next to her for about an hour. During this time, they each consumed alcoholic beverages and conversed on a first-name basis. Chiriboga testified that Tedder had told her that, if anyone asked her to explain this meeting, she should say that "it was just plain that he said that if he saw me in Northwoods, he would buy me a beer, and that was the end of it."

In the following week, appellant and Chiriboga had another conversation in which he advised her that he would be at the Northwoods on Friday evening. Again he offered to buy her a beer. Chiriboga replied that this would be acceptable; but, before going to the tavern on this occasion, she asked Sergeant Stephanie Canady of the squadron administrative office if there were Marine Corps orders concerning fraternization. Chiriboga told Canady that she was concerned because she had a date with an officer. At trial, she explained that she had been concerned that both she and Tedder might be violating some directive by their meeting.

Chiriboga then went to the Northwoods alone. She met Tedder at the bar where he and his friends purchased drinks for her. After some conversation and drinking, she accompanied him to a private club he belonged to. Later they drove to his house, where they had sexual intercourse.

Appellant again instructed Chiriboga to tell anyone who inquired that he had agreed to buy her a drink if he met her at the Northwoods but not to say anything further. When the Naval Investigative Service (NIS) commenced an investigation into his conduct, he told her not to discuss the events of the evening beyond their meeting at the Northwoods. In particular, he wanted her to deny that there had been any "date" or prearrangement between them on the night in question.

Penal statutes applicable to service members and military directives intended to govern their conduct must convey some notice of the standards of behavior they require. We have recognized that "not every social conduct between an officer and an enlisted man is or even can reasonably be prohibited." This Court has urged that appropriate directives be drafted to govern the relationships between officers and enlisted persons. In this way, notice would be provided.

The air force did not take this suggestion. Moreover, according to the determination of the Air Force Court of Military Review, there was no custom of the service in the air force which prohibited dating or consensual sexual intercourse with enlisted women who were not under the accused's command or supervision. Therefore, we held that, for want of constitutionally adequate notice an air force officer could not be prosecuted successfully under Articles 133 and 134 of the Uniform Code for fraternization with an enlisted person who was not under his command or supervision, when the alleged misconduct consisted only of consensual sexual intercourse.

The army, on the other hand, has issued some directives which give notice as to various prohibited relationships between officers and certain enlisted personnel. Thus, in *United States v. Mayfield,* 21 M.J. 418 (C.M.A. 1986), this Court affirmed the conviction of an officer for wrongfully fraternizing with a female enlisted trainee assigned to his company—although not under his direct supervision—by asking her for a date. Mayfield did not contend that he was unaware of the restrictions on the relationship he had attempted to establish. Moreover, he admitted on cross-examination that he had been well aware of the command policy which prohibited dating between the command cadre and the trainees.

The commandant of the Marine Corps has also attempted to provide guidance for his officers about the correct relationships with their subordinates. Paragraph 1100.4 of the Marine Corps Manual (1980) provides:

> Relations Between Officers and Enlisted Marines. Duty relationships and social and business contacts among Marines of different grades will be consistent with traditional standards of good order and discipline and the mutual respect that has always existed between Marines of senior grade and those of lesser grade. Situations which invite or give the appearance of familiarity or undue informality among Marines of different grades will be avoided or, if found to exist, corrected.

Subsequent paragraphs quote observations on leadership by former commandant, Major General John A. Lejeune, which appeared in the 1921 edition of the Marine Corps Manual. They compare the relationship between marine officers and enlisted persons to "that of teacher and scholar . . . partak[ing] of the nature of the relation between father and son." The manual also observes that a large portion of those persons who enlist "are under twenty-one years of age" and "in the formative period of their lives."

The Marine Corps Development and Education Command has prepared a lesson plan on fraternization; and this plan, which makes reference to the Marine Corps Manual, observes that certain relationships between an officer and an enlisted person—such as that which developed between appellant and Chiriboga—are inconsistent with good order and discipline. Moreover, the Court of Military Review found that the cus-

tom of the service which prohibited an intimate relationship between officers and enlisted persons still exists in the Naval Service. This finding was grounded on the publication of the Manual for Courts-Martial, United States, 1984, which specifically recognized wrongful fraternization as a serious offense, and on the prior case law in the naval service.

In his capacity as unit legal officer for the squadron, Tedder had some official duties that pertained to Chiriboga. Indeed, he first met her while performing those duties. Although the specification on fraternization under Article 134 does not allege that she was a "subordinate member" of his command, it appears that in some respects Tedder was her supervisor. Certainly he was in a position to affect her career by his recommendations as to appropriate action in connection with certain accusations that had been made against her.

As described in Lance Corporal Chiriboga's testimony, Tedder's own course of conduct made it clear that he did not believe that he could lawfully maintain an intimate sexual relationship with a woman marine who was in his unit. Although Tedder was well aware that he should not institute a sexual relationship with Lance Corporal Chiriboga, he did so anyway and thereby prejudiced good order and discipline. Therefore, the finding of guilty of the specification alleging wrongful fraternization with Chiriboga in violation of Article 134 is valid.

Although not included in the above condensed version of the case, Captain Tedder was also convicted of conduct unbecoming an officer (Article 133, UCMJ) for having enlisted female marines obtain dates for him. Was this an inappropriate use of subordinate personnel? Compare *Tedder* with *United States v. Robinson* in chapter 6. One of the issues in *Tedder* was whether the Marine Corps had a custom of prohibiting personal relationships among officers and enlisted. In reaching its decision, the court relied on regulations promulgated by the commandant of the Marine Corps. Note that in *Robinson* the Air Force Court of Military Review found there was no custom in the U.S. Air Force which prohibited dating or consensual sexual intercourse with enlisted women who were not under the accused's command or supervision. In *Tedder,* the accused was charged with fraternization under Article 134, UCMJ. Because of the difficulty in showing that particular associations violate the custom of the service, the U.S. Navy has issued general orders defining prohibited relationships.

OPNAVINST 5370.2

Chief of Naval Operations Instruction 5370.2 (OPNAVINST 5370.2) prohibits the following relationships:

(1) Any personal relationship between an officer and an enlisted member that is unduly familiar and does not respect differences in rank and grade; and
(2) When prejudicial to good order and discipline or of a nature to bring discredit on the naval service, personal relationships between officer members or between enlisted members that are unduly familiar and that do not respect differences in grade or rank.

The above explains that unduly familiar officer-enlisted relationships are always prohibited under OPNAVINST 5370.2. For an unduly familiar relationship between officer members or between enlisted members to be prohibited, however, it must prejudice good order and discipline or discredit the naval service. OPNAVINST 5370.2 explains that prejudice to good order and discipline or discredit to the service results from circumstances which:

(1) call into question a senior's objectivity;
(2) result in actual or apparent preferential treatment;
(3) undermine the authority of a senior; or
(4) compromise the chain of command.

What circumstances satisfy the above criteria? The instruction explains that unduly familiar relationships between officer members or between enlisted members in the same chain of command normally undermine the leadership authority of the senior and

compromise the chain of command, and that relationships between chief petty officers (E-7 to E-9) and junior enlisted (E-1 to E-6) at the same command (but not in the same direct chain of command) also typically prejudice good order and discipline or discredit the naval service. The instruction further provides that personal relationships that are unduly familiar between staff/student personnel at training commands are also prejudicial to good order and discipline. Relationships between officer members and between enlisted members outside of the situations described above must be analyzed on a case-by-case basis to determine if they are prejudicial to good order and discipline or discredit the naval service.

What activities are "unduly familiar?" OPNAVINST 5370.2 explains that dating, cohabitation, sexual relationships, and private business relationships are considered unduly familiar. Note that a fraternization case is not excused by a subsequent marriage between the offending parties. Note also that fraternization is a gender-neutral concept. Its focus is on the detriment to good order and discipline resulting from unduly familiar senior-subordinate relationships, not the gender of the members involved.

As discussed above, OPNAVINST 5370.2 is punitive in nature and violations of its provisions discussed above may be charged as violation of a lawful general order under Article 92, UCMJ. The secretary of the navy, in Article 1165 of the U.S. Navy Regulations, also prohibits unduly familiar relationships between officer and enlisted members and unduly familiar relationships between officer members and between enlisted members that are prejudicial to good order and discipline or of a nature to bring discredit on the naval service. Article 1165, U.S. Navy Regulations, is a lawful general order as well. May an officer be charged with both fraternization and conduct unbecoming an officer for engaging in a prohibited relationship with an enlisted person? See the discussion in the next section regarding Article 133, UCMJ, and *Parker v. Levy.*

Conduct Unbecoming an Officer

Paragraph 59b, Part 4, MCM, sets forth the elements of Article 133, UCMJ:

(1) That the accused did or omitted to do certain acts; and
(2) That, under the circumstances, these acts or omissions constituted conduct unbecoming an officer and gentleman.

Paragraph 59c, Part 4, MCM, defines a "gentleman" and attempts to explain the nature of conduct unbecoming an officer:

(1) Gentleman. As used in this article, "gentleman" includes both male and female commissioned officers, cadets, and midshipmen. The elements of this offense under Article 133 are quite broad.
(2) Nature of offense. Conduct violative of this article is action or behavior in an official capacity which, in dishonoring or disgracing the person as an officer, seriously compromises the officer's character as a gentleman, or action or behavior in an unofficial or private capacity which, in dishonoring or disgracing the officer personally, seriously compromises the person's standing as an officer. There are certain moral attributes common to the ideal officer and the perfect gentleman, a lack of which is indicated by acts of dishonesty, unfair dealing, indecency, indecorum, lawlessness, injustice, or cruelty. Not everyone is or can be expected to meet unrealistically high moral standards, but there is a limit of tolerance based on customs of the service and military necessity below which the personal standards of an officer, cadet, or midshipman cannot fall without seriously compromising the person's standing as an officer, cadet, or midshipman or the person's character as a gentleman. This article prohibits conduct by a commissioned officer, cadet, or midshipman which, taking all the circumstances into consideration, is thus compromising. This article includes acts made punishable by any other article, provided these acts amount to conduct unbecoming an officer and a gentleman. Thus, a commissioned officer who steals property violates both this article and Article 121. Whenever the offense charged is the same as a specific offense set forth in this

Manual, the elements of proof are the same as those set forth in the paragraph which treats that specific offense, with the additional requirement that the act or omission constitutes conduct unbecoming an officer and gentleman.

Article 133 has been attacked for being impermissibly vague in defining what constitutes unbecoming conduct. The Supreme Court addressed this issue in the following case.

PARKER V. LEVY
SUPREME COURT OF THE UNITED STATES
417 U.S. 733
JUNE 19, 1974
Opinion: Justice Rehnquist

Appellee Howard Levy, a physician, was a captain in the army stationed at Fort Jackson, South Carolina. From the time he entered on active duty in July 1965 until his trial by court-martial, he was assigned as Chief of the Dermatological Service of the United States Army Hospital at Fort Jackson. On June 2, 1967, appellee was convicted by a general court-martial of violations of Arts. 90, 133, and 134 of the UCMJ.

The facts upon which his conviction rests are virtually undisputed. The evidence admitted at his court-martial trial showed that one of the functions of the hospital to which appellee was assigned was that of training Special Forces aide men. As Chief of the Dermatological Service, appellee was to conduct a clinic for those aide men. In the late summer of 1966, it came to the attention of the hospital commander that the dermatology training of the students was unsatisfactory. After investigating the program and determining that appellee had totally neglected his duties, the commander called appellee to his office and personally handed him a written order to conduct the training. Appellee read the order, said that he understood it, but declared that he would not obey it because of his medical ethics. Appellee persisted in his refusal to obey the order, and later reviews of the program established that the training was still not being carried out.

During the same period of time, appellee made several public statements to enlisted personnel at the post, of which the following is representative:

The United States is wrong in being involved in the Vietnam War. I would refuse to go to Vietnam if ordered to do so. I don't see why any colored soldier would go to Vietnam: they should refuse to go to Vietnam and if sent should refuse to fight because they are discriminated against and denied their freedom in the United States, and they are sacrificed and discriminated against in Vietnam by being given all the hazardous duty and they are suffering the majority of casualties. If I were a colored soldier I would refuse to go to Vietnam and if I were a colored soldier and were sent I would refuse to fight. Special Forces personnel are liars and thieves and killers of peasants and murderers of women and children.

This Court has long recognized that the military is, by necessity, a specialized society separate from civilian society. We have also recognized that the military has, again by necessity, developed laws and traditions of its own during its long history. The differences between the military and civilian communities result from the fact that "it is the primary business of armies and navies to fight or be ready to fight wars should the occasion arise." *Toth v. Quarles,* 350 U.S. 11, 17 (1955).

Just as military society has been a society apart from civilian society, so "military law . . . is a jurisprudence which exists separate and apart from the law which governs in our federal judicial establishment." And to maintain the discipline essential to perform its mission effectively, the military has developed what "may not unfitly be called the customary military law" or "general usage of the military service." The Court has approved the enforcement of those military customs and usages by courts-martial from the early days of this Nation.

The differences, first between the military community and the civilian community, and second between military law and civilian law, continue in the present day under the Uniform Code of Military Justice. That code cannot be equated to a civilian criminal code. It, and the various versions of the Articles of War which have preceded it, regulate aspects of the conduct of members of the military which in the civilian sphere are left unregulated. While a civilian criminal code carves out a relatively small segment of potential conduct and declares it criminal, the Uniform Code of Military Justice essays more varied regulation of a much larger segment of the activities of the more tightly knit military community.

In civilian life there is no legal sanction—civil or criminal—for failure to behave as an officer and a gentleman; in the military world, Art. 133 imposes such a sanction on a commissioned officer. The code likewise imposes other sanctions for conduct that in civilian life is not subject to criminal penalties: disrespect toward superior commissioned officers, Art. 89; cruelty toward, or oppression or maltreatment of subordinates, Art. 93; negligent damaging, destruction, or wrongful disposition of military property of the United States, Art. 108; improper hazarding of a vessel, Art. 110; drunkenness on duty, Art. 112; and malingering, Art. 115.

But the other side of the coin is that the penalties provided in the code vary from death and substantial penal confinement at one extreme to forms of administrative discipline which are below the threshold of what would normally be considered a criminal sanction at the other. Though all of the offenses described in the code are punishable "as a court-martial may direct," and the accused may demand a trial by court-martial, Art. 15 of the code also provides for the imposition of nonjudicial "disciplinary punishments" for minor offenses without the intervention of a court-martial. The punishments imposable under that article are of a limited nature.

In short, the Uniform Code of Military Justice regulates a far broader range of the conduct of military personnel than a typical state criminal code regulates of the conduct of civilians; but at the same time the enforcement of that code in the area of minor offenses is often by sanctions which are more akin to administrative or civil sanctions than to civilian criminal ones.

The availability of these lesser sanctions is not surprising in view of the different relationship of the government to members of the military. It is not only that of lawgiver to citizen, but also that of employer to employee. Indeed, unlike the civilian situation, the government is often employer, landlord, provisioner, and lawgiver rolled into one. That relationship also reflects the different purposes of the two communities. While members of the military community enjoy many of the same rights and bear many of the same burdens as do members of the civilian community, within the military community there is simply not the same autonomy as there is in the larger civilian community. The military establishment is subject to the control of the civilian commander-in-chief and the civilian departmental heads under him, and its function is to carry out the policies made by those civilian superiors.

Perhaps because of the broader sweep of the Uniform Code, the military makes an effort to advise its personnel of the contents of the Uniform Code, rather than depending on the ancient doctrine that everyone is presumed to know the law. Article 137 of the Uniform Code requires that the provisions of the code be "carefully explained to each enlisted member at the time of his entrance on active duty, or within six days thereafter" and that they be "explained again after he has completed six months of active duty. . . ." Thus the numerically largest component of the services, the enlisted personnel, who might be expected to be a good deal less familiar with the Uniform Code than commissioned officers, are required by its terms to receive instructions in its provisions. Article 137 further provides that a complete text of the code and of the regulations prescribed by the president "shall be made available to any person on active duty, upon his request, for his personal examination."

With these very significant differences between military law and civilian law and between the military community and the civilian community in mind, we turn to appellee's challenges to the constitutionality of Arts. 133 and 134. Appellee urges that both Art. 133 and Art. 134 (the general article) are "void for vagueness" under the Due Process Clause of the Fifth Amendment and overbroad in violation of the First Amendment.

Each of these articles has been construed by the United States Court of Military Appeals or by other military authorities in such a manner as to at least partially narrow its otherwise broad scope. The United States Court of Military Appeals has stated that Art. 134 must be judged not in vacuo, but in the context in which the years have placed it. Article 134 does not make every irregular, mischievous, or improper act a court-martial offense, but its reach is limited to conduct that is directly and palpably—as distinguished from indirectly and remotely—prejudicial to good order and discipline. The article applies only to calls for active opposition to the military policy of the United States, and does not reach all disagreement with, or objection to, a policy of the government.

Levy had fair notice from the language of each article that the particular conduct which he engaged in was punishable. This is a case, then, in which the statutes by their terms or as authoritatively construed apply without question to certain activities, but whose application to other behavior is uncertain.

Void for vagueness simply means that criminal responsibility should not attach where one could not reasonably understand that his contemplated conduct is proscribed. In determining the sufficiency of the notice a statute must of necessity be examined in the light of the conduct with which a defendant is charged. Since appellee could have had no reasonable doubt that his public statements urging Negro enlisted men not to go to Vietnam if ordered to do so were both "unbecoming an officer and a gentleman," and "to the prejudice of good order and discipline in the armed forces," in violation of the provisions of Arts. 133 and 134, respectively, his challenge to them as unconstitutionally vague under the Due Process Clause of the Fifth Amendment must fail.

We likewise reject appellee's contention that Arts. 133 and 134 are facially invalid because of their "overbreadth." While the members of the military are not excluded from the protection granted by the First Amendment, the different character of the military community and of the military mission requires a different application of those protections. The fundamental necessity for obedience, and the consequent necessity for imposition of discipline, may render permissible within the military that which would be constitutionally impermissible outside it. Doctrines of First Amendment overbreadth asserted in support of challenges to imprecise language like that contained in Arts. 133 and 134 are not exempt from the operation of these principles.

There is a wide range of the conduct of military personnel to which Arts. 133 and 134 may be applied without infringement of the First Amendment. While there may lurk at the fringes of the articles, even in the light of their narrowing construction by the United States Court of Military Appeals, some possibility that conduct which would be ultimately held to be protected by the First Amendment could be included within their prohibition, we deem this insufficient to invalidate either of them at the behest of appellee. His conduct, that of a commissioned officer publicly urging enlisted personnel to refuse to obey orders which might send them into combat, was unprotected under the most expansive notions of the First Amendment. Articles 133 and 134 may constitutionally prohibit that conduct, and a sufficiently large number of similar or related types of conduct so as to preclude their invalidation for overbreadth.

The Supreme Court's holding in *Parker v. Levy* firmly established the constitutionality of Article 133 and Article 134, the general article. Although Captain Levy asserted that the articles were void for vagueness, the court concluded that he was on sufficient notice that his conduct was improper. In its discussion, the court noted that certain conduct is unbecoming because it violates the customs and usages of the military. Where else does custom establish law? See chapter 11.

The MCM provides the following specific examples of unbecoming conduct:

(1) Knowingly making a false official statement;
(2) Dishonorable failure to pay a debt;
(3) Cheating on an exam;
(4) Opening and reading a letter of another without authority;
(5) Using insulting or defamatory language to another officer in that officer's presence or about that officer to other military persons;
(6) Being drunk and disorderly in a public place;
(7) Public association with known prostitutes;
(8) Committing or attempting to commit a crime involving moral turpitude; and
(9) Failing without good cause to support the officer's family.

Outside these specific examples, how can an officer know if his or her conduct violates Article 133? The following case considers this issue.

UNITED STATES V. DONATO J. GUAGLIONE, FIRST LIEUTENANT, U.S. ARMY
UNITED STATES COURT OF MILITARY APPEALS
27 M.J. 268
NOVEMBER 16, 1988
Opinion: Everett, Chief Judge

This case had its beginnings in the late summer of 1984 at Bad Hersfeld, Federal Republic of Germany, when appellant's unit formed a softball team. The team included Guaglione, a number of other officers, a warrant officer, and several enlisted soldiers. Among the enlisted members were Privates First Class Kennedy, Diaz, and Sawyer. Despite the natural closeness engendered by such activity, proper military courtesy was observed; and the junior members of the team referred to appellant as "Lieutenant G." Neither Kennedy, Diaz, nor Sawyer was directly subordinate to appellant.

In September of that year the team entered a tournament sponsored by the unit's parent command. This contest was held in Darmstadt, some distance from their assigned installation. After the team had been eliminated on September 6, the members arranged car pools among themselves for the return trip to Bad Hersfeld; and Kennedy, Diaz, and Sawyer rode back with Lieutenant Guaglione. En route, the passengers bought and consumed an alcoholic beverage. Guaglione did not partake thereof—presumably because he was driving.

The parties stopped in Frankfurt for food. After consuming hamburgers at a fast-food outlet, they decided to visit the nearby "red light district." The houses of prostitution in this area were legal; and one witness at the trial described them as being "a tourist attraction." There was no evidence that the area had been declared off-limits by any military commander.

The four men remained for about an hour. During this period, Kennedy and Diaz partook of the services available. Guaglione entered two of the houses of prostitution; but, while there, he did nothing more than look and comment on the physical charms of the hostesses. After the visit to the brothels, the journey to Bad Hersfeld resumed.

Testifying in his own behalf, Guaglione denied any

criminal misconduct, although he admitted visiting the houses of prostitution. This visit he attributed to his own "personal curiosity," that is, "to see what those houses looked like, what was there, what was available." In this connection, he asserted that, although his enlisted passengers had been in the "red-light district" before, he had never before seen "legalized prostitution." Guaglione asserted that he had not allowed the soldiers to smoke marijuana or to visit his quarters. Although he admitted to preservice experimentation with marijuana while in high school and due to peer pressure, he denied use of the substance on September 6, 1984. Guaglione's defense attorneys presented evidence of his excellent military character and Sawyer's lack of credibility.

Appellant's battery and battalion commanders testified that his conduct in visiting the houses of prostitution had displayed "poor judgment" but had not demeaned him as an officer. The battalion commander, Lieutenant Colonel Leverett, an officer of some twenty-three years' military service, refused to describe appellant's conduct as "unbecoming" despite trial counsel's repeated attempts to so characterize it during cross-examination. Also, the former first sergeant of the battery to which Guaglione was assigned testified that, on the basis of his own experience and knowledge of the customs and standards of the army, appellant's act was only "poor judgment." This witness had served in the army for 27 years at the time of trial.

The government's only rebuttal witness was the brigade commander, Colonel A. W. Schulz. Testifying in response to a hypothetical question based on the facts of this case, he stated on direct examination, "I do not believe the conduct is acceptable." When asked whether the visit to the house of prostitution "rises to the level . . . that would disgrace him as an officer," he responded, "I think it comes very close. It might be very, very poor judgment and it certainly borders on conduct unbecoming."

In determining whether Guaglione's visit to the house of prostitution constituted unbecoming conduct, we accept the premise that a commissioned officer may be held to a higher standard of accountability for his conduct than an enlisted member or a civilian. However, not every delict or misstep warrants punishment under Article 133. In general, it must be so disgraceful as to render an officer unfit for service.

There is no evidence that Guaglione participated in any sexual activity while in the Frankfurt "red-light district" or that he encouraged any of the enlisted members to do so. They already were familiar with this district, while Guaglione had never seen "legalized prostitution" before. There is also no evidence that, while they were in the houses of prostitution, any of the three soldiers addressed Guaglione in any familiar way, failed to show him military courtesy, or committed a breach of military decorum. Moreover, no American commander had attempted to prohibit American service members from entering these brothels by declaring them off-limits; and they were lawful under German law.

Despite the high standards of accountability to which an officer is held, it still is necessary that, through custom, regulation, or otherwise, he be given notice that his conduct is unbecoming. In this connection, we recognize that participation on an athletic team tends to be an equalizer and that the members of the team tend to evaluate one another in terms of athletic ability rather than military rank. When officers and enlisted members play on the same team, it is inevitable that some relaxation of usual military decorum will occur and that there will be some modification of ordinary military relationships. Obviously, military authorities have come to the conclusion that, whatever the disadvantage of this relaxation may be, there are many offsetting advantages; and we are well aware that many military units have teams on which both officers and enlisted persons participate. The camaraderie that results under these circumstances must be taken into account in determining whether unlawful "fraternization" has occurred in violation of service custom.

With this in mind, we cannot ignore the testimony of Guaglione's own battery commander and battalion commander—persons from whom he would be expected to receive guidance as to his military responsibilities—that his conduct constituted no more than "poor judgment." Likewise, the first sergeant, with extensive military experience, was unwilling to characterize appellant's conduct as unbecoming. The testimony even of Colonel Schultz, appellant's brigade commander, who was a rebuttal witness, is so equivocal as to undermine the government's position.

We conclude that the government has failed to show that Guaglione had been given the requisite notice that his conduct would be considered "unbecoming." Accordingly, appellant's conviction for fraternizing in violation of Article 133 cannot stand.

Study Questions

Boatswain's Mate Third Class (BM3) Daniels and Boatswain's Mate Seaman (BMSN) Beam both were authorized liberty from 1630, 17 February (Friday) through 0730, 20 February (Monday), and they had plans to meet after liberty call before going out for the weekend. At about 1200 on Friday, Daniels decided that he had better things to do than to stay on board USS *Bert* berthed at Naval Station San Diego; therefore, he left the ship at 1200 and went to his and Beam's favorite off-base club. Beam waited until liberty call to leave the ship and showed up at the club at 1700. The guys were having a great time until Beam was arrested by the San Diego police at 2100, 18 February (Saturday night) for driving under the influence (DUI). The San Diego police notified the *Bert* at 2200, 18 February, of Beams' whereabouts. Beam was put in jail and remained there until he plead guilty to the DUI on 21 February (Tuesday). At 1600, 21 February, the police notified the *Bert* that Beam was available for pickup. Daniels arrived at the *Bert* at 0730, 20 February, ready for a full week of work.

1. Which of the following correctly states the period of BMSN Beam's unauthorized absence?

    a. 1630, 17 February–0730, 20 February

    b. 1630, 17 February–2200, 18 February

    c. 0730, 20 February–1600, 21 February

    d. 2200, 18 February–1600, 21 February

    e. 2200, 18 February–0730, 20 February

2. Which of the following correctly states the period of BM3 Daniel's unauthorized absence?

    a. 1630, 17 February–0730, 20 February

    b. 1200, 17 February–2200, 18 February

    c. 1200, 17 February–1630, 17 February

    d. 1200, 17 February–0730, 20 February

    e. He was never in an unauthorized absence status.

The USS *Nantucket,* located at Charleston, South Carolina, was scheduled to shift berths (piers) at Naval Station Charleston at 1300, Friday, 31 November. BM3 Helen Chambers was authorized liberty from 1630, 31 November until 0730, 3 December and had plans to go to Atlanta for the weekend. At 1200 on Friday, 31 November, BM3 Chambers intentionally left the ship early to avoid the mundane tasks associated with shifting berths and headed for Atlanta. Unbeknownst to BM3 Chambers, the ship's XO came over the 1MC (ship's public address system) at 1500 and announced to all hands that the *Nantucket* would be getting under way on Monday, 3 December at 0800 for a three-day training exercise. BM3 Chambers, who was having a great weekend in Atlanta, had every intention of returning by quarters at 0700 on Monday morning but was caught by a severe, unexpected ice storm that developed in Atlanta late Sunday afternoon. Despite her best efforts, she was not able to get back to Naval Station Charleston until 1600 on Monday, 3 December. Upon her arrival at the pier, she was surprised to find the *Nantucket* gone. BM3 Chambers immediately reported into the Squadron Duty Office.

3. Which of the following offenses did BM3 Chambers commit by leaving the *Nantucket* at 1200 on 31 November?

    a. Unauthorized Absence from Unit or Organization, Art 86, UCMJ.

    b. Missing Movement Through Design, Art 87, UCMJ.

    c. Missing Movement Through Neglect, Art 87, UCMJ.

    d. Both (a) and (b) above.

    e. None of the above.

4. Which of the following correctly states the period of BM3 Chambers's unauthorized absence?

    a. 1200, 31 November–1630, 31 November

    b. 1630, 31 November–1600, 3 December

    c. 0700, 3 December–1600, 3 December

    d. 1200, 31 November–0700, 3 December

    e. 1200, 31 November–1600, 3 December

5. What factors will tend to prove the crime of desertion?

6. Which of the following is *true* regarding the case of *United States v. Riofredo?*

    a. LCPL Riofredo successfully asserted the defense of impossibility.

    b. LCPL Riofredo successfully asserted the defense of mistake of fact.

    c. LCPL Riofredo unsuccessfully asserted the defense of duress.

    d. LCPL Riofredo unsuccessfully asserted the defense of impossibility.

    e. None of the above is true.

Per U.S. Navy Uniform Regulations, Admiral Jackson, Commander-in-Chief, U.S. Naval Forces, Europe (CINCUSNAVEUR), is a prescribing authority for uniform policy within the CINCUSNAVEUR area of responsibility. As a prescribing authority, Admiral Jackson has the authority to decide whether male sailors can wear earrings or nose rings off base while on liberty in the CINCUSNAVEUR area of responsibility. Pursuant to this authority, he signed and issued the following:

    a. The wearing of earrings or nose rings by male personnel in the naval service within the CINCUSNAVEUR area of responsibility is strictly prohibited. Male personnel are prohibited from wearing earrings and nose rings while on duty or while on leave or liberty. This prohibition applies irrespective of whether a member is in military or civilian attire.

    b. Violations of this directive may result in administrative or punitive action.

USS *Nashville* was in port in Holy Loch, Scotland. While on liberty out in town, Operations Specialist First Class (OS1) Brooks, a crew member of the *Nashville,* decided to wear his favorite set of gold earrings and a subtle (but stylish) silver and turquoise nose ring. OS1 Brooks was aware of the prohibition on wearing earrings in European foreign ports but had no idea that nose rings were not allowed.

7. Based on the above facts, which orders offenses, if any, did OS1 Brooks commit by wearing the earrings and nose ring?

The commanding officer of the USS *Nashville,* Commander Travis, USN (an O-5), had also promulgated his own written instruction on the subject. This order, NASHVILLEINST 5100.2a, dated 1 January 1995, also prohibited the wearing of earrings or nose rings while on liberty in foreign ports, and applied to all service members attached to or embarked on the *Nashville.* The instruction clearly stated that violations were punishable under the UCMJ. Shortly before the current deployment, Commander Travis included the provisions of NASHVILLEINST 5100.2a in several consecutive issues of the ship's plan of the day (POD). OS1 Brooks had been on leave immediately before the deployment and was unaware of the new instruction.

8. Which of the following statements is *true?*

    a. By violating NASHVILLEINST 5100.2a, OS1 Brooks is guilty of failure to obey an other lawful order, Art 92, UCMJ.

    b. By violating NASHVILLEINST 5100.2a, OS1 Brooks is guilty of willful disobedience of a superior commissioned officer, Art 90, UCMJ.

    c. NASHVILLEINST 5100.2a is not a lawful order because it does not serve a valid military purpose and is overly broad.

    d. Both (a) and (b) are true.

    e. OS1 Brooks is not guilty of violating NASHVILLEINST 5100.2a because he lacked actual knowledge of the instruction.

When OS1 Brooks returned to the Holy Loch Naval Station, he was still wearing the earrings and nose ring. Consequently, he was confronted by the gate guard, Master at Arms Third Class (MA3) Gill, an E-3, whose duties included enforcement of proper uniform standards. MA3 Gill immediately told OS1 Brooks to remove the earrings and nose ring. OS1 Brooks responded by screaming at MA3 Gill, "You stupid camouflaged piece of ———. There is no way I am taking out my earrings and nose ring. You are a worthless ———." MA3 Gill responded by asking OS1 Brooks the name of his division officer on board the *Nashville*. OS1 Brooks responded by screaming at the top of his lungs, "His name is LTJG Strait and he is the biggest ——— loser in the entire civilized world!" LTJG Strait was out in town on liberty at the time of the incident.

9. If OS1 Brooks is charged with disrespect toward a petty officer, Article 91, UCMJ, which of the following would be a *valid* defense?

a. His statements to MA3 Gill fit within the "purely private conversation" doctrine.

b. OS1 Brooks is senior to MA3 Gill.

c. The earrings and nose ring were legal; therefore, he was legally justified in chewing out MA3 Gill.

d. The wearing of the earrings and nose ring was legal; therefore, MA3 Gill was not properly in the execution of his office at the time.

e. None of the above would be a valid defense.

10. If OS1 Brooks is charged with disrespect toward a superior commissioned officer, Article 89, UCMJ, which of the following would be a *valid* defense?

a. LTJG Strait was not present to hear the statement.

b. His statement about LTJG Strait fits within the "purely private conversation" doctrine.

c. He did not intend the statement to be disrespectful.

d. LTJG Strait was on liberty and not in the execution of his office when the statement was made.

e. None of the above would be a valid defense.

11. What are the differences between the charges of disrespect toward a superior commissioned officer, Article 89, and disrespect toward a petty officer, Article 91?

Boatswain's Mate Chief (BMC) Biggins, USN, was the leading chief petty officer for the deck division on board the USS *Sandpiper,* under way in the Pacific. While inspecting the division berthing spaces one morning, he discovered three marijuana cigarettes on Boatswain's Mate Seaman Apprentice (BMSA) Hackett's rack. BMSA Hackett had purchased the marijuana cigarettes from Machinist's Mate Third Class (MM3) Mather the night before on the fantail of the *Sandpiper.* The marijuana had come from MM3 Mather's marijuana farm in the backyard of his off-base apartment. Prior to the deployment, MM3 Mather brought a large amount of marijuana on board the *Sandpiper* for himself and any of his shipmates who might want to buy some for their own use. BMC Biggins picked up the three marijuana cigarettes and turned them over to the master-at-arms (MAA).

12. Based on the above scenario, what offenses did BMSA Hackett commit?

13. Based on the above scenario, what offenses did MM3 Mather commit?

14. If BMC Biggins is charged with wrongful possession of marijuana, Article 112a, UCMJ, which of the following statements would be *true?*

a. He is guilty since he knew the substance was marijuana.

b. He is guilty since he knew he was in possession of marijuana.

c. He is not guilty since he took possession of the marijuana in the course of his official duties; such possession is not wrongful.

d. He is guilty since he should not have picked up the marijuana cigarettes in the first place. He should have left them on BMSA

Hackett's rack while he went to search for the MAA.

e. None of the above is true.

15. OPNAVINST 5370.2 is the navy's Fraternization Policy. What kind of order is the instruction? Describe the relationships it prohibits.

16. All of the following are examples of Conduct Unbecoming an Officer and Gentleman, Article 133, UCMJ, *except:*

a. An army first lieutenant tutors a fellow lieutenant in platoon leadership at the request of his battery commander but charges the lieutenant more than two thousand dollars for the professional "extra instruction" sessions.

b. A female ensign requests the assistance of her enlisted subordinates in getting dates with a male petty officer.

c. An army first lieutenant is a member of his unit's softball team, which includes several enlisted soldiers.

d. A midshipman at the Naval Academy cheats on his electrical engineering exam.

e. A navy lieutenant is drunk and disorderly at the annual Tailhook convention at the Las Vegas Hilton hotel.

CHAPTER SIX

GOVERNMENT ETHICS

Ethical government means much more than laws. It is a spirit, an imbued code of conduct, an ethos. . . . Laws and rules can never be fully descriptive of what an ethical person should do. . . . Compulsion by law is the most expensive way to make people behave.

—President's Commission on Federal Ethics Law Reform, *To Serve with Honor* (1989)

Introduction

As the above quotation implies, government ethics laws seek to compel government employees, both civilians and members of the armed forces, to behave ethically. Some have suggested, as is also implied above, that law alone, in the absence of a sense of personal honor, cannot effectively and efficiently promote and ensure ethical conduct. Conversely, for those who possess such a sense of honor, ethics laws become superfluous; such people behave ethically without regard to the compulsion of law. Perhaps a better view is that law and honor each gives force and power to the other, thus better inducing the ethical behavior that society desires. Whatever is true, however, ethics laws exist and are important to the naval officer in that he or she must comply with them and ensure that his or her subordinates do the same.

The rules in this area may seem sophisticated and complex, and sometimes even counterintuitive. To comply with ethics rules requires knowledge and understanding of the laws and regulations, and a feel for when to check the rule book before taking an action that may turn out to be inappropriate or even illegal. To begin the process of acquiring this required knowledge and understanding, this chapter traces the development of laws regulating conduct of government employees and discusses the purposes behind them. The discussion then focuses on the contemporary law of government ethics and reviews those laws and derivative regulations of frequent concern to naval personnel.

Development of Ethics Laws

Corruption in American government has existed since the establishment of the United States, and as a consequence, attempts to limit the conduct of government employees have also existed since that time. In the nineteenth century, extensive bribery and graft provoked the enactment of criminal laws addressing such abuses, particularly in the area of procurement fraud. Surprisingly, however, these statutes are not the primary source of contemporary government ethics laws, which focus on preventing conflicts of interest. Contemporary ethics law was born out of a desire to curb the use of public office for private gain. Professor A. Allen King explains in "Symposium Ethics in Government: Ethics in Government and the Vision of Public Service," *George Washington Law Review* 58 (1990): 419:

> Corruption has accompanied American political life from the founding of the Constitution. For example, Jefferson's Postmaster General lobbied openly for the advancement of land companies in which the Postmaster had invested. Moreover, the spoils system defined public employment in terms of patronage, where obligations to political patrons replaced other loyalties, and rebates of salary and requirements of personal service were commonly perceived as conditions of employment. Following the Civil War, the buying and selling of offices was commonplace, and the purchasers often used these offices for personal gain. Corruption served as one of the period's motifs.
>
> Bribery and graft, the crudest forms of corruption, provoked the enactment of criminal penalties and criminal statutes addressing these derelictions and specific abuses of governmental authority, particularly involving

procurement, in the mid-nineteenth century preceding and following the Civil War. The regulation of ethics in government, however, controlling conflicts of interest, as opposed to graft and bribery, is linked historically and conceptually to the civil service reform movement of the late nineteenth century and to the Civil Service Act of 1883.

> The spoils system invited, if not required, personal corruption, and placed the powers of government in the hands of persons who used and manipulated that power for their own gain. In addition, the lack of ethical principles in government permitted unfair and inequitable application of the laws, and subjected citizens to not only inefficient but abusive government as well.
>
> The reform movement sought to create politically neutral public employees by emphasizing competence and professionalism. It desired public employees able to perform their jobs free of requirements to support political officials and free of pressures to base government decisions on personal or partisan motives.

Thus the concept of "public service" by politically neutral employees has been the underlying premise of ethics laws since the passage of the Civil Service Act of 1883. The regulation of government employee behavior began to increase in the early 1960s with the passage of new statutes designed to address conflicts of interest in three important areas: (1) conflicting financial interests, (2) outside compensation, and (3) postgovernment service employment. In 1965 Congress delegated extensive authority to federal agencies to issue and enforce comprehensive ethics regulations. Consequently, from 1965 to 1993, federal employees (including military personnel) were governed to a large extent by their agency's own rules relating to ethics and standards of conduct. The Department of the Navy had its own standards of ethical conduct contained in an instruction issued by the secretary of the navy (the SECNAVINST 5370.2 series). Congress again modified existing ethics statutes and added new ethics laws by the Government Ethics Act of 1978. Each agency, however, retained authority to create its own ethics regulations within the statutory framework. Motivated in part by the unethical conduct of federal employees in the Iran-Contra affair, President George Bush established a commission to study federal ethics law. This commission recommended a single set of standards for all executive branch employees (including military personnel). The Office of Government Ethics (OGE) made this recommendation reality by issuing the Standards of Ethical Conduct for Employees of the Executive Branch, which became effective in February 1993. Pursuant to the OGE's Standards of Ethical Conduct, the Department of Defense (DOD) issued the Joint Ethics Regulation 5500.7R (JER) to supplement the OGE regulation. This instruction superseded the navy's ethics instruction, SECNAVINST 5370.2. The OGE and DOD regulations are discussed below.

In the last decade, public awareness regarding government ethics has heightened significantly because of well-publicized investigations into Whitewater, the potential misuse of FBI files by the White House, and the Iran-Contra affair. Before you study particular standards of conduct, consider the following facts concerning Lieutenant Colonel Oliver North's involvement in Iran-Contra. Do you think Lieutenant Colonel North acted unethically? Illegally? Does it matter which?

UNITED STATES V. OLIVER S. NORTH

UNITED STATES DISTRICT COURT FOR THE DISTRICT OF

COLUMBIA

713 F. SUPP. 1448 (D. D.C. 1989)

The evidence shows that, by May, 1986, defendant North had spent the prior 18 months or more in his secret effort "to keep the Contras together body and soul." Although he accomplished this goal in a number of different ways, a key part of North's project was to direct the opening up of a Southern front in Nicaragua with the assistance of Army General (Ret.) Richard Secord and his organization acting under North's direction. In 1986, North expanded the operation by enlisting General Secord to assist with the Iran initiative.

The North-Secord relationship thus had its locus in North's position as NSC staff member in Washington, D.C.

It was through this position that North directed both Contra-related and Iran-related business to Secord, and North's continued employment at the NSC was essential to the continuation of Secord's involvement in these projects.

In late April 1986, Secord told Glenn Robinette, a security consultant whose office is in Washington, that North and his family had been the object of threats. He solicited Robinette's assistance to "give some support" to North in this connection. On April 30, 1986, Robinette went to the North household, met Mrs. North, and walked through the North home to determine what "could be used" to provide the family with increased security. Robinette then "contacted several security equipment suppliers" to determine what equipment was available and how much it would cost.

On May 5, 1986, North, Secord, and Robinette met in North's office in Washington, D.C. Robinette at this time had completed his "preliminary review" and "was prepared to discuss what [Robinette] thought should be done" with respect to a security system. Robinette told North that he wanted to install a security system to "frighten away or scare any intruders or people coming to the home." At the end of the meeting, North "seemed to accept what [Robinette] told him as a preliminary plan, equipment and plans and procedures." North said "something to [the] effect" of "go ahead and keep working on it." Robinette accordingly continued his work on the system, and was recompensed for his time by Secord. On May 10, there was another meeting at which more specific plans were discussed, and the security system paid for entirely by Secord [using his own private, nongovernment funds], was installed [at North's private home] the following month.

General Secord was also charged with the federal crime of conspiracy to give and with giving a gratuity to a government official. In discussing General Secord's case, the court noted that the relevant federal law concerning giving and receiving gratuities concerned, among other things, the issue of whether General Secord gave things of value because of the official position held by Lieutenant Colonel North. See *United States v. Secord,* 726 F. Supp. 845 (D. D.C. 1989).

Look at the federal law excerpted below, Title 18

United States Code, Section 201 (1994). Does this affect your thinking as to Lieutenant Colonel North's behavior?

> 201. Bribery of public officials and witnesses. . . .
> (b)(2)(A) Whoever being a public official directly or indirectly, corruptly demands, seeks, receives, accepts, or agrees to receive or accept anything of value personally or for any other person or entity, in return for being influenced in the performance of any official act; or. . . .
> (c)(1)(B) Whoever being a public official directly or indirectly demands, seeks, receives, accepts, or agrees to receive or accept anything of value personally for or because of any official act performed or to be performed by such official or person; . . . shall be fined or imprisoned for not more than two years, or both.

In analyzing how the above excerpts from Section 201 of Title 18 apply to the *North* facts, it might be helpful to consider the reason for the rule. According to the United States Court of Appeals for the Fifth Circuit, one purpose of Section 201 is to reach any situation in which the judgment of a government agent might be clouded because of payments or gifts made to him by reason of his position, because even if corruption is not intended by either party, there may remain a tendency in such a situation for the government agent to provide conscious or unconscious preferential treatment to the gift. See *United States v. Evans,* 572 F.2d 455 (5th Cir. 1978). Would, or could, the gift of the security fence to Lieutenant Colonel North have clouded his judgment such that he might have provided General Secord's private business venture preferential treatment over competing private businesses seeking to do business with the government? Is there a potential appearance of impropriety that might affect the public confidence in honest and fair government?

Purpose of Ethics Laws

The above section discussed how ethics regulations developed out of concern over abuses by government employees motivated by conflicting private and public obligations, and how such abuses impaired government function. Professor King explains the potential effects of unethical behavior by government employees:

> Corruption and conflict of interest violations undercut public confidence in government because they indicate a bureaucracy out of control and raise the specter that public employees will use the power of government for their own purposes. Abuse of power and abuse of the public can follow closely upon one another. Therefore, bureaucracies have an interest in controlling and regulating corruption and conflicts of interest. If members of the bureaucracy cannot show self-restraint, other methods of control must be sought. (*George Washington Law Review* 58 [1990]: 432)

Do more ethics regulations mean more ethical employees? Professor King argues that the moral force implicit in the concept of public service as a public trust has diminished in the last twenty years, and he warns against the use of laws to make up for this loss of moral force. He argues this point as follows:

> Too great a reliance on legal regulation can have side effects, like a drug too frequently used. By converting ethical problems into legal ones, the law becomes the sole judge of propriety. What can be done becomes what should be done. If what is legal continues to seem improper, additional conduct is made illegal, reinforcing the perception that what is legal constitutes what is proper. Soon ethics has limited significance apart from legal command and enforcement structures and sanctions become increasingly important. (*George Washington Law Review* 58 [1990]: 432–33)

Do you agree with Professor's King's contention that the public service vision, that is, a moral or ethical code requiring public servants to act for the public good rather than for their own, has lost importance as the motivator of government employees to act ethically? What about the notion that the legal regulation of ethics actually damages the promotion of ethics in government? Consider the following statement of the former navy inspector general, Vice Admiral David Bennett:

> We have so many obscure and confusing directives that most of us are in violation of something most of the time. I'm not suggesting ignoring directives in our daily professional lives. A good approach is to ask ourselves: What are we really trying to do; what is the most efficient way to accomplish the task; what, if anything, do I need to change; whose endorsement or permission do I need; how do I explain it to my troops and my boss. Most of our tasks are relatively simple when reduced to their essence. The common sense approach almost always works. Living in fear of making an honest mistake or of being criticized is not why any of us was hired. Our fear should be that we won't have the courage of our convictions, won't be worthy of the trust of those we lead or won't be ready when we are needed (*Surface Sitrep* 10, no. 4 [August/September 1994]).

Sources and Enforcement of Current Ethics Laws and Regulations

As discussed above, there are several sources of ethics rules, including federal criminal statutes and regulations issued by the OGE and DOD.

Title 18 of the U.S. Code contains several statutes pertaining to bribery, corruption, and conflicts of interest. According to the federal courts, the purpose of these statutes (Title 18 U.S. Code, Sections 201–8) is to protect the government from corruption and self-interested financial dealing, and their function is to protect the public from corrupting influences that might be brought to bear upon government agents who are financially interested in business transactions which they are conducting on behalf of government. See *San Francisco v. United States,* 443 F. Supp 1116 (N.D. Cal. 1977) affirmed (9th Cir. 1980) 615 F.2d 498. For example, as to bribery, 18 U.S. Code, Section 201(b) (discussed above with respect to the *North* case) provides:

> Employees are prohibited from, directly or indirectly, giving, offering, promising, demanding, seeking, receiving, accepting, or agreeing to receive anything of value to influence any official act, to influence commission of fraud on the United States, to induce committing or omitting any act in violation of a lawful duty.

With regard to conflicts of interest, Sectin 208 of Title 18 prohibits federal employees from participating in any governmental activity in which they know that they have a private financial interest. This is not a new concept. For example, a 1942 Opinion of the Attorney General of the United States held that an army officer should not have been assigned to maintain liaison with a private corporation of which he was an officer and stockholder, because a person whose duty it was to serve the public should not have been put into a position in which he could also serve his selfish interests. Sec. 40 Op Atty. Gen. 168 (1942).

The Standards of Ethical Conduct issued by OGE in 1993 is a comprehensive ethics regulation applicable to all employees of the executive branch, including military officers. It incorporates the criminal conflict of interest statutes of Title 18 (such as the one quoted above) and sets forth numerous other standards of conduct. It also requires government agencies to "initiate appropriate disciplinary or corrective action in individual cases" and authorizes federal agencies, such as the DOD, to issue regulations supplementing its provisions, as well. Pursuant to this authorization, DOD issued the JER to supplement the OGE regulation in 1994. The JER explains and amplifies the OGE Standards of Ethical Conduct, as well as the criminal statutes in Title 18. It applies to all civilian employees and military personnel, including officers and midshipmen, and makes the OGE Standards of Ethical Conduct applicable to enlisted personnel as well. The JER covers such activities as gifts (giving and receiving), conflicts of interest, impartiality in performing duties, outside activities and employment, misuse of position, travel, gambling, political activities, honoraria, and postgovernment service employment.

The JER is a lawful general order which makes the failure to obey its rules a violation of Article 92,

UCMJ, punishable at court-martial, nonjudicial punishment, or addressed through nonpunitive measures (for example, nonpunitive letters of caution or letters of instruction). See chapters 4 and 5. As with all general orders, ignorance of the regulation is not a valid defense. As noted above, an ethics violation may subject the violator to separate federal criminal or civil sanctions as provided in the particular statute involved, as well. What other UCMJ articles apply to ethics violations? See chapter 5 and *United States v. Robinson* below.

Current Ethics Rules

General Principles and Standards

Although it is difficult, if not impossible, to know all the ethics rules, it is essential that the naval officer understand certain fundamental standards from which the more specific rules are derived. If he or she understands and applies these general ethical principles, it is unlikely that an unknowing violation of a more technical rule will occur. The following regulation from the OGE Standards of Ethical Conduct lays out the fourteen fundamental tenets of ethical conduct:

§ 2635.101 Basic obligation of public service.

General principles. The following general principles apply to every employee and may form the basis for the standards contained in this part. Where a situation is not covered by the standards set forth in this part, employees shall apply the principles set forth in this section in determining whether their conduct is proper.

(1) Public service is a public trust, requiring employees to place loyalty to the constitution, the laws and ethical principles above private gain.

(2) Employees shall not hold financial interests that conflict with the conscientious performance of duty.

(3) Employees shall not engage in financial transactions using nonpublic Government information or allow the improper use of such information to further any private interest.

(4) An employee shall not, except as permitted by this regulation, solicit or accept any gift or other item of monetary value from any person or entity seeking official action from, doing business with, or conducting activities regulated by the employee's agency, or whose interests may be substantially affected by the performance or nonperformance of the employee's duties.

(5) Employees shall put forth honest effort in the performance of their duties.

(6) Employees shall not knowingly make unauthorized commitments or promises of any kind purporting to bind the Government.

(7) Employees shall not use public office for private gain.

(8) Employees shall act impartially and not give preferential treatment to any private organization or individual.

(9) Employees shall protect and conserve Federal property and shall not use it for other than authorized activities.

(10) Employees shall not engage in outside employment or activities, including seeking or negotiating for employment, that conflict with official Government duties and responsibilities.

(11) Employees shall disclose waste, fraud, abuse and corruption to appropriate authorities.

(12) Employees shall satisfy in good faith their obligations as citizens, including all just financial obligations, especially those—such as federal, state, or local taxes—that are imposed by law.

(13) Employees shall adhere to all laws and regulations that provide equal opportunity for all Americans regardless of race, color, religion, sex, national origin, age, or handicap.

(14) Employees shall endeavor to avoid any actions creating the appearance that they are violating the law or the ethical standards set forth in this part. Whether particular circumstances create an appearance that the law or these standards have been violated shall be determined from the perspective of a reasonable person with knowledge of the relevant facts.

Do the above rules reflect the public service concept that motivated the civil service reform movement of the nineteenth century? Do you agree that a government employee who abides by the above standards will not run afoul of other, more specific ethics regulations? Consider some of the more specific rules set forth below.

Specific Ethics Rules

GIFTS BETWEEN SUPERIORS AND SUBORDINATES

As with the rest of society, military members commonly exchange gifts. Ethical problems arise, however, when the giving or receipt of a gift raises the appearance of favoritism. The OGE's Standards of Ethical Conduct regulate gifts as follows:

§ 2635.302.
(a) Gifts to superiors. Except as provided in this subpart, an employee may not:
(1) Directly or indirectly, give a gift to a or make a donation toward a gift for an official superior; or
(2) Solicit a contribution from another employee for a gift to either his own or the other employee's official superior.
(b) Gifts from employees receiving less pay. Except as provided in this subpart, an employee may not directly or indirectly, accept a gift from an employee receiving less pay than himself unless:
(1) The two employees are not in a subordinate-official superior relationship; and
(2) There is a personal relationship between the two employees that would justify the gift.
(c) Limitation on use of exceptions. Notwithstanding any exception provided in this subpart, an official superior shall not coerce the offering of a gift from a subordinate.

MISUSE OF OFFICIAL POSITION

One of the broadest ethics rules is the prohibition on government employees using their position or government property for personal benefit or for the benefit of relatives, friends, or other private organizations:

§ 2635.702 Use of public office for private gain.

An employee shall not use his public office for his own private gain, for the endorsement of any product, service or enterprise, or for the private gain of friends, relatives, or persons with whom the employee is affiliated in a nongovernmental capacity, including nonprofit organizations of which the employee is an officer or member, and persons with whom the employee has or seeks employment or business relations.
(a) Inducement or coercion of benefits. An employee shall not use or permit the use of his government position or title or any authority associated with his public office in a manner that is intended to coerce or induce another person, including a subordinate, to provide any benefit, financial or otherwise, to himself or to friends, relatives, or persons with whom the employee is affiliated in a nongovernmental capacity.
(b) Appearance of governmental sanction. An employee shall not use or permit the use of his government position or title or any authority associated with his public office in a manner that could reasonably be construed to imply that his agency or the government sanctions or endorses his personal activities or those of another.
(c) Endorsements. An employee shall not use or permit the use of his government position or title or any authority associated with his public office to endorse any product, service or enterprise except: . . .
(e) Use of terms of address and ranks. Nothing in this section prohibits an employee who is ordinarily addressed using a general term of address, such as "The Honorable," or a rank, such as a military or ambassadorial rank, from using that term of address or rank in connection with a personal activity.

This rule prohibits, among other things, use of public office to obtain private "benefits," "financial or otherwise," from subordinates. Consider the following case decided by the Air Force Court of Military Review regarding the definition of what is a "benefit" for purposes of ethics law.

UNITED STATES V. STAFF SERGEANT GORDON T. ROBINSON, JR., UNITED STATES AIR FORCE
UNITED STATES AIR FORCE COURT OF MILITARY REVIEW
37 M.J. 588
MAY 10, 1993
Opinion: Snider, Judge

Appellant was a shift supervisor of a software maintenance complex section located at Falcon AFB, Colorado. Airman K was a female airman assigned to appellant's shift. The work area contained tall mainframe computers as well as a room in the rear portion of the work area. The common practice was that a superior conducted counseling in the rear room, while other corrective action, such as brief oral rebukes or on-the-spot corrections, were provided behind the mainframes. This practice was followed to avoid embarrassment in front of peers.

On three to six occasions during duty hours, appellant appeared in the work area and asked Airman K to step behind the mainframes so he could talk to her.

After they went behind the mainframes, appellant proceeded to hug Airman K. On these occasions, appellant did not speak to Airman K at all (as he did during actual counseling), but merely smiled and walked away after hugging her. Appellant did not order, or demand, Airman K to step behind the mainframes, but Airman K stated she instinctively assumed appellant was acting in his superior and supervisory capacity when he asked her to step back there, as well as assuming it was for an official work purpose. She never asked the purpose of appellant's requests before responding, nor did she hesitate, for she did not desire to appear insubordinate to a superior. Airman K stated that, on each occasion, she remained rigid with her arms at her side, not responding in any manner, in hopes appellant would realize his actions were unwelcomed.

Appellant was charged with a violation of Air Force Regulation (AFR) 30-30, Standards of Conduct, Paragraph 8 (May 1989).

AFR 30-30, Paragraph 8, reads as follows:

Using official Air Force Position. Air force personnel must not use their air force positions to induce, coerce, or influence a person (including subordinates) in any way to provide any personal benefit, financial or otherwise, to themselves or others.

Appellant avers that acquiring the opportunity for the "sexual advances" alleged in the specification does not constitute a "personal benefit," and, therefore, no reasonable reading or interpretation of AFR 30-30 reaches the conduct of which he was convicted.

To support his averment, appellant emphasizes the fact that AFR 30-30 defines the term, "gratuity," but does not define "benefit." He argues that this fact reflects the drafters' intent to restrict AFR 30-30 to commercial or financial transactions. This assertion is plainly incorrect. Paragraph 8, by its very terms, clearly addresses benefits other than those of a financial nature. Further, none of our precedents construing AFR 30-30 suggest its reach is confined to financial or commercial situations and transactions.

The trial judge was entirely correct in applying the plain meaning of the term, "benefit," which includes "anything that is advantageous or for the good of a person or thing," as well as financial situations. *Random House College Dictionary*, rev. ed. (1980). Consequently, the charge alleges acts which fall within the terms of the regulation's prohibition and it placed appellant on notice of what he was required to defend against. We find it states an offense under Article 92, UCMJ.

The instant case is an example of the government proving the allegations without evidence of a blatant use of rank or position, or by showing stroking or cajolery, etc. However, the evidence clearly shows appellant used his official position to acquire Airman K's presence in a secluded location for unwelcomed hugs. Given the de facto supervisory, as well as the superior-subordinate relationship between them, appellant used the force of his position when he indicated his desire to speak with Airman K. Subtly directing her behind the mainframes to effect his desire to hug her out of the view of coworkers provided him a personal benefit in violation of AFR 30-30, Paragraph 8.

Do you agree with the court's conclusion? Compare the air force instruction with Section 2635.702 of the OGE Standards of Ethical Conduct (use of public office for private gain) discussed above. Would the same result be reached under both sections? Consider the following provision in the OGE Standards of Ethical Conduct:

§ 2635.705 Use of official time.
(b) Use of a subordinate's time. An employee shall not encourage, direct, coerce, or request a subordinate to use official time to perform activities other than those

required in the performance of official duties or authorized in accordance with law or regulation.

Could Staff Sergeant Robinson be convicted under this provision?

MISUSE OF GOVERNMENT PROPERTY
Related to the rules concerning misuse of position is the prohibition on using government property for other than official purposes:

§ 2635.704 Use of Government property.
(a) Standard. An employee has a duty to protect and conserve government property and shall not use such property, or allow its use, for other than authorized purposes.
(b) Definitions. For purposes of this section:
  (1) Government property includes any form of real or personal property in which the government has an ownership, leasehold, or other property interest as well as any right or other intangible interest that is purchased with government funds, including the services of contractor personnel. The term includes office supplies, telephone and other telecommunications equipment and services, the government mails, automated data processing capabilities, printing and reproduction facilities, government records, and government vehicles.
  (2) Authorized purposes are those purposes for which government property is made available to members of the public or those purposes authorized in accordance with law or regulation.

Should this section be read as broadly as the court in *Robinson* interpreted the air force regulation? Would it make any difference if the use of government property was for charitable or philanthropic purposes?

FINANCIAL RESPONSIBILITIES
Should the government regulate whether its employees handle their financial obligations in a responsible manner? If an employee does not, is it right for the government to prosecute the individual? Take a look at this section of the OGE Standards of Ethical Conduct:

§ 2635.809 Just financial obligations.
  Employees shall satisfy in good faith their obligations

as citizens, including all just financial obligations, especially those such as federal, state or local taxes that are imposed by law. For purposes of this section, a just financial obligation is a debt acknowledged by the employee or reduced to judgment by a court. In good faith means an honest intention to fulfill any just financial obligation in a timely manner. In the event of a dispute between an employee and an alleged creditor, this section does not require an agency to determine the validity or amount of the disputed debt or to collect a debt on the alleged creditor's behalf.

Will a provision such as Section 2635.809 cause employees to handle their money matters in a more responsible manner? See the section on Administrative Separation Procedures in chapter 4 regarding separation of navy members who exhibit a "set pattern of failure to pay just debts" (Naval Military Personnel Manual 3630600b [2][a]). Also look at Article 134, UCMJ (debt, dishonorable failure to pay).

GAMBLING
The military also places restrictions on gambling by its employees:
2-302. Gambling
a. A DoD employee shall not participate while on Federally-owned or leased property or while on duty [for military members, this means, in this context, present for duty] for the Federal government in any gambling activity except:
  (1) Activities necessitated by a DoD employee's law enforcement duties;
  (2) Activities by organizations composed of DoD employees or their dependents when transacted entirely among their own members and approved by the Head of the DoD Component or designee; or
  (3) Private wagers among DoD employees if based on a personal relationship and transacted entirely within assigned Federal government living quarters and within the limitations of local laws.

Based on the above, what fundraising activities are permitted on military installations? Note that military organizations are not permitted to have fund raising events such as casino nights, while Indian reservations (also on federal property) are allowed to run gambling casinos. What are the policy considerations in the two situations?

Conclusion

In concluding this discussion of ethics in government, consider the following remarks regarding the relationship between ethics, leadership, and military readiness, excerpted from a speech entitled "The Privilege of Leadership, the Courage of Character," given by Secretary of the Navy John Dalton at the U.S. Naval Academy on 29 April 1994:

> What is the tie between leadership and ethics? Between ethics and readiness? Quite simply, the main element of effective leadership is trust. To trust someone to be a leader to accept the changes and often the hardships they bring, requires the leader to be worthy of trust. We must trust the individual who we consider consistently able to act in an ethical, honest manner. And even if we can't always define every aspect of ethics and honesty, we know it when we see it.
>
> Without ethical leadership in our armed forces, there can be no trust by subordinates in the orders of their superiors. There can be none of the special esprit or bonding that we consider essential to the teamwork required for a sound defense. And there would be little confidence by the American people in the rightness of our actions. Without trust and confidence, there cannot be an effective military for America . . . that is the ultimate measure of readiness. . . .
>
> A leader stands for something . . . and that something is character. People choose to follow because they believe that that individual, that leader, has the personal principles to make the right choice, the ethical choice, when it comes to making a tough decision. They choose to follow because they believe that when faced with an ethical dilemma, their leader will make the decision that is in their best interests . . . not the leader's personal best interest . . . but in his or her follower's best interests. You do not have to believe in exactly the same things that the leader does . . . you don't have to have exactly the same perspective . . . no two people

have exactly the same thoughts. No, what makes people follow a leader, even if they disagree about this idea or that, is the belief that the leader will do his or her best for the collective good.

Are Secretary Dalton's views on the relationship between ethics, leadership, and readiness—that is, that ethics and honor require a military leader to place the interests of others before his or her own personal interests and in so doing inspire trust and confidence in those to be led—different from the purposes underlying ethics laws and regulations as discussed in this chapter?

Study Questions

1. Ensign Karen Anjinsan is good friends with her department head, Lieutenant Anita Toronaga. Lieutenant Toronaga is getting married and Ensign Anjinsan has chosen a twenty-five-dollar wedding gift for her. Ensign Anjinsan has also been asked by her coworkers to contribute toward a group gift for the lieutenant. The ensign may:

    a. Choose a gift worth ten dollars or less for Lieutenant Toronaga but not contribute toward the group gift.

    b. Not worry about the ethics rules because the lieutenant is a personal friend.

    c. Not give Lieutenant Toronaga a personal gift but contribute toward the group gift.

    d. Give the twenty-five-dollar wedding gift. She may also contribute toward the group gift.

2. The colonel, and battalion commanding officer, is retiring. His executive officer has invited all battalion officers (there are ten) and their spouses to a twenty-five-dollar per person dinner given in the colonels' honor and is collecting money to buy the shotgun that the colonel has always wanted. The executive officer may:

    a. Tell the officers they have to contribute thirty dollars for the shotgun and buy a twenty-five-dollar dinner ticket.

    b. Suggest a thirty-dollar contribution but make it clear that the officers may contribute whatever they want. Also, collect twenty-five dollars from anyone attending the dinner.

c. Not give the shotgun, but may suggest the officers take the colonel to a local deli for lunch.

d. Require the officers (including those not attending the dinner) to pay at least fifty-five dollars, since this is a "once-in-a-lifetime" event for the colonel.

3. A supply officer at a naval station is asked by a friend to determine why his firm's bid on a construction project at the naval station had not been accepted. At a department-level staff meeting, the supply officer employee raised as a matter for official inquiry the rejection of the bid and asked that the particular license be expedited. Is this a violation of government ethics law?

4. A department head on a destroyer is asked to provide a letter of recommendation for a former division officer in his department. The department head wants to use official stationery and sign the letter using his official title. Is this a problem? What if the recommendation is for a personal friend with whom he has not dealt with in the navy?

5. Can a commanding officer appear in a television commercial in which she endorses an appliance used in the galley of her ship, stating that it has been found by the navy to be safe for residential use?

6. May the judge advocate general of the navy use his official title or refer to his government position in a book jacket endorsement of a novel about organized crime written by an author whose work he admires? May he do so in a book review published in a newspaper?

7. May a sailor make a personal long-distance call charged to her personal calling card?

8. Chief Douglas is the sponsor for her daughter's high school debate team. The team does several special projects during the school year to finance the program's "extras." Many times Chief Douglas needs copies of letters and letter-sized posters for various reasons. She uses the office copier for these small items. She may:

a. Make twenty copies at a time and not exceed the fifty-copy deminimis limit per month.

b. Not use the copier for anything other than government-authorized copying required by her job.

c. Use the office copier to make copies on her own time (during lunch, or before or after work).

d. Copy only official debate team letters, but not posters and other publicity materials.

9. Commander Powell is involved in scouting with his children. A coleader suggested that Commander Powell borrow a projector from work for use at a scout meeting. He borrowed it on Friday and returned it first thing Monday morning. The commander also replaced a defective switch at his own expense while he had the projector. On Monday morning he told his executive officer what he had done. What should his executive officer do now?

a. She should be happy that he replaced the switch. It takes forever to get machinery repaired through normal procurement channels.

b. Insist that next time he should tell her before he borrows the projector.

c. She should tell him to be sure to return things he borrows in the original condition so as not to disrupt the government supply and repair systems.

d. She should make sure he knows that he should not use government equipment for personal use and require that he not do it again.

10. The computer of a disbursing officer at a marine base gives her access to a commercial service providing information for investors. May she use it for personal investment research?

11. May a navy command hold a raffle in which the proceeds are to pay for renovating the enlisted club?

12. May an executive officer of a marine battalion order his administrative clerk to type his personal correspondence during duty hours? What if the executive officer asks and the yeoman agrees to do the work? What if the arrangement is entirely voluntary and appropriate compensation is paid, and the yeoman types the correspondence at home on her own time? What if the compensation is inadequate?

CHAPTER SEVEN

SEARCH AND SEIZURE

When we assumed the soldier, we did not lay aside the citizen.

—George Washington, 26 June 1775

Introduction

The Fourth Amendment, contained in the Bill of Rights, guarantees:

> The right of the people to be secure in their persons, houses, papers, and effects, against unreasonable searches and seizures, shall not be violated, and no Warrants shall issue, but upon probable cause, supported by Oath or affirmation, and particularly describing the place to be searched, and the persons or things to be seized.

The Court of Military Appeals in *United States v. Jacoby,* 29 C.M.R. 244, 247 (C.M.A. 1960) stated:

> It is apparent that the protections in the Bill of Rights, except those which are expressly or by necessary implication inapplicable, are available to members of our armed forces.

As the quotation implies, the military environment modifies to some degree the protections of the Fourth Amendment. This is the case in large measure because the expectation of privacy in the military is different than in the civilian sector. This chapter focuses on the extent of the military's impact on the protections of the Fourth Amendment.

Fourth Amendment Requirements

Searches within the Fourth Amendment

The Fourth Amendment's protection against unreasonable search and seizure applies to examinations that meet certain requirements. The case below addresses how the Fourth Amendment applies to military members.

UNITED STATES V. ROBERT F. BAKER, STAFF SERGEANT,
U.S. ARMY
UNITED STATES COURT OF MILITARY APPEALS
30 M.J. 262
AUGUST 1, 1990
Opinion: Everett, Judge

Appellant was convicted of a charge that on April 22, 1988, he had stolen two stereo components worth $510 from the Army and Air Force Exchange Service in violation of Article 121, UCMJ.

The defense moved to suppress a box containing the two stereo components which were the subject of the larceny charge and claimed that this evidence was the product of an illegal search. Only one witness testified on this motion, Mrs. Mary Holmes, who was called by the prosecution. On April 22, 1988, she had been working "as an exchange detective" for the Army and Air Force Exchange System (AAFES) at Fort Lewis, Washington. When she first saw Sergeant Baker,

> He had a shopping cart which contained one huge packing box, brown packing box, and he was strolling from the stereo area by stationery and heading up towards the cashier's cage and the brown box was on top of the shopping cart, and then he had a stereo item on the very bottom of the shopping cart and was just pushing it down the aisle.

Mrs. Holmes followed him around and noticed Baker had gone over into the boys' area and pushed his shopping cart in between two racks of children's–little boys'—jeans.

> He proceeded to take the brown box off the top of the shopping cart and open it up and then take the stereo item

from underneath the shopping cart and tried to stick it inside this brown box, but the stereo item wouldn't fit. So, he put the stereo item back onto the bottom of the shopping cart and then he closed the big box back up and ran his hand over the tape that was on top of it and picked it up . . . and put it on top of the shopping cart again.

Subsequently, Baker repeated his effort to put the stereo item into the box; but again he was unsuccessful. "Then he took the stereo item and laid it kind of on the carpet and then he taped back up the brown box and placed it back on top of the shopping cart and instead of putting the stereo item back underneath the shopping cart, he placed it underneath" some clothing. Thereafter, he again placed the stereo item back in the cart; but, finally he "put it back on the shelf where all the like items were, and then he turned around and left out of the area and at [that] time I went, and kind of waited for him to come out on the mall."

After appellant had gone "through the central check out area and came out through the two main doors" into a mall area, Mrs. Holmes approached Baker and identified herself as an exchange detective. After telling him that she wished to "do a parcel . . . check of different items to make sure" the "cashiers with our new system in have properly rung up the merchandise," Mrs. Holmes told Baker, "I would like to check his package. And he handed me a small brown bag and I said, 'No,' I said, 'I'd like to check this big brown one here if I can.'" Baker claimed that it only contained his "wife's clothing," whereupon Mrs. Holmes asked him to go with her and two other exchange employees back into the store.

Mrs. Holmes testified that, according to the guidelines provided her, "we are just a detaining unit. We have no authority to apprehend—as a matter of fact, even when we go out on the mall and ask, and after we identify ourselves and ask for their ID card, they do not need to give it to us. They do not need to come with us. They can turn around and walk out the door and just act like we aren't even there. We have no authority whatsoever." Mrs. Holmes maintained that, as an exchange detective, she had no more "authority than any other store employee" and no more "than any other private citizen that would be in the area."

Military authorities controlled the Army and Air Force Exchange Service and the local post exchange at Fort Lewis. Accordingly, Mrs. Holmes position as a store detective at a base exchange was not private, but governmental in nature and military in purpose.

According to her own testimony, Mrs. Holmes was authorized only "to detain" and not "to apprehend" and had no "more authority than any other private citizen that would be in the area." But the protection of the Fourth Amendment is not limited to searches and seizures by investigators or law-enforcement personnel. It also extends to searches and seizures performed by many other governmental officials. We conclude that the search by Mrs. Holmes was not made by a private person. This, however, is only the beginning of the inquiry.

No Fourth Amendment protection is granted unless the person claiming it had a reasonable expectation of privacy.

By entering a post exchange to shop, a person does not automatically forfeit Fourth Amendment protection and become subject to inspection of his purse or wallet. This is particularly true when no sign or notice is posted to inform the customer that his belongings may be searched at the will of store detectives and when, unlike the situation with some public buildings, no published regulations give notice that the parcels of patrons may be inspected.

Although we conclude that the customer entering a post exchange or other government operated store has a privacy interest which entitles him to Fourth Amendment protection, we also recognize that the Fourth Amendment only safeguards against "unreasonable searches and seizures." Moreover, not every search or seizure is unreasonable because it is performed without a warrant or with less than probable cause.

We conclude that the search and seizure of Baker's brown box, as well as his physical detention, were "reasonable" for purposes of the Fourth Amendment. In our view, a person who brings a big box into a post exchange and opens it in a furtive or surreptitious manner has a reduced expectation of privacy in comparison with a customer who walks through the exchange with a sealed box or closed purse.

The opinion in *Baker* discussed who the Fourth Amendment restricts in conducting searches and in what situations a person has an expectation of privacy. Military Rule of Evidence 311 addresses these issues as well:

> Evidence obtained as a result of an unlawful search and seizure made by a person acting in a governmental capacity is inadmissible if the accused had a reasonable expectation of privacy in the person, place or property searched; the accused had a legitimate interest in the property or evidence seized when challenging a seizure; or the accused would otherwise have grounds to object to the search or seizure under the Constitution of the United States as applied to members of the armed forces.

Is Military Rule of Evidence 311 consistent with *Baker?* The next case considers where an expectation of privacy exists in the military.

UNITED STATES V. WILLIAM E. PORTT, JR., AIRMAN
FIRST CLASS, U.S. AIR FORCE
UNITED STATES COURT OF MILITARY APPEALS
21 M.J. 333
FEBRUARY 17, 1986
Opinion: Cox, Judge

Airman Scott Garner and Airman Ronald Coolidge were assigned to clean the security police guard-mount room on the morning of May 8, 1983. This room was used for briefings and contained desks, chairs, and small wall lockers. The lockers were assigned by request to individual security policemen who wanted one for their own use. Each user was required to provide a padlock for his locker at his own expense.

Airman Garner noticed that one of the lockers, A-44, was unlocked, with the padlock just hanging on it. He testified that he opened the locker because he was "curious" and observed only a mitten lying on top of a white piece of paper and what appeared to be a yellow shot record. He surmised that it was a "junk" locker and not assigned to anyone.

Airman Garner then removed the mitten and threw it at Airman Coolidge, who found a crushed soda can inside it. After examining the can, they suspected that it had been used as a device to smoke marijuana. Becoming nervous at the prospect of being found in the possession of contraband, they put the can back inside the mitten, returned the mitten to the locker, closed the door, and reported their findings to the flight chief. Law-enforcement authorities were notified and responded with a drug dog and handler, and a security police investigator.

Although the dog did not alert on locker A-44, the locker was opened by law-enforcement officials and searched, apparently to determine whose locker it was. Records of the locker assignments were kept on cards by the six flight chiefs, but the card reflecting the assignment of locker A-44 was unavailable at the time. Appellant's name appeared on the shot record discovered in the locker, which led the security police to appellant. Upon questioning, appellant admitted that locker A-44 was assigned to him, although he had not used it in six months, and confessed that he frequently used and distributed marijuana. Furthermore, he consented to a search of his barracks room, urine, and automobile.

Prior to pleas, appellant sought to suppress the resulting physical evidence and confessions as tainted by the illegal entry into his locker.

The question is whether the Fourth Amendment required the law-enforcement officials to obtain a search authorization before they opened the locker a second time and examined the contents. Appellant can successfully invoke the Fourth Amendment's prohibition against unreasonable searches only if he had a reasonable "expectation of privacy" in the locker which has been violated by the search that occurred. The determination of whether a reasonable expectation of privacy existed is a legal conclusion. In considering reasonableness, we must determine whether a person invoking the protection of the Fourth Amendment took normal precautions to maintain his privacy—that is, precautions customarily taken by those seeking privacy.

The Supreme Court has applied the two-point test articulated by Justice Harlan in *Katz v. United States,* 389 U.S. 347, 360 (1967), to determine whether an accused had a legitimate expectation of privacy:

> First that a person has exhibited an actual (subjective) expectation of privacy and, second, that the expectation be one that society is prepared to recognize as "reasonable."

We doubt that appellant maintained a subjective expectation of privacy in locker A-44. His failure to secure the lock, keep any valuables in it, or even go near the locker in six months indicates as much. Even if appellant satisfied the first part of Justice Harlan's test, however, the facts do not satisfy the second and most important part.

Generally, a warrantless search of a government locker assigned for the personal use of a military member, particularly if the locker were located in living quarters, would be unreasonable, as such lockers are in a class of effects in which there exists a legitimate expectation of privacy. The locker here, however, was located in a common area. Moreover, the initial private invasion of the locker revealed that it was an apparently abandoned "junk" locker, with the only contents being a crushed soda can inside a mitten and two scraps of paper. The law-enforcement officials were free to avail themselves of this information.

In addition to the information obtained through the private action, the law-enforcement officials knew that no name was on the locker and that it was left unlocked in a common area where all the other lockers were routinely locked. Thus, appellant had failed to take the most elementary precaution, one that was taken by the other locker users to maintain their privacy. Based on the facts as they existed at the time of the governmental intrusion into the locker, we conclude that appellant retained no reasonable expectation of privacy in the locker.

Compare *Portt* with the following case.

UNITED STATES V. JOHN V. BATTLES, STOREKEEPER SEAMAN APPRENTICE, U.S. NAVY
UNITED STATES COURT OF MILITARY APPEALS
25 M.J. 58
SEPTEMBER 24, 1987
Opinion: Sullivan, Judge

On Sunday, 9 September 1984, both Storekeeper Seaman Apprentice [SKSA] Battles and Seaman [SN] Troy W. Lipmyer were berthed in S-8 berthing on board USS *Enterprise.* At approximately 0200 that morning the commanding officer had ordered to be searched a postal package addressed to SN Lipmyer; when this package was opened, 92 hits of LSD were discovered. Subsequently, at approximately 0300–0400 the executive officer ordered a "health and comfort inspection" of S-8 berthing. SKSA Battles and other personnel sleeping in the berthing area were awakened, taken out of the berthing area into a void, searched and then ordered into their working spaces while the "inspection" was being conducted. During this "inspection" a box bearing SKSA Battles' name was found by a maintenance locker; when this box was opened, phenobarbital and USS *Enterprise* cigarette lighters were discovered inside.

The *Enterprise* executive officer, Captain Dantone, ordered the "health and comfort inspection"; he testified at SN Lipmyer's court-martial that:

> Prior to 9 September 1984 we had several masts that included people from S-8. I had several indicators from informants on the ship that there was a larger amount of drug activity in S-8 than we had throughout the rest of the ship; the names Battles and Babb were familiar to me well prior to the discovery of the phenobarbital; Battles had been to mast for drug use and I believe Babb had also and I interviewed them personally. So those two prior to this whole time were known to me to ha[ve] at least had involvement in drugs.

Appellant asserts that the "health and comfort inspection" noted above was no more than a subterfuge search designed to locate evidence for later use in disciplinary proceedings. In support of his contention, he notes the early hour of the inspection, its occurrence two hours after discovery of other drugs, the pre-existing suspicions with respect to appellant and his berthing mates, and the executive officer's intent to initiate disciplinary action against anyone violating drug laws. Appellant argues that these facts preclude a finding that a legitimate inspection occurred. His argument further implies that this search required probable cause, which was lacking and was so unreasonable as to otherwise violate the Fourth Amendment.

The first question we must ask is whether appellant had a reasonable expectation of privacy in berthing area S-8 on the USS *Enterprise* while this naval vessel was under way in the Pacific Ocean. Appellant shared this berthing area with approximately sixty other crew members. The berthing area was subject to a great deal of traffic during shift changes, as well as unit inspections and other operational demands. The box in which drugs were found was not located in the limited storage area assigned to appellant on board this ship but near a maintenance locker in a common space in the berthing area. In this context, we hold that appellant cannot reasonably claim that his expectation of privacy in berthing area S-8 was so great as to bar other naval personnel from accessing its common spaces. A berthing area on a naval ship is more like a workplace than a home or barrack's environment. We hold that operational realities and common sense dictate that, at the very least, appellant had no reasonable expectation of privacy in the common spaces of such a berthing area.

Appellant also had no reasonable expectation of privacy in the box which contained the illegal drugs. The box, with his name on it, was found in a common area near a maintenance locker, and it was unsealed and open. Its location and unprotected condition lead us to conclude that appellant failed to take reasonable precautions to insure his privacy rights in the contents of the box. As a result, we conclude that appellant relinquished any possible expectation of privacy in this box prior to its examination by the inspection team.

Probable Cause Searches

SEARCH AUTHORIZATIONS

If a sailor or marine has a reasonable expectation of privacy in a particular place, the Fourth Amendment protects that private area from an unreasonable search. The consequence of a privacy expectation is that a search authorization based upon probable cause is generally required. Miliary Rule of Evidence 315(d) describes who has the authority to issue search authorizations:

> Power to authorize. Authorization to search pursuant to this rule may be granted by an impartial individual in the following categories:
> (1) Commander. A commander or other person serving either in a position analogous to an officer in charge or a position of command, who has control over the place where the property or person to be searched is situated

or found, or if that place is not under military control, having control over persons subject to military law or the law of war; or

(2) Military judge. A military judge or magistrate if authorized under regulations prescribed by the Secretary of Defense or the Secretary concerned.

The above language indicates that the commander issuing a search authorization must be neutral and detached. When, if ever, is a commander impartial for purposes of the Fourth Amendment? The next case considers that issue.

UNITED STATES V. ELIJAH D. EZELL
UNITED STATES COURT OF MILITARY APPEALS
6 M.J. 307
APRIL 9, 1979
Opinion: Perry, Judge

We granted review in these cases to consider identical claims, made by the appellants, that evidence leading to their convictions was seized during searches authorized by commanding officers who, by reason of their involvement in ferreting out evidence of crime, were not neutral and detached magistrates and that hence the evidence was obtained in violation of the Fourth Amendment to the Constitution of the United States. It is claimed that military commanders are inherently devoid of neutrality and detachedness because of a conflict between their attendant duties as commanding officers and the requirement of the Fourth Amendment that search warrants be issued only by neutral and detached magistrates. We are, therefore, urged to rule that for these and other reasons commanding officers are per se disqualified to authorize searches and seizures of evidence of crime.

The fundamental inquiry in considering Fourth Amendment issues is whether or not a search or seizure is reasonable under all the circumstances. Inherent in the warrant requirement is the prerequisite that it be issued by a neutral and detached magistrate. The point of the Fourth Amendment, which often is not grasped by zealous officers, is not that it denies law enforcement the support of the usual inferences which reasonable men draw from evidence. Its protection consists in requiring that those inferences be drawn by a neutral and

detached magistrate instead of being judged by the officer engaged in the often competitive enterprise of ferreting out crime.

In these cases, the appellants contend that, for a variety of reasons, military commanders are inherently devoid of neutrality and detachedness. We are, therefore, urged to announce a per se rule of disqualification of the commander as an appropriate official to exercise the warrant authority of the Fourth Amendment. We proceed here to discuss that contention together with the various arguments of the parties.

The appellants contend that commanding officers are so involved in the business of investigating criminal conduct that they are devoid of neutrality and detachedness. The very objective of command, it is argued, is the maintenance of law, order, and discipline. Therefore, to effectuate that command objective, it is said that the commander necessarily becomes a law-enforcement official. The appellants remind us that commanding officers have the authority to arrest. We are also reminded that this Court has had occasion to pass upon conduct of the commander which underscores the law enforcement function of command. Indeed, it is clear that military commanders have statutory and manual authority to perform many functions that are properly classified as law enforcement in nature. Yet, under Paragraph 152 of the Manual for Courts-Martial, commanders are charged with the duty to authorize searches.

The military commander must himself or through subordinates perform a variety of duties. These included the concomitant authority to enforce the law, authorize prosecutions for offenses allegedly committed, maintain discipline, investigate crime, authorize searches and seizures, as well as train and fashion those under his command into a cohesive fighting unit. These duties provide the basis for a persuasive argument against the notion that he may at the same time be neutral and detached as contemplated by the Fourth Amendment. Indeed, no official in the civilian community having similarly combined functions could qualify as a neutral and detached magistrate under Fourth Amendment jurisprudence. We decline, however, to hold that military commanders are per se disqualified to act as neutral and detached magistrates.

Our declination results not only for the reasons previously stated but in deference to the president's designation of the commander as the authorized person to issue the search authorization.

We have recognized that the military commander is capable of neutrality when he is not actively involved in the investigative or prosecutorial functions which are otherwise clearly within the perimeters of command authority. We have also held that, when the military commander becomes personally involved as an active participant in the gathering of evidence or otherwise demonstrates personal bias or involvement in the investigative or prosecutorial process against the accused, that commander is devoid of neutrality and cannot validly perform the functions envisioned by Paragraph 152 of the Manual for Courts-Martial. These approaches, properly applied, will, we believe, continue to provide for the men and women of the armed services the protection of the Fourth Amendment.

Whether an authorization to search is made by a commanding officer, or by his delegate, the act of authorizing a search on the basis of probable cause is a judicial function. Consequently, the military officer's decision to authorize a search on probable cause must be made with a magistrate's neutrality and detachment. Or, to put it in the words of the MCM in describing the necessary quality of an officer delegated the power to authorize searches, the magistrate function in the military must be exercised by an impartial person. The search authority must be exercised with a judicial rather than a police attitude to the examination of the operative facts.

In light of what has been stated, we hold that obtaining information to be used as the basis for requesting authorization to search is a law-enforcement function and involvement in that information-gathering process would disqualify the commander from authorizing the search. Specifically included in this process are such actions as approving or directing the use of information, the use of drug detection dogs except in gate searches, the use of controlled buys, surveillance operations, and similar activities. It is noted that there is no constitutional requirement for judicial approval of any of these activities before they may be conducted.

Once the law enforcement agency decides that there is a sufficient basis for requesting search authorization, then the information available to them may be presented to the commander for his judicial determination. At this point the commander may require the agency to provide such additional information as he deems necessary. This would be an exercise of his judicial function since he is passing upon the sufficiency of a completed application. It must be emphasized that agencies must not use the request to search as a subterfuge by presenting a clearly deficient request so that the commander may help fill in the gaps. Finally, we consider that anyone present during the search is engaged in law-enforcement activities, so we expect that the commander will not be present at the scene of the search. Presence would indicate to us that the commander has been engaged in law-enforcement activities throughout his participation in the entire authorization process, except in very extraordinary situations, which we will deal with on a case-by-case basis.

Consider Military Rule of Evidence 315(d):

An otherwise impartial authorizing official does not lose that character merely because he or she is present at the scene of a search or is otherwise readily available to persons who may seek the issuance of a search authorization; nor does such an official lose impartial character merely because the official previously and impartially authorized investigative activities.

Is this language consistent with the decision in *Ezell?* Based on *Ezell*, when is a commander no longer neutral and detached?

The following case addresses the scope of a commander's authority to issue a search authorization.

UNITED STATES V. RAENELL A. CHAPPLE, DISBURSING CLERK
SEAMAN APPRENTICE, U.S. NAVY
UNITED STATES COURT OF MILITARY APPEALS
36 M.J. 410
APRIL 19, 1993
Opinion: Gierke, Judge

On January 5, 1988, several crew members of the USS *Belknap,* including Lieutenant Commander (LCDR) McConahy and Disbursing Clerk (DK3) Dacey, reported that their checks had been stolen and that checks drawn on their accounts had been forged and cashed at the USS *Belknap* disbursing office. The Naval Investigative Service (NIS) initiated an investigation and listed appellant as a suspect since he was assigned to the disbursing office during the time the stolen checks were negotiated. The NIS attempted to interview appellant, but he invoked his right to counsel.

On September 19, 1988, the NIS received the report of a handwriting examiner who opined that there were "strong indications" that appellant had forged one of the stolen checks belonging to DK3 Dacey. On September 22, 1988, appellant, wearing navy dungarees with "R. A. Chapple" stenciled on the shirt, presented LCDR McConahy's checkbook to a teller at the Navy Federal Credit Union in Naples, Italy. Appellant told the teller that LCDR McConahy was his boss and that LCDR McConahy had sent him to obtain additional checks. The teller took one of the deposit slips from the checkbook to verify LCDR McConahy's account, but when she returned appellant had departed the credit union. The teller reported what had happened to the credit union manager, who advised the teller that LCDR McConahy had reported his checks missing and had been transferred from the area approximately 6 months earlier. Appellant's actions at the credit union were reported to the NIS.

The NIS also learned that appellant lived off base with his fiance, Radioman Seaman (RMSN) Victoria Johns, in an apartment leased by RMSN Johns from an Italian landlord. Her lease was negotiated and prepared through the housing referral office operated by Naval Support Activity, Naples (NAVSUPPACT).

The NIS requested authorization from Captain Paron, USN, commanding officer, NAVSUPPACT, to search RMSN Johns' apartment for the stolen checks. After being provided with an affidavit relating the foregoing information and consulting with his staff judge advocate, Captain Paron authorized the search. Neither appellant nor RMSN Johns was assigned to NAVSUPPACT. Appellant was assigned to Commander Task Force 63 (CTF 63), and RMSN Johns was assigned to Naval Communications Area Master Station Mediterranean (NAVCAMSMED). However, Captain Paron

was designated by Commander-in-Chief, United States Naval Forces Europe Instruction (CINCUSNAVEURINST) 5450.21d as senior officer present (Administration) for Naples and the local coordinator for the Naples area, with responsibility for supporting both CTF 63 and NAVCAMSMED.

The NIS agents initially did not rely on the search authorization because RMSN Johns executed a written consent to the search of her apartment. However, she was not able to admit the NIS agents into the apartment because she had left her keys in the apartment. The NIS agents brought appellant to the apartment, ordered him to unlock the entrance, searched the apartment, and found the stolen checks.

At trial, appellant contested Captain Paron's authority to authorize a search of the apartment, arguing that Captain Paron was neither RMSN Johns' commander nor appellant's, and that he did not have authority over the property, which was a privately owned apartment leased and occupied by RMSN Johns.

Captain Paron's authority to authorize the search of RMSN Johns' apartment must be based on either his control over RMSN Johns' apartment or his command relationship with RMSN Johns or appellant. The sole authority relied upon by the government, both at trial and before this Court, is Captain Paron's responsibility under CINCUSNAVEURINST 5450.21d to operate a housing referral office. While that directive required Captain Paron to provide assistance to military personnel in finding and contracting for housing, it does not confer any authority over the property leased through the housing referral office.

Turning next to Captain Paron's command relationship with RMSN Johns and appellant, it is undisputed that Captain Paron was not in the chain of command for RMSN Johns' unit or appellant's. We hold that Captain Paron's law enforcement support responsibilities under CINCUSNAVEURINST 5450.21d do not make his position analogous to an officer in charge or a position of command. The directive tasks him to provide police and fire protection for supported units but does not vest him with command authority over those units. His responsibility is to support members of tenant and supported units, not to command them.

When a search is authorized by a commander, the authorization must specifically describe the place to be searched and the things to be seized. How particular must the search authorization be? This question is considered in the following case.

UNITED STATES V. ROBERT E. ABERNATHY, III, CORPORAL,
U.S. MARINE CORPS
UNITED STATES NAVY COURT OF MILITARY REVIEW
6 M.J. 819
DECEMBER 28, 1978
Opinion: Gladis, Judge

Appellant was convicted of one specification of selling military property without authority (two red toolboxes) and one specification of larceny of United States government property (one gray toolbox), in violation of Articles 108 and 121, UCMJ. The evidence presented by the prosecution at trial indicates that appellant sold the two red toolboxes to a Corporal (now Sergeant) Logan and had previously stated to Sergeant Logan that the two red toolboxes would be obtained from the warehouse [at] Camp Lejeune where appellant worked. Sergeant Logan, a military policeman, had provided information to the Naval Investigative Service concerning the forthcoming sale and had made the purchase with funds provided by the Naval Investigative Service. Sergeant Logan also provided information that other government property was located at appellant's quarters [at] Camp Lejeune. On the basis of this information, authorization to search appellant's quarters for "items of stolen government property and other items identified as contraband" was granted by the chief of staff for Marine Corps Base, Camp Lejeune. The gray toolbox was among the items seized from appellant's quarters.

The appellant contends that the search of his residence was illegal because the information upon which the command authorization was based was overbroad. The request for authorization to search appellant's residence and seize items of stolen U.S. government property and other material which might be identified as contraband recited that appellant had admitted to the informant stealing and selling various items of government property, that on the previous evening at his residence appellant had sold two toolboxes he had stolen

from his place of duty to the informant, and that the informant had observed an additional quantity of toolboxes of the same description at the residence. The authorization to search appellant's residence authorized seizure of items of stolen government property and other items identified as contraband.

In determining whether an authorization to search is overbroad resort may be had to the request. There is no room for a grudging or negative attitude by reviewing courts towards command authorizations. Requests must be tested and interpreted in a commonsense and realistic fashion. Technical requirements of elaborate specificity once exacted under common law pleadings have no proper place in this area. Examining the authorization in the light of the request, we construe the authorization to authorize only a search for the toolboxes observed by the informant and seizure of any contraband observed during the search for the toolboxes. The authorization was not overbroad and the seizure of the gray toolbox was legal.

Abernathy emphasizes that the request for the search will determine in large measure the specificity required in the search authorization. Where can a law enforcement official look in searching for the items described in the search authorization? The next decision ponders the legal scope of a search.

UNITED STATES V. SADAT-ABDUL JASPER,
PRIVATE FIRST CLASS, U.S. ARMY
UNITED STATES COURT OF MILITARY APPEALS
20 M.J. 112
MAY 28, 1985
Opinion: Cox, Judge

While appellant was working as a mail clerk in February 1980 at Kelly Barracks, Federal Republic of Germany, a package containing $95,000 in American Express funds was stolen from the mails. Appellant was questioned concerning the theft and consented to a search of his off-post apartment. No evidence incriminating appellant was found at that time.

In early June, appellant was informed that charges were pending against him for adultery; he had been living with Private First Class Gwendolyn Battle, a female soldier who was not his wife. Although he apparently was still a suspect in the theft from the mails, he was not then charged with larceny. On June 11, 1980, appellant went on ordinary leave, flying by commercial airline to the United States to "work on a divorce." He failed to return to his unit upon termination of his leave on June 24, 1980.

On July 25, 1980, appellant's unit commander sent Staff Sergeant Bennie Kos, the unit supply sergeant, with an inventory team to appellant's off-post apartment to inventory his effects, to box them up, and to transport them to the unit for storage and safekeeping. They obtained a key to the apartment from another soldier with whom appellant had left a key when he went on leave.

While at the apartment, Sergeant Kos found an opened envelope addressed to Major John V. Lewin from Captain and Mrs. David V. Olson. On the face of the envelope was an insured sticker and a customs tag with a notation that the envelope contained a chain. Sergeant Kos looked inside the envelope and read the enclosed letter, which indicated that a gold necklace had been forwarded in the envelope. No necklace was then in the envelope. Sergeant Kos took the letter and envelope to the unit and turned them over to the authorities. On the motion to suppress the letter and envelope, Sergeant Kos testified, in part, as follows:

> When we first went in, we went in there and weren't quite positive whether the stuff belonged to him or the landlord. What we done was we started with all the clothing and this type of stuff first, and went through and inventoried the majority of all the small stuff and later on went back and picked up the large items after we confirmed it with the landlady of what stuff was hers. I found the letter in the bedroom. It was laying on the floor, right next to the closet. I was pulling something out of the closet and there were other papers laying on the bottom of the closet, and as I slid it out these papers came out, and when I reached down and finished picking up the rest of the papers and stuff I noticed it laying there. I picked it up and inspected it and found out that the item was registered and it was not addressed to Jasper or Battle.

Staff Sergeant Kos then read the letter:

> Because I was curious to find out what reasoning he would have of having the mail there, and that's when I found

that it contained the necklace—or was to contain the necklace. I was not instructed to search for anything. We were sent there to inventory his personal effects by regulation.

The regulations on which trial counsel relied in this case required the unit commander to inventory the personal effects, clothing, and government property of a service member dropped from the rolls of the unit.

Because Sergeant Kos was properly in appellant's apartment to conduct an inventory, we must consider whether he exceeded the scope of that inventory by looking inside the envelope and reading the enclosed letter. In this case, the purposes of the inventory procedure were to identify, inventory, and transport appellant's belongings to the unit for storage. Although Sergeant Kos testified that he read the letter because he was "curious" after noticing that the envelope was registered and was not addressed to either appellant or the other person known to have occupied the apartment, his characterization of his subjective motive is not controlling. Rather, an objective assessment of the facts and circumstances known to him at the time is necessary to determine the reasonableness of his actions.

Sergeant Kos was there to inventory only property that actually belonged to appellant. The inventory team removed all property from the apartment that was determined to belong to appellant and left behind items determined to belong to the landlady. Because the envelope on its face did not belong to appellant and appeared to have contained something of value, opening the envelope and reading the letter was a reasonable way to establish ownership.

We conclude that the envelope and letter were discovered during a valid inventory that was conducted in a reasonable manner and the evidence was admissible.

In some cases, the time necessary to obtain a search authorization may result in the loss or destruction of the evidence. Military Rule of Evidence 315(g) addresses such exigent circumstances:

> Exigencies. A search warrant or search authorization is not required under this rule for a search based on probable cause when:
> (1) Insufficient time. There is a reasonable belief that the delay necessary to obtain a search warrant or search

authorization would result in the removal, destruction, or concealment of the property or evidence sought;

(2) Lack of communications. There is a reasonable military operational necessity that is reasonably believed to prohibit or prevent communication with a person empowered to grant a search warrant or authorization and there is a reasonable belief that the delay necessary to obtain a search warrant or search authorization would result in the removal, destruction, or concealment of the property or evidence sought;

(3) Search of operable vehicle. An operable vehicle is to be searched, except in the circumstances where a search warrant or authorization is required by the Constitution of the United States, this Manual, or these rules.

Note that while the exigent circumstances exception eliminates the search authorization requirement, it does not do away with the need for probable cause. Why are searches of automobiles per se exempt from the warrant requirement? Consider the following quotation from the United States Supreme Court in *Chambers v. Maroney,* 399 U.S. 42 (1970):

> The guaranty of freedom from unreasonable searches and seizures by the Fourth Amendment has been construed, practically since the beginning of the government, as recognizing a necessary difference between a search of a store, dwelling house or other structure in respect of which a proper official warrant readily may be obtained, and a search of a ship, motor boat, wagon or automobile, for contraband goods, where it is not practicable to secure a warrant because the vehicle can be quickly moved out of the locality or jurisdiction in which the warrant must be sought.

PROBABLE CAUSE

What is probable cause and when is it required? Military Rule of Evidence 315(f) addresses these issues:

Basis for search authorizations.

(1) Probable cause requirement. A search authorization issued under this rule must be based upon probable cause.

(2) Probable cause determination. Probable cause to search exists when there is a reasonable belief that the

person, property, or evidence sought is located in the place or on the person to be searched. A search authorization may be based upon hearsay evidence in whole or in part. A determination of probable cause under this rule shall be based upon any or all of the following:

(1) Written statements communicated to the authorizing officer;

(2) Oral statements communicated to the authorizing official in person, via telephone, or by other appropriate means of communication; or

(3) Such information as may be known by the authorizing official that would not preclude the officer from acting in an impartial fashion.

The factors used to determine whether probable cause exists are considered in the next case.

UNITED STATES V. KENNETH C. QUEEN, ELECTRONICS TECHNICIAN THIRD CLASS, U.S. NAVY
UNITED STATES NAVY–MARINE CORPS COURT OF MILITARY REVIEW
20 M.J. 817
JUNE 28, 1985
Opinion: Gregory, Senior Judge

The first question we consider is whether the military judge erred in denying the defense motion to suppress the fruits of a search of appellant's automobile located [at] Naval Station, Long Beach, California. Captain Barnhart, commanding officer, Naval Station, Long Beach, authorized the search on the basis of information provided by Lieutenant Commander Peck, executive officer of USS *John Young* (DD-973), the ship to which appellant was attached. Lieutenant Commander Peck had telephoned Captain Barnhart and advised him that several crew members had been recently threatened by appellant and were frightened since a crew member had previously seen a gun in appellant's car. LCDR Peck did not identify the crew members threatened or the informants; however, he did advise Captain Barnhart that one of these sailors who reported this was under oath and he (LCDR Peck) believed what he was hearing. Captain Barnhart was further advised that appellant lived aboard USS *John Young* and had not checked the gun in with the ship's armory. Captain Barnhart was not informed that these informants had been previously involved in drug transactions, had multiple nonjudicial punishments, were awaiting administrative discharge, one had been promised assistance toward a better discharge for information about drug dealing aboard the ship, and one was indebted to appellant. The search of appellant's automobile uncovered the dangerous weapon, the drugs and drug-related items, and the U.S. Navy tools.

In this case, Captain Barnhart was aware that crew members of *John Young* had reported threats involving use of a firearm and that another crew member had seen a weapon in appellant's vehicle about six weeks earlier. He also knew that appellant lived aboard *John Young* and had not checked a firearm into the ship's armory. From this, it was reasonable for Captain Barnhart to deduce that appellant did possess a firearm and that it would probably still be located in his vehicle. Captain Barnhart testified at trial that he also felt an expediency present because the vehicle was currently located [at] the Naval Station, it was late in the work day, and he could not be sure of appellant's intentions.

Captain Barnhart was not aware of the informants' poor reputations aboard *John Young*; however, he had been advised that the informants had come forward and reported these matters to their Executive Officer. The Court of Military Appeals has recognized the unique "truth-telling effect" of a service member giving information to a superior officer and the degree of accountability in military society not always found in civilian society.

We concede that the question of probable cause in this case is a close one. Examining the totality of circumstances surrounding the case, however, we find the information available to Captain Barnhart, including the accountability of the less than savory informants, sufficient to find probable cause for the ordered search.

The *Queen* case used the "totality of the circumstances" test to determine whether probable cause existed. The Supreme Court in *Illinois v. Gates* established this test as the method to assess whether probable cause exists that contraband or evidence of a crime will be found in a particular place. In what other situations is a "totality of the circumstances" test used? See *United States v. Goudy* below.

The Plain View Doctrine

As noted in the *Abernathy* case, an "agent executing a search warrant may lawfully seize contraband not described in the warrant which he observes." The Fourth Amendment, therefore, does not apply to evidence observed in "plain view." To seize items in plain view it is not necessary to have a search authorization, probable cause, or any other basis to conduct the search. The following case discusses the elements of the "plain view" doctrine.

UNITED STATES V. DONALD J. KALISKI, SECOND
LIEUTENANT, U.S. AIR FORCE
UNITED STATES COURT OF MILITARY APPEALS
37 M.J. 105
JUNE 1, 1993
Opinion: Gierke, Judge

A military judge sitting as a general court-martial convicted appellant, contrary to his pleas, of conduct unbecoming an officer by committing acts of adultery and sodomy with the wife of a staff sergeant, in violation of Article 133. The military judge sentenced appellant to a dismissal, forfeiture of $500.00 pay per month for 2 months, and a reprimand.

Appellant was a public affairs officer at Vandenberg Air Force Base, California. Mrs. S was employed by a local newspaper and regularly conducted business at the base public affairs office. She was married to a staff sergeant assigned to the base hospital and the mother of two children, ages 11 and 8.

Appellant's coworker and neighbor observed Mrs. S's car outside appellant's Bachelor Officer's Quarters (BOQ) on numerous occasions, suspected they were having an affair, and reported his suspicions to the security police on June 25, 1990. Appellant's BOQ was a duplex on Vandenberg Air Force Base, with a private entrance at the front and a sliding glass door leading to a private patio at the rear.

On Friday evening, June 29, 1990, appellant's neighbor called the security police to advise them that Mrs. S's car was once again parked outside appellant's BOQ. At about 10:15 P.M., two investigators, Staff Sergeants Hagans and Pennywitt, rode by appellant's quarters on bicycles while investigating an unrelated complaint of animal mutilation. They noticed Mrs. S's car parked in front of the BOQ, but the curtains were drawn and the interior appeared to be dark. When they rode by again at about 11:00 P.M., the scene was unchanged. They returned shortly before midnight and rode their bicycles into an open field behind appellant's BOQ. From a distance of about 60 feet they noticed a light and movement inside appellant's BOQ. Sergeant Pennywitt went to the front of the BOQ, determined that Mrs. S's car was still parked in front, and verified that they were looking into appellant's BOQ. Sergeant Pennywitt returned to the rear of the building. He and Hagans then advanced onto the patio, within three feet of the patio door, and peeked through an 8- to 10-inch gap in the curtains. They watched appellant and Mrs. S for about 35 minutes, during which they witnessed appellant and Mrs. S engaging in oral sodomy. Shortly after midnight, they saw Mrs. S looking directly at them. Thinking they had been seen peering through the curtains, they ran from the area, leaving their bicycles behind.

Sergeants Hagans and Pennywitt had been told "to handle the situation with a great deal of professionalism" because it involved an officer. They ran from the scene because they "didn't feel that [they] should go ahead and cause an embarrassing moment between an officer and an enlisted person's wife."

On the following Monday morning, the security police called Mrs. S to the police station and interviewed her. Sergeant Pennywitt testified that he told Mrs. S that they "were investigating an allegation with Lieutenant Kaliski and herself." He testified that he did not tell her that he had personally "observed the activity," but he told her that he and Sergeant Hagans "knew some things and that we wanted to interview her to confirm or deny it."

Sergeant Pennywitt testified that Mrs. S asked if they had observed her activity with appellant. Sergeant Pennywitt testified that he was "not real positive" whether he told Mrs. S what they had observed before or after her statement was written, but he "believe[d] it was after the statement was written." Mrs. S testified that on the night of June 29–30, while with appellant in his BOQ, she observed someone looking into the BOQ from the patio.

At trial appellant moved to suppress all evidence obtained from the surveillance of his BOQ and any evidence derived from the observations of the security police, including Mrs. S's testimony. The military judge found that "Sergeants Hagans and Pennywitt were not trespassing at the time they made their observations," and that the activities of appellant and Mrs. S "were in plain view."

The Fourth Amendment protects citizens from unreasonable governmental intrusion into their homes. A tenant has the same protection as an owner. Military law recognizes a privacy right in government quarters. The Fourth Amendment protects not only the interior of a home, but also the land "immediately adjacent" to the dwelling. Looking into the window of a private residence is a search. Where, as in this case, such a visual search occurs, the question is whether the search was reasonable. A plain view observation does not constitute an unreasonable search if made from a place where the observer has a right to be.

Sergeants Hagans and Pennywitt had no right to be on appellant's patio, peeking through his patio door. They were not in a public area, but on a private patio on which appellant had a reasonable expectation of privacy. When Sergeants Hagans and Pennywitt peeked through the almost-closed curtain in the middle of the night and observed his sexual activities with Mrs. S, they had no search authorization or other justification for their visual search of appellant's quarters. Accordingly, Sergeants Hagans and Pennywitt conducted an unlawful search of appellant's quarters.

Examinations Not within the Fourth Amendment

Inspections and Inventories

This analysis of Military Rule of Evidence 313 discusses inspections in the military in relation to the Fourth Amendment:

The intent of the Framers [of the Constitution], the language of the amendment itself, and the nature of military life render the application of the Fourth

Amendment to a normal inspection questionable. As the Supreme Court has often recognized: "Military personnel must be ready to perform their duty whenever the occasion arises. To ensure that they always are capable of performing their mission promptly and reliably, the military services 'must insist upon a respect for duty and a discipline without counterpart in civilian life.'" An effective armed force without inspections is impossible, a fact amply illustrated by the unfettered right to inspect vested in commanders throughout the armed forces of the world.

Military Rule of Evidence 313 defines an "inspection" and explains the admissibility of evidence obtained during the course of an inspection:

(a) Evidence obtained from inspections and inventories in the armed forces conducted in accordance with this rule is admissible.
(b) An "inspection" is an examination of the whole or part of a unit, organization, installation, vessel, aircraft, or vehicle, the primary purpose of which is to determine and to ensure the security, military fitness, or good order and discipline of the unit, organization, installation, vessel, aircraft, or vehicle. An inspection may include but is not limited to an examination to determine and to ensure that any or all of the following requirements are met: that the command is properly equipped, functioning properly, maintaining proper standards of readiness, sea or airworthiness, sanitation and cleanliness, and that personnel are present, fit, and ready for duty. An inspection also includes an examination to locate and confiscate unlawful weapons and other contraband.

When is an inspection not really an inspection for purposes of the Fourth Amendment? Military Rule of Evidence 313 describes the circumstances that make an inspection an unlawful search:

An examination made for the primary purpose of obtaining evidence for use in a trial by court-martial or in other disciplinary proceedings in not an inspection within the meaning of this rule. If a purpose of an examination is to locate weapons or contraband, and if: (1) the examination was directed immediately following a report of a specific offense in the unit, organization, installation, vessel, aircraft, or vehicle and was not previously scheduled; (2) specific individuals are selected for examination; or (3) persons examined are subjected to substantially different intrusions during the same examination, the prosecution must prove by clear and convincing evidence that the examination was an inspection within the meaning of this rule. Inspections shall be conducted in a reasonable manner. Inspections may utilize any reasonable natural or technological aid and may be conducted with or without notice to those inspected.

Use of an inspection as a guise to obtain evidence against a particular person is unlawful. The following case addresses that principle as it applies to berthing spaces on board ships.

UNITED STATES V. GREG S. THATCHER, PRIVATE,
U.S. MARINE CORPS
UNITED STATES COURT OF MILITARY APPEALS
28 M.J. 20
FEBRUARY 28, 1989
Opinion: Everett, Chief Judge

One Monday morning in January 1985, Corporal Cerullo, the Company Police Sergeant, discovered missing from the police shed "a gray metal tool box containing assorted tools, . . . a green army first-aid kit, containing his own assorted tools, and a green metal trunk (with a 'The Who' sticker on the side)." All of these items had been in the shed the previous Friday, but none had been logged out. After Cerullo had unsuccessfully searched the barracks' common areas, he reported the incident to Gunnery Sergeant McKay. Major Talbott, the company commander, joined the conversation, and both McKay's and Talbott's initial reaction was that the property probably had been misplaced. Further search of the police shed and the surrounding area, however, proved fruitless.

Noting that, previously, property had been removed from the police shed without being logged out properly, Talbott surmised that possibly one of the persons assigned to a working party that had been in the area the week before had checked out the property and had left it in a working area or in his room. The Court of

Military Review found factually that, at this point, Talbott "had no knowledge . . . whether the property had been stolen."

However, when Talbott was advised that Thatcher had been a member of the working party, he grimaced. Cerullo testified:

I went down the list and I told him that we'd had Private Thatcher. You know, he looked at me like, you know, he'd been in a lot of trouble before. You know, the major knows that he's been caught, not caught, but he's been, well, he has been caught but not charged with taking things.

As Talbott himself later testified, "It just seems like whenever something negative happens around the company, Private Thatcher's name is involved."

Talbott instructed Cerullo to check the possibility of a mixup with another marine, who he knew owned a trunk similar to the missing one. He also instructed McKay and Cerullo "to track these people down" who had been in the working party and "to look in their rooms to see if the tool boxes were in their rooms." As McKay put it, Talbott had "informed Corporal Cerullo and I to find out who was on the working party that week, and to go over into their rooms and search for the tools." McKay testified that "Cerullo relayed back to" him that "First Sergeant Poffenroth [had] stat[ed] something about 'Go over to Thatcher's room. He's been caught stealing before.'"

At this point, it should be noted that, for the preceding eight months, there had been a routine of conducting daily health-and-comfort inspections of this unit to check for cleanliness and to ensure that all pilferable items were secured in wall lockers. Usually, such inspections were done in the morning, but occasionally they were held during the lunch hour. All rooms were inspected, whether locked or unlocked and whether the occupants were present or away. During the inspections, McKay was not authorized to open or to break into secured wall lockers. Only if a wall locker was unlocked was he to enter it, and then only to identify to whom it belonged.

Talbott indicated at trial that he had intended his check of the working party personnel's rooms for the tools to be part of that day's health-and-comfort inspection. However, he conceded that he never formally advised McKay to conduct this check in connection with the daily inspection.

So, as Sherlock Holmes might have said, the game was afoot. Passing by a head (latrine) and another person's room, McKay and Cerullo went directly to Thatcher's room, where they knocked on the closed door. Before receiving a response, however, they entered the room and found Thatcher standing next to his open wall locker, packing the locker's contents into his open seabag in anticipation of his scheduled discharge the next day. While "inspecting" the room, McKay advised Thatcher that he was looking for the missing tools.

At this point, Cerullo spotted a green metal trunk with a "The Who" sticker on its side inside the open wall locker. After Cerullo had advised McKay of his discovery, McKay directed Thatcher to remove the trunk and to remove the trunk's contents. Inside, McKay discovered the gray metal tool box and tools and the green army first-aid kit and tools that they were looking for.

Later that same day, in the afternoon, the health-and-comfort inspection was conducted of the remainder of the barracks.

The government seeks to forestall any consideration of appellant's claim by contending that because his room was subject to a daily health-and-comfort inspection, Thatcher lacked any "legitimate expectation of privacy" therein against intrusion by command.

To the extent this theory implies that a commander's daily routine of inspecting the rooms of his subordinates automatically cancels any reasonable expectation of privacy by them with respect to their rooms, we reject the notion. The circumstance that one is subject to a lawful inspection does not preclude him from complaining about an inspection which violates the requirements imposed by the president. To accept the government's argument would obliterate service members' Fourth Amendment rights with respect to their rooms and their property; and in so doing, we would be overruling our established precedents recognizing those rights. In short, if an intrusion on privacy is really an "inspection," no reasonable expectation of privacy has been violated; but if the purported inspection is only a subterfuge for a search or is not properly conducted, then a violation has occurred.

Although the military judge conducted a meticulous

inquiry and applied the correct standard of proof, we disagree with his conclusion that the government established by the requisite "clear and convincing" evidence that the intrusion into Thatcher's room was a lawful military inspection rather than a prohibited criminal search without probable cause.

In the first place, Thatcher was the prime suspect with respect to the possible theft of the tools and boxes. He was awaiting imminent discharge from the Marine Corps, and he had been in the working party so he might have had an opportunity to steal the property. He was thought by his commander and others to have stolen things before, even though for some reason he had never been charged therewith. Indeed, Thatcher's reputation was such that Major Talbott, his commander, "grimaced" when he learned that Thatcher had been in the working party. Talbott knew that Thatcher always was involved somehow in any trouble in the unit.

Although the barracks was inspected daily, on this occasion McKay and Cerullo passed by the head and another room and went straight to Thatcher's room. Moreover, after the stolen property had been seized in Thatcher's room in the morning, no further examination of the barracks took place until that afternoon. Thus, it appears that when McKay and Cerullo went to the barracks, they had in mind not the routine daily inspection (which could have included looking for the missing items, if done in a neutral fashion) but instead a search of the suspect's quarters. This inference is supported by this testimony of Gunnery Sergeant McKay on direct examination:

> Q. Exactly what was it the commanding officer told you that morning?
> A. The commanding officer told Corporal Cerullo and myself, sir, to find out who was on the working parties and go over and search their rooms for the possible tools that were missing.

Furthermore, although both McKay and Cerullo gave detailed statements to the Naval Investigative Service (NIS) on the day after the stolen property was recovered, neither of those statements made any reference to an "inspection" or gave any indication that Cerullo and McKay were making an inspection rather than a search. According to McKay's testimony, he first mentioned an "inspection" in a conversation with trial counsel or defense counsel a few days before trial, and some two months after his earlier statement.

This evidence is not "clear and convincing," thus the government has failed to establish that the incriminating evidence was found as the result of a lawful inspection. Instead, that evidence is inadmissible because it was the product of an unlawful intrusion into Thatcher's room.

Military Rule of Evidence 313 states that an order to produce body fluids is an inspection subject to the same requirements as all inspections. The following case considers the lawfulness of the military's urinalysis program.

ELIZABETH SUSAN UNGER, LIEUTENANT, U.S. NAVY V.
DANIEL ZIEMNIAK, CAPTAIN, U.S. NAVY, MILITARY JUDGE
UNITED STATES COURT OF MILITARY APPEALS
27 M.J. 349
JANUARY 27, 1989
Opinion: Everett, Chief Judge

In August 1988, Lieutenant Unger was charged with willfully disobeying the lawful order of a superior commissioned officer that she comply with a Naval directive, OPNAV Instruction 5350.4a, by giving a urine sample under direct observation by a female enlisted service member.

Lieutenant Unger is a Naval Academy graduate with eight years of unblemished service. In July 1988, she was required to provide a urine sample at Great Lakes Naval Training Center in connection with the drug-testing program authorized by OPNAVINST 5350.4a. That directive calls for "direct observation" of the private parts of a person who is giving a urine specimen. Accordingly, a female chief petty officer insisted that Lieutenant Unger "disrobe from the waist down, sit on a toilet, and urinate into a collection bottle" while being observed from a distance of approximately eighteen inches. Lieutenant Unger refused to comply with the conditions, although, without direct observation, she provided a sample which ultimately tested negative for drugs.

Because of her refusal to be directly observed, Lieutenant Unger was given "a direct oral order from" her executive officer "to comply with OPNAVINST 5350.4a and provide another sample under direct visual observation of her "private parts." She refused this order because of her claimed constitutional rights to privacy and to freedom from unreasonable searches and seizures and also because, in her view, the direct observation by an enlisted person constituted fraternization and demeaned her status as an officer. Her refusal gave rise to the charge filed against her after she refused punishment under Article 15, UCMJ.

Lieutenant Unger insists that even if mandatory drug testing is reasonable, her superiors sought to make her provide a urine specimen under conditions that were humiliating and degrading. In effect, she is contending that, by use of a direct order, her military superiors were attempting to accomplish an unreasonable, and therefore unconstitutional, "seizure" of her urine.

In this connection, she insists that it was unreasonable to require that she give a urine specimen under "direct observation." As Lieutenant Unger emphasizes, "direct observation" is not required currently in civilian drug-testing programs, unless there is reason to believe that a particular individual to be tested may substitute a urine specimen. Moreover, until recently direct observation was only required in collecting the urine specimens of male service members, and alternate procedures were employed for female service members.

Undoubtedly, for many persons it is unpleasant and disagreeable to urinate while being directly observed by someone else. However, we also realize that there are cavities in the body where small quantities of urine can be secreted for purposes of substitution in the event of a drug test; and only by direct observation can this tactic be prevented. Indeed, many tricks have been used to avoid detection by compulsory urinalysis. There are reports of persons who sell drug-free urine to others who, in turn, will substitute pure urine for their own urine when a specimen is being collected. A leading athlete has described how he concealed some drug-free urine on his body for purposes of substitution if he was required by the National Football League to submit a urine specimen. Only recently, we reviewed the case of a female commissioned officer who had devised still another scheme to defeat the air force's drug-testing program. See *United States v. Norvell,* 26 M.J. 477 (C.M.A. 1988).

In view of the varied tactics which may be employed to evade drug testing, we conclude that it is not unreasonable per se for the navy to require "direct observation" when urine specimens are collected. Otherwise, the temptation and opportunity for evasion are too great.

Lieutenant Unger also complains that she was to be directly observed by an enlisted person while she provided the urine specimen. Although her pleadings are phrased in terms of fraternization, her real complaint is that, in the hierarchical military society, it is demeaning and degrading for an officer to be observed by an enlisted person while she performs an activity that typically is performed in private.

However disagreeable it may be for an officer to be observed under such circumstances by an enlisted person, we believe that the need to prevent evasion of the drug-testing program justifies the surveillance. We recognize the importance of maintaining the military hierarchical structure reflected in rank, but we doubt the practicality of requiring that a person giving a urine specimen be of lower rank than the observer.

Furthermore, to exempt officers entirely from the requirement of "direct observation" would ignore the lesson that officers, like enlisted persons, may yield to the temptation of drugs and use tricks to avoid detection. The armed services are sufficiently egalitarian that every person in the armed services may be required to provide a urine specimen under direct observation. Although rank has its privileges, favored treatment in drug testing is not one of them.

Lieutenant Unger insists that, for physiological and psychological reasons, the requirement for "direct observation" is more offensive and degrading for a female than for a male. We recognize that in the military context males and females are not totally fungible. Therefore, Congress has limited the use of women for combat purposes and does not require them to register for the draft. Furthermore, for many years, the armed services apparently allowed use of alternatives to the direct observation of females giving urine specimens.

Our conclusion, however, is that, even though as a policy matter the armed services could modify the current procedures for collecting urine from female service members, they may require direct observation for females as well as for males. In our opinion, such observation of females does not inevitably transmute collection of urine specimens into an unreasonable "seizure" of the urine.

Although we reject Lieutenant Unger's claim that direct observation of the collection of urine from females is unconstitutional, a caution is in order. Direct observation can be performed in different ways and from different distances. If the eyes of the observer are too close to the genitalia of the person giving the urine specimen, the process of obtaining this specimen would be unduly humiliating and degrading. Likewise, even though a male gynecologist may examine a woman's vagina for medical purposes, we believe it would be clearly unreasonable for male service members, even if medical corpsmen, to serve as "observers" of women who have been required to give urine specimens.

Lieutenant Unger argued that observation of her by an enlisted person constituted fraternization and demeaned her status as an officer. Does observation of an officer by an enlisted person during a urinalysis constitute an "unduly familiar" relationship? See the discussion of fraternization in chapter 5. Lieutenant Unger also argued that direct observation of females is more intrusive and degrading than for males. Is such a distinction viable in light of a gender-neutral approach to assignment of personnel in the U.S. Navy and Marine Corps?

Inventories

An inventory, like an inspection, is not a search under the Fourth Amendment if it is conducted for a legitimate purpose. Military Rule of Evidence 313(c) explains:

> Inventories. Unlawful weapons, contraband, or other evidence of crime discovered in the process of an inventory, the primary purpose of which is administrative in nature, may be seized. Inventories shall be conducted in a reasonable fashion. An examination made for the primary purpose of obtaining evidence for use in a trial by court-martial or in other disciplinary proceedings is not an inventory within the meaning of this rule.

Evidence discovered in the process of a proper inventory may be seized and admitted into evidence at court-martial. In *United States v. Jasper* above, the examination of the accused's off-base apartment overseas was an inventory that resulted from the accused's deserter status. Inventories of the property of deserters and confined personnel, and routine seabag examinations, are common types of inventories. When are these types of inspections unlawful?

Searches Not Requiring Probable Cause

Installations Overseas

Military Rule of Evidence 314 describes those searches not requiring probable cause. Included in that rule are searches on leaving or entering United States military property abroad:

> In addition to the authority to conduct inspections, a commander of a United States military installation, enclave, or aircraft on foreign soil, or in foreign or international airspace, or a United States vessel in foreign or international waters, may authorize appropriate personnel to search persons or the property of such persons upon entry to or exit from the installation, enclave, aircraft, or vessel to ensure the security, military fitness, or good order and discipline of the command. A search made for the primary purpose of obtaining evidence for use in a trial by court-martial or other disciplinary proceeding is not authorized.

The following case discusses the type of searches described above.

UNITED STATES V. JULIO E. RIVERA, AIRMAN FIRST CLASS,
U.S. AIR FORCE
UNITED STATES COURT OF MILITARY APPEALS
4 M.J. 215
FEBRUARY 20, 1978
Opinion: Fletcher, Chief Judge

Counsel for the appellant argue that the random gate search program utilized at Korat Royal Thai Air Force Base was constitutionally infirm because it was too vague, undefined, and unlimited in scope and application to pass muster under the Fourth Amendment. The heroin in question was the product of two separate seizures. On the night of August 31, 1974, the appellant arrived at gate one of the base riding in a civilian (Thai) taxi; the gate guard, at the direction of a Sergeant Blackmore, the handler for the marijuana detection dog stationed at the gate, directed the taxi driver to pull over to the side of the road and stop. The occupants were removed, and Sergeant Blackmore led the dog into the vehicle whereupon it "alerted" towards the back seat. The dog was led into the back seat area and it "alerted" even more strongly where the appellant had been sitting. Sergeant Blackmore then asked the two passengers for their military identification cards. The appellant, whose hands and legs were visibly shaking, was placed under apprehension after the dog "alerted" upon him, and taken to the gate guard shack and read his rights. A search of his pants pocket revealed a small plastic vial containing the heroin which was the basis for the first charge of possession of heroin.

On October 22, 1974, the appellant and another serviceman were entering the base through gate one; at Sergeant Blackmore's direction the civilian taxi was stopped and ordered to pull over to the side of the road. As the passengers alighted from the taxi, the marijuana dog "alerted" on the other serviceman; Sergeant Blackmore then proceeded to search the car. When the sergeant noticed the appellant, he took the dog out of the car and asked both the appellant and the other serviceman for their military identification cards. After the dog "alerted" on both men, Sergeant Blackmore informed both that they were being detained. At that point the appellant started to move behind the other passenger and appeared to Sergeant Blackmore to be attempting to place a white container in his mouth. After a struggle, the sergeant was able to force the appellant to spit out the pieces of the container, analysis of which revealed heroin.

I start with the proposition of the Supreme Court that searches made at the border, pursuant to the long-standing right of the sovereign to protect itself by stopping and examining persons and property crossing into the country, are reasonable simply because they occur at the border. This exception to the search warrant requirement is not based upon the doctrine of exigent circumstances, but instead is the result of historical recognition by both the Congress and the Court of the distinctions between those activities occurring at the border and those occurring elsewhere. The Supreme Court in *Boyd v. United States,* 116 U.S. 616 (1886), set forth the doctrinal basis for the exception by noting that from the commencement of our government, customs agents have had the power to make searches and seizures without the normal prerequisites of probable cause or a search warrant. The Court emphasized that the very Congress which proposed the Bill of Rights enacted the first customs statute granting such powers to those entrusted with protection of the international borders. Thus, travelers may be stopped in crossing an international boundary because of national self-protection reasonably requiring one entering the country to identify himself as entitled to come in, and his belongings as effects which may be lawfully brought in.

I recognize that a distinction between the problem posed by this case and that addressed by the Supreme Court is the absence of Congressional action granting this custom power to the military as to points of entry onto American installations in foreign countries. Yet I feel that the essential underlying rationale remains applicable, and that the factual similarities between an international border and the entrance onto an American military installation overseas compels adoption of the border search exception for this situation.

Examining the facts of this case, I am satisfied that the procedures utilized were reasonable and sufficiently non-intrusive to comply with the standards enunciated by the Supreme Court. The magnitude of the service's need to maintain the security of the installation on foreign soil and to combat an ever increasing drug traffic problem, when coupled with the reasonableness of the procedures persuade me that each search meets the requirements of the Fourth Amendment.

Note that searches at the entry or exit point of a base, aircraft, or ship located in the United States must be all-inclusive or random. These types of examinations are considered to be inspections. What difference is there between a search at an exit or entry point of a military installation overseas and an inspection? Is the purpose of both types of searches the same?

Government Property

Searches of government property are an everyday occurrence in the military. When do such searches run afoul of the Fourth Amendment? Military Rule of Evidence 314(d) considers that question:

> Searches of government property. Government property may be searched unless the person to whom the property is issued or assigned has a reasonable expectation of privacy therein at the time of the search. Under normal circumstances, a person does not have a reasonable expectation of privacy in government property that is not issued for personal use. Wall or floor lockers in living quarters issued for the purpose of storing personal possessions normally are issued for personal use; but the determination as to whether a person has a reasonable expectation of privacy in government property issued for personal use depends on the facts and circumstances at the time of the search.

The legality of a search of government property will turn on whether the item was issued for personal use as described above. What factors will bear on that determination? The next case considers that issue.

UNITED STATES V. FELIX A. MUNIZ, CAPTAIN, U.S. AIR FORCE
UNITED STATES COURT OF MILITARY APPEALS
23 M.J. 201
Opinion: Cox, Judge

Appellant was second in command of the 96th Munitions Maintenance Squadron, Dyess AFB, Texas. During the last week of September and the first week of October 1983, appellant's commander, Lieutenant Colonel John M. Rhoads, was on leave. Appellant was in charge of the squadron. Appellant, though married and the father of a young daughter, had evidently established some sort of relationship with Captain S, a female air force officer, not appellant's wife, who was stationed at Greenham Common RAF Base, England. Apparently, appellant made the acquaintance of this officer in Aviano, Italy, where they both had been stationed previously.

In late September 1983, during Lieutenant Colonel Rhoads' leave, appellant called Captain S and told her (falsely) that he had been granted leave and (accurately) that he would be coming to visit her for two weeks. Several days later, appellant told the unit first sergeant, Master Sergeant Thomas Little, that he had to go on leave to Puerto Rico because his uncle had died and he needed to care for his ailing mother (it was this statement that constituted the conduct-unbecoming charge). Indeed, it appears that appellant's uncle had recently died, but taking care of his mother was not what was animating appellant. His only purpose in saying this to Master Sergeant Little was to set the stage for his clandestine trip to England. To be consistent with the story he told his wife, appellant also asked the first sergeant to tell her, should she inquire, that he was on a temporary duty assignment. The reason given for requesting this service was purportedly to not upset her because of his uncle's death.

A few days later, but still before the commander returned, appellant filled out and signed a leave request indicating a leave address, without telephone number, in Puerto Rico (this action resulted in the false-official-document charge). Placing the document on the commander's desk for his signature, appellant departed for England only hours before the commander returned. In accordance with appellant's instructions, the first sergeant duly briefed the commander on the crisis; and the request was approved. But for an untimely ear infection, nobody might have been the wiser.

What appellant could not anticipate was that his infant daughter would develop an ear infection of such proportions as to require surgery. Confronted with this situation, Mrs. Muniz came in to see Lieutenant Colonel Rhoads to enlist his assistance in getting in touch with appellant. The exact degree of medical urgency is not documented in the record, and it does not appear that Rhoads was so informed. Nonetheless, the impression was unmistakably conveyed to Rhoads that the situation was serious and that it was urgent that Mrs. Muniz consult with appellant before giving her consent to the operation. As can be imagined, Rhoads and Little sprang into action.

Through Red Cross and security police channels, all efforts were employed to contact appellant at his supposed leave address in Puerto Rico. When it was discovered that the address appellant left was insufficient, they sent for appellant's file from the personnel office and got a better address. Of course, the efforts to contact him in Puerto Rico were to no avail, as he was in England. It is certain that appellant's relatives in Puerto Rico were actually contacted because Mrs. Muniz received at least one phone call from a relative in Puerto Rico asking why the security police were coming around looking for appellant. Having no idea at the time that her husband was supposedly in Puerto Rico, Mrs. Muniz became quite upset and called Lieutenant Colonel Rhoads about it. Again she impressed on him the urgency of contacting appellant.

Confronted with this turn of events, Rhoads and Little began to realize that appellant was not where he said he would be. Still motivated by the overriding need to put him in contact with his wife about his daughter, however, they began to play long shots. They both knew appellant had only recently arrived at the unit from his previous assignment in Italy. Master Sergeant Little also recalled that appellant had been receiving letters at the unit, through distribution, with an APO return number. Thinking that there might be a connection between his unexplained absence and the letters—or perhaps because they simply had nothing better to go on—the two "sleuths" decided to look in his office for the letters, on the chance that they might provide a clue. Not having any luck on the surfaces or in the unlocked drawers, they "jimmied" the lock on a drawer of appellant's credenza.

In the drawer, they found a stack of letters bearing an APO return address. According to their testimony, they merely copied the APO number, along with a "PSE box," leaving the letters in the drawer. Both Rhoads and Little insisted that they did not open the letters or even remove them from the drawer. As no sender's name appeared with the return address, they consulted a directory and found that the number corresponded to Greenham Common RAF Base, England. It so happened that another member of the unit, Staff Sergeant Prentiss, had also been assigned at Aviano. Rhoads and Little asked Prentiss if he knew of anyone who had been at Aviano but who was now at Greenham Common. Prentiss identified Captain S.

The effort then shifted to contacting Captain S. By dint of considerable persistence, they got through to her duty section but found that she was on leave (she was touring the country with appellant). They left the message that, if appellant were there, he was to call Lieutenant Colonel Rhoads or Mrs. Muniz immediately, as there had been an emergency. When appellant and Captain S returned from their travels several days later, they found the note; appellant promptly called Lieutenant Colonel Rhoads. By then, the surgery had been successfully completed, and appellant was so informed. Rhoads also ordered appellant to return to base, which he did.

The evidence taken regarding the privacy conditions in the office was also essentially uncontroverted. Appellant, as second in command, had a separate office. This office and the credenza therein were government property. The principal purpose of the facility was to conduct military business. Though the door to the office was lockable, both the commander and the first sergeant had access to it by key. The credenza was allocated to appellant's exclusive use. It had recently arrived at the unit and had come equipped with a set of keys. Appellant had never been asked to turn in any of the keys, and no unit policy had been formulated concerning the nature of items unit members might keep in their work areas. From time to time in the course of their official duties, various staff members would enter each other's work areas, notwithstanding the absence of the occupant, to obtain work products. Appellant's office had previously been so entered, despite his absence, for such purposes. No one had ever entered his locked credenza drawers.

Like the earlier civilian cases, our earlier military cases tended to emphasize the ownership interests in the property in question. It is now clear, however, in the civilian context that people can acquire legitimate expectations of privacy vis-à-vis law-enforcement authorities in property they do not own. Thus, the fact that the credenza was government-owned does not automatically exclude the possibility that appellant may have acquired a legitimate expectation of privacy in its contents.

We note that the credenza, like any other item of government property within the command, was subject at a moment's notice to a thorough inspection. That omnipresent fact of military life, coupled with the indisputable government ownership and the ordinarily nonpersonal nature of military offices, could have left appellant with only the most minimal expectation—or hope—of privacy in the drawer vis-à-vis his commander. This minimal expectation must be distinguished from an unquestionably greater expectation of privacy and security vis-à-vis the rest of the world.

Additionally, it should be borne in mind that Rhoads, above all, was appellant's military commander. That particular relationship imposes a much greater degree of responsibility—in both directions—than is true of most civilian analogs. As commander, Rhoads had a compelling duty to notify his subordinate of his child's trouble—if for no other reason than to permit him to return home and comfort her. Had Rhoads simply given up at the first dead end, had he merely contented himself with sitting on his hands and not even bothering to exert the minimal effort of breaking into this government-owned drawer, we would have had serious reservations about his fitness to command. A service member has a right to expect that, if he is killed in battle, his leaders will not willingly surrender his body to the enemy. He should have no less reason to trust that, if his dependents are in trouble, his leaders will exert every human effort to find him. By not being where he led his commander to believe he would be, appellant virtually invited his commander to look in his credenza drawer if it became necessary to contact him. Viewed in this light, it was really appellant's misconduct that dispersed whatever lingering remnants of privacy, vis-à-vis his commander, he may have retained in the drawer.

The issue in *Muniz* was whether the accused had an expectation of privacy in a locked desk. What factors did the court consider in making its ruling? Is there a privacy expectation in other types government property? See *United States v. Battles* above for a discussion of the privacy expectation in barracks. Could the court have upheld the search of Captain Muniz's locker as a lawful "emergency" search? Consider Military Rule of Evidence 314(i), which discusses the "emergency" exception:

Emergency searches to save life or for related purposes. In emergency circumstances to save life or for a related purpose, a search may be conducted of persons or property in a good faith effort to render immediate medical aid, to obtain information that will assist in the rendering of such aid, or to prevent immediate or ongoing personal injury.

Compare emergency searches with the exigent circumstances exception to the search authorization requirement discussed above. Do the two principles go hand in hand? Where does probable cause come into play in the exigent circumstances exception? In the O. J. Simpson murder trial, the police claimed that they feared for the safety of Mr. Simpson and his children. Is this a legitimate emergency under military law? Consider the following case.

UNITED STATES V. TECHNICAL SERGEANT MARVIN J. WALKER, UNITED STATES AIR FORCE
UNITED STATES AIR FORCE COURT OF MILITARY REVIEW
OCTOBER 3, 1985

On 5 January 1983, while on leave in the Philippines, the appellant was apprehended by Air Force Security Police for wrongful possession of marijuana. He was allowed to return to his duty station at Kadena Air Base the following day. On 10 January 1985 the OSI Superintendent of Investigative Operations on Kadena AB, Mr. Louis F. Breaux, Jr., received a telephone call from the Security Police Desk Sergeant that there was a possible homicide at an off-base residence of an air force member. Agent Breaux proceeded to the scene. The Security Police flight chief, other Security Police representatives, local law enforcement officials, the appellant's first sergeant, and hospital personnel were there when he arrived. The OSI agent learned that the situation involved the appellant, the same sergeant who was recently apprehended for possession of marijuana in the Philippines.

Meanwhile the medics were inside the appellant's residence rendering aid. The OSI agent looked through a window and saw the appellant lying in a bath tub. At about this time some medics came out and asked if they could move certain items to affect the appellant's removal from the apartment. Agent Breaux knew that a knife was either in the bath tub or near to it, however, since it was necessary to save the appellant's life he voiced no objections to the appellant's removal from his residence. Agent Breaux saw the medics remove the appellant from the apartment on a stretcher. He then proceeded to discuss the case with the Okinawan officials at the scene and did not enter the appellant's residence until 10 to 15 minutes after he had witnessed him removed therefrom. Agent Breaux then entered the apartment for the express purpose of investigating whether there had been a suicide or homicide attempt. The OSI Agent was asked by defense counsel "so your entrance then into the apartment was not to render any kind of emergency aid to, you know, in assistance to Sgt Walker, was it?" Answer: "no."

Given these facts, we find that the warrantless search of appellant's residence did not qualify as a search conducted pursuant to an emergency circumstance. In the case at bar, the OSI agent knew the appellant had already been removed from his residence by the medics when he entered some 10 to 15 minutes later. His stated delayed purpose in going into Sgt Walker's residence was clearly not a good faith effort to render immediate medical aid or to obtain information that would assist in the rendering of such aid, or to prevent immediate or ongoing personal injury, but to seek evidence to establish whether there had been a suicide attempt.

Consent

A valid consent to search does away with the need for a search authorization based on probable cause. When is a consent lawful? Who may give consent? Can the scope of the search be limited? Military Rule of Evidence 314(e) addresses these questions:

Consent searches.
(1) General rule. Searches may be conducted of any person or property with lawful consent.
(2) Who may consent. A person may consent to a search of his or her person or property, or both, unless control over such property has been given to another. A person may grant consent to search property when the person exercises control over that property.
(3) Scope of consent. Consent may be limited in any way by the person granting consent, including limitations in terms of time, place, or property and may be withdrawn at any time.

(4) Voluntariness. To be valid, consent must be given voluntarily. Voluntariness is a question to be determined from all the circumstances. Although a person's knowledge of the right to refuse to give consent is a factor to be considered in determining voluntariness, the prosecution is not required to demonstrate such knowledge as a prerequisite to establishing a voluntary consent. Mere submission to the color of authority of personnel performing law enforcement duties or acquiescence in an announced or indicated purpose to search is not a voluntary consent.

Whether a consent is lawful depends on the voluntariness of the permission to search. *United States v. Goudy* addresses the factors used to determine whether a consent is voluntary.

UNITED STATES V. STEPHEN A. GOUDY, LANCE CORPORAL, U.S. MARINE CORPS
UNITED STATES COURT OF MILITARY APPEALS
32 M.J. 88
FEBRUARY 5, 1991

Major Harrison, appellant's company commander, suspected that appellant had stolen a number of items of personal property belonging to other members of the unit. Apparently, appellant earlier had made incriminating statements to two people concerning their missing property, and Harrison was aware of these statements. Accordingly, he arranged for Sergeant Laird, an apprentice investigator with the Criminal Investigation Division, to come to his office to look into the matter.

When appellant arrived for work at 6:30 A.M., his supervisor advised him that he was to report to Major Harrison's office at 8:00 A.M.; in the meantime, he was told to carry out his normal duties but was admonished that he would be under the "strict guide" of one of the company's sergeants. Specifically, although appellant's usual routine was undisturbed, he was not to go anywhere or do anything except in the presence of the named sergeant.

At the appointed hour, the sergeant escorted appellant to Harrison's office, where appellant reported to his commander in the position of attention. Laird and Staff Sergeant Hudson, another investigator, also were in the room, and Harrison introduced them to appellant. Preliminarily, Harrison advised appellant that he suspected him of selling a television that did not belong to him and of stealing personal property of other marines in the barracks. He asked generally whether appellant understood his rights under Article 31 of the code, to which appellant replied that he did.

Harrison observed that the best way to clear up the matter would be to search appellant's room. He advised appellant that "he needed" his "consent" to do so and suggested that, if appellant "had nothing to hide, there was no reason" not to give that consent by signing a consent-to-search form. Appellant did ultimately sign the form. After Harrison had made the comments set out above, appellant responded, "'Okay,' or 'Yes,' something like that, in that nature," and Harrison "then . . . just gave him to" Laird. Laird described what happened at that point:

I filled it [the consent form] out and I went step-by-step over all this with him, telling him where to initial, where I had marked out parts that had nothing to do with what we were looking for. Had him read it, then I asked him, "Do you understand everything about this form?" [I told him] that he didn't have to give his consent to search because . . . the form says that you don't have to give your consent to search, and he said, "Okay." Finally, just before appellant signed the form, Laird again asked, "'Do you understand everything on this form?,' and he said, 'Yes.'"

Appellant acknowledged that he was not under arrest or apprehension at the time, only under escort. While Harrison's voice was "authoritative," appellant conceded that at no time did Harrison raise his voice, scream, or make any threats or promises. Laird described Harrison as "cool, calm, and collected. Just wanted to find out what was going on." Laird also testified that appellant's physical and mental appearance seemed normal at the time, with no indications that he was under the influence of any alcohol or drug that might impair his understanding.

If the government relies upon consent to justify the lawfulness of a search, it has the burden of proving that consent was freely and voluntarily given. Whether such consent was voluntary must be determined from the totality of the circumstances, and "must be shown by

clear and convincing evidence." The person's knowledge of the right to refuse consent and the fact that the person is in some form of custody at the time consent is requested are important factors to be considered. Neither, however, is fully determinative, one way or the other. To reiterate, the question of consent must be answered from the totality of the circumstances.

Appellant acknowledged to Harrison an awareness of his rights under Article 31, UCMJ. Certainly, Harrison's general inquiry in this regard would not be sufficient to meet the requirements for admissibility of a subsequent statement. In the context of a consent to search, however, it does suggest that appellant was alerted to the fact that this confrontation with his commander was one in which his rights as a criminal suspect would be respected.

By appellant's own admission, Harrison never overtly ordered appellant's compliance with his request for consent. We recognize that Goudy had been brought to Harrison's office under escort and that, under many circumstances, a request from a major in the Marine Corps likely would be met with a response of "aye, aye, sir."

However, granting appellant's plea to this Court to view these circumstances as an "implied order," even in the context just discussed in the first consideration above, would virtually establish a "bright-line" rule against a military commander's personally asking a subordinate for his consent to search unless the commander did so informally and without any of the usual trappings of military courtesy that accompany such a meeting. That is neither the law nor logic, much less both.

Beyond this, appellant was orally admonished by Laird that he did not have to give his consent, and the form which he signed reiterated that advice. Appellant claims that he did not read the form before signing it; if true, however, he omitted to do so at his own peril. In any event, he received the advice orally from Laird.

Harrison told Goudy that he needed his consent in order to search. Accordingly, other than appellant's "implied order" argument addressed above, there is no basis for a claim that appellant's consent was merely acquiescence to a claim of lawful authority. The message was clear: Appellant, by virtue of his consent, held the key to his privacy.

Goudy was a twenty-year-old high school graduate,

with a GT/GCT score of 129 and two years of experience in the Marine Corps. Moreover, his testimony at trial—at least so far as can be discerned from the printed pages—was well articulated and assertive, not at all reflective of an uncertain or submissive person. All this makes it even less likely that appellant—alerted to his statutory rights as a criminal suspect and forthrightly advised that he did not have to consent, would have merely rolled over in the face of an "implied order," as opposed to deciding for himself that his best chance lay in voluntarily consenting.

Nothing in Harrison's message or demeanor could have overcome appellant's own free choice. The commander was calm and his voice was conversational, not overbearing in any manner. Further, Harrison made no obvious or subtle threats or promises to induce appellant to do something that he had not decided for himself was in his own best interest.

Whether he believed that he was caught and might as well give up or whether he hoped to bluff his way out of the situation by agreeing to the search to demonstrate that he had nothing to hide—either way, it does not amount to coercion or any overwhelming of appellant's free choice.

Is it always best to attempt to obtain consent prior to conducting a search? What impact would the mental or physical condition of the person granting consent have on the decision to seek permission? From the prosecution's standpoint, written consent is preferable to oral consent. Does *Goudy* illustrate this point?

Incident to Apprehension

Military Rule of Evidence 314(g) discusses the authority to search following a lawful apprehension:

Searches incident to a lawful apprehension.
(1) General rule. A person who has been lawfully apprehended may be searched.
(2) Search for weapons and destructible evidence. A search may be conducted for weapons or destructible evidence in the area within the immediate control of a person who has been apprehended. The area within the person's "immediate control" is the area which the indi-

vidual searching could reasonably believe that the person apprehended could reach with a sudden movement to obtain such property; provided, that the passenger compartment of an automobile, and containers within the passenger compartment may be searched as a contemporaneous incident of the apprehension of an occupant of the automobile, regardless whether the person apprehended has been removed from the vehicle.

What is the purpose of the above rule? The following case demonstrates the mechanics of a search incident to an apprehension.

UNITED STATES V. ANDERSON WALLACE, JR.,
STAFF SERGEANT, U.S. ARMY
U.S. COURT OF MILITARY APPEALS
34 M.J. 353
JULY 30, 1992
Opinion: Wiss, Judge

The Army Criminal Investigation Command (CID) received an anonymous tip that Specialist Robin Farrar was distributing cocaine from her quarters. In response, the CID instructed Sergeant Sermons, who was a CID confidential source, to make friends with Farrar and to attempt to purchase cocaine from her.

At some point, a meeting between Sermons and Farrar for this purpose was arranged for March 10, 1989, and the CID made all necessary preparations for a controlled buy on that occasion. When Sermons arrived at Farrar's quarters, she advised him that she did not have the cocaine at the moment but that her source would arrive with it soon.

Shortly thereafter, surveilling agents saw a black man and woman drive up to Farrar's quarters in a car that agents learned was registered to appellant. The couple left the car and went into Farrar's quarters.

Inside, Sermons remained alone while the couple and Farrar went to the rear of the quarters. After a short period of time, Farrar returned to Sermons with two bags of cocaine, which Sermons bought. Sermons, however, did not see either of the couple in possession of the cocaine or see either one deliver it to Farrar.

Farrar was apprehended on April 26. During her interrogation, she gave two statements involving appellant in her drug operation and identifying him as the black male whom Sermons had seen on March 10. Apparently, some subsequent efforts were made to set up transactions in which appellant actually would deliver the drug to the agent/buyer, but none was successful. In any event, the CID finally decided to apprehend appellant, and on June 9, 1989, Agent Cobb sent for him. Command Sergeant Major Boseman escorted appellant to the CID office. The following direct examination of Agent Cobb reveals what happened upon appellant's arrival:

A. I told him he was under apprehension and I also asked him if he understood what those offenses meant, or if he understood what those offenses were and he nodded in the affirmative. He didn't say anything; he nodded in the affirmative.

Q. Was the accused free to leave your office at that point?

A. No.

Q. Did he seem surprised about what you were saying to him?

A. No, he did not.

Q. What happened next?

A. Uh, I told Staff Sergeant Wallace to empty his pockets, which he did. I told him to stand against the wall and I conducted a pat down search of his body.

Q. Then what did you do?

A. I sat him down, completed a interview worksheet on him, advised him of his rights for the offenses of wrongful possession, distribution of cocaine.

Q. Let's back up a little bit; did you search his wallet at all?

A. Yes, I did.

Q. When?

A. After he had been patted down.

Q. And what did you say to him?

A. I told Sergeant Wallace, I said "watch me as I go through your wallet," we do that sometimes—a lot of times there's currency in there and we don't want any problems or someone to say my money was missing after CID searched my wallet. He was on one side of the table; I was on the other.

Q. Why were you searching the wallet?

A. Any weapons, any destructible evidence that he might have had in the wallet at the time.

Q. I show you what have been marked as Prosecution Exhibits 1 through 4 for identification (hands documents to witness); can you tell me what those are?

A. These are photostatic copies of pieces of paper that I removed from Staff Sergeant Wallace's wallet on the day that he was apprehended in my office.

Q. Why did you seize these pieces of paper?

A. We had reason to believe that Sergeant Wallace was a distributor of cocaine, and from the dollar amounts and the names on it, it appeared to be a list of money that was owed for cocaine transaction or drug deals.

No rational conclusion can be permitted but that the search was incident to an apprehension. According to Agent Cobb's testimony, he sent for appellant for the very purpose of formally apprehending him; upon arrival, Cobb promptly informed appellant that he was under apprehension and the reasons therefore. Within seconds thereafter, appellant's pockets were emptied, his body patted down, and his wallet searched, all directed at locating any weapons or "destructible evidence." Appellant was then fingerprinted and finally taken to the Military Police Station for formal release to his unit. These circumstances leave no room at all to doubt Cobb's testimony that "the only reason" he had sent for appellant "was to apprehend him."

Appellant's contention that the search of his wallet was outside the lawful scope of a search incident to apprehension misses the mark. A search for weapons or destructible evidence "within the 'immediate control' area" of the arrestee—without regard to whether there is probable cause to believe that the person has a weapon or is about to destroy evidence—is reasonable, at least so long as the search is not "remote in time or place from the arrest."

In sum, then, we conclude that Agent Cobb had probable cause to apprehend appellant; that he did lawfully apprehend appellant; and that the challenged search of appellant's wallet was incident to the apprehension.

The U.S. Supreme Court in *New York v. Belton*, 453 U.S. 545 (1981), held that a lawful apprehension of a passenger in a vehicle authorizes a search of not only the entire passenger compartment of the vehicle but also any container found inside, whether open or closed. Even if the vehicle occupant is under arrest and outside the automobile, the passenger compartment and containers may be searched. Note that a search incident to an apprehension does not authorize the search of the vehicle's trunk, only the passenger compartment and containers located therein. Why are law enforcement officials given such broad authority to search a vehicle following an arrest? Compare the authority to search incident to an apprehension with the exigent circumstances exception to the warrant requirement. Is there ever a situation in which a search authorization is required to search a car?

Study Questions

1. Airman Hatfield is popularly known as a ready source of a illegal drugs. His commander has requested that NCIS investigate several rumors about Airman Hatfield. One day at 1245, Agent Helmsman of the NCIS hurriedly approaches the commanding officer with a request for authorization for a search of Airman Hatfield's car. He relates to the commanding officer that Petty Officer McCoy provided him with information that Airman Hatfield and a cohort were to replenish their supply of high-grade marijuana by meeting their supplier at lunch time. According to Petty Officer McCoy, they were to leave the ship at 1200 and drive around the base in a white 1966 Mustang until no one was watching and then make the transfer.

Helmsman reports that a records check has verified that Airman Hatfield owns a white 1966 Mustang. Furthermore, he and a person matching the description provided by Petty Officer McCoy were observed leaving the ship in the same car just a few minutes before 1200. The two returned to the pier in the Mustang at 1235. Both suspects are back on board the ship. Agent Helmsman says that since the vehicle returned it has been under constant supervision by other NCIS agents.

   a. What is the most important issue for the commander to consider in granting or denying Agent Helmsman's search request?

   b. What information regarding Petty Officer McCoy should the commanding officer elicit from Agent Helmsman? For what purpose?

   c. If the commanding officer is not satisfied that the information provided by Petty Officer McCoy is sufficient to constitute probable cause, what could NCIS do to bolster its information?

   d. The executive officer suggests that whether or not they have probable cause, it is all right to search Hatfield's car anywhere on base because of the signs posted at all gates: "Entry grants consent to search of all persons and vehicles on board this installation." Is this good advice?

   e. Suppose that Airman Hatfield eases through a stop sign and is apprehended for a traffic violation. May NCIS then search his car for drugs?

   f. Suppose a valid search of Airman Hatfield's car yields four pounds of high-quality marijuana laced with opium. Can Agent Helmsman then request authority to search Airman Hatfield's room in the barracks, arguing that it is only logical that if he has it in his car he probably has it in his barracks room as well?

   g. Suppose that the commanding officer concludes there is no probable cause to search Airman Hatfield's car. Agent Helmsman then seizes the initiative, and when Airman Hatfield returns to AIMD he asks Airman Hatfield for consent to search his car. What procedures should Agent Helmsman use to ensure he conducts a valid consent search?

2. What are the requirements for a legitimate seizure of property under the "plain view" doctrine?

3. Quarterdeck searches on a United States ship in a foreign port are considered equivalent to what other type of examination?

4. You are the duty officer of a shore command and your duties require you to make periodic "walk-through" inspections of the enlisted barracks. While walking through the barracks one evening, you smell what you believe to be the strong odor of marijuana emanating from behind the locked door of an en-

listed room. You notice that the bottom of the door appears to have been sealed off on the inside by something, perhaps a rolled-up rug. These observations, along with your experience, lead you reasonably to believe that marijuana is being consumed inside that particular room. What should you do?

a. Immediately call the commanding officer, inform him of all the facts, and wait for him to prepare his written search authorization based upon probable cause.

b. Immediately enter the barracks room using the duty officer's master key; once inside you may seize the marijuana and make the appropriate apprehensions.

c. Immediately knock on the door and wait for the occupants to open the door. Then advise them of their Article 31(b) rights and their right to consent to a search of their room.

d. Immediately knock on the door, but enter *only if* you hear a window being opened or a toilet being flushed.

e. Continue on with your walk through of the barracks, since the occupants of the room have a reasonable expectation of privacy in their barracks room.

Lieutenant Sharp was talking to his division chief, Electrician's Mate Chief (ETC) Hawkeye, on the messdecks of the USS *Ticonderoga* (CG-55). As he was talking, he saw a third class petty officer (PO3) pass something to the sailor sitting next to him at the table. Lieutenant Sharp did not know the name of the PO3, but he did recognize the other sailor as Fireman Smart. The PO3 looked suspicious to Lieutenant Sharp because he looked around several times and took great care to conceal the item that was being passed. Lieutenant Sharp was aware that several enlisted members of the *Ticonderoga* had recently been identified through the command's urinalysis program as abusers of cocaine.

5. Based on these facts, what may Lieutenant Sharp *lawfully* do?

a. Thoroughly search both sailors for weapons and destructible evidence.

b. Temporarily detain both sailors; he may then ask the PO3 to identify himself and to explain his suspicious conduct.

c. Apprehend the PO3 based on his reasonable suspicion that criminal activity "was afoot."

d. Immediately request that the commanding officer authorize an inspection of both sailors' berthing spaces.

e. None of the above; they would all be unlawful.

While Lieutenant Sharp was contemplating what he could lawfully do under the circumstances, Fireman Smart approached him. Fireman Smart was one of Lieutenant Sharp's most trustworthy and reliable subordinates. Fireman Smart told Lieutenant Sharp that the PO3 had just given him a small bag containing a white powdery substance that the PO3 claimed was cocaine. The PO3 had asked Fireman Smart to try it out as a free sample and had told Fireman Smart that if he liked it, there was plenty more where that came from since he had another half-ounce of cocaine in his locker. Fireman Smart then immediately handed Lieutenant Sharp the bag of cocaine. Based on Fireman Smart's report as well as the bag of cocaine, Lieutenant Sharp promptly and lawfully apprehended the PO3, who was still on the messdecks. The PO3 identified himself as Hull Technician Third Class (HT3) Felony. Lieutenant Sharp then conducted a thorough search of HT3 Felony that resulted in his seizure of two more bags of cocaine from HT3 Felony's pockets.

6. The two bags of cocaine seized from HT3 Felony's pockets are:

a. Inadmissible, since Lieutenant Sharp did not have probable cause to search HT3 Felony's pockets.

b. Admissible as the result of a search incident to a lawful apprehension.

c. Admissible as the result of a lawful "frisk" for drugs.

d. Inadmissible, since Lieutenant Sharp did not obtain proper search authorization.

e. Inadmissible, since HT3 Felony never consented to a search of his pockets.

After informing the commanding officer of the above events and the report of Fireman Smart, Lieutenant Sharp obtained verbal search authorization from the commanding officer to search HT3 Felony's locker on board the *Ticonderoga*. This search yielded a half-ounce of cocaine.

7. The half-ounce of cocaine seized from HT3 Felony's locker is:

a. Inadmissible, since HT3 Felony had a reasonable expectation of privacy in his locker.

b. Admissible as the result of a search incident to a lawful apprehension.

c. Inadmissible, since there were no exigent circumstances present.

d. Admissible as the result of a lawful search based on probable cause.

e. Admissible as the result of a lawful inspection of HT3 Felony's locker.

8. What is a valid purpose for a inspection? Are unlawful weapons, contraband, or other evidence of crime seized during the course of a lawful inspection, admissible at court-martial?

9. What are the requirements for a lawful command search? What is the role of the commander who has control over the place where the property or person to be searched is located? How does "probable cause" factor into a command search?

10. What are the requirements for a valid gate or quarterdeck inspection in the United States (purpose, procedure, and so on). May evidence seized during a valid gate or quarterdeck inspection be admitted in a trial by court-martial?

CHAPTER EIGHT

SELF-INCRIMINATION

Because of a subordinate military person's obligation to respond to the command of his superior, Congress enacted Article 31 [UCMJ] to serve as a protection against the inherent tendency of that relationship, either directly or subtly, to induce an accused to respond to a question by the superior.

—*United States v. Lewis,* 12 M.J. 205, 206–7 (C.M.A. 1982)

Introduction

The military requires strict adherence to authority on the part of its members. Consequently, military superiors generally expect subordinates to immediately respond to their inquiries. Because military leaders also perform significant law enforcement functions, there is a natural tension between the obligation to provide information and the privilege against self-incrimination. While service members are protected by both statutory and constitutional safeguards, the nature of the military nevertheless places significant day-to-day pressures on the privilege against self-incrimination. This chapter addresses the parameters of the right against self-incrimination in the armed forces and focuses on the effect that military life has on the protections of that right.

Sources of the Right against Self-Incrimination

The Fifth Amendment to the Constitution provides:

> No person . . . shall be compelled in any criminal case to be a witness against himself.

Article 31(a) of the UCMJ provides the following:

> No person subject to this chapter may compel any person to incriminate himself or to answer a question the answer to which may intend to incriminate him.

Is there a difference between Article 31(a) and the Fifth Amendment? The Court of Appeals for the Armed Forces in *United States v. Armstrong,* 9 M.J. 374 (C.M.A. 1980), stated, "The clearly manifested intent of Congress in enacting Article 31(a) was merely to afford the serviceperson a privilege against self-incrimination which parallel[s] the constitutional privilege." Does the statement in *Armstrong* mean that soldiers and sailors receive exactly the same protections as the rest of society? Can you think of a situation in which that would not be possible?

Scope of the Right against Self-Incrimination

Exactly what does the privilege against self-incrimination protect? Military Rule of Evidence 301(a) states:

> General Rule. The privileges against self-incrimination provided by the Fifth Amendment to the Constitution of the United States and Article 31 are applicable only to evidence of a testimonial or communicative nature.

The above rule codifies the Supreme Court's holdings to the effect that the privilege against self-incrimination only protects individuals from creating evidence against themselves. See *Schmerber v. California,* 384 U.S. 757 (1966). Because verbal or written statements or testimony are "created" by an accused in response to questioning by investigators or prosecutors, such evidence is subject to the safeguards of the Fifth Amendment. Whether the compulsion of other types of evidence violates the Fifth Amendment and Article 31(a) depends on its "testimonial or communicative nature." The following case considers this issue with respect to blood samples.

UNITED STATES V. RALPH M. ARMSTRONG,
SPECIALIST FIVE, U.S. ARMY
U.S. COURT OF MILITARY APPEALS
9 M.J. 370
OCT. 27, 1980
Opinion: Everett, Chief Judge

On the evening of January 29, 1978, appellant drove with three passengers in his Mercedes automobile to a night club in Bremerhaven, Germany. While there they consumed a substantial amount of beer. After they had departed the night club, appellant's automobile crashed into the rear of a trailer-container parked on a city street. The passenger seated beside the appellant on the front seat was killed; the other passengers were injured to various degrees.

Appellant ran from the scene of the accident and was apprehended in flight by the German police. Shortly thereafter, he was confronted by Sergeant Luis of the American military police who detected a strong odor of alcohol on appellant's breath. Luis accompanied the appellant to an American hospital. However, the appellant was advised that "if you refuse to take the blood alcohol test, your USAREUR permit would be revoked." Moreover, Luis explained to appellant that the German police could transport him to a German medical facility where a blood specimen could be drawn from him by force and, if necessary, used in any subsequent German court proceedings. Thereupon, appellant agreed to take the blood alcohol test.

Because of the need to treat other persons injured in the crash, a delay of some three hours occurred before the blood was drawn. Just before the appellant took the blood test, he was re-advised of his rights and once again agreed to submit to the test. Two blood specimens were taken—one for use by American military authorities and the other for the German police.

At trial, defense counsel objected to the receipt in evidence of the blood-test results.

Whether the words of Sergeant Luis would constitute compulsion for purposes of Article 31(a), UCMJ, need not be determined, for the statutory language providing that no person may be compelled to "incriminate himself" was not intended to go beyond the scope of the Fifth Amendment. Hence it has no relevancy to blood specimens or other body fluids since, under the currently dominant "testimonial compulsion" approach to interpretation of the Fifth Amendment, such evidence is not subject to self-incrimination safeguards as it lacks the qualities of a communication by the suspect.

Therefore, we conclude that, in enacting the compulsory self-incrimination provision of Article 31, Congress did not plan for blood samples to be covered by the privilege. Instead, the clearly manifested intent of Congress in enacting Article 31(a) was merely to afford to servicepersons a privilege against self-incrimination which paralleled the constitutional privilege. Accordingly, Article 31 did not apply to the taking of blood specimens from Armstrong since body fluids are not within the purview of the Fifth Amendment.

Warnings

Warnings Required under Miranda v. Arizona

The Supreme Court in *Miranda v. Arizona,* 384 U.S. 436, 444 (1966), held the following:

The prosecution may not use statements, whether exculpatory or inculpatory, stemming from custodial interrogation of the defendant unless it demonstrates the use of procedural safeguards effective to secure the privilege against self-incrimination. By custodial interrogation, we mean questioning initiated by law enforcement officers after a person has been taken into custody or otherwise deprived of his freedom of action in any significant way. As for the procedural safeguards to be employed, unless other fully effective means are devised to inform accused persons of their right of silence and to assure a continuous opportunity to exercise it, the following measures are required. Prior to any questioning, the person must be warned that he has a right to remain silent, that any statement he does make may be used as evidence against him, and that he has a right to the presence of an attorney, either retained or appointed. The defendant may waive effectuation of these rights, provided the waiver is made voluntarily, knowingly and intelligently. If, however, he indicates in any manner and at any stage of the process that he wishes to consult with an attorney before speaking there can be no questioning. Likewise, if the individual is alone and indicates in any manner that he does not wish to be in-

terrogated, the police may not question him. The mere fact that he may have answered some questions or volunteered some statements on his own does not deprive him of the right to refrain from answering any further inquiries until he has consulted with an attorney and thereafter consents to be questioned.

Following *Miranda,* the military was faced with the question of whether the sweeping changes in criminal procedure brought on by that decision applied to its personnel. The next case addressed that issue.

UNITED STATES V. MICHAEL L. TEMPIA, AIRMAN THIRD
CLASS, U.S. AIR FORCE
UNITED STATES COURT OF MILITARY APPEALS
16 U.S.C.M.A. 629; 37 C.M.R. 249
APRIL 25, 1967
Opinion: Ferguson, Judge

On May 1, 1966, accused accompanied an Airman Keitel to the base library. Upon request, Keitel pointed out the location of the latrine. Accused left Keitel in the reading room and returned in five or six minutes. From other testimony, it appears he went to the ladies' rest room, stood in its partially opened door, and made obscene proposals to three young girls. The victims left the library, returned with one of their parents and the Air Police, and pointed accused out in the reading room. Accused was asked "to come back to the office" by one of the policemen. He did so.

At the Air Police office, accused was advised by Agent Blessing that he was suspected of taking indecent liberties with children; of his rights under Article 31; and "'that you may consult with legal counsel if you desire.'" Agent McQuary assisted Agent Blessing in the interview. It was immediately terminated, as Tempia stated "'he wanted counsel.'" He was released from custody.

On May 3, 1966, Tempia was again called to the "OSI Office" where he was once more advised by Blessing, in the presence of Agent Feczer, of his rights and entitlement to consult with counsel. Accused "'stated he had not yet received legal counsel.'" Blessing thereupon called Major Norman K. Hogue, base staff judge advocate, and made an appointment for Tempia.

Blessing's interview with Tempia terminated at 8:50 A.M., and the latter proceeded to Major Hogue's office.

Hogue informed him he was the staff judge advocate and "that I could not accept an attorney-client relationship with him because if I did, it would disqualify me from acting in my capacity as staff judge advocate." He further stated to Tempia that he would nevertheless "advise him of his legal rights and explained to him that this was different than acting as his defense counsel in that I did not want to hear any of his story, but I would answer any legal questions he had after I explained some rights to him."

Major Hogue also told accused he could not make a military lawyer available to him "as his defense counsel during that OSI investigation," but that he had the right to employ civilian counsel; would be given a reasonable time to do so; and that civilian counsel would be entitled to appear with him at the investigation. In addition, Hogue advised him of his rights under Article 31, and explained those rights to him, but:

As I say, I told him no military lawyer would be appointed to represent him during the OSI investigation or any investigation by the law enforcement agents on this base. I told him that if charges are preferred in his case, referred to trial by special court-martial or general court-martial, where it's referred to an investigation under Article 32b, he would be furnished a military lawyer at that time, one certified under Article 27b of the Uniform Code of Military Justice.

Following his session with Major Hogue, Tempia returned to the Office of Special Investigations, at 9:24 A.M. He "was then called in . . . readvised of his rights, readvised of the nature of the investigation and of his rights to seek legal counsel the second time." He stated he had consulted with Major Hogue, and did not desire further counsel as "they could not help him. . . . He said, 'They didn't do me no good.'" Thereafter, he was interrogated by Blessing and Feczer, to whom he began to dictate his confession.

The government urges upon us the proposition that the accused was not in custody, and, hence, the need for appropriate advice and assistance did not arise. We may at once dispose of this contention. The accused was apprehended on May 1, 1966; freed to seek counsel; recalled for interrogation on May 3, 1966; an appointment was made for him with Major Hogue, following which, he immediately returned to the Office of Special

Investigations, where his interrogation was successfully completed. The test to be applied is not whether the accused, technically, has been taken into custody, but absent that, whether he has been "otherwise deprived of his freedom of action in any significant way." Here, the accused was clearly summoned for interrogation. Had he not obeyed, he would have undoubtedly subjected himself to being penalized for a failure to repair. In the military, unlike civil life, a suspect may be required to report and submit to questioning quite without regard to warrants or other legal process. It ignores the realities of that situation to say that one ordered to appear for interrogation has not been significantly deprived of his freedom of action. Hence, we conclude there was "custodial interrogation" in this case.

The accused was fully advised of his rights under Article 31 and of his right to consult with counsel. On indicating a desire to speak with counsel, he was initially freed and, ultimately, on May 3, was referred to Major Hogue for further advice concerning his rights. But that officer went no further than to emphasize to the accused that he could not form an attorney-client relationship with him; to advise him again of his rights under Article 31; and to inform him he could retain civilian counsel at his own expense, who could appear at his interrogation. He specifically told accused no military lawyer would be appointed "to represent him during the OSI investigation or any investigation by the law enforcement agents on this base."

Miranda squarely points out "the person must be warned that he has a right to remain silent, that any statement he does make may be used as evidence against him, and that he has a right to the presence of an attorney, either retained or appointed." In addition, if the accused "indicates in any manner and at any stage of the process that he wishes to consult with an attorney before speaking there can be no questioning. Likewise, if the individual is alone and indicates in any manner that he does not wish to be interrogated, the police may not question him."

Undoubtedly, the advice given Tempia under Article 31, sufficed to inform him both of his right to remain silent and the purpose for which any statement he might make could be used. The advice as to counsel, however, was deficient. First, accused was only warned by the agents that he was entitled to consult with counsel. When Major Hogue elaborated on this proposition, he limited the availability of counsel to private attorneys employed by the accused at his own expense. He specifically told accused no attorney would be appointed to represent him in any law enforcement investigation. This is exactly contrary to the information which, under *Miranda* must be preliminarily communicated to the accused.

Article 31(b) Warnings

The military justice system has a long history of providing warnings to service members; much longer, in fact, than most civilian criminal systems. The 1917 Manual for Courts-Martial, for example, recognized the inherently coercive atmosphere that may exist between superiors and subordinates and advised investigators to "warn the person investigated that he need not answer any question that might tend to incriminate him." By 1921, the Manual for Courts-Martial expanded the protection by requiring investigators and other military superiors to give warnings regarding self-incrimination. Under the Elston Act of 1948 and the 1949 Manual for Courts-Martial, a failure to provide warnings caused the exclusion of an accused's statement at court-martial, unless the government could show that the accused was otherwise aware of the right to remain silent. This tradition of broad protections against self-incrimination played a significant role in the adoption of Article 31(b):

> No person subject to this chapter may interrogate, or request any statement from an accused or a person suspected of an offense without first informing him of the nature of the accusation and advising him that he does not have to make any statement regarding the offense of which he is accused or suspected and that any statement made by him may be used as evidence against him in a trial by court-martial.

The language of Article 31(b) indicates that an accused must be warned if he or she is "suspected" of an offense. In contrast, *Miranda* warnings are necessary when an accused is undergoing "custodial inter-

rogation." Also, the Article 31(b) warning does not mention the right to counsel, while *Miranda* provides the right to have an attorney present during questioning. Which, if either, provides greater protection? Which warning will likely occur first?

Note that the military courts construe Articles 31(a) and (b) in significantly different ways. The Court of Military Appeals explained in *United States v. Ravenel,* 26 M.J. 344, 349 (C.M.A. 1988):

> This Court clearly is on record that, while Article 31(a) and the Fifth Amendment coincide in scope and while Article 31(b) was enacted to serve the purpose of avoiding coerced statements in violation of both provisions, unique factors in the military environment unknown in the civilian setting lead us to interpret Article 31(b) as being broader in the scope of its protection than is the mandate of *Miranda.* Both the subtleties of the superior-subordinate relationship and the conditioned response, consciously created from the first day of basic training, to respond almost unthinkingly to the wishes of a military superior can permit no other result.

Thus, the military courts hold that Article 31(a) is identical in scope to the Fifth Amendment, but that the protections of Article 31(b) are broader than those in *Miranda.* How is Article 31(b) broader in its protections than *Miranda?* Does the answer hinge on when a person must be warned under Article 31(b)?

WHEN ARTICLE 31(B) WARNINGS ARE REQUIRED

Following enactment of Article 31(b), the military courts initially construed the provision in a literal manner. In *United States v. Wilson,* 8 C.M.R. 48, 54–55 (C.M.A. 1953), the Court of Military Appeals concluded that a "person suspected of an offense" must be warned without regard to the purpose or nature of the questioning. Do you foresee problems with such a rigid standard? In *United States v. Duga,* 10 M.J. 206 (C.M.A. 1981), the Court of Military Appeals addressed the "literal interpretation" standard established in *Wilson* as follows:

Careful consideration of the history of the requirement of the warning, compels a conclusion that its purpose is to avoid impairment of the constitutional guarantee against compulsory self-incrimination. Because of the effect of superior rank or official position upon one subject to military law, the mere asking of a question under certain circumstances is the equivalent of a command. A person subjected to these pressures may rightly be regarded as deprived of his freedom to answer or to remain silent. Under such circumstances, we do not hesitate to reverse convictions whenever the accused has been deprived of the full benefit of the rights granted him by Congress. By the same token, however, it is our duty to see to it that such rights are not extended beyond the reasonable intendment of the code at the expense of substantial justice and on the grounds that are fanciful or unsubstantial.

Based on the above reasoning, the Court of Military Appeals held that Article 31(b) "applies only to situations in which, because of military rank, duty, or other similar relationship, there might be subtle pressure on a suspect to respond to an inquiry." When would such a situation exist? The following case considers that issue.

UNITED STATES V. AIRMAN JOHN G. LOUKAS,
UNITED STATES AIR FORCE
COURT OF MILITARY APPEALS
29 M.J. 385
FEBRUARY 13, 1990
Opinion: Sullivan, Judge

The appellant was the loadmaster aboard a C-130 flight bound for Trinidad, Bolivia, where it was to receive certain unspecified cargo. The assistant crew chief, who was alone in the empty cargo section with the appellant at one point in the flight, noticed that the latter was acting in a decidedly irrational manner, pointing and calling out to invisible persons. The appellant handed the assistant crew chief his sidearm, a .38 calibre pistol, while urging that he take it. The assistant crew chief did so and reported the incident to his immediate superior, the aforementioned SSgt Dryer. SSgt Dryer confronted the appellant and observed that he was continuing to hallucinate. This behavior and the appel-

lant's general appearance, caused SSgt Dryer to suspect that the appellant was under the influence of a drug. He was concerned for the security of the aircraft and its crew. Accordingly, he asked whether the appellant had taken drugs. The appellant responded that he had not. SSgt Dryer asked in a more insistent tone what the appellant had taken, or words to that effect. The appellant, in reply, acknowledged that he had used cocaine the evening before.

Sergeant Dryer was the crew chief of an operational military aircraft who was similarly responsible for the plane's safety and that of its crew, including the accused, his military subordinate. In addition, his questioning of the accused was limited to that required to fulfill his operational responsibilities, and there was no evidence suggesting his inquiries were designed to evade constitutional or codal rights. The unquestionable urgency of the threat and immediacy of the crew chief's response underscore the legitimate operational nature of his queries. Under our precedents, the prosecution satisfactorily showed that Article 31 warnings were not required in this operational context.

The reasoning in *Loukas* has been construed to mean that absent a law enforcement or disciplinary purpose an investigation is exempt from Article 31(b). In a recent case, the Court of Military Appeals concluded that an army pediatrician did not have to give Article 31(b) warnings to an accused when questioning him about injuries to his four-year-old son. See *United States v. Bowerman*, 39 M.J. 219 (C.M.A. 1994). Based on these precedents, when are Article 31(b) warnings required? When are they not? See chapter 4 concerning the applicability of Article 31(b) at nonjudicial punishment and administrative separation hearings.

WHO MUST PROVIDE ARTICLE 31(B) WARNINGS
The above discussion tells us generally when warnings are necessary based on the purpose of the questioning. However, the UCMJ provides that only persons subject to the UCMJ must comply with Article 31. Active duty personnel are always subject to the UCMJ and therefore have to abide by Article 31 at all times. Military Rule of Evidence 305(b)(1) also ex-

plains that "'a person subject to the code' includes a person acting as a knowing agent of a military unit or of a person subject to the code." Who is a "knowing agent"? As a general rule, civilian and foreign law enforcement personnel are not agents of the military. The military courts hold, however, that civilians who act as "instruments of the military" are subject to Article 31 requirements. See *United States v. Quillen*, 27 M.J. 312 (C.M.A. 1988) (exchange store detective required to provide Article 31[b] warnings to soldier suspected of shoplifting). Would this include persons who work for the Naval Criminal Investigative Service?

Remedies

What happens to evidence that is obtained in contravention of Article 31 or the Fifth Amendment? Article 31(d) explains the remedy for a violation of the protections contained in the UCMJ:

> No statement obtained from any person in violation of this article . . . may be received in evidence against him in a trial by court-martial.

Like Article 31, a violation of the Fifth Amendment renders evidence inadmissible at court-martial. This prohibition on the introduction of evidence is known as the "exclusionary rule." It applies to the unlawful compulsion of evidence in violation of Article 31(a) and the Fifth Amendment and a failure to provide *Miranda* or Article 31(b) warnings. Does the exclusionary rule apply at forums other than courts-martial, such as administrative proceedings? See chapter 4.

A failure to comply with Article 31 is also a violation of the UCMJ. Article 98 provides that "any person . . . who . . . knowingly and intentionally fails to enforce or comply with any provision of this chapter regulating the proceedings before, during, or after trial of an accused; shall be punished as a court-martial may direct." The intent of Congress in enacting Article 98 was to protect the procedural rights of service members, and, in particular, to enforce respect

for the right against self-incrimination. Is it feasible to enforce this provision? Do you think prosecutions for violations of Article 98 are common?

Study Questions

1. Which, if either, provides broader protections, Article 31(a) or the Fifth Amendment?

2. Which of the following may lawfully be required of a suspect *without* advising the suspect of his or her rights under Article 31(b), UCMJ?

    a. Provide fingerprints.

    b. Provide urine samples.

    c. Submit to the taking of a blood sample.

    d. Provide voice exemplars (samples).

    e. All of the above may lawfully be required.

3. When must a *Miranda* warning be provided to a service member? How is "custodial interrogation" defined by the Supreme Court? Why is it important?

4. What is the difference between *Miranda* warnings and Article 31(b) advisements? When are Article 31(b) warnings required? Does the purpose of the questioning affect whether Article 31(b) applies?

5. Before requesting a statement from a service member whom a naval officer suspects has committed an offense under the UCMJ (but who is not in custody or otherwise being deprived of his freedom of action in any significant way), she must first do which of the following:

    a. Inform him of the nature of the offense.

    b. Advise him that he does not have to make any statement regarding the offense and that any statement he does make may be used against him in trial by court-martial.

    c. Inform him he has the right to consult with counsel before questioning and to have counsel present during questioning.

    d. Both steps (a) and (b) must be taken.

    e. All of the steps above must be taken.

6. What is the "exclusionary rule"? Where and when does it apply?

CHAPTER NINE

MILITARY INVESTIGATIONS

One of the primary purposes of conducting investigations of any type is to identify ways to improve the effectiveness and efficiency of the Department or of its components. Investigations alone, however, do not achieve that purpose. Put differently, investigations are means, not ends.

—JAG Manual 0203

Introduction

The number and types of investigations conducted by the military is rivaled by few institutions. This is due in large measure to the tight control that the military must maintain over its personnel and property. Investigations of damage to personnel or property, as well as probes into violations of laws and regulations, are just some of the types of inquiries that the services conduct. While military investigations serve different purposes, many of these probes share similar characteristics. This chapter will discuss the most common varieties of investigations conducted in the armed forces, and the relationship between those inquiries.

Criminal Investigations

The U.S. Navy and Marine Corps divide criminal offenses into two categories: major and minor. This distinction is important not only because it has an impact on the forum where the offense is adjudicated (see chapters 4 and 5) but also because it determines the command, organization, or agency that will conduct the inquiry.

Major Criminal Offenses

SECNAVINST 5520.3 describes the responsibility for investigating major criminal offenses in the U.S. Navy and Marine Corps:

> Within the Department of the Navy, the Naval Criminal Investigative Service (NCIS) is primarily responsible for investigating actual, suspected or alleged major criminal offenses committed against a person, the United States Government, or private property, including the attempts or conspiracies to commit such offenses. A major criminal offense (felony) is defined for purposes of this instruction as one punishable under the Uniform Code of Military Justice by confinement for a term of more than 1 year, or similarly framed federal statutes, state, local or foreign laws or regulation. Incidents of actual, suspected or alleged major criminal offenses coming to command attention must be immediately referred to NCIS whether occurring on or off an installation or ship and regardless of whether they are being investigated by state, local or other authorities. The referral to NCIS should be made before any substantive investigative steps are considered by the command, such as interrogation of suspect(s) or conducting searches of property, as to which individuals have an expectation to privacy, unless such steps are necessary to protect life or property or to prevent the destruction of evidence.

Why is there a concern that commands will conduct an inquiry into a major offense prior to notifying NCIS? Note that the Fourth Amendment may require the exclusion of evidence which is derived from illegally obtained evidence. See chapter 7. Is NCIS concerned that its investigation of a major offense will be tainted by mistakes made by the command involved?

SECNAVINST 5520.3 also explains how criminal investigations among different agencies are coordinated:

> A major criminal offense may constitute a violation of both military and civil law, and may involve both military personnel and civilians. Primary or concurrent jurisdiction may also rest with another agency outside of the Department of the Navy. Only NCIS has the authority to make investigative referrals in these instances. When Department of the Navy commands or personnel are contacted by other law enforcement organizations in connection with investigative matters, the matter must be referred to NCIS for coordination. This policy includes inquiries by federal, state, local and foreign law enforcement or investigative agencies when the matter involves security or major criminal offenses, as previously defined.

The above section discusses jurisdiction of the military and civilian agencies. Does jurisdiction of courts-martial depend on the location of the crime? See the discussion of jurisdiction over offenses and *United States v. Solario* in chapter 3.

Minor Criminal Offenses

SECNAVINST 5520.3 provides guidance on investigation of minor offenses:

> A minor criminal offense is one punishable under the UCMJ by confinement of one year or less, or carrying similar punishment by federal, state, local or foreign statute or regulation, and lacking any of the considerations enumerated in the discussion of major criminal offenses.
>
> Use of Command Investigators. Many navy and marine corps commands maintain an investigative capability. Use of command investigators for criminal and security investigations shall be limited to minor offenses, as defined in this instruction, except when NCIS has declined jurisdiction. This stipulation does not preclude command investigations in those instances where NCIS is not investigating or where the offense is purely military in nature (e.g., unauthorized absence).

Note that "command investigators" are personnel specifically trained in criminal investigative techniques. In the navy these personnel are usually master-at-arms. In addition to command investigators, officers and senior enlisted also conduct inquiries into minor offenses. These "preliminary inquiries" provide the information necessary to dispose of cases at nonjudicial punishment or through nonpunitive measures. As with NCIS agents and command investigators, preliminary inquiry officers gather evidence of the suspected offense. However, they also provide information regarding an accused's military performance and behavior and any other information that will provide the command with a full understanding of both the case and the accused. A preliminary inquiry officer also makes a specific recommendation concerning disposition and punishment of the suspected offense. See figures 4-2 and 4-3 in chapter 4. A preliminary inquiry officer normally interviews all material witnesses as well as the accused. How does the Fourth Amendment apply to a search conducted by a preliminary inquiry officer? What about the Fifth Amendment or Article 31, UCMJ? See chapters 4, 7, and 8.

Intelligence and Security Investigations

SECNAVINST 5520.3 explains the nature of criminal intelligence investigations:

> Criminal intelligence operations are defined as formalized programs targeting persons or organizations whose criminal activity significantly affects the naval establishment, or those activities designed to gain information of a criminal intelligence nature for law enforcement purposes. A high degree of specialized training and experience is necessary for the successful accomplishment of these operations, and, to the extent that they are undertaken within the Department of the Navy, they will be done exclusively by NCIS, regardless of location.

The following case considers the constitutional implications of an investigation into the compromise of classified information.

UNITED STATES V. CLAYTON J. LONETREE, SERGEANT, U.S. MARINE CORPS
U.S. COURT OF MILITARY APPEALS
35 M.J. 396
SEPTEMBER 28, 1992
Sentelle, Circuit Judge

Sergeant Clayton Lonetree was a Marine Corps embassy guard on duty in Moscow when he met Soviet agent Violetta Seina in a subway station. He began a romantic liaison with Seina and eventually passed confidential information to a Soviet agent named Yefimov (a.k.a. "Uncle Sasha"). Ignorant of his activities, the Marine Corps transferred Lonetree to guard duty at the U.S. Embassy in Vienna, where he continued his contact with the Soviets through an agent named Lyssove (a.k.a. "George"). His double life came to an end on December 14, 1986, when, in the first of a series of meetings with two Vienna-station U.S. intelligence agents known as "Big John" and "Little John" ("the Johns"), Lonetree disclosed his involvement with the Soviet agents.

The Naval Investigative Service (NIS) took over questioning Lonetree from the Johns on December 24, 1986, and obtained a more detailed account of the information Lonetree had passed to the Soviets. Based on Lonetree's confessions to the Johns and the NIS, as well as verification through a U.S. government agent known as "John Doe" of Lonetree's relationship with George, a general court-martial found Lonetree guilty of conspiracy to commit espionage, disobeying navy security regulations, disclosing the identities of covert agents, willfully communicating information in violation of the Federal Espionage Act, and committing espionage.

Lonetree argued that his confessions should have been suppressed because they were induced by false promises of confidentiality made by the Johns, promises the Johns violated by sharing Lonetree's statements with the NIS. It is uncontroverted that Lonetree first approached Big John at the U.S. Embassy in Vienna on December 14, 1986, and explained that he had become "deeply involved" with Soviet agents. Big John had his subordinate, Little John, maintain a dialogue with Lonetree, during which Lonetree provided ever-increasing details about his work and contacts with the Soviets. The prosecution concedes that "in the interest of gaining Lonetree's trust Little John assured appellant that any information would be treated as 'confidential.'" Despite this assurance, the Johns divulged Lonetree's confidences to NIS investigating agents brought in to interrogate Lonetree and testified at Lonetree's trial about the statements he made.

Consistent with both military and civilian authority, for an inducement to be unlawful and thus render the resulting confession involuntary, an inducement must be made by someone acting in a law enforcement capacity or in a position superior to the person making the confession. Lonetree does not attempt to convince us that the Johns were somehow his superiors, asserting instead that, because Little John was a U.S. government official, his false promissory inducement was unlawful. As explained above, though, Lonetree needs to show more than that the Johns were affiliated with the U.S. government; he must show that the Johns were acting in a law enforcement capacity when they made their inductive promise of confidentiality. The Johns displayed none of the indicia of law enforcement actors: They did not engage in custodial or coercive discussions with Lonetree; they made clear they did not represent the command or law enforcement entities; and they did not attempt to restrict Lonetree's movements or suggest they possessed the authority to do so. In fact, all the meetings between Lonetree and the Johns were arranged with Lonetree's approval, and he even cancelled one scheduled meeting. Lonetree does not refute this. Because Lonetree does not provide a scintilla of evidence indicating that the Johns were engaged in a law enforcement activity when they made their promise of confidentiality, we hold that Lonetree's confession was voluntary, so it was properly admitted at his court-martial.

The *Lonetree* case refers to Article 31(d), which provides in part that "no statement obtained from any person in violation of this article, or through the use of coercion, unlawful influence, or unlawful inducement may be received in evidence against him in a trial by court-martial." The case also discusses Article 31(b). When are rights warnings under 31(b) necessary? See chapter 8. Is the court's holding in *Lonetree* consistent with *United States v. Loukas* in chapter 8?

There are also special requirements for investigating compromises of classified documents. OP-NAVINST 5510.1 requires an immediate preliminary inquiry in every case in which classified information has been "lost, compromised or subjected to compromise." Following completion of the preliminary

inquiry, the command with custodial responsibility over the material must convene a JAG Manual investigation and notify NCIS if it suspects that a compromise of classified information may have occurred and that one or more of the following conditions are also true: (1) the probability of harm to the national security cannot be discounted, (2) significant security weaknesses may have been revealed, or (3) punitive disciplinary action is contemplated.

A JAG Manual investigation of a possible compromise addresses all aspects of the possible security violation, including accountability, procedures, and harm to the national security. JAG Manual investigations are discussed in the next section.

Administrative Investigations

The U.S. Navy and Marine Corps also conduct inquiries primarily focused not on criminal culpability, but on issues such as efficient command administration, claims for or against the government, safety, training, leadership, and injuries to personnel. These inquiries serve to collect and record information and are purely advisory in nature. The findings of such inquiries do not constitute final determinations or legal judgments, and their recommendations are not binding. The report of an administrative investigation may, however, become the basis for actions such as reevaluation of operational practices or standards, redesign and improvement of material, modification or adoption of instructions, regulations, and procedures, disciplinary action and reply to inquiries concerning incidents of public interest. The types of inquiries discussed in this section are all administrative in nature; however, each variety of investigation (JAG Manual investigations, line of duty determinations, and safety inquiries) serve a different purpose.

JAG Manual Investigations

Chapter 2 of the JAG Manual contains the regulations concerning administrative fact-finding bodies

(JAG Manual investigations). There are three types of administrative fact-finding bodies: command investigations, litigation report investigations, and courts or boards of inquiries. Before deciding which variety of fact-finding body to convene, a preliminary inquiry into the matter is usually necessary. JAG Manual 0204 describes a preliminary inquiry:

> Purpose. A preliminary inquiry serves as an analytical tool to determine whether additional investigation is warranted and, if so, how it is to be conducted. The preliminary inquiry is the foundation for the subsequent exercise of the convening authority's discretion and is not intended to develop facts extensively or to serve as a medium for analyzing facts.
>
> Method. A convening authority may conduct a preliminary inquiry personally or through designees. The preliminary inquiry may be accomplished in any manner considered sufficient by the convening authority. No particular format is required, but the convening authority may choose to document the outcome in writing.

The preliminary inquiry is a screening method to determine if a JAG Manual investigation is necessary. As noted above, there are three types of JAG Manual investigations. JAG Manual 0209a describes the most common of these inquiries, the command investigation:

> A command investigation functions to gather, analyze, and record relevant information about an incident or event of primary interest to command authorities. Most investigations will be of this nature. Command investigations may, for example, be used to inquire into
> (1) significant property losses (minor property losses may be adequately documented through other means in most cases), other than damage to or destruction of public quarters since such incidents are likely to result in claims against or for the Government and, consequently, require a litigation-report investigation;
> (2) incidents in which a member of the naval service, as a result of possible misconduct, incurs a disease or injury that may result in a permanent disability or a physical inability to perform duty for a period exceeding 24

hours (distinguished from a period of hospitalization for evaluation or observation);
> (3) deaths of military personnel, or of civilian personnel occurring aboard an activity under military control, apparently caused by suicide or under other unusual circumstances; and
> (4) aircraft incidents, groundings, floodings, fires, and collisions not determined to be major incidents.

Paragraph 0209c describes the responsibilities of commanders to convene command investigations:

> (1) Generally, an officer in command (including an officer-in-charge) is responsible for initiating command investigations into incidents occurring within, or involving personnel of, the command.
> (2) If a commander believes that the investigation of an incident is impractical or inappropriate for the command to investigate, another command may be requested to conduct the investigation.
> (3) Whenever more than one command is involved in an incident requiring investigation, a single investigation should be conducted. Such an investigation may be convened by the officer in command of any of the activities concerned, and all the activities shall cooperate in the investigation.

Paragraph 0209e provides the procedures for conducting a command investigation:

> (1) A command investigation
>   (a) is convened in writing;
>   (b) is conducted by one or more persons in the Department;
>   (c) collects evidence by personal interviews, telephone inquiries, or written correspondence;
>   (d) is documented in writing in the manner prescribed by the CA in the convening order;
>   (e) does not involve hearings; and
>   (f) may contain sworn statements signed by witnesses.

Line officers without significant training in investigations and legal matters usually conduct command investigations. What are the advantages/disadvantages of using such investigators? In certain situations, the investigating officer must interview persons suspected of violations of the UCMJ. Should the investigating officer advise such persons of the right to remain silent under Article 31(b)? Does it make any difference that a JAG Manual investigation is an administrative inquiry? See chapter 8.

Following completion of a command investigation, the commander convening the inquiry may act on the results of the inquiry in one of several ways. JAG Manual 0209g sets forth the commander's options:

A convening authority may determine that the investigation is of no interest to anyone outside the command, and, unless otherwise directed by superior authority, may choose to treat it as an internal report. If the convening authority intends to forward the report of investigation:

(1) Upon receiving a command investigation report, the convening authority shall review or have the report reviewed, and either endorse the report in writing or return it to the investigating officer for further investigation. In the endorsement, the convening authority may approve, disapprove, modify, or add to the findings of fact, opinions, and recommendations. The convening authority may also concur in or disagree with recommendations which the convening authority cannot implement at the convening authority's level. If the convening authority did not require opinions and recommendations in the convening order, then the convening authority shall state such opinions and make such recommendations as deemed appropriate. The convening authority shall also indicate what corrective action, if any, is warranted and has been or will be taken.

(2) The convening authority shall retain a copy of the report and forward the original, through the chain-of-command (including area coordinators when appropriate), to the officer who exercises general court-martial convening authority over the convening authority.

Based on the above, when will a commander treat a command investigation as an internal report? Do you think commanders generally prefer keeping inquiries internal? The JAG Manual also provides specific requirements for the investigation of certain types of incidents (for example, aircraft accidents, vehicle ac-

cidents, ship groundings and collisions, and stranding of ships). See JAG Manual 0226–0227 and 0230–0237 for the requirements of investigating these specific varieties of incidents.

The second variety of JAG Manual inquiry, the litigation report investigation, is described in JAG Manual 0210:

Purpose. [W]hen an incident or event is likely to result in claims or civil litigation against or for DON or the United States . . . the primary purpose of the resulting investigation is often to prepare to defend the legal interests of the Department and the United States. A command should contact a judge advocate at the earliest opportunity prior to commencing a litigation-report investigation to determine if a litigation-report investigation is the appropriate type of investigation to be conducted under the circumstances. Investigations into such incidents must be conducted under the direction and supervision of a judge advocate, and be protected from disclosure to anyone who does not have an official need to know.

Comparison with Command Investigations:
(1) Unlike a command investigation, a litigation-report investigation must be
(a) convened only after consultation with a cognizant judge advocate;
(b) conducted under the direction and supervision of that judge advocate;
(c) conducted primarily in anticipation of claims or litigation; and
(d) forwarded to the Judge Advocate General.
(2) Like a command investigation, a litigation-report investigation
(a) may not be used to investigate a major incident;
(b) may not have designated parties; and
(c) does not involve hearings.

Why do litigation-report inquiries involve naval lawyers? What types of incidents may result in a claim for or against the government? JAG Manual 0210e describes the procedures for conducting a litigation report investigation:

(1) A litigation-report investigation shall

(a) be convened in writing;

(b) be conducted by one or more persons in DON under the direction and supervision of the cognizant judge advocate;

(c) collect evidence by personal interviews, telephone inquiries, written correspondence, or other means;

(d) be documented in writing in the manner prescribed by the cognizant judge advocate; and

(e) shall *not* contain statements signed by witnesses. (Signed statements are subject to discovery and release to opposing parties in civil litigation even if provided to an attorney.)

(2) During the course of a litigation-report investigation, the investigating officer shall be guided by the cognizant judge advocate and shall consult frequently as the investigation progresses.

The third variety of JAG Manual investigation, the court or board of inquiry, is a formal procedure to investigate "major incidents." Following the gun turret explosion on board USS *Iowa* in 1989, the navy convened a one-officer inquiry (then known as an informal investigation) to probe into the tragedy. The two-star admiral conducting the inquiry concluded that the explosion was most probably caused by a detonation device placed in the turret by a troubled sailor. The media and Congress criticized both the findings of the investigation and the navy's selection of a relatively informal fact-finding procedure to delve into the incident. The navy subsequently revised the JAG Manual to ensure that a court or board of inquiry is convened for all events considered to be "major" and for serious and significant acts.

The JAG Manual defines a "major incident":

An extraordinary incident occurring during the course of official duties resulting in multiple deaths, substantial property loss, or substantial harm to the environment where the circumstances suggest a significant departure from the expected level of professionalism, leadership, judgment, communication, state of material readiness, or other relevant standard. Substantial property loss or other harm is that which greatly exceeds what is normally encountered in the course of day to

day operations. These cases are often accompanied by national public and press interest and significant congressional attention. They may also have the potential of undermining public confidence in the Naval service. That the case is a major incident may be apparent when it is first reported or as additional facts become known.

JAG Manual 0211b describes a court of inquiry:

(1) Convened by persons authorized to convene general courts-martial or so designated by the secretary of the navy.

(2) Consists of at least three commissioned officers as members and also has appointed legal counsel for the court. It may also include advisors appointed to assist the members.

(3) Convened by written appointing order.

(4) Uses a hearing procedure. Takes all testimony under oath and records all open proceedings verbatim, except arguments of counsel, whether or not directed to do so in the appointing order.

(5) Designates as parties persons subject to the UCMJ whose conduct is subject to inquiry.

(6) Designates as parties persons subject to the UCMJ or employed by the Department of Defense who have a direct interest in the subject under inquiry and request to be so designated.

(7) Has the power to order military personnel to appear, testify, and produce evidence, and the power to subpoena civilian witnesses to appear, testify, and produce evidence.

Less formal than a court of inquiry is a board of inquiry. JAG Manual 0211c details the characteristics of a board of inquiry:

(1) Convened by persons authorized to convene general courts-martial.

(2) Consists of one or more commissioned officers, and should have appointed legal counsel for the board.

(3) Convened by written appointing order, which should direct that all testimony be taken under oath and all open proceedings, except counsel's argument, recorded verbatim. Persons whose conduct is subject to inquiry or who have a direct interest in the subject of the inquiry may be designated parties by the convening

authority in the appointing order. The convening authority may also authorize the board to designate parties during the proceedings.

(4) Uses a hearing.

(5) Does not possess power to subpoena civilian witnesses . . . but can order naval personnel to appear, testify, and produce evidence.

The responsibility for convening courts and boards of inquiry is discussed in JAG Manual 0211e:

(1) The officer exercising general court-martial convening authority over the command most involved in a major or serious incident, if a flag or general officer, or the first flag or general officer in the chain-of-command, or any superior flag officer in the chain-of-command, will immediately take cognizance over the case as the convening authority.

(2) Whenever more than one command is involved in a major or serious incident requiring formal investigation, a single investigation shall be conducted. The common superior commander shall convene the investigation in such cases, unless that officer's conduct or performance of duty may be subject to inquiry, in which case the next superior in the chain-of-command shall convene the investigation.

Based on the above, what are the differences between a court of inquiry and a board of inquiry? Consider which investigative body has the power to subpoena civilians. Note that a court of inquiry must designate persons as "party," and a board of inquiry may do so. The JAG Manual defines a "party" and explains the rights of a person so designated:

Party. A "party" is an individual . . . whose conduct is either the subject of the inquiry or has a direct interest in the inquiry.

Subject to inquiry. A person's conduct or performance of duty is "subject to inquiry" when the person is involved in the incident or event under investigation in such a way that either disciplinary action may follow, that his rights or privileges may be adversely affected, or that his personal reputation or professional standing may be jeopardized.

Direct interest. A person has a "direct interest" in the subject of inquiry:

(1) When the findings, opinions, or recommendations of the fact-finding body may, in view of his relation to the incident or circumstances under investigation, reflect questionable or unsatisfactory conduct or performance of duty; or

(2) When the findings, opinions, or recommendations may relate to a matter over which the person has a duty or right to exercise official control.

Rights. A person duly designated a party before a fact-finding body shall be advised of and accorded the following rights:

(1) To be given due notice of such designation.

(2) To be present during the proceedings, but not when the investigation is cleared for deliberations.

(3) To be represented by counsel.

(4) To examine and to object to the introduction of physical and documentary evidence and written statements.

(5) To object to the testimony of witnesses and to cross-examine witnesses other than his own.

(6) To introduce evidence.

(7) To testify as a witness.

(8) To refuse to incriminate himself; and, if accused or suspected of an offense, to be informed of the nature of the accusation and advised that he does not have to make any statement regarding the offense of which he is accused or suspected; and that any statement made by him may be used as evidence against him in a trial by court-martial.

(9) To make a voluntary statement, oral or written, to be included in the record of proceedings.

(10) To make an argument at the conclusion of presentation of evidence.

(11) To be properly advised concerning the Privacy Act of 1974.

(12) To challenge members.

Compare the procedural protections afforded a party in an administrative proceeding with an accused at court-martial. Who has more rights? See chapter 3.

Line of Duty Determinations

When service members incur an injury that might result in permanent disability or that results in the physical inability to perform duty for a period exceeding twenty-four hours, a finding concerning the member's responsibility for the injury is necessary. For members of the naval service, these findings are known as line of duty determinations.

JAG Manual 0222a explains why line of duty determinations are necessary:

> Line of duty/misconduct determinations are extremely important since they control several personnel actions, the most important of which is the awarding of disability retirement and severance pay. These determinations will also effect extensions of enlistment; changes in longevity, severance, and retirement pay multipliers; forfeitures of pay; reserve incapacitation pay and medical care entitlement; and benefits administered by the Department of Veterans Affairs.

JAG Manual 0221a provides the specifics on when line of duty findings are required:

> If a member incurs a disease or injury that may result in a permanent disability or that results in the member's physical inability to perform duty for a period exceeding 24 hours (as distinguished from a period of hospitalization for evaluation or observation), then determining whether the disease or injury was incurred in the line of duty or as the result of misconduct is very important. An injury or disease suffered by a member of the naval service will, however, be presumed to have been incurred in the line of duty and not as a result of misconduct unless contrary findings are made.

JAG Manual 0229 discusses the relationship of line of duty determinations to disciplinary actions:

> An adverse line of duty/misconduct determination is not a punitive measure. If warranted, commanders should take independent disciplinary action. Similarly, a favorable line of duty/misconduct determination does not preclude separate disciplinary action. Nor is such a favorable determination relevant or binding on the issue of guilt or innocence of the member in a separate disciplinary proceeding.

JAG Manual 0223 sets forth when an injury is incurred not in the line of duty:

> (1) as a result of the member's own misconduct;
> (2) while avoiding duty by deserting;
> (3) while absent without leave and such absence materially interfered with the performance of required military duties . . . ;
> (4) while confined under sentence of a court-martial that included an unremitted dishonorable discharge; or
> (5) while confined under sentence of a civil court following conviction of an offense that is defined as a felony by the law of the jurisdiction where convicted.

"Misconduct" as that term is used in line of duty determinations is explained in JAG Manual 0224:

> Generally. "Misconduct," as used in this chapter, is a term of art. It is more than just inappropriate behavior. An injury or disease is the result of a member's misconduct if it is either intentionally incurred or is the result of willful neglect which demonstrates a reckless disregard for the foreseeable and likely consequences of the conduct involved. Simple or ordinary negligence, or carelessness, standing alone, does not constitute misconduct. The fact that the conduct violates law, regulation, or order, or is engaged in while intoxicated, does not, of itself, constitute a basis for a misconduct determination.
>
> Presumption. An injury or disease suffered by a member of the naval service is presumed to have been incurred in the line of duty and not to be the result of misconduct. Clear and convincing evidence is required to overcome this presumption.

"Clear and convincing evidence" is a higher standard of proof than preponderance of the evidence, but less than beyond a reasonable doubt. See chapters 3 and 4. Why is there a more difficult burden in line of duty cases than in nonjudicial punishment? See JAG Manual 0222 above which addresses the ramifications of a not in the line of duty finding.

JAG Manual 0225 discusses the relationship between misconduct and line of duty:

> For purposes of these regulations, "misconduct" can never be "in line of duty." Hence, a finding or determination that an injury was incurred as a result of the member's own misconduct must be accompanied by a

finding or determination that the member's injury was incurred "not in line of duty." It is permissible, however, to find that an injury was incurred "not as a result of misconduct" and "not in line of duty." As an example, a member who is absent without authority may be injured by a felonious assault or struck by a vehicle driven by a drunken driver. Obviously, the injury was incurred through no fault of the member, but if the absence materially interfered with the performance of his required military duties a finding of "not in line of duty" must result.

Possible Findings. The only possible combinations of findings are:

(1) "In line of duty" and "not due to the member's own misconduct";

(2) "Not in line of duty" and "not due to the member's own misconduct"; and

(3) "Not in line of duty" and "due to the member's own misconduct."

Which of the above findings is favorable for the service member? Which is not? Note that the above section references the connection between unauthorized absence and line of duty determinations. JAG Manual 0225c specifically addresses this issue:

(1) Whether absence without leave materially interferes with the performance of required military duties necessarily depends upon the facts of each situation, applying a standard of reality and common sense. No definite rule can be formulated as to what constitutes "material interference." Generally speaking, absence in excess of 24 hours constitutes a material interference unless evidence to the contrary exists. Similarly, an absence of shorter duration will not be considered a material interference unless there is clear and convincing evidence to establish the contrary.

Note that under 10 U.S.C., Section 1207, a service member is ineligible for physical disability retirement or physical disability severance benefits if the disability was incurred during a period of unauthorized absence, regardless of the length of such absence and regardless of whether such absence constituted a material interference with the performance of required military duties.

The method of investigating line of duty cases and the means of recording the findings is addressed in JAG Manual 0230:

Each injury or disease requiring line of duty/misconduct determinations must be the subject of a preliminary inquiry. If, however, following a preliminary inquiry the conditions set forth in subparagraph c below are met, then the member's command need not convene an investigation and need not report the line of duty/misconduct determinations separately.

Entry in Health or Dental Record. An investigation need not be convened and a report need not be forwarded concerning misconduct and line of duty when, in the opinion of the medical officer (or senior representative of a medical department), with the concurrence of the commanding officer, the injury or disease was incurred "in line of duty" and "not as a result of the member's own misconduct" and appropriate entries to this effect have been made in the member's health or dental record.

Command Investigations. A command must convene an investigation and make findings concerning misconduct and line of duty when

(1) the injury was incurred under circumstances which suggest a finding of "misconduct" might result. These circumstances include, but are not limited to, all cases in which a qualifying injury was incurred

(a) while the member was using illegal drugs;

(b) while the member's blood alcohol content was of .10 percent by volume or greater. This does not preclude the convening of an investigation if the blood-alcohol percentage is lower than .10, if the circumstances so indicate; and

(c) as a result of a bona fide suicide attempt;

(2) the injury was incurred under circumstances that suggest a finding of "not in line of duty" might result;

(3) there is a reasonable chance of permanent disability and the commanding officer considers the convening of an investigation essential to ensure an adequate official record is made concerning the circumstances surrounding the incident.

Because an adverse line of duty finding may result in the loss of pay and other benefits, service members may choose to remain silent when questioned about an injury. JAG Manual 0221b explains this right:

> Any person in the Armed Forces, prior to being asked to sign any statement relating to the origin, incidence, or aggravation of any disease or injury that he or she has suffered, shall be advised of the right not to sign such a statement. The spirit of this section will be violated if a person, in the course of an investigation, obtains the member's oral statements and reduces them to writing, unless the above advice was given first. Compliance with this section must be documented.

Note that injury warnings are in addition to Article 31(b) warnings. Is the injury warning a constitutional right, or is it required solely by statute or administrative regulation? See chapter 8.

Safety and Mishap Investigations

Apart from criminal and JAG Manual inquiries, the U.S. Navy and Marine Corps also conduct investigations that focus solely on safety issues. JAG Manual 0244 explains the relationship between safety investigations and other types of probes:

> Mishap Investigation Reports. For the sole purpose of safety and mishap prevention, the Chief of Naval Operations has issued special instructions . . . for the conduct, analysis, and review of investigations of mishaps that occur aboard ships or submarines. These investigations are conducted by mishap investigation boards appointed for that purpose and the results are documented in mishap investigation reports.
>
> JAGMAN Investigations. When an afloat mishap results in death or serious injury, extensive damage to government property, or the possibility exists that a claim may be filed by or against the Government, a JAGMAN investigation shall be appointed to investigate and determine the cause and responsibility for the mishap, nature and extent of any injuries, description of all damage to property, and any and all attendant circumstances. These JAGMAN investigations are in addition to, and separate from, the mishap investigation boards.

OPNAVINST 5102.1 discusses how mishap interviews are conducted and the restrictions that exist on the results of this type on inquiry:

> Individuals interviewed during investigations conducted under this instruction shall not testify under oath and shall be advised that their statements (oral or written) are for one purpose only, the prevention of further mishaps. That assurance is necessary to obtain complete and candid information regarding the circumstances surrounding a mishap. Information obtained during any investigation conducted under this instruction shall not be the basis for any administrative, regulatory, disciplinary, or criminal proceeding within the Department of the Navy.

Aircraft mishap investigations serve a similar purpose as inquiries of incidents on board ships and submarines. OPNAVINST 3750.6 explains:

> The purpose of aircraft mishap investigations is hazard detection, to identify the cause factors of the mishap and the damage and/or injury occurring in the course of the mishap. Cause factors of mishaps, and cause factors of injury and damage occurring in the course of a mishap, can be two different matters, but both are the subject of aircraft mishap investigations. Other, less important reasons for conducting aircraft mishap investigations include determination of the extent of damage and injury resulting from the mishap and demonstration of the safety commitment of the organization conducting the investigation. All naval aircraft mishap investigations are conducted solely for safety purposes.

Statements gathered during the course of safety investigations are privileged from disclosure and from use in disciplinary proceedings. Paragraph 606 of OPNAVINST 3750.6 explains the privilege and its purpose in relation to aircraft mishap investigations:

> The mishap investigation shall not be used for the following:
> (1) In making any determination affecting the interest of an individual making a statement under an assurance of confidentiality or involved in a mishap.
> (2) As evidence or to obtain evidence in determining

the misconduct or line of duty status of killed or injured personnel.

(3) As evidence to determine the responsibility of personnel from the standpoint of discipline.

(4) As evidence to assert affirmative claims on behalf of the government.

(5) As evidence to determine the liability of the government for property damage caused by a mishap.

(6) As evidence before administrative bodies, such as Naval Aviator/Naval Flight Officer Evaluation Boards (USN) or Field Flight Performance Boards (USMC).

(7) In any other punitive or administrative action taken by the Department of the Navy.

Why are safety inquires privileged from disclosure? The late Admiral Mike Boorda, former Chief of Naval Operations, explained the nature and significance of privileged safety investigations as it related to the inquiry into the death of the navy's first female combat pilot, Lieutenant Kara Hultgreen. The safety report of the crash causing her death was released to the media without authority. He stated:

> Most of you have probably seen the continuing accounts of the investigations into last fall's F-14 crash that killed LT Hultgreen. As you know JAG Manual investigations and aviation mishap reports are very different approaches with very different objectives. They deal with the same facts and because of that, should agree (they do in this case but they are also different). The JAG Manual report establishes cause and accountability. The aviation mishap report is much more detailed and, because it is intended to serve aviation safety and instructional needs, it examines every factor and reports in the bluntest of terms. . . . One or more people have taken it upon themselves to release all or part of one of the navy's most consistently safeguarded investigation reports, the aviation mishap report. The effectiveness and integrity of the entire mishap safety investigation process rests on our ability to have a frank discussion of accident causes and what might be done to prevent such accidents in the future. Those doing mishap reports must be free to discuss in very direct terms not only what happened but all the things that might have been done to prevent or lessen the mishap.

Admiral Boorda emphasized the importance of maintaining the confidentiality and privileged nature of safety inquiries. Based on his comments, what is the effect of an improper release of a mishap investigation? Outside of the safety investigation situation, communications by service personnel are normally not privileged from use in future disciplinary proceedings. However, certain relationships do protect against such use. For example, attorney-client communications are privileged, as are discussions with clergy personnel and between spouses. See Military Rules of Evidence 501–504. Note, however, that the doctor-patient privilege does not currently exist in the military.

Study Questions

1. Who investigates major criminal offenses in the U.S. Navy and Marine Corps? Who handles the inquiry into minor violations?

2. What is the purpose of criminal intelligence operations? How are such investigations different from criminal inquiries?

3. What are the three types of JAG Manual investigations? When should a preliminary inquiry be done prior to convening a JAG Manual investigation?

4. Who has authority to convene a command investigation? Litigation report investigation? A court or board of inquiry?

5. When is a command investigation appropriate? What is the purpose of such an inquiry?

6. What is a "major incident?" Which fact-finding body should inquire into a major incident?

7. While on patrol in the Atlantic Ocean, the USS *Caine* collides with an oil tanker. Admiral Queeg convenes an investigation and appoints one rear admiral and two captains to look into the incident. The fact-finding body has subpoena power, and a JAG officer is assigned to act as the legal advisor. This type of administrative fact-finding body is:

a. A formal investigation.

b. A command investigation.

c. An informal investigation.

d. A court of inquiry.

e. A litigation report investigation.

Postal Clerk Third Class (PC3) Claven and Disbursing Clerk Third Class (DK3) Peterson are both attached to the USS *Boston,* homeported in Norfolk, Virginia. One evening while on liberty together, they stopped at a convenience store and purchased two six-packs of beer. After the beer was gone, PC3 Claven kept the party going by smoking some crack cocaine. While stopped at a red light just outside the Norfolk city limits, DK3 Peterson's car was crushed from behind by an "eighteen-wheeler" whose driver had fallen asleep at the wheel. Both DK3 Peterson and PC3 Claven had been wearing their seat belts but nevertheless suffered severe injuries as a result of the force of the impact. They were taken to Portsmouth Naval Hospital for treatment, but PC3 Claven died from his injuries shortly after their arrival. The autopsy on PC3 Claven revealed a blood alcohol content (BAC) of .21 percent and the presence of cocaine metabolite in his bloodstream. DK3 Peterson survived but was hospitalized for several months for treatment of his injuries. DK3 Peterson is now permanently disabled and will require extensive physical therapy. Laboratory analysis of DK3 Peterson's blood revealed a BAC of .19 percent, well above the legal limit in Virginia.

8. What is the proper line of duty (LOD)/misconduct determination for PC3 Claven?

a. In the LOD, not due to misconduct.

b. Not in the LOD, not due to misconduct.

c. Not in the LOD, due to misconduct.

d. In the LOD, due to misconduct.

e. No LOD/misconduct determination should be made.

9. What is the proper line of duty (LOD)/misconduct determination for DK3 Peterson?

a. In the LOD, not due to misconduct.

b. Not in the LOD, not due to misconduct.

c. Not in the LOD, due to misconduct.

d. In the LOD, due to misconduct.

e. No LOD/misconduct determination should be made.

10. What are the three possible line of duty/misconduct determinations? When is each type appropriate? When should a command investigation be used to record a line of duty determination?

11. How does unauthorized absence affect the line of duty status of an injured service member?

12. What is the purpose of safety investigations? How are they different from criminal investigations and JAG Manual inquires? For what purpose can a safety investigation be used?

CHAPTER TEN

APPREHENSION AND RESTRAINT

When a judge orders a man into confinement without a charge against him, he deprives him of liberty without due process of law; and in doing so violates the earliest and most important guaranty of constitutional freedom. . . . There must be some great and most serious defect in the administration of the law when such things can take place, and the matter is one which concerns every member of the political community; for if constitutional principles fail to protect the most humble of the people, they protect no one.

—*Miner v. Post & Tribune Co.,* 49 Mich. 358, 13 N.W. 773 (1882)

The military's need to maintain good order and discipline requires that service personnel perform many functions typically handled by police or law enforcement officials in the civilian sector. Apprehension and restraint are good examples of this unique aspect of military law. Because of order and discipline considerations, the military delegates the authority to apprehend or restrain service members to a broad segment of its personnel. To ensure that this important authority is used properly, extensive procedures and limitations affecting apprehension and restraint exist. This chapter discusses the authority and grounds to restrict the movement of service members, as well as the consequences of resisting or challenging such restrictions.

Apprehending or restraining a service member also has important ramifications from both a constitutional and procedural standpoint. For example, confining a service member begins the running of several procedural clocks, including the accused's statutory and constitutional right to a speedy trial. This chapter also addresses the procedural implications related to apprehension and restraint.

Apprehension

Rules for Court-Martial 302(a)(1) defines "apprehension" as "the taking of a person into custody." An "apprehension" in a military setting is not synonymous with a civilian "arrest." In fact, an apprehension often occurs well before what is considered an arrest in civilian criminal law. Why is this the case? How are an arrest, an apprehension, and a detention distinct? Why is the fact that they are distinct important? See the discussion below of each of these types of restraints.

Authority to Apprehend

RCM 302(b) describes who possesses the authority to apprehend in the military:

> The following officials may apprehend any person subject to trial by court-martial:
> (1) Military law enforcement officials. Security police, military police, master at arms personnel, members of the shore patrol, and persons designated by proper authorities to perform military criminal investigative, guard, or police duties, whether subject to the code or not, when, in each of the foregoing instances, the official making the apprehension is in the execution of law enforcement duties;
> (2) Commissioned, warrant, petty, and noncommissioned officers. All commissioned, warrant, petty, and noncommissioned officers on active duty or inactive duty training;
> (3) Civilians authorized to apprehend deserters. . . . any civilian officer having authority to apprehend offenders under laws of the United States or of a State, Territory, Commonwealth, or possession, or the District of Columbia, when the apprehension is of a deserter from the armed forces.

Based on the above section, commissioned and warrant officers may be apprehended by noncommissioned or petty officers. Do you foresee a problem with enlisted personnel apprehending officers? Does it help or hurt good order and discipline to give this important authority to junior personnel? The discussion to RCM 302 explains that "noncommissioned and petty officers not otherwise performing law enforcement duties should not apprehend a commissioned officer unless directed to do so by a commissioned officer or in order to prevent disgrace to the service of the escape of one who has committed a serious offense." This same rule applies to NCIS agents as well. See JAG Manual 0168. Note that enlisted personnel who are not petty officers or noncommissioned officers may only apprehend if they are performing law enforcement duties.

Grounds and Procedures to Apprehend

RCM 302(c) sets forth the bases and procedures for apprehending persons:

> Grounds for apprehension. A person subject to the code or trial thereunder may be apprehended for an offense triable by court-martial upon probable cause to apprehend. Probable cause to apprehend exists when there are reasonable grounds to believe that an offense has been or is being committed and the person to be apprehended committed or is committing it. Persons authorized to apprehend (commissioned, warrant, petty, and noncommissioned officers) may also apprehend persons subject to the code who take part in quarrels, frays, or disorders, wherever they occur.

RCM 302(c) provides authority to apprehend service members who are involved in disturbances. Why is this provision necessary? What remedies are available to a service member who is wrongly apprehended? See Article 138, UCMJ (complaint of wrongs).

Recall that a civilian arrest is different than an military apprehension. RCM 302(d) describes how an apprehension occurs:

> (1) In general. An apprehension is made by clearly notifying the person to be apprehended that the person is in custody. This notice should be given orally or in writing, but it may be implied by the circumstances.

(2) Warrants. Neither warrants nor any other authorization shall be required for an apprehension under these rules except as required in subsection (e)(2) of this rule.
(3) Use of force. Any person authorized under these rules to make an apprehension may use such force and means as reasonably necessary under the circumstances to effect the apprehension.

The authority of military personnel to apprehend may depend on the location of the person to be apprehended. RCM 302(e) spells out where military apprehensions can occur:

(1) In general. An apprehension may be made at any place, except:
(2) Private dwellings. A private dwelling includes dwellings, on or off a military installation, such as single family houses, duplexes, and apartments. The quarters may be owned, leased, or rented by the residents, or assigned, and may be occupied on a temporary or permanent basis. "Private dwelling" does not include the following, whether or not subdivided into individual units: Living areas in military barracks, vessels, aircraft, vehicles, tents, bunkers, field encampments, and similar places. No person may enter a private dwelling for the purpose of making an apprehension under these rules unless:
  (A) Pursuant to consent . . . ;
  (B) Under exigent circumstances . . . ;
  (C) In the case of a private dwelling which is military property or under military control, or nonmilitary property in a foreign country,
    (i) if the person to be apprehended is a resident of the private dwelling, there exists, at the time of the entry, reason to believe that the person to be apprehended is present in the dwelling, and the apprehension has been authorized by an official upon a determination that probable cause to apprehend the person exists; or
    (ii) if the person to be apprehended is not a resident of the private dwelling, the entry has been authorized by an official . . . upon a determination that probable cause exists to apprehend the person and to believe that the person to be apprehended is or will be present at the time of the entry.

Probable cause that an offense has been or is being committed provides the basis for an apprehension. "Offenses" as used in RCM 302 refers only to crimes under the UCMJ. Apprehension of service members for civilian crimes sometimes occurs on board military installations as well. This usually happens through coordination with the base or unit commander by civilian law enforcement authorities. Note that civilian authorities must have an arrest warrant and agree to deliver the member back to his or her unit once the charges are resolved before a sailor or marine will be delivered. See Article 14, UCMJ; JAG Manual 0603, 0607.

Except in private dwellings, a warrant is not required to apprehend a service member. This rule is a codification of longstanding military law. See *United States v. Kinane,* 1 M.J. 309 (C.M.A. 1976); *United States v. Sanford,* 12 M.J. 170 (C.M.A. 1981). Is this inconsistent with the Fourth Amendment protection against unlawful searches and seizures? RCM 302(e)(2) defines a "private dwelling" for purposes of the warrant requirement. This definition is based upon those areas where service members are considered to have an expectation of privacy. See chapter 7 regarding constitutional restraints on search and seizure. If a warrant is not needed to apprehend a service member located in a barracks, does this also do away with the need for probable cause? RCM 302(d)(3) authorizes the use of force to apprehend. Does this include the use of "deadly force?"

Apprehension and Custody Offenses

APPREHENSION OFFENSES

Article 95, UCMJ, makes it a crime for a service member to

(1) resist apprehension;
(2) flee from apprehension;
(3) break arrest; or
(4) escape from custody or confinement.

In reading the following facts from *United States v. Burgess,* 32 M.J. 446 (C.M.A. 1991), consider which offenses, if any, the accused committed under Article 95:

On June 9, 1989, in Clarksville, Tennessee, accused met with a prospective cocaine buyer. Unbeknownst to him, the buyer actually was an undercover agent of the CID (Criminal Investigation Department) who was part of a drug suppression team investigating accused's recent drug activity. The rendezvous took place in the parking lot of a local retail store; both the accused and the agent remained in their respective cars during the meeting. A surveillance team consisting of military agents and Tennessee State Police was also at the site, waiting and prepared to apprehend the accused when the drug deal was completed.

The accused and the agent had previously negotiated the sale of one ounce of cocaine, but when accused noticed a police car near the scene, he became hesitant. The agent suggested that they move elsewhere (each man still remained in his own automobile), and the accused agreed. The two cars began to move; the accused's car followed the agent's.

As this was occurring, the surveillance team watched for the undercover agent's prearranged sign, the illumination of the brake lights on the agent's car, indicating that the deal was done and that they should act. Consequently, when the agent's car moved and the brake lights brightened, the surveillance team incorrectly assumed that the signal had been given, and they moved in to arrest accused. One CID agent "jumped out of a vehicle and yelled, 'Police, you're under arrest!'"

The accused ignored the agent and drove off in his car. He was immediately pursued by several military and state police vehicles, with sirens blaring and lights flashing.

Was the accused in *Burgess* ever apprehended? Did he resist apprehension or flee from apprehension? Was he ever "in custody" for purposes of Article 95? Will such a determination turn on whether the accused was "apprehended" as that term is defined in the military? See the discussion below regarding escape from custody.

Note that a person attempting to apprehend must be authorized to do so. Consequently, a reasonable belief that the person attempting to apprehend lacks authority to do so is a defense to a charge of resisting apprehension. It is not, however, a valid defense for the accused to resist apprehension on the basis that

no grounds existed for the apprehension, that is, he or she had not committed an offense. What do you think is the reasoning behind this distinction?

ESCAPE FROM CUSTODY OR CONFINEMENT

The following discussion from *United States v. Ellsey*, 37 C.M.R. 75 (1966) addresses the differences between the offenses of escape from custody and escape from confinement:

> The accused was taken from the battalion adjutant's office by a guard, who was there furnished with a written confinement order directing his incarceration in the brig. En route to the confinement facility, accused was accompanied to his barracks in order to pack his gear. While at the latter place, accused evaded his guard and disappeared. Based on these facts, the accused was convicted of escape from confinement. It is urged that the statute creates but the single offense of escape which may be proven to be committed regardless of the allegations from either custody or confinement, both being mere forms of physical restraint.
>
> Confinement is defined by the UCMJ as "the physical restraint of a person." It may be imposed upon an enlisted person only by a commissioned officer, and by a warrant officer, petty officer, or noncommissioned officer only when such authority is conferred upon them by a commanding officer. It may be imposed upon a commissioned or warrant officer or civilian "only by a commanding officer to whose authority he is subject."
>
> On the other hand, custody is defined only inferentially by the code, which declares "apprehension is the taking of a person into custody." The MCM elaborates on this by declaring:
>
> > Custody is that restraint of free locomotion which is imposed by lawful apprehension. The restraint may be corporeal and forcible or, once there has been a submission to apprehension or a forcible taking into custody, it may consist of control exercised in the presence of the prisoner by official acts or orders.
>
> Unlike confinement, "Any person authorized under regulations governing the armed forces" may apprehend members of the services and thus impose the sta-

tus of custody upon them. So, also, may officers, warrant officers, and noncommissioned officers quell disorders and "apprehend persons subject to this chapter who take part therein." In short, "there is a clear distinction between the authority to apprehend and the authority to arrest or confine." Moreover, those empowered to apprehend are only authorized "to secure the custody of an alleged offender until proper authority may be notified."

Thus, it will be seen that custody and confinement are entirely different in nature. The first results from apprehension and lasts "until proper authority may be notified." It may be imposed by any person empowered by departmental regulations. Confinement, on the other hand, absent authorization by a commanding officer, may be ordered only by a commissioned officer. Its execution before and after trial is subjected to strict control. Finally, while custody may of necessity be maintained by physical restraint, it also suffices to utilize no more than moral suasion. Hence, far from being identical to confinement, it is an altogether different condition.

Applied to the facts before us, the fatal variance between the evidence and the "charge" upon which the accused was tried becomes apparent. The accused had been duly ordered into confinement. It appears he was then taken into custody for delivery to the confinement facility. Before that delivery could be effected and confinement actually imposed upon him, the accused made his escape. Hence, his offense was breach of lawful custody of his guard and not of a confinement in which he never entered. Poetically speaking, "Stone walls do not a prison make, nor iron bars a cage"; practically and legally, they do.

Based on the above discussion, what is the difference between escape from custody and escape from confinement? Why was the distinction between the two offenses important in *Ellsey*?

BREAKING ARREST AND RESTRICTION

The following case discusses the difference between the offenses of breaking arrest under Article 95 and breaking restriction under Article 134.

UNITED STATES V. BASCOM BROOKS HUGHES, AIRMAN APPRENTICE, U.S. NAVY
UNITED STATES NAVY BOARD OF REVIEW
11 C.M.R. 600
JUNE 5, 1953
Opinion: Albrink, McNemar, and Lauerman, Judges

The accused was convicted of a violation of the UCMJ, Article 95, in that he broke arrest at U.S. Naval Air Technical Training Center, Norman, Oklahoma.

A prosecution's witness testified that he was the athletic officer of the center and that while on duty on 3 January 1953 as officer of the day he put the accused under arrest by having him read and sign a certain form, and giving the accused a copy thereof. On cross-examination the defense had the witness identify the piece of paper involved, and it was received into evidence as Defense Exhibit "A."

This exhibit reads:

1. You are hereby notified that you have been:
(a) Restricted to the limits of the Naval Air Technical Training Center.

2. You will report to the CMAA, NATTC at Barracks #39 for instructions upon receipt and acknowledgment of this notice.

3. While in restraint, you will not indulge in the use of intoxicating beverages of any kind.

4. You are warned not to violate the terms of restraint or you will be subject to severe disciplinary action.

Arrest and restriction are separate forms of authorized restraint; breach of arrest is pleaded under Article 95, UCMJ, and breach of restriction is pleaded under Article 134, UCMJ; breach of arrest has a greater maximum legal limit of punishment than breach of restriction; breach of restriction is a lesser included offense of breach of arrest. Notification to the accused of the imposition of restraint, of the type of restraint being imposed, and of the limits of the restraint as well as a legal power to impose restraint of the type used are parts of the element of due imposition of restraint common to both arrest and restriction. Such notice should be clear and unambiguous, and the accused should not be compelled to speculate as to his status. We are of the opinion that if a person being placed under restraint is simultaneously given a written notification pertaining to his status, the written notice governs, unless there is an express cancellation or negation, either written or oral, of the provisions thereof. Defense Exhibit "A" clearly imposes only restriction, and the charge should be reduced to the lesser included offense of breach of restriction, a violation of Article 134, UCMJ.

What is the distinction between arrest and restriction? See the discussion below regarding pretrial restraint. Why was the distinction between the two crimes important in *Hughes?* Which is more commonly used, restriction or arrest?

Pretrial Restraint

RCM 304(a) describes the types of restraint imposable prior to disposition of an offense:

> (1) Conditions on liberty. Conditions on liberty are imposed by orders directing a person to do or refrain from doing specified acts. Such conditions may be imposed in conjunction with other forms of restraint or separately.
> (2) Restriction in lieu of arrest. Restriction in lieu of arrest is the restraint of a person by oral or written orders directing the person to remain within specified limits; a restricted person shall, unless otherwise directed, perform full military duties while restricted.
> (3) Arrest. Arrest is the restraint of a person by oral or written order not imposed as punishment, directing the person to remain within specified limits; a person in the status of arrest may not be required to perform full military duties such as commanding or supervising personnel, serving as guard, or bearing arms.
> (4) Confinement. Pretrial confinement is physical restraint, imposed by order of competent authority, depriving a person of freedom pending disposition of offenses.

RCM 304(b) also explains who has authority to impose restraint prior to disposition of an offense:

> (1) Of civilians and officers. Only a commanding officer to whose authority the civilian or officer is subject may order pretrial restraint of that civilian or officer.
> (2) Of enlisted persons. Any commissioned officer may order pretrial restraint of any enlisted person.
> (3) Delegation of authority. The authority to order pretrial restraint of civilians and commissioned and

warrant officers may not be delegated. A commanding officer may delegate to warrant, petty, and noncommissioned officers authority to order pretrial restraint of enlisted persons of the commanding officer's command or subject to the authority of that commanding officer.

RCM 304(c) explains when pretrial restraint is appropriate:

> When a person may be restrained. No person may be ordered into restraint before trial except for probable cause. Probable cause to order pretrial restraint exists when there is a reasonable belief that:
> (1) An offense triable by court-martial has been committed;
> (2) The person to be restrained committed it; and
> (3) The restraint ordered is required by the circumstances.

What factors should be considered in deciding on appropriate pretrial restraint? Possible flight prior to trial is often a factor. Is the likelihood that the service member will commit another offense pertinent? What about violent or suicidal tendencies on the part of the accused? See RCM 305, discussed below.

Note that pretrial restraint may not be used as punishment. The remedy for a violation of this rule is meaningful sentence relief. This means that the military judge should reduce the sentence to compensate for the unlawful pretrial restraint. See *United States v. Pringle,* 41 C.M.R. 324 (C.M.A. 1970); *United States v. Nelson,* 39 C.M.R. 177 (1969). What factors should the judge consider in crafting appropriate relief? See the discussion below regarding illegal pretrial confinement.

Pretrial Confinement

Confinement is the most serious type of pretrial restraint. It is physical restraint depriving a person of freedom pending disposition of charges. RCM 305(d) explains the procedural rules regarding pretrial confinement:

> When a person may be confined. No person may be ordered into pretrial confinement except for probable

cause. Probable cause to order pretrial confinement exists when there is a reasonable belief that:

(1) An offense triable by court-martial has been committed;

(2) The person confined committed it; and

(3) Confinement is required by the circumstances.

Compare the above rules with the procedures for other types of pretrial restraint. See RCM 304, discussed above. Confinement prior to disposition of an alleged offense triggers significant procedural rights for the confinee. RCM 305(e) describes those protections:

Advice to the accused upon confinement. Each person confined shall be promptly informed of:

(1) The nature of the offenses for which held;

(2) The right to remain silent and that any statement made by the person may be used against the person;

(3) The right to retain civilian counsel at no expense to the United States, and the right to request assignment of military counsel; and

(4) The procedures by which pretrial confinement will be reviewed.

How do the above rights compare with an accused at court-martial? See chapter 3. Should a prisoner have the right to counsel? RCM 305(f) addresses that issue:

Military counsel. If requested by the prisoner, military counsel shall be provided to the prisoner before the initial review of the basis for confinement. Counsel may be assigned for the limited purpose of representing the accused only during the pretrial confinement proceedings before charges are referred. If assignment is made for this limited purpose, the prisoner shall be so informed. Unless otherwise provided by regulations of the Secretary concerned, a prisoner does not have a right under this rule to have military counsel of the prisoner's own selection.

Compare the right to counsel following pretrial confinement with an accused's counsel rights at court-martial. See chapter 3. In which situation does an accused have greater right to counsel?

RCM 305(h) addresses the review of a decision to place a member in pretrial confinement:

Notification and action by commander.

(1) Report. Unless the commander of the prisoner ordered the pretrial confinement, the commissioned, warrant, noncommissioned, or petty officer to whose charge the prisoner was committed shall, within 24 hours after that commitment, cause to be made a report to the commander which shall contain the name of the prisoner, the offenses charged against the prisoner, and the name of the person who ordered or authorized confinement.

(2) Action by commander.

(A) Decision. Not later than 72 hours after ordering a prisoner into pretrial confinement, or after receipt of a report that a member of the commander's unit or organization has been confined, the commander shall decide whether pretrial confinement will continue.

(B) Requirements for confinement. The commander shall direct the prisoner's release from pretrial confinement unless the commander believes upon probable cause, that is, upon reasonable grounds, that:

(i) An offense triable by a court-martial has been committed;

(ii) The prisoner committed it; and

(iii) Confinement is necessary because it is foreseeable that:

(a) The prisoner will not appear at a trial, pretrial hearing, or investigation, or

(b) The prisoner will engage in serious criminal misconduct; and

(iv) Less severe forms of restraint are inadequate.

A commander's decision to impose pretrial confinement is subject to review under RCM 305(i):

Procedures for review of pretrial confinement.

(1) In general. A review of the adequacy of probable cause to believe the prisoner has committed an offense and of the necessity for continued pretrial confinement shall be made within seven days of the imposition of confinement.

(2) By whom made. The review under this subsection shall be made by a neutral and detached officer appointed in accordance with regulations prescribed by the secretary concerned.

What is the remedy if it is determined that pretrial confinement was illegally imposed? RCM 305(k) considers that situation:

Remedy. The remedy for [illegal pretrial confinement] shall be an administrative credit against the sentence adjudged for any confinement served as the result of such noncompliance. Such credit shall be computed at the rate of one day credit for each day of confinement served as a result of such noncompliance. This credit is to be applied in addition to any other credit the accused may be entitled as a result of pretrial confinement served. This credit shall be applied first against any confinement adjudged. If no confinement is adjudged, or if the confinement adjudged is insufficient to offset all the credit to which the accused is entitled, the credit . . . shall be applied against hard labor without confinement, restriction, fine, and forfeiture of pay, in that order, if adjudged. For purposes of this subsection, one day of confinement shall be equal to 1 day of total forfeiture or a like amount of fine. The credit shall not be applied against any other form of punishment.

The above rules are designed to ensure that service members are not improperly confined. This explains the extensive review that occurs in pretrial confinement cases. If a member is a flight risk, then pretrial confinement is normally appropriate. "Serious criminal misconduct" is more difficult to determine. RCM 305 states that it includes intimidation of witnesses, seriously injuring others, or other offenses which pose a serious threat to the safety of the community or to the effectiveness, morale, discipline, readiness, or safety of the command, or to the national security of the United States. Does this clarify the issue?

Compare the remedies described above in RCM 305(k) for illegal pretrial confinement with the remedies for a speedy trial violation discussed below. RCM 305 does not provide a remedy for illegal confinement in cases in which the accused is acquitted or not awarded any of the punishments listed in 305(k). Are there any other remedies available to the accused? See Article 138, UCMJ.

How does a ship or unit at sea comply with the procedural rules governing pretrial confinement? Which takes priority, the rights of the accused or the operational requirements of his or her command? RCM 305(m)(2) provides an exception for confinement on board a vessel at sea:

At sea. [The rules relating to counsel and review of pretrial confinement] shall not apply in the case of a person on board a vessel at sea. In such situations, confinement on board the vessel at sea may continue only until the person can be transferred to a confinement facility ashore. Such transfer shall be accomplished at the earliest opportunity permitted by the operational requirements and mission of the vessel.

Speedy Trial

The Sixth Amendment to the Constitution provides that "in all criminal prosecutions, the accused shall enjoy the right to a speedy and public trial." The military has established its own rules to ensure that an accused's right to a speedy trial are not violated. RCM 707 describes those rules:

(a) In general. The accused shall be brought to trial within 120 days after the earlier of:
   (1) Preferral of charges;
   (2) The imposition of restraint.

What happens if the government fails to the speedy clock rule? RCM 707(d) explains:

Remedy. A failure to comply with the right to a speedy trial will result in a dismissal of the affected charges. This dismissal will be with or without prejudice to the government's right to reinstitute court-martial proceedings against the accused for the same offense at a later date. The charges must be dismissed with prejudice where the accused has been deprived of his or her constitutional right to a speedy trial.

The purpose of RCM 707 is to apply speedy trial rights under the Sixth Amendment to the military. The time limit to bring an accused in pretrial confinement to trial under RCM 707 was at one time only ninety days. The 120-day rule in RCM 707 now applies to all types of restraint, including pretrial confinement. What factors would cause the government to fail to try an accused in 120 days? The general rule is that the government is accountable for all time prior to trial unless a competent authority grants a delay. Military judges and convening authorities are required to make an independent determination as to whether there is good cause for a pretrial delay and to grant such delays for only so long as is necessary under the circumstances.

Until recently, the military courts held that when an accused has been held in pretrial confinement for more than ninety days, a presumption arose that the accused's right to a speedy trial had been violated. In such cases, the government had to demonstrate due diligence in bringing the case to trial. *United States v. Burton,* 44 C.M.R. 166 (C.M.A. 1971). This rule resulted in a number of dismissals based on speedy trial grounds. See, for example, *United States v. Pyburn,* 48 C.M.R. (C.M.A. 1974). Note that when an accused is released from pretrial restraint for a significant period, he or she will be treated as if no restraint had been imposed. Therefore, unless restraint is reimposed, the 120-day period will run from the date of preferral of charges, regardless of whether that event occurs before or after the accused was released from restraint. Based on this rule, are there situations in which the government would want or need to release an accused from pretrial confinement?

Commanding officers are given authority to restrict the liberty of members in foreign countries without having to use disciplinary procedures. This is part of the "liberty risk program" discussed in chapter 4. The following case considers liberty risk as a form of pretrial restraint for purposes of speedy trial.

UNITED STATES V. BOBBY J. WILKES, LANCE CORPORAL,
U.S. MARINE CORPS
UNITED STATES NAVY–MARINE CORPS COURT OF MILITARY
REVIEW
27 M.J. 571
SEPTEMBER 21, 1988
Opinion: Riley, Senior Judge

As a result of a previous unauthorized absence, the appellant, on 24 December 1986, received nonjudicial punishment which included restriction for 30 days. Appellant had served 19 days of that restriction when he left without authorization once again. On 5 February 1987, appellant surrendered to military authorities in Albany, Georgia. Appellant returned to his unit (Communications Company, H and S Battalion, Camp Kinser, Okinawa) on 8 February 1987, and on the next day he began serving the remainder of the previously imposed restriction. On the last day of that restriction (19 February 1987), appellant was interviewed by agents of the Naval Investigative Service (NIS). In that interview, he confessed to writing 33 bad checks totaling over $10,000. Later that day, Lieutenant Ubalde, the appellant's acting executive officer, after learning of appellant's bad check offenses and his unauthorized absence, placed him on pretrial restriction. Appellant remained in that status until 24 February 1987, when he was placed in a "liberty risk" status, restricting him to the limits of the base. He remained in that status until his trial began 125 days later on 30 June 1987.

Before this Court, appellant argues that the liberty risk program in this instance was used as a subterfuge to avoid the strict accountability of RCM 707. The government, on the other hand, argues that the appellant was placed in the liberty risk program in order to help him with an alcohol abuse problem and to avoid alcohol-related incidents involving the appellant and foreign nationals.

On 24 February, appellant was placed on the liberty risk program which, in essence, did nothing more than change the name of his continuing restriction. He still had to muster every four hours during non-working hours. At trial, appellant's commanding officer, Major Glenn, testified that he had interviewed the appellant upon appellant's arrival at Camp Kinser in December 1986. In that interview, appellant told him that he had an alcohol problem and had recently completed a voluntary rehabilitation course at the Naval Hospital on Okinawa. Major Glenn stated that the liberty risk status was imposed because appellant "had all the indications of a recovering alcoholic" and, because the command wanted to protect the appellant from any alcohol-related problems in the surrounding community.

In answering the military judge's questions, however, Major Glenn gave some revealing information about his concept of the liberty risk program vis-à-vis pretrial restriction:

Q. Major Glenn, are you aware, or were you at the time as commanding officer, that there's a difference between restriction imposed as a punishment for nonjudicial punishment and restriction imposed as a form of pretrial restraint?

A. Oh, yes, sir.

Q. Did you ever impose restriction in your company as a form of pretrial restraint during your time as a company commander?

A. That's a very touchy situation, sir, and the reason I have always used the liberty risk program because of the legal ramifications; and I can't recall ever putting someone on restriction without the result of nonjudicial punishment.

Q. Are you saying, sir, that if you applied restriction as a pretrial restraint, that the restriction with regard to confines, as you have described it, would be less?

A. That's a hard one for me to answer because like I said, sir, I cannot recall putting anyone on restriction prior to a resolution of any judicial proceedings. I try and stay away from awarding a restriction without the punishment being awarded at my level or the punishment being awarded at the battalion commander's level or as a result of court-martial. The liberty risk program is an administrative tool that I have used quite a bit.

Major Glenn further testified that he had neither seen nor heard of appellant having been involved in any alcohol-related incidents either on base or in the surrounding community. Additionally, there was never any indication, oral or written, to the appellant about when his liberty risk status would terminate. Instead, the liberty risk restrictions remained in effect until 30 June 1987, the date of his trial.

While we may not agree with appellant's categorization of his assignment to the liberty risk program as a subterfuge to avoid speedy trial problems, we are not convinced that concern for the appellant's safety and the maintenance of good international relations were the primary motivations behind the liberty risk restrictions. That is, while there may have been a genuine concern on the part of the commanding officer about

appellant's suspected alcohol problem, we find that the liberty risk status was not imposed primarily for such purposes. It was imposed primarily to ensure his presence at trial, and, as such, did not stop the speedy trial clock, which continued to run uninterrupted for 131 days. This violated the 120-day rule of RCM 707.

Study Questions

1. Define "apprehension" as used in the military. Who has the authority to apprehend?

2. What are the grounds for apprehending a service member? How is an apprehension made? When, if ever, is a warrant required to apprehend?

3. What constitutes actively resisting apprehension?

4. What is the difference between escape from custody and escape from confinement? Why is the distinction significant?

5. What is the difference between breaking arrest and breaking restriction?

6. What are the permissible types of pretrial restraint? Who has the authority to impose pretrial restraint? When should it be used?

7. When is pretrial confinement appropriate? What are a pretrial confinee's rights? How is pretrial confinement reviewed? What is the remedy for unlawful pretrial confinement?

8. How long does the military have to bring a service member to trial? When does the speedy trial clock begin? How does release from pretrial restraint affect the speedy trial clock?

9. Which of the following will not start the "speedy trial clock?"

a. The preferral of charges against the accused.

b. Placing the accused on pretrial restriction.

c. Placing conditions on the liberty of the accused.

d. Placing the accused in pretrial confinement.

e. Both (a) and (c).

CHAPTER ELEVEN

INTERNATIONAL LAW

International law is part of our law.

> —United States Supreme Court

The sources of military jurisdiction include . . .
international law.

> —Preamble, Manual for Courts-Martial

At all times, commanders shall observe, and require their commands to observe, the principles of international law. Where necessary to fulfill this responsibility, a departure from other provisions of Navy Regulations is authorized.

> —Article 0705, United States Navy Regulations (1990)

Introduction

Although scholars, philosophers, and academicians sometimes debate whether such a thing as international law truly exists in the same sense as we think of domestic criminal and civil law, there can be no doubt that there occurs in the international community a body of norms, rules, processes, and institutions by which conduct in the international arena is measured, judged, and to some degree, governed. The naval services of the United States operate within this international legal system and are one of the many and varied actors in that system. Others include states such as the United States itself, international organizations such as the United Nations (UN) and the North Atlantic Treaty Organization (NATO), and international nongovernmental organizations such as the International Committee of the Red Cross, Greenpeace, Amnesty International, and Human Rights Watch. Actors in the international legal system also include transnational corporations and businesses, and in a growing number of cases, individual persons, such as those seeking relief in domestic and international courts for violations of the international law of human rights, in particular those prohibiting torture, genocide, and crimes against humanity. This latter development represents a significant departure from the classical view of international law as concerned only with the actions of states with respect to each other and which reached the conduct of individual persons only to the extent to which a state might desire to perceive an injury to one of its nationals as an injury to the state itself.

International tribunals, both courts, such as the UN's International Court of Justice (ICJ), and arbitral tribunals, such as the Iran–United States Claims Tribunal, are also among the cast of players upon the international stage, yet it is largely because many of these courts and tribunals do not provide particularly effective enforcement mechanisms for violations of international law, or for resolutions of disputes by and among the other actors in the international system, at least not to the same degree as do criminal and civil courts in the domestic legal system, that some scholars argue that the norms and rules of the international system cannot be considered "law." Even these skeptical scholars, however, must recognize that the international system relies heavily in its operation upon the language and process of law. Indeed, most students of the system, which draws its rules of normative behavior from, among others, two explicitly legal primary sources—treaties and customary law—in the end agree that a system of international law does exist, and that this legal system significantly influences the behavior of the players within it. In fact, even in the absence of strong and effective judicial enforcement, nations tend to comply with international law, although often on a basis that seems to the casual observer to be essentially voluntary. In the event of apparent noncompliance, however, violators often attempt to justify their conduct as permitted by some exception to, or interpretation of, international law, which manifests the tangibility of the law even as an attempt is made to escape its effect.

Why do nations generally comply with international law and worry about it when they do not? *The Commander's Handbook on the Law of Naval Opera-*

tions, a naval warfare publication produced by the Department of the Navy, suggests the following reason:

> International law provides stability in international relations and an expectation that certain acts and omissions will effect predictable consequences. If one nation violates the law, it may expect that others will reciprocate. Consequently, failure to comply with international law ordinarily involves greater political and economic costs than does observance. In short, nations comply with international law because it is in their interest to do so.

Certainly, the United States has historically found support of the international legal system to be in its national interest. Indeed, as noted in the quotes above, the naval services require by explicit regulation that commanders observe and comply with the principles of international law. These principles include, for example, those of the international law of the sea, the law of armed conflict, and the laws regulating the use of force by states, all subjects of particular interest to professional military officers. Study and understanding of those specific principles, however, requires first an exposure to some basic concepts that provide the foundation for, and context of, international law in its broader sense. A good place to start is with the sources of international law: treaties and customary law.

Sources of International Law

Sources—Generally

The American Law Institute, in its 1987 *Restatement of the Law, Third, Foreign Relations Law of the United States,* lists the following sources of international law:

> (1) A rule of international law is one that has been accepted as such by the international community of states
>   (a) in the form of customary law;
>   (b) by international agreement; or
>   (c) by derivation from general principles common to the major legal systems of the world.

(2) Customary international law results from a general and consistent practice of states followed by them from a sense of legal obligation.

(3) International agreements create law for the states parties thereto and may lead to the creation of customary international law when such agreements are intended for adherence by states generally and are in fact widely accepted.

(4) General principles common to the major legal systems, even if not incorporated or reflected in customary law or international agreement, may be invoked as supplementary rules of international law where appropriate.

So, we see that the primary sources of international law are international agreements, often called treaties, which bind only the parties to them as if parties to a contract, and customary laws. Customary international laws are rules that have evolved from the practice of nations—that is, from what states actually do and say about what they do—when that practice somehow comes to involve a perception that the practice is required by law. Customary law generally binds all states, while treaty law binds only those states party to the treaty.

Treaties

Article 6 of the Constitution of the United States declares, in part, that "all Treaties made, or which shall be made, under the authority of the United States shall be the supreme Law of the land." The kind of treaty referred to here is an international agreement made in accordance with Article 2, Section 2 of the Constitution—that is, pursuant to the president's power "by and with the consent of the Senate to make Treaties, provided two thirds of the Senators present concur." The definition of a treaty under international law, however, is much broader than that implied by the Constitution; international obligations, legally binding in the international system, may arise from international agreements that have not been ratified by the Senate and that therefore cannot be considered treaties in the sense of Article 6 of the Constitu-

tion. Executive agreements made by the president, for example, although not treaties under Article 6 of the Constitution, may be considered treaties under international law. Consider the following two definitions of a "treaty" under international law.

The Vienna Convention on the Law of Treaties, itself a treaty, one which entered into force in 1980 with 59 nations party to it (not including the United States), states that a "'treaty' means an international agreement concluded between States in written form and governed by international law, whether embodied in a single instrument or in two or more related instruments and whatever its particular designation." Contrast this with the following excerpt from Section 301 of the *Restatement:*

(1) "international agreement" means an agreement between two or more states or international organizations that is intended to be legally binding and is governed by international law;

(2) "party" means a state or international organization that has consented to be bound by the international agreement and for which the agreement is in force.

Comment:

a. Various designations of agreements. The terminology used for international agreements is varied. Among the terms used are: treaty, convention, agreement, protocol, covenant, charter, statute, act, declaration, concordat, exchange of notes, agreed minute, memorandum of agreement, memorandum of understanding, and modus vivendi. Whatever their designation, all agreements have the same legal status, except as their provisions or the circumstances of their conclusion indicate otherwise.

b. Form of agreement. While most international agreements are in writing, written form is not essential to their binding character. The Vienna Convention specifies that it applies only to written agreements, but under customary international law oral agreements are no less binding although their terms may not be readily susceptible of proof. . . .

f. International organizations and agreements. . . . The Vienna Convention applies only to agreements between states . . . The Vienna Convention does not apply to agreements between a state and an international organization, or between two international organizations, but the rules stated in this Part apply to such agreements also. . . .

The sources of international law, as we have said, include treaties and customary law, and here we see that a treaty, the Vienna Convention, and customary law, as reported by the *Restatement,* provide slightly differing definitions of exactly what a treaty is. The Vienna Convention excludes unwritten international agreements from its definition of a treaty, while the *Restatement* argues that oral agreements may form binding treaties under international law. Moreover, the Vienna Convention defines as treaties only those written agreements concluded between states, while the *Restatement's* view of customary law would have it include among treaties those agreements concluded between a state and an international organization—between a state and the UN for example. The critical element common to both, however, implicit in the Vienna Convention and explicit in the *Restatement,* is that the parties to the treaty intend to have made a legally binding agreement.

Examples of treaties important to the student of naval law include the Charter of the United Nations, the various Geneva Conventions relevant to the law of armed conflict, and the Third United Nations Convention on the Law of the Sea. Another very commonly encountered kind of treaty is the Status of Forces Agreement (SOFA), versions of which govern the use of military facilities and areas used by the United States in foreign countries, such as those in Japan, Korea, the United Kingdom, and the several states of the European continent. SOFAs generally permit U.S. military personnel stationed in these foreign countries to drive with their U.S. driver's licenses, to bring their household goods and automobiles into the country without paying customs duties, and to be exempt from paying income taxes to the host government. In addition, SOFAs usually include terms governing the exercise of criminal ju-

risdiction over service members and their families who may commit crimes while stationed abroad. An example typical of such provisions is that found in the SOFA between the United States and Japan:

1. Subject to the provisions of this Article,
   (a) the military authorities of the United States shall have the right to exercise within Japan all criminal and disciplinary jurisdiction conferred on them by the law of the United States;
   (b) the authorities of Japan shall have jurisdiction over members of the United States armed forces, the civilian component, and their dependents with respect to offenses committed within the territory of Japan and punishable by the law of Japan. . . .
3. In cases where the right to jurisdiction is concurrent the following rules shall apply:
   (a) The military authorities of the United States shall have the primary right to exercise jurisdiction over members of the United States armed forces or the civilian component in relation to
      (i) offenses solely against the property or security of the United States, or offenses solely against the person or property of another member of the United States armed forces or the civilian component or of a dependent;
      (ii) offenses arising out of any act or omission done in the performance of official duty.
   (b) In the case of any other offense the authorities of Japan shall have the primary right to exercise jurisdiction.

The effect of this kind of SOFA criminal jurisdiction provision is to subject U.S. service members and their family members to trial in foreign courts for any crimes they commit under the host country's criminal law, when the crimes involve nationals of the host country. In appropriate cases, convicted service members may serve sentences in the host country's jail. The United States will have primary jurisdiction only over UCMJ offenses not criminal under host-country law—such as unauthorized absence, for example—and over offenses involving only U.S. personnel, such as an assault by one service member upon another or upon the family of another. The United States would also have primary jurisdiction over actions that would be crimes under host-country law in cases in which the actions are "done in the performance of official duty." The two cases below provide examples of how the process can work in these latter two circumstances.

WILSON, SECRETARY OF DEFENSE V. GIRARD
SUPREME COURT OF THE UNITED STATES
354 U.S. 524
JULY 11, 1957

Girard, a Specialist Third Class in the United States Army, was engaged on January 30, 1957, with members of his cavalry regiment in a small unit exercise at Camp Weir range area, Japan. Japanese civilians were present in the area, retrieving expended cartridge cases. Girard and another Specialist Third Class were ordered to guard a machine gun and some items of clothing that had been left nearby. Girard had a grenade launcher on his rifle. He placed an expended 30-caliber cartridge case in the grenade launcher and projected it by firing a blank. The expended cartridge case penetrated the back of a Japanese woman gathering expended cartridge cases and caused her death.

A Security Treaty between Japan and the United States, signed September 8, 1951, was ratified by the Senate on March 20, 1952, and proclaimed by the president effective April 28, 1952. Article 3 of the Treaty authorized the making of Administrative Agreements between the two governments concerning "the conditions which shall govern the disposition of armed forces of the United States of America in and about Japan. . . ." Expressly acting under this provision, the two Nations, on February 28, 1952, signed an Administrative Agreement covering, among other matters, the jurisdiction of the United States over offenses committed in Japan by members of the United States armed forces, and providing that jurisdiction in any case might be waived by the United States. This Agreement became effective on the same date as the Security Treaty (April 28, 1952) and was considered by the Senate before consent was given to the Treaty.

The United States claimed the right to try Girard upon the ground that his act, as certified by his commanding officer, was "done in the performance of official duty" and therefore the United States had primary jurisdiction. Japan insisted that it had proof that Girard's action was without the scope of his official duty and therefore that Japan had the primary right to try him.

A sovereign nation has exclusive jurisdiction to punish offenses against its laws committed within its borders, unless it expressly or impliedly consents to surrender its jurisdiction. . . . Japan's cession to the United States of jurisdiction to try American military personnel for conduct constituting an offense against the laws of both countries was conditioned by the covenant of Article 17, Section 3, Paragraph (c) of the Protocol that "the authorities of the State having the primary right shall give sympathetic consideration to a request from the authorities of the other State for a waiver of its right in cases where that other State considers such waiver to be of particular importance."

The issue for our decision is therefore narrowed to the question whether, upon the record before us, the Constitution or legislation subsequent to the Security Treaty prohibited the carrying out of this provision authorized by the Treaty for waiver of the qualified jurisdiction granted by Japan. We find no constitutional or statutory barrier to the provision as applied here. In the absence of such encroachments, the wisdom of the arrangement is exclusively for the determination of the Executive and Legislative Branches. [Girard lost his case. He was tried and convicted in Japanese court of bodily injury resulting in death, and served a comparatively light sentence].

Is the administrative agreement that defines the boundaries of criminal jurisdiction in this case a "treaty" within the meaning of Article 6 of the Constitution, or is it an executive agreement (that is, a treaty as defined by international law, but not for the purposes of Article 6 of the Constitution)? Why do you think the Japanese government took the position that Girard's action was not "in the performance of his official duty?" On what foundation could the United States rest its argument to the contrary? Consider the American commanding officer's Certificate as to Official Duty and the Japanese response:

COMPANY F, 8TH CAVALRY REGIMENT
7 FEBRUARY 1957
SUBJECT: CERTIFICATE AS TO OFFICIAL DUTY
THRU: PROVOST MARSHAL, REGIONAL CAMP WHITTINGTON
TO: CHIEF PROCURATOR, MAEBASHI DISTRICT, MAEBASHI
CITY, HONSHU, JAPAN

1. Pursuant to the provisions of Paragraph 43 of the Agreed Views of the Criminal Jurisdiction Subcommittee with respect to the Protocol amending Article 17 of the Administrative Agreement between the United States and Japan, I certify that Girard, William S., Specialist Third Class, was in the performance of his official duty at 1350 hours, 30 January 1957, Camp Weir Range Area, when he was involved in the following incident: On 30 January 1957, 2nd Battalion, 8th Cavalry Regiment, was engaged in routine training at Camp Weir Range Area. Company F was conducting blank firing exercises. Specialist Third Class Girard was instructed by his platoon leader to move near a position near an unguarded machine gun to guard the machine gun and items of field equipment that were in the immediate area. Girard, following instructions, moved to the designated position near the machine gun. While performing his duties as guard, he fired an expended cartridge case, as a warning, which struck and killed Sakai, Naka, Kami-Shinden, Somamura, Gumma Prefecture, who had entered the range area for the purpose of gathering expended cartridge cases.

2. The United States will exercise jurisdiction in this case, unless notification is given immediately that proof to the contrary exists.

3. Should this incident result in trial of the above individual by general court-martial, you will be notified of the date of trial in accordance with the provisions of Paragraph 45 of the above mentioned Agreed Views.

CARL C. ALLIGOOD
1ST LT. INFANTRY
COMMANDING
MAEBASHI DISTRICT PUBLIC
PROCURATOR'S OFFICE
MAEBASHI, 9 FEBRUARY 1957

To: Mr. Carl C. Alligood, 1st Lt Infantry, Command, F Co., 2nd Bn 8th Cavalry Regiment
Re: Notification of the existence of the contrary proof.

Dear Sir:
Reference is made to the letter from you dated on 8 February 1957, regarding to the "On Duty" status of the case involving SP3 Girard S. William, which we received on 8 February 1957.

This is to inform you that this office considers the proof contrary thereto exists, basing upon our examinations.
/s/ Nagami Sakai
Chief Procurator
Maebashi Public Procurator's Office
[The Japanese summary of the facts was as follows:]

He (Girard) and Nickel went to the gun and, about 13.15 hrs he picked up and threw expended cartridge cases in the direction of the slope south of the hill, and, beckoning Hidehara Onozeki (male) and Naka Sakai (female) who had been at a place in the south-west of Hill 655 to gather empty cartridge cases, etc., cried out to them 'Papa-San, daijobu,' 'Mama-San, daijobu' ('Old man, O.K., old lady, O.K.'), etc. in Japanese and thus let the 2 Japanese pick up expended cartridge cases he had thrown. Then he, pointing to the nearby hole for Naka Sakai, cried out to her in Japanese 'Mama-San, takusan-ne' ('Old lady, plenty more!'), and hinting thereby that there remained some expended cartridge cases in it, induced her to go to the hole. But, at that moment, Hideharu Onozeki who was picking up expended cartridge cases on the said slope became suspicious of the suspects behaviour and tried to run away. Then the suspect suddenly shouted to Onoseki 'Ge-Rou! Hey!' and fired a blank shot towards him, placing an expended cartridge case in the grenade launcher attached to the rifle which he had carried with him. Then he cried out 'Ge-Rou! Hey!' to Naka Sakai who was in the hole, and, when he saw her running off towards the north slope of the hill, he, holding the stock of the rifle under his arm, fired standing a blank shot toward her about eight (8) meters away with an expended cartridge case put in the grenade launcher, just in the same manner as he had done to Hideharu Onozeki, as the result of which he made her sustain a penetrating wound on the left side of her back which proved fatal on the spot because of the loss of blood resulting from a cut in the main artery."

SP3 William S. Girard, the suspect in this case, had

been instructed to guard a machine gun and equipment at the time of occurrence of the case. It is evident, however, as shown in the above finding of facts, that the incident arose when he, materially deviating from the performance of such duty of his, wilfully threw expended cartridge cases away towards Naka Sakai and Hideharu Onozeki, and, thus inviting them to come near to him, he fired towards them. Therefore, the incident is not considered to have arisen out of an act or omission done in the performance of official duty.

What happens when the crime involves only Americans, and not, as in the *Girard* case, a national of the host country? In the following case, the civilian wives of active duty service members overseas were tried by courts-martial for murder of their husbands. Each argued that trial by court-martial denied them their constitutional right to trial by jury. The government argued that trial by court-martial was authorized and required by the SOFAs with the host countries in which the crimes had occurred.

REID, SUPERINTENDENT OF DISTRICT OF COLUMBIA JAIL V. COVERT
SUPREME COURT OF THE UNITED STATES
354 U.S. 1
JUNE 10, 1957
Opinion: Black, Justice

These cases raise basic constitutional issues of the utmost concern. They call into question the role of the military under our system of government. They involve the power of Congress to expose civilians to trial by military tribunals, under military regulations and procedures, for offenses against the United States thereby depriving them of trial in civilian courts, under civilian laws and procedures and with all the safeguards of the Bill of Rights. These cases are particularly significant because for the first time since the adoption of the Constitution wives of soldiers have been denied trial by jury in a court of law and forced to trial before courts-martial.

Mrs. Clarice Covert killed her husband, a sergeant in the United States Air Force, at an airbase in England. Mrs. Covert, who was not a member of the armed ser-

vices, was residing on the base with her husband at the time. She was tried by a court-martial for murder under Article 118 of the Uniform Code of Military Justice (UCMJ). The trial was on charges preferred by air force personnel and the court-martial was composed of air force officers. The court-martial asserted jurisdiction over Mrs. Covert under Article 2 of the UCMJ, which provides: "The following persons are subject to this code: Subject to the provisions of any treaty or agreement to which the United States is or may be a party or to any accepted rule of international law, all persons serving with, employed by, or accompanying the armed forces without the continental limits of the United States."

Mrs. Dorothy Smith killed her husband, an army officer, at a post in Japan where she was living with him. She was tried for murder by a court-martial and despite considerable evidence that she was insane was found guilty and sentenced to life imprisonment. She was then confined in a federal penitentiary in West Virginia. Her father, respondent here, filed a petition for habeas corpus in a District Court for West Virginia. The petition charged that the court-martial was without jurisdiction because Article 2 of the UCMJ was unconstitutional insofar as it authorized the trial of civilian dependents accompanying servicemen overseas.

At the beginning we reject the idea that when the United States acts against citizens abroad it can do so free of the Bill of Rights. The United States is entirely a creature of the Constitution. Its power and authority have no other source. It can only act in accordance with all the limitations imposed by the Constitution. When the government reaches out to punish a citizen who is abroad, the shield which the Bill of Rights and other parts of the Constitution provide to protect his life and liberty should not be stripped away just because he happens to be in another land. This is not a novel concept. To the contrary, it is as old as government.

At the time of Mrs. Covert's alleged offense, an executive agreement was in effect between the United States and Great Britain which permitted United States' military courts to exercise exclusive jurisdiction over offenses committed in Great Britain by American servicemen or their dependents. For its part, the United States agreed that these military courts would be willing and able to try and to punish all offenses against the laws of Great Britain by such persons. In all material respects, the same situation existed in Japan when Mrs. Smith killed her husband. Even though a court-martial does not give an accused trial by jury and other Bill of Rights protections, the government contends that Art. 2 of the UCMJ, insofar as it provides for the military trial of dependents accompanying the armed forces in Great Britain and Japan, can be sustained as legislation which is necessary and proper to carry out the United States' obligations under the international agreements made with those countries. The obvious and decisive answer to this, of course, is that no agreement with a foreign nation can confer power on the Congress, or on any other branch of government, which is free from the restraints of the Constitution. The [executive agreement then] in effect in Great Britain and the other North Atlantic Treaty Organization nations, as well as in Japan, [was] the NATO Status of Forces Agreement . . . which by its terms gives the foreign nation primary jurisdiction to try dependents accompanying American servicemen for offenses which are violations of the law of both the foreign nation and the United States. The foreign nation has exclusive criminal jurisdiction over dependents for offenses which only violate its laws. However, the Agreement contains provisions which require that the foreign nations provide procedural safeguards for our nationals tried under the terms of the Agreement in their courts. Apart from those persons subject to the Status of Forces and comparable agreements and certain other restricted classes of Americans, a foreign nation has plenary criminal jurisdiction, of course, over all Americans—tourists, residents, businessmen, government employees and so forth—who commit offenses against its laws within its territory.

Article 6, the Supremacy Clause of the Constitution, declares: "This Constitution, and the Laws of the United States which shall be made in Pursuance thereof; and all Treaties made, or which shall be made, under the Authority of the United States, shall be the supreme Law of the Land." There is nothing in this language which intimates that treaties and laws enacted pursuant to them do not have to comply with the provisions of the Constitution. Nor is there anything in the debates which accompanied the drafting and ratifi-

cation of the Constitution which even suggests such a result. These debates as well as the history that surrounds the adoption of the treaty provision in Article 6 make it clear that the reason treaties were not limited to those made in "pursuance" of the Constitution was so that agreements made by the United States under the Articles of Confederation, including the important peace treaties which concluded the Revolutionary War, would remain in effect. It would be manifestly contrary to the objectives of those who created the Constitution, as well as those who were responsible for the Bill of Rights—let alone alien to our entire constitutional history and tradition—to construe Article 6 as permitting the United States to exercise power under an international agreement without observing constitutional prohibitions. In effect, such construction would permit amendment of that document in a manner not sanctioned by Article 5. The prohibitions of the Constitution were designed to apply to all branches of the national government and they cannot be nullified by the Executive or by the Executive and the Senate combined.

This Court has also repeatedly taken the position that an Act of Congress, which must comply with the Constitution, is on a full parity with a treaty, and that when a statute which is subsequent in time is inconsistent with a treaty, the statute to the extent of conflict renders the treaty null. It would be completely anomalous to say that a treaty need not comply with the Constitution when such an agreement can be overridden by a statute that must conform to that instrument.

In summary, we conclude that the Constitution in its entirety applied to the trials of Mrs. Smith and Mrs. Covert.

If civilian family members of active duty service members abroad cannot be tried by court-martial, must they be tried by host-country courts for offenses against other members of the military community, when those offenses violate host-country criminal law? What other options does an overseas base commander have with respect to civilians who misbehave on an overseas installation?

The preceding discussion illustrated the effect that treaty law has on the activities of military personnel at nearly every level of day-to-day life, as well as al-luding to its effect upon activities related to military operations at sea, during armed conflict, and involv-ing the threat or use of force in operations other than war. Perhaps an even more important and encom-passing source of law in the international legal sys-tem, however, is customary law. *The Commander's Handbook on the Law of Military Operations,* for ex-ample, unequivocally declares, "Customary interna-tional law is the principal source of international law and is binding upon all nations."

Customary International Law

What exactly is customary international law? Article 38 of the Statute of the International Court of Justice states that "the Court, whose function is to decide in accordance with international law such disputes as are submitted to it, shall apply . . . international cus-tom, as evidence of a general practice accepted as law." In this definition, the custom is not itself a law, but evidence of the existence of a law—that is, because the court can observe a custom, it may infer that the custom exists out of some sense in the international community that the custom developed and is adhered to out of a belief that it is a matter of law. What the court—or anyone else seeking to establish a particu-lar rule of customary international law—really looks for, then, is evidence of a perceived legal obligation. Perceived by whom? By states, and by the many other players in the international system. If the actors in the international system perceive a certain practice to be a matter of law and behave in a manner consis-tent with such a perception, then the perception be-comes the reality. The perception and the consistent behavior resulting from, and contributing to it, if ob-servable, in fact become the law. This then is the essence of customary international law—a practice so commonly followed that it may be considered custom-ary, when followed out of a sense of legal obligation.

As noted in the reporter's notes to Section 102 of the *Restatement,* the concept is essentially circular:

There have been philosophical debates about the very basis of the definition: how can practice build law? Most troublesome conceptually has been the circularity in the suggestion that law is built by practice based on a sense of legal obligation: how it can be asked, can there be a sense of legal obligation before the law from which the legal obligation derives has matured? Such conceptual difficulties, however, have not prevented acceptance of customary law essentially as here defined. . . . Perhaps the definition reflects a later stage in the history of international law when governments found practice and sense of obligation already in evidence, and accepted them without inquiring as to the original basis of that sense of legal obligation.

Thus, notwithstanding the "which came first?" co-nundrum inherent in the concept, a practice engaged in as a matter of custom may provide very persuasive evidence that the "custom" is at the same time a law and indeed exists by virtue of this very fact. Proving that a custom establishes a rule of international law requires more, however, than simply asserting that it occurs. It requires analysis of the practice of states and other players in the international system; that is, looking at what they actually do. The process of proof also requires analysis of what they say about what they do; what is said provides evidence of whether or not the players perceive a legal obligation. Sources of evidence relevant to this inquiry include, as noted in Article 38 of the Statute of the Interna-tional Court of Justice, "judicial decisions and the teachings of the most highly qualified publicists of the various nations," as well as diplomatic correspon-dence, press releases, opinions of legal advisors, mili-tary manuals, rules of engagement, previous or re-lated treaties, policy statements, domestic legislation, and statements of international organizations.

The following case represents an example of how such an analysis might be conducted. In the case of *The Paquete Habana,* the U.S. Supreme Court found itself challenged by the need to decide whether the customary international law of armed conflict per-mitted U.S. warships to target Cuban coastal fishing vessels during the Spanish-American War. As you read this opinion, note the evidence considered by the Court in resolving this question. Note also the role played by rules of engagement in the Court's analysis, how those rules are related to the international law of armed conflict, and the relationship of principles of humanity and of military necessity to that law.

THE PAQUETE HABANA
SUPREME COURT OF THE UNITED STATES
175 U.S. 677
JANUARY 8, 1900 DECIDED

Mr. Justice Gray delivered the opinion of the court.

These are two appeals from decrees of the District Court of the United States for the Southern District of Florida, condemning two fishing vessels and their cargoes as prizes of war.

Each vessel was a fishing smack, running in and out of Havana, and regularly engaged in fishing on the coast of Cuba; sailed under the Spanish flag; was owned by a Spanish subject of Cuban birth, living in the city of Havana; was commanded by a subject of Spain, also residing in Havana; and her master and crew had no interest in the vessel, but were entitled to shares, amounting in all to two thirds, of her catch, the other third belonging to her owner. Her cargo consisted of fresh fish, caught by her crew from the sea, put on board as they were caught, and kept and sold alive. Until stopped by the blockading squadron, she had no knowledge of the existence of the war, or of any blockade. She had no arms or ammunition on board, and made no attempt to run the blockade after she knew of its existence, nor any resistance at the time of the capture.

The *Paquete Habana* was a sloop, 43 feet long on the keel, and of 25 tons burden, and had a crew of three Cubans, including the master, who had a fishing license from the Spanish government . . . She left Havana March 25, 1898; sailed along the coast of Cuba . . . and there fished for twenty-five days . . . within the territorial waters of Spain; and then started back for Havana, with a cargo of about 40 quintals of live fish. On April 25, 1898, about two miles off Mariel, and eleven miles from Havana, she was captured by the United States gunboat *Castine*.

The *Lola* was a schooner, 51 feet long on the keel, and of 35 tons burden, and had a crew of six Cubans, including the master, and no commission or license. She left Havana April 11, 1898, and proceeded to Campeachy Sound off Yucatan, fished there eight days, and started back for Havana with a cargo of about 10,000 pounds of live fish. On April 26, 1898, near Havana, she was stopped by the United States steamship *Cincinnati*, and was warned not to go into Havana, but was told that she would be allowed to land at Bahia Honda. She then changed her course, and put for Bahia Honda, but on the next morning, when near that port, was captured by the United States steamship *Dolphin*.

Each vessel was thereupon sold by auction; the *Paquete Habana* for the sum of $490; and the *Lola* for the sum of $800. . . .

We are . . . brought to the consideration of the question whether, upon the facts appearing in these records, the fishing smacks were subject to capture by the armed vessels of the United States during the recent war with Spain.

By an ancient usage among civilized nations, beginning centuries ago, and gradually ripening into a rule of international law, coast fishing vessels, pursuing their vocation of catching and bringing in fresh fish, have been recognized as exempt, with their cargoes and crews, from capture as prize of war.

International law is part of our law, and must be ascertained and administered by the courts of justice of appropriate jurisdiction, as often as questions of right depending upon it are duly presented for their determination.

For this purpose, where there is no treaty, and no controlling executive or legislative act or judicial decision, resort must be had to the customs and usages of civilized nations; and, as evidence of these, to the works of jurists and commentators, who by years of labor, research and experience, have made themselves peculiarly well acquainted with the subjects of which they treat. Such works are resorted to by judicial tribunals, not for the speculations of their authors concerning what the law ought to be, but for trustworthy evidence of what the law really is.

[Our] review of the precedents and authorities on the subject appears to us abundantly to demonstrate that at the present day, by the general consent of the civilized nations of the world, and independently of any express treaty or other public act, it is an established rule of international law, founded on considerations of humanity to a poor and industrious order of men, and of the mutual convenience of belligerent States, that coast fishing vessels, with their implements and supplies, cargoes and crews, unarmed, and honestly pursuing their peaceful calling of catching and bringing in fresh fish, are exempt from capture as prizes of war.

The exemption, of course, does not apply to coast fishermen or their vessels, if employed for a warlike purpose, or in such a way as to give aid or information to the enemy; nor when military or naval operations create a necessity to which all private interests must give way.

This rule of international law is one which prize courts, administering the law of nations, are bound to take judicial notice of, and to give effect to, in the absence of any treaty or other public act of their own government in relation to the matter.

To this subject, in more than one aspect, are singularly applicable the words uttered by Mr. Justice Strong, speaking for this court:

> Undoubtedly, no single nation can change the law of the sea. That law is of universal obligation, and no statute of one or two nations can create obligations for the world. Like all the laws of nations, it rests upon the common consent of civilized communities. It is of force, not because it was prescribed by any superior power, but because it has been generally accepted as a rule of conduct. . . . It is recognition of the historical fact that by common consent of mankind these rules have been acquiesced in as of general obligation. Of that fact, we think, we may take judicial notice. Foreign municipal laws must indeed be proved as facts, but it is not so with the law of nations.

The position taken by the United States during the recent war with Spain was quite in accord with the rule of international law, now generally recognized by civilized nations, in regard to coast fishing vessels.

On April 21, 1898, the secretary of the navy gave instructions to Admiral Sampson, commanding the North Atlantic Squadron, to "immediately institute a blockade of the north coast of Cuba." The blockade was immediately instituted accordingly. On April 22, the president issued a proclamation, declaring that the United States had instituted and would maintain that blockade, "in pursuance of . . . the law of nations applicable to such cases."

On April 26, 1898, the president issued another proclamation, which, after reciting the existence of the war, as declared by Congress, contained this further recital: "It being desirable that such war should be conducted upon principles in harmony with the present views of nations and sanctioned by their recent practice." This recital was followed by specific declarations of certain rules for the conduct of the war by sea, making no mention of fishing vessels. But the proclamation clearly manifests the general policy of the government to conduct the war in accordance with the principles of international law sanctioned by the recent practice of nations.

On April 28, 1898 (after the capture of the two fishing vessels now in question), Admiral Sampson telegraphed to the secretary of the navy as follows:

> I find that a large number of fishing schooners are attempting to get into Havana from their fishing grounds near the Florida reefs and coasts. They are generally manned by excellent seamen, belonging to the maritime inscription of Spain, who have already served in the Spanish navy, and who are liable to further service. As these trained men are naval reserves, have a semi-military character, and would be most valuable to the Spaniards as artillerymen, either afloat or ashore, I recommend that they should be detained prisoners of war, and that I should be authorized to deliver them to the commanding officer of the army at Key West.

To that communication the secretary of the navy, on April 30, 1898, guardedly answered: "Spanish fishing vessels attempting to violate blockade are subject, with crew, to capture, and any such vessel or crew considered likely to aid enemy may be detained."

The Admiral's despatch assumed that he was not authorized, without express order, to arrest coast fishermen peaceably pursuing their calling; and the necessary implication and evident intent of the response of the Navy Department were that Spanish coast fishing vessels and their crews should not be interfered with, so long as they neither attempted to violate the blockade, nor were considered likely to aid the enemy.

The *Paquete Habana,* as the record shows, was a fishing sloop of twenty-five tons burden. She had no arms or ammunition on board; she had no knowledge of the blockade, or even of the war, until she was stopped by a blockading vessel; she made no attempt to run the blockade, and no resistance at the time of the capture; nor was there any evidence whatever of likelihood that she or her crew would aid the enemy.

In the case of the *Lola,* the only differences in the facts were that she was a schooner of thirty-five tons burden, and had a crew of six men, including the master; that after leaving Havana, and proceeding some two hundred miles along the coast of Cuba, she went on, about a hundred miles farther, to the coast of Yucatan, and there fished for eight days; and that, on her return, when near Bahia Honda, on the coast of Cuba, she was captured, with her cargo of live fish, on April 27, 1898. These differences afford no ground for distinguishing the two cases.

Upon the facts proved in either case, it is the duty of this court, sitting as the highest prize court of the United States, and administering the law of nations, to declare and adjudge that the capture was unlawful.

Professional military officers might note that the case of the *Paquete Habana* is a case which, at bottom, is one concerned with the law of armed conflict; and in deciding a legal issue born of war, the Court made pronouncements about principles of international law applicable not only to legal issues associated with war but also to those associated with the international legal system in its broadest sense. This result is not at all novel; much of modern international law derives from international legal principles first developed out of an effort to ameliorate the violence, suffering, and destruction associated with war by using law to induce limits. Indeed, perhaps the seminal work of modern international law, written in 1625 by Dutch scholar Hugo Grotius, often called "father of international law," is entitled *The Law of War and Peace.* In the *Paquete Habana* the Court considered treaties as evidence of customary international law. What is the relationship between a treaty and customary international law?

The comments to Section 102 of the *Restatement* make two points relevant to understanding the relationship between treaties and customary international law:

International agreements constitute practice of states and as such contribute to the growth of customary law . . . Some multilateral agreements may come to be law for non-parties that do not actively dissent. That may be the effect where a multilateral agreement is designed for adherence by states generally, is widely accepted, and not rejected by a significant number of important states. A wide network of similar bilateral arrangements on a subject may constitute practice and also result in customary law.

Multilateral agreements open to all states . . . are increasingly used for general legislation, whether to make new law, as in human rights . . . or for codifying and developing customary law.

In another judicial decision born out of issues of armed attack, self-defense, force, and violence, the International Court of Justice elaborated upon and applied these concepts in a modern context. In 1984 Nicaragua sued the United States in the ICJ, alleging the United States had, among other things, engaged in an illegal armed attack against Nicaragua's territorial sovereignty and political independence, in violation of both the Charter of the United Nations and customary international law. Although the United States did not consent to the exercise of jurisdiction by the ICJ and, in fact, refused to participate in the trial on the merits of the case, the ICJ's lengthy and comprehensive opinion is often cited in support of the broad and fundamental international law principles discussed.

INTERNATIONAL COURT OF JUSTICE; JUDGMENT ON MERITS IN CASE CONCERNING MILITARY AND PARAMILITARY ACTIVITIES IN AND AGAINST NICARAGUA NICARAGUA V. UNITED STATES, ICJ REPORTS, P. 14

On 9 April 1984 the Ambassador of the Republic of Nicaragua to the Netherlands filed in the Registry of the Court an Application instituting proceedings against the United States of America in respect of a dispute concerning responsibility for military and paramilitary activities in and against Nicaragua:

(a) That the United States, in recruiting, training, arming, equipping, financing, supplying and otherwise encouraging, supporting, aiding, and directing military and paramilitary actions in and against Nicaragua, has violated and is violating its express charter and treaty obligations to Nicaragua, and in particular, its charter and treaty obligations under Article 2(4) of the United Nations Charter.

(b) That the United States, in breach of its obligation under general and customary international law, has violated and is violating the sovereignty of Nicaragua by:

— armed attacks against Nicaragua by air, land and sea;

— incursions into Nicaraguan territorial waters;

— aerial trespass into Nicaraguan airspace;

— efforts by direct and indirect means to coerce and intimidate the government of Nicaragua.

(c) That the United States, in breach of its obligation under general and customary international law, has used and is using force and the threat of force against Nicaragua.

(d) That the United States, in breach of its obligation under general and customary international law, has intervened and is intervening in the internal affairs of Nicaragua.

(e) That the United States, in breach of its obligation under general and customary international law, has infringed and is infringing the freedom of the high seas and interrupting peaceful maritime commerce.

(f) That the United States, in breach of its obligation under general and customary international law, has killed, wounded and kidnapped and is killing, wounding and kidnapping citizens of Nicaragua.

(g) That, in view of its breaches of the foregoing legal obligations, the United States is under a particular duty to cease and desist immediately from all use of force—whether direct or indirect, overt or covert—against Nicaragua, and from all threats of force against Nicaragua; from all violations of the sovereignty, territorial integrity or political independence of Nicaragua, including all intervention, direct or indirect, in the internal affairs of Nicaragua; from all support of any kind—including the provision of training, arms, ammunition, finances, supplies, assistance, direction or any other form of support—to any nation, group, organization, movement or individual engaged or planning to engage in military or paramilitary actions in or against Nicaragua; from all efforts to restrict, block or endanger access to or from Nicaraguan ports; and from all killings, woundings and kidnappings of Nicaraguan citizens.

There can be no doubt that the issues of the use of force and collective self-defence raised in the present proceedings are issues which are regulated both by customary international law and by treaties, in particular the United Nations Charter.

As regards the suggestion that the areas covered by the two sources of law are identical, the Court observes that the United Nations Charter, the convention to which most of the United States argument is directed, by no means covers the whole area of the regulation of the use of force in international relations. On one essential point, this treaty itself refers to pre-existing customary international law; this reference to customary law is contained in the actual text of Article 51, which mentions the "inherent right" of individual or collective self-defence, which "nothing in the present Charter shall impair" and which applies in the event of an armed attack. The Court therefore finds that Article 51 of the Charter is only meaningful on the basis that there is a "natural" or "inherent" right of self-defence, and it is hard to see how this can be other than of a customary nature, even if its present content has been confirmed and influenced by the Charter. Moreover the Charter, having itself recognized the existence of this right, does not go on to regulate directly all aspects of its content. For example, it does not contain any specific rule whereby self-defence would warrant only measures which are proportional to the armed attack and necessary to respond to it, a rule well established in customary international law. Moreover, a definition of the "armed attack" which, if found to exist, authorizes the exercise of the "inherent right" of self-defence, is not provided in the Charter, and is not part of treaty law. It cannot therefore be held that Article 51 is a provision which "subsumes and supervenes" customary international law. It rather demonstrates that in the field in question, the importance of which for the present dispute need hardly be stressed, customary international law continues to exist alongside treaty law. The areas governed by the two sources of law thus do not overlap exactly, and the rules do not have the same content.

This could also be demonstrated for other subjects, in particular for the principle of non-intervention.

Even if the customary norm and the treaty norm were to have exactly the same content, this would not be a reason for the Court to hold that the incorporation of the customary norm into treaty-law must deprive the customary norm of its applicability as distinct from that of the treaty norm. The existence of identical rules in international treaty law and customary law has been clearly recognized by the Court in the North Sea Continental Shelf cases. To a large extent, those cases turned on the question whether a rule enshrined in a treaty also existed as a customary rule, either because the treaty had merely codified the custom, or caused it to "crystallize," or because it had influenced its subsequent adoption. The Court found that this identity of content in treaty law and in customary international law did not exist in the case of the rule invoked, which appeared in one article of the treaty, but did not suggest that such identity was debarred as a matter of principle: on the contrary, it considered it to be clear that certain other articles of the treaty in question "were . . . regarded as reflecting, or as crystallizing, received or at least emergent rules of customary international law." More generally, there are no grounds for holding that when customary international law is comprised of rules identical to those of treaty law, the latter "supervenes" the former, so that the customary international law has no further existence of its own.

There are a number of reasons for considering that, even if two norms belonging to two sources of international law appear identical in content, and even if the States in question are bound by these rules both on the level of treaty-law and on that of customary international law, these norms retain a separate existence. This is so from the standpoint of their applicability. In a legal dispute affecting two States, one of them may argue that the applicability of a treaty rule to its own conduct depends on the other State's conduct in respect of the application of other rules, on other subjects, also included in the same treaty. For example, if a State exercises its right to terminate or suspend the operation of a treaty on the ground of the violation by the other party of a "provision essential to the accomplishment of the object or purpose of the treaty" (in the words of

Art. 60, para. 3(b), of the Vienna Convention on the Law of Treaties), it is exempted, vis-à-vis the other State, from a rule of treaty-law because of the breach by that other State of a different rule of treaty-law. But if the two rules in question also exist as rules of customary international law, the failure of the one State to apply the one rule does not justify the other State in declining to apply the other rule. Rules which are identical in treaty law and in customary international law are also distinguishable by reference to the methods of interpretation and application. A State may accept a rule contained in a treaty not simply because it favours the application of the rule itself, but also because the treaty establishes what that State regards as desirable institutions or mechanisms to ensure implementation of the rule. Thus, if that rule parallels a rule of customary international law, two rules of the same content are subject to separate treatment as regards the organs competent to verify their implementation, depending on whether they are customary rules or treaty rules. The present dispute illustrates this point.

It will therefore be clear that customary international law continues to exist and to apply, separately from international treaty law, even where the two categories of law have an identical content. . . . so far from having constituted a marked departure from a customary international law which still exists unmodified, the Charter gave expression in this field to principles already present in customary international law, and that law has in the subsequent four decades developed under the influence of the Charter, to such an extent that a number of rules contained in the Charter have acquired a status independent of it. The essential consideration is that both the Charter and the customary international law flow from a common fundamental principle outlawing the use of force in international relations.

In view of this conclusion, the Court has next to consider what are the rules of customary international law applicable to the present dispute. For this purpose, it has to direct its attention to the practice and *opinio juris* of States; as the Court recently observed,

> It is of course axiomatic that the material of customary international law is to be looked for primarily in the actual practice and *opinio juris* of States, even though multilateral conventions may have an important role to play in record-

ing and defining rules deriving from custom, or indeed in developing them.

It is not to be expected that in the practice of States the application of the rules in question should have been perfect, in the sense that States should have refrained, with complete consistency, from the use of force or from intervention in each other's internal affairs. The Court does not consider that, for a rule to be established as customary, the corresponding practice must be in absolutely rigorous conformity with the rule. In order to deduce the existence of customary rules, the Court deems it sufficient that the conduct of States should, in general, be consistent with such rules, and that instances of State conduct inconsistent with a given rule should generally have been treated as breaches of that rule, not as indications of the recognition of a new rule. If a State acts in a way prima facie incompatible with a recognized rule, but defends its conduct by appealing to exceptions or justifications contained within the rule itself, then whether or not the State's conduct is in fact justifiable on that basis, the significance of that attitude is to confirm rather than to weaken the rule.

What multilateral treaties did the ICJ look to in its analysis of customary international law? What was the relationship between these treaties and customary law? What effect does the creation of a multilateral treaty have on customary law? Do developments in customary law influence treaty formation? What is the potential effect of widely accepted multilateral treaties on nonparties to those treaties? If a particular rule of international law is substantially the same in a multilateral treaty as it is in customary law, what incentives exist for states to sign on to the treaty? In this regard, consider that the International Court of Justice is an institution created by the UN Charter.

Among the several important points discussed in the *Nicaragua* case is one only alluded to there, but here deserving of further discussion. The ICJ noted that practice need not be universally followed to be considered general. Wide acceptance is sufficient. What happens when a state does not actively engage in a generally followed practice but does not actually object either? Such states are said to acquiesce to the practice. Comment (b) to Section 102 of the *Restatement* states that "inaction may constitute state practice, as when a state acquiesces in acts of another state that affect its legal rights." Thus silence in a circumstance in which one might be expected to object amounts to tacit acceptance, and acceptance constitutes practice. What about states that actively dissent and object to a practice, either by diplomatic notes or other means to publicize their dissent, or by deliberately engaging in some contrary practice? Can these dissenters, by objecting, prevent a rule of customary international law from forming? Or does their dissent have some less comprehensive effect? Comment (d) to Section 102 says, "Although customary law may be built by the acquiescence as well as by the actions of states . . . and become generally binding on all states, in principle a state that indicates its dissent from a practice while the law is still in the process of development is not bound by that rule even after it matures."

The conceptual effects of objection and acquiescence upon developing customary international law have influenced the oceans policy of the United States with respect to the international law of the sea. Consider this excerpt from *Excessive Maritime Claims,* a book published as volume 66 of the *Naval War College International Law Studies* series:

It is accepted international law and practice that, to prevent changes in or derogations from rules of law, States must persistently object to actions by other States that seek to change those rules. Protest 'must, at the very least, be repeated' and 'must be supported by conduct which opposes the presentations of the claimant state.' Naturally, States are not required to adopt a course of conduct which virtually negates the rights reserved by the protest. Consequently, States will not be permitted to acquiesce in emerging new rules of law and later claim exemption from them at will.

Acquiescence is the tacit acceptance of a certain legal position as a result of a failure to make a reservation of rights at the appropriate juncture. For acquiescence to arise, a claim must have been made and accepted. The claim must be made in a manner, and in such circumstances, that the other State has been placed on notice of that claim. The conduct that allegedly constitutes acquiescence, or tacit acceptance of that claim, likewise must be clear and unequivocal. The failure to make a timely protest in circumstances where it reasonably could have been expected to do so may constitute tacit acceptance of that claim.

Where the claim protested against has the effect of taking away a nation's right to use portions of the oceans, mere preservation of one's legal right to operate there is of little practical value when one chooses not to operate there except in extraordinary circumstances. Avoiding areas where a country needs to operate, or could be expected to operate, in the absence of the illegal claim gives both practical and legal effect to the excessive claim.

One of the four Geneva Conventions of 1949 establishes rules of international law requiring humane treatment of prisoners of war (POWs). Many of these treaty law principles coexist with virtually identical rules of customary international law. Suppose the United States is engaged in armed conflict with another country and that country is violating international law by maltreating American POWs in its custody, claiming that these captives are international criminals undeserving of POW status. Why should the United States comply with the Geneva Conventions in its treatment of any POWs it may hold when the enemy is not? What should the United States do about the violations committed by the other side?

Suppose a state announces that a portion of the ocean off of its coast is permanently closed to foreign shipping unless permission is asked and received from that state's government. Should the United States acquiesce to that claim? What happens if it does and then other states make similar claims? Brazil, Iran, and India have all announced that foreign warships must request permission to operate in the waters extending two hundred miles from these states' coasts. A number of other countries make outright claims of two-hundred-mile territorial seas and purport to restrict foreign naval operations in those waters. If the United States considers these claims excessive and not supportable under the customary international law of the sea, what should it do? What could happen if the United States does nothing?

Conclusion

The sources of international law include international agreements and customary international law. Customary international law is formed of practice combined with *opinio juris,* that is, a perception that the practice is legally obligatory. Action is practice, and it therefore has a profound influence on the development and formation of customary international law. Action may take the form of agreement to treaties, and also of military operations and the rules of engagement associated with them. The conduct of the naval services of the United States in action thus actually influences the development of international law. Failure to act, if considered acquiescence, may have similar consequences. Thus the naval services in action—and at rest—affect the development and evolution of the customary international law of the sea and of the customary international law of armed conflict. Conversely, existing international law provides a context within which the naval services must operate. The following chapters discuss in further detail the law of armed conflict and the interaction between international law and the military activities of the United States' naval services.

Study Questions

1. What are the sources of international law?
2. Why do states comply with international law?
3. What is the difference between the Vienna Convention definition of a treaty and the customary international law definition? U.S. law definition and international law definition?

4. How is customary international law formed?

5. What provides evidence of the existence of a rule of customary international law?

6. How does treaty law affect the development of customary international law?

7. To whom or what does treaty law apply? What about customary international law?

8. What are SOFAs? What do they typically say about foreign criminal jurisdiction?

9. Why is it important for a state to object by action and deed to claims of right under customary international law with which it does not agree?

10. To whom does international law apply?

11. What effect can military rules of engagement have upon international law? Vice versa?

CHAPTER TWELVE

THE LAW OF ARMED CONFLICT

War is . . . an act of force to compel the enemy to do our will. . . . Attached to force are certain self-imposed, imperceptible limitations hardly worth mentioning, known as international law and custom, but they scarcely weaken it.

—Carl Von Clausewitz, *On War* (1818)

Decisions were impacted by legal considerations at every level, [the law of war] proved invaluable in the decision-making process.

—General Colin Powell,
discussing the role of the law of war
in the Gulf War (1991)

Introduction

The Law of Armed Conflict (LOAC), sometimes also called the law of war or international humanitarian law, attempts to limit the force, violence, destruction, and suffering inherent in war. Yet war, considered conceptually and in its platonically ideal state, according to Carl Von Clausewitz, author of the brilliant and paradigmatic *On War,* "is an act of force, and there is no logical limit to the application of that force." Once started, reasoned Clausewitz, war must lead to extremes, and in the extreme, war, unfettered by any external constraints, is a "clash of forces freely operating and obedient to no law but their own"—a kind of autonomous natural phenomenon, like fire or lightening or nuclear explosion—a "pulsation of violence," "a blind natural force," "composed of primordial violence, hatred and enmity." Pure war, once unleashed, will always be total war, that is, "a complete, untrammeled, absolute manifestation of violence," which will "rule by the laws of its own nature," replacing whatever human objectives that might have motivated its ignition with its own consuming greed for all encompassing violence and destruction.

Perhaps Abraham Lincoln had a similar insight—
that the often limited aims of humans in war may be
transformed in unpredictable ways by the very forces
they let loose in pursuit of those aims—when he gave
his Second Inaugural Address, with the American
Civil War all but over, saying:

> Neither party expected for the war, the magnitude or
> the duration, which it has already attained. Neither an-
> ticipated that the cause of the conflict might cease with,
> or even before, the conflict itself should cease. Each
> looked for an easier triumph, and a result less funda-
> mental and astounding. . . . The prayers of both could
> not be answered; that of neither has been answered
> fully. The Almighty has His own purposes.

Thus Lincoln observed, as had Clausewitz, that war
appears sometimes to behave as an independent phenomenon, perhaps with intentions of its own, capable of growing by itself and according to its own puz-
zling rules, beyond the powers of control over its
violence and destruction possessed by those who release its forces. In considering the transformation of
the great war of his own personal experience, Lincoln
saw a divine hand. Clausewitz, however, looked beyond his own personal experience—the total wars of
the Napoleonic era—and made a historical examination of the question. His first and most fundamental
insight resulted: the observation that the pure and total war predicted by theory—the war of complete,
untrammeled, and absolute violence—is the historical exception, not the rule. He noted that, in practice, "warfare . . . eludes the strict theoretical requirement that extremes of force be applied." What, he
wondered, imposes the limits on war that, in most
cases, prevents its escalation to the theoretical extreme?

His answer was the now famous declaration that
"all wars can be considered acts of policy." He elaborated that "war is not a mere act of policy but a true
political instrument, a continuation of political activity by other means." Wars, reasoned Clausewitz,
are defined by the political aims or objectives of those
at war. According to Clausewitz, this political element,
can, to some degree, subordinate the blind natural
forces and uncertainties of war to the power of human
reason. The political element is a critical barrier that
can keep war from exploding into its pure form of absolute and unlimited violence. "The degree of force
that must be used against the enemy depends on the
scale of political demands of either side." Limited objectives may require only limited force.

Unlimited objectives, however, tend to produce
unlimited or total war, because when the sole aim of
a war is to "overthrow the opponent," "the closer will
war approach its abstract concept, the more important will be the destruction of the enemy, the more
closely will the military aims and the political objects
of war coincide." Policy, thought Clausewitz, determines the character of war. "As policy becomes more
ambitious and vigorous, so will war, and this may
reach the point where war attains its absolute form."

Clausewitz had experienced this, he thought, in
the Napoleonic wars of his own experience, when
"war, untrammeled by any conventional restraints,
had broken loose in all its elemental fury." But, he
observed,

> It is no more likely that war will always be so monu-
> mental in character than that the ample scope it has
> come to enjoy will again be severely restricted. A theory,
> then, that dealt exclusively with absolute war would ei-
> ther have to ignore any case in which the nature of war
> had been deformed by outside influence, or else it
> would have to dismiss them all as misconstrued. This
> cannot be what theory is for. Its purpose is to demon-
> strate what war is in practice, not what its ideal nature
> ought to be.

Most wars, Clausewitz observed, are not total or unlimited wars. The political objective of the states involved in most wars is more limited than total defeat
of the enemy, and limited political objectives tend to
influence the military objectives, so as to also limit
the force, violence, and destruction associated with
these limited wars. He reasoned:

Thus policy converts the overwhelmingly destructive element of war into a mere instrument. The terrible two handed sword that should be used with total strength to strike once and no more, becomes the lightest rapier—sometimes even a harmless foil fit only for thrusts and feints and parries.

There is a risk, however, even in the use of limited war as a means of political intercourse. Although the objective of war may be, in its conception, political, using "the sword in place of the pen," war, noted Clausewitz, "does not on that account cease to think according to its own laws." Once set in motion, war tends toward total, absolute, and pure violence, unless restrained by external forces. If the restraints to escalation set in place by adherence to political objectives slip, then war burns free. When political and military objectives become disconnected, when military objectives subsume political ones, when political objectives do not lend themselves to accomplishment by means of war, or when military success produces expanded political objectives, war tends to escalate according to its own laws—and the theoretical natural laws of war demand that "it march relentlessly toward the absolute." In the words of Clausewitz, "If we look at war in this light, we do not need to lose sight of the absolute: on the contrary, we must constantly bear it in mind."

Perhaps this was the phenomenon Lincoln was describing in his Second Inaugural Address—he had seen a war begun with limited objectives, intended to be fought with limited means, escalate into a total war fought with all the means available at the time. In the twentieth century, we have seen total war burn free at least twice, in the two world wars, the second ending with such "a complete, untrammeled, absolute manifestation of violence" as neither Clausewitz nor Lincoln could have ever imagined. In the post-Hiroshima world the risk of escalation to total war fought with all means available to opposing forces is unacceptable. In today's thermonuclear world, with its capacity for biological and chemical warfare as well as nuclear, there can be no winner of such a total war. Either war must cease as a means of political intercourse, or what wars must be, must be fought for limited political objectives and with limited military means. Political restraints that tend to limit war cannot be permitted to slip.

Although for Clausewitz, international law imposed only "imperceptible limitations hardly worth mentioning" on force, violence, and destruction in war, in today's world international law is an important political and military restraint on war, as General Colin Powell noted in the remark quoted at the head of this chapter. It provides a means by which the international culture seeks to prevent war when possible, and when it is not, to prevent its escalation, to contain it while fighting efficiently and effectively—and where necessary, violently—while at the same time keeping political and military objectives closely and appropriately related. Again in the words of Clausewitz:

> If, then, civilized nations do not put their prisoners to death or devastate cities and countries, it is because intelligence plays a larger part in their methods of warfare and has taught them more effective ways of using force than the crude expression of instinct.

Thus, notwithstanding his dismissal of international law as a significant restraint on force in war, Clausewitz might have agreed that laws requiring humane treatment of prisoners of war, protection of noncombatant civilians, and prohibiting indiscriminate targeting of cities, among others, in addition to being humane, tend to make the use of force more economical, disciplined, and effective, and therefore more useful in the accomplishment of underlying political objectives. These kinds of laws tend to dampen the accelerating chain reaction of reciprocally more extreme force and violence through which war escalates out of control; they inhibit the growth of the implacable anger and bitter enmity that demands total destruction and unconditional surrender of a defeated enemy when a negotiated peace might in fact be more expedient and less destructive even for the victor, that exhorts humans at war to fight on desperately and viciously even in the face of inevitable defeat, causing them to prefer death and destruction to negotiated submission, and that makes peace, achieved sometimes more as a matter of momentary exhaustion than of satisfaction, often unstable and difficult to maintain. They help keep military objectives limited, so that limited political aims are not transformed by obedience to war's own natural laws, and they help focus the use of force so that it is economical and disciplined, and therefore more effective and efficient in accomplishing its objectives.

In essence, what we are saying is that, in our world of intercontinental ballistic missiles and multiple thermonuclear warheads, without law, war hazards disaster—the risk of escalation and its result is unacceptable—but that with law, war, when necessary and unavoidable, when forced upon us against our will, can be contained and directed to work effectively to accomplish narrowly limited aims. Law helps keep military and political objectives limited, linked, and closely tied, and so helps restrain escalation from limited war to total war, while at the same time tending to enhance the operational effectiveness of the military forces involved. Law is a critical link in the chain by which policy keeps leashed the wild dogs of war, and with which they are trained to attack under direction of their human master, and not according to their own feral appetites.

As alluded to above, the Law of Armed Conflict involves two related but separate conceptual territories. The first describes when it is legal to go to war, sometimes called *jus ad bellum,* and the second what it is legal to do in war, sometimes called *jus in bello.* Our discussion will begin with the first, which under modern law requires an examination of the 1946 Judgement of the International Military Tribunal at Nuremberg, and of the Charter of the United Nations—both of which limit war by limiting the objectives for which it may be begun. As you read this section, ask yourself what political objectives are now legal and appropriate for accomplishment by means of war.

The Justice of War *(Jus ad Bellum)*

It is fair to say that modern international law in this area—that is, the international law governing when a state may go to war—was born at Nuremberg, where the International Military Tribunal tried Germans accused of certain crimes against international law committed before and during the Second World War. Consider this condensed excerpt from *The Significance of Nuremberg for Modern International Law,* by Fred L. Morrison, originally published in volume 149 of *Military Law Review:*

Nuremberg is the visible symbol of the transition from a Westphalian system of state sovereignty to an international system that took place in the middle of this century. In a sense, it represents the foundation of modern thinking about international law, with an emphasis on the maintenance of peace.

The judgement of Nuremberg is one of the formative events for the international law of our day. It has transformed the legal and political basis for the exercise of public authority in the modern world. Unabashed claims of national sovereignty, stimulated by the nation-state system recognized at Westphalia, have been modified by universalist claims for peace, human rights, and limitations on the use of force articulated in the Nuremberg principles.

Nuremberg is, of course, not only a city, it is a concept. It encompasses London (and the Charter of the War Crimes Tribunal drafted there), Tokyo (and the Principal Eastern Theater Trials), San Francisco (and the drafting of the Charter), Lake Success (and the initial United Nations meetings), as the locations of the subsidiary trials of World War II, and a host of other decisions and events that we accept as part of our modern common learning about international law. Other international agreements and understandings led to it—the various Hague Conventions, the Covenant of the League of Nations, the Kellogg-Briand Pact, the various treaties of nonaggression in the interwar period. And others succeeded it—the Genocide Convention, the Universal Declaration of Human Rights, and other instruments of the modern era. But the years 1945–46 were the critical point of change, and the adoption of the Charter and the judgement of Nuremberg were the high points of that change in the international order.

Nuremberg marks a paradigm shift . . . from a Westphalian system of state sovereignty to an increasingly international set of community norms. To understand the world before Nuremberg, one must first understand the world before [the 1648 Treaty of] Westphalia. Before 1648, the Pope and Emperor had claimed spiritual power and temporal authority to control the exercise of political power. Neither of them had been completely successful, especially for the preceding century, but both continued to have some aura of supremacy. After Westphalia, neither the Pope nor the Emperor, nor anybody else, had "jurisdiction" over the local sovereign, however petty and mean that sovereign might be. The world after Westphalia was a world of state sovereignty. International law accepted the permissibility of wars of colonial conquest; indeed, it accepted wars among self-styled "civilized" states so long as the requisite formalities had been observed. Rules limiting those uses of force were binding only in so far as they had been accepted—and not yet repudiated—by one of the nation states.

The Covenant of the League of Nations [in 1919] did not in terms prohibit war—it only provided temporary and procedural relief. The Kellogg-Briand Pact prohibited war as an instrument of national policy, but it was only a treaty, binding on its signatories, not a principle of generally applicable law. Although there was some controversy about whether these rules articulated newly emerging general principles of law and there was growing sentiment among international lawyers against "unjust wars" or wars of aggression, that sentiment had not yet been fully absorbed into the body of knowledge at the time of the Nuremberg proceedings.

The authors of the Nuremberg Charter—and the judges at Nuremberg itself—had to transform this system of unlimited state sovereignty . . . Nuremberg symbolized the end of a notion of unlimited national sovereignty and the emergence of a new international set of norms binding the state, despite the command of the national sovereign. It was the clearest symbol that a paradigm shift was taking place.

The world after Nuremberg was very different from the world before. The decisions of 1945–46 erased any lingering doubts about the illegality of aggressive war.

On the question of the use of military forces, the United Nations Charter articulated the principal limitations in Articles 1 and 2, in providing that:

> The purposes of the United Nations are . . . to take effective collective measures for the prevention and removal of threats to the peace, and for the suppression of acts of aggression or other breaches of the peace.
>
> All members shall refrain in their international relations from the threat or use of force against the territorial integrity or political independence of any state, or in any manner inconsistent with the Purpose of the United Nations.

The Nuremberg Charter and the war crimes trials are considered more fully in the next chapter. For our purposes here, however, consider Article 6(a) of the Charter of the Tribunal:

> (a) Crimes against Peace: namely, planning, preparation, initiation, or waging a war of aggression, or a war in violation of international treaties, agreements or assurances, or participation in a common plan or conspiracy for accomplishment of any of the foregoing.

What political objectives does this permit war to be used as a means to obtain? Consider these excerpts from the Charter of the United Nations:

> Article 2(3): All members shall settle their international disputes by peaceful means in such a manner that international peace and security, and justice, are not endangered.
>
> Article 2(7): Nothing contained in the present Charter shall authorize the United Nations to intervene in matters which are essentially within the domestic jurisdiction of any state. . . . but this principle shall not prejudice the application of enforcement measures under Chapter 7.
>
> Chapter 7: Action with Respect to Threats to the Peace, Breaches of the Peace, and Acts of Aggression—
>
> Article 39: The Security Council shall determine the existence of any threat to the peace, breach of the peace, or act of aggression and shall make recommendations, or decide what measures shall be taken in accordance with Articles 41 and 42, to maintain or restore international peace and security.

Article 41: The Security Council may decide what measures not involving the use of armed force are to be employed to give effect to its decisions, and it may call upon the Members of the United Nations to apply such measures. These may include complete or partial interruption of economic relations and of rail, sea, air, postal, radio and other means of communication, and the severance of diplomatic relations.

Article 42: Should the Security Council consider that measures provided for in Article 41 would be inadequate or have proved to be inadequate, it may take such action by air, sea or land forces as may be necessary to maintain or restore international peace and security. Such action may include demonstrations, blockade, and other operations by air, sea, or land forces of members of the United Nations.

Article 51: Nothing in the present Charter shall impair the inherent right of individual or collective self-defense if an armed attack occurs against a Member of the United Nations . . .

Acceptable—that is, legal—political objectives of war under the UN Charter appear to include at least maintenance or restoration of international peace and security, and self-defense against armed attack. What about intervention by use of force to stop a state from committing human rights abuses against its own citizens, such as the Iraqi chemical attacks on their own Kurdish populations that occurred in the 1980s? To prevent border crossings by large numbers of fleeing refugees, such as in the cases of Cuba and Haiti in the 1990s? To obtain territory? To alter the political system in a particular country? To stop or control a civil war, such as the one in Bosnia-Herzegovina, or the efforts of the so-called Chechen Republic to secede from Russia? To stop starvation and suffering, such as occurred in Somalia in 1992? To stop or deter international terrorism? To prevent an attack, such as the Israeli preemptive strike that began the Six-Day War in 1967?

A critical question is what exactly triggers the right to self-defense? The International Court of Justice (ICJ), in the case of *Nicaragua v. United States,* a part

of which you read in the last chapter, has taken a very narrow view, holding that only an "armed attack" triggers the right of national self-defense, and defining "armed attack" rather narrowly. Review the excerpt of that opinion in the last chapter, and then consider this additional excerpt.

Must a nation, in effect, "take the first hit," or should it be able to exercise its right of self-defense in response to an "imminent threat of armed attack?" The court says it expresses no view on that issue. Is that true? According to the ICJ, what constitutes an "armed attack"? What is the difference between "intervention" and "armed attack," and how does that difference affect the right of self-defense? May a state respond with force to unlawful intervention in its internal affairs by an outside state? What if, for example, one state is providing logistical and training support for subversive or terrorist forces who then infiltrate the other? May that second state use force against the first? Does the court see a difference between an "armed attack" and "the use of force"? Do you find the court's discussion of that question persuasive?

Additionally, note the court's discussion of the right of collective self-defense. When may one state come to the defense of another? Does the court's opinion tend to place limits on the use of force—that is, to narrow the legally acceptable political objectives—or to broaden them? Which is the better approach, narrow or broad?

NICARAGUA V. UNITED STATES, ICJ REPORTS 1986, P. 14

The general rule prohibiting force allows for certain exceptions. In view of the arguments advanced by the United States to justify the acts of which it is accused by Nicaragua, the Court must express a view on the content of the right of self-defence, and more particularly the right of collective self-defence. First, with regard to the existence of this right, it notes that in the language of Article 51 of the United Nations Charter, the inherent right which any State possesses in the event of an armed attack, covers both collective and individual self-defence. Thus, the Charter itself testifies to the existence of the right of collective self-defence in customary international law. Moreover, just as the wording of certain General Assembly declarations adopted by States demonstrates their recognition of the principle of the prohibition of force as definitely a matter of customary international law, some of the wording in those declarations operates similarly in respect of the right of self-defence (both collective and individual). Thus, in the declaration on the Principles of International Law concerning Friendly Relations and Co-operation among States in accordance with the Charter of the United Nations, the reference to the prohibition of force is followed by a paragraph stating that:

> nothing in the foregoing paragraphs shall be construed as enlarging or diminishing in any way the scope of the provisions of the Charter concerning cases in which the use of force is lawful.

This resolution demonstrates that the States represented in the General Assembly regard the exception to the prohibition of force constituted by the right of individual or collective self-defence as already a matter of customary international law.

With regard to the characteristics governing the right of self-defence, since the Parties consider the existence of this right to be established as a matter of customary international law, they have concentrated on the conditions governing its use. In view of the circumstances in which the dispute has arisen, reliance is placed by the Parties only on the right of self-defence in the case of an armed attack which has already occurred, and the issue of the lawfulness of a response to the imminent threat of armed attack has not been raised. Accordingly the Court expresses no view on that issue. The Parties also agree in holding that whether the response to the attack is lawful depends on observance of the criteria of the necessity and the proportionality of the measures taken in self-defence. Since the existence of the right of collective self-defence is established in customary international law, the Court must define the specific conditions which may have to be met for its exercise, in addition to the conditions of necessity and proportionality to which the Parties have referred.

In the case of individual self-defence, the exercise of this right is subject to the State concerned having been the victim of an armed attack. Reliance on collective self-defence of course does not remove the need for this. There appears now to be general agreement on the nature of the acts which can be treated as constituting armed attacks. In particular, it may be considered to be agreed that an armed attack must be understood as including:

> not merely action by regular armed forces across an international border, but also "the sending by or on behalf of a State of armed bands, groups, irregulars or mercenaries, which carry out acts of armed force against another State of such gravity as to amount to" (inter alia) an actual armed attack conducted by regular forces, "or its substantial involvement therein."

This description, contained in Article 3, Paragraph (g) of the Definition of Aggression annexed to General Assembly Resolution 3314, may be taken to reflect customary international law.

The Court sees no reason to deny that, in customary law, the prohibition of armed attacks may apply to the sending by a State of armed bands to the territory of another State, if such an operation, because of its scale and effects, would have been classified as an armed attack rather than as a mere frontier incident had it been carried out by regular armed forces.

But the Court does not believe that the concept of "armed attack" includes not only acts by armed bands where such acts occur on a significant scale but also assistance to rebels in the form of the provision of weapons or logistical or other support. Such assistance may be regarded as a threat or use of force, or amount to intervention in the internal or external affairs of other States.

It is also clear that it is the State which is the victim of an armed attack which must form and declare the view that it has been so attacked. There is no rule in customary international law permitting another State to exercise the right of collective self-defence on the basis of its own assessment of the situation. Where collective self-defence is invoked, it is to be expected that the State for whose benefit this right is used will have declared itself to be the victim of an armed attack.

The question remains whether the lawfulness of the use of collective self-defence by the third State for the benefit of the attacked State also depends on a request addressed by that State to the third State. A provision of the Charter of the Organization of American States is here in point: and while the Court has no jurisdiction to consider that instrument as applicable to the dispute, it may examine it to ascertain what light it throws on the content of customary international law. The Court notes that the Organization of American States Charter includes, in Article 3(f), the principle that: "an act of aggression against one American State is an act of aggression against all the other American States" and a provision in Article 27 that

> every act of aggression by a State against the territorial integrity or the inviolability of the territory or against the sovereignty or political independence of an American State shall be considered an act of aggression against the other American States.

Furthermore, by Article 3, Paragraph 1, of the Inter-American Treaty of Reciprocal Assistance, signed at Rio de Janeiro on 2 September 1947, the High-Contracting Parties

> agree that an armed attack by any State against an American State shall be considered as an attack against all the American States and, consequently, each one of the said Contracting Parties undertakes to assist in meeting the attack in the exercise of the inherent right of individual or collective self-defence recognized by Article 51 of the Charter of the United Nations;

and under Paragraph 2 of that Article,

> On the request of the State or States directly attacked and until the decision of the Organ of Consultation of the Inter-American System, each one of the Contracting Parties may determine the immediate measures which it may individually take in fulfillment of the obligation contained in the preceding paragraph and in accordance with the principle of continental solidarity.

The Court observes that the Treaty of Rio de Janeiro provides that measures of collective self-defence taken by each State are decided "on the request of the State or States directly attacked." It is significant that this requirement of a request on the part of the attacked State appears in the treaty particularly devoted to these matters of mutual assistance; it is not found in the more general text (the Charter of the Organization of American States), but Article 28 of that Charter provides for

the application of the measures and procedures laid down in "the special treaties on the subject."

At all events, the Court finds that in customary international law, whether of a general kind or that particular to the inter-American legal system, there is no rule permitting the exercise of collective self-defence in the absence of a request by the State which regards itself as the victim of an armed attack. The Court concludes that the requirement of a request by the State which is the victim of the alleged attack is additional to the requirement that such a State should have declared itself to have been attacked.

To justify certain activities involving the use of force, the United States has relied solely on the exercise of its right of collective self-defence. . . . The Court must [also] enquire whether there is any justification for the activities in question, to be found not in the right of collective self-defence against an armed attack, but in the right to take counter-measures in response to conduct of Nicaragua which is not alleged to constitute an armed attack. It will examine this point in connection with an analysis of the principle of non-intervention in customary international law.

The principle of non-intervention involves the right of every sovereign State to conduct its affairs without outside interference; though examples of trespass against this principle are not infrequent, the Court considers that it is part and parcel of customary international law. As the Court has observed: "Between independent States, respect for territorial sovereignty is an essential foundation of international relations," and international law requires political integrity also to be respected. Expressions of an opinio juris regarding the existence of the principle of non-intervention in customary international law are numerous and not difficult to find. The existence in the opinio juris of States of the principle of non-intervention is backed by established and substantial practice. It has moreover been presented as a corollary of the principle of the sovereign equality of States. A particular instance of this is General Assembly Resolution 2625, the Declaration on the Principles of International Law concerning Friendly Relations and Co-operation among States. In the Corfu Channel case, when a State claimed a right of intervention in order to secure evidence in the territory of another State for submission to an international tribunal, the Court observed that

> the alleged right of intervention as the manifestation of a policy of force, such as has, in the past, given rise to most serious abuses and such as cannot, whatever be the present defects in international organization, find a place in international law. Intervention is perhaps still less admissible in the particular form it would take here; for, from the nature of things, it would be reserved for the most powerful States, and might easily lead to perverting the administration of international justice itself.

Notwithstanding the multiplicity of declarations by States accepting the principle of non-intervention, there remain two questions: first, what is the exact content of the principle so accepted, and secondly, is the practice sufficiently in conformity with it for this to be a rule of customary international law?

As regards the first problem—that of the content of the principle of non-intervention—the Court will define only those aspects of the principle which appear to be relevant to the resolution of the dispute.

In this respect it notes that, in view of the generally accepted formulations, the principle forbids all States or groups of States to intervene directly or indirectly in the internal or external affairs of other States. A prohibited intervention must accordingly be one bearing on matters in which each State is permitted, by the principle of State sovereignty, to decide freely.

One of these is the choice of a political, economic, social and cultural system, and the formulation of foreign policy. Intervention is wrongful when it uses methods of coercion in regard to such choices, which must remain free ones.

The element of coercion, which defines, and indeed forms the very essence of, prohibited intervention, is particularly obvious in the case of an intervention which uses force, either in the direct form of military action, or in the indirect form of support for subversive or terrorist armed activities within another State. As noted above (Paragraph 191), General Assembly Resolution 2625 equates assistance of this kind with the use of force by the assisting State when the acts committed in another State "involve a threat or use of force." These forms of action are therefore wrongful in the light of both the principle of non-use of force, and that of non-intervention. In view of the nature of Nicaragua's complaints against the United States, and those expressed by the United States in regard to Nicaragua's conduct towards El Salvador, it is primarily acts of intervention of this kind with which the Court is concerned in the present case.

However, before reaching a conclusion on the nature of prohibited intervention, the Court must be satisfied that State practice justifies it. There have been in recent years a number of instances of foreign intervention for the benefit of forces opposed to the government of another State. The Court is not here concerned with the process of decolonization; this question is not in issue in the present case. It has to consider whether there might be indications of a practice illustrative of belief in a kind of general right for States to intervene, directly or indirectly, with or without armed force, in support of an internal opposition in another State, whose cause appeared particularly worthy by reason of the political and moral values with which it was identified. For such a general right to come into existence would involve a fundamental modification of the customary law principle of non-intervention.

In considering the instances of the conduct above described, the Court has to emphasize that, as was observed in the North Sea Continental Shelf cases, for a new customary rule to be formed, not only must the acts concerned "amount to a settled practice," but they must be accompanied by the *opinio juris sive necessitatis.* Either the States taking such action or other States in a position to react to it, must have behaved so that their conduct is

> evidence of a belief that this practice is rendered obligatory by the existence of a rule of law requiring it. The need for such a belief, i.e., the existence of a subjective element, is implicit in the very notion of the *opinio juris sive necessitatis.*

The Court has no jurisdiction to rule upon the conformity with international law of any conduct of States not parties to the present dispute, or of conduct of the Parties unconnected with the dispute; nor has it authority to ascribe to States legal views which they do not themselves advance. The significance for the Court of cases of State conduct prima facie inconsistent with the principle of non-intervention lies in the nature of the ground offered as justification. Reliance by a State on a novel right or an unprecedented exception to the principle might, if shared in principle by other States, tend towards a modification of customary international law. In fact however the Court finds that States have not justified their conduct by reference to a new right of intervention or a new exception to the principle of its prohibition. The United States authorities have on some occasions clearly stated their grounds for intervening in the affairs of a foreign State for reasons connected with, for example, the domestic policies of that country, its ideology, the level of its armaments, or the direction of its foreign policy. But these were statements of international policy, and not an assertion of rules of existing international law.

In particular, as regards the conduct towards Nicaragua which is the subject of the present case, the United States has not claimed that its intervention, which it justified in this way on the political level, was also justified on the legal level, alleging the exercise of a new right of intervention regarded by the United States as existing in such circumstances. As mentioned above, the United States has, on the legal plane, justified its intervention expressly and solely by reference to the "classic" rules involved, namely, collective self-defence against an armed attack. Nicaragua, for its part, has often expressed its solidarity and sympathy with the opposition in various States, especially in El Salvador. But Nicaragua too has not argued that this was a legal basis for an intervention, let alone an intervention involving the use of force.

The Court therefore finds that no such general right of intervention, in support of an opposition within another State, exists in contemporary international law. The Court concludes that acts constituting a breach of the customary principle of non-intervention will also, if they directly or indirectly involve the use of force, constitute a breach of the principle of non-use of force in international relations.

When dealing with the rule of the prohibition of the use of force, the Court considered the exception to it constituted by the exercise of the right of collective self-defence in the event of armed attack. Similarly, it must now consider the following question: if one State acts towards another State in breach of the principle of non-intervention, may a third State lawfully take such action by way of counter-measures against the first State as would otherwise constitute an intervention in its internal affairs?

A right to act in this way in the case of intervention would be analogous to the right of collective self-defence in the case of an armed attack, but both the act which gives rise to the reaction, and that reaction itself, would in principle be less grave.

Since the Court is here dealing with a dispute in which a wrongful use of force is alleged, it has primarily to consider whether a State has a right to respond to intervention with intervention going so far as to justify a use of force in reaction to measures which do not constitute an armed attack but may nevertheless involve a use of force. It might however be suggested that, in such a situation, the United States might have been permitted to intervene in Nicaragua in the exercise of some right analogous to the right of collective self-defence, one which might be resorted to in a case of intervention short of armed attack.

The Court has recalled above that for one State to use force against another, on the ground that that State has committed a wrongful act of force against a third State, is regarded as lawful, by way of exception, only when the wrongful act provoking the response was an armed attack. Thus the lawfulness of the use of force by a State in response to a wrongful act of which it has not itself been the victim is not admitted when this wrongful act is not an armed attack. In the view of the Court, under international law in force today—whether customary international law or that of the United Nations system—States do not have a right of "collective" armed response to acts which do not constitute an "armed attack." Furthermore, the Court has to recall that the United States itself is relying on the "inherent right of self-defence" but apparently does not claim that any such right exists as would, in respect of intervention, operate in the same way as the right of collective self-defence in respect of an armed attack.

The Court considers that in international law, if one State, with a view to the coercion of another State, supports and assists armed bands in that State whose purpose is to overthrow the government of that State, that amounts to an intervention by the one State in the internal affairs of the other, whether or not the political objective of the State giving such support and assistance is equally far-reaching. It is for this reason that the Court has only examined the intentions of the United States Government so far as they bear on the question of self-defence.

The Court therefore finds that the support given by the United States, up to the end of September 1984, to the military and paramilitary activities of the contras in Nicaragua, by financial support, training, supply of weapons, intelligence and logistic support, constitutes a clear breach of the principle of non-intervention.

The Court has already indicated its conclusion that the conduct of the United States towards Nicaragua cannot be justified by the right of collective self-defence in response to an alleged armed attack on one or other of Nicaragua's neighbours. So far as regards the allegations of supply of arms by Nicaragua to the armed opposition in El Salvador, the Court has indicated that while the concept of an armed attack includes the despatch by one State of armed bands into the territory of another State, the supply of arms and other support to such bands cannot be equated with armed attack. Nevertheless, such activities may well constitute a breach of the principle of the non-use of force and an intervention in the internal affairs of a State, that is, a form of conduct which is certainly wrongful, but is of lesser gravity than an armed attack.

While an armed attack would give rise to an entitlement to collective self-defence, a use of force of a lesser degree of gravity cannot, as the Court has already observed (Paragraph 211 above), produce any entitlement to take collective counter-measures involving the use of force. The acts of which Nicaragua is accused, even assuming them to have been established and imputable to that State, could only have justified proportionate counter-measures on the part of the State which had been the victim of these acts, namely El Salvador, Honduras or Costa Rica. They could not justify counter-measures taken by a third State, the United States, and particularly could not justify intervention involving the use of force.

Many commentators and international lawyers argue for a broader interpretation of the right of national self-defense than that taken by the ICJ. Consider these condensed excerpts from an article originally published in volume 126 of *Military Law Review,* by Judge Abraham D. Sofaer, who was the legal adviser at the U.S. Department of State during the Reagan administration. In particular, note Judge Sofaer's discussion of necessity and proportionality, which are the two fundamental legal limitations on the use of force in the national self-defense. Does his view broaden or limit the legally acceptable political objectives of the use of force?

The law has played—and must continue to play—an important role in marking the limits and conditions on measures used to protect our national security against state-sponsored terror. Many proposed military actions were considered and rejected during recent years on legal grounds. That must and will continue to occur. But the law must not be allowed improperly to interfere with legitimate national security measures. In important respects, it is doing so today. My purpose here is to review areas in which unwarranted limitations are being imposed on counter-terrorist actions, under both international law and U.S. domestic law, and to explain some of the dangers such limitations may pose.

In the realm of international law, several legal concepts have been invoked that would impose serious limits on strategic flexibility. The most significant of these is the narrow view of self-defense recently espoused by the International Court of Justice (ICJ) in *Nicaragua v. United States.* Narrow views of self-defense give terrorists and their state sponsors substantial advantages in their war against the democracies.

To the extent these limitations are not in fact mandated by the U.N. Charter, customary principles of international law, or the U.S. Constitution, they are indefensible. State-sponsored terrorism poses a threat to our national security, to which the United States must respond effectively. To succeed in this effort, our nation's policy planners and military strategists are entitled to as much flexibility as possible in combatting an enemy that accepts no limits based on law, but only those imposed by an effective defense. As lawyers, we have a special responsibility to identify and to revise or reject unjustifiable legal restrictions on our nation's capacity to protect its security. The president and other national security leaders will naturally regard any use of force with great caution, and good judgment may counsel against some such actions even where the law allows them. But the law should not be distorted or manipulated to dictate restraints in circumstances where judgment is the proper measure.

The use of force is governed in international law by the U.N. Charter, which in article 2(4) obligates all members "to refrain in their international relations from the threat or use of force against the territorial integrity or political independence of any state." The Charter expressly provides, however, in article 51, that "nothing in the present Charter shall impair the inherent right of individual or collective self-defense if an armed attack occurs against a Member of the United Nations, until the Security Council has taken measures necessary to maintain international peace and security."

The United States has always assumed that these Charter provisions, and the understandings and customary practice that help define their meaning, provide a workable set of rules to deal with the array of needs that potentially require the use of force, including such threats as state-supported terrorism and insurgencies. General Assembly interpretive declarations make clear that "force" means physical violence, not other forms of coercion. But they also indicate that aggression includes both direct and indirect complicity in all forms of violence, not just conventional hostilities. The United States has long assumed that the inherent right of self-defense potentially applies against any illegal use of force, and that it extends to any group or State that can properly be regarded as responsible for such activities.

These assumptions are supported in customary practice. A substantial body of authority exists, however, which advocates positions that, if adhered to by the U.S., would largely undermine this or any other nation's capacity to defend itself against state-sponsored terrorism. The principal limitations proposed in these sources are: a) an unrealistically limited view of the meaning of "armed attack"; b) artificially restrictive views of necessity and proportionality; c) restrictions on the situations in which terrorist groups or States can be held responsible for terrorist actions; and d) absolute deference to the principle of territorial integrity.

A. ARMED ATTACK

Article 51 preserves the right to self-defense "if an armed attack occurs against a Member." This language suggests to some writers that force can be used in self-defense only to defend against an "armed attack" that "occurs" "against [the territory of] a Member." Proponents of this restrictive view of self-defense would greatly limit the extent to which force can lawfully be used to prevent or to deter future attacks and to defend against attacks upon the citizens or property of a member, outside its territory, that cannot be said to threaten its "territorial integrity or political independence."

A disturbing instance of this reasoning is found in the ICJ's decision in *Nicaragua v. United States*. The ICJ declined to find that Nicaragua had engaged in "aggression," although the court either found or assumed that Nicaragua had supplied arms to the rebels in El Salvador for several years. The court concluded that a limited intervention of this sort cannot justify resort to self-defense, because customary law only allows the use of force in self-defense against an "armed attack," and an armed attack does not include "assistance to rebels in the form of the provision of weapons or logistical or other support." This ruling is without support in customary international law or the practice of nations, which could not be read to deprive a State of the right to defend itself against so serious a form of aggression. Recognizing this, the ICJ came up with the following solution: a State is not permitted to resort to "self-defense" against aggression short of armed attack, but it may be able to take what the court called "proportionate countermeasures." While a State that is the victim of a terrorist attack based on such support by another State may seek to resort to "countermeasures," the fact that the court refused to treat such support as a basis for self-defense erroneously suggests it is necessarily a less serious form of aggression than a conventional attack, and thus a less legitimate basis for the defensive use of force.

The United States rejects the notion that the U.N. Charter supersedes customary international law on the right of self-defense. Article 51 characterizes that right as "inherent" in order to prevent its limitation based on any provision in the Charter. We have always construed the phrase "armed attack" in a reasonable manner, consistent with a customary practice that enables any State effectively to protect itself and its citizens from every illegal use of force aimed at the State. Professor Schachter, among other prominent scholars, supports the view that attacks on a State's citizens in foreign countries can sometimes properly be regarded as armed attacks under the Charter. "When such attacks are aimed at the government or intended to change a policy of that state, the attacks are reasonably considered as attacks on the state in question. In some cases, attacks on non-nationals who have ethnic or religious affiliations with a state opposed by the terrorists should be regarded as attacks on the state."

A sound construction of article 51 would allow any State, once a terrorist "attack occurs" or is about to occur, to use force against those responsible for the attack in order to prevent the attack or to deter further attacks unless reasonable ground exists to believe that no further attack will be undertaken. In 1984 Secretary Shultz described this policy as an "active defense." "From a practical standpoint," he said, "a purely passive defense does not provide enough of a deterrent to terrorism and the states that sponsor it." Later that year he described why an active defense was needed to deter: We must reach a consensus in this country that our responses should go beyond passive defense to consider means of active prevention, preemption, and retaliation. Our goal must be to prevent and deter future terrorist acts, and experience has taught us over the years that one of the best deterrents to terrorism is the certainty that swift and sure measures will be taken against those who engage in it. We should take steps toward carrying out such measures. There should be no moral confusion on this issue. Our aim is not to seek revenge but to put an end to violent attacks against innocent people, to make the world a safer place to live for all of us. Clearly the democracies have a moral right, indeed a duty, to defend themselves.

Deterrence is a key principle under the Charter. A view of the meaning of "armed attack" that restricts it to conventional, ongoing uses of force on the territory of the victim State would as a practical matter immunize those who attack sporadically or on foreign territory, even though they can be counted on to attack specific States repeatedly.

The notion that self-defense relates only to a use of force that materially threatens a State's "territorial integrity or political independence," as proscribed in article 2(4), ignores the Charter's preservation of the "inherent" scope of that right. Nations—including the U.S.—have traditionally defended their military personnel, citizens, commerce, and property from attacks even when no threat existed to their territory or independence. The military facilities, vessels, and embassies of a nation have long been considered its property, and for some purposes its territory. Attacks on a nation's citizens cannot routinely be treated as attacks on the nation itself; but where an American is attacked because he is American, in order to punish the U.S. or to coerce the U.S. into accepting a political position, the attack is one in which the U.S. has a sufficient interest to justify extending its protection through necessary and proportionate actions. No nation should be limited to using force to protect its citizens, from attacks based on their citizenship, to situations in which they are within its boundaries.

B. NECESSITY AND PROPORTIONALITY

The U.S. is committed to using force in its self-defense only when necessary, and only to the extent it is proportionate to the threat defended against. Our uses of force during the Reagan Administration met these tests. In fact, military planners were not infrequently accused of having too greatly limited our actions, particularly against Iran in the Persian Gulf.

Writers seeking to impose the strictest possible limits on self-defense, who generally claim for purposes of defining self-defense that customary law has been superseded, nonetheless turn to precedents in customary law for definitions of necessity and proportionality. Particularly popular is Secretary of State Daniel Webster's description of anticipatory self-defense in The Caroline dispute.

A State, he wrote, must demonstrate a "necessity for self-defense, instant, overwhelming, leaving no choice of means, and no moment for deliberation" and must do "nothing unreasonable or excessive; since the act, justified by the necessity of self-defense, must be limited by that necessity, and kept clearly within it."

This statement exaggerates the test of necessity in a situation where that issue was dicta. More fundamentally, moreover, the Caroline test was applied when war was still a permissible option for States that had actually been attacked. Webster's statement therefore related, in that context, to situations in which no prior attack or other act of war had occurred.

An unrealistically strict view of necessity and proportionality was most recently advanced by the ICJ in *Nicaragua v. United States*. The court held that, because certain American actions were taken "several months after the major offensive of the armed opposition against the government of El Salvador had been completely repulsed," the measures were unnecessary, and it was possible to "eliminate the main danger of the Salvadoran government without the United States embarking on activities in and against Nicaragua." As to proportionality, the court said it could not regard the actions relating to the mining of Nicaraguan ports and attacks on port and oil installations as satisfying proportionality, and that United States help to the contras persisted too long after any aggression by Nicaragua could have reasonably been presumed to have continued. Judge Schwebel detailed in his opinion the depredations in which insurgents in El Salvador had engaged, which were very similar to those that the United States allegedly supported. He explained that an action is proportional when it is necessary to end and to repulse an attack, not just when it corresponds exactly to the acts of aggression. Mining of the harbors and attacks on oil installations could have been expected to restrict the flow of arms from Nicaragua's harbors and therefore to diminish Nicaragua's capacity to continue its aggression.

C. RESPONSIBILITY FOR AGGRESSION

Most significantly, the court cannot safely impose a standard on States that requires them to abstain from the exercise of self-defense on the assumption that no new offensive will be undertaken by an aggressor who retains the capacity to attack or to support an attack. Courts must leave such delicate and dangerous predictions within the reasonable discretion of individuals assigned the responsibility for protecting their nationals. Sound military strategy must govern such tactical decisions, not retrospective second-guessing of judges.

The limitations of necessity and proportionality are traditional, civilizing constraints on the use of force. Respect for such traditional doctrine is undermined,

however, when States are expected to accept too high a degree of risk of substantial injury before being allowed to defend themselves or to accept a continuation of unlawful aggression because of a tit-for-tat limit on military response. The law should not be construed to prevent military planners from implementing measures they reasonably consider necessary to prevent unlawful attacks.

The ICJ has recently provided States that assist terrorist groups with important support in their attempt to evade responsibility for the terrorist conduct of such groups in other States. In *Nicaragua v. United States* the court ruled that U.S. support for the contras was not extensive enough to make the U.S. responsible for the contras' actions in Nicaragua. (The U.S. was held responsible only for its own actions, such as the mining of the harbors.) The extent of U.S. support for the contras found by the court was significant, however, and included financing for food and clothing, military training, arms, and tactical assistance. The court concluded, nonetheless, that these forms of support were insufficient to hold the U.S. accountable, because the contras remained autonomous: "The Court does not consider that the assistance given by the United States to the contras warrants the conclusion that these forces are subject to the United States to such an extent that any acts they have committed are imputable to that State."

The United States at no time during the Nicaragua litigation advanced as a defense for its support for the contras the claim that it had no responsibility for their actions. Any U.S. support for the contras was based on the belief that such support is legitimate as a measure of collective self-defense in light of Nicaragua's support of communist revolutions in El Salvador, Honduras, and eventually all of Central America. The court's ruling in the litigation had the effect of relieving the U.S. of liability for contra activities and thereby limiting the effect of the court's ruling on liability. But the long-run consequences of this ruling will be as pernicious to peaceful relations among States as the court's rulings limiting the scope of self-defense. The rulings on self-defense will have the effect of restricting the effectiveness of responses to aggression and thereby will encourage aggression by reducing the deterrent capacity of States. The ruling on State responsibility will have the effect of reducing the costs imposed on States for supporting aggression and for assisting groups they know intend to engage in unlawful acts.

Here, too, the court had no basis in established practice or custom to limit so drastically the responsibility of States for the foreseeable consequences of their support of groups engaged in illegal actions, whether the actions are called "armed resistance" or whether the perpetrators are called terrorists. Established principles of international law and many specific decisions and actions strongly support the principle that a State violates its duties under international law if it supports or even knowingly tolerates within its territory activities constituting aggression against another State. As Judge Schwebel noted in his dissent in *Nicaragua,* the U.N. Definition of Aggression proscribes not only the "sending" of "armed bands, groups, irregulars, or mercenaries" to carry out "acts of armed force" but also any "substantial involvement therein." He pointed out that Nicaragua had been substantially involved in the acts of armed force by the Salvadoran insurgents.

The ultimate remedy for a State's knowingly harboring or assisting terrorists who attack another State or its citizens is self-defense. In December 1985 several airline passengers were killed by terrorists in simultaneous attacks at the Rome and Vienna airports, including five Americans; many more were wounded. Some of the terrorists had in their possession Tunisian passports taken by Libyan authorities from Tunisian workers excluded from Libya. In addition, immediately after these attacks, in which eleven-year-old Natasha Simpson and other civilians were killed, Qadhafi of Libya publicly hailed the killers as "heroes." These facts, together with Qadhafi's record of activities and statements, led the U.S. to impose on Libya all remaining sanctions short of force and to make clear that Libya would be held responsible for the actions of terrorists whom it supported. President Reagan announced:

> By providing material support to terrorist groups which attack U.S. citizens, Libya has engaged in armed aggression against the United States under established principles of international law, just as if he [Qadhafi] had used its own armed forces. . . . If these [economic and political] steps do not end Qadhafi's terrorism, I promise you that further steps will be taken.

In a speech at the National Defense University on January 15, 1986, Secretary Shultz repeated the point:

> There should be no confusion about the status of nations that sponsor terrorism against Americans and American property. There is substantial legal authority for the view that a state which supports terrorist or subversive attacks against another state, or which supports or encourages terrorist planning and other activities within its own territory, is responsible for such attacks. Such conduct can amount to an ongoing armed aggression against the other state under international law.

Despite these warnings, the U.S. learned in April 1986 that Libya was involved in two major terrorist incidents against Americans during that month and that Libya was in the process of planning others. In Paris, terrorists who were acting in part on Libya's behalf or with its support planned to attack persons lined up for visas at the U.S. Embassy. The attack contemplated—with automatic rifles and grenades—would have resulted in substantial loss of life, but it was thwarted through excellent intelligence work by U.S. and French services. Another attack was planned against a disco in Berlin that was frequented by U.S. military personnel. Efforts to thwart this attack were unsuccessful, and a bomb exploded in the disco on April 5, 1986, killing at least one civilian and two U.S. servicemen and injuring some fifty others. Intelligence established Libya's culpability, as well as its plans for further attacks. This led to President Reagan's decision to bomb terrorist-related targets in Libya.

The case for holding Libya responsible for the Berlin disco bombing and for a pattern of other prior and planned terrorist actions was very strong. Some particularly sensitive aspects of the case were made public, at a substantial price in terms of U.S. intelligence capabilities. The president decided in that instance, after public statements had already been made by other officials revealing a source of our information, that a degree of public disclosure was appropriate. While members of the press and some others have raised questions about the sufficiency of the case against Libya, they did so largely on the ground that other evidence pointed to Syria as having been involved. In general, however, the case against Libya was accepted, and numerous States showed the seriousness with which they regarded this matter by cutting the staffs at Libya's embassies in their countries, thereby materially reducing Libya's capacity to assist terrorists and to engage in other illegal activity.

We, however, recognize and strongly support the principle that a state subjected to continuing terrorist attacks may respond with appropriate use of force to defend against further attacks. This is an aspect of the inherent right of self-defense recognized in the U.N. Charter. We support this principle regardless of attacker and regardless of victim. It is the collective responsibility of sovereign states to see that terrorism enjoys no sanctuary, no safe haven, and that those who practice it have no immunity from the responses their acts warrant. Moreover, it is the responsibility of each state to take appropriate steps to prevent persons or groups within its sovereign territory from perpetrating such acts.

V. CONCLUSION

The battle to influence the law and to ensure that it serves the interests of freedom and the civilized world is therefore far from some abstract exercise. It is a struggle to determine whether the rule of law will prevail. It is baseless to contend that the United States no longer supports the rule of law merely because it is engaged in this struggle. We are not struggling against the rule of law, but for a rule of law that reflects our values and methods: the values of custom, tolerance, fairness, and equality; and the methods of reasoned, consistent, and principled analysis. We must oppose strenuously the adoption of rules of law that we cannot accept, because of the very fact that we take law so seriously.

We have no cause to doubt the propriety of this effort. The rules of law that we advocate enhance our capacity to defend our national security, but that hardly makes them inappropriate or unsound. Why should the law, for example, give its blessing to rules that

* limit a nation's right to defend itself to situations in which its territory or political independence is threatened, thereby preventing it from defending its citizens abroad?

* enable States to avoid responsibility, in accordance with traditional, universally accepted standards, for providing sanctuary and support to groups known to be engaged in terrorist acts?

* grant absolute and overriding weight in all situations to the interest of territorial integrity?

Secretary Shultz said that the free nations "cannot afford to let the Orwellian corruption of language hamper our efforts to defend ourselves, our interests, or our friends." The same is true of law. We must not allow the corruption of international law, such as the effort to legitimize "wars of national liberation" or to diminish the inherent right of self-defense, to hamper our national security efforts. Rather, we must ensure that the law is, in fact, on our side, and that, while its proper restraints are respected and effectively implemented, no artificial barrier is allowed to inhibit the legitimate exercise of power in dealing with the threat of state-sponsored terrorism.

Judge Sofaer cites the attack by the United States on Libya in 1986 as an example of a legal use of force in national self-defense from terrorist attacks on United States citizens abroad. He states that, although some questioned the legitimacy of the attack, "in general, however, the case against Libya was accepted." For yet another point of view, read "Just War Doctrine's Complementary Role in the International Law of War," by Professor William V. O'Brien (*U.S. Naval College International Law Studies 1995,* vol. 67, *Legal and Moral Constraints on Low-Intensity Conflict,* ed. A. R. Coll, J. S. Ord, and S. A. Rose). Professor O'Brien states, "No Security Council action condemning the U.S. 1986 raid against Libya was possible [the U.S. had a veto] but, with the exception of the United Kingdom, Council members held to the strict version [of self-defense] and denied the U.S. claim of self-defense. The U.S. action was condemned by the General Assembly."

While the exact boundaries of legitimate national self-defense may be somewhat fuzzy, it is clear that war for the purpose of aggression and dispute resolution is illegal, and that the use of force to defend against aggression is lawful. In a 1974 General Assembly resolution (UNGA Resolution 3314), the United Nations defined illegal aggression as including but not limited to bombardment; blockade; land, sea, or air attack; and sponsoring terrorists, mercenaries, or irregular combatants against another state.

As a general rule, self-defense in response to aggression is legal when the threat is "immediate" or "imminent" and action is "necessary" and "proportional." The Standing Rules of Engagement for U.S. Forces (appendix 6) defines "necessity" as when "a hostile act occurs or a force or terrorist unit exhibits hostile intent," and "proportionality" as "the force used must be reasonable in intensity, duration, and magnitude, based on all the facts known to the commander at the time, to decisively counter the hostile act or hostile intent and ensure the continued safety of US forces."

Did the U.S. attack on Libya meet these criteria? Was there an immediate or imminent threat of aggression against the United States as defined by the UN General Assembly? If so, was there a necessity for a U.S. armed attack in response? Was the U.S. armed attack proportional?

Once armed conflict begins, regardless of whether or not one side is an illegal aggressor, international law considers the conduct of military operations by both sides to be regulated by the law of armed conflict governing the means and methods of war, sometimes referred to as *jus in bello*.

Justice in War (*Jus in Bello*)

A school of thought known as military realism argues that *inter aram silent leges,* that is, "in war the laws are silent." General William Tecumseh Sherman, a top Union army general during the American Civil War, renowned for burning Atlanta and the subsequent devastating "March to the Sea" through Georgia, put it this way: "War is cruelty, and you cannot refine it; and those who brought cruelty on our country deserve all the curses and maledictions a people can pour out." The realist argues that there are and should be no limits to the use of force in war, and that the aggressor, who is at fault for immorally and illegally beginning the conflict, should not benefit from limits on means and methods of warfare imposed upon a righteous defender, who after all, has the

moral high ground and the ethical and legal imperative to win and defeat aggression at all costs and by any means necessary: the ends justify the means. Although the realist's view has its attractions, its fatal flaw lies in the risk of escalation to total war and human disaster inherent in modern warfare without limits.

Some argue that the answer is to refrain from the use of force no matter what—this is the pacifist view, which argues, essentially, that nothing is allowable. This view, like the realist view, suffers from the same fatal flaw: in the extreme case, it can lead to human disaster. A pacifist community will very likely not survive in the face of determined human aggression. National self-defense from aggression must therefore be permitted, yet must not be permitted to escalate to total war. This is the bridge from *jus ad bellum* to *jus in bello.* When law fails to prevent armed conflict, law nevertheless hopes to limit that conflict so that the aggressor suffers defeat, without escalation to total war, and with good prospects for an early return to stable peace. This is to the benefit of the law abiding defender, because a war without limits leaves little spoils for the "victor."

The law of armed conflict is based on one basic principle and four precepts. It regulates who can be killed and with what weapons they may be killed. The basic principle, one of customary law, is stated in Article 22 of the Annex to the 1907 Hague Convention IV Respecting the Laws and Customs of War on Land: "The right of belligerents to adopt means and methods of injuring the enemy is not unlimited." The four precepts, all derived from the basic principle that means and methods of warfare are not unlimited, are those of humanity, necessity, proportionality, and discrimination. Some sources add a fifth precept, that of chivalry. Consider the following explanation from *The Commander's Handbook on the Law of Naval Operations:*

General Principles of the Law of Armed Conflict:
   The law of armed conflict seeks to prevent unnecessary suffering and destruction by controlling and mitigating the harmful effects of hostilities through mini-

mum standards of protection to be accorded to combatants and to noncombatants. To that end, the law of armed conflict provides that:

1. Only that degree and kind of force, not otherwise prohibited by the law of armed conflict, required for the partial or complete submission of the enemy with a minimum expenditure of time, life, and physical resources may be applied.

2. The employment of any kind or degree of force not required for the purpose of the partial or complete submission of the enemy with a minimum expenditure of time, life, and physical resources is prohibited.

3. Dishonorable (treacherous) means, dishonorable expedients, and dishonorable conduct during armed conflict are forbidden.

The law of armed conflict is not intended to impede the waging of hostilities. Its purpose is to ensure that the violence of hostilities is directed toward the enemy's forces and is not used to cause purposeless, unnecessary human misery and physical destruction. In that sense, the law of armed conflict complements and supports the principles of warfare embodied in the military concepts of objective, mass, economy of force, surprise, and security. Together, the law of armed conflict and the principles of warfare underscore the importance of concentrating forces against critical military targets while avoiding the expenditure of personnel and resources against persons, places, and things that are militarily unimportant.

The following excerpt elaborates on the concept of military necessity:

Military Necessity. The law of armed conflict provides that only that degree and kind of force, not otherwise prohibited by the law of armed conflict, required for the partial or complete submission of the enemy with a minimum expenditure of time, life, and physical resources may be applied. This principle, often referred to as "military necessity," is a fundamental concept of restraint designed to limit the application of force in armed conflict to that which is in fact required to carry out a lawful military purpose. Too often it is misunderstood and misapplied to support the application of mil-

itary force that is excessive and unlawful under the misapprehension that the "military necessity" of mission accomplishment justifies the result. While the principle does recognize that some amount of collateral damage and incidental injury to civilians and civilian objects may occur in an attack upon a legitimate military objective, it does not excuse the wanton destruction of life and property disproportionate to the military advantage to be gained from the attack.

In describing the principles of humanity and discrimination, *The Commander's Handbook* states:

Indiscriminate Effect. Weapons that are incapable of being controlled so as to be directed against a military target are forbidden as being indiscriminate in their effect. Drifting armed contact mines and long-range unguided missiles (such as the German V-1 and V-2 rockets of World War II) fall into this category. A weapon is not indiscriminate simply because it may cause incidental or collateral civilian casualties, provided such casualties are not foreseeably excessive in light of the military advantage expected to be gained. An artillery round that is capable of being directed with a reasonable degree of accuracy at a military target is not an indiscriminate weapon simply because it may miss its mark or inflict collateral damage. Conversely, uncontrolled balloon-borne bombs, such as those released by the Japanese against the west coast of the United States and Canada in World War II, lack that capability of direction and are, therefore, unlawful.

Unnecessary Suffering. Antipersonnel weapons are designed to kill or disable enemy combatants and are lawful notwithstanding the death, pain, and suffering they inflict. Weapons that are designed to cause unnecessary suffering or superfluous injury are, however, prohibited because the degree of pain or injury, or the certainty of death, they produce is needlessly or clearly disproportionate to the military advantage to be gained by their use. Poisoned projectiles and dum-dum bullets fall into this category, because there is little military advantage to be gained by ensuring the death of wounded personnel through poisoning or the expanding effect of soft-nosed or unjacketed lead ammunition. Similarly, using materials that are difficult to detect or are undetectable by field x-ray equipment, such as glass or clear plastic, as the injuring mechanism in military ammunition is prohibited, since they unnecessarily inhibit the treatment of wounds. Use of such materials as incidental components in ammunition, e.g., as wadding or packing, is not prohibited.

The concept of proportionality is illustrated by the rule governing infliction of collateral damage. This rule balances military necessity against the inhumanity caused by a particular operation and concludes that the military advantage gained must outweigh the associated harm to noncombatants or nonmilitary property:

Incidental Injury and Collateral Damage. It is not unlawful to cause incidental injury or death to civilians, or collateral damage to civilian objects, during an attack upon a legitimate military objective. Incidental injury or collateral damage should not, however, be excessive in light of the military advantage anticipated by the attack. Naval commanders must take all practicable precautions, taking into account military and humanitarian considerations, to keep civilian casualties and damage to the absolute minimum consistent with mission accomplishment and the security of the force. In each instance, the commander must determine whether incidental injuries and collateral damage would be excessive, on the basis of an honest and reasonable estimate of the facts available to him. Similarly, the commander must decide, in light of all the facts known or reasonably available to him, including the need to conserve resources and complete the mission successfully, whether to adopt an alternative method of attack, if reasonably available, to reduce civilian casualties and damage.

As noted, the Law of Armed Conflict limits the means of injuring the enemy. Poison, or poisoned weapons, for example, are prohibited, as are arms, projectiles, or material calculated to cause unnecessary suffering (sometimes translated from the original French as "superfluous injury"). These rules limit the kinds of weapons that may be used. Other rules limit who may be killed and what may be targeted. *The Commander's Handbook on the Law of Naval Operations* has this to say about targeting:

Principles of Lawful Targeting.

The law of naval targeting is premised upon the three fundamental principles of the law of armed conflict:

1. The right of belligerents to adopt means of injuring the enemy is not unlimited.

2. It is prohibited to launch attacks against the civilian population as such.

3. Distinctions must be made between combatants and noncombatants, to the effect that noncombatants be spared as much as possible.

These legal principles governing targeting generally parallel the military principles of objective, mass, and economy of force. The law requires that only objectives of military importance be attacked but permits the use of sufficient mass to destroy those objectives. At the same time, unnecessary (and wasteful) collateral destruction must be avoided to the extent possible and, consistent with mission accomplishment and the security of the force, unnecessary human suffering prevented. The law of naval targeting, therefore, requires that all reasonable precautions must be taken to ensure that only military objectives are targeted so that civilians and civilian objects are spared as much as possible the ravages of war.

Only military objectives may be attacked. "Military objectives are those objects which, by their nature, location, purpose, or use, effectively contribute to the enemy's war-fighting or war-sustaining capability and whose total or partial destruction, capture, or neutralization would constitute a definite military advantage to the attacker under the circumstances at the time of the attack." Civilians and civilian objects may not be attacked:

Civilian objects consist of all civilian property and activities other than those used to support or sustain the enemy's war-fighting capability. Attacks on installations such as dikes and dams are prohibited if their breach or destruction would result in the loss of civilian lives disproportionate to the military advantage to be gained. Similarly, the intentional destruction of food, crops, livestock, drinking water, and other objects indispensable to the survival of the civilian population, for the specific purpose of denying the civilian population of their use, is prohibited.

Civilians are noncombatants, and so may not be attacked. Other categories of noncombatants immune from attack include the wounded, sick and shipwrecked, medical personnel and chaplains, parachutists descending from disabled aircraft (but not paratroopers descending to attack), and prisoners of war. For example, the 1907 Hague Convention states "it is especially forbidden—To kill or wound an enemy who, having laid down his arms, or having no longer means of defence, has surrendered at discretion." Thus, soldiers who have surrendered are not lawful targets—they are "noncombatants," and may not be killed. Conversely, noncombatants who engage in hostile acts against combatants are considered "unlawful combatants": they may not be lawfully killed (except in self-defense) and they may not lawfully kill. See appendix 5.

Combatants, as defined by *The Commander's Handbook,* include "all members of the regularly organized armed forces of a party to the conflict (except medical personnel, chaplains, civil defense personnel, and members of the armed forces who have acquired civil defense status) as well as irregular forces who are under responsible command and subject to internal military discipline, carry their arms openly, and otherwise distinguish themselves clearly from the civilian population."

The following edited opinion of the Supreme Court of the United States discusses the consequence of action as an unlawful combatant. As you read the opinion, consider whether there is any advantage to a legal entitlement to treatment as a Prisoner of War as opposed to as an unlawful combatant. What happens to unlawful combatants who are captured?

EX PARTE QUIRIN
SUPREME COURT OF THE UNITED STATES
317 U.S. 1
JULY 31, 1942
Chief Justice Stone delivered the opinion of the Court.

After the declaration of war between the United States and the German Reich, petitioners received training at a sabotage school near Berlin, Germany, where they were instructed in the use of explosives and in methods of secret writing. Thereafter petitioners, with a German citizen, Dasch, proceeded from Germany to a seaport in Occupied France, where petitioners Burger, Heinck and Quirin, together with Dasch, boarded a German submarine which proceeded across the Atlantic to Amagansett Beach on Long Island, New York. The four were there landed from the submarine in the hours of darkness, on or about June 13, 1942, carrying with them a supply of explosives, fuses, and incendiary and timing devices. While landing they wore German Marine Infantry uniforms or parts of uniforms. Immediately after landing they buried their uniforms and the other articles mentioned, and proceeded in civilian dress to New York City.

The remaining four petitioners at the same French port boarded another German submarine, which carried them across the Atlantic to Ponte Vedra Beach, Florida. On or about June 17, 1942, they came ashore during the hours of darkness, wearing caps of the German Marine Infantry and carrying with them a supply of explosives, fuses, and incendiary and timing devices. They immediately buried their caps and the other articles mentioned, and proceeded in civilian dress to Jacksonville, Florida, and thence to various points in the United States.

All were taken into custody in New York or Chicago by agents of the Federal Bureau of Investigation. All had received instructions in Germany from an officer of the German High Command to destroy war industries and war facilities in the United States, for which they or their relatives in Germany were to receive salary payments from the German government. They also had been paid by the German government during their course of training at the sabotage school and had received substantial sums in United States currency, which were in their possession when arrested. The currency had been handed to them by an officer of the German High Command, who had instructed them to wear their German uniforms while landing in the United States.

From the very beginning of its history this Court has recognized and applied the law of war as including that part of the law of nations which prescribes, for the conduct of war, the status, rights and duties of enemy nations as well as of enemy combatants. By universal agreement and practice, the law of war draws a distinction between the armed forces and the peaceful populations of belligerent nations and also between those who are lawful and unlawful combatants. Lawful combatants are subject to capture and detention as prisoners of war by opposing military forces. Unlawful combatants are likewise subject to capture and detention, but in addition they are subject to trial and punishment by military tribunals for acts which render their belligerency unlawful.

The spy who secretly and without uniform passes the military lines of a belligerent in time of war, seeking to gather military information and communicate it to the enemy, or an enemy combatant who without uniform comes secretly through the lines for the purpose of waging war by destruction of life or property, are familiar examples of belligerents who are generally deemed not to be entitled to the status of prisoners of war, but to be offenders against the law of war subject to trial and punishment by military tribunals.

Our government, by thus defining lawful belligerents entitled to be treated as prisoners of war, has recognized that there is a class of unlawful belligerents not entitled to that privilege, including those who, though combatants, do not wear "fixed and distinctive emblems." By a long course of practical administrative construction by its military authorities, our government has likewise recognized that those who during time of war pass surreptitiously from enemy territory into our own, discarding their uniforms upon entry, for the commission of hostile acts involving destruction of life or property, have the status of unlawful combatants punishable as such by military commission. This precept of the law of war has been so recognized in practice both here and abroad, and has so generally been accepted as valid by authorities on international law that we think it must be regarded as a rule or principle of the law of war recognized by this government.

The petitioners were charged with "being enemies of the United States and acting for . . . the German Reich, a belligerent enemy nation, secretly and covertly passed, in civilian dress, contrary to the law of war, through the military and naval lines and defenses of the United States . . . and went behind such lines, contrary to the law of war, in civilian dress . . . for the purpose of committing . . . hostile acts, and, in particular, to destroy certain war industries, war utilities and war materials within the United States."

This specification so plainly alleges violation of the law of war as to require but brief discussion of petitioners' contentions. As we have seen, entry upon our territory in time of war by enemy belligerents, including those acting under the direction of the armed forces of the enemy, for the purpose of destroying property used or useful in prosecuting the war, is a hostile and warlike act. It subjects those who participate in it without uniform to the punishment prescribed by the law of war for unlawful belligerents.

Modern warfare is directed at the destruction of enemy war supplies and the implements of their production and transportation, quite as much as at the armed forces. Every consideration which makes the unlawful belligerent punishable is equally applicable whether his objective is the one or the other. The law of war cannot rightly treat those agents of enemy armies who enter our territory, armed with explosives intended for the destruction of war industries and supplies, as any the less belligerent enemies than are agents similarly entering for the purpose of destroying fortified places or our Armed Forces.

By passing our boundaries for such purposes without uniform or other emblem signifying their belligerent status, or by discarding that means of identification after entry, such enemies become unlawful belligerents subject to trial and punishment.

Unlawful combatants are subject to trial and punishment for acts of war that would be lawful for combatants; combatants, however, are not, so long as they comply with the law of armed conflict and commit no crimes. Thus, a combatant who kills another combatant, even from ambush and not in self-defense, has committed no crime, while the same action undertaken by a noncombatant is murder. Combatants who are captured are not subject to trial and punishment for their lawful acts of war, and must be treated as prisoners of war. Even prisoners of war, however, may be tried and punished for their unlawful acts. Consider the case of General Manuel Noriega, a Panamanian captured by the United States in Panama, and tried in the United States as a common criminal for his involvement in illegal drug running. As you read the court's opinion, note the requirements imposed by the Geneva Convention of 1949 for the humane treatment of prisoners of war.

UNITED STATES V. NORIEGA
UNITED STATES DISTRICT COURT FOR THE SOUTHERN
DISTRICT OF FLORIDA
808 F. SUPP. 791
DECEMBER 8, 1992

Defendant contends that the Geneva Convention Relative to the Treatment of Prisoners of War ("Geneva III"), August 12, 1949, is applicable law that the Court must recognize. Defendant urges further that whether or not the U.S. government classifies General Noriega as a prisoner of war ("POW"), he is one, in fact, and must be afforded all the benefits of that status.

Before the Court are several questions, but the ultimate one appears to be whether or not the Geneva Convention prohibits incarceration in a federal penitentiary for a prisoner of war convicted of common crimes against the United States. To resolve this issue the Court must consider: is Geneva III applicable to this case; and, if so, which of its provisions apply to General Noriega's confinement and what do they require?

APPLICABILITY OF GENEVA III:

Before examining in detail the various provisions of Geneva III, the Court must address whether the treaty has any application to the case at bar. Geneva III is an international treaty designed to protect prisoners of war from inhumane treatment at the hands of their captors. Regardless of whether it is legally enforceable under the present circumstances, the treaty is undoubtedly a valid international agreement and "the law of the land" in the United States. As such, Geneva III applies to any POW captured and detained by the United States, and the U.S. government has—at minimum—an international obligation to uphold the treaty.

A. NORIEGA'S PRISONER OF WAR STATUS
Article 2

The present Convention shall apply to all cases of declared war or of any other armed conflict which may arise between two or more of the High Contracting Parties, even if the state of war is not recognized by one of them. The Convention shall also apply to all cases of partial or total occupation of the territory of a High Contracting Party.

The Convention applies to an incredibly broad spectrum of events. The government has characterized the deployment of U.S. Armed Forces to Panama on December 20, 1989, as the "hostilities" in Panama. However the government wishes to label it, what occurred in late 1989–early 1990 was clearly an "armed conflict" within the meaning of Article 2. Armed troops intervened in a conflict between two parties to the treaty. While the text of Article 2 itself does not define "armed conflict," the Red Cross Commentary to the Geneva Conventions of 1949 states that:

Any difference arising between two states and leading to the intervention of members of the armed forces is an armed conflict within the meaning of Article 2. . . . It makes no difference how long the conflict lasts, how much slaughter takes place, or how numerous are the participating forces; it suffices for the armed forces of one Power to have captured adversaries falling within the scope of Article 4.

In addition, the government has professed a policy of liberally interpreting Article 2:

The United States is a firm supporter of the four Geneva Conventions of 1949. . . . As a nation, we have a strong desire to promote respect for the laws of armed conflict and to secure maximum legal protection for captured members of the U.S. Armed Forces. Consequently, the United States has a policy of applying the Geneva Conventions of 1949 whenever armed hostilities occur with regular foreign armed forces, even if arguments could be made that the threshold standards for the applicability of the Conventions contained in common Article 2 are not met. In this respect, we share the views of the International Committee of the Red Cross that Article 2 of the Conventions should be construed liberally.

Article 4

A. Prisoners of war, in the sense of the present Convention, are persons belonging to one of the following categories, who have fallen into the power of the enemy:

> (1) Members of the armed forces of a Party to the conflict. . . .

Geneva III's definition of a POW is easily broad enough to encompass General Noriega. It is not disputed that he was the head of the PDF, and that he has "fallen into the power of the enemy." Subsection 3 of Article 4 states that captured military personnel are POWs even if they "profess allegiance to a government or an authority not recognized by the Detaining Power."

Article 5

The present Convention shall apply to the persons referred to in Article 4 from the time they fall into the power of the enemy and until their final release and repatriation. Should any doubt arise as to whether persons, having committed a belligerent act and having fallen into the hands of the enemy, belong to any of the categories enumerated in Article 4, such persons shall enjoy the protection of the present Convention until such time as their status has been determined by a competent tribunal.

B. "LAW OF THE LAND"

The Geneva Convention applies to this case because it has been incorporated into the domestic law of the United States. A treaty becomes the "supreme law of the land" upon ratification by the United States Senate. Geneva III was ratified by a unanimous Senate vote on July 6, 1955. Thus, Geneva III is a properly ratified treaty which the United States must uphold. The government acknowledges that Geneva III is "the law of the land."

C. ENFORCEMENT

1. Article 78 Right of Protest

There are potentially two enforcement avenues available to a POW who feels his rights under the Geneva Convention have been violated. The first is the right to complain about the conditions of confinement to the military authorities of the Detaining Power or to representatives of the Protecting Power or humanitarian organizations. This right is established in Article 78 of Geneva III, and cannot be renounced by the POW or revoked or unnecessarily limited by the Detaining Power.

Article 78

Prisoners of war shall have the right to make known to the military authorities in whose power they are, their requests regarding the conditions of captivity to which they are subjected. They shall also have the unrestricted right to apply to the representatives of the Protesting Powers either through their prisoners' representative or, if they consider it necessary, direct, in order to draw their attention to any points on which they may have complaints to make regarding their conditions of captivity. These requests and complaints shall not be limited nor considered to be a part of the correspondence quota referred to in Article 71. They must be transmitted immediately. Even if they are recognized to be unfounded, they may not give rise to any punishment. Prisoners' representatives may send periodic reports on the situation in the camps and the needs of the prisoners of war to the representatives of the Protecting Powers.

In theory, by calling attention to violations of the Convention the prisoner of war will embarrass the government into rectifying any unacceptable conditions to which he is being subjected. However, the obvious weakness of this complaint procedure is that it has no real teeth. Incentive for the government to comply with the treaty stems from its eagerness to be looked upon favorably by others, and, it is hoped, from its desire simply to do what is proper under the circumstances. However, if we truly believe in the goals of the Convention, a more substantial and dependable method must also be available, if necessary, to protect the POW's rights. Recourse to the courts of the Detaining Power seems an appropriate measure, where available.

After all, the ultimate goal of Geneva III is to ensure humane treatment of POWs—not to create some amorphous, unenforceable code of honor among the signatory nations. "It must not be forgotten that the Conventions have been drawn up first and foremost to protect individuals, and not to serve State interests."

The Court can envision numerous situations in which the Article 78 right of protest may not adequately protect a POW who is not being afforded all of the applicable safeguards of Geneva III. If in fact the United States holds Geneva III in the high regard that it claims, it must ensure that its provisions are enforceable by the POW entitled to its protections.

Controlling Provisions of Geneva III

The Court's final task is to determine which provisions of Geneva III are relevant to an individual who is both a prisoner of war and a convicted felon. While these characteristics are not mutually exclusive, the combination of the two in one person creates a novel and somewhat complicated situation with respect to the application of Geneva III.

The essential dispute between Noriega and the government is whether to rely on Articles 21 and 22 or on Article 108 in determining where to place the general. The defense argues that Articles 21 and 22, which explicitly prohibit placing POWs in penitentiaries, apply to General Noriega. The government contends that Article 108 controls, and allows the United States to incarcerate a POW serving a criminal sentence anywhere U.S. military personnel convicted of similar offenses could be confined, including penitentiaries.

Some concern has been expressed about the potential inconsistency between these provisions. However, a careful reading of the various Articles in their proper context proves that no inconsistency exists. Simply stated, Articles 21 and 22 do not apply to POWs convicted of common crimes against the Detaining Power. The Convention clearly sets POWs convicted of crimes apart from other prisoners of war, making special provision for them in Articles 82–108 on "penal and disciplinary sanctions."

Articles 21 and 22

Article 21

The Detaining Power may subject prisoners of war to internment. It may impose on them the obligation of not leaving, beyond certain limits, the camp where they are interned, or if the said camp is fenced in, of not going outside its perimeter. Subject to the provisions of the present Convention relative to penal and disciplinary sanctions, prisoners of war may not be held in close confinement except where necessary to safeguard their health and then only during the continuation of the circumstances which make such confinement necessary.

Article 22

Prisoners of war may be interned only in premises located on land and affording every guarantee of hygiene and healthfulness. Except in particular cases which are justified by the interest of the prisoners themselves,

they shall not be interned in penitentiaries. Articles 21 and 22 appear at the beginning of Chapter 1—"General Observations"—of Section 2—"Internment of Prisoners of War." This chapter of Geneva III deals with the internment of POWs who have not been convicted of crimes, and is thus inapplicable to General Noriega. Defendant's reliance on these Articles is misplaced; if anything, they make clear that POWs convicted of crimes are subject to a different set of rules than other prisoners of war. Article 22's general prohibition against internment of POWs in penitentiaries is limited by Article 21's acknowledgement that all general requirements regarding the treatment of POWs are "subject to the provisions of the present Convention relative to penal and disciplinary sanctions." This reference to Articles 82–108 shows that the articles in Section 2, Chapter 1 do not apply to POWs serving judicial sentences.

Further support for this argument is the use of the term "internment" throughout Section 2, Chapter 1, as opposed to the terms "detention," "confinement," or "imprisonment" used in the penal sanctions Articles. The Commentary elaborates on this point:

> The concept of internment should not be confused with that of detention. Internment involves the obligation not to leave the town, village, or piece of land, whether or not fenced in, on which the camp installations are situated, but it does not necessarily mean that a prisoner of war may be confined to a cell or room. Such confinement may only be imposed in execution of penal or disciplinary sanctions, for which express provision is made in Section 6, Chapter 3.

Thus, Article 22 prohibits internment—but not imprisonment—of POWs in penitentiaries. For these reasons, it is the opinion of this Court that Articles 21 and 22 do not apply to General Noriega.

B. Article 108

The government has argued that the Geneva Convention "explicitly and unambiguously" authorizes the United States to incarcerate Noriega in a penitentiary, so long as he is not treated more harshly than would be a member of the U.S. armed forces convicted of a similar offense.

Paragraph 1 of Article 108 reads:

> Sentences announced on prisoners of war after a conviction has become duly enforceable, shall be served in the same establishments and under the same conditions as in

the case of members of the armed forces of the Detaining Power. These conditions shall in all cases conform to the requirements of health and humanity.

Pursuant, then, to paragraph 1 it appears that General Noriega could technically be incarcerated in a federal penitentiary without violating the Geneva Convention. However, this should not be the end of the inquiry. The real issue is whether federal penitentiaries in general or any particular federal penitentiary can afford a prisoner of war the various protections due him under the Geneva Convention.

The government has argued that because all federal penal facilities must satisfy the Eighth Amendment prohibition on cruel and unusual punishment, any facility is at least theoretically "humane." This misses the point, however, that the Geneva III standard of humane treatment is not the same as the Constitutional standard embodied in the Eighth Amendment. The Eighth Amendment establishes a minimum level of treatment. As long as the United States meets that minimum standard, it can operate within the confines of the Eighth Amendment. The Geneva Convention, on the other hand, delineates some fairly specific benefits for POWs which may not always be required by the Eighth Amendment.

Article 108 requires that the conditions in any facility in which a POW serves his sentence "shall in all cases conform to the requirements of health and humanity." Interpreting the language of these provisions is not always easy. The Commentary to Article 108 says reference should be made to Articles 25 and 29, which lay down minimum standards of accommodation for POWs.

Article 25 provides, in relevant part:

Conditions shall make allowance for the habits and customs of the prisoners and shall in no case be prejudicial to their health. The premises . . . shall be entirely protected from dampness and adequately heated and lighted.

Article 29 provides, in relevant part:

Prisoners of war shall have for their use, day and night, conveniences which conform to the rules of hygiene and are maintained in a constant state of cleanliness.

In addition, Article 108 dictates that the POW must be allowed to "receive and despatch correspondence, to receive at least one relief parcel monthly, to take regular exercise in the open air, to have the medical care required by [his] state of health, and the spiritual assistance [he] may desire. Many of these terms are vague. For example, what is "regular" exercise? Reasonable people may differ on what these provisions require. However, given the United States' asserted commitment to protecting POWs and promoting respect for the laws of armed conflict through liberal interpretation of the Geneva Conventions, vague or ambiguous terms should always be construed in the light most favorable to the prisoner of war.

C. OTHER APPLICABLE ARTICLES
Paragraph 3 of Article 108 states:

In any case, prisoners of war sentenced to a penalty depriving them of their liberty shall retain the benefit of the provisions of Articles 78 and 126 of the present Convention. . . . Penalties to which they may be subjected shall be in accordance with the provisions of Article 87, third paragraph.

The government concedes that the three Articles cited within the text of Article 108—78, 87, and 126—also apply to General Noriega. ("Defendant correctly contends that a sentenced prisoner of war retains prisoner of war status for purposes of correspondence, health and spiritual care, and exercise").

Paragraph 3 of Article 87 prohibits collective punishment for individual acts, corporal punishment, imprisonment in premises without daylight and, in general, any form of torture or cruelty. Again, some of these terms are vague, but because of the U.S. commitment to construing the Geneva Conventions liberally, and because it is imperative that the United States set a good example in its treatment of POWs, ambiguous terms must be construed in the light most favorable to the POW.

Article 126 creates an almost unrestricted grant of authority for representatives of the Protecting Power and international humanitarian organizations to supervise the treatment of POWs wherever and in whatever type of facility they may be held.

The government argues that Article 108's reference to Articles 78, 87, and 126 is an express limitation on Noriega's rights—that these are the only Articles that apply to POWs incarcerated for common crimes. Defendant counters that 108 is just a floor, so while POWs may not be treated worse than U.S. soldiers convicted of similar crimes, frequently they must be treated better. Noriega asserts that Article 108 must be read in conjunction with Article 85 which states that "prisoners of war prosecuted under the laws of the Detaining Power for acts committed prior to capture shall retain, even if convicted, the benefits of the present Convention." The Commentary supports Noriega's position that he continues to be entitled to the Convention's general protections:

> The Convention affords important safeguards to prisoners of war confined following a judicial sentence. Some of these safeguards result from general provisions applicable to all the conditions relating to internment, such as Article 13 (humane treatment), Article 14 (respect for the person of prisoners . . .), Article 16 (equality of treatment). Other provisions refer expressly to the execution of penalties and specifically prohibit cruelty, any attack on a prisoner's honour (Article 87), and discriminatory treatment (Article 88). . . . Confinement does not involve any suppression of the principal safeguards afforded to prisoners of war by the present Convention, and the number of provisions rendered inapplicable by the fact of . . . confinement is therefore small. . . . In fact, these articles (78, 87, 126) are among the provisions which are not rendered inapplicable by confinement. Because of their greater importance, however, . . . special reference was made to them.

It thus appears that a convicted POW is entitled to the basic protections of Geneva III for as long as he remains in the custody of the Detaining Power. Throughout the Commentary to Article 108, reference is made to Articles other than the three specifically named in the text. The logical conclusion is that judicial confinement serves to abrogate only those protections fundamentally inconsistent with incarceration.

This Court finds that, at a minimum, all of the Articles contained in Section 1, General Provisions, should apply to General Noriega, as well as any provisions relating to health. By their own terms, Articles 82–88 (the General Provisions section of the Penal and Disciplinary Sanctions chapter) and 99–108 (Judicial Proceedings subsection) apply.

In addition, the Court would once again note that the stated U.S. policy is to err to the benefit of the POW. In order to set the proper example and avoid diminishing the trust and respect of other nations, the U.S. government must honor its policy by placing General Noriega in a facility that can provide the full panoply of protections to which he is entitled under the Convention.

CONCLUSION

The Defendant Noriega is plainly a prisoner of war under the Geneva Convention III. He is, and will be, entitled to the full range of rights under the treaty, which has been incorporated into U.S. law. Nonetheless, he can serve his sentence in a civilian prison to be designated by the Attorney General or the Bureau of Prisons so long as he is afforded the full benefits of the Convention.

Whether or not those rights can be fully provided in a maximum security penitentiary setting is open to serious question. For the time being, however, that question must be answered by those who will determine Defendant's place and type of confinement. In this determination, those charged with that responsibility must keep in mind the importance to our own troops of faithful and, indeed, liberal adherence to the mandates of Geneva III. Regardless of how the government views the Defendant as a person, the implications of a failure to adhere to the Convention are too great to justify departures.

In the turbulent course of international events—the violence, deceit, and tragedies which capture the news—the relatively obscure issues in this case may seem unimportant. They are not. The implications of a less-than-strict adherence to Geneva III are serious and must temper any consideration of the questions presented.

Why does the court consider adherence to the convention so important? What are the implications of a failure to adhere? Note also that prisoners of war are noncombatants. How does this affect the actions of prisoners of war seeking to escape? See Paragraph 11.7 of *The Commander's Handbook* (prisoners of war are subject to punishment for causing death or injury in the course of an escape attempt).

Conclusion

The Law of Armed Conflict seeks to limit the destructive potential of war by narrowing the lawful justifications for resort to force, and by limiting the means and methods of war once begun. Nations may resort to war only in self-defense, or pursuant to authorization of the United Nations in support of its efforts to maintain international peace and security. Once engaged in international armed conflict, international law requires that force be limited to that required by military necessity, with regard to the principles of humanity, discrimination, and proportionality. The means and methods of war are not unlimited. Only combatants may engage in war, and only combatants and other military objectives may be targeted, although collateral damage may be permissible if proportional to the military advantage to be gained by destruction of the lawful target. Failure to comply with these legal restrictions in war may result in prosecution for war crimes.

Study Questions

1. What are the lawful bases for use of force by one state against another?

2. What triggers the right of national self-defense under Article 51 of the UN Charter?

3. Define armed attack. How does the definition of the International Court of Justice differ from Judge Sofaer's?

4. Who defines threats to international peace and security? What action[s] is/are authorized in response to a declared threat?

5. Define a noncombatant; list examples. May these people be intentionally targeted?

6. Define a combatant.

7. Describe lawful military objectives that may be targeted.

8. What is an unlawful combatant, and what is the consequence of becoming one?

9. What is collateral damage, and when is it legally acceptable?

10. What kind of weapons are unlawful? Why?

11. Explain how treatment of a prisoner of war differs from the treatment of an unlawful combatant; from a common criminal.

CHAPTER THIRTEEN

WAR CRIMES

If the nations which command the great physical forces of the world want the society of nations to be governed by the rule of law, these principles [of the Nuremberg Charter] may contribute to that end. If those who have the power of decision revert to the concept of unlimited and irresponsible sovereignty, neither this nor any charter will save the world from international lawlessness.

—Justice Robert H. Jackson, preface to his official report as U.S. representative to the Nuremberg Trials (1949)

Nature of War Crimes

The term "war crime" is the technical expression for a violation of the law of war. The laws governing the conduct of armed conflict limit the means and methods of warfare. These laws derive from international treaties (conventions) and custom. While not always an easy undertaking, determining whether conduct constitutes a war crime is achievable in most circumstances. The true difficulty in studying war crimes comes with understanding the political aspects of war crimes cases. Unlike domestic criminal cases, prosecution of persons for violations of the law of war requires evidence of guilt, plus the right international situation and necessary political will to carry through with the case. The result is an inconsistent history of war crimes prosecutions that may lead one to question the relevance of the law in this area. Perhaps a better view, however, is to recognize that war crimes law does exist and that an understanding of the rules will enable military officers and their subordinates to comply with those regulations. A comprehension of war crimes law will also facilitate an insight into the political circumstances and considerations that affect decisions by nations to try or not try suspected war criminals.

Development of War Crimes Law

Serious legal consideration of the conduct of belligerents during war did not begin until the second half of the nineteenth century. The Union army enacted General Order 100, known as the Lieber Code during the American Civil War. This set of laws sought to codify international law on the treatment of prisoners of war and noncombatants. The humanitarian principles contained in the code provided a substantial basis for subsequent international conventions concerning the conduct of war. The Declaration of St. Petersburg of 1868 sought to limit the use of projectiles over a certain weight. The 1907 Hague Convention IV went further and placed restrictions on the use of certain inhumane weapons during armed conflict and limited the means of conducting warfare. See appendix 5 for full text. Following World War I, the international community ratified several conventions concerning the conduct of war. The use of poisonous gases during World War I resulted in the 1925 Geneva Protocol for the Prohibition of the Use in War of Gases and Bacteriological Methods. The 1929 Geneva Conventions provided protections for prisoners of war and the wounded and sick, as well. The 1928 General Treaty for the Renunciation of War (known as the Kellogg-Briand Pact) sought to eliminate the use of aggressive war as an instrument of foreign policy.

While international agreements and custom set up principles for the conduct of armed conflict, the war crimes trials following the end of World War I were the first large-scale attempt to try persons for actions occurring during war. Such trials had occurred, however, on a sporadic basis up to that time. For example, during the Boer War of 1899–1902, the British tried and convicted several Boers of acts contrary to the usages of war. The British also convicted three Australian soldiers of shooting Boer prisoners in the well-known case of Lieutenant Charles Morant. Following the end of World War I, the Treaty of Versailles prohibited extradition of persons accused of war crimes. The Allies, therefore, agreed to permit cases against Germans to be tried by a German court at Leipzig, Germany. Department of the Army Pamphlet 27-161-2, *International Law,* describes the results of those trials:

> The trials resulted in six convictions and six acquittals. Most of the acquittals resulted from a failure of the court to accept certain evidence as credible. Disappointment was expressed over the comparatively light sentences meted out but also over the fact the trials dealt almost exclusively with treatment of shipwrecked survivors of submarine activity and with the treatment of prisoners of war. No trials were held on the actual conduct of hostilities, such as the use of weapons and the destruction of life and property in combat. Another objection was the fact that the court itself was under pressure from the German press and public. Both were very hostile to the trials. For example, after the sentence was announced in the *Llandovery Castle* case the British observers had to leave by a side door under police escort.

The offenses charged at Leipzig ranged from torpedoing a hospital ship to killing prisoners of war. The most severe punishment awarded at the trials was confinement for four years.

At the close of World War II, the victorious Allied nations undertook an aggressive program for the punishment of war criminals. This program began with the establishment of an international military tribunal for the trial of senior German officers and leaders in Nuremberg, Germany. The trials at Nuremberg lasted nine and a half months. The tribunal held 403 open sessions, heard evidence from 113 witnesses, and considered more than 1,900 interrogatory responses and affidavits.

Following the trials of German leaders at Nuremberg, the Allies established a second international tribunal to try senior Japanese officials. Known as the International Military Tribunal for the Far East, this court tried twenty-eight high-ranking Japanese leaders. The tribunal convicted twenty-five of the accused, with two of the defendants dying during the

Defendant	Findings	Sentence
Goering	Guilty	Hanging
Hess	Guilty	Life
Ribbentrop	Guilty	Hanging
Fritzsche	Not Guilty	
Keitel	Guilty	Hanging
Kaltenbrunner	Guilty	Hanging
Rosenberg	Guilty	Hanging
Frank	Guilty	Hanging
Frick	Guilty	Hanging
Streicher	Guilty	Hanging
Funk	Guilty	Life
Schacht	Not Guilty	
Von Neurath	Guilty	15 years
Doenitz	Guilty	10 years
Raeder	Guilty	Life
Von Schiroch	Guilty	20 years
Sauckel	Guilty	Hanging
Jodl	Guilty	Hanging
Bormann	Guilty (tried in absentia)	Hanging
Von Papen	Not Guilty	
Seyss-Inquart	Guilty	Hanging
Speer	Guilty	20 years
Krupp	Not tried because of old age	
Ley	Suicide	

Figure 13-1

proceedings and one judged unfit to stand trial. Seven of the defendants were hanged, sixteen were sentenced to life imprisonment, and the remainder were sentenced to long prison terms. Following the dramatic and well-publicized hearings at Nuremberg and Tokyo, the Allies tried other suspected war criminals using various types of tribunals, commissions, and courts. The United States established military tribunals and commissions in various places in Europe and Asia. There is no complete list of all the war crimes trials held following World War II; however, it is safe to estimate that the Allies tried more than twenty-four thousand persons on war crimes charges.

The experiences of World War II led the world community to codify specific international rules pertaining to war crimes in the Geneva Conventions of 1949. These conventions set forth a list of serious war crimes, termed "grave breaches." Apart from the World War II war crimes trials, prosecution of individuals for war crimes has occurred sporadically since 1945. The United States tried service members for

crimes in Vietnam. See *United States v. Calley* in the section on Responsibility for War Crimes below, and in Panama, see *United States v. Freed* (first sergeant charged with murder for shooting a Panamanian prisoner acquitted at general court-martial).

Recently, the United Nations commenced war crimes trials for atrocities committed during the conflict in Bosnia-Herzegovina. Because the peace-keeping forces in the former Yugoslavia have been reluctant to arrest suspected war criminals, the United Nations tribunal has yet to try any senior Serbian officials. Do you agree that the greatest impediment to trying suspected war criminals in the former Yugoslavia is not the law, but political considerations? Is it easier to conduct war crimes prosecutions if there is a clear victor in the conflict? The Russians are alleged to have committed war atrocities in Chechnya. Do the international rules regarding war crimes apply to that conflict?

Defining War Crimes

The Charter of the International Military Tribunal at Nuremberg contained the following categories of crimes:

1. Crimes Against Peace. Planning, preparation, initiation, or waging of a declared or undeclared war of aggression, or war otherwise in violation of international treaties, agreements, or assurances.

2. War Crimes. The traditional violations of the laws or customs of war.

3. Crimes Against Humanity. A collective category of major felonious crimes committed against any civilian population before or during an armed conflict.

The categories of war crimes used in the Nuremberg trials evolved from both customary and conventional law. See chapter 11, which describes the sources of the law of war. The crime of waging aggressive war, however, was not articulated as an offense until the end of World War II. Although the Kellogg-Briand Pact of 1928 renounced war as an instrument of national policy, neither it nor its predecessors declared aggressive wars to be illegal under international law. At the time of the trials, the charge of crimes against peace raised serious *ex poste facto* issues that were resolved in favor of the prosecution. U.S. Supreme Court Justice Robert H. Jackson, the senior prosecutor for the United States at Nuremberg, believed that the criminalization of aggression was the most important aspect of the trials. Note, however, that of the twenty-four accused at Nuremberg, only one was found guilty solely of crimes against peace and only two were convicted solely of crimes against humanity.

Article 2 of the United Nations Charter provides:

> All Members shall settle their international disputes by peaceful means in such a manner that international peace and security, and justice, are not endangered.
> All Members shall refrain in their international relations from the threat or use of force against the territorial integrity or political independence of any state.

Do the above provisions outlaw aggression? In other words, if an individual were tried for crimes against peace, as in the Nuremberg cases, would he or she be charged with violating Article 2 of the United Nations Charter? If no, is there a law that proscribes aggressive war? After the World War II war crimes trials, are crimes against peace now part of customary international law? The world community charged that Iraq had committed a war crime by waging aggressive war against Kuwait. Did Iraq's invasion violate the proscription on waging wars of aggression? If yes, then why have there been no war crimes trials involving Iraq?

Article 50, 1949 Geneva Convention for the Amelioration of the Condition of the Wounded and Sick in Armed Forces in the Field, lists the following grave breaches of the convention:

> Grave breaches to which the preceding Article relates shall be those involving any of the following acts, if committed against persons or property protected by the Convention: willful killing, torture or inhuman treatment, including biological experiments, willfully causing great suffering or serious injury to body or health, and extensive destruction and appropriation of property, not justified by military necessity and carried out unlawfully and wantonly.

The above list is not exhaustive of all serious war crimes. For example, Iraq's intentional release of oil into the Persian Gulf during the Gulf War is generally considered a grave breach offense. Genocide, the destruction of a national, ethnic, racial, or religious group, was outlawed by the Geneva Convention on the Prevention and Punishment of the Crime of Genocide. This offense is viewed as a grave breach of the law of war as well.

Violations of the law of war not amounting to grave breaches constitute "simple breaches." See appendix 4 concerning the distinction between simple and grave breaches. Army Pamphlet 27-10, *The Law of Land Warfare,* provides examples of simple breaches of the law of war:

1. Making use of poisoned or otherwise forbidden arms or ammunition;

2. Treacherous request for quarter;

3. Maltreatment of dead bodies;

4. Firing on localities which are undefended and without military significance;

5. Abuse of or firing on the flag of truce;

6. Misuse of protected emblems;

7. Use of civilian clothing by troops to conceal their military character during battle;

8. Compelling prisoners of war to perform prohibited labor;

9. Killing without trial spies or other persons who have committed hostile acts.

Responsibility for War Crimes

The prosecutions at Nuremberg and in the Far East at the conclusion of World War II raised the issue of who is legally responsible for the commission of war crimes. The following case addresses that issue.

IN RE YAMASHITA
SUPREME COURT OF THE UNITED STATES
327 U.S. 1
FEBRUARY 4, 1946
Opinion: Stone, Chief Justice

Prior to September 3, 1945, petitioner was the commanding general of the Fourteenth Army Group of the Imperial Japanese Army in the Philippine Islands. On that date he surrendered to and became a prisoner of war of the United States Army Forces in Baguio, Philippine Islands. On October 8, 1945, petitioner, after pleading not guilty to the charge, was held for trial before a military commission of five army officers appointed by order of General Styer.

The charge. Neither congressional action nor the military orders constituting the commission authorized it to place petitioner on trial unless the charge preferred against him is of a violation of the law of war. The charge, so far as now relevant, is that petitioner, between October 9, 1944, and September 2, 1945, in the Philippine Islands,

> while commander of armed forces of Japan at war with the United States of America and its allies, unlawfully disregarded and failed to discharge his duty as commander to control the operations of the members of his command, permitting them to commit brutal atrocities and other high crimes against people of the United States and of its allies and dependencies, particularly the Philippines; and he . . . thereby violated the laws of war.

The prosecution alleges a series of acts, one hundred and twenty-three in number, committed by members of the forces under petitioner's command during the period mentioned. The first item specifies the execution of "a deliberate plan and purpose to massacre and exterminate a large part of the civilian population of Batangas Province, and to devastate and destroy public, private and religious property therein, as a result of which more than 25,000 men, women and children, all unarmed noncombatant civilians, were brutally mistreated and killed, without cause or trial, and entire set-tlements were devastated and destroyed wantonly and without military necessity." Other items specify acts of violence, cruelty and homicide inflicted upon the civilian population and prisoners of war, acts of wholesale pillage and the wanton destruction of religious monuments.

It is not denied that such acts directed against the civilian population of an occupied country and against prisoners of war are recognized in international law as violations of the law of war. But it is urged that the charge does not allege that petitioner has either committed or directed the commission of such acts, and consequently that no violation is charged as against him. But this overlooks the fact that the gist of the charge is an unlawful breach of duty by petitioner as an army commander to control the operations of the members of his command by "permitting them to commit" the extensive and widespread atrocities specified. The question then is whether the law of war imposes on an army commander a duty to take such appropriate measures as are within his power to control the troops under his command for the prevention of the specified acts which are violations of the law of war and which are likely to attend the occupation of hostile territory by an uncontrolled soldiery, and whether he may be charged with personal responsibility for his failure to take such measures when violations result. That this was the precise issue to be tried was made clear by the statement of the prosecution at the opening of the trial.

It is evident that the conduct of military operations by troops whose excesses are unrestrained by the orders or efforts of their commander would almost certainly result in violations which it is the purpose of the law of war to prevent. Its purpose to protect civilian populations and prisoners of war from brutality would largely be defeated if the commander of an invading army could with impunity neglect to take reasonable measures for their protection. Hence the law of war presupposes that its violation is to be avoided through the control of the operations of war by commanders who are to some extent responsible for their subordinates.

[International law] plainly imposed on petitioner, who at the time specified was military governor of the Philippines, as well as commander of the Japanese forces, an affirmative duty to take such measures as were within his power and appropriate in the circumstances to protect prisoners of war and the civilian population.

We do not make the laws of war but we respect them so far as they do not conflict with the commands of Congress or the Constitution. There is no contention that the present charge, thus read, is without the support of evidence, or that the commission held petitioner responsible for failing to take measures which were beyond his control or inappropriate for a commanding officer to take in the circumstances. We do not here appraise the evidence on which petitioner was convicted. We do not consider what measures, if any, petitioner took to prevent the commission, by the troops under his command, of the plain violations of the law of war detailed in the bill of particulars, or whether such measures as he may have taken were appropriate and sufficient to discharge the duty imposed upon him. These are questions within the peculiar competence of the military officers composing the commission and were for it to decide. It is plain that the charge on which petitioner was tried charged him with a breach of his duty to control the operations of the members of his command, by permitting them to commit the specified atrocities. This was enough to require the commission to hear evidence tending to establish the culpable failure of petitioner to perform the duty imposed on him by the law of war and to pass upon its sufficiency to establish guilt.

A frequent defense in war crimes trials is that the accused was ordered by a superior to commit the offense. For example, in the *Dover Castle* case of World War I, Karl Neumann, the commander of the German submarine that torpedoed the British hospital ship, *Dover Castle,* raised the defense that he was simply following the orders of the German Admiralty in sinking the vessel. The court at Leipzig held that the "Admiralty Staff was the highest service authority over the accused. He was in duty bound to obey their orders in service matters. So far as he did that, he was free from criminal responsibility. Therefore, he cannot be held responsible for sinking the Hospital Ship *Dover Castle* according to orders." The next case considers the defense of superior orders raised by an accused charged with shooting civilians.

UNITED STATES V. FIRST LIEUTENANT
WILLIAM L. CALLEY, JR., U.S. ARMY
UNITED STATES ARMY COURT OF MILITARY REVIEW
46 C.M.R. 1131
FEBRUARY 16, 1973
Opinion: Alley, Judge

On 16 March 1968 Lieutenant Calley was the 1st platoon leader in C Company, 1st Battalion, 20th Infantry, 11th Light Infantry Brigade, as he had been since he arrived in the Republic of Vietnam in December 1967. The 11th Brigade was assigned to the American Division, itself only formally activated in October 1967.

The American Division was assigned a tactical area of operation along the South China Sea Coast from Quang Ngai Province north into Quang Nam Province. That area, approximately 150 kilometers from north to south, was divided among the three constituent brigades, the 11th Brigade receiving the southern-most portion. With the exception of the area in the vicinity of Quang Ngai City, which had been assigned to 2nd Republic of Vietnam Army (ARVN) Division, the 11th Brigade area of operation ran from Duc Pho District north to Binh Son District, and inland for approximately 30 kilometers.

In January 1968, appellant's company; A Company, 3d Battalion, 1st Infantry; and B Company, 4th Battalion, 3d Infantry, were chosen by the brigade commander to compose Task Force Barker. A supporting field artillery battery was organized from the assets of three existing batteries of the brigade's organic field artillery battalion. The Task Force area of operation, designated Muscatine, was located north of the Song Diem-Diem and east of Highway 1 northward for approximately 12 kilometers to Binh Son. Its operations were conducted from two fire support bases, Uptight and Dottie (Task Force Barker Headquarters).

During operations in the southern sector of its area of operation, the units of Task Force Barker drew fire from enemy forces which would withdraw south of the Song Diem-Diem. After the Tet offensive in early February 1968 Task Force Barker requested and received authority temporarily to extend its area of operation south of the river into Son My village. Intelligence reports had indicated that the 48th Viet Cong Battalion maintained its base camp in the My Lai (1), or Pinkville, area of Song My. The village reportedly had been controlled by the Viet Cong for twenty years. Prior efforts by friendly forces to enter the area had been sternly resisted. When Task Force Barker made sweeps into Son My later in February, it met only limited success. At the cost of moderate casualties it destroyed some enemy supplies and fortifications, but was unable decisively to engage the main enemy force.

C Company, appellant's unit, had not experienced much combat prior to 16 March 1968. In its three months of overseas duty, two of which were with Task Force Barker, its operations had consisted of uneventful patrolling, attempted ambushes, providing defense for the fire bases, and providing blocking forces for Task Force missions. The casualties it had sustained were mainly from mines and booby traps. While moving into a blocking position on 25 February 1968 the company became ensnared in a mine field, suffering two killed and thirteen wounded. Appellant was not on this operation, for he had just returned from a three day incountry rest and recuperation leave. On 14 March 1968, a popular sergeant in the second platoon was killed and three others were wounded by a booby trap.

The next day, Captain Medina, commander of C Company, was notified that his company would engaged in an upcoming offensive action. He was briefed at Task Force headquarters, then called his officers and men together on the evening of 15 March 1968 for a unit briefing. The content of the briefing (a matter of some dispute as will subsequently be discussed) essentially was that the next morning the unit would engage the 48th VC Battalion, from whom it could expect heavy resistance and by whom it would be outnumbered by more than two to one. C Company was to be inserted by airlift to the west of My Lai (4), sweep through it, and continue toward My Lai (1) or Pinkville (Appendices A and C). There they would be joined in a night defensive position by B Company of the Task Force, which would be conducting a similar operation from south to north into My Lai (1), and by A Company which would be in a blocking position north of the river.

The concept of the operation for C Company was for the 1st and 2nd platoons to sweep rapidly through My Lai (4) and the 3rd platoon to follow. The 3rd platoon would thoroughly search the hamlet and destroy all that could be useful to the enemy. A demolition team of engineers was attached to assist in the destruction of enemy bunkers and facilities.

This was to be the unit's first opportunity to engage decisively the elusive enemy they had been pursuing since their arrival in South Vietnam. The men, as is normal in an untried unit, faced the operation with both anticipation and fear, mindful of the recent casualties taken in less perilous missions.

C Company was transported by helicopter from LZ Dottie about six miles southeast to My Lai (4) in two lifts. The first lift was completed at approximately 0730 hours; the second lift at 0747 hours. The insertion was preceded by five minutes of preparatory fires of 105 howitzer high explosive rounds and by gunship fire. The insertion, although within 100 meters of the western edge of My Lai (4), was not opposed by hostile fire. In formation with the first and second platoons on line from north to south, the third platoon in reserve and the mortar platoon remaining with the rear to provide support if needed, C Company laid heavy suppressive fires into the subhamlet as the first and second platoons began the assault.

Despite expectations of heavy resistance based upon specific intelligence briefings, C Company moved through My Lai (4) without receiving any fire. The only unit casualty on 16 March 1968 was one self-inflicted wound. No mines or booby traps were detonated. Lead elements of the company had no occasion to call for mortar fire from the weapons platoon; the forward observer with C Company had no occasion to call for any fire from artillery units in direct support. In My Lai (4), the unit encountered only unarmed, unresisting, frightened old men, women, and children, and not the expected elements of the 48th Viet Cong Battalion. The villagers were found in their homes eating breakfast and beginning their morning chores.

The members of C Company reacted to the unexpected absence of opposition in diverse ways. Some continued the mission as if the enemy was in fact being engaged. Most recognized the difference between actual and expected circumstances, so while continuing with the destruction of foodstuffs, livestock, and buildings, reverted to the unit standing operating procedures on collecting and evacuating Vietnamese. Many soldiers took no action at all, but stood passively by while others destroyed My Lai (4). A few, after witnessing inexplicable acts of violence against defenseless villagers, affirmatively refused to harm them.

No single witness at appellant's trial observed all that transpired at My Lai (4). The testimony of the 92 witnesses was shaded by the lapse of time between 16 March 1968 and the commencement of trial in November 1970. Even in the voluminous record, all that happened is not fully revealed. One reason for vagueness and confusion in testimony offered by both sides is that the operation itself was confused, having been planned on the basis of faulty intelligence and conducted with inexperienced troops without adequate command control.

With this caveat as to the evidence, we come to the events which led to charges against appellant. Twenty out of the twenty-seven persons who were members of Lieutenant Calley's understrength platoon on 16 March 1968 testified at his court-martial.

The first platoon arrived on the first lift about 0730 hours. Its initial task was to provide perimeter defense for the insertion of the remainder of the company. After the company was on the ground and organized for assault, the first platoon moved toward My Lai (4) in formation.

After the first platoon's movement through My Lai (4), which took from ninety minutes to two hours to cover only a third of a mile, the majority of the platoon formed a perimeter defense about fifty to one hundred meters east of the ditch on the east side of the subhamlet. The rest of C Company more thoroughly searched and destroyed My Lai (4). The first platoon remained in its defensive position for another two hours or so until after the company had taken a lunch break. C Company then continued its mission with less eventful forays into two other subhamlets of Song My village. At one time later in the afternoon C Company was ordered by the brigade commander to return to My Lai (4) to verify reports of civilian casualties; but after an estimate of twenty-eight killed was radioed in by Captain Medina, that order was countermanded by the division commander.

As previously described, some of the villagers rooted out of their homes were placed in a group guarded by Private First Class Paul Meadlo and Private First Class

Dennis Conti. Private First Class Dursi, who was about fifteen feet from Private First Class Meadlo watching his own group of Vietnamese, saw Lieutenant Calley come onto the trail and heard him ask Meadlo "if he could take care of that group." A couple of minutes later the appellant returned and, as Dursi remembered, yelled to Meadlo, "why haven't you wasted them yet?" Private First Class Dursi turned and started to move his group down the trail when he heard M-16 fire from his rear.

Private First Class Conti recounted that Lieutenant Calley told him and Meadlo "to take care of the people," left, and returned:

> Then he came out and said, "I thought I told you to take care of them." Meadlo said, "We are. We are watching them" and he said "No, I mean kill them."

The Ditch. It is not disputed that during midmorning on 16 March 1968 a large number of unresisting Vietnamese were placed in a ditch on the eastern side of My Lai (4) and summarily executed by American soldiers. We can best begin a recital of the tragic facts and circumstances surrounding this offense by examining the appellant's testimony.

Lieutenant Calley testified that after he passed PFC Meadlo for the second time at the trail, he moved toward Sergeant Mitchell's location in the southeastern part of My Lai (4). He found him near a ditch that ran through that sector. He walked up the ditch until he broke into a clearing. There he discovered some of his men firing upon Vietnamese in another ditch. Lieutenant Calley admitted that he also fired with them and told Meadlo to get his people over to the ditch or, if he couldn't move them, to "waste them." He then went north to check out the positions of his men.

Charles Sledge confirmed some of those movements of his platoon leader. However, Sledge remembers important events differently. He heard someone shout that Sergeant Mitchell had some people at a ditch; moved there; saw twenty to thirty Vietnamese women, children, and a few old men; saw Lieutenant Calley and Sergeant Mitchell shove these Vietnamese down into the ditch and fire into them from four or five feet. The victims screamed and fell. A helicopter landed nearby. Lieutenant Calley went to it to talk with the aviator and returned to say to Sledge, "He don't like the way

I'm running the show, but I'm the boss here."

Other members of the first platoon saw Vietnamese placed into a ditch and appellant and others fire into it. Some members of the third platoon also saw the bloody bodies. Also, the observations of witnesses who were in the supporting helicopters portray a telling, and ghastly, overview of the slaughter at the ditch. Aviators and crew members saw from the air numbers of bodies they variously estimated from about thirty to about one hundred. One aviator, a Lieutenant (then Warrant Officer) Thompson, actually landed near the scene three times. The second time, he spoke with someone, who from the evidence must have been Lieutenant Calley. Thompson succeeded in evacuating a few living Vietnamese despite appellant's deprecations. The evidence from others is certainly persuasive that Lieutenant Calley boasted, "I'm the boss here," after he spoke with an aviator.

According to Specialist Four Sledge, five or ten minutes after Lieutenant Calley returned from speaking with a helicopter aviator, he and Calley encountered a forty to fifty year old man dressed in white robes as they moved north up the ditch. Appellant repeatedly questioned the man, "Viet Cong adou?" (Are you Viet Cong), to which the man continually replied, "No vice." Suddenly Lieutenant Calley shot the man in the face at point blank range, blowing half his head away. Immediately after this incident Sledge remembered that:

> Someone hollered, 'there's a child,' you know, running back toward the village. Lieutenant Calley ran back, I don't know if it was a girl or boy but it was a little baby, and he grabbed it by the arm and threw it into the ditch and fired.

Legal Responsibility. In an argument of extraordinary scope, appellant asks us to hold that the deaths of the My Lai villagers were not legally requitable in that the villagers had no right to continued life cognizable in our law. The two premises for this view are first, that the history of operations around Pinkville discloses villager sympathy and support for the Viet Cong, so extensive and enduring as to constitute all the villagers as belligerents themselves; and second, that appellant's superiors had determined the belligerent status of the villagers before the operation of 16 March, i.e., as belligerents, the villagers were not entitled to the protections of

peaceful civilian status under the Geneva Convention Relative to the Protection of Civilian Persons in Time of War, or of prisoner of war status because they did not organize under a responsible commander, bear a fixed distinctive sign recognizable at a distance, carry arms openly, and conduct their own operations in accordance with the laws of war, the four minima which must be satisfied by irregular belligerents in order to be regarded as prisoners of war under Article 4, Geneva Convention Relative to the treatment of Prisoners of War.

This argument is tainted by several fallacies. One is that participation in irregular warfare is done by individuals, although they may organize themselves for the purpose. Slaughtering many for the presumed delicts of a few is not a lawful response to the delicts. We do not know whether the findings specifically included the deaths of infants in arms or children of toddler age, but the fallacy is clear when it is recalled that villagers this young were indiscriminately included in the general carnage. A second fallacy is that the argument is in essence a plea to permit summary execution as a reprisal for irregular villager action favoring the Viet Cong. Reprisal by summary execution of the helpless is forbidden in the laws of land warfare. It is not the law that the villagers were either innocent civilians or eligible for prisoner of war status or liable to summary execution. Whether an armed conflict be a local uprising or a global war, summary executions as in My Lai (4) are not justifiable.

Granting his own sanity, appellant also contends that he was nevertheless not guilty of murder because he did not entertain the requisite mens rea. He claims that his acts were justified because of the orders given to him; or, if the orders and his response do not constitute a complete defense, he is at most guilty of manslaughter.

Responding to a question during direct examination asking why he gave Meadlo the order, "If he couldn't get rid of them to 'waste them,'" Lieutenant Calley replied, "Because that was my order. That was the order of the day, sir." The appellant stated he received that order from Captain Medina, "The night before in the company briefings, the platoon leaders' briefing, the following morning before we lifted off, and twice there in the village."

Captain Medina, who was called as a witness at the

request of the court members, gave a different version of his remarks to the company on the eve of the operation:

> The briefing that I conducted for my company was that C Company had been selected to conduct a combat assault operation onto the village of My Lai (4) beginning with LZ time 0730 hours on the morning of the 16th of March, 1968. I gave them the enemy situation, intelligence reports where the 48th VC Battalion was located in the village of My Lai (4). I told them that the VC Battalion numbered approximately 250 to 280 men and that we would be outnumbered approximately two to one, and that we could expect a hell of a good fight and that we probably would be engaged. I told them that even though we were outnumbered that we had a double coverage of gunships that were being provided and that the artillery was being placed onto the village and that this would help make up for the difference in ratio between the enemy forces and our company. I told the people that this would give them a chance to engage the 48th VC Battalion, that the 48th VC Battalion was the one that we had been chasing around the Task Force Barker area of operation, and that we would finally get a chance to engage them in combat, and that we would be able to destroy the 48th VC Battalion. . . . The information that I gave also in the briefing to the company was that the 48th VC Battalion was located at the village of My Lai (4), and that the intelligence reports also indicated that the innocent civilians or noncombatants would be gone to market at 0700 hours in the morning. This was one reason why the artillery preparation was being placed onto the village at 0720 hours with the combat assault LZ time 0730 hours. I did not make any reference to the handling of prisoners.

Captain Medina recalled that someone at the company briefing asked, "Do we kill women and children," and that his reply was, "No, you do not kill women and children. You must use common sense. If they have a weapon and are trying to engage you, then you can shoot back, but you must use common sense."

If the members found that appellant fabricated his claim of obedience to orders, their finding has abundant support in the record. If they found his claim of acting in obedience to orders to be credible, he would nevertheless not automatically be entitled to acquittal. Not every order is exonerating.

The trial judge's instructions under which he submitted the issues raised by evidence of obedience to or-

ders were entirely correct. After fairly summarizing the evidence bearing on the question, he correctly informed the members as a matter of law that any order received by appellant directing him to kill unresisting Vietnamese within his control or within the control of his troops would have been illegal; that summary execution of detainees is forbidden by law. A determination of this sort, being a question of law only, is within the trial judge's province.

The instructions continued:

> The question does not rest there, however. A determination that an order is illegal does not, of itself, assign criminal responsibility to the person following the order for acts done in compliance with it. Soldiers are taught to follow orders, and special attention is given to obedience of orders on the battlefield. Military effectiveness depends upon obedience to orders. On the other hand, the obedience of a soldier is not the obedience of an automaton. A soldier is a reasoning agent, obliged to respond, not as a machine, but as a person. The law takes these factors into account in assessing criminal responsibility for acts done in compliance with illegal orders.
>
> The acts of a subordinate done in compliance with an unlawful order given him by his superior are excused and impose no criminal liability upon him unless the superior's order is one which a man of ordinary sense and understanding would, under the circumstances, know to be unlawful, or if the order in question is actually known to the accused to be unlawful.

The trial judge amplified these principles by specifying the burden of proof and the logical sequence for consideration of the questions to be resolved. The members were told that if they found beyond a reasonable doubt that appellant actually knew the orders under which he asserted he operated were illegal, the giving of the orders would be no defense; that the final aspect of the obedience question was more objective in nature, namely, that if orders to kill unresisting detainees were given, and if appellant acted in response thereto being unaware that the orders were illegal, he must be acquitted unless the members were satisfied beyond a reasonable doubt that a man of ordinary sense and understanding would have known the orders to be unlawful.

The instructions were sound and the members' findings correct. An order of the type appellant says he received is illegal. Its illegality is apparent upon even cursory evaluation by a man of ordinary sense and understanding. A finding that it is not exonerating should not be disturbed. Appellant's attempts to distinguish these cases fail. More candidly, he argues that they are all wrongly decided insofar as they import the objective standard of an order's illegality as would have been known by a man of ordinary sense and understanding. The argument is essentially that obedience to orders is a defense which strikes at mens rea; therefore in logic an obedient subordinate should be acquitted so long as he did not personally know of the order's illegality. Precedent aside, we would not agree with the argument. Heed must be given not only to subjective innocence-through-ignorance in the soldier, but to the consequences for his victims. Also, barbarism tends to invite reprisal to the detriment of our own force or disrepute which interferes with the achievement of war aims, even though the barbaric acts were preceded by orders for their commission. Casting the defense of obedience to orders solely in subjective terms of mens rea would operate practically to abrogate those objective restraints which are essential to functioning rules of war. The court members, after being given correct standards, properly rejected any defense of obedience to orders.

First Lieutenant Calley was originally sentenced to life imprisonment. The reviewing authority reduced the prison term to twenty years; the sentence was then mitigated to ten years by the secretary of the army. First Lieutenant Calley was released on parole prior to serving his entire ten-year term. Captain Medina, First Lieutenant Calley's superior, was also tried for the murders at My Lai. At trial, the military judge instructed the jury regarding the culpability of Captain Medina:

After taking or issuing an order, a commander must remain alert and make timely adjustments as required by a changing situation. Furthermore, a commander is also responsible if he has actual knowledge that troops or other persons subject to his control are in the process of committing or are about to commit a war crime and he wrongfully fails to take the necessary and reasonable

steps to insure compliance with the law of war. *You will observe that these legal requirements placed upon a commander require actual knowledge plus a wrongful failure to act.* Thus mere presence at the scene without knowledge will not suffice. That is, the commander-subordinate relationship alone will not allow an inference of knowledge. While it is not necessary that a commander actually see an atrocity being committed, *it is essential that he know that his subordinates are in the process of committing atrocities or about to commit atrocities* [emphasis added].

Captain Medina was acquitted of the charges. Was the instruction to the jury in the *Medina* case in line with *Yamishita*? What are the differences in the two cases? Of the twenty-five soldiers charged with war crimes or related acts arising out of the My Lai incident, none, except First Lieutenant Calley, were convicted at court-martial. Does this present the same problem raised by the Leipzig trials following World War I?

Prosecution of War Crimes

Article 49 of the 1949 Geneva Convention for the Amelioration of the Conditions of the Wounded and Sick in Armed Forces in the Field provides:

The High Contracting Parties undertake to enact any legislation necessary to provide effective penal sanctions for persons committing, or ordering to be committed, any of the grave breaches of the present Convention defined in the following Article.

Each High Contracting Party shall be under the obligation to search for persons alleged to have committed, or to have ordered to be committed, such grave breaches, and shall bring such persons, regardless of their nationality, before its own courts. It may also, if it prefers, and in accordance with the provisions of its own legislation, hand such persons over for trial to another High Contracting Party concerned, provided such High Contracting Party has made out a *prima facie case.*

Each High Contracting Party shall take measures necessary for the suppression of all acts contrary to the provisions of the present Convention other than the grave breaches defined in the following Article.

The United States satisfies its obligations described in the above section in several ways. The jurisdiction to try persons suspected of war crimes is addressed in the UCMJ:

Art. 18. Jurisdiction of general courts-martial

General courts-martial also have jurisdiction to try any person who by the law of war is subject to trial by a military tribunal and may adjudge any punishment permitted by the law of war.

Art. 21. Jurisdiction of courts-martial not exclusive.

The provisions of this chapter conferring jurisdiction upon courts-martial do not deprive military commissions, provost courts, or other military tribunals of concurrent jurisdiction with respect to offenders or offenses that by statute or by the law of war may be tried by military commissions, provost courts, or other military tribunals.

Based on the above provisions, forums other than courts-martial still have authority to hear war crimes cases. In what situations would the use of such forums be appropriate/advisable? Consider the following action taken by the United Nations with respect to the former Yugoslavia:

The Security Council,

Expressing once again its grave concern at continuing reports of widespread and flagrant violations of international humanitarian law occurring within the territory of the former Yugoslavia, and especially in the Republic of Bosnia and Herzegovina, including reports of mass killings, massive, organized and systemic rape of women, and the continuance of the practice of "ethnic cleansing," including for the acquisition and the holding of territory,

Believing, that the establishment of an international tribunal and the prosecution of persons responsible for the above-mentioned violations of international humanitarian law will contribute to ensuring that such violations are halted and effectively redressed,

Decides hereby to establish an international tribunal for the sole purpose of prosecuting persons responsible for serious violations of international humanitarian law in the territory of the former Yugoslavia.

To satisfy its obligations under the Geneva Conventions, the United States military requires training of all of its personnel on the law of war. Also, the Department of Defense requires the prompt reporting and investigation of alleged war crimes, as well as the appropriate disposition of such cases. See Department of Defense Directive 5100.77.

Study Questions

1. What is a war crime? What is the difference between a grave and simple breach of the law of war?

2. What are the sources of war crimes law?

3. Which of the following categories of individuals may be held liable for war crimes?

   a. Individuals who actually commit war crimes.

   b. Individuals who order the commission of war crimes.

   c. Superiors who did not know, but reasonably should have known, of the commission of war crimes by forces under their command, and failed to take action to stop them.

   d. All of the above.

   e. (a) and (b) only.

4. Which of the following statements is *false* regarding "grave breaches" of the law of war?

   a. They consist of serious violations such as willful killing, torture, or inhumane treatment of protected persons.

   b. Signatories to the Geneva Conventions have an affirmative duty to search for and bring to trial persons alleged to have committed grave breaches.

   c. The statute of limitations for prosecuting grave breaches is five years from the date of the offense.

   d. U.S. service members who commit grave breaches are subject to prosecution under the UCMJ for the specific offending conduct (murder, rape, destruction of property, and so on).

   e. None of the above; they are all true statements.

5. Upon discovery of war crime activities, the discovering nation has the responsibility to

    a. Prosecute the war criminal.

    b. Declare the war criminal as an undesirable and deport them.

    c. Turn over the war criminal to another nation for prosecution.

    d. Either (a) or (c).

    e. Either (a) or (c), but only if the prosecution occurs within five years, the statute of limitations period for grave breaches of the Geneva Conventions.

6. When, if ever, will the defense that the accused was following orders be successful? Could the defense ever work for killing noncombatants?

7. What other forums besides general courts-martial have jurisdiction to try suspected war criminals? What is the policy of the United States regarding prosecution of its own service members for war crimes?

APPENDIXES

CONSTITUTION OF THE UNITED STATES

We the People of the United States, in Order to form a more perfect Union, establish Justice, insure domestic Tranquility, provide for the common defence, promote the general Welfare, and secure the Blessings of Liberty to ourselves and our Posterity, do ordain and establish this Constitution of the United States of America.

Article I

Section 1. All legislative Powers herein granted shall be vested in a Congress of the United States, which shall consist of a Senate and a House of Representatives.

Section 2. The House of Representatives shall be composed of Members chosen every second year by the people of the several states, and the Electors in each State shall have the Qualifications requisite for Electors of the most numerous Branch of the State Legislature.

No person shall be a Representative who shall not have attained to the Age of twenty-five Years, and been seven Years a Citizen of the United States, and who shall not, when elected, be an Inhabitant of that State in which he shall be chosen.

When vacancies happen in the Representation from any state, the Executive Authority thereof shall issue Writs of Election to fill such Vacancies.

The House of Representatives shall choose the Speaker and other officers; and shall have the sole power of Impeachment.

Section 3. The Senate of the United States shall be composed of two Senators from each State chosen by the Legislature thereof, for six Years and each Senator shall have one Vote.

Immediately after they shall be assembled in Consequence of the first Election, they shall be divided as equally as may be into three Classes. The Seats of the Senators of the first Class shall be vacated at the Expiration of the second Year, of the second Class at the Expiration of the fourth Year, and of the third Class at the Expiration of the sixth Year, so that one third may be chosen every second Year; and if Vacancies happen by Resignation, or otherwise during the Recess of the Legislature of any State, the Executive thereof may make temporary Appointments until the next Meeting of the Legislature, which shall then fill such Vacancies.

No person shall be a Senator who shall not have attained to the Age of thirty Years, and been nine Years a Citizen of the United States, who shall not, when elected, be an Inhabitant of that State for which he shall be chosen.

The Vice-President of the United States shall be President of the Senate, but shall have no Vote unless they be equally divided.

The Senate shall choose their other Officers, and also a President pro tempore, in the Absence of the Vice-President, or when he shall exercise the Office of President of the United States.

The Senate shall have the sole Power to try all Impeachments. When sitting for that Purpose, they shall be on Oath or Affirmation. When the President of the United States is tried, the Chief Justice shall preside: And no Person shall be convicted without the Concurrence of two-thirds of the Members present.

Judgement in Cases of Impeachment shall not extend further than to removal from Office and disqualification to hold and enjoy any Office of honor, Trust or Profit under the United States; but the Party convicted shall nevertheless be liable and subject to Indictment, Trial, Judgment and Punishment, according to Law.

Section 4. The Times, Places and Manner of holding Elections for Senators and Representatives, shall be prescribed in each State by the Legislature thereof: but the Congress may at any time by Law make or alter such Regulations, except as to the Places of choosing Senators.

The Congress shall assemble at least once in every Year, and such Meeting shall be on the first Monday in December, unless they shall by Law appoint a different Day.

Section 5. Each House shall be the Judge of the Elections, Returns and Qualifications of its own Members, and a Majority of each shall constitute a Quorum to do Business; but a smaller Number may adjourn from day to day, and may be authorized to compel the Attendance of absent Members, in such Manner, and under such Penalties as each House may provide.

Each House may determine the Rules of its Proceedings, punish its Members for disorderly Behaviour, and with the Concurrence of two-thirds, expel a Member.

Each House shall keep a Journal of its Proceedings, and from time to time publish the same, excepting such Parts as may in their Judgment require Secrecy; and the Yeas and Nays of the Members either House on any question shall, at the Desire of one fifth of those Present be entered on the Journal.

Neither House, during the Session of Congress shall, without the Consent of the other, adjourn for more than three days, nor to any other Place than that in which the two Houses shall be sitting.

Section 6. The Senators and Representatives shall receive a Compensation for their Services, to be ascertained by Law, and paid out of the Treasury of the United States. They shall in all Cases, except Treason, Felony and Breach of the Peace, be privileged from Arrest during their Attendance at the Session of their respective Houses, and in going to and returning from the same; and for any Speech or Debate in either House, they shall not be questioned in any other Place.

No Senator or Representative shall, during the Time for which he is elected, be appointed to any Civil Office under the Authority of the United States, which shall have been created, or the Emoluments whereof shall have been increased during such time; and no Person holding any Office under the United States, shall be a Member of either House during his Continuance in Office.

Section 7. All Bills for raising Revenue shall originate in the House of Representatives; but the Senate may propose or concur with Amendments as on other Bills.

Every Bill which shall have passed the House of Representatives and the Senate, shall, before it become a Law, be presented to the President of the United States; if he approve he shall sign it, but if not he shall return it, with his Objections to that House in which it shall have originated, who shall enter the Objections at large on their Journal, and proceed to reconsider it. If after such Reconsideration two-thirds of that House shall agree to pass the Bill, it shall be sent, together with the Objections, to the other House, by which it shall likewise be reconsidered, and if approved by two-thirds of that House, it shall become a Law. But in all such Cases the Votes of Both Houses shall be determined by Yeas and Nays, and the Names of the Persons voting for and against the Bill shall be entered on the Journal of each House respectively. If any Bill shall not be returned by the President within ten Days (Sundays excepted) after it shall have been presented to him, the Same shall be a Law, in like Manner as if he had signed it, unless the Congress by their Adjournment prevent its Return, in which Case it shall not be a Law.

Every Order, Resolution, or Vote to which the Concurrence of the Senate and House of Representatives may be necessary (except on a question of Adjournment) shall be presented to the President of the United States; and before the Same shall take Effect, shall be approved by him, or being disapproved by him, shall be repassed by two thirds of the Senate and House of Representatives, according to the Rules and Limitations prescribed in the Case of a Bill.

Section 8. The Congress shall have Power To lay and collect Taxes, Duties, Imposts and Excises, to pay the Debts and provide for the common Defence and general Welfare of the United States; but all Duties, Imposts and Excises shall be uniform throughout the United States.

To borrow Money on the credit of the United States;

To regulate Commerce with foreign Nations, and among the several States, and with the Indian Tribes;

To establish an uniform rule of Naturalization, and uniform Laws on the subject of Bankruptcies throughout the United States;

To coin Money, regulate the Value thereof, and of foreign coin, and fix the Standard of Weights and Measures;

To provide for the Punishment of counterfeiting the Securities and current Coin of the United States;

To establish Post Offices and post Roads;

To promote the Progress of Science and useful Arts, by securing for limited Times to Authors and Inventors the exclusive Right to their respective Writings and Discoveries;

To constitute Tribunals inferior to the supreme Court;

To define and punish Piracies and Felonies committed on the high Seas, and Offenses against the Law of Nations;

To declare War, grant Letters of Marque and Reprisal, and make Rules concerning Captures on Land and Water;

To raise and support Armies, but no Appropriation of Money to that use shall be for a longer Term than two Years;

To provide and maintain a Navy;

To make Rules for the Government and Regulation of the land and naval Forces;

To provide for calling forth the Militia to execute the Laws of the Union, suppress Insurrections and repel Invasions;

To provide for organizing, arming, and disciplining, the Militia, and for governing such Part of them as may be employed in the Service of the United States, reserving to the States respectively, the Appointment of the Officers, and the Authority of training the Militia according to the discipline prescribed by Congress;

To exercise exclusive Legislation in all Cases whatsoever, over such District (not exceeding ten Miles square) as may, by Cession of particular States, and the Acceptance of Congress, become the Seat of the Government of the United States, and to exercise like Authority over all Places purchased by the Consent of the Legislature of the States in which the Same shall be, for the Erection of Forts. Magazines, Arsenals, dock-Yards, and other needful Buildings; And

To make all Laws which shall be necessary and proper for carrying into Execution the foregoing Powers, and all other Powers vested by the Constitution in the Government of the United States, or in any Department or Officer thereof.

Section 9. The Migration or Importation of such Persons as any of the States now existing shall think proper to admit, shall not be prohibited by the Congress prior to the Year one thousand eight hundred and eight, but a Tax or duty may be imposed on such Importation, not exceeding ten dollars for each Person.

Privilege of the Writ of Habeas Corpus shall not be suspended, unless when in Cases of Rebellion or Invasion the public Safety require it.

No Bill of Attainder or ex post facto Law shall be passed.

No Capitation, or other direct, Tax shall be laid, unless in Proportion to the Census or Enumeration herein before directed to be taken.

No Tax or Duty shall be laid on Articles exported from any State.

No Preference shall be given by any Regulation of Commerce or Revenue to the Ports of one State over those of another: nor shall Vessels bound to, or from, one State, be obliged to enter, clear, or pay Duties in another.

No Money shall be drawn from the Treasury, but in Consequence of Appropriations made by Law; and a regular Statement and Account of the Receipts and Expenditures of all public Money shall be published from time to time.

No Title of Nobility shall be granted by the United States: And no Person holding any Office of Profit or Trust under them, shall, without the Consent of the Congress, accept of any present, Emolument, Office, or Title, of any kind whatever, from any King, Prince, or foreign State.

Section 10. No State shall enter into any Treaty, Alliance, or Confederation; grant Letters of Marque and Reprisal; coin Money; emit Bills of Credit; make any Thing but gold and silver Coin a Tender in Payment of Debts; pass any Bill of Attainder, ex post facto Law, or Law impairing the Obligation of Contracts, or grant any Title of Nobility.

No State shall, without the Consent of the Congress, lay any Imposts or Duties on Imports or Exports, except what may be absolutely necessary for executing its inspection Laws; and the net Produce of all Duties and Imports, laid by any State on Imports or Exports, shall be for the Use of the Treasury of the United States; all such Laws shall be subject to the Revision and Control of the Congress.

No State shall, without the Consent of Congress, lay any Duty of Tonnage, keep Troops, or Ships of War in time of Peace, enter into any Agreement or Compact with another State, or with a foreign Power, or engage in War, unless actually invaded, or in such imminent Danger as will not admit of delay.

Article II

Section 1. The executive Power shall be vested in a President of the United States and, together with the Vice President, chosen for the same Term, be elected as follows.

Each State shall appoint, in such Manner as the Legislature thereof may direct, a Number of Electors, equal to the whole Number of Senators and Representatives to which the State may be entitled in the Congress: but no Senator or Representative, or Person holding an Office of Trust or Profit under the United States, shall be appointed an Elector.

The Electors shall meet in their respective States, and vote by Ballot for two Persons, of whom one at least shall not be an Inhabitant of the same State with themselves. And they shall make a List of all the Persons voted for, and of the Number of Votes for each; which List they shall sign and certify, and transmit sealed to the Seat of the Government of the United States, directed to the President of the Senate. The President of the Senate shall, in the Presence of the Senate and House of Representatives, open all the Certificates, and the Votes shall then be counted. The Person having the greatest Number of Votes shall be the President, if such Number be a Majority of the whole Number of Electors appointed; and if there be more than one who have such Majority, and have an equal Number of Electors appointed; and if there be more than one who have such Majority, and have an equal Number of Votes, then the House of Representatives shall immediately choose by Ballot one of them for President; and if no Person have a Majority, then from the five highest on the List the said House shall in like Manner choose the President. But in choosing the President, the Votes shall be taken by States, the Representation from each State having one Vote; a quorum for this Purpose shall consist of a Member or Members from two thirds of the States, and a Majority of all the states shall be necessary to a choice. In every case, after the Choice of the President, the Person having the greatest Number of Votes of the Electors shall be the Vice President. But if there should remain two or more who have equal Votes, the Senate shall choose from them by Ballot the Vice President.

The Congress may determine the Time of the choosing the Electors, and the Day on which they shall give their Votes; which Day shall be the same throughout the United States.

No Person except a natural born Citizen, or a Citizen of the United States, at the time of the Adoption of this Constitution, shall be eligible to the Office of President; neither shall any Person be eligible to that Office who shall not have attained to the Age of thirty five Years, and been fourteen Years a Resident within the United States.

In Case of the Removal of the President from Office, or his Death, Resignation, or Inability to discharge the Powers and Duties of the said Office, the Same shall devolve on the Vice President, and the Congress may by Law provide for the Case of Removal, Death, Resignation or Inability, both of the President and Vice President, declaring what Officer shall then act as President, and such Officer shall act accordingly, until the Disability be removed, or a President be elected.

The President shall, at stated Times, receive for his Services, a Compensation, which shall neither be increased nor diminished during the Period for which he shall have been elected, and he shall not receive within a Period any other Emolument from the United States, or any of them.

Before he enter on the Execution of his Office, he shall take the following Oath or Affirmation: "I do solemnly swear (or affirm) that I will faithfully execute the Office of President of the United States, and will to the best of my Ability, preserve, protect and defend the Constitution of the United States."

Section 2. The President shall be Commander in Chief of the Army and Navy of the United States, and of the Militia of the several States, when called into the actual Service of the United States; he may require the Opinion, in writing of the principal Officer in each of the executive Departments, upon any Subject relating to the Duties of their respective Offices, and he shall have power to grant Reprieves and Pardons for Offenses against the United States, except in Cases of Impeachment.

He shall have Power, by and with the Advice and Consent of the Senate, to make Treaties, provided two thirds of the Senators present concur; and he shall nominate, and by and with the Advice and Consent of the Senate, shall appoint Ambassadors, other public Ministers and Consuls, Judges of the Supreme Court, and all other Officers of the United States, whose Appointments are not herein otherwise provided for, and which shall be established by Law. But the Congress may by law vest the Appointment of such inferior Officers, as they think proper, in the President alone, in the Courts of Law, or in the Heads of Departments.

The President shall have Power to fill up all Vacancies that may happen during the Recess of the Senate, by granting Commissions which shall expire at the End of their Session.

Section 3. He shall from time to time give to the Congress Information of the State of the Union, and recommend to their Consideration such Measures as he shall judge neces-

sary and expedient; he may, on extraordinary Occasions, convene both Houses, or either of them, and in Case of Disagreement between them, with Respect to the Time of Adjournment, he may adjourn them to such Time as he shall think proper; he shall receive Ambassadors and other public Ministers; he shall take Care that the Laws be faithfully executed, and shall Commission all the Officers of the United States.

Section 4. The President, Vice President and all civil Officers of the United States, shall be removed from Office on Impeachment for, and Conviction of, Treason, Bribery, or other high Crimes and Misdemeanors.

Article III

Section 1. The judicial Power of the United States shall be vested in one Supreme Court, and in such inferior courts as the Congress may from time to time ordain and establish. The Judges, both of the Supreme and inferior Courts, shall hold their Offices during good Behavior, and shall, at stated Times, receive for their Services a Compensation which shall not be diminished during their Continuance in Office.

Section 2. The judicial Power shall extend to all Cases, in Law and Equity, arising under this Constitution, the Laws of the United States, and Treaties made, or which shall be made, under their Authority; to all Cases affecting Ambassadors, other public Ministers, and Consuls; to all Cases of admiralty and maritime Jurisdiction; to Controversies to which the United States shall be a Party; to Controversies between two or more States, between a State and Citizens of another State, between Citizens of different States, between Citizens of the same State claiming Lands under Grants of different States, and between a State or the Citizens thereof, and foreign States, Citizens, or Subjects.

In all Cases affecting Ambassadors, other public Ministers and Consuls, and those in which a State shall be a Party, the Supreme Court shall have original Jurisdiction. In all the other Cases before mentioned, the Supreme Court shall have appellate Jurisdiction, both as to Law and Fact, with such Exceptions and under such Regulations as the Congress shall make.

The Trial of all Crimes, except in Cases of Impeachment, shall be by Jury; and such Trial shall be held in the State where the said Crimes shall have been committed; but when not committed within any State the Trial shall be at such Place or Places as the Congress may by Law have directed.

Section 3. Treason against the United States shall consist only in levying War against them, or in adhering to their Enemies, giving them Aid and Comfort. No Person shall be convicted of Treason unless on the Testimony of two Witnesses to the same overt Act, or on Confession in open Court.

The Congress shall have Power to declare the Punishment of Treason, but no Attainder of Treason shall work Corruption of Blood, or Forfeiture except during the Life of the Person attained.

Article IV

Section 1. Full Faith and Credit shall be given in each State to the public Act, Records, and judicial Proceedings of every other State. And the Congress may, by general Laws, prescribe the Manner in which such Acts, Records, and Proceedings shall be proved, and the Effect thereof.

Section 2. The Citizens of each State shall be entitled to all Privileges and Immunities of Citizens in the several States.

A Person charged in any State with Treason, Felony, or other Crime, who shall flee from Justice, and be found in another State, shall, on Demand of the executive Authority of the State from which he fled, be delivered up, to be removed to the State having Jurisdiction of the Crime.

No Person held to Service or Labor in one State, under the Laws thereof, escaping into another, shall, in Consequence of any Law or Regulation therein, be discharged from such Service or Labor, but shall be delivered up on Claim of the Party to whom such Service or Labor may be due.

Section 3. New States may be admitted by the Congress into this Union; but no new State shall be formed or erected within the Jurisdiction of any other State, nor any State be formed by the Junction of two or more States, or Parts of States, without the Consent of the Legislatures of the States concerned as well as of the Congress.

The Congress shall have Power to dispose of and make all needful Rules and Regulations respecting the Territory or other Property belonging to the United States; and nothing in this Constitution shall be so construed as to Prejudice any Claims of the United States, or of any particular State.

Section 4. The United States shall guarantee to every State in this Union a Republican Form of Government, and shall protect each of them against Invasion; and on Application of the Legislature, or of the Executive (when the Legislature cannot be convened), against domestic Violence.

Article V

The Congress, whenever two thirds of both House shall deem it necessary, shall propose Amendments to this Constitution, or, on the Application of the Legislatures of two thirds of the several States, shall call a Convention for proposing Amendments, which, in either Case, shall be valid, to all intents and Purposes, as Part of this Constitution, when ratified by the Legislatures of three fourths of the several States, or by Conventions in three fourths thereof, as the one or the other Mode of Ratification may be proposed by the Congress; Provided that no Amendment which may be made prior to the Year One thousand eight hundred and eight shall in any Manner affect the first and fourth Clauses in the Ninth Section of the first Article; and that no State, without its Consent, shall be deprived of its equal Suffrage in the Senate.

Article VI

All Debts contracted and Engagements entered into, before the Adoption of this Constitution, shall be as valid against the United States under this Constitution, as under the Confederation.

This Constitution, and the Laws of the United States which shall be made in Pursuance thereof, and all Treaties made, or which shall be made, under the Authority of the United States, shall be the supreme Law of the Land; and the Judges in every State shall be bound thereby, Anything in the Constitution or Laws of any State to the Contrary notwithstanding.

The Senators and Representatives before mentioned, and the Members of the several State Legislatures, and all executive and judicial Officers, both of the United States and of the several States, shall be bound, by Oath or Affirmation, to support this Constitution; but no religious Test shall ever be required as a Qualification to any Office or public Trust under the United States.

Article VII

The Ratification of the Conventions of nine States shall be sufficient for the Establishment of this Constitution between the States so ratifying the Same.

Articles in Addition to, and Amendment of, the Constitution of the United States of America, Proposed by Congress, and Ratified by the Legislatures of the Several States Pursuant to the Fifth Article of the Original Constitution

Amendment I

Congress shall make no law respecting an establishment of religion, or prohibiting the free exercise thereof; or abridging the freedom of speech, or of the press; or the right of the people peaceably to assemble, and to petition the Government for a redress of grievances.

Amendment II

A well-regulated Militia being necessary to the security of a free State, the right of the people to keep and bear Arms, shall not be infringed.

Amendment III

No Soldier shall, in time of peace, be quartered in any house, without the consent of the Owner; nor in time of war, but in a manner to be prescribed by law.

Amendment IV

The right of the people to be secure in their persons, houses, papers, and effects, against unreasonable searches and seizures, shall not be violated; and no Warrants shall issue, but upon probable cause, supported by Oath or affirmation, and particularly describing the place to be searched and the persons or things to be seized.

Amendment V

No person shall be held to answer for a capital, or otherwise infamous, crime, unless on a presentment or indictment of a Grand Jury, except in cases arising in the land or naval forces, or in the Militia, when in actual service, in time of War, or public danger; nor shall any person be subject, for the same offence, to be twice put in jeopardy of life or limb; nor shall be compelled in any criminal case to be a witness against himself nor be deprived of life, liberty, or property, without due process of law; nor shall private property be taken for public use, without just compensation.

Amendment VI

In all criminal prosecutions, the accused shall enjoy the right to a speedy and public trial, by an impartial jury of the State and district wherein the crime shall have been committed, which district shall have been previously ascertained by law; and to be informed of the nature and cause of the accusation; to be confronted with the witnesses against him; to have compulsory process for obtaining witnesses in his favor; and to have the Assistance of Counsel for his defence.

Amendment VII

In Suits at common law, where the value in controversy shall exceed twenty dollars, the right of trial by jury shall be preserved; and no fact, tried by a jury, shall be otherwise reexamined in any Court of the United States than according to the rules of the common law.

Amendment VIII

Excessive bail shall not be required, nor excessive fines imposed, nor cruel and unusual punishment inflicted.

Amendment IX

The enumeration in the Constitution of certain rights shall not be construed to deny or disparage others retained by the people.

Amendment X

The powers not delegated to the United States by the Constitution, nor prohibited by it to the States, are reserved to the States respectively or to the people.

Amendment XI

The Judicial power of the United States shall not be construed to extend to any suit in law or equity, commenced or prosecuted against one of the United States by Citizens of another State or by Citizens or Subjects of any Foreign State.

Amendment XII

The Electors shall meet in their respective States, and vote by ballot for President and Vice-President, one of whom, at least, shall not be an inhabitant of the same State with themselves; they shall name in their ballots the person voted for as President, and in distinct ballots the person voted for as Vice-President; and they shall make distinct lists of all persons voted for as President, and of all persons voted for as Vice-President, and of the number of votes for each, which lists they shall sign, and certify, and transmit, sealed, to the seat of the government of the United States, directed to the President of the Senate; the President of the Senate shall, in the presence of the Senate and the House of Representatives, open all the certificates, and the votes shall then be counted; the person having the greatest num-

ber of votes for President shall be the President, if such number be a majority of the whole number of Electors appointed; and if no person have such a majority, then, from the persons having the highest numbers, not exceeding three on the list of those voted for a President, the House of Representatives shall choose immediately, by ballot, the President. But in choosing the President, the votes shall be taken by States, the representation from each State having one vote; a quorum for this purpose shall consist of a member or members from two-thirds of the States, and a majority of all the States shall be necessary to a choice. And if the House of Representatives shall not choose a President, whenever the right of choice shall devolve upon them, before the fourth day of March next following, the Vice-President shall act as President, as in case of death, or other constitutional disability of the President. The person having the greatest number of votes as Vice-President, shall be the Vice-President, if such number be a majority of the whole number of Electors appointed; and if no person have a majority, then, from the two highest numbers on the list, the Senate shall choose the Vice-President; a quorum for the purpose shall consist of two-thirds of the whole number of Senators; a majority of the whole number shall be necessary to a choice. But no person constitutionally ineligible to the office of President shall be eligible to that of Vice-President of the United States.

Amendment XIII

Section 1. Neither slavery nor involuntary servitude, except as a punishment for crime, whereof the party shall have been duly convicted, shall exist within the United States, or any place subject to their jurisdiction.

Section 2. Congress shall have power to enforce this article by appropriate legislation.

Amendment XIV

Section 1. All persons born or naturalized in the United States, and subject to the jurisdiction thereof, are citizens of the United States and of the State wherein they reside. No State shall make or enforce any law which shall abridge the privileges or immunities of citizens of the United States; nor shall any State deprive any person of life, liberty, or property, without due process of law, nor deny any person within its jurisdiction the equal protection of the laws.

Section 2. Representatives shall be apportioned among the several States according to their respective numbers, counting the whole number of persons in each State, excluding Indians not taxed. But when the right to vote at any election for the choice of electors for President and Vice-President of the United States, Representatives in Congress, the Executive and Judicial officers of a State, or the members of the Legislature thereof, is denied to any of the male inhabitants of such State, being twenty one years of age, and citizens of the United States, or in any way abridged, except for participation in rebellion or other crime, the basis of representation therein shall be reduced in the proportion which the number of such male citizens shall bear to the whole number of male citizens twenty one years of age in such State.

Section 3. No person shall be a Senator or Representative in Congress, or elector of President and Vice President, or hold any office, civil or military, under the United States, or under any State, who, having previously taken an oath, as a Member of Congress, or as an officer of the United States, or as a member of any State legislature, or as an executive or judicial officer of any State, to support the Constitution of the United States, shall have engaged in insurrection or rebellion against the same, or given aid or comfort to the enemies thereof. But Congress may, by a vote of two thirds of each House, remove such disability.

Section 4. The validity of the public debt of the United States, authorized by law, including debts incurred for payment of pensions and bounties for services in suppressing insurrection or rebellion, shall not be questioned. But neither the United States nor any State shall assume or pay any debt or obligation incurred in aid of insurrection or rebellion against the United States, or any claim for the loss or emancipation of any slave; but all such debts, obligations, and claims shall be held illegal and void.

Section 5. The Congress shall have power to enforce, by appropriate legislation, the provisions of this article.

Amendment XV

Section 1. The right of citizens of the United States to vote shall not be denied or abridged by the United States or by any State on account of race, color, or previous condition of servitude.

Section 2. The Congress shall have power to enforce this article by appropriate legislation.

Amendment XVI

The Congress shall have power to lay and collect taxes on incomes, from whatever source derived, without apportionment among the several States and without regard to any census or enumeration.

Amendment XVII

The Senate of the United States shall be composed of two Senators from each State, elected by the people thereof, for six years; and each Senator shall have one vote. The electors in each State shall have the qualifications requisite for electors of the most numerous branch of the State legislatures.

When vacancies happen in the representation of any State in the Senate, the executive authority of such State shall issue writs of election to fill such vacancies: Provided, That the legislature of any State may empower the executive thereof to make temporary appointment until the people fill the vacancies by election as the legislature may direct.

This amendment shall not be so construed as to affect the election or term of any Senator chosen before it becomes valid as part of the Constitution.

Amendment XVIII

Section 1. After one year from the ratification of this article the manufacture, sale or transportation of intoxicating liquors within, the importation thereof into, or the exportation thereof from the United States and all territory subject to the jurisdiction thereof for beverage purposes is hereby prohibited.

Section 2. The Congress and the several States shall have concurrent power to enforce this article by appropriate legislation.

Section 3. This article shall be inoperative unless it shall have been ratified as an amendment to the Constitution by the legislatures of the several States, as provided in the Constitution, within seven years of the date of the submission hereof to the States by Congress.

[Repealed by Amendment XXI.]

Amendment XIX

The right of citizens of the United States to vote shall not be denied or abridged by the United States or by State on account of sex.

Congress shall have power to enforce this article by appropriate legislation.

Amendment XX

Section 1. The terms of the President and Vice President shall end at noon on the 20th day of January, and the terms of Senators and Representatives at noon on the 3d day of January, of the years in which such terms would have ended if this article had not ratified; and the terms of their successors shall then begin.

Section 2. The Congress shall assemble at least once in every year, and such meeting shall begin at noon on the 3d day of January, unless they shall by law appoint a different day.

Section 3. If, at the time fixed for the beginning of the term of the President, the President-elect shall have died, the Vice President-elect shall become President. If a President shall not have been chosen before the time fixed for the beginning of his term, or if the President-elect shall have failed to qualify, then the Vice President-elect shall act as President until a President shall have qualified; and the Congress may by law provide for the case wherein neither a President-elect nor a Vice President-elect shall have qualified, declaring who shall then act as President, or the

manner in which one who is to act shall be selected, and such person shall act accordingly until a President or Vice President shall have qualified.

Section 4. The Congress may by law provide for the case of the death of any of the persons from whom the House of Representatives may choose a President whenever the right of choice shall have devolved upon them, and for the case of the death of any of the persons from whom the Senate may choose a Vice President whenever the right of choice shall have devolved upon them.

Section 5. Sections 1 and 2 shall take effect on the 15th day of October following the ratification of this article.

Section 6. This article shall be inoperative unless it shall have been ratified as an amendment to the Constitution by three fourths of the several States within seven years from the date of its submission.

Amendment XXI

Section 1. The eighteenth article of amendment to the Constitution of the United States is hereby repealed.

Section 2. The transportation or importation into any State, Territory, or possession of the United States for delivery or use therein of intoxicating liquors, in violation of the laws thereof, is hereby prohibited.

Section 3. This article shall be inoperative unless it shall have been ratified as an amendment to the Constitution by conventions in the several States, as provided in the Constitution, within seven years from the date of the submission hereof to the States by the Congress.

Amendment XXII

Section 1. No person shall be elected to the office of the President more than twice, and no person who has held the office of President, or acted as President, for more than two years of a term to which some other person was elected President shall be elected to the office of the President more than once. But this Article shall not apply to any person holding the office of President when this Article was proposed by the Congress, and shall not prevent any person who may be holding the office of President, or acting as President, during the term within which this Article becomes operative from holding the office of President or acting as President during the remainder of such term.

Section 2. This article shall be inoperative unless it shall have been ratified as an amendment to the Constitution by the legislatures of three-fourths of the several States within seven years from the date of its submission to the States by the Congress.

Amendment XXIII

Section 1. The District constituting the seat of Government of the United States shall appoint in such manner as the Congress may direct:

A number of electors of President and Vice President equal to the whole number of Senators and Representatives in Congress to which the District would be entitled if it were a State, but in no event more than the least populous State; they shall be considered, for the purposes of the election of President and Vice President, to be electors appointed by a State; and they shall meet in the District and perform such duties as provided by the twelfth article of amendment.

Section 2. The Congress shall have power to enforce this article by appropriate legislation.

Amendment XXIV

Section 1. The right of citizens of the United States to vote in any primary or other election for President or Vice President, for electors for President or Vice President, or for Senator or Representative in Congress, shall not be denied or abridged by the United States or any State by reason of failure to pay any poll tax or other tax.

Section 2. The Congress shall have power to enforce this article by appropriate legislation.

Amendment XXV

Section 1. In case of the removal of the President from office or of his death or resignation, the Vice President shall become President.

Section 2. Whenever there is a vacancy in the office of the Vice President, the President shall nominate a Vice President who shall take office upon confirmation by a majority vote of both Houses of Congress.

Section 3. Whenever the President transmits to the President pro tempore of the Senate and the Speakers of the House of Representatives his written declaration that he is unable to discharge the powers and duties of his office, and until he transmits to them a written declaration to the contrary, such powers and duties shall be discharged by the Vice President as Acting President.

Section 4. Whenever the Vice President and a majority of either the principal officers of the executive departments or of such other body as Congress may by law provide, transmit to the President pro tempore of the Senate and the Speaker of the House of Representatives their written declaration that the President is unable to discharge the powers and duties of his office, the Vice President shall immediately assume the powers and duties of the office as Acting President.

Thereafter, when the President transmits to the President pro tempore of the Senate and the Speaker of the House of Representatives his written declaration that no inability exists, he shall resume the powers and duties of his office unless the Vice President and a majority of either principal officers of the executive department or of such other body as Congress may by law provide, transmit within four days to the President pro tempore of the Senate and the Speaker of the House of Representatives their written declaration that the President is unable to discharge the powers and duties of his office. Thereupon Congress shall decide the issue, assembling within forty eight hours for that purpose if not in session. If the Congress, within twenty one days after Congress is required to assemble, determines by two thirds vote of both Houses that the President is unable to discharge the powers and duties of his office, the Vice President shall continue to discharge the same as Acting President; otherwise, the President shall resume the powers and duties of his office.

Amendment XXVI

Section 1. The right of citizens of the United States, who are eighteen years of age or older, to vote shall not be denied or abridged by the United States or by any State on account of age.

Section 2. The Congress shall have the power to enforce this article by appropriate legislation.

Amendment XXVII

No law, varying the compensation for the services of the Senators and Representatives, shall take effect until an election of the Representatives shall have intervened.

APPENDIX TWO

UNIFORM CODE OF MILITARY JUSTICE

Subchapter I. General Provisions

Art. 1. Definitions

In this chapter.

(1) The term "Judge Advocate General" means, severally, the Judge Advocates General of the Army, Navy, and Air Force and, except when the Coast Guard is operating as a service in the Navy, the General Counsel of the Department of Transportation.

(2) The Navy, the Marine Corps, and the Coast Guard when it is operating as a service in the Navy, shall be considered as one armed force.

(3) The term "commanding officer" includes only commissioned officers.

(4) The term "officer in charge" means a member of the Navy, the Marine Corps, or the Coast Guard designated as such by appropriate authority.

(5) The term "superior commissioned officer" means a commissioned officer superior in rank or command.

(6) The term "cadet" means a cadet of the United States Military Academy, the United States Air Force Academy, or the United States Coast Guard Academy.

(7) The term "midshipman" means a midshipman of the United States Naval Academy and any other midshipman on active duty in the naval service.

(8) The term "military" refers to any or all of the armed forces.

(9) The term "accuser" means a person who signs and swears to charges, any person who directs that charges nominally be signed and sworn to by another, and any other person who has an interest other than an official interest in the prosecution of the accused.

(10) The term "military judge" means an official of a general or special court-martial detailed in accordance with article 26.

(11) The term "law specialist" means a commissioned officer of the Coast Guard designated for special duty (law).

(12) The term "legal officer" means any commissioned officer of the Navy, Marine Corps, or Coast Guard designated to perform legal duties for a command.

(13) The term "judge advocate" means—

(A) an officer of the Judge Advocate General's Corps of the Army or the Navy;

(B) an officer of the Air Force or the Marine Corps who is designated as a judge advocate; or

(C) an officer of the Coast Guard who is designated as a law specialist.

(14) The term "record," when used in connection with the proceedings of a court-martial, means—

(A) an official written transcript, written summary, or other writing relating to the proceedings; or

(B) an official audiotape, videotape, or similar material from which sound, or sound and visual images, depicting the proceedings may be reproduced.

Art. 2. Persons subject to this chapter

(a) The following persons are subject to this chapter:

(1) Members of a regular component of the armed forces, including those awaiting discharge after expiration of their terms of enlistment; volunteers from the time of their muster or acceptance into the armed forces; inductees from the time of their actual induction into the armed forces; and other persons lawfully called or ordered into, or to duty in or for training in, the armed forces, from the dates when they are required by the terms of the call or order to obey it.

(2) Cadets, aviation cadets, and midshipmen.

(3) Members of a reserve component while on inactive-duty training, but in the case of members of the Army National Guard of the United States or the Air National Guard of the United States only when in Federal service.

(4) Retired members of a regular component of the armed forces who are entitled to pay.

(5) Retired members of a reserve component who are receiving hospitalization from an armed force.

(6) Members of the Fleet Reserve and Fleet Marine Corps Reserve.

(7) Persons in custody of the armed forces serving a sentence imposed by a court-martial.

(8) Members of the National Oceanic and Atmospheric Administration, Public Health Service, and other organizations, when assigned to and serving with the armed forces.

(9) Prisoners of war in custody of the armed forces.

(10) In time of war, persons serving with or accompanying an armed force in the field.

(11) Subject to any treaty or agreement to which the United States is or may be a party or to any accepted rule of international law, persons serving with, employed by, or accompanying the armed forces outside the United States and outside the Commonwealth of Puerto Rico, Guam, and the Virgin Islands.

(12) Subject to any treaty or agreement to which the United States is or may be a party or to any accepted rule of international law, persons within an area leased by or otherwise reserved or acquired for the use of the United States which is under the control of the Secretary concerned and which is outside the United States and outside the Canal Zone, the Commonwealth of Puerto Rico, Guam, and the Virgin Islands.

(b) The voluntary enlistment of any person who has the capacity to understand the significance of enlisting in the armed forces shall be valid for purposes of jurisdiction under subsection (a) and a change of status from civilian to member of the armed forces shall be effective upon the taking of the oath of enlistment.

(c) Notwithstanding any other provision of law, a person serving with an armed force who—

(1) submitted voluntarily to military authority;

(2) met the mental competence and minimum age qualifications of sections 504 and 505 of this title at the time of voluntary submission to military authority;

(3) received military pay or allowances; and

(4) performed military duties;

is subject to this chapter until such person's active service has been terminated in accordance with law or regulations promulgated by the secretary concerned.

(d)(1) A member of a reserve component who is not on active duty and who is made the subject of proceedings under article 15 or article 30 with respect to an offense against this chapter may be ordered to active duty involuntarily for the purpose of

(A) investigation under section 832 of this title (article 32);

(B) trial by court-martial; or

(C) nonjudicial punishment under section 815 of this title (article 15).

(2) A member of a reserve component may not be ordered to active duty under paragraph (1) except with respect to an offense committed while the member was—

(A) on active duty; or

(B) on inactive-duty training, but in the case of members of the Army National Guard of the United States or the Air National Guard of the United States only when in Federal service.

(3) Authority to order a member to active duty under paragraph (1) shall be exercised under regulations prescribed by the President.

(4) A member may be ordered to active duty under

paragraph (1) only by a person empowered to convene general courts-martial in a regular component of the armed forces.

(5) A member ordered to active duty under paragraph (1), unless the order to active duty was approved by the secretary concerned, may not

(A) be sentenced to confinement; or

(B) be required to serve a punishment consisting of any restriction on liberty during a period other than a period of inactive duty training or active duty (other than active duty ordered under paragraph (1)).

Art. 3. Jurisdiction to try certain personnel

(a) Subject to article 43, a person who is in a status in which the person is subject to this chapter and who committed an offense against this chapter while formerly in a status in which the person was subject to this chapter is not relieved from amenability to the jurisdiction of this chapter for that offense by reason of a termination of that person's former status.

(b) Each person discharged from the armed forces who is later charged with having fraudulently obtained his discharge is, subject to article 43, subject to trial by court-martial on that charge and is after apprehension subject to this chapter while in the custody of the armed forces for that trial. Upon conviction of that charge he is subject to trial by court-martial for all offenses under this chapter committed before the fraudulent discharge.

(c) No person who has deserted from the armed forces may be relieved from amenability to the jurisdiction of this chapter by virtue of a separation from any later period of service.

(d) A member of a reserve component who is subject to this chapter is not, by virtue of the termination of a period of active duty or inactive-duty training, relieved from amenability to the jurisdiction of this chapter for an offense against this chapter committed during such period of active duty or inactive-duty training.

Art. 4. Dismissed officer's right to trial by court-martial

(a) If any commissioned officer, dismissed by order of the President, makes a written application for trial by court-martial setting forth, under oath, that he has been wrongfully dismissed, the President, as soon as practicable, shall convene a general court-martial to try that officer on the charges on which he was dismissed. A court-martial so convened has jurisdiction to try the dismissed officer on those charges, and he shall be considered to have waived the right to plead any statute of limitations applicable to any offense with which he is charged. The court-martial may, as part of its sentence, adjudge the affirmance of the dismissal, but if the court-martial acquits the accused or if the sentence adjudged, as finally approved or affirmed, does not include dismissal or death, the Secretary concerned shall substitute for the dismissal ordered by the President a form of discharge authorized for administrative issue.

(b) If the President fails to convene a general court-martial within six months from the preparation of an application for trial under this article, the Secretary concerned shall substitute for the dismissal order by the President a form of discharge authorized for administrative issue.

(c) If a discharge is substituted for a dismissal under this article, the President alone may reappoint the officer to such commissioned grade and with such rank as, in the opinion of the President, that former officer would have attained had he not been dismissed. The reappointment of such a former officer shall be without regard to the existence of a vacancy and shall affect the promotion status of other officers only insofar as the President may direct. All time between the dismissal and the reappointment shall be considered as actual service for all purposes, including the right to pay and allowances.

(d) If an officer is discharged from any armed force by administrative action or is dropped from the rolls by order of the President, he has no right to trial under this article.

Art. 5. Territorial applicability of this chapter

This chapter applies in all places.

Art. 6. *Judge Advocates and legal officers*

(a) The assignment for duty of judge advocates of the Army, Navy, Air Force, and Coast Guard shall be made upon the recommendation of the Judge Advocate General of the armed force of which they are members. The assignment for duty of judge advocates of the Marine Corps shall be made by direction of the Commandant of the Marine Corps. The Judge Advocate General or senior members of his staff shall make frequent inspection in the field in supervision of the administration of military justice.

(b) Convening authorities shall at all times communicate directly with their staff judge advocates or legal officers in matters relating to the administration of military justice; and the staff judge advocate or legal officer of any command is entitled to communicate directly with the staff judge advocate or legal officer of a superior or subordinate command, or with the Judge Advocate General.

(c) No person who has acted as member, military judge, trial counsel, assistant trial counsel, defense counsel, assistant defense counsel, or investigating officer in any case may later act as a staff judge advocate or legal officer to any reviewing authority upon the same case.

(d)(1) A judge advocate who is assigned or detailed to perform the functions of a civil office in the Government of the United States of this title may perform such duties as may be requested by the agency concerned, including representation of the United States in civil and criminal cases.

(2) The Secretary of Defense, and the Secretary of Transportation with respect to the Coast Guard when it is not operating as a service in the Navy, shall prescribe regulations providing that reimbursement may be a condition of assistance by judge advocates assigned or detailed under article 973(b)(2)(B) of this title.

Art. 6a. *Investigation and disposition of matters pertaining to the fitness of military judges*

(a) The President shall prescribe procedures for the investigation and disposition of charges, allegations, or information pertaining to the fitness of a military judge or military appellate judge to perform the duties of the judge's position. To the extent practicable, the procedures shall be uniform for all armed forces.

(b) The President shall transmit a copy of the procedures prescribed pursuant to this section to the Committees on Armed Services of the Senate and the House of Representatives.

Subchapter II. Apprehension and Restraint

Art. 7. *Apprehension*

(a) Apprehension is the taking of a person into custody.

(b) Any person authorized under regulations governing the armed forces to apprehend persons subject to this chapter or to trial thereunder may do so upon reasonable belief that an offense has been committed and that the person apprehended committed it.

(c) Commissioned officers, warrant officers, petty officers, and noncommissioned officers have authority to quell quarrels, frays and disorders among persons subject to this chapter and to apprehend persons subject to this chapter who take part therein.

Art. 8. *Apprehension of deserters*

Any civil officer having authority to apprehend offenders under the laws of the United States or of a State, Territory, Commonwealth, or possession, or the District of Columbia may summarily apprehend a deserter from the armed forces and deliver him into the custody of those forces.

Art. 9. *Imposition of restraint*

(a) Arrest is the restraint of a person by an order, not imposed as a punishment for an offense, directing him to remain within certain specified limits. Confinement is the physical restraint of a person.

(b) An enlisted member may be ordered into arrest or confinement by any commissioned officer by an order, oral or written, delivered in person or through other persons subject to this chapter. A commanding officer may authorize warrant officers, petty officers, or noncommissioned officers to order enlisted members of his command or subject to his authority into arrest or confinement.

(c) A commissioned officer, a warrant officer, or a civilian subject to this chapter or to trial thereunder may be ordered into arrest or confinement only by a commanding officer to whose authority he is subject, by an order, oral or written, delivered in person or by another commissioned officer. The authority to order such persons into arrest or confinement may not be delegated.

(d) No person may be ordered into arrest or confinement except for probable cause.

(e) Nothing in this article limits the authority of persons authorized to apprehend offenders to secure the custody of an alleged offender until proper authority may be notified.

Art. 10. Restraint of persons charged with offenses

Any person subject to this chapter charged with an offense under this chapter shall be ordered into arrest or confinement, as circumstances may require; but when charged only with an offense normally tried by a summary court-martial, he shall not ordinarily be placed in confinement. When any person subject to this chapter is placed in arrest or confinement prior to trial, immediate steps shall be taken to inform him of the specific wrong of which he is accused and to try him or to dismiss the charges and release him.

Art. 11. Reports and receiving of prisoners

(a) No provost marshal, commander or a guard, or master at arms may refuse to receive or keep any prisoner committed to his charge by a commissioned officer of the armed forces, when the committing officer furnishes a statement, signed by him, of the offense charged against the prisoner.

(b) Every commander of a guard or master at arms to whose charge a prisoner is committed shall, within twenty-four hours after that commitment or as soon as he is relieved from guard, report to the commanding officer the name of the prisoner, the offense charged against him, and the name of the person who ordered or authorized the commitment.

Art. 12. Confinement with enemy prisoners prohibited

No member of the armed forces may be placed in confinement in immediate association with enemy prisoners or other foreign nationals not members of the armed forces.

Art. 13. Punishment prohibited before trial

No person, while being held for trial, may be subjected to punishment or penalty other than arrest or confinement upon the charges pending against him, nor shall the arrest or confinement imposed upon him be any more rigorous than the circumstances required to insure his presence, but he may be subjected to minor punishment during that period for infractions of discipline.

Art. 14. Delivery of offenders to civil authorities

(a) Under such regulations as the Secretary concerned may prescribe, a member of the armed forces accused of an offense against civil authority may be delivered, upon request, to the civil authority for trial.

(b) When delivery under this article is made to any civil authority of a person undergoing sentence of a court-martial, the delivery, if followed by conviction in a civil tribunal, interrupts the execution of the sentence of the court-martial, and the offender after having answered to the civil authorities for his offense shall, upon the request of competent military authority, be returned to military custody for the completion of his sentence.

Subchapter III. Non-Judicial Punishment

Art. 15. Commanding Officer's non-judicial punishment

(a) Under such regulations as the President may prescribe, and under such additional regulations as may be prescribed by the Secretary concerned, limitations may be placed on the powers granted by this article with respect to the kind and amount of punishment authorized, the categories of commanding officers and warrant officers exercising command authorized to exercise those powers, the applicability of this article to an accused who demands trial by court-martial, and the kinds of courts-martial to which the case may be referred upon such a demand. However, except in the case of a member attached to or embarked in a vessel, punishment may not be imposed upon any member of the armed forces under this article if the member has, before the imposition of such punishment, demanded trial by court-martial in lieu of such punishment. Under similar regulations, rules may be prescribed with respect to the suspension of punishments authorized hereunder. If authorized by regulations of the Secretary concerned, a commanding officer exercising general court-martial jurisdiction or an officer of general or flag rank in command may delegate his powers under this article to a principal assistant.

(b) Subject to subsection (a) any commanding officer may, in addition to or in lieu of admonition or reprimand, impose one or more of the following disciplinary punishments for minor offenses without the intervention of a court-martial—

(1) upon officers of his command—

(A) restriction to certain specified limits, with or without suspension from duty, for not more than 30 consecutive days;

(B) if imposed by an officer exercising general court-martial jurisdiction or an officer of general or flag rank in command

(i) arrest in quarters for not more than 30 consecutive days;

(ii) forfeiture of not more than one-half of one month's pay per month for two months;

(iii) restriction to certain specified limits, with or without suspension from duty, for not more than 60 consecutive days;

(iv) detention of not more than one-half of one month's pay per month for three months;

(2) upon other personnel of his command—

(A) if imposed upon a person attached to or embarked in a vessel, confinement on bread and water or diminished rations for not more than three consecutive days;

(B) correctional custody for not more than seven consecutive days;

(C) forfeiture of not more than seven days' pay;

(D) reduction to the next inferior pay grade, if the grade from which demoted is within the promotion authority of the officer imposing the reduction or any officer subordinate to the one who imposes the reduction;

(E) extra duties, including fatigue or other duties, for not more than 14 consecutive days;

(F) restriction to certain specified limits, with or without suspension from duty, for not more than 14 consecutive days;

(G) detention of not more than 14 days' pay;

(H) if imposed by an officer of the grade of major or lieutenant commander, or above

(i) the punishment authorized under clause (A);

(ii) correctional custody for not more than 30 consecutive days;

(iii) forfeiture of not more than one-half of one month's pay per month for two months;

(iv) reduction to the lowest or any intermediate pay grade, if the grade from which demoted is within the promotion authority of the officer imposing the reduction or any officer subordinate to the one who imposes the reduction, but an enlisted member in a pay grade above E4 may not be reduced more than two pay grades;

(v) extra duties, including fatigue or other duties, for not more than 45 consecutive days;

(vi) restriction to certain specified limits, with or without suspension from duty, for not more than 60 consecutive days;

(vii) detention of not more than one-half of one month's pay per month for three months.

Detention of pay shall be for a stated period of not more than one year but if the offender's term of service expires earlier, the detention shall terminate upon that expiration. No two or more of the punishments of arrest in quarters, confinement on bread and water or diminished rations, correctional custody, extra duties, and restriction may be combined to run consecutively in the maximum amount imposable for each. Whenever any of those punishments are combined to run consecutively, there must be an apportionment. In addition, forfeiture of pay may not be combined with detention of pay without an apportionment. For the purpose of this subsection, "correctional custody" is the physical restraint of a person during duty or nonduty hours and may include extra duties, fatigue duties, or hard labor. If practicable, correctional custody will not be served in immediate association with persons awaiting trial or held in confinement pursuant to trial by court-martial.

(c) An officer in charge may impose upon enlisted members assigned to the unit of which he is in charge such of the punishments authorized under subsection (b)(2)(A)–(G) as the Secretary concerned may specifically prescribe by regulation.

(d) The officer who imposes the punishment authorized in subsection (b), or his successor in command, may, at any time, suspend probationally any part or amount of the unexecuted punishment imposed and may suspend probationally a reduction in grade or a forfeiture imposed under subsection (b), whether or not executed.

In addition, he may, at any time, remit or mitigate any part or amount of the unexecuted punishment imposed and may set aside in whole or in part the punishment, whether executed or unexecuted, and restore all rights, privileges and property affected. He may also mitigate reduction in grade to forfeiture or detention of pay. When mitigating—

(1) arrest in quarters to restriction;

(2) confinement on bread and water or diminished rations to correctional custody;

(3) correctional custody or confinement on bread and water or diminished rations to extra duties or restriction, or both; or

(4) extra duties to restriction;

the mitigated punishment shall not be for a greater period than the punishment mitigated. When mitigating forfeiture of pay to detention of pay, the amount of the detention shall not be greater than the amount of the forfeiture. When mitigating reduction in grade to forfeiture or detention of pay, the amount of the forfeiture or detention shall not be greater than the amount that could have been imposed initially under this article by the officer who imposed the punishment mitigated.

(e) A person punished under this article who considers his punishment unjust or disproportionate to the offense may, through the proper channel, appeal to the next superior authority. The appeal shall be promptly forwarded and decided, but the person punished may in the meantime be required to undergo the punish-

ment adjudged. The superior authority may exercise the same powers with respect to the punishment imposed as may be exercised under subsection (d) by the officer who imposed the punishment. Before acting on an appeal from a punishment of—

(1) arrest in quarters for more than seven days;

(2) correctional custody for more than seven days;

(3) forfeiture of more than seven days' pay;

(4) reduction of one or more pay grades from the fourth or a higher pay grade;

(5) extra duties for more than 14 days;

(6) restriction for more than 14 days; or

(7) detention of more than 14 days' pay;

the authority who is to act on the appeal shall refer the case to a judge advocate or a lawyer of the Department of Transportation for consideration and advice, and may so refer the case upon appeal from any punishment imposed under subsection (b).

(f) The imposition and enforcement of disciplinary punishment under this article for any act or omission is not a bar to trial by court-martial for a serious crime or offense growing out of the same act or omission, and not properly punishable under this article; but the fact that a disciplinary punishment has been enforced may be shown by the accused upon trial, and when so shown shall be considered in determining the measure of punishment to be adjudged in the event of a finding of guilty.

(g) The Secretary concerned may, by regulation, prescribe the form of records to be kept of proceedings under this article and may also prescribe that certain categories of those proceedings shall be in writing.

Subchapter IV. Court-Martial Jurisdiction

Art. 16. Courts-martial classified

The three kinds of courts-martial in each of the armed forces are—

(1) general courts-martial, consisting of—

(A) a military judge and not less than five members; or

(B) only a military judge, if before the court is assembled the accused, knowing the identity of the military judge and after codefense counsel, requests orally on the record or in writing a court composed only of a military judge and the military judge approves;

(2) special courts-martial, consisting of—

(A) not less than three members; or

(B) a military judge and not less than three members; or

(C) only a military judge, if one has been detailed to the court, and the accused under the same conditions as those prescribed in clause (1)(B) so requests; and

(3) summary courts-martial, consisting of one commissioned officer.

Art. 17. Jurisdiction of courts-martial in general

(a) Each armed force has court-martial jurisdiction over all persons subject to this chapter. The exercise of jurisdiction by one armed force over personnel of another armed force shall be in accordance with regulations prescribed by the President.

(b) In all cases, departmental review after that by the officer with authority to convene a general court-marital for the command which held the trial, where that review is required under this chapter, shall be carried out by the department that includes the armed force of which the accused is a member.

Art. 18. Jurisdiction of general courts-martial

Subject to article 17, general courts-martial have jurisdiction to try persons subject to this chapter for any offense made punishable by this chapter and may, under such limitations as the President may prescribe, adjudge any punishment not forbidden by this chapter, including the penalty of death when specifically authorized by this chapter. General courts-martial also have jurisdiction to try any person who by the law of war is subject to trial by a military tribunal and may adjudge any punishment permitted by the law of war. However, a general court-marital of the kind specified in article 16(1)(B) shall not have jurisdiction to try any person for any offense for which the death penalty may be adjudged unless the case has been previously referred to trial as a noncapital case.

Art. 19. Jurisdiction of special courts-martial

Subject to article 17, special courts-martial have jurisdiction to try persons subject to this chapter for any noncapital offense made punishable by this chapter and, under such regulations as the President may prescribe, for capital offenses. Special courts-martial may, under such limitations as the President may prescribe, adjudge any punishment not forbidden by this chapter except death, dishonorable discharge, dismissal, confinement for more than six months, hard labor without confinement for more than three months, forfeiture of pay exceeding two-thirds pay per month, or forfeiture of pay for more than six months. A bad-conduct discharge may not be adjudged unless a complete record of the proceedings and testimony has been made, counsel having the qualifications prescribed under article 27(b) was detailed to represent the accused, and a military judge was detailed to the trial, except in any case in which a military judge could not be detailed to the trial because of physical conditions or military exigencies. In any such case in which a military judge was not detailed to the trial, the convening authority shall make a detailed written statement, to be appended to the record, stating the reason or reasons a military judge could not be detailed.

Art. 20. Jurisdiction of summary courts-martial

Subject to article 17, summary courts-martial have jurisdiction to try persons subject to this chapter, except officers, cadets, aviation cadets, and midshipmen, for any noncapital offense made punishable by this chapter. No person with respect to whom summary courts-martial have jurisdiction may be brought to trial before a summary court-martial if he objects thereto. If objection to trial by summary court-martial is made by an accused, trial may be ordered by special or general court-martial as may be appropriate. Summary courts-martial may, under such limitations as the President may prescribe, adjudge any punishment not forbidden by this chapter except death, dismissal, dishonorable or bad-conduct discharge, confinement for more than one month, hard labor without confinement for more than 45 days, restriction to specified limits for more than two months, or forfeiture of more than two-thirds of one month's pay.

Art. 21. *Jurisdiction of courts-martial not exclusive*

The provisions of this chapter conferring jurisdiction upon courts-martial do not deprive military commissions, provost courts, or other military tribunals of concurrent jurisdiction with respect to offenders or offenses that by statute or by the law of war may be tried by military commissions, provost courts, or other military tribunals.

Subchapter V. Composition of Courts-Martial

Art. 22. *Who may convene general courts-martial*

(a) General courts-martial may be convened by—
  (1) the President of the United States;
  (2) the Secretary of Defense;
  (3) the commanding officer of a unified or specified combatant command;
  (4) the Secretary concerned;
  (5) the commanding officer of a Territorial Department, an Army Group, an Army, an Army Corps, a division, a separate brigade, or a corresponding unit of the Army or Marine Corps;
  (6) the commander in chief of a fleet; the commanding officer of a naval station or larger shore activity of the Navy beyond the United States;
  (7) the commanding officer of an air command, an air force, an air division, or a separate wing of the Air Force or Marine Corps;
  (8) any other commanding officer designated by the Secretary concerned; or
  (9) any other commanding officer in any of the armed forces when empowered by the President.
(b) If any such commanding officer is an accuser, the court shall be convened by superior competent authority, and may in any case be convened by such authority if considered desirable by him.

Art. 23. *Who may convene special courts-martial*

(a) Special courts-martial may be convened by—
  (1) any person who may convene a general court-martial;

  (2) the commanding officer of a district, garrison, fort, camp, station, Air Force base, auxiliary air field, or other place where members of the Army or the Air Force are on duty;
  (3) the commanding officer of a brigade, regiment, detached battalion, or corresponding unit of the Army;
  (4) the commanding officer of a wing, group, or separate squadron of the Air Force;
  (5) the commanding officer of any naval or Coast Guard vessel, shipyard, base, or station; the commanding officer of any Marine brigade, regiment, detached battalion, or corresponding unit; the commanding officer of any Marine barracks, wing, group, separate squadron, station, base, auxiliary air field, or other place where members of the Marine Corps are on duty;
  (6) the commanding officer of any separate or detached command or group of detached units of any of the armed forces placed under a single commander for this purpose; or
  (7) the commanding officer or officer in charge of any other command when empowered by the Secretary concerned.
(b) If any such officer is an accuser, the court shall be convened by superior competent authority, and may in any case be convened by such authority if considered advisable by him.

Art. 24. *Who may convene summary courts-martial*

(a) Summary courts-martial may be convened by—
  (1) any person who may convene a general or special court-martial;
  (2) the commanding officer of a detached company or other detachment of the Army;
  (3) the commanding officer of a detached squadron or other detachment of the Air Force; or
  (4) the commanding officer or officer in charge of any other command when empowered by the Secretary concerned.
(b) When only one commissioned officer is present with a command or detachment he shall be the summary court-martial of that command or detachment and shall hear and determine all summary court-martial

cases brought before him. Summary courts-martial may, however, be convened in any case by superior competent authority when considered desirable by him.

Art. 25. Who may serve on courts-martial

(a) Any commissioned officer on active duty is eligible to serve on all courts-martial for the trial of any person who may lawfully be brought before such courts for trial.

(b) Any warrant officer on active duty is eligible to serve on general and special courts-martial for the trial of any person, other than a commissioned officer, who may lawfully be brought before such courts for trial.

(c)(1) Any enlisted member of an armed force on active duty who is not a member of the same unit as the accused is eligible to serve on general and special courts-martial for the trial of any enlisted member of an armed force who may lawfully be brought before such courts for trial, but he shall serve as a member of a court only if, before the conclusion of a session called by the military judge under article 39(a) prior to trial or, in the absence of such a session, before the court is assembled for the trial of the accused, the accused personally has requested orally on the record or in writing that enlisted members serve on it. After such a request, the accused may not be tried by a general or special court-marital the membership of which does not include enlisted members in a number comprising at least one-third of the total membership of the court, unless eligible enlisted members cannot be obtained on account of physical conditions or military exigencies. If such members cannot be obtained, the court may be assembled and the trial held without them, but the convening authority shall make a detailed written statement, to be appended to the record, stating why they could not be obtained.

(2) In this article, "unit" means any regularly organized body as defined by the Secretary concerned, but in no case may it be a body larger than a company, squadron, ship's crew, or body corresponding to one of them.

(d)(1) When it can be avoided, no member of an armed force may be tried by a court-martial any member of which is junior to him in rank or grade.

(2) When convening a court-martial, the convening authority shall detail as members thereof such members of the armed forces as, in his opinion, are best qualified for the duty by reason of age, education, training, experience, length of service, and judicial temperament. No member of an armed force is eligible to serve as a member of a general or special court-martial when he is the accuser or a witness for the prosecution or has acted as investigating officer or as counsel in the same case.

(e) Before a court-martial is assembled for the trial of a case, the convening authority may excuse a member of the court from participating in the case. Under such regulations as the Secretary concerned may prescribe, the convening authority may delegate his authority under this subsection to his staff judge advocate or legal officer or to any other principal assistant.

Art. 26. Military judge of a general or special court-martial

(a) A military judge shall be detailed to each general court-martial. Subject to regulations of the Secretary concerned, a military judge may be detailed to any special court-martial. The Secretary concerned shall prescribe regulations providing for the manner in which military judges are detailed for such courts-martial and for the persons who are authorized to detail military judges for such courts-martial. The military judge shall preside over each open session of the court-martial to which he has been detailed.

(b) A military judge shall be a commissioned officer of the armed forces who is a member of the bar of a Federal court or a member of the bar of the highest court of a State and who is certified to be qualified for duty as a military judge by the Judge Advocate General of the armed force of which such military judge is a member.

(c) The military judge of a general court-martial shall be designated by the Judge Advocate General, or his designee, of the armed force of which the military judge is a member for detail in accordance with regulations prescribed under subsection (a). Unless the court-martial was convened by the President or the Secretary concerned, neither the convening authority nor any member of his staff shall prepare or review any report concerning the effectiveness, fitness, or efficiency of the military judge so detailed, which relates to his performance of duty as a military judge. A commissioned officer who is certified to be qualified for duty as a military judge of a general court-martial may perform such duties only when he is assigned and directly responsible to the Judge Advocate General, or his designee, of which the military judge is a member and may perform duties of a judicial or nonjudicial nature other than those relating to his primary duty as a military judge of a general court-martial when such duties are assigned to him by or with the approval of that Judge Advocate General or his designee.

(d) No person is eligible to act as military judge in a case if he is the accuser or a witness for the prosecution or has acted as investigating officer or a counsel in the same case.

(e) The military judge of a court-martial may not consult with the members of the court except in the presence of the accused, trial counsel, and defense counsel, nor may he vote with the members of the court.

Art. 27. *Detail of trial counsel and defense counsel*

(a)(1) Trial counsel and defense counsel shall be detailed for each general and special court-martial. Assistant trial counsel and assistant and associate defense counsel may be detailed for each general and special court-martial. The Secretary concerned shall prescribe regulations providing for the manner in which counsel are detailed for such courts-martial and for the persons who are authorized to detail counsel for such courts-martial.

(2) No person who has acted as investigating officer, military judge, or court member in any case may act later as trial counsel, assistant trial counsel, or, unless expressly requested by the accused, as defense counsel or assistant or associate defense counsel in the same case. No person who has acted for the prosecution may act later in the same case for the defense, nor may any person who has acted for the defense act later in the same case for the prosecution.

(b) Trial counsel or defense counsel detailed for a general court-martial—

(1) must be a judge advocate who is a graduate of an accredited law school or is a member of the bar of a Federal court or of the highest court of a State; or must be a member of the bar of a Federal court or of the highest court of a State; and

(2) must be certified as competent to perform such duties by the Judge Advocate General of the armed force of which he is a member.

(c) In the case of a special court-martial—

(1) the accused shall be afforded the opportunity to be represented at the trial by counsel having the qualifications prescribed under article 27(b) unless counsel having such qualifications cannot be obtained on account of physical conditions or military exigencies. If counsel having such qualifications cannot be obtained, the court may be convened and the trial held but the convening authority shall make a detailed written statement, to be appended to the record, stating why counsel with such qualifications could not be obtained;

(2) if the trial counsel is qualified to act as counsel before a general court-martial, the defense counsel detailed by the convening authority must be a person similarly qualified; and

(3) if the trial counsel is a judge advocate or a member of the bar of a Federal court or the highest court of a State, the defense counsel detailed by the convening authority must be one of the foregoing.

Art. 28. *Detail or employment of reporters and interpreters*

Under such regulations as the Secretary concerned may prescribe, the convening authority of a court-martial, military commission, or court of inquiry shall detail or employ qualified court reporters, who shall record the proceedings of and testimony taken before that court or commission. Under like regulations the convening authority of a court-martial, military commission, or court of inquiry may detail or employ interpreters who shall interpret for the court or commission.

Art. 29. *Absent and additional members*

(a) No member of a general or special court-martial may be absent or excused after the court has been assembled for the trial of the accused unless excused as a result of a challenge, excused by the military judge for physical disability or other good cause, or excused by order of the convening authority for good cause.

(b) Whenever a general court-martial, other than a general court-martial composed of a military judge only, is reduced below five members, the trial may not proceed unless the convening authority details new members sufficient in number to provide not less than five members. The trial may proceed with the new members present after the recorded evidence previously introduced before the members of the court has been read to the court in the presence of the military judge, the accused, and counsel for both sides.

(c) Whenever a special court-martial, other than a special court-martial composed of a military judge only, is reduced below three members, the trial may not proceed unless the convening authority details new members sufficient in number to provide not less than three members. The trial shall proceed with the new members present as if no evidence had previously been introduced at the trial, unless a verbatim record of the evidence previously introduced before the members of the court or a stipulation thereof is read to the court in the presence of the military judge, if any, the accused, and counsel for both sides.

(d) If the military judge of a court-martial composed of a military judge only is unable to proceed with the trial because of physical disability, as a result of a challenge, or for other good cause, the trial shall proceed, subject to any applicable conditions of article 16(1)(B) or (2)(C), after the detail of a new military judge as if no evidence had previously been introduced, unless a verbatim record of the evidence previously introduced or a stipulation thereof is read in court in the presence of the new military judge, the accused, and counsel for both sides.

Subchapter VI. Pre-Trial Procedure

Art. 30. Charges and specifications

(a) Charges and specifications shall be signed by a person subject to this chapter under oath before a com-

missioned officer of the armed forces authorized to administer oaths and shall state—

(1) that the signer has personal knowledge of, or has investigated, the matters set forth therein; and

(2) that they are true in fact to the best of his knowledge and belief.

(b) Upon the preferring of charges, the proper authority shall take immediate steps to determine what disposition should be made thereof in the interest of justice and discipline, and the person accused shall be informed of the charges against him as soon as practicable.

Art. 31. Compulsory self-incrimination prohibited

(a) No person subject to this chapter may compel any person to incriminate himself or to answer any question the answer to which may tend to incriminate him.

(b) No person subject to this chapter may interrogate, or request any statement from an accused or a person suspected of an offense, without first informing him of the nature of the accusation and advising him that he does not have to make any statement regarding the offense of which he is accused or suspected and that any statement made by him may be used as evidence against him in a trial by court-martial.

(c) No person subject to this chapter may compel any person to make a statement or produce evidence before any military tribunal if the statement or evidence is not material to the issue and may tend to degrade him.

(d) No statement obtained from any person in violation of this article, or through the use of coercion, unlawful influence, or unlawful inducement, may be received in evidence against him in a trial by court-martial.

Art. 32. Investigation

(a) No charge or specification may be referred to a general court-martial for trial until a thorough and impartial investigation of all the matters set forth therein has been made. This investigation shall include inquiry as to the truth of the matter set forth in the charges, consideration of the form of charges, and a recommendation as to the disposition which should be made of the case in the interest of justice and discipline.

(b) The accused shall be advised of the charges against him and of his right to be represented at that investigation by counsel. The accused has the right to be represented at that investigation as provided in article 38 and in regulations prescribed under that section. At that investigation full opportunity shall be given to the accused to cross-examine witnesses against him if they are available and to present anything he may desire in his own behalf, either in defense or mitigation, and the investigation officer shall examine available witnesses requested by the accused. If the charges are forwarded after the investigation, they shall be accompanied by a statement of the substance of the testimony taken on both sides and a copy thereof shall be given to the accused.

(c) If an investigation of the subject matter of an offense has been conducted before the accused is charged with the offense, and if the accused was present at the investigation and afforded the opportunities for representation, cross-examination, and presentation prescribed in subsection (b), no further investigation of that charge is necessary under this article unless it is demanded by the accused after he is informed of the charge. A demand for further investigation entitles the accused to recall witnesses for further cross-examination and to offer any new evidence in his own behalf.

(d) The requirements of this article are binding on all persons administering this chapter but failure to follow them does not constitute jurisdictional error.

Art. 33. Forwarding of charges

When a person is held for trial by general court-martial the commanding officer shall, within eight days after the accused is ordered into arrest or confinement, if practicable, forward the charges, together with the Investigation and allied papers, to the officer exercising general court-martial jurisdiction. If that is not practicable, he shall report in writing to that officer the reasons for delay.

Art. 34. Advice of staff judge advocate and reference for trial

(a) Before directing the trial of any charge by general court-martial, the convening authority shall refer it to his staff judge advocate for consideration and advice. The convening authority may not refer a specification under a charge to a general court-martial for trial unless he has been advised in writing by the staff judge advocate that—

(1) the specification alleges an offense under this chapter;

(2) the specification is warranted by the evidence indicated in the report of investigation under article 32 (if there is such a report); and

(3) a court-martial would have jurisdiction over the accused and the offense.

(b) The advice of the staff judge advocate under subsection (a) with respect to a specification under a charge shall include a written and signed statement by the staff judge advocate

(1) expressing his conclusions with respect to each matter set forth in subsection (a); and

(2) recommending action that the convening authority take regarding the specification.

If the specification is referred for trial, the recommendation of the staff judge advocate shall accompany the specification.

(c) If the charges or specifications are not formally correct or do not conform to the substance of the evidence contained in the report of the investigating officer, formal corrections, and such changes in the charges and specifications as are needed to make them conform to the evidence, may be made.

Art. 35. Service of charges

The trial counsel to whom court-martial charges are referred for trial shall cause to be served upon the accused a copy of the charges upon which trial is to be had. In time of peace no person may, against his objection, be brought to trial or be required to participate by himself or counsel in a session called by the military judge under article 39(a), in a general court-martial case within a period of five days after the service of charges upon him, or in a special court-martial within a period of three days after the service of the charges upon him.

Subchapter VII. Trial Procedure

Art. 36. President may prescribe rules

(a) Pretrial, trial, and post-trial procedures, including modes of proof, for cases arising under this chapter triable in courts-martial, military commissions and other military tribunals, and procedures for courts of inquiry, may be prescribed by the President by regulations which shall, so far as he considers practicable, apply the principles of law and the rules of evidence generally recognized in the trial of criminal cases in the United States district courts, but which may not be contrary to or inconsistent with this chapter.

(b) All rules and regulations made under this article shall be uniform insofar as practicable.

Art. 37. Unlawfully influencing action of court

(a) No authority convening a general, special, or summary court-martial, nor any other commanding officer, may censure, reprimand, or admonish the court or any member, military judge, or counsel thereof, with respect to the findings or sentence adjudged by the court, or with respect to any other exercises of its or his functions in the conduct of the proceedings. No person subject to this chapter may attempt to coerce or, by any unauthorized means, influence the action of a court-martial or any other military tribunal or any member thereof, in reaching the findings or sentence in any case, or the action of any convening, approving, or reviewing authority with respect to his judicial acts. The foregoing provisions of the subsection shall not apply with respect to (1) general instructional or informational courses in military justice if such courses are designed solely for the purpose of instructing members of a command in the substantive and procedural aspects of courts-martial, or (2) to statements and instructions given in open court by the military judge, president of a special court-martial, or counsel.

(b) In the preparation of an effectiveness, fitness, or efficiency report or any other report or document used in whole or in part for the purpose of determining whether a member of the armed forces is qualified to be advanced, in grade, or in determining the assignment or transfer of a member of the armed forces or in determining whether a member of the armed forces should be retained on active duty, no person subject to this chapter may, in preparing any such report (1) consider or evaluate the performance of duty of any such member of a court-martial, or (2) give a less favorable rating or evaluation of any member of the armed forces because of the zeal with which such member, as counsel, represented any accused before a court-martial.

Art. 38. Duties of trial counsel and defense counsel

(a) The trial counsel of a general or special court-martial shall prosecute in the name of the United States, and shall, under the direction of the court, prepare the record of the proceedings.

(b)(1) The accused has the right to be represented in his defense before a general or special court-martial or at an investigation under article 32 as provided in this subsection.

(2) The accused may be represented by civilian counsel if provided by him.

(3) The accused may be represented—

(A) by military counsel detailed under article 27; or

(B) by military counsel of his own selection if that counsel is reasonably available (as determined under regulations prescribed under paragraph (7)).

(4) If the accused is represented by civilian counsel, military counsel detailed or selected under paragraph (3) shall act as associate counsel unless excused at the request of the accused.

(5) Except as provided under paragraph (6), if the accused is represented by military counsel of his own selection under paragraph (3)(B), any military counsel detailed under paragraph (3)(A) shall be excused.

(6) The accused is not entitled to be represented by more than one military counsel. However, the person authorized under regulations prescribed under section 827 of this title (article 27) to detail counsel, in his sole discretion—

(A) may detail additional military counsel as assistant defense counsel; and

(B) if the accused is represented by military counsel of his own selection under paragraph (3)(B), may approve a request from the accused that military counsel detailed under paragraph (3)(A) act as associate defense counsel.

(7) The Secretary concerned shall, by regulation, define "reasonably available" for the purpose of paragraph (3)(B) and establish procedures for determining whether the military counsel selected by an accused under that paragraph is reasonably available. Such regulations may not prescribe any limitation based on the reasonable availability of counsel solely on the grounds that the counsel selected by the accused is from an armed force other than the armed force of which the accused is a member. To the maximum extent practicable, such regulations shall establish uniform policies among the armed forces while recognizing the differences in the circumstances and needs of the various armed forces. The Secretary concerned shall submit copies of regulations prescribed under this paragraph to the Committees on Armed Services of the Senate and House of Representatives.

(c) In any court-martial proceeding resulting in a conviction, the defense counsel—

(1) may forward for attachment to the record of proceedings a brief of such matters as he determines should be considered in behalf of the accused on review (including any objection to the contents of the record which he considers appropriate);

(2) may assist the accused in the submission of any matter under article 60 of this title; and

(3) may take other action authorized by this chapter.

(d) An assistant trial counsel of a general court-martial may, under the direction of the trial counsel or when he is qualified to be a trial counsel as required by article 27, perform any duty imposed by law, regulation, or the custom of the service upon the trial counsel of the court. An assistant trial counsel of a special court-martial may perform any duty of the trial counsel.

(e) An assistant defense counsel of a general or special court-martial may, under the direction of the defense counsel or when he is qualified to be the defense counsel as required by article 27, perform any duty imposed by law, regulation, or the custom of the service upon counsel for the accused.

Art. 39. Sessions

(a) At any time after the service of charges which have been referred for trial to a court-martial composed of a military judge and members, the military judge may, subject to article 35, call the court into session without the presence of the members for the purpose of—

(1) hearing and determining motions raising defenses or objections which are capable of determination without trial of the issues raised by a plea of not guilty;

(2) hearing and ruling upon any matter which may be ruled upon by the military judge under this chapter, whether or not the matter is appropriate for later consideration or decision by the members of the court;

(3) if permitted by regulations of the Secretary concerned, holding the arraignment and receiving the pleas of the accused; and

(4) performing any other procedural function which may be performed by the military judge under this chapter or under rules prescribed pursuant to section 836 of this title (article 36) and which does not require the presence of the members of the court. These proceedings shall be conducted in the presence of the accused, the defense counsel, and the trial counsel and shall be made a part of the record. These proceedings may be conducted notwithstanding the number of members of the court and without regard to article 29.

(b) When the members of a court-martial deliberate or vote, only the members may be present. All other proceedings, including any other consultation of the members of the court with counsel or the military judge, shall be made a part of the record and shall be in the presence of the accused, the defense counsel, the trial counsel, and in cases in which a military judge has been detailed to the court, the military judge.

Art. 40. Continuances

The military judge or a court-martial without a military judge may, for reasonable cause, grant a continuance to any party for such time, and as often, as may appear to be just.

Art. 41. Challenges

(a)(1) The military judge and members of a general or special court-martial may be challenged by the accused or the trial counsel for cause stated to the court.

The military judge, or, if none, the court, shall determine the relevance and validity of challenges for cause, and may not receive a challenge to more than one person at a time. Challenges by the trial counsel shall ordinarily be presented and decided before those by the accused are offered.

(2) If exercise of a challenge for cause reduces the court below the minimum number of members required by article 16, all parties shall (notwithstanding article 29) either exercise or waive any challenge for cause then apparent against the remaining members of the court before additional members are detailed to the court. However, peremptory challenges shall not be exercised at that time.

(b)(1) Each accused and the trial counsel are entitled initially to one peremptory challenge of the members of the court. The military judge may not be challenged except for cause.

(2) If exercise of a peremptory challenge reduces the court below the minimum number of members required by article 16, the parties shall (notwithstanding article 29) either exercise or waive any remaining peremptory challenge (not previously waived) against the remaining members of the court before additional members are detailed to the court.

(c) Whenever additional members are detailed to the court, and after any challenges for cause against such additional members are presented and decided, each accused and the trial counsel are entitled to one peremptory challenge against members not previously subject to peremptory challenge.

Art. 42. Oaths

(a) Before performing their respective duties, military judges, members of general and special courts-martial, trial counsel, assistant trial counsel, defense counsel, assistant or associate defense counsel, reporters, and interpreters shall take an oath to perform their duties faithfully. The form of the oath, the time and place of the taking thereof, the manner of recording the same, and whether the oath shall be taken for all cases in which these duties are to be performed or for a particular case, shall be as prescribed in regulations of the Secretary concerned. These regulations may provide that an oath to perform faithfully duties as a military judge, trial counsel, assistant trial counsel, defense counsel, associate defense counsel may be taken at any time by any judge advocate or other person certified to be qualified or competent for the duty, and if such an oath is taken it need not again be taken at the time the judge advocate, or other person, is detailed to that duty.

(b) Each witness before a court-martial shall be examined on oath.

Art. 43. Statute of limitations

(a) A person charged with absence without leave or missing movement in time of war, or with any offense punishable by death, may be tried and punished at any time without limitation.

(b)(1) Except as otherwise provided in this section (article), a person charged with an offense is not liable to be tried by court-martial if the offense was committed more than five years before the receipt of sworn charges and specifications by an officer exercising summary court-martial jurisdiction over the command.

(2) A person charged with an offense is not liable to be punished under article 15 if the offense was committed more than two years before the imposition of punishment.

(c) Periods in which the accused is absent without authority or fleeing from justice shall be excluded in computing the period of limitation prescribed in this article.

(d) Periods in which the accused was absent from territory in which the United States has the authority to apprehend him, or in the custody of civil authorities, or in the hands of the enemy, shall be excluded in computing the period of limitation prescribed in this article.

(e) For an offense the trial of which in time of war is certified to the President by the Secretary concerned to be detrimental to the prosecution of the war or inimical to the national security, the period of limitation prescribed in this article is extended to six months after the termination of hostilities as proclaimed by the President or by a joint resolution of Congress.

(f) When the United States is at war, the running of any statute of limitations applicable to any offense under this chapter—

(1) involving fraud or attempted fraud against the United States or any agency thereof in any manner, whether by conspiracy or not;

(2) committed in connection with the acquisition, care, handling, custody, control, or disposition of any real or personal property of the United States; or

(3) committed in connection with the negotiation, procurement, award, performance, payment, interim financing, cancellation, or other termination or settlement, of any contract, subcontract, or purchase order which is connected with or related to the prosecution of the war, or with any disposition of termination inventory by any war contractor or Government agency;

is suspended until three years after the termination of hostilities as proclaimed by the President or by a joint resolution of Congress.

(g)(1) If charges or specifications are dismissed as defective or insufficient for any cause and the period prescribed by the applicable statute of limitations—

(A) has expired; or

(B) will expire within 180 days after the date of dismissal of the charges and specifications, trial and punishment under new charges and specifications are not barred by the statute of limitations if the conditions specified in paragraph (2) are met.

(2) The conditions referred to in paragraph (1) are that the new charges and specifications must—

(A) be received by an officer exercising summary court-martial jurisdiction over the command within 180 days after the dismissal of the charges or specifications; and

(B) allege the same acts or omissions that were alleged in the dismissed charges or specifications (or allege acts or omissions that were included in the dismissed charges or specifications).

Art. 44. Former jeopardy

(a) No person may, without his consent, be tried a second time for the same offense.

(b) No proceeding in which an accused has been found guilty by court-martial upon any charge or specification is a trial in the sense of this article until the finding of guilty has become final after review of the case has been fully completed.

(c) A proceeding which, after the introduction of evidence but before a finding, is dismissed or terminated by the convening authority or on motion of the prosecution for failure of available evidence or witnesses without any fault of the accused is a trial in the sense of this article.

Art. 45. Pleas of the accused

(a) If an accused after arraignment makes an irregular pleading, or after a plea of guilty sets up matter inconsistent with the plea, or if it appears that he has entered the plea of guilty improvidently or through lack of understanding of its meaning and effect, or if he fails or refuses to plead, a plea of not guilty shall be entered in the record, and the court shall proceed as though he had pleaded not guilty.

(b) A plea of guilty by the accused may not be received to any charge or specification alleging an offense for which the death penalty may be adjudged. With respect to any other charge or specification to which a plea of guilty has been made by the accused and accepted by the military judge or by a court-martial without a military judge, a finding of guilty of the charge or specification may, if permitted by regulations of the Secretary concerned, be entered immediately without vote. This finding shall constitute the finding of the court unless the plea of guilty is withdrawn prior to announcement of the sentence, in which event the proceedings shall continue as though the accused had pleaded not guilty.

Art. 46. Opportunity to obtain witnesses and other evidence

The trial counsel, the defense counsel, and the court-martial shall have equal opportunity to obtain witnesses and other evidence in accordance with such regulations as the President may prescribe. Process issued in court-martial cases to compel witnesses to appear and testify and to compel the production of other evidence shall be similar to that which courts of the United States having criminal jurisdiction may lawfully issue and shall run to any part of the United States, or the Territories, Commonwealths, and possessions.

Art. 47. Refusal to appear or testify

(a) Any person not subject to this chapter who—

(1) has been duly subpoenaed to appear as a witness before a court-martial, military commission, court of inquiry, or any other military court or board, or before any military or civil officer designated to take a deposition to be read in evidence before such a court, commission, or board;

(2) has been duly paid or tendered the fees and mileage of a witness at the rates allowed to witnesses attending the courts of the United States; and

(3) willfully neglects or refuses to appear, or refuses to qualify as a witness or to testify or to produce any evidence which that person may have been legally subpoenaed to produce;

is guilty of an offense against the United States.

(b) Any person who commits an offense named in subsection (a) shall be tried on information in a United States district court or in a court of original criminal jurisdiction in any of the Territories, Commonwealths, or possessions of the United States, and jurisdiction is conferred upon those courts for that purpose. Upon conviction, such a person shall be punished by a fine of not more than $500, or imprisonment for not more than six months, or both.

(c) The United States attorney or the officer prosecuting for the United States in any such court of original criminal jurisdiction shall, upon the certification of the facts to him by the military court, commission, court of inquiry, or board, file an information against and prosecute any person violating this article.

(d) The fees and mileage of witnesses shall be advanced or paid out of the appropriations for the compensation of witnesses.

Art. 48. Contempts

A court-martial, provost court, or military commission may punish for contempt any person who uses any menacing word, sign, or gesture in its presence, or who disturbs its proceedings by any riot or disorder. The punishment may not exceed confinement for 30 days or a fine of $100, or both.

Art. 49. Depositions

(a) At any time after charges have been signed as provided in article 30, any party may take oral or written depositions unless the military judge or court-martial without a military judge hearing the case or, if the case is not being heard, an authority competent to convene a court-martial for the trial of those charges forbids it for good cause. If a deposition is to be taken before charges are referred for trial, such an authority may designate commissioned officers to represent the prosecution and the defense and may authorize those officers to take the deposition of any witness.

(b) The party at whose instance a deposition is to be taken shall give to every other party reasonable written notice of the time and place for taking the deposition.

(c) Depositions may be taken before and authenticated by any military or civil officer authorized by the laws of the United States or by the laws of the place where the deposition is taken to administer oaths.

(d) A duly authenticated deposition taken upon reasonable notice to the other parties, so far as otherwise admissible under the rules of evidence, may be read in evidence or, in the case of audiotape, videotape, or similar material, may be played in evidence before any military court or commission in any case not capital, or in any proceeding before a court of inquiry or military board, if it appears

(1) that the witness resides or is beyond the State, Territory, Commonwealth, or District of Columbia in which the court, commission, or board is ordered to sit, or beyond 100 miles from the place of trial or hearing;

(2) that the witness by reason of death, age, sickness, bodily infirmity, imprisonment, military necessity, nonamenability to process, or other reasonable cause,

is unable or refuses to appear and testify in person at the place of trial or hearing; or

(3) that the present whereabouts of the witness is unknown.

(e) Subject to subsection (d), testimony by deposition may be presented by the defense in capital cases.

(f) Subject to subsection (d), a deposition may be read in evidence or, in the case of audiotape, videotape, or similar material, may be played in evidence in any case in which the death penalty is authorized but is not mandatory, whenever the convening authority directs that the case be treated as not capital, and in such a case a sentence of death may not be adjudged by the court-martial.

Art. 50. *Admissibility of records of courts of inquiry*

(a) In any case not capital and not extending to the dismissal of a commissioned officer, the sworn testimony, contained in the duly authenticated record of proceedings of a court of inquiry, of a person whose oral testimony cannot be if otherwise admissible under the rules of evidence, be read in evidence by any party before a court-martial or military commission if the accused was a party before the court of inquiry and if the same issue was involved or if the accused consents to the introduction of such evidence.

(b) Such testimony may be read in evidence only by the defense in capital cases or cases extending to the dismissal of a commissioned officer.

(c) Such testimony may also be read in evidence before a court of inquiry or a military board.

Art. 50a. *Defense of lack of mental responsibility*

(a) It is an affirmative defense in a trial by court-martial that, at the time of the commission of the acts constituting the offense, the accused, as a result of a severe mental disease or defect, was unable to appreciate the nature and quality or the wrongfulness of the acts. Mental disease or defect does not otherwise constitute a defense.

(b) The accused has the burden of proving the defense of lack of mental responsibility by clear and convincing evidence.

(c) Whenever lack of mental responsibility of the accused with respect to an offense is properly at issue, the military judge, or the president of a court-martial without a military judge, shall instruct the members of the court as to the defense of lack of mental responsibility under this section and shall charge them to find the accused—

(1) guilty;

(2) not guilty; or

(3) not guilty only by reason of lack of mental responsibility.

(d) Subsection (c) does not apply to a court-martial composed of a military judge only. In the case of a court-martial composed of a military judge only, whenever lack of mental responsibility of the accused with respect to an offense is properly at issue, the military judge shall find the accused—

(1) guilty;

(2) not guilty; or

(3) not guilty only by reason of lack of mental responsibility.

(e) Notwithstanding the provisions of article 52, the accused shall be found not guilty only by reason of lack of mental responsibility if—

(1) a majority of the members of the court-martial present at the time the vote is taken determines that the defense of lack of mental responsibility has been established; or

(2) in the case of court-martial composed of a military judge only, the military judge determines that the defense of lack of mental responsibility has been established.

Art. 51. *Voting and rulings*

(a) Voting by members of a general or special court-martial on the findings and on the sentence, and by members of a court-martial without a military judge upon questions of challenge, shall be by secret written ballot. The junior member of the court shall count the votes. The count shall be checked by the president, who shall forthwith announce the result of the ballot to the members of the court.

(b) The military judge and, except for questions of challenge, the president of a court-martial without a military judge shall rule upon all questions of law and all interlocutory questions arising during the proceedings. Any such ruling made by the military judge upon any question of law or any interlocutory question other than the factual issue of mental responsibility of the accused, or by the president of a court-martial without a military judge upon any question of law other than a motion for a finding of not guilty, is final and constitutes the ruling of the court. However, the military judge or the president of a court-martial without a military judge may change his ruling at any time during the trial. Unless the ruling is final, if any member objects thereto, the court shall be cleared and closed and the question decided by a voice vote as provided in article 52, beginning with the junior in rank.

(c) Before a vote is taken on the findings, the military judge or the president of a court-martial without a military judge shall, in the presence of the accused and counsel, instruct the members of the court as to the elements of the offense and charge them—

(1) that the accused must be presumed to be innocent until his guilt is established by legal and competent evidence beyond reasonable doubt;

(2) that in the case being considered, if there is a reasonable doubt as to the guilt of the accused, the doubt must be resolved in favor of the accused and he must be acquitted;

(3) that, if there is reasonable doubt as to the degree of guilt, the finding must be in a lower degree as to which there is no reasonable doubt; and

(4) that the burden of proof to establish the guilt of the accused beyond reasonable doubt is upon the United States.

(d) Subsections (a), (b), and (c) do not apply to a court-martial composed of a military judge only. The military judge of such a court-martial shall determine all questions of law and fact arising during the proceedings and, if the accused is convicted, adjudge an appropriate sentence. The military judge of such a court-martial shall make a general finding and shall in addition on request find the facts specially. If an opinion or memorandum of decision is filed, it will be sufficient if the findings of fact appear therein.

Art. 52. *Number of votes required*

(a)(1) No person may be convicted of an offense for which the death penalty is made mandatory by law, except by the concurrence of all the members of the court-martial present at the time the vote is taken.

(2) No person may be convicted of any other offense, except as provided in article 45(b) or by the concurrence of two-thirds of the members present at the time the vote is taken.

(b)(1) No person may be sentenced to suffer death, except by the concurrence of all the members of the court-martial present at the time the vote is taken and for an offense in this chapter expressly made punishable by death.

(2) No person may be sentenced to life imprisonment or to confinement for more than ten years, except by the concurrence of three-fourths of the members present at the time the vote is taken.

(3) All other sentences shall be determined by the concurrence of two-thirds of the members present at the time the vote is taken.

(c) All other questions to be decided by the members of a general or special court-martial shall be determined by a majority vote, but a determination to reconsider a finding of guilty or to reconsider a sentence, with a view toward decreasing it, may be made by any lesser vote which indicates that the reconsideration is not opposed by the number of votes required for that finding or sentence. A tie vote on a challenge disqualifies the member challenged. A tie vote on a motion for a finding of not guilty or on a motion relating to the question of the accused's sanity is a determination against the accused. A tie vote on any other question is a determination in favor of the accused.

Art. 53. *Court to announce action*

A court-martial shall announce its findings and sentence to the parties as soon as determined.

Art. 54. *Record of trial*

(a) Each general court-martial shall keep a separate record of the proceedings in each case brought before it, and the record shall be authenticated by the signature of the military judge. If the record cannot be authenticated by the military judge by reason of his death, disability, or absence, it shall be authenticated by the signature of the trial counsel or by that of a member if the trial counsel is unable to authenticate it by reason of his death, disability, or absence. In a court-martial consisting of only a military judge the record shall be authenticated by the court reporter under the same conditions which would impose such a duty on a member under the subsection.

(b) Each special and summary court-martial shall keep a separate record of the proceedings in each case, and the record shall be authenticated in the manner required by such regulations as the President may prescribe.

(c)(1) A complete record of the proceedings and testimony shall be prepared—

(A) in each general court-martial case in which the sentence adjudged includes death, a dismissal, a discharge, or (if the sentence adjudged does not include a discharge) any other punishment which exceeds that which may otherwise be adjudged by a special court-martial; and

(B) in each special court-martial case in which the sentence adjudged includes a bad-conduct discharge.

(2) In all other court-martial cases, the record shall contain such matters as may be prescribed by regulations of the President.

(d) A copy of the record of the proceedings of each general and special court-martial shall be given to the accused as soon as it is authenticated.

Subchapter VIII. Sentences

Art. 55. Cruel and unusual punishments prohibited

Punishment by flogging, or by branding, marking, or tattooing on the body, or any other cruel or unusual punishment, may not be adjudged by a court-martial or inflicted upon any person subject to this chapter. The use of irons, single or double, except for the purpose of safe custody, is prohibited.

Art. 56. Maximum limits

The punishment which a court-martial may direct for an offense may not exceed such limits as the President may prescribe for that offense.

Art. 57. Effective date of sentences

(a) No forfeiture may extend to any pay or allowances accrued before the date on which the sentence is approved by the person acting under article 60(c).

(b) Any period of confinement included in a sentence of a court-martial begins to run from the date the sentence is adjudged by the court-martial, but periods during which the sentence to confinement is suspended or deferred shall be excluded in computing the service of the term of confinement.

(c) All other sentences of courts-martial are effective on the date ordered executed.

(d) On application by an accused who is under sentence to confinement that has not been ordered executed, the convening authority or, if the accused is no longer under his jurisdiction, the officer exercising general court-martial jurisdiction over the command to which the accused is currently assigned, may in his sole discretion defer service of the sentence to confinement. The deferment shall terminate when the sentence is ordered executed. The deferment may be rescinded at any time by the officer who granted it or, if the accused is no longer under his jurisdiction, by the officer exercising general court-martial jurisdiction over the command to which the accused is currently assigned.

(e)(1) In any case in which a court-martial sentences a person referred to in paragraph (2) to confinement, the convening authority may postpone the service of the sentence to confinement, without the consent of that person, until after permanently released to the armed forces by a state or foreign country referred to in that paragraph.

(2) Paragraph (1) applies to a person subject to this chapter who—

(A) While in the custody of a state or foreign country is temporarily returned by that state or foreign country to the armed forces for trial by court-martial; and

(B) After the court-martial, is returned to that state or foreign country under the authority of a mutual agreement or treaty, as the case may be.

(3) In this subsection, the term "state" means a state of the United States, the District of Columbia, a territory, or a possession of the United States.

Art. 58. Execution of confinement

(a) Under such instructions as the Secretary concerned may prescribe, a sentence of confinement adjudged by a court-martial or other military tribunal, whether or not the sentence includes discharge or dismissal, and whether or not the discharge or dismissal has been executed, may be carried into execution by confinement in any place of confinement under the control of any of the armed forces or in any penal or correctional institution under the control of the United States, or which the United States may be allowed to use. Persons so confined in a penal or correctional institution not under the control of one of the armed forces are subject to the same discipline and treatment as persons confined or committed by the courts of the United States or of the State, Territory, District of Columbia, or place in which the institution is situated.

(b) The omission of the words "hard labor" from any sentence of a court-martial adjudging confinement does not deprive the authority executing that sentence of the power to require hard labor as a part of the punishment.

Art. 58a. Sentences: reduction in enlisted grade upon approval

(a) Unless otherwise provided in regulations to be prescribed by the Secretary concerned, a court-martial sentence of an enlisted member in a pay grade above E-1, as approved by the convening authority, that includes—

(1) a dishonorable or bad-conduct discharge;
(2) confinement; or
(3) hard labor without confinement;

reduces that member to pay grade E-1, effective on the date of that approval.

(b) If the sentence of a member who is reduced in pay grade under subsection (a) is set aside or disapproved, or, as finally approved, does not include any punishment named in subsection (a)(1), (2), or (3), the rights and privileges of which he was deprived because of that reduction shall be restored to him and he is entitled to the pay and allowances to which he would have been entitled for the period the reduction was in effect, had he not been so reduced.

Subchapter IX. Post-Trial Procedure and Review of Courts-Martial

Art. 59. Error of law; lesser included offense

(a) A finding or sentence of court-martial may not be held incorrect on the ground of an error of law unless the error materially prejudices the substantial rights of the accused.

(b) Any reviewing authority with the power to approve or affirm a finding of guilty may approve or affirm, instead, so much of the finding as includes a lesser included offense.

Art. 60. Action by the convening authority

(a) The findings and sentence of a court-martial shall be reported promptly to the convening authority after the announcement of the sentence.

(b)(1) The accused may submit to the convening authority matters for consideration by the convening authority with respect to the findings and the sentence. Except in a summary court-martial case, such a submission shall be made within 10 days after the accused has been given an authenticated record of trial and, if applicable, the recommendation of the staff judge advocate or legal officer under subsection (d). In a summary court-martial case, such a submission shall be made within seven days after the sentence is announced.

(2) If the accused shows that additional time is required for the accused to submit such matters, the convening authority or other person taking action under this section, for good cause, may extend the

applicable period under paragraph (1) for not more than an additional 20 days.

(3) In a summary court-martial case, the accused shall be promptly provided a copy of the record of trial for use in preparing a submission authorized by paragraph (1).

(4) The accused may waive his right to make a submission to the convening authority under paragraph (1). Such a waiver must be made in writing and may not be revoked. For the purposes of subsection (c)(2), the time within which the accused may make a submission under this subsection shall be deemed to have expired upon the submission of such a waiver to the convening authority.

(c)(1) The authority under this section to modify the findings and sentence of a court-martial is a matter of command prerogative involving the sole discretion of the convening authority. Under regulations of the Secretary concerned, a commissioned officer commanding for the time being, a successor in command, or any person exercising general court-martial jurisdiction may act under this section in place of the convening authority.

(2) Action on the sentence of a court-martial shall be taken by the convening authority or by another person authorized to act under this section. Subject to regulations of the Secretary concerned, such action may be taken only after consideration of any matters submitted by the accused under subsection (b) or after the time for submitting such matters expires, whichever is earlier. The convening authority or other person taking such action, in his sole discretion, may approve, disapprove, commute, or suspend the sentence in whole or in part.

(3) Action on the findings of a court-martial by the convening authority or other person acting on the sentence is not required. However, such person, in his sole discretion, may—

(A) dismiss any charge or specification by setting aside a finding of guilty thereto; or

(B) change a finding of guilty to a charge or specification to a finding of guilty to an offense that is a lesser included offense of the offense stated in the charge or specification.

(d) Before acting under this section on any general

court-martial case or any special court-martial case that includes a bad-conduct discharge, the convening authority or other person taking action under this section shall obtain and consider the written recommendation of his staff judge advocate or legal officer. The convening authority or other person taking action under this section shall refer the record of trial to his staff judge advocate or legal officer, and the staff judge advocate or legal officer shall use such record in the preparation of his recommendation. The recommendation of the staff judge advocate or legal officer shall include such matters as the President may prescribe by regulation and shall be served on the accused, who may submit any matter in response under subsection (b). Failure to object in the response to the recommendation or to any matter attached to the recommendation waives the right to object thereto.

(e)(1) The convening authority or other person taking action under this section, in his sole discretion, may order a proceeding in revision or a rehearing.

(2) A proceeding in revision may be ordered if there is an apparent error or omission in the record or if the record shows improper or inconsistent action by a court-martial with respect to the findings or sentence that can be rectified without material prejudice to the substantial rights of the accused. In no case, however, may a proceeding in revision—

(A) reconsider a finding of not guilty of any specification or a ruling which amounts to a finding of not guilty;

(B) reconsider a finding of not guilty of any charge, unless there has been a finding of guilty under a specification laid under that charge, which sufficiently alleges a violation of some article of this chapter; or

(C) increase the severity of some article of the sentence unless the sentence prescribed for the offense is mandatory.

(3) A rehearing may be ordered by the convening authority or other person taking action under this section if he disapproves the findings and sentence and states the reasons for disapproval of the findings. If such person disapproves the findings and sentence and does not order a rehearing, he shall dismiss the charges. A rehearing as to the findings may not be or-

dered where there is a lack of sufficient evidence in the record to support the findings. A rehearing as to the sentence may be ordered if the convening authority or other person taking action under this subsection disapproves the sentence.

Art. 61. *Waiver or withdrawal of appeal*

(a) In each case subject to appellate review under article 66 or 69(a), except a case in which the sentence as approved under article 60(c) includes death, the accused may file with the convening authority a statement expressly waiving the right of the accused to such review. Such a waiver shall be signed by both the accused and by defense counsel and must be filed within 10 days after the action under article 60(c) is served on the accused or on defense counsel. The convening authority or other person taking such action, for good cause, may extend the period for such filing by not more than 30 days.

(b) Except in a case in which the sentence as approved under article 60(c) includes death, the accused may withdraw an appeal at any time.

(c) A waiver of the right to appellate review or the withdrawal of an appeal under this section bars review under article 66 or 69(a).

Art. 62. *Appeal by the United States*

(a)(1) In a trial by court-martial in which a military judge presides and in which a punitive discharge may be adjudged, the United States may appeal an order or ruling of the military judge which terminates the proceedings with respect to a charge or specification or which excludes evidence that is substantial proof of a fact material in the proceeding. However, the United States may not appeal an order or ruling that is, or that amounts to, a finding of not guilty with respect to the charge or specification.

(2) An appeal of an order or ruling may not be taken unless the trial counsel provides the military judge with written notice of appeal from the order or ruling within 72 hours of the order or ruling. Such notice shall include a certification by the trial counsel that the appeal is not taken for the purpose of delay

and (if the order or ruling appealed is one which excludes evidence) that the evidence excluded is substantial proof of a fact material in the proceeding.

(3) An appeal under this section shall be diligently prosecuted by appellate Government counsel.

(b) An appeal under this section shall be forwarded by a means prescribed under regulations of the President directly to the Court of Criminal Appeals and shall, whenever practicable, have priority over all other proceedings before that court. In ruling on an appeal under this section, the Court of Criminal Appeals may act only with respect to matters of law, notwithstanding article 66(c).

(c) Any period of delay resulting from an appeal under this section shall be excluded in deciding any issue regarding denial of a speedy trial unless an appropriate authority determines that the appeal was filed solely for the purpose of delay with the knowledge that it was totally frivolous and without merit.

Art. 63. *Rehearings*

Each rehearing under this chapter shall take place before a court-martial composed of members not members of the court-martial which first heard the case. Upon a rehearing the accused may not be tried for any offense of which he was found not guilty by the first court-martial, and no sentence in excess of or more severe than the original sentence may be approved, unless the sentence is based upon a finding of guilty of an offense not considered upon the merits in the original proceedings, or unless the sentence prescribed for the offense is mandatory. If the sentence approved after the first court-martial was in accordance with a pretrial agreement and the accused at the rehearing changes his plea with respect to the charges or specifications upon which the pretrial agreement was based, or otherwise does not comply with the pretrial agreement, the approved sentence as to those charges or specifications may include any punishment not in excess of that lawfully adjudged at the first court-martial.

Art. 64. *Review by a judge advocate*

(a) Each case in which there has been a finding of guilty that is not reviewed under article 66 or 69(a) shall be reviewed by a judge advocate under regulations of the Secretary concerned. A judge advocate may not review a case under this subsection if he has acted in the same case as an accuser, investigating officer, member of the court, military judge, or counsel or has otherwise acted on behalf of the prosecution or defense. The judge advocate's review shall be in writing and shall contain the following:

　(1) Conclusions as to whether—

　　(A) the court had jurisdiction over the accused and the offense;

　　(B) the charge and specification stated an offense; and

　　(C) the sentence was within the limits prescribed as a matter of law.

　(2) A response to each allegation of error made in writing by the accused.

　(3) If the case is sent for action under subsection (b), a recommendation as to the appropriate action to be taken and an opinion as to whether corrective action is required as a matter of law.

(b) The record of trial and related documents in each case reviewed under subsection (a) shall be sent for action to the person exercising general court-martial jurisdiction over the accused at the time the court was convened (or to that person's successor in command) if—

　(1) the judge advocate who reviewed the case recommends corrective action;

　(2) the sentence approved under article 60(c) extends to dismissal, a bad-conduct or dishonorable discharge, or confinement for more than six months; or

　(3) such action is otherwise required by regulations of the Secretary concerned.

(c)(1) The person to whom the record of trial and related documents are sent under subsection (b) may—

　　(A) disapprove or approve the findings or sentence, in whole or in part;

　　(B) remit, commute, or suspend the sentence in whole or in part;

　　(C) except where the evidence was insufficient at the trial to support the findings, order a rehearing on the findings, on the sentence, or on both; or

　　(D) dismiss the charges.

　(2) If a rehearing is ordered but the convening authority finds a rehearing impracticable, he shall dismiss the charges.

　(3) If the opinion of the judge advocate in the judge advocate's review under subsection (a) is that corrective action is required as a matter of law and if the person required to take action under subsection (b) does not take action that is at least as favorable to the accused as that recommended by the judge advocate, the record of trial and action thereon shall be sent to the Judge Advocate General for review under section 869(b) of this title (article 69(b)).

Art. 65. Disposition of records

(a) In a case subject to appellate review under article 66 or 69(a) in which the right to such review is not waived, or an appeal is not withdrawn, under article 61, the record of trial and action thereon shall be transmitted to the Judge Advocate General for appropriate action.

(b) Except as otherwise required by this chapter, all other records of trial and related documents shall be transmitted and disposed of as the Secretary concerned may prescribe by regulation.

Art. 66. Review by Court of Criminal Appeals

(a) Each Judge Advocate General shall establish a Court of Criminal Appeals which shall be composed of one or more panels, and each such panel shall be composed of not less than three appellate military judges. For the purpose of reviewing court-martial cases, the court may sit in panels or as a whole in accordance with rules prescribed under subsection (f). Any decision of a panel may be reconsidered by the court sitting as a whole in accordance with such rules. Appellate military judges who are assigned to a Court of Criminal Appeals may be commissioned officers or civilians, each of whom must be a member of a bar of a Federal court or the highest court of a State. The Judge Advocate General shall designate as chief judge late military judges of the Court of Criminal Appeals established by him. The chief judge shall determine on which panels of the court the appellate judges assigned to the court will serve and which military judge assigned to the court will act as the senior judge on each panel.

(b) The Judge Advocate General shall refer to a Court of Criminal Appeals the record in each case of trial by court-martial—

(1) in which the sentence, as approved, extends to death, dismissal of a commissioned officer, cadet, or midshipman, dishonorable or bad-conduct discharge, or confinement for one year or more; and

(2) except in the case of a sentence extending to death, the right to appellate review has not been waived or an appeal has not been withdrawn under article 61.

(c) In a case referred to it, the Court of Criminal Appeals may act only with respect to the findings and sentence as approved by the convening authority. It may affirm only such findings of guilty and the sentence or such part or amount of the sentence, as it finds correct in law and fact and determines, on the basis of the entire record, should be approved. In considering the record, it may weigh the evidence, judge the credibility of witnesses, and determine controverted questions of fact, recognizing that the trial court saw and heard the witnesses.

(d) If the Court of Criminal Appeals sets aside the findings and sentence, it may, except where the setting aside is based on lack of sufficient evidence in the record to support the findings, order a rehearing. If it sets aside the findings and sentence and does not order a rehearing, it shall order that the charges be dismissed.

(e) The Judge Advocate General shall, unless there is to be further action by the President, the Secretary concerned, the Court of Appeals for the Armed Forces, or the Supreme Court, instruct the convening authority to take action in accordance with the decision of the Court of Criminal Appeals. If the Court of Criminal Appeals has ordered a rehearing but the convening authority finds a rehearing impracticable, he may dismiss the charges.

(f) The Judge Advocate General shall prescribe uniform rules of procedure for Courts of Criminal Appeals and shall meet periodically to formulate policies and procedure in regard to review of court-martial cases in the office of the Judge Advocate General and by Courts of Criminal Appeals.

(g) No member of a Court of Criminal Appeals shall be required, or on his own initiative be permitted, to prepare, approve, disapprove, review, or submit, with respect to any other member of the same or another Court of Criminal Appeals, an effectiveness, fitness, or efficiency report, or any other report or document used in whole or in part for the purpose of determining whether a member of the armed forces is qualified to be advanced in grade, or in determining the assignment or transfer of a member of the armed forces, or in determining whether a member of the armed forces shall be retained on active duty.

(h) No member of a Court of Criminal Appeals shall be eligible to review the record of any trial if such member served as investigating officer in the case or served as a member of the court-martial before which such trial was conducted, or served as military judge, trial or defense counsel, or reviewing officer of such trial.

Art. 67. Review by the Court of Appeals for the Armed Forces

(a) The Court of Appeals for the Armed Forces shall review the record in—

(1) all cases in which the sentence, as affirmed by a Court of Criminal Appeals, extends to death;

(2) all cases reviewed by a Court of Criminal Appeals which the Judge Advocate General orders sent to the Court of Appeals for the Armed Forces for review; and

(3) all cases reviewed by a Court of Criminal Appeals in which, upon petition of the accused and on good cause shown, the Court of Appeals for the Armed Forces has granted a review.

(b) The accused may petition the Court of Appeals for the Armed Forces for review of a decision of a Court of Criminal Appeals within 60 days from the earlier of—

(1) the date on which the accused is notified of the decision of the Court of Criminal Appeals; or

(2) the date on which a copy of the decision of the Court of Criminal Appeals, after being served on appellate counsel of record for the accused (if any), is deposited in the United States mails for delivery by first class certified mail to the accused at an address provided by the accused or, if no such address has

been provided by the accused, at the latest address listed for the accused in his official service record. The Court of Appeals for the Armed Forces shall act upon such a petition promptly in accordance with the rules of the court.

(c) In any case reviewed by it, the Court of Appeals for the Armed Forces may act only with respect to the findings and sentence as approved by the convening authority and as affirmed or set aside as incorrect in law by the Court of Criminal Appeals. In a case which the Judge Advocate General orders sent to the Court of Appeals for the Armed Forces, that action need be taken only with respect to the issues raised by him. In a case reviewed upon petition of the accused, that action need be taken only with respect to issues specified in the grant of review. The Court of Appeals for the Armed Forces shall take action only with respect to matters of law.

(d) If the Court of Appeals for the Armed Forces sets aside the findings and sentence, it may, except where the setting aside is based on lack of sufficient evidence in the record to support the findings, order a rehearing. If it sets aside the findings and sentence and does not order a rehearing, it shall order that the charges be dismissed.

(e) After it has acted on a case, the Court of Appeals for the Armed Forces may direct the Judge Advocate General to return the record to the Court of Criminal Appeals for further review in accordance with the decision of the Court. Otherwise, unless there is to be further action by the President or the Secretary concerned, the Judge Advocate General shall instruct the convening authority to take action in accordance with that decision. If the court has ordered a rehearing, but the convening authority finds a rehearing impracticable, he may dismiss the charges.

Art. 67a. Review by the Supreme Court

(a) Decisions of the United States Court of Appeals for the Armed Forces are subject to review by the Supreme Court by writ of certiorari as provided in section 1259 of title 28. The Supreme Court may not review by a writ of certiorari under this section any action of the Court of Appeals for the Armed Forces in refusing to grant a petition for review.

(b) The accused may petition the Supreme Court for a writ of certiorari without prepayment of fees and costs or security therefor and without filing the affidavit required by section 1915(a) of title 28.

Art. 68. Branch offices

The Secretary concerned may direct the Judge Advocate General to establish a branch office with any command. The branch office shall be under an Assistant Judge Advocate General who, with the consent of the Judge Advocate General, may establish a Court of Criminal Appeals with one or more panels. That Assistant Judge Advocate General and any Court of Criminal Appeals established by him may perform for that command under the general supervision of the Judge Advocate General, the respective duties which the Judge Advocate General and a Court of Criminal Appeals established by the Judge Advocate General would otherwise be required to perform as to all cases involving sentences not requiring approval by the President.

Art. 69. Review in the office of the Judge Advocate General

(a) The record of trial in each general court-martial that is not otherwise reviewed under article 66 shall be examined in the office of the Judge Advocate General if there is a finding of guilty and the accused does not waive or withdraw his right to appellate review under article 61. If any part of the findings or sentence is found to be unsupported in law or if reassessment of the sentence is appropriate, the Judge Advocate General may modify or set aside the findings or sentence or both.

(b) The findings or sentence, or both, in a court-martial case not reviewed under subsection (a) or under article 66 may be modified or set aside, in whole or in part, by the Judge Advocate General on the ground of newly discovered evidence, fraud on the court, lack of jurisdiction over the accused or the offense, error prejudicial to the substantial rights of the accused, or the appropriateness of the sentence. If such a case is considered upon application of the accused, the application must be filed in the office of the Judge Advocate General by the accused on or before the last day of the two-year period beginning on the date the sentence is approved under article 60(c), unless the accused establishes good cause for failure to file within that time.

(c) If the Judge Advocate General sets aside the findings or sentence, he may, except when the setting aside is based on lack of sufficient evidence in the record to support the findings, order a rehearing. If he sets aside the findings and sentence and does not order a rehearing, he shall order that the charges be dismissed. If the Judge Advocate General orders a rehearing but the convening authority finds a rehearing impractical, the convening authority shall dismiss the charges.

(d) A Court of Criminal Appeals may review, under article 66—

(1) any court-martial case which (A) is subject to action by the Judge Advocate General under this section, and (B) is sent to the Court of Criminal Appeals by order of the Judge Advocate General; and,

(2) any action taken by the Judge Advocate General under this section in such case.

(e) Notwithstanding article 66, in any case reviewed by a Court of Criminal Appeals under this section, the Court may take action only with respect to matters of law.

Art. 70. Appellate counsel

(a) The Judge Advocate General shall detail in his office one or more commissioned officers as appellate Government counsel, and one or more commissioned officers as appellate defense counsel, who are qualified under article 27(b)(1).

(b) Appellate Government counsel shall represent the United States before the Court of Criminal Appeals or the Court of Appeals for the Armed Forces when directed to do so by the Judge Advocate General. Appellate Government counsel may represent the United States before the Supreme Court in cases arising under this chapter when requested to do so by the Attorney General.

(c) Appellate defense counsel shall represent the accused before the Court of Criminal Appeals, the Court of Appeals for the Armed Forces, or the Supreme Court—

(1) when requested by the accused;

(2) when the United States is represented by counsel; or

(3) when the Judge Advocate General has sent the case to the Court of Appeals for the Armed Forces.

(d) The accused has the right to be represented before the Court of Criminal Appeals, the Court of Appeals for the Armed Forces, or the Supreme Court by civilian counsel if provided by him.

(e) Military appellate counsel shall also perform such other functions in connection with the review of court-martial cases as the Judge Advocate General directs.

Art. 71. Execution of sentence; suspension of sentence

(a) If the sentence of the court-martial extends to death, that part of the sentence providing for death may not be executed until approved by the President. In such a case, the President may commute, remit, or suspend the sentence, or any part thereof, as he sees fit. That part of the sentence providing for death may not be suspended.

(b) If in the case of a commissioned officer, cadet, or midshipman, the sentence of a court-martial extends to dismissal, that part of the sentence providing for dismissal may not be executed until approved by the Secretary concerned or such Under Secretary or Assistant Secretary as may be designated by the Secretary concerned. In such a case, the Secretary, Under Secretary or Assistant Secretary, as the case may be, may commute, remit, or suspend the sentence, or any part of the sentence, as he sees fit. In time of war or national emergency he may commute a sentence of dismissal to reduction to any enlisted grade. A person so reduced may be required to serve for the duration of the war or emergency and six months thereafter.

(c)(1) If a sentence extends to death, dismissal, or a dishonorable or bad-conduct discharge and if the right of the accused to appellate review is not waived, and an appeal is not withdrawn, under article 61, that part of the sentence extending to death, dismissal, or a dishonorable or bad-conduct discharge may not be executed until there is a final judgment as to the legality of the proceedings (and with respect to death or dismissal, approval under subsection (a) or (b), as appropriate). A judgment as to legality of the proceedings is final in such cases when review is completed by a Court of Criminal Appeals and—

(A) the time for the accused to file a petition for review by the Court of Appeals for the Armed Forces has expired and the accused has not filed a timely petition for such review and the case is not otherwise under review by that Court;

(B) such a petition is rejected by the Court of Appeals for the Armed Forces; or

(C) review is completed in accordance with the judgment of the Court of Appeals for the Armed Forces and—

(i) a petition for a writ of certiorari is not filed within the time limits prescribed by the Supreme Court;

(ii) such a petition is rejected by the Supreme Court; or

(iii) review is otherwise completed in accordance with the judgment of the Supreme Court.

(2) If a sentence extends to dismissal or a dishonorable or bad-conduct discharge and if the right of the accused to appellate review is waived, or an appeal is withdrawn, under article 61, that part of the sentence extending to dismissal or a bad-conduct or dishonorable discharge may not be executed until review of the case by a judge advocate (and any action of that review) under article 64 is completed. Any other part of a court-martial sentence may be ordered executed by the convening authority or other person acting on the case under article 60 when approved by him under that section.

(d) The convening authority or other person acting on article 60 may suspend the execution of any sentence or part thereof, except a death sentence.

Art. 72. Vacation of suspension

(a) Before the vacation of the suspension of a special court-martial sentence which as approved includes a bad-conduct discharge, or of any general court-martial sentence, the officer having special court-martial jurisdiction over the probationer shall hold a hearing on the alleged violation of probation. The probationer shall be represented at the hearing by counsel if he so desires.

(b) The record of the hearing and the recommendation of the officer having special court-martial jurisdiction shall be sent for action to the officer exercising general court-martial jurisdiction over the probationer. If he vacates the suspension, any unexecuted part of the sentence, except a dismissal, shall be executed, subject to applicable restrictions in article 71(c). The vacation of the suspension of a dismissal is not effective until approved by the Secretary concerned.

(c) The suspension of any other sentence may be vacated by any authority competent to convene, for the command in which the accused is serving or assigned, a court of the kind that imposed the sentence.

Art. 73. Petition for a new trial

At any time within two years after approval by the convening authority of a court-martial sentence, the accused may petition the Judge Advocate General for a new trial on the grounds of newly discovered evidence or fraud on the court. If the accused's case is pending before a Court of Criminal Appeals or before the Court of Appeals for the Armed Forces, the Judge Advocate General shall refer the petition to the appropriate court for action. Otherwise the Judge Advocate General shall act upon the petition.

Art. 74. Remission and suspension

(a) The Secretary concerned and, when designated by him, any Under Secretary, Assistant Secretary, Judge Advocate General, or commanding officer may remit or suspend any part or amount of the unexecuted part of any sentence, including all uncollected forfeitures other than a sentence approved by the President.

(b) The Secretary concerned may, for good cause, substitute an administrative form of discharge for a discharge or dismissal executed in accordance with the sentence of a court-martial.

Art. 75. Restoration

(a) Under such regulations as the President may prescribe, all rights, privileges, and property affected by an executed part of a court-martial sentence which has been set aside or disapproved, except an executed dismissal or discharge, shall be restored unless a new trial or rehearing is ordered and such executed part is included in a sentence imposed upon the new trial or rehearing.

(b) If a previously executed sentence of dishonorable or bad-conduct discharge is not imposed on a new trial, the Secretary concerned shall substitute therefore a form of discharge authorized for administrative issuance unless the accused is to serve out the remainder of this enlistment.

(c) If a previously executed sentence of dismissal is not imposed on a new trial, the Secretary concerned shall substitute therefore a form of discharge authorized for administrative issue, and the commissioned officer dismissed by the sentence may be reappointed by the President alone to such commissioned grade and with such rank as in the opinion of the President that former officer would have attained had he not been dismissed. The reappointment of such a former officer shall be without regard to the existence of a vacancy and shall affect the promotion status of other officers only insofar as the President may direct. All time between the dismissal and the reappointment shall be considered as actual service for all purposes, including the right to pay and allowances.

Art. 76. Finality of proceedings, findings, and sentences

The appellate review of records of trial provided by this chapter, the proceedings, findings, and sentences of courts-martial as approved, reviewed, or affirmed as required by this chapter, and all dismissals and discharges carried into execution under sentences by courts-martial following approval, review, or affirmation as required by this chapter, are final and conclusive. Orders publishing the proceedings of courts-martial and all action taken pursuant to those proceedings are binding upon all departments, courts, agencies, and officers of the United States, subject only to action upon a petition for a new trial as provided in article 73 and to action by the Secretary concerned as provided in article 74, and the authority of the President.

Art. 76a. Leave required to be taken pending review of certain court-martial convictions

Under regulations prescribed by the Secretary concerned, an accused who has been sentenced by a court-martial may be required to take leave pending completion of action under this subchapter if the sentence, as approved under article 60, includes an unsuspended dismissal or an unsuspended dishonorable or bad-conduct discharge. The accused may be required to begin such leave on the date on which the sentence is approved under article 60 or at any time after such date, and such leave may be continued until the date which action under this subchapter is completed or may be terminated at any earlier time.

Subchapter X. Punitive Articles

Art. 77. Principals

Any person punishable under this chapter who
(1) commits an offense punishable by this chapter, or aids, abets, counsels, commands, or procures its commission; or
(2) causes an act to be done which if directly performed by him would be punishable by this chapter;
is a principal.

Art. 78. Accessory after the fact

Any person subject to this chapter who, knowing that an offense punishable by this chapter has been committed, receives, comforts, or assists the offender in order to hinder or prevent his apprehension, trial, or punishment shall be punished as a court-martial may direct.

Art. 79. Conviction of lesser included offense

An accused may be found guilty of an offense necessarily included in the offense charged or of an attempt to commit either the offense charged or an offense necessarily included therein.

Art. 80. Attempts

(a) An act, done with specific intent to commit an offense under this chapter amounting to more than mere preparation and tending, even though failing, to effect its commission, is an attempt to commit that offense.

(b) Any person subject to this chapter who attempts to commit any offense punishable by this chapter shall be punished as a court-martial may direct, unless otherwise specifically prescribed.

(c) Any person subject to this chapter may be convicted of an attempt to commit an offense although it appears on the trial that the offense was consummated.

Art. 81. Conspiracy

Any person subject to this chapter who conspires with any other person to commit an offense under this chapter shall, if one or more of the conspirators does an act to effect the object of the conspiracy, be punished as a court-martial may direct.

Art. 82. Solicitation

(a) Any person subject to this chapter who solicits or advises another or others to desert in violation of article 85 or mutiny in violation of article 94 shall, if the offense solicited or advised is attempted or committed, be punished with the punishment provided for the commission of the offense, but, if the offense solicited or advised is not committed or attempted, he shall be punished as a court-martial may direct.

(b) Any person subject to this chapter who solicits or advises another or others to commit an act of misbehavior before the enemy in violation of article 99 or sedition in violation of article 94 shall, if the offense solicited or advised is committed, be punished with the punishment provided for the commission of the offense, but, if the offense solicited or advised is not committed, he shall be punished as a court-martial may direct.

Art. 83. Fraudulent enlistment, appointment, or separation

Any person who

(1) procures his own enlistment or appointment in the armed forces by knowingly false representation or deliberate concealment as to his qualifications for the enlistment or appointment and receives pay or allowances thereunder; or

(2) procures his own separation from the armed forces by knowingly false representation or deliberate concealment as to his eligibility for that separation;

shall be punished as a court-martial may direct.

Art. 84. Unlawful enlistment, appointment, or separation

Any person subject to this chapter who effects an enlistment or appointment in or a separation from the armed forces of any person who is known to him to be ineligible for that enlistment, appointment, or separation because it is prohibited by law, regulation, or order shall be punished as a court-martial may direct.

Art. 85. Desertion

(a) Any member of the armed forces who—

(1) without authority goes or remains absent from his unit, organization, or place of duty with intent to remain away therefrom permanently;

(2) quits his unit, organization, or place of duty with intent to avoid hazardous duty or to shirk important service; or

(3) without being regularly separated from one of the armed forces enlists or accepts an appointment in the same or another one of the armed forces without fully disclosing the fact that he has not been regularly separated, or enters any foreign armed service except when authorized by the United States;

is guilty of desertion.

(b) Any commissioned officer of the armed forces who, after tender of his resignation and before notice of its acceptance, quits his post or proper duties without leave and with intent to remain away therefrom permanently is guilty of desertion.

(c) Any person found guilty of desertion or attempt to desert shall be punished, if the offense is committed in time of war, by death or such other punishment as a court-martial may direct, but if the desertion or attempt to desert occurs at any other time, by such punishment, other than death, as a court-martial may direct.

Art. 86. *Absence without leave*

Any member of the armed forces who, without authority—
(1) fails to go to his appointed place of duty at the time prescribed;
(2) goes from that place; or
(3) absents himself or remains absent from his unit, organization, or place of duty at which he is required to be at the time prescribed;
shall be punished as a court-martial may direct.

Art. 87. *Missing movement*

Any person subject to this chapter who through neglect or design misses the movement of a ship, aircraft, or unit with which he is required in the course of duty to move shall be punished as a court-martial may direct.

Art. 88. *Contempt toward officials*

Any commissioned officer who uses contemptuous words against the President, the Vice President, Congress, the Secretary of Defense, the Secretary of a military department, the Secretary of Transportation, or the Governor or legislature of any State, Territory, Commonwealth, or possession in which he is on duty or present shall be punished as a court-martial may direct.

Art. 89. *Disrespect toward superior commissioned officer*

Any person subject to this chapter who behaves with disrespect toward his superior commissioned officer shall be punished as a court-martial may direct.

Art. 90. *Assaulting or willfully disobeying superior commissioned officer*

Any person subject to this chapter who—
(1) strikes his superior commissioned officer or draws or lifts up any weapon or offers any violence against him while he is in the execution of his office; or
(2) willfully disobeys a lawful command of his superior commissioned officer;

shall be punished, if the offense is committed in time of war, by death or such other punishment as a court-martial may direct, and if the offense is committed at any other time, by such punishment, other than death, as a court-martial may direct.

Art. 91. *Insubordinate conduct toward warrant officer, noncommissioned officer, or petty officer*

Any warrant officer or enlisted member who
(1) strikes or assaults a warrant officer, noncommissioned officer, or petty officer, while that officer is in the execution of his office;
(2) willfully disobeys the lawful order of a warrant officer, noncommissioned officer, or petty officer; or
(3) treats with contempt or is disrespectful in language or deportment toward a warrant officer, noncommissioned officer, or petty officer while that officer is in the execution of his office;
shall be punished as a court-martial may direct.

Art. 92. *Failure to obey order or regulation*

Any person subject to this chapter who—
(1) violates or fails to obey any lawful general order or regulation;
(2) having knowledge of any other lawful order issued by a member of the armed forces, which it is his duty to obey, fails to obey the order; or
(3) is derelict in the performance of his duties;
shall be punished as a court-martial may direct.

Art. 93. *Cruelty and maltreatment*

Any person subject to this chapter who is guilty of cruelty toward, or oppression or maltreatment of, any person subject to his orders shall be punished as a court-martial may direct.

Art. 94. *Mutiny or sedition*

(a) Any person subject to this chapter who—
(1) with intent to usurp or override lawful military authority, refuses, in concert with any other person,

to obey orders or otherwise do his duty or creates any violence or disturbance is guilty of mutiny;

(2) with intent to cause the overthrow or destruction of lawful civil authority, creates, in concert with any other person, revolt, violence, or other disturbance against that authority is guilty of sedition;

(3) fails to do his utmost to prevent and suppress a mutiny or sedition being committed in his presence, or fails to take all reasonable means to inform his superior commissioned officer or commanding officer of a mutiny or sedition which he knows or has reason to believe is taking place, is guilty of a failure to suppress or report a mutiny or sedition.

(b) A person who is found guilty of attempted mutiny, sedition, or failure to suppress or report a mutiny or sedition shall be punished by death or such other punishment as a court-martial may direct.

Art. 95. Resistance, breach of arrest, and escape

Any person subject to this chapter who resists apprehension or breaks arrest or who escapes from custody or confinement shall be punished as a court-martial may direct.

Art. 96. Releasing prisoner without proper authority

Any person subject to this chapter who, without proper authority, releases any prisoner committed to his charge, or who through neglect or design suffers any such prisoner to escape, shall be punished as a court-martial may direct, whether or not the prisoner was committed in strict compliance with law.

Art. 97. Unlawful detention

Any person subject to this chapter who, except as provided by law, apprehends, arrests, or confines any person shall be punished as a court-martial may direct.

Art. 98. Noncompliance with procedural rules

Any person subject to this chapter who

(1) is responsible for unnecessary delay in the disposition of any case of a person accused of an offense under this chapter; or

(2) knowingly and intentionally fails to enforce or comply with any provision of this chapter regulating the proceedings before, during, or after trial of an accused; shall be punished as a court-martial may direct.

Art. 99. Misbehavior before the enemy

Any person subject to this chapter who before or in the presence of the enemy—

(1) runs away;

(2) shamefully abandons, surrenders, or delivers up any command, unit, place, or military property which it is his duty to defend;

(3) through disobedience, neglect, or intentional misconduct endangers the safety of any such command, unit, place, or military property;

(4) casts away his arms or ammunition;

(5) is guilty of cowardly conduct;

(6) quits his place of duty to plunder or pillage;

(7) causes false alarms in any command, unit, or place under control of the armed forces;

(8) willfully fails to do his utmost to encounter, engage, capture, or destroy, combatants, vessels, aircraft, or any other thing, which it is his duty so to encounter, engage, capture, or destroy; or

(9) does not afford all practicable relief and assistance to any troops, combatants, vessels, or aircraft of the armed forces belonging to the United States or their allies when engaged in battle; shall be punished by death or such other punishment as a court-martial may direct.

Art. 100. Subordinate compelling surrender

Any person subject to this chapter who compels or attempts to compel the commander of any place, vessel, aircraft, or other military property, or of any body of members of the armed forces, to give it up to an enemy or to abandon it, or who strikes the colors or flag to any enemy without proper authority, shall be punished by death or such other punishment as a court-martial may direct.

Art. 101. Improper use of countersign

Any person subject to this chapter who in time of war discloses the parole or countersign to any person not entitled to receive it or who gives to another who is entitled to receive and use the parole or countersign a different parole or countersign from that which, to his knowledge, he was authorized and required to give, shall be punished by death or such other punishment as a court-martial may direct.

Art. 102. *Forcing a safeguard*

Any person subject to this chapter who forces a safeguard shall suffer death or such other punishment as a court-martial may direct.

Art. 103. *Captured or abandoned property*

(a) All persons subject to this chapter shall secure all public property taken from the enemy for the service of the United States, and shall give notice and turn over to the proper authority without delay all captured or abandoned property in their possession, custody, or control.

(b) Any person subject to this chapter who—

(1) fails to carry out the duties prescribed in subsection (a);

(2) buys, sells, trades, or in any way deals in or disposes of captured or abandoned property, whereby he receives or expects any profit, benefit, or advantage to himself or another directly or indirectly connected with himself; or

(3) engages in looting or pillaging;

shall be punished as a court-martial may direct.

Art. 104. *Aiding the enemy*

Any person who—

(1) aids, or attempts to aid, the enemy with arms, ammunition, supplies, money, or other things; or

(2) without proper authority, knowingly harbors or protects or gives intelligence to, or communicates or corresponds with or holds any intercourse with the enemy, either directly or indirectly;

shall suffer death or such other punishment as a court-martial or military commission may direct.

Art. 105. *Misconduct as prisoner*

Any person subject to this chapter who, while in the hands of the enemy in time of war—

(1) for the purpose of securing favorable treatment by his captors acts without proper authority in a manner contrary to law, custom, or regulation, to the detriment of others of whatever nationality held by the enemy as civilian or military prisoners; or

(2) while in a position of authority over such persons maltreat them without justifiable cause;

shall be punished as a court-martial may direct.

Art. 106. *Spies*

Any person who in time of war is found lurking as a spy or acting as a spy in or about any place, vessel, or aircraft, within the control or jurisdiction of any of the armed forces, or in or about any shipyard, any manufacturing or industrial plant, or any other place or institution engaged in work in aid of the prosecution of the war by the United States, or elsewhere, shall be tried by a general court-martial or by a military commission and on conviction shall be punished by death.

Art. 106a. *Espionage*

(a)(1) Any person subject to this chapter who, with intent or reason to believe that it is to be used to the injury of the United States or to the advantage of a foreign nation, communicates, delivers, or transmits, or attempts to communicate, deliver, or transmit, to any entity described in paragraph (2), either directly or indirectly, any thing described in paragraph (3) shall be punished as a court-martial may direct, except that if the accused is found guilty of an offense that directly concerns (A) nuclear weaponry, military spacecraft or satellites, early warning systems, or other means of defense or retaliation against large scale attack, (B) war plans, (C) communications intelligence or cryptographic information, or (D) any other major weapons system or major element of defense strategy, the accused shall be punished by death or such other punishment as a court-marital may direct.

(2) An entity referred to in paragraph (1) is—

(A) a foreign government;

(B) a faction or party or military or naval force within a foreign country, whether recognized or unrecognized by the United States; or

(C) a representative, officer, agent, employee, subject, or citizen of such a government, faction, party, or force.

(3) A thing referred to in paragraph (1) is a document, writing, code book, signal book, sketch, photograph, photographic negative, blueprint, plan, map, model, note, instrument, appliance, or information relating to the national defense.

(b)(1) No person may be sentenced by court-martial to suffer death for an offense under this section (article) unless—

(A) the members of the court-martial unanimously find at least one of the aggravating factors set out in subsection (c); and

(B) the members unanimously determine that any extenuating or mitigating circumstances are substantially outweighed by any aggravating circumstances, including the aggravating factors set out under subsection (c).

(2) Findings under this subsection may be based on—

(A) evidence introduced on the issue of guilt or innocence;

(B) evidence introduced during the sentencing proceeding; or

(C) all such evidence.

(3) The accused shall be given broad latitude to present matters in extenuation and mitigation.

(c) A sentence of death may be adjudged by a court-martial for an offense under this section (article) only if the members unanimously find, beyond a reasonable doubt, one or more of the following aggravating factors:

(1) The accused has been convicted of another offense involving espionage or treason for which either a sentence of death or imprisonment for life was authorized by statute.

(2) In the commission of the offense, the accused knowingly created a grave risk of substantial damage to the national security.

(3) In the commission of the offense, the accused knowingly created a grave risk of death to another person.

(4) Any other factor that may be prescribed by the President by regulations under Article 36.

Art. 107. False official statements

Any person subject to this chapter who, with intent to deceive, signs any false record, return, regulation, order, or other official document, knowing it to be false, or makes any other false official statement knowing it to be false, shall be punished as a court-marital may direct.

Art. 108. Military property of United States—Loss, damage, destruction, or wrongful disposition

Any person subject to this chapter who, without proper authority—

(1) sells or otherwise disposes of;

(2) willfully or through neglect damages, destroys, or loses; or

(3) willfully or through neglect suffers to be lost, damaged, sold, or wrongfully disposed of;

any military property of the United States, shall be punished as a court-martial may direct.

Art. 109. Property other than military property of United States—Waste, spoilage, or destruction

Any person subject to this chapter who willfully or recklessly wastes, spoils, or otherwise willfully and wrongfully destroys or damages any property other than military property of the United States shall be punished as a court-martial may direct.

Art. 110. Improper hazarding of vessel

(a) Any person subject to this chapter who willfully and wrongfully hazards or suffers to be hazarded any vessel of the armed forces shall suffer death or such punishment as a court-martial may direct.

(b) Any person subject to this chapter who negligently

hazards or suffers to be hazarded any vessel of the armed forces shall be punished as a court-martial may direct.

Art. 111. Drunken or reckless operation of a vehicle, aircraft, or vessel

Any person subject to this chapter who—
(1) operates or physically controls any vehicle, aircraft, or vessel in a reckless or wanton manner or while impaired by a substance described in article 112a(b), or (2) operates or is in actual physical control of any vehicle, aircraft, or vessel while drunk or when the alcohol concentration in the person's blood or breath is 0.10 grams of alcohol per 100 milliliters of blood or 0.10 grams of alcohol per 210 liters of breath, as shown by chemical analysis, shall be punished as a court-martial may direct.

Art. 112. Drunk on duty

Any person subject to this chapter other than a sentinel or lookout, who is found drunk on duty, shall be punished as a court-martial may direct.

Art. 112a. Wrongful use, possession, etc., of controlled substances

(a) Any person subject to this chapter who wrongfully uses, possesses, manufactures, distributes, imports into the customs territory of the United States, exports from the United States, or introduces into an installation, vessel, vehicle, or aircraft used by or under the control of the armed forces a substance described in subsection (b) shall be punished as a court-martial may direct.
(b) The substances referred to in subsection (a) are the following:
(1) Opium, heroin, cocaine, amphetamine, lysergic acid diethylamide, methamphetamine, phencyclidine, barbituric acid, and marijuana and any compound or derivative of any such substance.
(2) Any substance not specified in clause (1) that is listed on a schedule of controlled substances prescribed by the President for the purposes of this article.
(3) Any other substance not specified in clause (1) or contained on a list prescribed by the President under clause (2) that is listed in schedules I through V of section 202 of the Controlled Substances Act (21 USC 812).

Art. 113. Misbehavior of sentinel

Any sentinel or lookout who is found drunk or sleeping upon his post or leaves it before being regularly relieved, shall be punished, if the offense is committed in time of war, by death or such other punishment as a court-martial may direct, but if the offense is at any other time, by such punishment other than death as a court-martial may direct.

Art 114. Dueling

Any person subject to this chapter who fights or promotes, or is concerned in or connives at fighting a duel, or who, having knowledge of a challenge sent or about to be sent, fails to report the fact promptly to the proper authority, shall be punished as a court-martial may direct.

Art. 115. Malingering

Any person subject to this chapter who for the purpose of avoiding work, duty, or service—
(1) feigns illness, physical disablement, mental lapse, or derangement; or
(2) intentionally inflicts self-injury;
shall be punished as a court-martial may direct.

Art. 116. Riot or breach of peace

Any person subject to this chapter who causes or participates in any riot or breach of the peace shall be punished as a court-martial may direct.

Art. 117. Provoking speeches or gestures

Any person subject to this chapter who uses provoking or reproachful words or gestures towards any other person subject to this chapter shall be punished as a court-martial may direct.

Art. 118. Murder

Any person subject to this chapter who, without justification or excuse, unlawfully kills a human being, when he—
(1) has a premeditated design to kill;
(2) intends to kill or inflict great bodily harm;
(3) is engaged in an act which is inherently dangerous to another and evinces a wanton disregard of human life; or
(4) is engaged in the perpetration or attempted perpetration of burglary, sodomy, rape, robbery, or aggravated arson;
is guilty of murder, and shall suffer such punishment as a court-martial may direct, except that if found guilty under clause (1) or (4), he shall suffer death or imprisonment for life as a court-martial may direct.

Art. 119. Manslaughter

(a) Any person subject to this chapter who, with an intent to kill or inflict great bodily harm, unlawfully kills a human being in the heat of sudden passion caused by adequate provocation is guilty of voluntary manslaughter and shall be punished as a court-martial may direct.
(b) Any person subject to this chapter who, without an intent to kill or inflict great bodily harm, unlawfully kills a human being—
(1) by culpable negligence; or
(2) while perpetrating or attempting to perpetrate an offense, other than those named in clause (4) of article 118, directly affecting the person;
is guilty of involuntary manslaughter and shall be punished as a court-martial may direct.

Art. 120. Rape and carnal knowledge

(a) Any person subject to this chapter who commits an act of sexual intercourse, by force and without consent, is guilty of rape and shall be punished by death or such other punishment as a court-martial may direct.

(b) Any person subject to this chapter who, under circumstances not amounting to rape, commits an act of sexual intercourse with a female not his wife who has not attained the age of sixteen years, is guilty of carnal knowledge and shall be punished as a court-martial may direct.
(c) Penetration, however slight, is sufficient to complete either of these offenses.

Art. 121. Larceny and wrongful appropriation

(a) Any person subject to this chapter who wrongfully takes, obtains, or withholds, by any means, from the possession of the owner or of any other person any money, personal property, or article of value of any kind—
(1) with intent permanently to deprive or defraud another person of the use and benefit of property or to appropriate it to his own use or the use of any person other than the owner, steals that property and is guilty of larceny; or
(2) with intent temporarily to deprive or defraud another person of the use and benefit of property or to appropriate it to his own use or the use of any person other than the owner;
is guilty of wrongful appropriation.
(b) Any person found guilty of larceny or wrongful appropriation shall be punished as a court-martial may direct.

Art. 122. Robbery

Any person subject to this chapter who with intent to steal takes anything of value from the person or in the presence of another, against his will, by means of force or violence or fear of immediate or future injury to his person or property or to the person or property of a relative or member of his family or of anyone in his company at the time of the robbery, is guilty of robbery and shall be punished as a court-martial may direct.

Art. 123. Forgery

Any person subject to this chapter who, with intent to defraud—
(1) falsely makes or alters any signature, to, or any part of, any writing which would, if genuine, apparently im-

pose a legal liability on another or change his legal right or liability to his prejudice; or

(2) utters, offers, issues, or transfers such a writing, known by him to be so made or altered;

is guilty of forgery and shall be punished as a court-martial may direct.

Art. 123a. Making, drawing, or uttering check, draft, or order without sufficient funds

Any person subject to this chapter who—

(1) for the procurement of any article or thing of value, with intent to defraud; or

(2) for the payment of any past due obligation, or for any other purpose, with intent to deceive;

makes, draws, utters, or delivers any check, draft, or order for the payment of money upon any bank or other depository, knowing at the time that the maker or drawer has not or will not have sufficient funds in, or credit with, the bank or other depository for the payment of that check, draft, or order in full upon its presentment, shall be punished as a court-martial may direct. The making, drawing, uttering, or delivering by a maker or drawer of a check, draft or order, payment of which is refused by the drawee because of insufficient funds of the maker or drawer in the drawee's possession or control, is prima facie evidence of his intent to defraud or deceive and of his knowledge of insufficient funds in, or credit with, that bank or other depository, unless the maker or drawer pays the holder the amount due within five days after receiving notice, orally or in writing, that the check, draft, or order was not paid on presentment. In this section, the word "credit" means an arrangement or understanding, express or implied, with the bank or other depository for the payment of that check, draft, or order.

Art. 124. Maiming

Any person subject to this chapter who, with intent to injure, disfigure, or disable, inflicts upon the person of another an injury which

(1) seriously disfigures his person by a mutilation thereof;

(2) destroys or disables any member or organ of his body; or

(3) seriously diminishes his physical vigor by the injury of any member or organ;

is guilty of maiming and shall be punished as a court-martial may direct.

Art. 125. Sodomy

(a) Any person subject to this chapter who engages in unnatural carnal copulation with another person of the same or opposite sex or with an animal is guilty of sodomy. Penetration, however slight, is sufficient to complete the offense.

(b) Any person found guilty of sodomy shall be punished as a court-martial may direct.

Art. 126. Arson

(a) Any person subject to this chapter who willfully and maliciously burns or sets on fire an inhabited dwelling, or any other structure, movable or immovable, wherein to the knowledge of the offender there is at the time a human being, is guilty of aggravated arson and shall be punished as court-martial may direct.

(b) Any person subject to this chapter who willfully and maliciously burns or sets fire to the property of another, except as provided in subsection (a), is guilty of simple arson and shall be punished as a court-martial may direct.

Art. 127. Extortion

Any person subject to this chapter who communicates threats to another person with the intention thereby to obtain anything of value or any acquittance, advantage, or immunity is guilty of extortion and shall be punished as a court-martial may direct.

Art. 128. Assault

(a) Any person subject to this chapter who attempts or offers with unlawful force or violence to do bodily harm to another person, whether or not the attempt or offer is consummated, is guilty of assault and shall be punished as a court-martial may direct.

(b) Any person subject to this chapter who—

(1) commits an assault with a dangerous weapon or other means or force likely to produce death or grievous bodily harm; or

(2) commits an assault and intentionally inflicts grievous bodily harm with or without a weapon;

is guilty of aggravated assault and shall be punished as a court-martial may direct.

Art. 129. Burglary

Any person subject to this chapter who, with intent to commit an offense punishable under articles 118–128, breaks and enters, in the nighttime, the dwelling house of another, is guilty of burglary and shall be punished as a court-martial may direct.

Art. 130. Housebreaking

Any person subject to this chapter who unlawfully enters the building or structure of another with intent to commit a criminal offense therein is guilty of housebreaking and shall be punished as a court-martial may direct.

Art. 131. Perjury

Any person subject to this chapter who in a judicial proceeding or in a course of justice willfully and corruptly—

(1) upon a lawful oath or in any form allowed by law to be substituted for an oath, gives any false testimony material to the issue or matter of inquiry; or

(2) in any declaration, certificate, verification, or statement under penalty or perjury as permitted under section 1746 of title 28, United States Code, subscribes any false statement material to the issue or matter of inquiry;

is guilty of perjury and shall be punished as a court-martial may direct.

Art. 132. Frauds against the United States

Any person subject to this chapter—

(1) who, knowing it to be false or fraudulent—

(A) makes any claim against the United States or any officer thereof; or

(B) presents to any person in the civil or military service thereof, for approval or payment, any claim against the United States or any officer thereof;

(2) who, for the purpose of obtaining the approval, allowance, or payment of any claim against the United States or any officer thereof—

(A) makes or uses any writing or other paper knowing it to contain any false or fraudulent statements;

(B) makes any oath to any fact or to any writing or other paper knowing the oath to be false; or

(C) forges or counterfeits any signature upon any writing or other paper, or uses any such signature knowing it to be forged or counterfeited;

(3) who, having charge, possession, custody, or control of any money, or other property of the United States, furnished or intended for the armed forces thereof, knowingly delivers to any person having authority to receive it, any amount thereof less than that for which he receives a certificate or receipt; or

(4) who, being authorized to make or deliver any paper certifying the receipt of any property of the United States furnished or intended for the armed forces thereof, makes or delivers to any person without having full knowledge of the truth of the statements therein contained and with intent to defraud the United States;

shall, upon conviction, be punished as a court-martial may direct.

Art. 133. Conduct unbecoming an officer and a gentleman

Any commissioned officer, cadet, or midshipman who is convicted of conduct unbecoming an officer and a gentleman shall be punished as a court-martial may direct.

Art. 134. General article

Though not specifically mentioned in this chapter, all disorders and neglects to the prejudice of good order and discipline in the armed forces, all conduct of a nature to bring discredit upon the armed forces, and crimes and offenses not capital, of which persons subject to this chapter may be guilty, shall be taken cognizance of by a general, special, or summary court-martial, according to the nature and degree of the offense, and shall be punished at the discretion of that court.

Subchapter XI. Miscellaneous Provisions

Art. 135. Courts of inquiry

(a) Courts of inquiry to investigate any matter may be convened by any person authorized to convene a general court-martial or by any other person designated by the Secretary concerned for that purpose, whether or not the persons involved have requested such an inquiry.

(b) A court of inquiry consists of three or more commissioned officers. For each court of inquiry the convening authority shall also appoint counsel for the court.

(c) Any person subject to this chapter whose conduct is subject to inquiry shall be designated as a party. Any person subject to this chapter or employed by the Department of Defense who has a direct interest in the subject of inquiry has the right to be designated as a party upon request to the court. Any person designated as a party shall be given due notice and has the right to be present, to be represented by counsel, to cross-examine witnesses, and to introduce evidence.

(d) Members of a court of inquiry may be challenged by a party, but only for cause stated to the court.

(e) The members, counsel, the reporter, and interpreters of courts of inquiry shall take an oath to faithfully perform their duties.

(f) Witnesses may be summoned to appear and testify and be examined before courts of inquiry, as provided for courts-martial.

(g) Courts of inquiry shall make findings of fact but may not express opinions or make recommendations unless required to do so by the convening authority.

(h) Each court of inquiry shall keep a record of its proceedings, which shall be authenticated by the signatures of the president and counsel for the court and forwarded to the convening authority. If the record cannot be authenticated by the president, it shall be signed by a member in lieu of the president. If the record cannot be authenticated by the counsel for the court, it shall be signed by a member in lieu of the counsel.

Art. 136. Authority to administer oaths and to act as notary

(a) The following persons on active duty or performing inactive-duty training may administer oaths for the purposes of military administration, including military justice:

(1) All judge advocates.

(2) All summary courts-martial.

(3) All adjutants, assistant adjutants, acting adjutants, and personnel adjutants.

(4) All commanding officers of the Navy, Marine Corps, and Coast Guard.

(5) All staff judge advocates and legal officers, and acting or assistant staff judge advocates and legal officers.

(6) All other persons designated by regulations of the armed forces or by statute.

(b) The following persons on active duty or performing inactive-duty training may administer oaths necessary in the performance of their duties:

(1) The president, military judge, trial counsel, and assistant trial counsel for all general and special courts-martial.

(2) The president and the counsel for the court of any court of inquiry.

(3) All officers designated to take a deposition.

(4) All persons detailed to conduct an investigation.

(5) All recruiting officers.

(6) All other persons designated by regulations of the armed forces or by statute.

Art. 137. Articles to be explained

(a)(1) The sections of this title (articles of the Uniform Code of Military Justice) specified in paragraph (3) shall be carefully explained to each enlisted member at the time of (or within six days after)—

(A) the member's initial entrance on active duty; or

(B) the member's initial entrance into a duty status with a reserve component.

(2) Such sections (articles) shall be explained again—

(A) after the member has completed six months of active duty or, in the case of a member of a reserve component, after the member has completed basic or recruit training; and

    (B) at the time when the member reenlists.

  (3) This subsection applies with respect to articles 2, 3, 7–15, 25, 27, 31, 38, 55, 77–134, and 137–139.

(b) The text of the Uniform Code of Military Justice and of the regulations prescribed by the President under such Code shall be made available to a member on active duty or to a member of a reserve component, upon request by the member, for the member's personal examination.

Art. 138. Complaints of wrongs

Any member of the armed forces who believes himself wronged by his commanding officer, and who, upon due application to that commanding officer, is refused redress, may complain to any superior commissioned officer, who shall forward the complaint to the officer exercising general court-martial jurisdiction over the officer against whom it is made. The officer exercising general court-martial jurisdiction shall examine into the complaint and take proper measures for redressing the wrong complained of; and he shall, as soon as possible, send to the Secretary concerned a true statement of that complaint, with the proceedings had thereon.

Art. 139. Redress of injuries to property

(a) Whenever complaint is made to any commanding officer that willful damage has been done to the property of any person or that his property has been wrongfully taken by members of the armed forces, he may, under such regulations as the Secretary concerned may prescribe, convene a board to investigate the complaint. The board shall consist of from one to three commissioned officers and, for the purpose of that investigation, it has power to summon witnesses and examine them upon oath, to receive depositions or other documentary evidence, and to assess the damages sustained against the responsible parties. The assessment of damages made by the board is subject to the approval of the commanding officer, and in the amount approved by him shall be charged against the pay of the offenders.

The order of the commanding officer directing charges herein authorized is conclusive on any disbursing officer for the payment by him to the injured parties of the damages as assessed and approved.

(b) If the offenders cannot be ascertained, but the organization or detachment to which they belong is known, charges totaling the amount of damages assessed and approved may be made in such proportion as may be considered just upon the individual members thereof who are shown to have been present at the scene at the time the damages complained of were inflicted, as determined by the approved findings of the board.

Art. 140. Delegation by the President

The President may delegate any authority vested in him under this chapter, and provide for the subdelegation of any such authority.

Subchapter XII. Court of Appeals for the Armed Forces

Art. 141. Status

There is a court of record known as the United States Court of Appeals for the Armed Forces. The court is established under article I of the Constitution. The court is located for administrative purposes only in the Department of Defense.

Art. 142. Judges

(a) Number. The United States Court of Appeals for the Armed Forces consists of five judges.

(b) Appointment; qualification.

  (1) Each judge of the court shall be appointed from civilian life by the President, by and with the advice and consent of the Senate, for a specified term determined under paragraph (2). A judge may serve as a senior judge as provided in subsection (e).

  (2) The term of a judge shall expire as follows:

    (A) In the case of a judge who is appointed after March 31 and before October 1 of any year, the term shall expire on September 30 of the year in which the fifteenth anniversary of the appointment occurs.

(B) In the case of a judge who is appointed after September 30 of any year and before April 1 of the following year, the term shall expire fifteen years after such September 30.

(3) Not more than three of the judges of the court may be appointed from the same political party, and no person may be appointed to be a judge of the court unless the person is a member of the bar of a Federal court or the highest court of a State.

(4) For purposes of appointment of judges to the court, a person retired from the armed forces after 20 or more years of active service (whether or not such person is on the retired list) shall not be considered to be in civilian life.

(c) Removal. Judges of the court may be removed from office by the President, upon notice and hearing, for—

(1) neglect of duty;

(2) misconduct; or

(3) mental or physical disability.

A judge may not be removed by the President for any other cause.

MANUAL FOR COURTS-MARTIAL (MCM) MAXIMUM PUNISHMENT CHART

Article	Offense	Discharge	Confinement	Forfeitures
82	Solicitation			
	If solicited offense not committed:			
	Solicitation to desert[1]	DD, BCD	3 yrs.[1]	Total
	Solicitation to mutiny[1]	DD, BCD	10 yrs.[1]	Total
	Solicitation to commit act of misbehavior before enemy[1]	DD, BCD	10 yrs.[1]	Total
	Solicitation to commit act of sedition[1]	DD, BCD	10 yrs.[1]	Total
83	Fraudulent enlistment, appointment	DD, BCD	2 yrs.	Total
	Fraudulent separation	DD, BCD	5 yrs.	Total
84	Effecting unlawful enlistment, appointment, separation	DD, BCD	5 yrs.	Total
85	Desertion			
	Intent to avoid hazardous duty, shirk important service[1]	DD, BCD	5 yrs.[1]	Total
	Other cases			
	Terminated by apprehension	DD, BCD	3 yrs.[1]	Total
	Otherwise terminated	DD, BCD	2 yrs.[1]	Total
86	Absence without leave			
	Failure to go, going from place of duty	None	1 mo.	2/3 1 mo.
	Absence from unit, organization, etc.			
	Not more than 3 days	None	1 mo.	2/3 1 mo.
	More than 3, not more than 30 days	None	6 mos.	2/3 6 mos.
	More than 30 days	DD, BCD	1 yr.	Total
	More than 30 days and terminated by apprehension	DD, BCD	1 yr., 6 mos.	Total

Note: 1. Suspended in time of war.

Article	Offense	Discharge	Confinement	Forfeitures
	Absence from guard or watch	None	3 mos.	2/3 3 mos.
	Absence from guard or watch with intent to abandon	BCD	6 mos.	Total
	Absence with intent to avoid maneuvers, field exercises	BCD	6 mos.	Total
87	Missing movement			
	Through design	DD, BCD	2 yrs.	Total
	Through neglect	BCD	1 yr.	Total
88	Contempt toward officials	Dismissal	1 yr.	Total
89	Disrespect toward superior commissioned officer	BCD	1 yr.	Total
90	Assaulting, willfully disobeying superior commissioned officer		1 yr.	Total
	Striking, drawing or lifting up any weapon or offering any violence toward superior commissioned officer execution of duty[1]	DD, BCD	10 yrs.[1]	Total
	Willfully disobeying lawful order of superior commissioned officer[1]	DD, BCD	5 yrs.[1]	Total
91	Insubordinate conduct toward warrant, noncommissioned, petty officer			
	Striking or assaulting:			
	Warrant officer	DD, BCD	5 yrs.	Total
	Superior noncommissioned officer	DD, BCD	3 yrs.	Total
	Other noncommissioned or petty officer	DD, BCD	1 yr.	Total
	Willfully disobeying:			
	Warrant officer	DD, BCD	2 yrs.	Total
	Noncommissioned or petty officer	BCD	1 yr.	Total
	Contempt, disrespect toward:			
	Warrant officer	BCD	9 mos.	Total
	Superior noncommissioned or petty officer	BCD	6 mos.	Total
	Other noncommissioned or petty officer	None	3 mos.	2/3 3 mos.
92	Failure to obey order, regulation			
	Violation, failure to obey general order or regulation	DD, BCD	2 yrs.	Total
	Violation, failure to obey other order	BCD	6 mos.	Total
	Dereliction in performance of duties			
	Through neglect, culpable inefficiency	None	3 mos.	2/3 3 mos.
	Willful	BCD	6 mos.	Total
93	Cruelty, maltreatment of subordinates	DD, BCD	1 yr.	Total
94	Mutiny & sedition	Death, DD, BCD	Life	Total

Article	Offense	Discharge	Confinement	Forfeitures
95	Resisting apprehension, breach of arrest; escape			
	Resisting apprehension	BCD	1 yr.	Total
	Breaking arrest	BCD	6 mos.	Total
	Escape from custody, pretrial confinement, or confinement on bread and water or diminished rations	DD, BCD	1 yr.	Total
	Escape from post-trial confinement	DD, BCD	5 yrs.	Total
96	Releasing prisoner without proper authority	DD, BCD	2 yrs.	Total
	Suffering prisoner to escape through neglect	BCD	1 yr.	Total
	Suffering prisoner to escape through design	DD, BCD	2 yrs.	Total
97	Unlawful detention	DD, BCD	3 yrs.	Total
98	Noncompliance with procedural rules, etc.			
	Unnecessary delay in disposition of case	BCD	6 mos.	Total
	Knowingly, intentionally failing to comply, enforce code	DD, BCD	5 yrs.	Total
99	Misbehavior before enemy	Death, DD, BCD	Life	Total
100	Subordinate compelling surrender	Death, DD, BCD	Life	Total
101	Improper use of countersign	Death, DD, BCD	Life	Total
102	Forcing safeguard	Death, DD, BCD	Life	Total
103	Captured, abandoned property; failure to secure, etc.			
	Of value of $100.00 or less	BCD	6 mos.	Total
	Of value of more than $100.00	DD, BCD	5 yrs.	Total
	Looting, pillaging	DD, BCD	Life	Total
104	Aiding the enemy	Death, DD, BCD	Life	Total
105	Misconduct as prisoner	DD, BCD	Life	Total
106	Spying	Mandatory Death, DD, BCD	Not applicable	Total
106a	Espionage	Death, DD, BCD	Life	Total
107	False official statements	DD, BCD	5 yrs.	Total
108	Military property; loss, damage, destruction, disposition			
	Selling, otherwise disposing			
	Of value of $100 or less	BCD	1 yr.	Total
	Of value of more than $100.00	DD, BCD	10 yrs.	Total
	Any firearm, explosive, or incendiary device	DD, BCD	10 yrs.	Total
	Damaging, destroying, losing or suffering to be lost, damaged, destroyed, sold, or wrongfully disposed:			

Article	Offense	Discharge	Confinement	Forfeitures
	Through neglect, of a value of:			
	$100.00 or less	None	6 mos.	2/3 6 mos.
	More than $100.00	BCD	1 yr.	Total
	Willfully, of a value of			
	$100.00 or less	BCD	1 yr.	Total
	More than $100.00	DD, BCD	10 yrs.	Total
	Any firearm, explosive, or incendiary device	DD, BCD	10 yrs.	Total
109	Property other than military property of U.S.: loss, damage, destruction, disposition:			
	Wasting, spoiling, destroying, or damaging property of a value of:			
	$100.00 or less	BCD	1 yr.	Total
	More than $100.00	DD, BCD	5 yrs.	Total
110	Hazarding a vessel			
	Willfully and wrongfully	Death, DD, BCD	Life	Total
	Negligently	DD, BCD	2 yrs.	Total
111	Drunken driving			
	Resulting in personal injury	DD, BCD	1 yr., 6 mos.	Total
	Other cases	BCD	6 mos.	Total
112	Drunk on duty	BCD	9 mos.	Total
112a	Wrongful use, possession, etc. of controlled substances			
	Wrongful use, possession, manufacture, or introduction of:			
	Amphetamine, cocaine, heroin, lysergic acid diethylamide, marijuana (except possession of less than 30 grams or use), methamphetamine, opium, phencyclidine, secobarbital, andSchedule I, II, and III controlled substances	DD, BCD	5 yrs.	Total
	Marijuana (possession of less than 30 grams or use), phenobarbital, and Schedule IV and V controlled substances	DD, BCD	2 yrs.	Total
	Wrongful distribution of, or, with intent to distribute, wrongful possession, manufacture, introduction, or wrongful importation of or exportation of:			
	Amphetamine, cocaine, heroin, lysergic acid diethylamide, marijuana, methamphetamine, opium, phencyclidine, secobarbital, and Schedule I, II, and III controlled substances	DD, BCD	15 yrs.	Total

Article	Offense	Discharge	Confinement	Forfeitures
	Phenobarbital and Schedule IV and V controlled substances	DD, BCD	10 yrs.	Total
113	Misbehavior of sentinel or lookout			
	In time of war	Death, DD, BCD	Life	Total
	In other time:			
	While receiving special pay	DD, BCD	10 yrs.	Total
	Other places	DD, BCD	1 yr.	Total
114	Dueling	DD, BCD	1 yr.	Total
115	Malingering			
	Feigning illness, etc.			
	In time of war, or while receiving special pay under 37 U.S.C. 310	DD, BCD	3 yrs.	Total
	Other	DD, BCD	1 yr.	Total
	Intentional self-inflicted injury			
	In time of war, or while receiving special pay	DD, BCD	10 yrs.	Total
	Other	DD, BCD	5 yrs.	Total
116	Riot	DD, BCD	10 yrs.	Total
	Breach of peace	None	6 mos.	2/3 6 mos.
117	Provoking speech, gestures	None	6 mos.	2/3 6 mos.
118	Murder			
	Article 118(1) or (4)	Death, mandatory minimum life, DD, BCD	Life	Total
	Article 118(2) or (3)	DD, BCD	Life	Total
119	Manslaughter			
	Voluntary	DD, BCD	10 yrs.	Total
	Involuntary	DD, BCD	3 yrs.	Total
120	Rape	Death, DD, BCD	Life	Total
	Carnal knowledge	DD, BCD	15 yrs.	Total
121	Larceny			
	Of military property of a value of $100.00 or less	BCD	1 yr.	Total
	Of property other than military property with a value of $100.00 or less	BCD	6 mos.	Total
	Of military property of a value of more than $100.00 or of any military motor vehicle, aircraft, vessel, firearm, or explosive	DD, BCD	10 yrs.	Total

Article	Offense	Discharge	Confinement	Forfeitures
	Of property other than military property of a value of more than $100.00 or any motor vehicle, aircraft, vessel, firearm, or explosive	DD, BCD	5 yrs.	Total
	Wrongful appropriation			
	Of value of $100.00 or less	None	3 mos.	2/3 3 mos.
	Of value of more than $100.00	BCD	6 mos.	Total
	Of vehicle, aircraft, vessel	DD, BCD	2 yrs.	Total
122	Robbery			
	Committed with a firearm	DD, BCD	15 yrs.	Total
	Other cases[1]	DD, BCD	10 yrs.	Total
123	Forgery	DD, BCD	5 yrs.	Total
123a	Checks, etc., insufficient funds, intent to deceive			
	To procure anything of value of:			
	$100.00 or less	BCD	6 mos.	Total
	More than $100.00	DD, BCD	5 yrs.	Total
	For payment of past due obligation, and other cases	BCD	6 mos.	Total
124	Maiming	DD, BCD	7 yrs.	Total
125	Sodomy			
	By force and without consent	DD, BCD	20 yrs.	Total
	With child under age of 16 years	DD, BCD	20 yrs.	Total
	Other cases	DD, BCD	5 yrs.	Total
126	Arson			
	Aggravated	DD, BCD	20 yrs.	Total
	Other cases, where property value is:			
	$100.00 or less	DD, BCD	1 yr.	Total
	More than $100.00	DD, BCD	5 yrs.	Total
127	Extortion	DD, BCD	3 yrs.	Total
128	Assaults			
	Simple assault	None	3 mos.	2/3 3 mos.
	Assault consummated by battery	BCD	6 mos.	Total
	Assault upon commissioned officer of U.S. or friendly power not in execution of office	DD, BCD	3 yrs.	Total
	Assault upon warrant officer, not in execution of office	DD, BCD	1 yr., 6 mos.	Total
	Assault upon noncommissioned or petty officer not in execution of office	BCD	6 mos.	Total

Article	Offense	Discharge	Confinement	Forfeitures
	Assault upon, in execution of office, person serving as sentinel, lookout, security policeman, military policeman, shore patrol, master at arms, or civil law enforcement	DD, BCD	3 yrs.	Total
	Assault consummated by battery upon child under age of 16 years	DD, BCD	2 yrs.	Total
	Assault with dangerous weapon or means likely to produce grievous bodily harm or death:			
	Committed with loaded firearm	DD, BCD	8 yrs.	Total
	Other cases	DD, BCD	3 yrs.	Total
	Assault in which grievous bodily harm is intentionally inflicted:			
	With a loaded firearm	DD, BCD	10 yrs.	Total
	Other cases	DD, BCD	5 yrs.	Total
129	Burglary	DD, BCD	10 yrs.	Total
130	Housebreaking	DD, BCD	5 yrs.	Total
131	Perjury	DD, BCD	5 yrs.	Total
132	Frauds against the United States			
	Offenses under article 132(1) or (2)	DD, BCD	5 yrs.	Total
	Offenses under article 132(3) or (4)			
	$100.00 or less	BCD	6 mos.	Total
	More than $100.00	DD, BCD	5 yrs.	Total
133	Conduct unbecoming officer	Dismissal	1 yr. or as prescribed	Total
134	Abusing public animal	None	3 mos.	2/3 3 mos.
	Adultery	DD, BCD	1 yr.	Total
	Assault, indecent	DD, BCD	5 yrs.	Total
	Assault			
	With intent to commit murder or rape	DD, BCD	20 yrs.	Total
	With intent to commit voluntary manslaughter, robbery, sodomy, arson, or burglary	DD, BCD	10 yrs.	Total
	With intent to commit housebreaking	DD, BCD	5 yrs.	Total
	Bigamy	DD, BCD	2 yrs.	Total
	Bribery	DD, BCD	5 yrs.	Total
	Graft	DD, BCD	3 yrs.	Total
	Burning with intent to defraud	DD, BCD	10 yrs.	Total
	Check, worthless, making and uttering—by dishonorably failing to maintain funds	BCD	6 mos.	Total

Article	Offense	Discharge	Confinement	Forfeitures
	Cohabitation, wrongful	None	4 mos.	2/3 4 mos.
	Correctional custody, escape from	DD, BCD	1 yr.	Total
	Correctional custody, breach of	BCD	6 mos.	Total
	Debt, dishonorably failing to pay	BCD	6 mos.	Total
	Disloyal statements	DD, BCD	3 yrs.	Total
	Disorderly conduct			
	Under such circumstances as to bring discredit	None	4 mos.	2/3 4 mos.
	Other cases	None	1 mo.	2/3 1 mo.
	Drunkenness			
	Aboard ship or under such circumstances as to bring discredit	None	3 mos.	2/3 3 mos.
	Other cases	None	1 mos.	2/3 1 mo.
	Drunk and disorderly			
	Aboard ship	BCD	6 mos.	Total
	Under such circumstances as to bring discredit	None	6 mos.	2/3 6 mos.
	Other cases	None	3 mos.	2/3 3 mos.
	Drinking liquor with prisoner	None	3 mos.	2/3 3 mos.
	Drunk prisoner	None	3 mos.	2/3 3 mos.
	Drunkenness—incapacitating oneself for performance of duties through prior indulgence in intoxicating liquor or drugs	None	3 mos.	2/3 3 mos.
	False or unauthorized pass offenses			
	Possessing or using with intent to defraud or deceive, or making, altering, counterfeiting, tampering with, or selling	DD, BCD	3 yrs.	Total
	All other cases	BCD	6 mos.	Total
	False pretenses, obtaining services under			
	Of a value of $100.00 or less	BCD	6 mos.	Total
	Of a value of more than $100.00	DD, BCD	5 yrs.	Total
	False swearing	DD, BCD	3 yrs.	Total
	Firearm, discharging—through negligence	None	3 mos.	2/3 3 mos.
	Firearm, discharging—willfully, under such circumstances as to endanger human life	DD, BCD	1 yr.	Total
	Fleeing scene of accident	BCD	6 mos.	Total
	Fraternization	Dismissal	2 yrs.	Total
	Gambling with subordinates	None	3 mos.	2/3 3 mos.
	Homicide, negligent	BCD	1 yr.	Total

Article	Offense	Discharge	Confinement	Forfeitures
	Impersonation			
	With intent to defraud	DD, BCD	3 yrs.	Total
	All other cases	BCD	6 mos.	Total
	Indecent act, liberties with child	DD, BCD	7 yrs.	Total
	Indecent exposure	BCD	6 mos.	Total
	Indecent language			
	Communicated to chid under 16 yrs	DD, BCD	2 yrs.	Total
	Other cases	BCD	6 mos.	Total
	Indecent acts with another	DD, BCD	5 yrs.	Total
	Jumping from vessel into the water	BCD	6 mos.	Total
	Kidnapping	DD, BCD	Life	Total
	Mail, taking, opening, secreting, destroying, or stealing	DD, BCD	5 yrs.	Total
	Mails, depositing or causing to be deposited obscene matters in	DD, BCD	5 yrs.	Total
	Misprision of serious offense	DD, BCD	3 yrs.	Total
	Obstructing justice	DD, BCD	5 yrs.	Total
	Wrongful interference with an adverse administrative proceeding	DD, BCD	5 yrs.	Total
	Pandering	DD, BCD	5 yrs.	Total
	Prostitution	DD, BCD	1 yr.	Total
	Parole, violation of	BCD	6 mos.	2/3 6 mos.
	Perjury, subornation of	DD, BCD	5 yrs.	Total
	Public record, altering, concealing, removing, mutilating, obliterating, or destroying			
	Quarantine, breaking	None	6 mos.	2/3 6 mos.
	Restriction, breaking	None	1 mo.	2/3 1 mo.
	Seizure, destruction, removal, or disposal of property to prevent	DD, BCD	1 yr.	Total
	Sentinel, lookout			
	Disrespect to	None	3 mos.	2/3 3 mos.
	Loitering or wrongfully sitting on post by			
	In time of war or while receiving special pay	DD, BCD	2 yrs.	Total
	Other cases	BCD	6 mos.	Total
	Soliciting another to commit an offense			

Article	Offense	Discharge	Confinement	Forfeitures
	Stolen property, knowingly receiving, buying, concealing			
	Of a value of $100.00 or less	BCD	6 mos.	Total
	Of a value of more than $100.00	DD, BCD	3 yrs.	Total
	Straggling	None	3 mos.	2/3 3 mos.
	Testify, wrongfully refusing to	DD, BCD	5 yrs.	Total
	Threat, bomb, or hoax	DD, BCD	5 yrs.	Total
	Threat, communicating	DD, BCD	3 yrs.	Total
	Unlawful entry	BCD	6 mos.	Total
	Weapon, concealed, carrying	BCD	1 yr.	Total
	Wearing unauthorized insignia, decoration, badge, ribbon, device, or lapel button	BCD	6 mos.	Total

SUMMARY OF THE 1949 GENEVA CONVENTIONS

CONTENTS

CHAPTER ONE
COMMON PROVISIONS OF THE
GENEVA CONVENTIONS

I. INTRODUCTION

In the aftermath of World War II, the world's nations recognized that the Geneva Red Cross Convention of 1929, which had been enacted to protect the wounded, sick and prisoners, had numerous shortcomings. In 1949, four new conventions were adopted to protect the victims of war; collectively, these are known as "The Geneva Conventions for the Protection of War Victims". The individual conventions are:

> Geneva Convention for the Amelioration of the Condition of the Wounded and Sick in Armed Forces in the Field (abbreviated GWS).

> Geneva Convention for the Amelioration of the Condition of the Wounded, Sick and Shipwrecked Members of Armed Forces at Sea (abbreviated GWS SEA).

> Geneva Convention Relative to the Treatment of Prisoners of War (abbreviated GPW).

> Geneva Convention Relative to the Protection of Civilian Persons in Time of War (abbreviated GC).

These conventions are the most comprehensive code of that segment of Law of Armed Conflict (LOAC) that deals with war victims, and they are among the most widely accepted of all international laws. As of 1987, 170 nations were U.N. members and 163 nations were parties to the Geneva Conventions. Included among these parties are the United States and the former Soviet Union.

The four conventions share a common purpose: the protection of war victims and those who aid war victims. The Geneva Conventions were not intended for the direct regulation of hostilities, although there is unquestionably some indirect effect on the conduct of military operations. "War victims" include civilians who are taking no part in the hostilities and those former combatants who are rendered "hors de combat" ("out of the combat") because of sickness, wounds, shipwreck, or being taken prisoner. The primary focus of the conventions is the protection of these war victims while they are in the hands of the enemy, it

being presumed that they do not need the protection of international law while they are under the control of their own government. "Persons who aid war victims" include medical personnel, chaplains, and Red Cross or neutral personnel who use their good offices to assist in the care and treatment of war victims.

II. COMMON PROVISIONS OF THE FOUR GENEVA CONVENTIONS

While dealing with separate subjects, the four conventions share a number of common provisions, the most notable of which are discussed below.

A. Applicability of the Conventions

When does the law set forth in the conventions apply? The simple answer is that it applies in all *international armed conflicts*. Identifying which conflicts fall within this category is not so simple. Obviously, a declared war such as World War II is such a conflict, although it is worthwhile to note that a formal declaration of war is *not* necessary to have an international armed conflict. Also included in this category would be any armed conflict, no matter how small or insignificant, between two (or more) parties to the conventions, or between a party and another nation not a party if the latter announces it will adhere in actual practice to the terms of the conventions. Clearly, a conflict wholly internal in its nature, such as one involving skirmishes with rebel insurgents, is not within the category. But consider what happens when a rebellion ripens into a full scale revolution, with different factions holding territory and claiming independence from the other (and announcing acceptance of the Geneva Conventions). Now the conflict more closely resembles an international armed conflict than it does an internal rebellion. And what about other conflicts such as "Peace-Keeping Operations" (Beirut, the Sinai); "Humanitarian Rescue Operations" (Grenada, the Iran hostage rescue attempt); and "responses" to international terrorism (the capture of the *Achille Lauro* hijackers, the Israeli strikes against P.L.O. targets)? Government officials are quick to claim publicly that these are not "wars", seemingly removing them from the category of "international armed conflicts". But out in the field an "armed conflict" is undeniably underway. Bottom line: always assume that the conventions apply in any action involving foreign (non-American) forces. Unless and until a *specific* renunciation of the application of the Geneva Conventions to a particular conflict is announced by the U.S. government, consider that the conventions do apply.

B. Article 3. "Mini-Convention"

What about conflicts *not* of an international character? Do the Geneva Conventions apply? Article 3, in all four conventions, known as the "mini-convention", applies in such conflicts to provide minimal humanitarian protection for the victims of war. This article mandates "humane treatment" for wounded, sick and "non-participants" in the conflict (including members of an armed force who lay down their arms). Article 3 outlaws such acts as murder, torture, hostage taking, and other cruel, humiliating and degrading treatment. While enemy soldiers who are taken prisoner are entitled to humane treatment, it is important to note that, under the "mini-convention", they are not vested with POW status. Therefore, unlike POWs, prisoners captured during a non-international conflict may be tried and punished for their acts of warfare. The "mini-convention" seeks to curb abuses in this area by mandating that sentences may be carried out only after a judgment of guilt by a regularly constituted court (no summary punishments, no sham tribunals) at which the prisoner has been afforded "indispensable judicial guarantees." This vague language (which judicial guarantees are "indispensable" among civilized nations?) leaves room for differences among nations, and you might expect that the rights afforded an accused before a court in Iraq or North Korea would differ markedly from those afforded in U.S. courts. This illustrates something encountered frequently throughout the conventions: provisions are not always specific in their drafting nor perfect in their applicability. Of course, this is to be expected when preparing a document to the satisfaction of a community of sovereign nations. Nevertheless, the conventions do represent a considerable achievement, in that the world's nations have agreed that victims of any war, whether it be international or non-international in character, do have basic rights which ought to be respected.

C. Special Agreements Altering the Conventions

Parties to a conflict may enter into special agreements, but these may only expand upon rights afforded to protected persons by the conventions. Provisions within the conventions will not be overridden, nor will protection thereunder be restricted or renounced, by any agreement between the parties. In addition, individuals may not renounce their rights under *any* circumstances. The absolute nature of the nonrenunciation provision is designed to eliminate instances in which a ruthless captor might torture a prisoner into signing a statement purporting to renounce his or her protection under the conventions.

D. Protecting Powers and Humanitarian Organizations

Neutral nations and humanitarian organizations are interested in adherence to the conventions by warring powers, perhaps for no other reason than the belief that a conflict fought under humane rules stands a better chance of being resolved with a lasting peace than does an inhumane, savage war. The parties to a conflict are obligated to respect the efforts of such nations and organizations as they act in the capacity of a "Protecting Power." "Protecting Powers" are watchdogs; each party to a conflict may designate a Protecting Power to act on its behalf, monitoring compliance with the terms of the conventions and reporting its observations to its sponsor nation. Protecting Powers also lend their "good offices to attempt resolution of disputes involving the parties to the conflict. Any impartial humanitarian organization may undertake relief efforts for war victims, even while not serving as a Protecting Power. It should be noted that such efforts are subject to the consent of the parties to the conflict. Of course, because these efforts further the spirit of the Geneva conventions, they should usually be welcomed.

E. Obligations to Publish and Enforce the Conventions

Signatories to the Geneva Conventions are obligated to publish and enforce the provisions of the conventions. For example, in order to prevent violations, nations must educate their citizens in the principles of the conventions. The course you are now taking is one way in which the U.S.

seeks to fulfill this treaty obligation. Also, nations are obliged to take such other actions as may be necessary to suppress all violations of the conventions. Chief among these would be to legislate penalties for offenses and establish courts or other tribunals to enforce such legislation; hopefully, the presence of such statutes and courts would deter misconduct. In the case of "grave breaches," which are the most serious violations of the conventions, the use of the phrase "effective penal sanctions" contemplates harsh penalties such as death, life imprisonment, or imprisonment for a significant period of years. U.S. service members who violate the terms of the conventions are subject to prosecution under the Uniform Code of Military Justice (UCMJ) for the specific offending conduct (murder, rape, larceny, destruction of property, etc.).

"Grave breaches" of the conventions are those involving any of the following acts, if committed against protected persons or property: willful killing, torture or inhumane treatment, including biological experiments; willfully causing great suffering or serious injury to body or health; unlawful deportation or transfer or unlawful confinement of a protected person; compelling a protected person to serve in the forces of a hostile Power; willfully depriving a protected person of the right to a fair trial; taking of hostages; and extensive destruction and appropriation of property not justified by military necessity.

Unfortunately, the existence of penal sanctions and the threat of prosecution do not deter all violations. Offenses sometimes occur, and when they do, there is an obligation to take action against the offenders. Alleged violations are to be investigated and, if of a continuing nature, halted immediately. Offenders should be tried and punished as warranted by the circumstances. Special obligations exist in the case of grave breaches. All parties to the conventions have an affirmative duty to search for and bring to trial persons alleged to have ordered or committed these heinous offenses. Because grave breaches have no statute of limitations, these obligations may continue, perhaps for years following the end of the conflict, until the offender dies or is brought to trial.

CHAPTER TWO
PROTECTION OF PRISONERS OF WAR

I. INTRODUCTION

Throughout much of history, members of a military force captured by the enemy had no substantial rights. Prisoners were largely at the mercy of their captors; they were mistreated, tortured, enslaved, held for ransom and killed. Even after it became the custom to keep prisoners alive, the lack of any accepted standard of treatment led to abuses. For example, during the American Revolution thousands of American prisoners died due to poor conditions on British prison ships, some of which were located in Baltimore harbor. This experience led the fledgling United States government to have an intense interest in the rights of prisoners of war. One of our first international agreements, a 1785 treaty with the Kingdom of Prussia, contained detailed rules to improve the treatment of POWs. These rules were later incorporated into other treaties.

General Order No. 100, also known as the "Lieber Code," promulgated during the American Civil War by the Union Army, contained 48 articles dealing with prisoners of war. This was the first attempt at codifying the laws, rules and customs which made up the international law on prisoners of war. The humanitarian principles contained in this document provided a significant basis for the treatment of prisoners of war in Hague Convention IV of 1907, in the 1929 Geneva Convention Relative to the Treatment of Prisoners of War, and in the present source treaty for POW rights, the Geneva Convention of 1949 Relative to the Treatment of Prisoners of War (abbreviated GPW).

There are two practical reasons why, as a member of the armed forces, you should be familiar with the rights and obligations of prisoners of war under the GPW.

First, in any combat situation you must be ready to capture and control enemy prisoners until they are sent to permanent POW camps. The GPW provides the basic humanitarian rules for treatment of prisoners. Fear of mistreatment is a significant deterrent to surrender; decent treatment of prisoners may encourage the enemy to surrender.

The second reason is also related to duty, but in a more personal way. If you should ever become a POW, knowing your rights and duties under GPW could help you deal effectively with your captors. Such knowledge could also help you insist on proper treatment for your subordinates in the POW chain of command.

II. PERSONS ENTITLED TO POW STATUS

The protected status of being a POW lasts from the time a person is captured until their final release and repatriation. Article 4 of the GPW defines six categories of persons as being entitled to POW treatment upon capture. These are:

A. Members of Armed Forces

This is the most obvious and the principal group protected under GPW. This category also includes any corps or force incorporated into the armed forces during time of war; but, this category does *not* include military chaplains or military medical personnel. Rather than becoming POWs upon capture, they become "retained persons." This special status is discussed in Chapter four.

B. Members of Resistance Movements

During World War II, the Allied Commanders in Europe recognized the French Resistance forces as a component of the Allied forces, and demanded POW treatment for its captured members. The Germans, on the other hand, had treated captured members of the French Resistance as unlawful combatants. GPW seeks to clarify the status of resistance forces in a manner that attempts a balance between a humanitarian concern for the plight of captured belligerents and the legitimate concern of operational commanders for the protection of their regular troops from the attacks of irregular forces. First, you should note that, under GPW, resistance movements are *not* the type of "militia or volunteer corps" which could become incorporated into the regular armed forces during time of war. Second, to obtain the entitlement to POW status upon capture, a resistance movement must meet the following four criteria:

1. The force must have a command structure, with a commander who is responsible for subordinates. This condition is fulfilled if the movement is commanded by a commissioned officer of the armed forces of that nation or by some other person who occupies a similar position of responsibility, as evidenced by documents, badges or other identification. It must be clear that individual soldiers are not operating on their own, but rather are accountable for their actions to a superior.

2. Personnel must wear a fixed, distinctive insignia recognizable at a distance. The wearing of a complete uniform is not necessary to satisfy this requirement. The purpose of the requirement is to make the belligerent forces distinguishable from the general civilian population, and any emblem or insignia that accomplishes this purpose is sufficient.

3. Personnel must carry their arms openly. Again, this will distinguish the members of the resistance force from the general civilian population.

4. The force must conduct its operations in accordance with the LOAC. This condition is satisfied if the resistance movement, as a whole, complies with the LOAC. The fact that an individual member has committed a war crime will not strip the entire group of POW status.

Embodied in the four criteria above is a decided concern with the ability to distinguish true civilians from resistance members. Of course, because the openness suggested in these criteria would run counter to the secrecy under which many resistance groups operate, it is possible that they would elect not to abide by these requirements. The choice rests with the commander: any member of a resistance group which does not satisfy the four criteria enjoys no legal right under international law to POW status. Therefore, if captured, he or she may be tried and punished as a criminal for assault, murder, property damage or other acts hostile to the enemy.

C. Members of a Regular Armed Force of a Government Not Recognized by the Detaining Power

During World War II, a debate arose about the correct status of General Charles de Gaulle's forces which were under the authority of the French National Liberation Committee. Were they legitimate belligerents, entitled upon capture to POW status? Or were they unlawful combatants, entitled to be tried and punished for their acts of warfare? The Germans did not recognize the FNLC as a legitimate government, and therefore contended that those forces were not operating under the direct authority of a party to the conflict. Eventually, through the intercession of the International Committee of the Red Cross (ICRC), the Germans granted POW status to captured members of these French forces. Consistent with this action, GPW Article 4 now clarifies that such forces are entitled to POW status.

D. Civilian Personnel Who Accompany the Armed Forces

Civilians such as news correspondents, supply contractors, tech reps, and welfare service personnel (such as Bob Hope's USO show) are entitled to POW status if captured. The enemy may choose to afford *better* treatment (i.e., release) to these persons and may indeed do so with news correspondents and welfare service personnel for the favorable propaganda value involved.

E. Civilian Aircraft Crews and Merchant Marine Crews

Whether or not directly supporting the war effort, these crews will be entitled to no worse than POW treatment if captured. Again, they may receive *better* treatment; for example, a civilian aircraft crew may be released and allowed to continue with its flight once the belligerent has determined that the flight is in no way aiding the enemy's war effort.

F. Levee en Masse

This occurs when civilians spontaneously rise up to defend their homeland against the invading force. Undoubtedly, they will not have the organization nor satisfy the "fixed, distinctive sign" requirement necessary to qualify them for POW treatment as a "resistance movement." Nevertheless, they will be entitled to POW status in the event of their capture if they carry their arms openly and generally adhere to the LOAC in their operations. You should note that a *levee en masse* lasts only until the defenders are sub-

dued or their homeland becomes occupied by the invaders. A civilian living in *occupied* territory enjoys no legal right to engage in acts of warfare against the occupying enemy; when captured, such a civilian may be tried and punished for his or her actions.

The determination of who is entitled to POW status is not made by the capturing forces in the field. Rather, in doubtful cases it is made by a tribunal which reviews any relevant evidence which may assist in an accurate resolution of the issue. During the Vietnam war, the U.S. conducted these tribunals on a regular basis; the tribunal consisted of not less than three officers, at least one of whom had to be a judge advocate or a military lawyer familiar with the Geneva Conventions. These tribunals tended to be liberal in granting POW status, even for enemy personnel who did not fit well into any of the six categories found in GPW Article 4. This was done for a political reason rather than for legal reasons: recognizing that U.S. servicemen were being taken prisoner by the enemy, it was hoped that vesting captured enemy personnel with POW status would encourage reciprocal, favorable treatment for captured Americans.

Since the capturing troops are relieved of any responsibility for determining POW status, the task of field personnel is greatly simplified. Any person captured by U.S. troops, even those persons clearly not entitled to POW status, are to be treated humanely. They should be thoroughly searched, secured (blindfolding and handcuffing during transit away from the battle zone is permissible) and removed from the front. Above all, you may not torture or execute any captured persons. All prisoners must be handled with care.

III. PERSONS NOT ENTITLED TO POW STATUS

A. Persons Not in One of the Six Groups

Any person who commits hostile acts and who is *not* included in one of the categories above, is not entitled to POW status. In addition, such persons lack the immunity of a soldier for their hostile acts, and may be tried and punished for murder, assault, or destruction of property, as the case may be. Note that resistance fighters whose units cannot meet the four criteria discussed above fall into this category, as do terrorists.

B. Losing POW Status

Persons normally entitled to POW status may *lose* their right to that status by their actions.

1. Spies

Spies are discussed in NWP 9, paragraph 12.8.

2. Out of Uniform

Traditionally, the wearing of a uniform was considered a prerequisite to POW status if the prisoner was taken on the battlefield. GPW makes no mention of this exclusion, but it seems to have persisted in practice. Soldiers fighting while not wearing their own nation's uniform are traditionally not entitled to POW status and therefore could be tried as common criminals for their violent acts. There are, however, three situations in which a person not wearing a uniform on capture clearly is entitled to POW status.

a. Three exceptions

(1) Away from the battle zone: A person captured far from the battle zone on leave or liberty could hardly be required to be in uniform.

(2) Evaders: Evading soldiers are entitled to wear any clothing they desire. An "evading" soldier is one who has been cut off from his unit behind enemy lines, and is merely trying to sneak back to his own forces. If he engages in intelligence gathering or sabotage, however, he becomes a spy and forfeits his POW status.

(3) Escaping POWs: Escaping POWs are entitled to wear any clothing they desire, and will not forfeit their POW status. Again, they are not entitled to engage in intelligence gathering or sabotage without forfeiting their POW status.

IV. PROTECTION OF POWS

The overall goal and emphasis of GPW is clearly the humane treatment of prisoners. No power is obliged to (but all warring nations do) hold POWs. The Geneva Conventions are exceedingly clear that if POWs are taken, the international community expects the captor nation to maintain humane standards and bear all of the costs involved.

A. Humane Treatment at All Times

POWs must at all times be humanely treated and are entitled to respect for their persons and their honor. This includes protection from acts of violence, intimidation and public curiosity.

This is absolutely required regardless of the financial costs involved. Also, the killing or mistreatment of POWs is not permitted for any reason, even when their presence retards the captor's movement, diminishes his power of resistance, or endangers his own self-preservation.

This obligation cannot be avoided by transferring POWs to another nation. Transferring POWs is permissible, but only if the original capturing state ensures that the receiving state complies fully with GPW. Furthermore, if the receiving state does not comply, then the original capturing state must retake custody of the POWs.

B. Interrogation of POWs

The capturing state is required to report the capture of each individual POW it detains. To facilitate this reporting requirement, every prisoner of war, when questioned on the subject, is bound to give his full name, rank, date of birth, and serial number or equivalent information. It is also for this reason that each nation is required to furnish its forces with personal identification cards. These cards are not to be taken by the capturing state. Indeed, if a POW does not have an ID card, the capturing state must issue one to the POW. This is the only information a prisoner is required to furnish.

No physical or mental torture, or any other form of coercion may be inflicted on prisoners of war to secure from them information of any kind whatever. Prisoners of war who refuse to answer may not be threatened, insulted, or abused.

C. Personal Effects

All personal effects (except weapons, military equipment and military documents) shall remain in the possession of prisoners of war. Personal effects and articles used for their clothing or feeding shall remain in their possession, even if such effects and articles are part of their regulation military equipment.

Badges of rank and nationality, decorations, and articles of personal or sentimental value may not be taken from prisoners of war. Money and other valuables carried by prisoners of war may not be taken away from them except by order of an officer, and then only for reasons of security. If taken, a receipt must be given to the POW and the items returned upon repatriation.

D. Evacuation of POWs

POWs must be evacuated, as soon as possible after their capture, to camps located far enough from the combat zone for them to be out of danger. They shall not be unnecessarily exposed to danger during evacuation. They must be transported under conditions no worse than the conditions the capturing power uses in transporting its own troops.

V. CONDITIONS OF INTERNMENT

A. POW Camp Location

POW camps may only be located on land, and shall be located in an area that is conducive to the health and hygiene of the POWs. POWs shall not be interned in penitentiaries.

No prisoner of war may at any time be sent to or detained in areas where he or she may be exposed to fire, nor may his or her presence be used to "shield" lawful targets from enemy attack.

Whenever military considerations permit, prisoner of war camps shall be marked with the letters "PW" or "PG" so as to be clearly visible from the air. Only prisoner of war camps shall be marked as such.

B. Parole

Parole is a traditional practice of releasing prisoners in return for their promise not to fight again in the current war; however, no POW can be compelled to accept parole. It was taken quite seriously in the past, to the point that the British actually returned one of their officers who violated his parole to the Germans during World War I. Parole is of obvious benefit to the prisoner, but it can also be a great benefit to the detaining power. The purpose of holding prisoners is to keep them from continuing to fight against you. If you can accomplish that end without the expense and difficulty of maintaining POW camps, so much the better. Partially for that reason, and partially because parole is difficult to enforce and subject to abuse by both sides, United States military personnel generally are not allowed to accept parole.

C. Quarters

Prisoners of war shall be quartered under conditions as favorable as those for the forces of the Detaining Power who are billeted in the same area. These conditions shall make allowance for the habits and customs of the prisoners and *shall in no case* be prejudicial to their health. Separate dormitories shall be provided for female POWs.

Note that prisoner housing standards are tied to those of the captor's troops in the area. If the captor's troops are poorly housed, prisoners may be as well, provided the housing is not so poor as to be unhealthy.

D. Food

The GPW states that food must be "sufficient in quantity, quality, and variety" to keep the prisoners in good health. Further, the detaining power must consider the dietary habits of prisoners. Prisoners must have adequate mess halls and kitchens where they can assist in preparing their own food. The captor must also furnish prisoners with sufficient, safe drinking water. Restricting food as a form of mass punishment is forbidden.

E. Clothing

The detaining power must provide outer clothing, underwear, footwear, and work clothing. It must mend or replace these items regularly. If possible, the detaining power supplies clothing from stocks of uniforms captured from the prisoners' own forces.

F. Health and Medical Care

The Conventions include detailed provisions for meeting the health and medical needs of prisoners. They insure at least a minimum standard of health. For example, camps must include adequate heads, showers, and laundry facilities. The captor "shall be bound to take all sanitary measures necessary to insure the cleanliness and healthfulness of camps and to prevent epidemics." And "Every camp shall have an adequate infirmary." Here, prisoners should receive treatment, preferably by medical personnel from their own captured forces. Sick call occurs regularly; medical inspections, at least monthly. Periodic X-ray examinations for tuberculosis and tests for other infectious and contagious diseases should be made. All needed medical care must be furnished and it is free of charge to the POW.

G. Religious and Recreational Activities

Prisoners may attend services of their faith and otherwise practice their religion. The Conventions require provision for physical exercise. This includes outdoor sports and games. Intellectual and educational activities must be encouraged whenever possible.

H. Mail

As soon as possible after capture, prisoners are to be allowed to inform their families of their whereabouts and health. This is to be done within a week after prisoners reach a POW camp. Usually this message is sent on a standard "capture card." The detaining power also forwards a copy of this card to the Central Prisoner of War Information Agency. This is a clearing house operated by the International Committee of the Red Cross in Geneva. Whenever a prisoner transfers to another camp or hospital, the detaining power must notify this agency. Prisoners have the right to send letters as frequently as the captor's censorship and postal facilities allow. They may also receive letters and relief packages forwarded through neutral agencies.

I. Camp Information

Every POW camp must have copies of the Geneva Conventions, in the prisoners' own language, posted in places where prisoners can read them. All camp notices, regulations, and orders must be in a language prisoners understand.

VI. POW LABOR

GPW does allow the Detaining Power to utilize POW labor, but there are a great number of detailed provisions in GPW concerning POW labor. This resulted because of the abuses on both sides during WWII. For instance, the Nazis used Russian and other POWs as slave labor, often simply working them until they died. On the other hand, the Allies used German POWs to remove mines in areas formerly occupied by the Nazis. As you might expect, many were killed in explosions.

General guidelines for POW labor include the following:

- Only POWs who are physically fit may work.

- Commissioned officers may not be compelled to work, but if they volunteer, they may do supervisory work.

- Noncommissioned officers may be required to perform supervisory work.

- Other enlisted personnel may be required to do manual labor.

- POW labor may not be used for military purposes except for work connected with camp administration, installation and maintenance.

- If additional food, clothing, medical care, training, etc., is required in order for the POW to perform his work, this must be furnished by the Detaining Power. Also, the POW must be paid for his labor.

- Working conditions can be no worse for the POWs than that enjoyed by the citizens of the Detaining Power employed in similar work.

- Unless a volunteer, no POW may be tasked to perform labor which is unhealthy or dangerous (such as clearing mines).

VII. PRISONER DISCIPLINE

A. Disciplinary Punishment

Disciplinary punishment is intended to punish infractions of camp rules and minor crimes. The procedure for disciplinary punishment is similar to that for nonjudicial punishment under the UCMJ. A hearing before the POW camp commandant is all that is required prior to implementing the punishment.

The disciplinary punishments applicable to prisoners of war are the following (all have a 30-day maximum):

1. A fine which shall not exceed 50 percent of the advances of pay and working pay which the prisoner of war would otherwise receive.

2. Discontinuance of privileges granted over and above the treatment provided for by the present Convention.

3. Fatigue duties not exceeding two hours daily (cannot be imposed on officers).

4. Confinement

In no case shall disciplinary punishments be inhuman, brutal or dangerous to the health of prisoners of war. The maximum of thirty days provided above may not be exceeded, even if the prisoner of war is answerable for several acts at the same time when he is awarded punishment, whether such acts are related or not.

B. Judicial Punishment

Judicial punishment refers to potentially severe punishment awarded by a court. It is reserved for serious offenses, which could include war crimes. GPW requires that disciplinary punishment should be used whenever possible.

If judicial punishment is used, then the POW can be sentenced only if the trial court and the procedures used in court are the same as those that would be used for a member of the detaining power's own armed forces. However, in no event may a POW be tried unless the court and procedures used guarantee at least the *minimum* generally recognized standards of independence, impartiality and due process. Minimum due process includes the right to assistance of lawyer counsel; to the assistance of an interpreter

and a fellow prisoner; to the calling of witnesses; and, if convicted, the right to appeal.

The use of the death penalty is discouraged, though not prohibited. If a death sentence is pronounced, at least six months must elapse before the sentence can be carried out. This allows for maximum diplomatic efforts to take place to prevent execution, if possible. Considerations of reciprocity have often prevented the execution of POWs.

One of the most extensively debated subjects at the 1949 Geneva Conference was whether a POW who is prosecuted for a precapture crime—in particular, offenses against the laws of war—should enjoy the benefits of POW status. It was determined that "Prisoners of war prosecuted under the laws of the Detaining Power for acts committed prior to capture shall retain, even if convicted, the benefits of the present Convention." According to this article, POW status is retained, regardless of the crime of which the prisoner is convicted. The former Soviet Union and many of its former satellite states made a reservation to this provision. They reserved the right to deny POW status to convicted war criminals. While the United States has rejected this reservation as contrary to international law, the existence of this reservation demonstrates the importance many governments attach to allegations of war crimes.

C. Escape

The GPW recognizes that all POWs have the right to attempt escape. While such attempts may be punished, the disciplinary punishment system must be used, thereby limiting the extent of punishment. In addition, *non-violent* acts committed in aid of an escape attempt are subject to the same limitations. Such non-violent offenses include offenses against public property; theft without intention of self-enrichment; making and using false papers; and the wearing of civilian clothing. *Violent* acts committed during an escape or an escape attempt may be dealt with through judicial punishment. The use of weapons against prisoners of war, especially against those who are escaping or attempting to escape, is an extreme measure, which under the GPW can only be used after appropriate warnings and as a last resort.

The escape of a prisoner of war shall be deemed to have succeeded when he or she has done one of the following:

1. joined his or her own armed forces or those of an allied power;

2. left the territory under the control of the Detaining Power and its allies, i.e., reached neutral territory;

3. joined a ship flying the flag of his or her country or of an allied Power.

Prisoners of war who have successfully escaped and who are subsequently recaptured, shall not be liable to any punishment for their previous escape.

CHAPTER THREE

PROTECTION OF CIVILIANS
I. INTRODUCTION AND BACKGROUND

During World Wars I and II, civilians caught in the conflict could look to only one international convention for protection: Hague Convention IV Respecting the Laws and Customs of War on Land. To its credit, that convention sought to establish specific protection for civilians who were under military occupation. The enemy was required to respect family lives, rights and property; pillage and collective punishments were forbidden; and enemy civilians could not be compelled to provide military information or swear allegiance to the occupying power. However, the experiences of two world wars highlighted the limitations of that convention. Those few general provisions pertained only in the case of a formal military occupation. Few articles in the convention could be applied to govern the treatment of civilians in situations other than an occupation, and of those, the terms were unclear, ambiguous, incomplete, and, in some cases, not mandatory. Even in occupied territory, there were no established rules for the trial and punishment of civilians, and no procedures detailed for their internment. Rather than condemning the Hague Convention for these shortcomings, it is well to recall that it was concluded in 1907 when hostilities were confined to the area close to the front, and when widespread guerilla war was not common. Total war,

which exposed the civilian population of whole countries to similar dangers as those faced by the Armed Forces, required more comprehensive treatment than that provided in Hague IV. From this recognition evolved the Geneva Convention of 1949 Relative to the Protection of Civilian Persons in Time of War (hereafter abbreviated GC), the first international convention devoted exclusively to the codification of the rights of civilians during an armed conflict. GC is the longest of the four Geneva Conventions, with 159 articles. In understanding the substantive provisions of this convention, it is useful to visualize GC as containing three distinct sub-agreements: the first is Article 3; the second is general protection for entire populations (Articles 13–26); and the third is "protected persons" (Articles 27–141).

II. ARTICLE 3: PROTECTION OF CIVILIANS IN A NON-INTERNATIONAL CONFLICT

Recall that this article (the so-called "mini-convention"), discussed in Chapter One of this handout, provides basic humanitarian protection to noncombatants and former combatants who have laid down their arms or otherwise been rendered *hors de combat* due to sickness, wounds, detention or any other cause. The basic rights provided are protection from being used as a hostage, protection from humiliating and degrading treatment, protection from all types of torture and violence (including murder), and protection from summary punishment and executions.

Remember: this article is applicable *only* in conflicts "not of an international character".

III. ARTICLES 13–26: GENERAL PROTECTION OF ENTIRE POPULATIONS AGAINST CERTAIN CONSEQUENCES OF WAR

While this portion of GC applies broadly (to "the whole of the population"), the actual protections provided are very few and, in some cases, are not mandatory.

A. Protect and Respect the Civilian Population

The provisions of GC Articles 13–26 apply to protect the entire populations of the warring opponents from the hardships of war, but the articles do not provide much in the way of specific, binding protection for those populations. Articles 16 and 24 do obligate the parties to "respect and protect" certain civilians: the wounded and sick; the shipwrecked and those otherwise exposed to grave danger; the infirm (usually thought of as invalids and the aged); expectant mothers; and orphaned children (under age 15). The phrase "protect and respect," refers to protection from such outrages as murder, torture, rape, medical or biological experiments, and cruel treatment of a like nature. Children must be cared for ("not left to their own resources") and educated. Also, those under 12 must be given some type of identity card or badge. After World War II, the problem of orphaned and separated children was immense, and no doubt spurred agreement among nations that specific procedures for safeguarding and identifying children be included in GC.

GC expresses concern for the plight of families, but the only *obligation* placed on parties to the convention is limited to *facilitating* personal communication among family members. This obligation serves to help re-unite dispersed family members.

B. Civilian Medical Facilities and Personnel

GC Articles 13–26 also address the issue of respect for civilian medical facilities and personnel. The establishment of hospital and safety zones for the benefit of certain civilians (those being the wounded, sick, aged, children under 15, expectant mothers and mothers of children under 7) is *optional* with a party to the conflict; respect for individual civilian hospitals, however, is *mandatory under all circumstances*. Furthermore, civilian medical personnel, hospital administrators and staff, and medical convoys on land or at sea shall likewise be respected and protected from attack. To facilitate identification of these persons and places, they should prominently display the appropriate emblem (usually a red cross or red crescent on a white background).

However, civilian hospitals, medical convoys, and medical personnel may be attacked *if* they are being used for military (vice humanitarian) purposes. Note that treating military personnel in a civilian hospital does *not* constitute using the hospital for a military purpose. All wounded and sick, whether civilian or military, are entitled to treatment as a basic humanitarian right. With respect to an attack on a hospital which is being used for military purposes, an attack shall not commence until after the enemy has been warned regarding the misuse of the hospital and then been given a reasonable opportunity to cease the offending military activities. This kind of procedure is fine in situations like that encountered by the U.S. when the North Vietnamese were abusing the protected status of the Boch Mai Hospital: after our protests and warnings were ignored, we bombed the SAM launching sites which had been co-located with the hospital. Of course, this incidentally damaged the hospital in the process. You should note that no protection exists for a hospital from which you are taking live fire. You need not convey any protests or warnings nor wait "a reasonable time limit" for the enemy to cease and desist. Your inherent right of self defense permits you to fire upon the building immediately. It was this situation which existed in Grenada when U.S. troops fired upon the Richmond Hill Institute.

C. Neutralized Zones

Any party to a conflict may propose the establishment, in the regions where fighting is taking place, of neutralized zones intended to shelter from the effects of war both the combatant and non-combatant wounded and sick, plus civilian persons who take no part in hostilities, and who, while they reside in the zones, perform no work of a military character.

When all parties concerned have agreed upon the geographical position, administration, food supply and supervision of the proposed neutralized zone, a written agreement shall be concluded and signed. The agreement shall fix the beginning and the duration of the neutralization of the zone.

D. Siege

GC encourages parties to the conflict to endeavor to conclude local agreements for the removal from besieged or encircled areas, of the wounded, sick, infirm, and aged persons, children and maternity cases, and for the passage of ministers of all religions, medical personnel and medical equipment on their way to such areas.

GC encourages a besieging force to allow the free passage of all consignments of medical and hospital stores and objects necessary for religious worship intended only for civilians, and to allow the free passage of all consignments of essential foodstuffs and clothing intended for children under fifteen, expectant mothers and maternity cases.

The obligation to allow free passage of these consignments is subject to the condition that the besieging force is satisfied that the consignments will not be diverted from their intended, limited destination, and that allowing the consignments will not result in a definite advantage to the military efforts or economy of the enemy.

Note that these provisions do *not* obligate the parties to institute neutralized zones, or to permit the removal of certain persons from besieged areas, or to allow medical and religious supplies, clothing and foodstuffs intended only for civilian use to pass into the hands of the adverse party. These provisions are purely voluntary; they are "urged," not "mandated." As with any voluntary provision, a military commander should carefully evaluate what effect, if any, compliance would have on the accomplishment of the assigned military objective. Consider this: if you were a siege commander, how would permitting wounded, sick, infirmed, children and maternity cases to leave the besieged area affect your objective, the capitulation of the enemy force?

IV. ARTICLES 27–141: PROTECTED PERSONS

To understand GC Articles 27–141 regarding protected persons, it is essential that you first understand who is a "protected person" for purposes of this convention.

A. Persons Entitled to "Protected Persons" Status

The civilians protected by GC Articles 27–141 are those civilians who find themselves in the hands of the enemy or of an occupying power. Also, certain citizens of neutral states are "protected persons" if their state does not have "normal diplomatic relations" with the nation in which

that citizen is located. Of course, being members of "the whole of the population," these people would also receive the limited protection of GC Articles 13–26. It is vital to note that an enemy civilian living in his own *unoccupied* territory is *not* a "protected person" under GC. It is presumed that such a civilian will be protected by his own government, and will benefit from its own domestic laws. Thus, there is no need for international law to intervene. International law (in the form of GC) is intended to ensure respect and protection for people who may not benefit from domestic laws: i.e., those civilians who find themselves under enemy control. Also, persons protected under one of the other Geneva Conventions are not considered "protected persons" under GC.

B. Humane Treatment Required at All Times

GC Article 27 provides in part, "Protected persons are entitled, in all circumstances, to respect for their persons, their honor, their family rights, their religious convictions and practices, and their manners and customs. They shall at all times be humanely treated, and shall be protected especially against all acts of violence or threats thereof and against insults and public curiosity."

Succinctly stated, GC Article 27 provides that *in all circumstances,* "protected persons" shall be treated humanely. This means they shall be protected from murder, torture, rape, enforced prostitution, insults, public ridicule, and any form of physical or mental coercion. Protection against these heinous crimes is not the only obligation imposed. The detaining power is obligated also to respect "protected persons," their honor, customs, religion and family rights. It should be obvious that these provisions were intended to address many of the crimes perpetrated against civilians in World War II: the "Rape of Manila," in which thousands of captured civilians were murdered, mutilated, raped and tortured; the use of captured civilians for medical experiments; denying civilians the means to earn a living; uprooting, dispersing or relocating families throughout Europe; and, of course, the Holocaust. A liberal application of the general obligations of respect and humane treatment embodied in the first paragraph of Article 27 likely would obviate the need for further treaty provisions, but experience has shown that, in time of war, "literal" vice "liberal" interpretations are likely. Therefore, many specific protections are stated in the succeeding GC articles, including prohibitions against collective penalties, pillage, hostage taking, and reprisals.

C. Collective Penalties, Pillage and Hostages Prohibited

Collective penalties, supposedly outlawed by Hague IV, were utilized during World War II. GC clearly outlaws them by permitting punishment *only* for offenses personally committed and by requiring a trial before the punishment is administered. Pillage is also proscribed. If "protected persons" and their family rights are to be respected, it seems only natural that their property should be respected and not plundered by the conquering invader. Similarly, a proscription against the use of protected civilians as hostages is consistent with the obligation to respect and to protect against torture, cruelty and collective punishments.

D. Reprisals Prohibited

The GC clearly outlaws acts of revenge taken against protected civilians under the care of the detaining power. The history of warfare is unfortunately dotted with instances in which entire populations of villages, or portions thereof, have been tortured and murdered and had their villages razed as vengeance for acts, whether lawful or criminal, committed against the detaining power. These acts of vengeance against a captive civilian populace are indefensible and unquestionably illegal.

Note: The GC's prohibition against reprisal actions involving *protected* civilians should not be confused with *lawful* reprisals designed to induce the enemy to comply with the LOAC. *See* NWP-9 section 6.2.3.

V. OTHER SECTIONS OF GC

Other protections afforded by the GC include, similar to POWs, that "protected persons" cannot be used to shield a legitimate target from attack. It is a law of war violation to attempt to shield a target by surrounding it with protected persons and conversely, the presence of protected persons does not render the target immune from attack.

GC further provides that any party to the conflict into whose hands protected persons may fall, is responsible for the treatment accorded to them by its agents, irrespective of any individual responsibility which may be incurred. You will recall that in 1982 the Israeli occupation forces in Lebanon delegated some security responsibilities to Phalangist Christian Militia (PCM) allied to their cause. In September of that year, the PCM massacred hundreds of Palestinian refugees at the Shatila and Sabra refugee camps, which were located in an area of West Beirut under Israeli occupation. After initial denials, the Israeli government accepted partial responsibility for this brutality. Under the GC, they had no alternative. As the occupying power, Israel had the ultimate responsibility for the proper treatment of "protected persons" under its occupation.

VI. THE COMMON CAVEAT THROUGHOUT GC: THE SECURITY OF THE DETAINING POWER

Throughout GC are provisions which recognize that the detaining or occupying power's ability to maintain control and security must not be compromised. Even Article 27, one of the most powerful articles in the convention with respect to the humane treatment of civilians, states that the Parties to the conflict may "take such measures of control and security in regard to protected persons as may be necessary as a result of the war." Although these frequent caveats to GC provisions clearly authorize detaining or occupying powers some latitude in dealing with protected persons (when necessary for security), they must be read in harmony with the bulk of the convention which mandates respect for protected persons in all circumstances. A protected person who engages in activities hostile to the detaining power continues to be a "protected person"; however, he or she may no longer be entitled to *all* of the rights and privileges that normally accrue to one with that status. Rather, rights and privileges *of that individual* are to be affected (recall the stricture against collective punishments). Note also that the withholding or modification should be limited to only so much as is necessary to maintain security; there is no wholesale forfeiture of all rights, and particularly no forfeiture of the rights associated with a fair trial on the offense charged. Finally, note also that full rights and privileges shall be restored at the earliest possible date. In order to avail oneself of the full protection of GC, the protected person owes a duty to the detaining power to be, in essence, a law abiding and non-hostile person. The protected person who violates this obligation can expect to forfeit some, but not all, of his or her protection under GC.

CHAPTER FOUR
THE WOUNDED, SICK AND SHIPWRECKED CONVENTIONS

I. INTRODUCTION AND BACKGROUND

In June, 1859, 39,000 troops were slain at the battle of Solferino in Northern Italy. Moved by the suffering he witnessed there, Henri Dunant wrote the book *Un Souvenir De Solferino* and, as a result of its publication, an International Congress was held at Geneva in 1863 and 1864 to examine the plight of wounded soldiers in the field. The result was the first Geneva Convention, adopted in 1864, to improve the condition of sick and wounded soldiers. The convention was updated in 1906 and again in 1929; and in 1949, two conventions were enacted which are still in force today. They are the Geneva Convention of 1949 for the Amelioration of the Condition of the Wounded and Sick in Armed Forces in the Field (abbreviated GWS), and the Geneva Convention of 1949 for Amelioration of the Condition of the Wounded, Sick and Shipwrecked Members of Armed Forces at Sea (abbreviated GWS SEA).

Stated generally, these conventions provide protection for armed forces personnel who are rendered *hors de combat* ("out of the combat") owing to sickness, wounds or shipwreck; protection for chaplains and military medical personnel who minister to the needs of those *hors de combat* personnel; and protection for the places where medical care is provided and for medical equipment and supplies. Obviously, GWS deals with situations on land and GWS SEA deals with those peculiar problems of medical care at sea; however, there is a considerable amount of overlap. This chapter will analyze the protection afforded by these conventions.

II. PROTECTION FOR CERTAIN PERSONS

A. The Wounded, Sick, and Shipwrecked

Not all wounded, sick and shipwrecked persons are protected by these conventions. For example, wounded or sick civilians are not within the scope of these conventions (recall that they are entitled to certain protection under GC). The persons who are protected by GWS and GWS SEA are the same six categories of people who are entitled to POW status under GPW and who are, in addition, wounded, sick, or shipwrecked. Upon capture by the enemy, they are entitled to POW status.

The definitions accorded the terms "wounded" and "sick" are not technical. A wound is any injury, incurred in battle or otherwise, which requires treatment. Sickness is an illness, vice an injury. "Shipwrecked," on the other hand, is a somewhat technical term. It refers to any person who has suffered the loss of his fighting platform and is now helpless and requires assistance to better his lot. Using the definition offered above, consider the case of personnel who are forced into the water from a disabled amphibious landing vehicle. If they continue to advance toward the beach, it cannot be said that they are "helpless" or that they require your assistance to better their lot. They have lost only their means of transport to the beach. Such personnel are not "shipwrecked," and the obligations of respect and protection which are owed to shipwrecked persons are not applicable. Finally, a "shipwrecked" person includes a person from an aircraft downed at sea.

The first duty thrust upon the parties to a conflict under GWS and GWS SEA is to search for and collect the dead, wounded and shipwrecked. In GWS SEA, the duty clearly attaches "after each engagement," and not during the battle itself. On the other hand, under GWS, the duty exists "at all times, and particularly after an engagement." Does this mean there is an obligation under GWS to commit personnel to search and collection operations during the heat of battle? Not at all. If, given the continuing battle, it is impractical or impossible to carry out a search and collection evolution, no violation of GWS has occurred. Even after an engagement, when the obligation surely arises on land or at sea, no violation of the law occurs if it is impossible to discharge this obligation owing to the nature of a unit or its mission. Mere inconvenience, on the other hand, is no excuse for refusing to undertake search and collection efforts after the enemy has disengaged and your unit has the opportunity for reasonably secure movement. Therefore, despite some differing language, the actual obligations under each convention are quite similar. Other measures, such as armistices and local agreements, for the benefit of wounded and sick persons are *not* mandated; they are certainly encouraged, but their implementation is dependent upon the voluntary assent of both sides.

Both GWS and GWS SEA make it clear that protected persons are to be "respected and protected under all circumstances." Once again, that broad, general language has been fleshed out by examples in the paragraphs which follow: no murder, no torture, and no medical experimentation. Also, the detaining power is responsible for providing such medical care as is possible, utilizing available personnel and supplies. Of particular interest is the priority of medical treatment. The GWS and GWS SEA require that all wounded personnel, regardless of nationality, be treated in order of *medical* priority. The common medical procedure which is used to prioritize patients for treatment is called "triage." Roughly stated, this procedure allocates resources first to those who are likely to survive *only* if immediate medical assistance is provided. Next to receive care are those not in need of immediate attention to survive (i.e., lesser wounds), and last in line are those who are unlikely to survive even with medical care (i.e., the mortal wounds). Nationality is *not* an element of the triage process. The practice of treating all Americans first, regardless of the severity of their wounds, would be a violation of these conventions.

B. Obligations Regarding Dead Combatants

GWS and GWS SEA require the parties to a conflict to notify the ICRC's Central Information Bureau (CIB) of the death of individual enemy combatants, and to forward the deceased enemy combatants' personal property to the CIB for return to next-of-kin. The parties are also required to provide dead combatants a dignified funeral, burial, or cremation and, if earthen graves are dug, appropriate markings so the graves may later be located. Compliance with these procedures can eliminate the fear and uncer-

tainty associated with a person being listed as "missing in actions" for a lengthy period of time.

C. Medical Personnel and Chaplains

If captured, chaplains and military medical personnel (recall that civilian medical personnel are protected under GC) are not POWs. Rather, they are considered "retained" personnel. This status allows all of the rights and benefits which would accrue to a POW, *plus* whatever additional freedom of the camp is necessary to permit the retained person to minister to the medical and spiritual needs of the POWs. It should be noted that the presence of medical personnel of the same nationality as prisoners does not relieve the detaining power of its obligation to ensure appropriate medical care for wounded and sick POWs.

Captured chaplains or medical personnel should be retained only so long as their humanitarian services are required for the benefit of other prisoners. If their services are not needed, they should be repatriated at the earliest practicable opportunity. This rule is designed to advance the overall objective of humanity permeating the conventions: imprisoning these persons without a need for their services diminishes the amount of assistance available to the wounded, sick and shipwrecked, while allowing chaplains and medical personnel to circulate freely increases the amount of care available.

Only full time medical personnel are given the special status of "retained personnel." Members of the armed forces who are part-time medical personnel, such as those specially trained to be orderlies or stretcher bearers if the need arises, but whose full-time duties are not medical duties, are POWs, not "retained personnel." However, they are to be allowed to continue performing medical duties after capture if they were so employed at the time of capture.

D. Loss of Protected Status

Both GWS and GWS SEA impose the general obligations of respect and protection for protected persons "in all circumstances." These general obligations also include a prohibition against intentionally firing on the wounded, sick and shipwrecked, and chaplains and medical personnel. This is a significant exemption from the general rule of warfare that enemy military personnel are lawful targets whenever and wherever they are found. However, if one of these protected persons engages in acts harmful to the enemy, that person has lost his or her protection.

Persons *hors de combat* (wounded, sick and shipwrecked) who fall into enemy hands sacrifice their usual right to engage in acts of war against the enemy in exchange for the protection of GPW and GWS or GWS SEA, as appropriate. If the protected person engages in acts of war, it should be apparent that the detaining power will be allowed to defend itself with appropriate means, which may include firing upon the transgressor.

Medical personnel likewise may not resist capture or engage in other acts harmful to the enemy (caring for the wounded is dot an "act harmful to the enemy," it is a "humanitarian" act). Two consequences may result from medical personnel engaging in "military" (vice "humanitarian") activities. First, the individual risks death or injury from being fired upon by the enemy. Second, if captured. the individual risks loss of "retained" status and becomes merely a POW because that person was not "exclusively" engaged in medical activities. A third consequence is also possible: the offending individual would risk prosecution for a war crime if they misused a protected symbol, such as the red cross.

III. PROTECTION FOR CERTAIN PLACES

A. Hospitals and Other Medical Units

Military medical facilities, be they hospitals (NRMC Bethesda) or mobile medical units (M*A*S*H 4077), may not be intentionally attacked. To facilitate this immunity and to guard against incidental damage to such facilities, they *should not* be co-located with legitimate targets. This admonition is frequently ignored. Many U.S. military hospitals are located in large military complexes which are themselves valid military objectives. Obviously, if such complexes were attacked, hospitals could expect to be damaged even if the hospital were not intentionally targeted; such "incidental damage" would *not* be a violation of the LOAC.

Military medical facilities are *not* immune from capture. If captured, the humanitarian character of the facility and its personnel should remain unchanged after capture until such time as the capturing power has removed the wounded and sick to another facility.

B. Sickbays on Vessels

Sickbays are treated in much the same way as hospitals and mobile medical units. However, the obligation not to attack the medical area is softened considerably ("shall be . . . spared as far as possible."), in recognition of the necessary co-location of a sickbay aboard a legitimate target.

C. Special Rules: Hospital Ships

Military hospital ships enjoy the same immunity from attack as hospitals and other medical units. However, it is important to note that, unlike other medical facilities, hospital ships *may not be captured!*

Not only may hospital ships not be captured, but the religious and medical personnel onboard, and the ship's crew, may not be captured. The purpose in this broad protection is to keep hospital ships in circulation for the benefit of *all* the wounded, sick, and shipwrecked. However, this immunity from capture does *not* extend to the actual wounded and sick combatants onboard, who may be taken prisoner by the enemy so long as they are fit to move and so long as the enemy has the facilities available at hand to ensure continued care.

For a ship to receive the protection of being a hospital ship, the enemy must be notified at least 10 days in advance that the ship is being so used, and must be provided a description of the ship including gross tonnage, length, and the number of masts and funnels. In addition, hospital ships must be painted white and marked with several large red crosses or crescents.

Since the enemy is prohibited from destroying or capturing hospital ships, just what rights does the belligerent have over those vessels? Basically, there are two: the right of "visit and search" and the right of "control."

"Visit and search," discussed more fully in NWP 9, involves stopping and boarding a vessel for the purpose of inspecting its true character. If a search of a vessel reveals that it truly is a hospital ship, then the vessel will be permitted to proceed. Of course, if the search reveals that the vessel is engaged in hostile, vice humanitarian activities, such as ferrying troops or ammunition, the vessel will lose its immunity and be subject to capture.

The right of "control" includes the power to order a hospital ship to stand off, to take a certain course and speed, to control certain communications, and even to detain the vessel for a period of up to seven days. For example, a belligerent may wish to employ any of these measures to maintain the secrecy of certain information about ships in company, or formation course and speed, which have been or could be observed by a nearby enemy hospital ship.

There are certain obligations placed upon the nation which operates a hospital ship. Assistance is to be provided to *all* wounded, sick and shipwrecked, regardless of nationality. Recall that only medical reasons will determine the order of medical care to be given. Hospital ships shall not be put to any "military" (vice "humanitarian") purpose. Violation of this provision by a hospital ship risks loss of the protection described earlier.

D. Loss of Protection for Medical Facilities

Hospitals and mobile medical units remain protected so long as they do not commit, outside of their humanitarian activities, acts harmful to the enemy. If acts harmful to the enemy occur, then a hospital or mobile medical unit may be attacked, but only after a warning has been given and the hospital or mobile medical unit fails to heed the warning. This warning requirement does not apply if giving a warning is impractical, such as when taking live fire from an anti-aircraft battery positioned on the hospital roof.

Some people mistakenly believe that by merely possessing weapons, medical personnel forfeit their protected status. The bearing of sidearms by doctors and nurses for self-defense does not change the humanitarian character of a medical facility or of the medical personnel therein. Neither does the posting of armed sentries at a medical facility. The GWS and GWS SEA recognize that individuals may need to defend themselves or their patients from wartime threats other than the threat of capture by the enemy. So long as weapons are not used to resist capture of the medical facility (which would, of course, be an "act harmful to the enemy"), the facility and its personnel remain protected. One caveat: sentries and medical personnel should carry "defensive" weapons only. The use of tanks, artillery, mortars and .50 caliber machine guns in and around a "medical facility" will cause the enemy much suspicion and will dramatically increase the likelihood of an enemy attack. A medical facility will also not lose its protected status due to the presence of arms and ammunition collected from the sick and wounded.

Hospital ships and sickbays of vessels are entitled to all of these same protections. In addition, note that neither the fact that the crews of ships or sickbays are armed for the maintenance of order, for their own defense or the defense of the sick and wounded; nor the presence on board of apparatus exclusively intended to facilitate navigation or communications will deprive them of protection. It is important to note that hospital ships *may not use* secret codes for communicating. The reason for this prohibition is obviously to prevent a hospital ship from being misused as a spy ship.

IV. PROTECTION OF CERTAIN THINGS

A. Medical Supplies

Under the LOAC, captured enemy military property may be put to use by the possessor or it may be destroyed to deny its possible recapture and use by the enemy. However, special rules exist for captured medical supplies. Material from mobile medical units "shall be reserved for the care of wounded and sick." No exceptions are indicated for this rule. A similar, but not identical rule for hospital buildings and hospital supplies requires that they be used for the treatment of wounded and sick after capture. However, this rule does allow their use for other purposes when "urgent military necessity" requires and when other arrangements have been made for the satisfactory care of the wounded and sick. In no case may medical supplies be destroyed in order to deny their use by the enemy.

B. Medical Transports

Medical transports on land shall not be intentionally attacked so long as they are being used for humanitarian purposes, but they may be captured. Captured land transports may be used for non-medical purposes on the condition that any wounded and sick are otherwise first cared for.

Medical transports at sea may be treated similarly to hospital ships. They are subject to visit and search but may not be attacked or captured. However, there is a significant qualifier to obtain this immunity as a medical transport. Notice of the voyage of the medical transport ship must be given to the enemy and the enemy must approve its voyage. These voyages, if they occur at all, likely will occur under the auspices of the ICRC or some neutral nation.

C. Special Rule: Medical Aircraft

Medical aircraft are given very limited protection. They may be fired upon *unless* they are flying at heights, at times, and on routes agreed to *in advance* between the belligerents. Therefore, a helicopter bearing a large red cross usually will *not* be protected when it enters a combat zone to pick up wounded, since it is unlikely that the belligerents have agreed in advance to its appearance. For medical aircraft on agreed upon flights, they shall obey every summons to land. In the event of a landing thus imposed, the aircraft with its occupants may continue its flight after examination, if any. The difference in this special rule for medical aircraft, and the general spirit of respect and protection for medical transports, apparently stems from a deep-rooted mistrust of enemy airborne platforms in the aftermath of World War II, which saw the advent of massive destruction from the skies. In 1949, the world's nations just did not feel comfortable granting an across-the-board immunity to aircraft bearing a medical emblem. *U.S. Rule*: U.S. forces are required to respect and protect the enemy's medical aircraft, even if the craft is not on an agreed upon flight, *if* the aircraft can be recognized as an aircraft being used on a legitimate medical mission. See NWP 9, paragraph 8.2.3.

V. IDENTIFICATION OF PROTECTED PERSONS, PLACES AND THINGS

Under both GWS and GWS SEA, to facilitate identification of medical persons, places and things, a clearly visible red symbol on a white background should be displayed. The only sanctioned symbols are the red cross, the red crescent (used by Islamic countries), and the red lion and sun (the emblem of the Shah of Iran). Iran now uses the red crescent, but has reserved the right to use the lion and sun symbol. Israel uses the red Star of David, which, while not sanctioned, was nevertheless respected in recent Israeli conflicts. These emblems are pictured in NWP 9. The purpose of the emblem is ease of identification. Its display is *not* a prerequisite to protection. If you know that a building is a hospital, it deserves respect even though it does not bear a red cross or crescent.

The conventions prescribe that medical personnel shall display the emblem on an armlet worn on the left arm. Buildings and transports shall bear the emblem in such a manner that it is clearly visible in all directions, including from the air. Hospital ships are to be painted white on all exterior surfaces, and shall display the emblem so it is visible in all directions, including from the air.

The display of the medical emblem is controlled by "competent military authority." Such authority may direct the camouflaging or even the removal of the emblem. While such directives are not violations of the LOAC, the military commander should consider the risks of attack and destruction when these emblems are not used.

HAGUE CONVENTION NO. IV RESPECTING THE LAWS AND CUSTOMS OF WAR ON LAND 18 OCTOBER 1907

Considering that, while seeking means to preserve peace and prevent armed conflicts between nations, it is likewise necessary to bear in mind the case where an appeal to may be brought about by events which their solicitude could not avert;

Animated by the desire to serve, even in this extreme case, the interests of humanity and the ever progressive needs of civilization;

Thinking it important, with this object, to revise the general laws and customs of war, either with a view to defining them with greater precision or to confining them within such limits as would mitigate their severity as far as possible;

Have deemed it necessary to complete and render more precise in certain particulars the work of the First Peace Conference, which, following on the Brussels Conference of 1874, and inspired by the ideas dictated by a wise and generous forethought, adopted provisions intended to define and govern the usages of war on land.

According to the views of the High Contracting Parties, these provisions, the wording of which has been inspired by the desire to diminish the evils of war, so far as military requirements permit, are intended to serve as a general rule of conduct for the belligerents in their mutual relations and in their relations with the inhabitants.

It has not, however, been found possible at present to concert Regulations covering all the circumstances which arise in practice;

On the other hand, the High Contracting Parties clearly do not intend that unforeseen cases should, in the absence of a written undertaking, be left to the arbitrary judgment of military commanders.

Until a more complete code of the laws of war has been issued, the High Contracting Parties deem it expedient to declare that, in cases not included in the Regulations adopted by them, the inhabitants and the belligerents remain under the protection and the rule of the principles of the law of nations, as they result from the usages established among civilized peoples, from the laws of humanity, and from the dictates of the public conscience.

They declare that it is in this sense especially that Articles 1 and 2 of the Regulations adopted must be understood.

The High Contracting Parties, wishing to conclude a fresh Convention to this effect, have appointed the following as their Plenipotentiaries:

[Here follow the names of the Plenipotentiaries.]

Who, after having deposited their full powers, found in good and due form, have agreed upon the following:

ARTICLE 1.

The Contracting Powers shall issue instructions to their armed land forces which shall be in conformity with the Regulations respecting the Laws and Customs of War on Land, annexed to the present Convention.

ARTICLE 2.

The provisions contained in the Regulations referred to in Article 1, as well as in the present Convention, do not apply except between Contracting Powers, and then only if all the belligerents are parties to the Convention.

ARTICLE 3.

A belligerent party which violates the provisions of the said Regulations shall, if the case demands, be liable to pay compensation. It shall be responsible for all acts committed by persons forming part of its armed forces.

ARTICLE 4.

The present Convention, duly ratified, shall replace as between the Contracting Powers, the Convention of the 29th July, 1899, respecting the Laws and Customs of War on Land.

The Convention of 1899 remains in force as between the Powers which signed it, and which do not also ratify the present Convention.

ARTICLE 5.

The present Convention shall be ratified as soon as possible.

The ratifications shall be deposited at The Hague.

The first deposit of ratifications shall be recorded in a *procès-verbal* signed by the Representatives of the Powers which take part therein and by the Netherlands Minister for Foreign Affairs.

The subsequent deposits of ratifications shall be made by means of a written notification, addressed to the Netherlands Government and accompanied by the instrument of ratification.

A duly certified copy of the *procès-verbal* relative to the first deposit of ratifications, of the notifications mentioned in the preceding paragraph, as well as of the instruments of ratification, shall be immediately sent by the Nether-

lands Government, through the diplomatic channel, to the Powers invited to the Second Peace Conference, as well as to the other Powers which have adhered to the Convention. In the cases contemplated in the preceding paragraph the said Government shall at the same time inform them of the date on which it received the notification.

ARTICLE 6.

Non-Signatory Powers may adhere to the present Convention.

The Power which desires to adhere notifies in writing its intention to the Netherlands Government, forwarding to it the act of adhesion, which shall be deposited in the archives of the said Government.

This Government shall at once transmit to all the other Powers a duly certified copy of the notification as well as of the act of adhesion, mentioning the date on which it received the notification.

ARTICLE 7.

The present Convention shall come into force, in the case of the Powers which were parties to the first deposit of ratifications, sixty days after the date of the *procès-verbal* of this deposit, and, in the case of the Powers which ratify subsequently or which adhere, sixty days after the notification of their ratification or of their adhesion has been received by the Netherlands Government.

ARTICLE 8.

In the event of one of the Contracting Powers wishing to denounce the present Convention, the denunciation shall be notified in writing to the Netherlands Government, which shall at once communicate a duly certified copy of the notification to all the other Powers, informing them of the date on which it was received.

The denunciation shall only have effect in regard to the notifying power, and one year after the notification has reached the Netherlands Government.

ARTICLE 9.

A register kept by the Netherlands Ministry for Foreign Affairs shall give the date of the deposit of ratifications made in virtue of Article 5, paragraphs 3 and 4, as well as the date on which the notifications of adhesion (Article 6, paragraph 2) or of denunciation (Article 8, paragraph 1) were received.

Each Contracting Power is entitled to have access to this register and to be supplied with duly certified extracts.

In faith of which the Plenipotentiaries have appended their signatures to the present Convention.

Done at The Hague, the 18th October, 1907, in a single original, which shall remain deposited in the archives of the Netherlands Government, and duly certified copies of which shall be sent, through the diplomatic channel, to the Powers which have been invited to the Second Peace Conference.

ANNEX TO THE CONVENTION. REGULATIONS RESPECTING THE LAWS AND CUSTOMS OF WAR ON LAND

SECTION I. ON BELLIGERENTS.

CHAPTER I. The Qualifications of Belligerents.*

ARTICLE 1.

The laws, rights, and duties of war apply not only to armies, but also to militia and volunteer corps fulfilling the following conditions:

1. To be commanded by a person responsible for his subordinates;

2. To have a fixed distinctive emblem recognizable at a distance;

3. To carry arms openly; and

4. To conduct their operations in accordance with the laws and customs of war.

In countries where militia or volunteer corps constitute the army, or form part of it, they are included under the denomination "army."

ARTICLE 2.

The inhabitants of a territory which has not been occupied, who, on the approach of the enemy, spontaneously

*For the most recent provisions relating to prisoners of war, see Geneva Convention Relative to the Treatment of Prisoners of War of 12 August 1949.

take up arms to resist the invading troops without having had time to organize themselves in accordance with Article 1, shall be regarded as belligerents if they carry arms openly and if they respect the laws and customs of war.

ARTICLE 3.

The armed forces of the belligerent parties may consist of combatants and noncombatants. In the case of capture by the enemy, both have a right to be treated as prisoners of war.

CHAPTER II. Prisoners of War.

ARTICLE 4.

Prisoners of war are in the power of the hostile Government, but not of the individuals or corps who capture them.

They must be humanely treated.

All their personal belongings, except arms, horses, and military papers, remain their property.

ARTICLE 5.

Prisoners of war may be interned in a town, fortress, camp, or other place, under obligation not to go beyond certain fixed limits; but they can only be placed in confinement as an indispensable measure of safety and only while the circumstances which necessitate the measure continue to exist.

ARTICLE 6.

The State may utilize the labour of prisoners of war according to their rank and aptitude, officers excepted. The tasks shall not be excessive and shall have no connection with the operations of the war.

Prisoners may be authorized to work for the public service, for private persons, or on their own account.

Work done for the State is paid at the rates in force for work of a similar kind done by soldiers of the national army, or, if there are none in force, at a rate according to the work executed.

When the work is for other branches of the public service or for private persons the conditions are settled in agreement with the military authorities.

The wages of the prisoners shall go towards improving their position, and the balance shall be paid them at the time of their release, after deducting the cost of their maintenance.

ARTICLE 7.

The Government into whose hands prisoners of war have fallen is charged with their maintenance.

In the absence of a special agreement between the belligerents, prisoners of war shall be treated as regards food, quarters, and clothing on the same footing as the troops of the Government who captured them.

ARTICLE 8.

Prisoners of war shall be subject to the laws, regulations, and orders in force in the army of the State in whose power they are. Any act of insubordination justifies the adoption towards them of such measures of severity as may be considered necessary .

Escaped prisoners who are retaken before being able to rejoin their own army or before leaving the territory occupied by the army which captured them are liable to disciplinary punishment.

Prisoners who, after succeeding in escaping, are again taken prisoners, are not liable to any punishment on account of the previous flight.

ARTICLE 9.

Every prisoner of war is bound to give, if he is questioned on the subject, his true name and rank, and if he infringes this rule, he is liable to have a curtailment of the advantages accorded to prisoners of his class.

ARTICLE 10.

Prisoners of war may be set at liberty on parole if the laws of their country allow, and, in such cases, they are bound, on their personal honour, scrupulously to fulfil, both towards their own Government and the Government by whom they were made prisoners, the engagements they have contracted.

In such cases their own Government is bound neither to require of nor accept from them any service incompatible with the parole given.

ARTICLE 11.

A prisoner of war cannot be compelled to accept his liberty on parole; similarly the hostile Government is not obliged to accede to the request of the prisoner to be set at liberty on parole.

ARTICLE 12.

Prisoners of war liberated on parole and recaptured bearing arms against the Government to whom they had pledged their honour, or against the allies of that Government, forfeit their right to be treated as prisoners of war, and can be brought before the Courts.

ARTICLE 13.

Individuals who follow an army without directly belonging to it, such as newspaper correspondents and reporters, sutlers and contractors, who fall into the enemy's hands and whom the latter thinks fit to detain, are entitled to be treated as prisoners of war, provided they are in possession of a certificate from the military authorities of the army which they were accompanying.

ARTICLE 14.

An information bureau for prisoners of war is instituted on the commencement of hostilities in each of the belligerent States, and, when necessary, in neutral countries which have received belligerents in their territory. The function of this bureau is to reply to all inquiries about the prisoners, to receive from the various services concerned all the information respecting internments and transfers, releases on parole, exchanges, escapes, admissions into hospital, deaths, as well as other information necessary to enable it to make out and keep up to date an individual return for each prisoner of war. The bureau must state in this return the regimental number, name and surname, age, place of origin, rank, unit, wounds, date and place of capture, internment, wounding, and death, as well as any observations of a special character. The individual return shall be sent to the Government of the other belligerent after the conclusion of peace.

It is likewise the function of the information bureau to receive and collect all objects of personal use, valuables, letters, etc., found on the field of battle or left by prisoners who have been released on parole, or exchanged, or who have escaped, or died in hospitals or ambulances, and to forward them to those concerned.

ARTICLE 15.

Relief societies for prisoners of war, which are properly constituted in accordance with the laws of their country and with the object of serving as the channel for charitable effort shall receive from the belligerents, for themselves and their duly accredited agents every facility for the efficient performance of their humane task within the bounds imposed by military necessities and administrative regulations. Agents of these societies may be admitted to the places of internment for the purpose of distributing relief, as also to the halting places of repatriated prisoners, if furnished with a personal permit by the military authorities, and on giving an undertaking in writing to comply with all measures of order and police which the latter may issue.

ARTICLE 16.

Information bureaus enjoy the privilege of free postage. Letters, money orders, and valuables, as well as parcels by post, intended for prisoners of war, or dispatched by them, shall be exempt from all postal duties in the countries of origin and destination, as well as in the countries they pass through.

Presents and relief in kind for prisoners of war shall be admitted free of all import or other duties, as well as of payments for carriage by the State railways.

ARTICLE 17.

Officers taken prisoners shall receive the same rate of pay as officers of corresponding rank in the country where they are detained, the amount to be ultimately refunded by their own Government.

ARTICLE 18.

Prisoners of war shall enjoy complete liberty in the exercise of their religion, including attendance at the services of whatever Church they may belong to, on the sole condition that they comply with the measures of order and police issued by the military authorities.

ARTICLE 19.

The wills of prisoners of war are received or drawn up in the same way as for soldiers of the national army.

The same rules shall be observed regarding death certificates as well as for the burial of prisoners of war, due regard being paid to their grade and rank.

ARTICLE 20.

After the conclusion of peace, the repatriation of prisoners of war shall be carried out as quickly as possible.

CHAPTER III. The Sick and Wounded.

ARTICLE 21.

The obligations of belligerents with regard to the sick and wounded are governed by the Geneva Convention.*

SECTION II. HOSTILITIES.

CHAPTER I. Means of Injuring the Enemy, Sieges, and Bombardments.

ARTICLE 22.

The right of belligerents to adopt means of injuring the enemy is not unlimited.

ARTICLE 23.

In addition to the prohibitions provided by special Conventions, it is especially forbidden—

a. To employ poison or poisoned weapons;

b. To kill or wound treacherously individuals belonging to the hostile nation or army.

c. To kill or wound an enemy who, having laid down his arms, or having no longer means of defence, has surrendered at discretion;

d. To declare that no quarter will be given;

e. To employ arms, projectiles, or material calculated to cause unnecessary suffering;

---

*For the most recent provisions relating to the treatment of sick and wounded, *see* the Geneva Convention for the Amelioration of the Condition of the Wounded and Sick in Armed Forces in the Field and the Geneva Convention for Amelioration of the Condition of the Wounded, Sick and Shipwrecked Members of Armed Forces at Sea, 12 August 1949.

f. To make improper use of a flag of truce, of the national flag, or of the military insignia and uniform of the enemy, as well as the distinctive badges of the Geneva Convention

g. To destroy or seize the enemy's property, unless such destruction or seizure be imperatively demanded by the necessities of war;

h. To declare abolished, suspended, or inadmissible in a Court of law the rights and actions of the nationals of the hostile party.

A belligerent is likewise forbidden to compel the nationals of the hostile party to take part in the operations of war directed against their own country, even if they were in the belligerent's service before the commencement of the war.

ARTICLE 24.

Ruses of war and the employment of measures necessary for obtaining information about the enemy and the country are considered permissible.

ARTICLE 25.

The attack or bombardment, by whatever means, of towns, villages, dwellings, or buildings which are undefended is prohibited.

ARTICLE 26.

The officer in command of an attacking force must, before commencing a bombardment, except in cases of assault, do all in his power to warn the authorities.

ARTICLE 27.

In sieges and bombardments all necessary measures must be taken to spare, as far as possible, buildings dedicated to religion, art, science, or charitable purposes, historic monuments, hospitals, and places where the sick and wounded are collected, provided they are not being used at the time for military purposes.

It is the duty of the besieged to indicate the presence of such buildings or places by distinctive and visible signs, which shall be notified to the enemy beforehand.

ARTICLE 28.

The pillage of a town or place, even when taken by assault, is prohibited.

CHAPTER II. Spies.

ARTICLE 29.

A person can only be considered a spy when, acting clandestinely or on false pretenses, he obtains or endeavours to obtain information in the zone of operations of a belligerent, with the intention of communicating it to the hostile party.

Thus, soldiers not wearing a disguise who have penetrated into the zone of operations of the hostile army, for the purpose of obtaining information, are not considered spies. Similarly, the following are not considered spies: Soldiers and civilians, carrying out their mission openly, intrusted with the delivery of despatches intended either for their own army or for the enemy's army. To this class belong likewise persons sent in balloons for the purpose of carrying despatches and, generally, of maintaining communications between the different parts of an army or a territory.

ARTICLE 30.

A spy taken in the act shall not be punished without previous trial.

ARTICLE 31.

A spy who, after rejoining the army to which he belongs, is subsequently captured by the enemy, is treated as a prisoner of war, and incurs no responsibility for his previous acts of espionage.

CHAPTER III. Parlementaires.

ARTICLE 32.

A person is regarded as a parlementaire who has been authorized by one of the belligerents to enter into communication with the other, and who advances bearing a white flag. He has a right to inviolability, as well as the trumpeter, bugler or drummer, the flag-bearer and interpreter who may accompany him.

ARTICLE 33.

The commander to whom a parlementaire is sent is not in all cases obliged to receive him.

He may take all the necessary steps to prevent the parlementaire taking advantage of his mission to obtain information.

In case of abuse, he has the right to detain the parlementaire temporarily.

ARTICLE 34.

The parlementaire loses his rights of inviolability if it is proved in a clear and incontestable manner that he has taken advantage of his privileged position to provoke or commit an act of treachery.

CHAPTER IV. Capitulations.

ARTICLE 35.

Capitulations agreed upon between the contracting parties must take into account the rules of military honour.

Once settled, they must be scrupulously observed by both parties.

CHAPTER V. Armistices.

ARTICLE 36.

An armistice suspends military operations by mutual agreement between the belligerent parties. If its duration is not defined, the belligerent parties may resume operations at any time, provided always that the enemy is warned within the time agreed upon, in accordance with the terms of the armistice.

ARTICLE 37.

An armistice may be general or local. The first suspends the military operations of the belligerent States everywhere; the second only between certain fractions of the belligerent armies and within a fixed radius .

ARTICLE 38.

An armistice must be notified officially and in good time to the competent authorities and to the troops. Hostilities are suspended immediately after the notification, or on the date fixed.

ARTICLE 39.

It rests with the contracting parties to settle, in the terms of the armistice, what communications may be held in the theatre of war with the inhabitants and between the inhabitants of one belligerent State and those of the other.

ARTICLE 40.

Any serious violation of the armistice by one of the parties gives the other party the right of denouncing it, and even, in cases of urgency, of recommencing hostilities immediately.

ARTICLE 41.

A violation of the terms of the armistice by private persons acting on their own initiative only entitles the injured party to demand the punishment of the offenders or, if necessary; compensation for the losses sustained.

SECTION III. MILITARY AUTHORITY OVER THE TERRITORY OF THE HOSTILE STATE.

ARTICLE 42.

Territory is considered occupied when it is actually placed under the authority of the hostile army.

The occupation extends only to the territory where such authority has been established and can be exercised.

ARTICLE 43.

The authority of the legitimate power having in fact passed into the hands of the occupant, the latter shall take all the measures in his power to restore, and ensure as far as possible, public order and safety, while respecting, unless absolutely prevented, the laws in force in the country.

ARTICLE 44.

A belligerent is forbidden to force the inhabitants of occupied territory to furnish information about the army of the other belligerent, or about its means of defence.

ARTICLE 45.

It is forbidden to compel the inhabitants of occupied territory to swear allegiance to the hostile Power.

ARTICLE 46.

Faraily honour and rights, the lives of persons, and private property, as well as religious convictions and practice, must be respected.

Private property cannot be confiscated.

ARTICLE 47. Pillage is formally forbidden.

ARTICLE 48.

If, in the territory occupied, the occupant collects the taxes, dues, and tolls imposed for the benefit of the State, he shall do so, as far as is possible in accordance with the rules of assessment and incidence in force, and shall in consequence be bound to defray the expenses of the administration of the occupied territory to the same extent as the legitimate Government was so bound.

ARTICLE 49.

If, in addition to the taxes mentioned in the above Article, the occupant levies other money contributions in the occupied territory, this shall only be for the needs of the army or of the administration of the territory in question.

ARTICLE 50.

No general penalty, pecuniary or otherwise, shall be inflicted upon the population on account of the acts of individuals for which they cannot be regarded as jointly and severally responsible.

ARTICLE 51.

No contribution shall be collected except under a written order, and on the responsibility of a Commander-in-chief.

The collection of the said contribution shall only be effected as far as possible in accordance with the rules of assessment and incidence of the taxes in force.

For every contribution a receipt shall be given to the contributors.

ARTICLE 52.

Requisitions in kind and services shall not be demanded from municipalities or inhabitants except for the needs of the army of occupation. They shall be in proportion to the resources of the country, and of such a nature as not to involve the population in the obligation of taking part in operations of the war against their country.

Such requisitions and services shall only be demanded on the authority of the commander in the locality occupied.

Contributions in kind shall as far as possible be paid for in cash; if not, a receipt shall be given and the payment of the amount due shall be made as soon as possible.

ARTICLE 53.

An army of occupation can only take possession of cash, funds, and realizable securities which are strictly the property of the State, depôts of arms, means of transport, stores and supplies, and, generally, all movable property belonging to the State which may be used for operations of the war.

All appliances, whether on land, at sea, or in the air, adapted for the transmission of news, or for the transport of persons or things, exclusive of cases governed by naval law, depôts of arms, and, generally, all kinds of ammunition of war, may be seized, even if they belong to private individuals, but must be restored and compensation fixed when peace is made.

ARTICLE 54.

Submarine cables connecting an occupied territory with a neutral territory shall not be seized or destroyed except in the case of absolute necessity. They must likewise be restored and compensation fixed when peace is made.

ARTICLE 55.

The occupying State shall be regarded only as administrator and usufructuary of public buildings, real estate, forests, and agricultural estates belonging to the hostile State, and situated in the occupied country. It must safeguard the capital of these properties, and administer them in accordance with the rules of usufruct.

ARTICLE 56.

The property of municipalities, that of institutions dedicated to religion, charity and education, the arts and sciences, even when State property, shall be treated as private property.

All seizure or destruction of, or wilful damage to, institutions of this character, historic monuments, works of art and science, is forbidden, and should be made the subject of legal proceedings.

STANDING RULES OF ENGAGEMENT FOR U.S. FORCES

1. Purpose and Scope

a. The purpose of these Standing Rules of Engagement (SROE) is to provide implementation guidance on the inherent right and obligation of self-defense and the application of force for mission accomplishment. The SROE establish fundamental policies and procedures governing the actions to be taken by U.S. force commanders during all military operations, contingencies, or prolonged conflicts. In order to provide uniform training and planning capabilities, this document is authorized for distribution to commanders at all levels to be used as fundamental guidance for training and directing their forces.

b. Except as augmented by supplemental rules of engagement for specific operations, missions, or projects, the policies and procedures established herein remain in effect until rescinded.

c. U.S. forces operating with multinational forces:

(1) U.S. forces assigned to the operational control (OPCON) of a multinational force will follow the ROE of the multinational force unless otherwise directed by the National Command Authorities (NCA). U.S. forces will be assigned and remain OPCON to a multinational force only if the combatant commander and higher authority determine that the ROE for that multinational force are consistent with the policy guidance on unit self-defense

and with the rules for individual self-defense contained in this document.

(2) When U.S. forces, under U.S. OPCON, operate in conjunction with a multinational force, reasonable efforts will be made to effect common ROE. If such ROE cannot be established, U.S. forces will exercise the right and obligation of self-defense contained in this document while seeking guidance from the appropriate combatant command. To avoid mutual interference, the multinational forces will be informed prior to U.S. participation in the operation of the U.S. forces' intentions to operate under these SROE and to exercise unit self-defense.

(3) Participation in multinational operations may be complicated by varying national obligations derived from international agreements; i.e., other members in a coalition may not be signatories to treaties that bind the United States, or they may be bound by treaties to which the United States is not a party. U.S. forces still remain bound by U.S. treaty obligations even if the other members in a coalition are not signatories to a treaty and need not adhere to its terms.

d. Commanders of U.S. forces subject to international agreements governing their presence in foreign countries (e.g., Status of Forces Agreements) are relieved of the inherent authority and obligation to use all necessary means available and to take all appropriate action for unit self-defense.

e. U.S. forces in support of operations not under operational or tactical control of a combatant commander or performing missions under direct control of the National Command Authority (NCA), Military Departments, or other U.S. government departments/agencies (i.e., marine security guards, certain special security forces) will operate under use-of-force or ROE promulgated by those departments or agencies.

f. U.S. Coast Guard (USCG) units and units under USCG OPCON conducting law enforcement operations, and USCG personnel using their law enforcement authority, will follow the use-of-force policy issued by the Commandant, USCG. Nothing in the USCG use-of-force policy negates a commander's inherent authority and obligation to use all necessary means available to take all appropriate action for unit self-defense in accordance with these SROE.

g. The guidance in this document does not cover U.S. forces deployed to assist federal and local authorities during times of civil disturbance within the territorial jurisdiction of any state, the District of Columbia, Commonwealths of Puerto Rico and the Northern Marianas, U.S. possessions, and U.S. territories. Forces in these situations will follow use-of-force policy found in DoD Civil Disturbance Plan, "Garden Plot" (Appendix 1 to Annex C of Garden Plot).

h. U.S. forces deployed to assist foreign, federal, and local authorities in disaster assistance missions, such as earthquakes and hurricanes, will follow use-of-force guidelines as set forth in the mission's execute order and subsequent orders.

i. U.S. forces will always comply with the Law of Armed Conflict. However, not all situations involving the use of force are armed conflicts under international law. Those approving operational rules of engagement must determine if the internationally recognized Law of Armed Conflict applies. In those circumstances when armed conflict, under international law, does not exist, Law of Armed Conflict principles may nevertheless be applied as a matter of national policy. If armed conflict occurs, the actions of U.S. forces will be governed by both the Law of Armed Conflict and rules of engagement.

2. Policy

a. THESE RULES DO NOT LIMIT A COMMANDER'S INHERENT AUTHORITY AND OBLIGATION TO USE ALL NECESSARY MEANS AVAILABLE AND TO TAKE ALL APPROPRIATE ACTION IN SELF-DEFENSE OF THE COMMANDER'S UNIT AND OTHER U.S. FORCES IN THE VICINITY.

b. U.S. national security policy serves to protect the United States, U.S. forces, and in certain circumstances, U.S. citizens and their property, U.S. commercial assets, and other designated non-U.S. forces, foreign nationals, and their property from hostile attack. U.S. national security policy is guided, in part, by the need to maintain a stable international environment compatible with U.S. national security interests. In addition, U.S. national security interests guide out global objectives of deterring armed attack against the United States across the range of military operations, defeating an attack should deterrence fail, and preventing or neutralizing hostile efforts to intimidate or coerce the United States by the threat or use of armed force or terrorist actions. Deterrence requires clear and evident capability and resolve to fight at any level of conflict and, if necessary, to increase deterrent force capabilities and posture deliberately so that any potential aggressor will assess its own risks as unacceptable. U.S. policy, should deterrence fail, provides flexibility to respond to crises with options that:

(1) Are proportional to the provocation.

(2) Are designed to limit the scope and intensity of the conflict.

(3) Will discourage escalation.

(4) Will achieve political and military objectives.

3. Intent

These SROE are intended to:

a. Provide general guidelines on self-defense and are applicable worldwide to all echelons of command.

b. Provide guidance governing the use of force consistent with mission accomplishment.

c. Be used in operations other than war, during transition from peacetime to armed conflict or war, and during armed conflict in the absence of superseding guidance.

4. Combatant Commanders' SROE

a. Combatant commanders may augment these SROE as necessary to reflect changing political and military policies, threats, and missions specific to their AOR. When specific standing rules governing the use of force in a combatant commander's AOR are required that are different from these SROE, they will be submitted to the Chairman of the Joint Chiefs of Staff for NCA approval as necessary and promulgated by the Joint Staff as an Annex to Enclosure C of these SROE.

b. Combatant commanders will distribute these SROE to subordinate commanders and units for compliance. The mechanism for disseminating ROE supplemental measures is set forth in Enclosure B.

5. Definitions

a. **Inherent Right of Self-Defense.** A commander has the authority and obligation to use all necessary means available and to take all appropriate action to defend that commander's unit and other U.S. forces in the vicinity from a hostile act or demonstration of hostile intent. Neither these rules nor the supplemental measures activated to augment these rules, limit this inherent right and obligation. At all times, however, the requirements of necessity and proportionality as amplified in these SROE will be the basis for the judgment of the commander as to what constitutes an appropriate response to a particular hostile act or demonstration of hostile intent.

b. **National Self-Defense.** National self-defense is the act of defending the United States, U.S. forces, and in certain circumstances, U.S. citizens and their property, U.S. commercial assets, and other designated non-U.S. forces, foreign nationals and their property, from a hostile act or hostile intent. Once a force or terrorist unit is declared hostile by appropriate authority exercising the right and obligation of national self-defense (see paragraph 2 of Appendix A to Enclosure A), individual U.S. units do not need to observe a hostile act or determine hostile intent before engaging that force.

NOTE: **Collective Self-Defense.** Collective self-defense, as a subset of national self-defense, is the act of defending other designated non-U.S. forces, personnel and their property from a hostile act or demonstration of hostile intent. Only the NCA may authorize U.S. forces to exercise collective self-defense.

c. **Unit Self-Defense.** Unit self-defense is the act of defending a particular unit of U.S. forces, including elements or personnel thereof, and other U.S. forces in the vicinity, against a hostile act or hostile intent. The need to exercise unit self-defense may arise in many situations such as localized low-level conflicts, humanitarian efforts, peace enforcement actions, terrorists response, or prolonged engagements. Individual self-defense is a subset of unit self-defense; see the glossary for a definition of individual self-defense.

d. **Elements of Self-Defense.** The application of armed force in self-defense requires the following two elements:

(1) **Necessity.** A hostile act occurs or a force or terrorist unit exhibits hostile intent.

(2) **Proportionality.** The force used must be reasonable in intensity, duration and magnitude, based on all facts known to the commander at the time, to decisively counter the hostile act or hostile intent and to ensure the continued safety of U.S. forces.

e. **Hostile Act.** A hostile act is an attack or other use of force by a foreign force or terrorist unit (organization or individual) against the United States, U.S. forces, and in certain circumstances, U.S. citizens, their property, U.S. commercial assets, and other designated non-U.S. forces, foreign nationals and their property. It is also force used directly to preclude or impede the mission and/or duties of U.S. forces, including the recovery of U.S. personnel and vital U.S. Government property. When a hostile act is in progress, the right exists to use proportional force, including armed force, in self-defense by all necessary means available to deter or neutralize the potential attacker or, if necessary, to destroy the threat. (See definitions in the Glossary for amplification.)

f. **Hostile Intent.** Hostile intent is the threat of imminent use of force by a foreign force or terrorist unit (organization or individual) against the United States, U.S. forces, and in certain circumstances, U.S. citizens, their property, U.S. commercial assets, or other designated non-

U.S. forces, foreign nationals and their property. When hostile intent is present, the right exists to use proportional force, including armed force, in self-defense by all necessary means available to deter or neutralize the potential attacker or, if necessary, to destroy the threat. (See definitions in the Glossary for amplification.)

g. **Hostile Force.** Any force or terrorist unit (civilian, paramilitary, or military), with or without national designation, that has committed a hostile act, demonstrated hostile intent, or has been declared hostile.

6. Declaring Forces Hostile

Once a force is declared hostile by appropriate authority, U.S. units need not observe a hostile act or a demonstration of hostile intent before engaging that force. The responsibility for exercising the right and obligation of national self-defense and declaring a force hostile is a matter of the utmost importance demanding considerable judgment of command. All available intelligence, the status of international relationships, the requirements of international law, the possible need for a political decision, and the potential consequences for the United States must be carefully weighed. Exercising the right and obligation of national self-defense by competent authority is in addition to and does not supplant the right and obligation to exercise unit self-defense. The authority to declare a force hostile is limited as amplified in Appendix A to Enclosure A.

7. Authority to Exercise Self-Defense

a. **National Self-Defense.** The authority to exercise national self-defense is outlined in Appendix A to Enclosure A.

b. **Collective Self-Defense.** Only the NCA may authorize the exercise of collective self-defense.

c. **Unit Self-Defense.** A unit commander has the authority and obligation to use all necessary means available and to take all appropriate action to defend the unit, including elements and personnel thereof, or other U.S. forces in the vicinity, against a hostile act or hostile intent. In defending against a hostile act or hostile intent under these SROE, unit commanders should use only that degree of force necessary to decisively counter the hostile act or hostile intent and to ensure the continued safety of U.S. forces.

8. Action in Self-Defense

a. **Means of Self-Defense.** All necessary means available and all appropriate actions may be used in self-defense. The following guidelines apply for unit or national self-defense:

(1) **Attempt to Control Without the Use of Force.** The use of force is normally a measure of last resort. When time and circumstances permit, the potentially hostile force should be warned and given the opportunity to withdraw or cease threatening actions. (See Appendix A to Enclosure A for amplification.)

(2) **Use Proportional Force to Control the Situation.** When the use of force in self-defense is necessary, the nature, duration, and scope of the engagement should not exceed that which is required to decisively counter the hostile act or hostile intent and to ensure the continued safety of U.S. forces or other protected personnel or property.

(3) **Attack to Disable or Destroy.** An attack to disable or destroy a hostile force is authorized when such action is the only prudent means by which a hostile act or hostile intent can be prevented or terminated. When such conditions exist, engagement is authorized only until the hostile force no longer poses an imminent threat.

b. **Immediate Pursuit of Hostile Foreign Forces.** In self-defense, U.S. forces may pursue and engage a hostile force that has committed a hostile act or demonstrated hostile intent and that remains an imminent threat. (See Appendix A to Enclosure A for amplification.)

c. **Defending U.S. Citizens, Property, and Designated Foreign Nationals.**

(1) **Within a Foreign Nation's U.S. Recognized Territory or Territorial Airspace.** A foreign nation has the principal responsibility for defending U.S. citizens and property within these areas. (See Appendix A to Enclosure A for amplification.)

(2) **At Sea.** Detailed guidance is contained in Annex A to Appendix B of this Enclosure.

(3) **In International Airspace.** Protecting civil aircraft in international airspace is principally the responsibility of the nation of registry. Guidance for certain cases of actual or suspected hijacking of airborne U.S. or foreign civil air-

craft is contained in MCM-102-92, 24 July 1992, "Hijacking of Civil Aircraft."

(4) **Terrorism.** Terrorist attacks are usually undertaken by civilian or paramilitary organizations, or by individuals under circumstances in which a determination of hostile intent may be difficult. The definitions of hostile act and hostile intent set forth above will be used in situations where terrorist attacks are likely. The term "hostile force" includes terrorist units when used in this document. When circumstances and intelligence dictate, supplemental ROE will be issued to meet this special threat.

(5) **Piracy.** Piracy is defined as an illegal act of violence, depredation (i.e., plundering, robbing, or pillaging), or detention in or over international waters committed for private ends by the crew or passengers of a private ship or aircraft against another ship or aircraft or against persons or property on board such ship or aircraft. U.S. warships and aircraft have an obligation to repress piracy on or over international waters directed against any vessel, or aircraft, whether U.S. or foreign flagged. If a pirate vessel or aircraft fleeing from pursuit proceeds into the territorial sea, archipelagic waters, or superjacent airspace of another country every effort should be made to obtain the consent of nation sovereignty to continue pursuit. Where circumstances permit, commanders will seek guidance from higher authority before using armed force to repress an act of piracy.

d. **Operations Within or in the Vicinity of Hostile Fire or Combat Zones Not Involving the United States.**

(1) U.S. forces should not enter, or remain in, a zone in which hostilities (not involving the United States) are imminent or occurring between foreign forces unless directed by proper authority.

(2) If a force commits a hostile act or demonstrates hostile intent against U.S. forces in a hostile fire or combat zone, the commander is obligated to act in unit self-defense in accordance with SROE guidelines.

e. **Right of Assistance Entry.**

(1) Ships, or under certain circumstances aircraft, have the right to enter a foreign territorial sea or archipelagic waters and corresponding airspace without the permission of the coastal or island state to engage in legitimate efforts to render emergency assistance to those in danger or distress from perils of the sea.

(2) Right of assistance extends only to rescues where the location of those in danger is reasonably well known. It does not extend to entering the territorial sea, archipelagic waters, or national airspace to conduct a search.

(3) For ships and aircraft rendering assistance on scene, the right and obligation of self-defense extends to and includes persons, vessels, or aircraft being assisted. The right of self-defense in such circumstances does not include interference with legitimate law enforcement actions of a coastal nation. However, once received on board the assisting ship or aircraft, persons assisted will not be surrendered to foreign authority unless directed by the NCA.

(4) Further guidance for the exercise of the right of assistance entry is contained in the CJCS Instruction 2410.01, 20 July 1993, "Guidance for the Exercise of Right of Assistance Entry."

Persian Gulf—A port quarter view of the guided missile frigate USS *Stark* listing to port after being struck by an Iraqi-launched exocet missile (18 May 87). Misunderstanding of the rules of engagement by the *Stark's* crew contributed to the ship's vulnerability to attack. Photo courtesy of U.S. Naval Institute.

DESERT SHIELD/DESERT STORM RULES OF ENGAGEMENT

DESERT SHIELD

RULES OF ENGAGEMENT

THESE ARE PEACETIME RULES OF ENGAGEMENT. NOTHING IN THESE RULES LIMITS THE RIGHTS OF INDIVIDUAL SOLDIERS TO DEFEND THEMSELVES OR THE RIGHTS AND RESPONSIBILITIES OF LEADERS TO DEFEND THEIR UNITS.

A. You may not conduct offensive military operations (raids, ambushes, etc.).

B. You may use force in self-defense in response to attacks or threats of imminent attack against U.S. or host nation forces, citizens, property, or commercial assets.

C. You are not permitted to enter the land, sea, or airspace of other countries—besides the host nation.

D. If you inadvertently enter territorial land, sea, or airspace of another country, you may use force in self-defense to withdraw.

E. You may not seize property of others to accomplish your mission in peacetime.

F. Proper contracting processes must be followed to obtain supplies and other items necessary to accomplish the mission.

G. Treat all persons and property with respect and dignity. Remember we are at peace.

REMEMBER

1. WE ARE NOT AT WAR.

2. THESE RULES ARE IN EFFECT UNLESS HOSTILITIES BEGIN.

3. KNOW THE WARTIME ROE AND FOLLOW THEM IF HOSTILITIES BEGIN.

CULTURAL DOs AND DON'Ts

DO:

A. Be friendly and courteous. A handshake accompanied with the phrase Al-Salaama 'Alaykum (Peace be upon you) is the most common form of greeting.

B. If you smoke (most Arab men do), offer to share cigarettes with those present.

C. Sit properly in chairs: upright with feet on the ground.

D. When in doubt, observe locals and imitate their behavior.

E. Avoid contact with Arab women. If introduced, be polite but do not stare or engage in any lengthy conversations.

DON'T:

A. Make critical comparisons of your religion vs. Islam.

B. Ask an Arab not to smoke.

C. Point your finger or use your index finger to beckon people; it is considered demeaning.

D. Use alcohol.

E. Possess or use pornographic or sexually explicit material.

DESERT STORM

RULES OF ENGAGEMENT

ALL ENEMY MILITARY PERSONNEL AND VEHI-CLES TRANSPORTING THE ENEMY OR THEIR SUPPLIES MAY BE ENGAGED SUBJECT TO THE FOLLOWING RESTRICTIONS:

A. Do not engage anyone who has surrendered, is out of battle due to sickness or wounds, is shipwrecked, or is an aircrew member descending by parachute from a disabled aircraft.

B. Avoid harming civilians unless necessary to save U.S. lives. Do not fire into civilian populated areas or buildings which are not defended or being used for military purposes.

C. Churches, Shrines, Schools, Museums, National Monuments, and any other historical or cultural sites will not be engaged except in self-defense.

D. Hospitals will be given special protection. Do not engage hospitals unless the enemy uses the hospital to commit acts harmful to U.S. forces, and then only after giving a warning and allowing a reasonable time to expire before engaging, if the tactical situation permits.

E. Booby traps may be used to protect friendly positions or to impede the progress of enemy forces. They may not be used on civilian personal property. They will be recov-ered or destroyed when the military necessity for their use no longer exists.

F. Looting and the taking of war trophies are prohibited.

G. Avoid harming civilian property unless necessary to save U.S. lives. Do not attack traditional civilian objects, such as houses, unless they are being used by the enemy for military purposes and neutralization assists in mission accomplishment.

H. Treat all civilians and their property with respect and dignity. Before using privately owned property, check to see if publicly owned property can substitute. No requisitioning of civilian property, including vehicles, without permission of a company level commander and without giving a receipt. If an ordering officer can contract the property, then do not requisition it.

I. Treat all prisoners humanely and with respect and dignity.

J. ROE Annex to the OPLAN provides more detail. Conflicts between this card and the OPLAN should be resolved in favor of the OPLAN.

REMEMBER

1. FIGHT ONLY COMBATANTS.

2. ATTACK ONLY MILITARY TARGETS.

3. SPARE CIVILIAN PERSONS AND OBJECTS.

4. RESTRICT DESTRUCTION TO WHAT YOUR MISSION REQUIRES.

APPENDIX 8

MILITARY JUSTICE TERMS

ACC	Accused		FORF	Forfeiture of Pay
ACMR	Army Court of Military Review		GCM	General Court-Martial
AFCMR	Air Force Court of Military Review		HL w/o C	Hard Labor without Confinement
BCD	Bad Conduct Discharge		INST	Instruction
B&W	Bread and Water		IMC	Individual Military Counsel
CA	Convening Authority		JAG	Judge Advocate General of the Navy
CAAF	Court of Appeals for the Armed Forces		JAGC	Judge Advocate Generals' Corps
CCA	Court of Criminal Appeals		JAGMAN	Manual of the Judge Advocate General
CC or CCU	Correctional Custody Unit		LN	Legalman
CGCMR	Coast Guard Court of Military Review		LOD	Line of Duty
CHL	Confinement at Hard Labor		MAA	Master-At-Arms
CMC	Commandant, USMC		MCM	Manual for Courts-Martial
CMO	Court-Martial Order		MJ	Military Judge
CMR	Court of Military Review		MJR	Military Justice Reports
CNO	Chief of Naval Operations		MAST	Captain's Mast
CO	Commanding Officer or Convening Order		MILPERSMAN	Naval Military Personnel Manual
			NAVREGS	Navy Regulations
CMA	Court of Military Appeals		NMCMR	Navy-Marine Corps Court of Military Review
CPO	Chief Petty Officer			
C-M	Court-Martial		NCO	Non-Commissioned Officer
CWO	Chief Warrant Officer		NCIS	Naval Criminal Investigative Service
DC	Defense Counsel		NLSO	Naval Legal Service Office
DD	Dishonorable Discharge		NJP	Nonjudicial Punishment
DIMRATS	Diminished Rations		OIC	Officer-in-Charge
DO	Division Officer		OTH	Other than Honorable Discharge
ED	Extra Duty		PIO	Preliminary Inquiry Officer
EMI	Extra Military Instruction		PO	Petty Officer
E&M	Extenuation and Mitigation		RIR	Reduction in Rate

REST	Restriction		SPCM	Special Court-Martial
PTIO	Pre-trial Investigating Officer		TAD	Temporary Additional Duty
SCM	Summary Court-Martial		TC	Trial Counsel
SECNAV	Secretary of the Navy		UA	Unauthorized Absence
SJA	Staff Judge Advocate		UCMJ	Uniform Code of Military Justice
SOFA	Status of Forces Agreement		VA	Veteran's Administration
SP	Shore Patrol		XO	Executive Officer

BIBLIOGRAPHY

American Law Institute. *Restatement of the Law, Third, Foreign Relations Law of the United States.* 1987.

American State Papers Military Affairs. 1832.

Byrne, Edward M. *Military Law.* Annapolis, Md.: Naval Institute Press, 1970.

Clausewitz, Carl von. *On War.* Edited by Peter Paret and Daniel Moran. Princeton, N.J.: Princeton University Press, 1992.

Generous, William T. *Swords and Scales.* Port Washington, N.Y.: Kennikat Press, 1973.

Grotius, Hugo. *The Law of War and Peace.* Indianapolis: Bobbs-Merrill, 1925.

King, Allen A. "Ethics in Government and the Vision of Public Service." *George Washington Law Review* 58 (1990): 417.

Morrison, Fred L. "The Significance of Nuremberg for Modern International Law." *Military Law Review* 149 (1995): 207.

Nunn, Sam. "The Fundamental Principles of the Supreme Court's Jurisprudence in Military Cases." *Wake Forest Law Review* 29 (1994): 559.

Snededeker, James. *A Brief History of Courts-Martial.* Annapolis, Md.: Naval Institute Press, 1954.

Sofaer, Abraham D. "Terrorism, the Law, and the National Defense." *Military Law Review* 126 (1989): 89.

Valle, James E. *Rocks and Shoals.* Annapolis, Md.: Naval Institute Press, 1980.

Van de Water, Frederic F. *The Captain Called It Mutiny.* New York: Washburn, 1954.

INDEX

ABOUT THE AUTHORS

Lieutenant Commander Filbert is an active duty Navy judge advocate. He earned a B.A. in history (with honors) from the University of Missouri; J.D. (with distinction) from the University of Missouri; and graduated from the Naval War College (with highest distinction). He has served as a prosecutor, assistant legal officer on an aircraft carrier; assistant professor of law at the U.S. Naval Academy; and as the speechwriter for the chief of naval operations. He is currently enrolled in the masters of law program (trial advocacy) at Temple University and is also serving as a special assistant U.S. attorney in the eastern district of Pennsylvania. Lieutenant Commander Filbert has published articles on several topics, including self-incrimination, search and seizure, military punishments, prison law, and criminal defenses.

Lieutenant Commander Kaufman is an active duty Navy judge advocate, currently assigned to the staff of the commander in chief, United States Pacific Fleet, as international and operational law counsel. Recently selected for promotion to commander, his previous assignments include duty as law section head and assistant professor at the U.S. Naval Academy, as legal officer on an aircraft carrier, as assistant counsel to the vice chief of naval operations, and as trial and defense counsel. He has taught international law as an adjunct professor at the University of Baltimore School of Law. He graduated from Emory University with a B.S. in biology, received his J.D. degree summa cum laude from the University of Baltimore School of Law (where he also served as editor in chief of the law review), and earned his LL.M. at Harvard Law School.

The **Naval Institute Press** is the book-publishing arm of the U.S. Naval Institute, a private, nonprofit, membership society for sea service professionals and others who share an interest in naval and maritime affairs. Established in 1873 at the U.S. Naval Academy in Annapolis, Maryland, where its offices remain today, the Naval Institute has members worldwide.

Members of the Naval Institute support the education programs of the society and receive the influential monthly magazine *Proceedings* and discounts on fine nautical prints and on ship and aircraft photos. They also have access to the transcripts of the Institute's Oral History Program and get discounted admission to any of the Institute-sponsored seminars offered around the country. Discounts are also available to the colorful bimonthly magazine *Naval History*.

The Naval Institute's book-publishing program, begun in 1898 with basic guides to naval practices, has broadened its scope in recent years to include books of more general interest. Now the Naval Institute Press publishes about 100 titles each year, ranging from how-to books on boating and navigation to battle histories, biographies, ship and aircraft guides, and novels. Institute members receive discounts of 20 to 50 percent on the Press's nearly 600 books in print.

Full-time students are eligible for special half-price membership rates. Life memberships are also available.

For a free catalog describing Naval Institute Press books currently available, and for further information about joining the U.S. Naval Institute, please write to:

Membership Department
U.S. Naval Institute
118 Maryland Avenue
Annapolis, MD 21402-5035
Telephone: (800) 233-8764
Fax: (410) 269-7940
Web address: www.usni.org